Postcards & Trains
Travel USA by Train

By JC Gacilo

National Library of Canada Cataloguing in Publication Data

Gacilo, J. C., 1966-
    Postcards and trains : travel USA by train / J C Gacilo ; edited by
Necitas N. Garcia and Casey Stone.
Includes bibliographical references.
ISBN 1-4120-0257-5
    I. Garcia, Necitas N. II. Stone, Casey III. Title.
E158.G234 2003   917.304'929   C2003-902389-3

This book was published _on-demand_ in cooperation with Trafford Publishing.
On-demand publishing is a unique process and service of making a book available for retail sale to the public taking advantage of on-demand manufacturing and Internet marketing.
On-demand publishing includes promotions, retail sales, manufacturing, order fulfilment, accounting and collecting royalties on behalf of the author.

Suite 6E, 2333 Government St., Victoria, B.C. V8T 4P4, CANADA
Phone   250-383-6864   Toll-free   1-888-232-4444 (Canada & US)
Fax   250-383-6804   E-mail   sales@trafford.com
Web site   www.trafford.com   TRAFFORD PUBLISHING IS A DIVISION OF TRAFFORD HOLDINGS LTD.
Trafford Catalogue #03-0626   www.trafford.com/robots/03-0626.html

10   9   8   7   6   5   4   3

Postcards & Trains
Travel USA by Train

Written By:

JC Gacilo

Edited by:
Casey Stone & Necitas Nobleza Garcia

About the Author

JC Gacilo has a degree, awards, and academic honors in Tourism and a Master in Business Administration. He has worked in entertainment, education, and various tourism industries internationally and has attended various international tourism training events and seminars. He is a member of the Pacific Asia Travel Association Young Tourism Professionals (PATAYTP) and is a supporter of the US Association of Train Travel (Chicago).

Mr. Gacilo speaks several languages and has traveled the world extensively. In preparation to write this book he spent more than a year traveling the United States by train, visiting 48 States, major cities, towns, and national parks logging more than 35,000 miles of US train travel. He is currently working as a Market Analyst, pursuing a degree in law, and living in Los Angeles, California.

Acknowledgment

Thanks to many generous and kind people who helped and assisted me in writing this book: Janelle of Niagara Falls, Nell of St. Louis, the staff of the Los Angeles City Library, Vic and Mrs. Sanches of Los Angeles, Ruggie of Guam, Patrick of Macau, my mother for her endless support and love, Amtrak's accommodating staff, train associations and tourism organizations, and finally to Casey without his generous support I would have not completed this book. Thank you all!

I dedicate this book to the thousands of Americans who are preserving the great American railways for their endless efforts in ensuring that part of the great American heritage will flourish for future generations.

Notice/Disclaimer

Information given in this book is current as of the time of writing. Postcards and Trains US train travel book will be revised from time to time in order to provide readers and travelers the most up-to-date information possible. However, things change fast: prices, fares, schedules, and even contacts and addresses change frequently, especially in the US.

Any current information you wish to share is most welcome. Please contact the author at ustraintravel@postcardsandtrains.com or visit Postcards & Trains website at <<http://www.postcardsandtrains.com>>.

Neither the author nor the publisher accepts any responsibility for loss, injury, or inconvenience caused to any person who uses this book.

Table of Contents

Contents at Glance

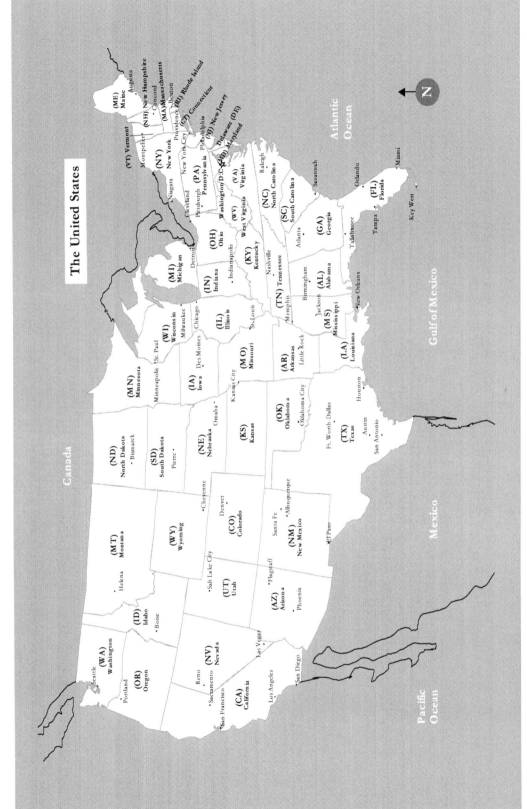

The United States

*I*ntroduction

Postcards stand for travel destinations and sites, while *Trains* refers to the experience of traveling via train. *Postcards and Trains- Travel USA by Train* is a complete travel guide and travel reference, with comprehensive destinations, accommodations, and transportation information. This book focuses mainly on destinations a traveler will experience while following the path of US train travel routes. Unlike other train travel books, which mostly focus on the train itself, the focal points of this book are the destinations and the unique opportunities of train travel.

Postcards and Trains details more than 500 destinations (cities, towns, national parks and natural wonders) and covers all 48 states and the District of Columbia. In addition, the book includes 4 main parts: Facts about the US, Facts about US Train Travel, Tips for Travelers, and the Train Travel Destinations. The latter part includes destination backgrounds, local transportation, places to see, what to expect, list of accommodations, etc. In addition there are illustrations, US and State Maps, US Train Route Maps, a rich photo collection of destination highlights, and a list of useful websites and telephone numbers. In the "Useful Information and Tips" section, among many other tips, there is information on Railroad Parks and Museum in the US and list of US train sales representative worldwide .

Here are some reasons why you should travel by train:

- ➢ Train travel is cheap and economical using special fares and passes.
- ➢ Most train depots are located in the center of towns and cities, making it easier to access major tourist sights, accommodations, and city's major facilities; train depots are usually connected to most major local transportation services (city bus lines and subways) making it cheaper to explore the city. (Imagine spending $20 to $60 for taxis if traveling by air).
- ➢ You'll have a chance to see what most visitors never have a chance to see and experience: natural wonders and the beautiful rural landscape and wildlife of North America.
- ➢ Comfortable train accommodations, services, romantic dinners and unique train experience.
- ➢ One of the safest modes of transport.
- ➢ Chance to meet and learn from locals and make new friends.
- ➢ You'll experience one of the US's cultural heritages, train travel.

What are you waiting for? Grab your bag, hop on the train and "Welcome Aboard" ......Don't forget your postcards!

Chapter-1

Facts about the US

Geography

The United States is the World's third-largest country (after Russia and Canada), with a land area of 3,537,441 sq. miles (5,695,280 sq. kilometers). It borders Canada (for 5,513 miles or 8,893 kilometers) to the north and Mexico (for 2,062 miles or 3,326 kilometers) to the south. The US has 12,353 miles (19,924 km) of water coastline, the Pacific Ocean on the west and the Atlantic Ocean on the East. The lowest point of the US is Death Valley, 282 feet below sea level, located in California, while the highest point is Mount McKinley at 20,320 ft in Alaska.

Landscape

The US is rich in natural beauty and wonders: Rocky Mountains, Mt. Rainer, Grand Canyon, Yosemite Valley, Yellowstone, Sequoia Park, and great deserts in the west and the pacific regions; Big Bend, hot springs, great plains in the Midwest; and great falls, valleys, rivers, and beautiful low mountains in the east. The US has it all!

US Brief Statistic Data

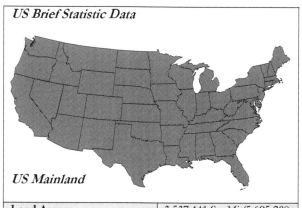

US Mainland

Land Area	3,537,441 Sq. Mi (5,695,280 sq. Km)
Population	281,421,906
Capital	Washington D.C.
Number of States	50
Largest States	Texas
Most Populated States	California (33,871,648)
World Land Area (1990)	6.2%
Northernmost point:	Point Barrow, Alaska
Easternmost point:	West Quoddy Head, Maine
Southernmost point:	Ka Lae (South Cape), Hawaii
Westernmost point	Cape Wrangell, Alaska
Highest point:	Mt. McKinley, Alaska (20,320 ft)
Lowest point:	Death Valley, California (282 ft below sea level)

Climate

The United States is a vast country that covers a huge span of latitude and various altitudes with very diverse climatic zones. Temperatures could reach as high as 120 degrees F (50 degrees C) during summer to as low as -40 degrees F (-40 degrees C) during winter.

The Northern Pacific Coast is a cooler region with much rainfall while the Southern Pacific Coast has moderate temperatures most of the year. High mountain, plateau, and desert areas have extreme temperatures. The Northern Midwest section of the US has very cold winter temperatures and warm temperatures during summer, while the Southern Midwest has a relatively moderate climate with relatively high humidity and less severe winter. The North

2

Eastern part of the US has cool winters and warm summers while the South Eastern US has a much milder winter, longer summer, and more tropical weather.

Time

Mainland United States (not including Alaska and Hawaii) is divided in four time zones: Pacific Time, Mountain Time, Central Time, and Eastern Time. Each time zone differs only by one hour, thus a person going to the east should add one hour to his/her time and if going to the west should subtract one hour of his/her time when passing each time zone boundary. Daylight Saving Time or DST begins in the United States at exactly 2 a.m. of the first Sunday of April and reverts to standard time at 2 a.m. of the last Sunday of October. You should set your watch or clock an hour ahead during DST and revert it during Standard time. The State of Arizona, Hawaii, and some parts of Indiana do not observe Daylight Saving Time.

Natural Resources

Temperature Conversion Table	
Fahrenheit	Celsius
150	66
140	60
130	54
120	49
110	43
100	37.8
98	36.7
95	35
90	32.2
85	29.4
80	26.7
75	23.9
70	21.1
60	15.6
50	10
40	4.4
30	-1.1
20	-6.7
10	-12.2
0	-17.8
-10	-23.3
-20	-28.9
-30	-34.4

Gold, silver, copper, iron, lead, nickel, mercury, molybdenum, tungsten, phosphates, uranium, bauxite, potash, coal, zinc, petroleum, natural gas, timber, amongst others.

Government

The US Government is a Federal Republic with a strong democratic tradition, governed in accordance with its Constitution which was first drawn up in 1787. The capital is Washington, DC with administrative division of 50 states. The Legal system is based on English common law. There are several political parties, mainly Democratic Party and Republican Party, and few other groups or parties.

Economy

The world strongest and richest economy, the US has the largest and most technologically influential economy in the world and is marked by steady growth, low inflation, low unemployment, and fast development in technology. The US economy makes up one quarter of world economic output, and its GDP purchasing power parity in 2000 is estimated at $9.963 trillion, with GDP real growth rate of 5%, and GDP per capita of $36,200.

The US is the leading industrial power in the world, with highly diversified and technologically advanced industries such as petroleum, chemical, steel, aerospace, automotive manufacturing, telecommunications, electronics, food processing, consumer goods, timber, mining, tourism, and services.

As of the year 2000 there is an estimated 140.9 million (including unemployed) labor force in the US, of which 30.2% are managerial and professional, 29.2% are technical, sales, and administrative support, 13.5% are in services, 24.6% in manufacturing, mining, transportation, crafts farming, and forestry, and 2.5% marine-related industry, with an unemployment rate of 4%. Despite its economic success, an estimated 12.7% of the population is living below the poverty line as of 1999.

Recent studies suggest that there is a growing gap between the rich, poor and the middleclass. According to a study conducted by the Federal Reserve, the richest 1 percent of the U.S. population owns nearly 40 percent of the nation's wealth. The top 20 percent of the population own more than 80 percent of the nation's wealth, while the lowest-earning 20 percent of the population earn only 5.7 percent of all the after-tax income paid to individuals in the United States each year. This suggests that despite its huge and strong economy, the US has the most unequal distribution of income and wealth compared to other industrialized countries of the world.

Demographic

The US has a population of approximately 281,421,906, of which 49.1% are male and 50.9% are female. 75.1% of the population is white, 12.5% Hispanic, 12.3% black, 3.6% Asian, and the rest are American Indian and Islanders. The average American life expectancy is 77.26 years (male 74.37 years, female 80.05 years).

Largest Cities in the United States by Population	
New York City, NY	8,008,278
Los Angeles, CA	3,694,820
Chicago, IL	2,896,016
Houston, TX	1,953,631
Philadelphia, PA	1,517,550
Phoenix, AZ	1,321,045
San Diego, CA	1,223,400
Dallas, TX	1,188,580
San Antonio, TX	1,144,646
Detroit, MI	951,270
Source: US 2000 census	

56% of Americans are Protestant, 28% Roman Catholic, 2% Jewish and the rest are Amish, Muslim, Hindu, Buddhist, or other religions. English and Spanish are widely spoken in the US.

Major US Holidays	
New Year's Day	January 1
Martin Luther King Day	January 15
Inauguration Day	January 20
Lincoln's Birthday	February 12
Washington's Birthday	February 22
Good Friday	Friday before Easter
Memorial Day	May 30
Independence Day	July 4
Labor Day	First Monday in September
Columbus Day	October 12
Veterans Day	November 11
Election Day	Tuesday after first Monday of November
Thanksgiving Day	Fourth Thursday in November
Christmas Day	December 25

Brief Chronology of the US History	
Date/Year	-Event(s)

Oct 12, 1492	-Christopher Columbus discovered America
Apr 2, 1513	-Juan Ponce De Leon founded the first colony in St. Augustine, Florida
Jul 4, 1776	-The US Declaration of Independence from Britain
Sep 3, 1783	-Britain and the United States signed the Treaty of Paris
Apr 30, 1789	-George Washington became the first President of the United States
Dec 12, 1800	-The capital of United States was moved to Washington, D.C.
Mar 4, 1801	-Thomas Jefferson became the third President of the United States
Jun 18, 1812	-The American Revolutionary war against Britian
Sep 20, 1814	-The Star-Spangled Banner became the official US National Anthem
Dec 24, 1814	-The United States and Britain signed the Treaty of Ghent
May 13, 1846	-The American/Mexican war
Feb 2, 1848	-The United States and Mexico signed the treaty of Guadalupe Hidalgo
Mar 4, 1861	-Abraham Lincoln became the sixteenth President of the United States
May 6, 1861	-President Lincoln officially declared a state of rebellion in the US southern states
May 21, 1861	-Richmond, VA became the capital of the Confederate States
Jul 3, 1863	-The Union army won the Battle Gettysburg
Mar 30, 1867	-The US acquired Alaska from Russia for $7.2 million
May 10, 1869	-The US Transcontinental Railroad met in Promontory Point, Utah
Apr 20, 1898	-The American/Spanish war
Jul 7, 1898	-The United States took possession of Hawaii
Dec 10, 1898	-The United States and Spain signed the Treaty of Paris
Feb 6, 1899	-The United States took possession of the Philippines, Guam, and Puerto Rico
Aug 4, 1916	-The US acquired the West Indies and the Virgin Islands for $25 million
Aug 25, 1916	-The US National Park Service was established
Mar 2, 1917	-Puerto Rico became US territory
Apr 6, 1917	-The United States joined World War I
Oct 29, 1929	-The beginning of the Great Depression
Mar 4, 1933	-Franklin Roosevelt became the thirty-second President of the United States
Dec 7, 1941	-Japan attacked Pearl Harbor, Hawaii
Dec 8, 1941	-The US joined World War II
Jun 6, 1944	-The allied invasion landed at Normandy ("D-Day")
Jan 12, 1945	-The Americans liberated the Philippines
Aug 6, 1945	-The US dropped the first atomic bomb on Hiroshima, Japan
Sep 2, 1945	-Japan surrendered, ending World War II
Oct 17, 1946	-The birth of the Cold War
Jan 20, 1961	-John Kennedy became the thirty-fifth President of the United States
Nov 22, 1963	-President John Kennedy was assassinated in Dallas, Texas
Apr 17, 1961	-The US invaded the Bay of Pigs, Cuba
Oct 22, 1962	-The Russia removed its missiles from Cuba
Jul 20, 1969	-Neil Armstrong landed on the Moon
Jan 27, 1973	-The United States and Vietnam signed a Peace Treaty, in Paris
Aug 9 1974	-President Nixon stepped down from his presidency as a result of the "Watergate" scandal
Nov 4, 1979	-Iranians stormed the US Embassy in Tehran and held 52 hostages
Jan 20, 1981	-The American hostages were freed
Nov 1986	-The "Iran-Contra Affair" scandal of the Regan Administration
Aug 2, 1990	-Iraqi forces launched a surprise invasion of Kuwait
Feb 23, 1991	-United Nations ground force led by the United States liberated Kuwait from Iraq
Feb 28, 1991	-The United Nations and Iraq signed a cease-fire agreement
Feb 1, 1992	-The United States and Russia officially ended the Cold War
Aug 7, 1998	-Terrorists destroyed American Embassies in Tanzania and Kenya
Sep 11, 2001	-WTC in New York City was attacked and destroyed, America declared war on terrorism
Mar 19,2003	-US invaded Iraq to remove Saddam Hussein's government

Brief History of US Railroading

The Birth of Railroad in the US

The development of the railroad in the US opened a new era in the history of American expansion and the building of a nation. The Railroad has played a significant role in securing the success of the Union, by delivering the union army and linking and unifying the states. But it was the rapidly growing population of Eastern America in the 19th century, followed by the ever-increasing movement of commerce and industries that drove the need to find faster ways of transportation. The story of American railroading began.

During the early days, Eastern America relied on the widespread river system and unpaved roads for commercial transportation and the movement of goods. However, the success of traveling on these systems was greatly dependent on Mother Nature's kindness: rivers need to reach navigable points or wait for ice to melt, while muddy streets need to wait for sludge to dry up.

It wasn't until the war of 1812 that the first construction of paved road was initiated. By 1820 there were more than 5000 miles of paved roads in the states of New York and Pennsylvania extending throughout the eastern region.

In spite of the expanded and improved road systems, people were dissatisfied with the hardship and slow speed travel they experienced on stagecoaches. And for commerce, the lack of an effective transportation system which was fast, economical, and reliable prevented perishable goods from being transported at an affordable price.

Rivers and canals, which were cheaper to construct than roads, allowed convenient boat travel, and were popular for a time. By 1830, there were more than 1,200 miles of canals spreading across the eastern region. One classic example was the 364-mile Erie canal which extended from Buffalo to Albany (New York) and was completed in 1825 (part of the canal is still preserved and can be visited in Buffalo, New York). On the other hand, the freezing of rivers and canals during winter and the inability to travel during the monsoon season (due to strong water currents) made Americans look for a more effective transportation solution.

The Americans turned to the railway system. In 1828 construction of the first 13-mile rail track connecting Baltimore and Ellicott City started. The following year the United States' first steam-powered locomotive, the "Stourbridge Lion," made history in Quincy, Massachusetts using the Delaware and Hudson tracks. The first scheduled train powered by steam engine was in 1830 by South Carolina's the "Best Friend of Charleston" with 141 passengers on board for a 6-mile journey.

ther railroad lines followed and continued to thrive around the eastern region. Between the 1840s and 1850s railroad tracks increased from 3,000 to 9,000 miles connecting most of the eastern states of the US. And by the early 1860s, at the beginning of the American civil war, there were estimated 30,000 miles of railroads in the US. Along with the railroad expansion, other infrastructure and development came; new settlements, roads, and bridges followed the path of the railroad.

In 1848 the first service train operated by "Galena" and "Chicago Union" rolled out of the city of Chicago, and by 1856 Chicago was linked to Mississippi, Ohio, and Missouri. The same year, the first railroad bridge crossing Mississippi river was completed. In the western region the "Sacramento Valley" was the first railway opened and George Pullman introduced his new type of upper and lower berth sleeping cars, the "Pullmans."

Railroads played a significant part during the American civil war of 1862: 30,000 men lead by General Braxton Bragg of the confederate army traveled 800 miles of track from Mississippi to Tennessee for almost a week by train. The following year more confederate troops were moved by train to reinforce Gen. Braxton Bragg troops in Chattanooga.

In retaliation, 23,000 Union troops were moved by train to Chattanooga in the surprisingly short time of less than ten days. The civil war was one of the bloodiest moments of American history. At the end of the civil war in 1865 almost half of the railroad systems in the southeastern region, including railroad bridges, were destroyed. In the state of Georgia alone the Confederate army used more than 1,000 tons of railroad track as building material for military artillery and war weaponry. This destruction of the railroad system in the south gave the opportunity to revitalize the railroad industry and help bring the railways into their glory.

Railroad West Expansion

Following the US acquisition of California from Mexico and the discovery of gold in the region in 1849, congress approved funding for the survey of possible railroad routes to connect eastern and western United States. In 1862 President Lincoln signed the Pacific Railway Bill, giving birth to the first transcontinental railroad in the US. It stated that Union Pacific would start at the Missouri River and build westward, while the Central Pacific Railroad would start east of Sacramento and build eastward.

Central Pacific hired thousand of Chinese immigrant workers while its counterpart in the east used mostly former army soldiers and Irish immigrants. It is indisputable that these men are responsible for building one of America's greatest achievements of modern engineering, the "Great West Railroad." On May 10, 1869 both east and west railroad lines finally met in Promontory Point, Utah uniting the whole of the United States by railroad for the first time. The event was celebrated by the famous "Golden Spike" ceremony performed by striking (driving into place) the final 17.6 carats gold spike.

The America's quest to tame the west was finally realized; with this expansion follows the mass migration of people, supported by the government. Land was given to encourage western migration, and farmers were given free cattle in exchange for their westward migration.

More than 1,700 miles of railroad was laid. New towns, cities and settlements were established, and in 1871 over 170 million acres of land had been granted to many railroad companies based on the government "Land Grants" of 1850. The grant was established to encourage the expansion and development of the railroad and land settlement in the western region in exchange for some government privileges and reserved federal government rights to use the railroads when needed, especially during wartime. Thus in 1880 there were 70,000 miles of railroad added, and the railroad standard of 4'-8" gauge was adopted.

There were many other railway developments by that time. The launching of the Pullman Palace Car in the 1870s introduced the first luxurious passenger cars with on-board gourmet meals, dinning cars with chandeliers and air-conditioned cars. The air-brake introduced by George Westinghouse in 1872 became a standard device in train passenger cars. The automatic coupler in 1873 and the automatic block signal control in 1890 were developed amongst other advances.

Most historians attribute the late 1800s and the early 1900s as the golden age of passenger trains. Back then the only comfortable and quick way of interstate travel was via train. The increasing middle and upper class population led to the growing need for luxurious train travel, so many luxurious liners and added train amenities never seen before were introduced. Some of the most popular were the "Pennsylvania Limited" introduced in 1887 and the "Pennsylvania Special" introduced in 1902, both using the popular Pullman Palace Cars traveling 908 miles of track between Chicago and New York City in just 20 hours.

Other known luxury liners were: the "Florida Special," established in 1888, serving tourists traveling between New York and Miami; the "1911 Panama Limited," an all deluxe passenger sleeping car serving tourists traveling between Chicago and New Orleans. In the west were the "New Coast Limited," "Orient Limited," and the "Olympian" amongst others. The growing popularity of the railway continued uninterrupted: by 1920 passenger train ridership reached more than 1 billion.

The government assumed control of the railway during World War I to move war machines, equipment, and to transport troops from both sides of the country. By the end of the war many train operators were bankrupt or on the brink of financial trouble. In addition, in 1921 congress passed the Federal Highway Act starting the development of the new interstate highway system. The train industry was approaching a new dark era.

The federal act triggered a massive car craze; as a result many car companies expanded and increased car manufacturing. Another factor that contributed to the decline of interstate train rider-ship was the American economic depression. By 1930 train interstate passenger rider-ship dropped by more than 41 percent and many local train services were cancelled giving way to other modes of transportation such as motorcars or "doodlebugs" and bus service which had been recently introduced.

In a desperate attempt to save the railroad industry, train designers introduced new "streamlined" trains. A futuristic, colorful, and attractive design coupled with much faster diesel engines were the key features of these new trains. The diesel powered "Zephyr 9900" and the gasoline powered "M 10,000" were introduced in 1934 providing services between Burlington, Chicago, and Quincy. Following the Zephyr's successful debut other streamliners came, mostly carrying the name Zephyr or a name of a famous American city. By the end of the 1930s there were 90 diesel streamliner trains in the US increasing the speed and comfort of train travel. Today the "Zephyr 9900" is permanently displayed at "Chicago's famous Museum of Science and Industry".

The results were promising: passenger rider-ship increased up to 38 percent, still only half of the train passenger rider-ship of the 20s. In 1949 the "California Zephyr" introduced the dome car, or the sightseers, running between Chicago and San Francisco. The new car gave passengers an enjoyable view as they rode through the Rocky Mountains. And in 1956 the "El Capitan" traveling between Chicago and Los Angeles introduced the newly improved wider car windows, new utilities, and two-story high-level cars.

In spite of all efforts, the railroad industry continued to decline with many train operators filing for bankruptcy. Those who remained enjoyed temporary benefits during the first two years of World War II. After the Second World War high operating costs, high equipment investment costs, and low rider-ship combined with competition from the emerging aviation industry and Americans' growing love for cars, the railway industry suffered its biggest blow.

The ailing railway industry was further threatened by the massive cut in the frequency of many interstate passenger train services, and by the end of 1956 more than 1,200 passenger train services was canceled (mostly long-haul routes). Lastly, the bankruptcy of Penn Central Railroad in 1970 threatened the survival of the eastern railroad system in the US, including the capital Washington DC railroad service, and most importantly the survival of a part of America's heritage: the train industry. It was then realized the strong need for creating a new and effective solution to revitalize the dying American railways.

The Birth of the New Era

In an effort to save America's railroad industry, President Nixon signed the legislation creating the National Railroad Passenger Corporation, popularly known as Amtrak, in October 1970. On May 1st of the following year Amtrak began service. Amtrak took over all but three passenger railroad services around the US. The three remaining were Rock Island Railroad, Southern Railways, and the Denver and Rio Grande which soon gave up all their services. At the beginning Amtrak inherited a fleet of old-fashioned and poorly maintained train cars and engines, operating 1,200 cars and 300 locomotives with 25 employees serving 314 destinations.

Amtrak purchased its first new passenger cars and locomotive by the mid 1970s and continuously improved its equipment, schedules, and consistency hoping to boost passenger rider-ship. In 1976 Amtrak acquired the North East Corridor 456 mile-track between Boston and Washington D.C. and later introduced its first high speed train the "Metro-liner" serving the northeast corridor. However, Amtrak remained greatly dependent on heavy government subsidies for its operation, and as a result of Congress' inability to secure funding for Amtrak, many long distance interstate routes were again eliminated during the first two decades of its operation.

The Reagan Administration had strongly expressed its opposition to Amtrak's heavy financial reliance on government funding, and threatened to cut Amtrak's badly-needed yearly subsidy. In the end, the congress voted to continue federal support of Amtrak. Although the former Bush administration did not exactly condemn the ailing Amtrak, his administration cut down most federal monetary support and subsidies.

On the contrary, the Clinton administration strongly expressed its support of the Nation's only interstate passenger train and regarded Amtrak as a solution to America's growing highway and airport congestion problems. Hence, the Clinton administration recommended to congress a 13% increase in government subsidies giving Amtrak a chance to develop and introduce more services and product lines. Still Amtrak has to meet its deadline of 2003 for independence from government subsidies.

Introducing "Amtrak"

Amtrak (from "American" and "Track"), officially called the National Railroad Passenger Corporation, began service on May 1st 1971 with service from New York to Philadelphia. In its first year of operation Amtrak served 184 train schedules, serving 314 destinations. Today Amtrak operates over 22,000 route-miles and serves more than 500 stations in 46 states (all states except Wyoming, South Dakota, Alaska, and Hawaii). Alternatively, Wyoming is served by Amtrak Thruway Motor-Coaches. In addition, Amtrak is still the only passenger train company that operates and serves inter-state services across the US.

Generally Amtrak uses railroad tracks owned by freight operators across the US. Amtrak owns only 730 route miles of track, which is about 3% of the total rail system in the US, mostly between Boston, Washington DC, and Michigan; 26.5 miles of railroad tunnels (18 tunnels), and 1,165 bridges totaling 61 miles of railroad track.

As of this writing Amtrak owns and operates some 436 locomotives: 360 diesels and 76 electric and high-speed train (the Acela). Currently, Amtrak runs 2,188 railroad cars of which 66 are first class and business class cars, 173 are sleeper cars, 743 are coach cars, 65 are lounge, café, and dinette cars, 83 are dining cars, 65 are dormitory and crew cars, and the rest of the remaining fleet are for baggage, mail, and express cars

Amtrak heavy maintenance facilities are located in Wilmington and Bear (Delaware), Beech Grove, Chicago, Indiana, Niagara Falls, New York City, Rensselaer (NY), Boston, Washington DC, Hialeah (FL), New Orleans, Seattle, Oakland, and Los Angeles.

During fiscal year 2000 Amtrak served 22.5 million passengers, an increase of 3 million in passenger rider-ship since 1996, and earned $1.1 billion in ticket revenue. Today there are more than 60,000 travelers that use Amtrak each day and in 2001 Amtrak served more than 23.5 million passengers across the US. During weekdays, Amtrak operates up to 265 trains (100 trains in intercity business unit and 48 trains in the Amtrak West business unit (Washington, Oregon, and California)), not including commuter trains.

In an attempt to meet congressional subsidy deadline of 2003, Amtrak is determined to boost rider-ship, schedules, and services. Aside from its expanding express and mail services, Amtrak has recently acquired its first 109 of the planned 350 car fleets of refrigerated railcars to carry perishable goods across the US.

In addition, Amtrak is continuously modernizing its fleet: the "View-liners" have replaced the aging Heritage sleepers; the new double-decker car the "Pacific Surf liner" will replace the three-decade old Am fleet and Horizon, serving the San Luis Obispo and San Diego routes, and the gleaming European-made Talgo was added to the fleet serving the US northern Pacific routes. The continuing upgrading of Amtrak's fleet has revitalized the experience and convenience of passenger train travel in the region.

The year 2000 introduction of Acela, high-speed (150 mph) train service in the northeast United States, offers hope that Amtrak will continue to improve its image and survive. Elsewhere in the world other high-speed trains such as the Japanese Shinkansen and the French TGV enjoy unprecedented popularity and success in passenger rider-ship and have become the symbol of train technological advancement and prosperity in the two countries. Amtrak is optimistic that the introduction of the same high-speed train technology in the US will revolutionize the image and boost rider-ship of America's least preferred means of transportation.

During the first month of Acela's operation, it attracted more than 11,000 passengers and boasts 94% on-time arrival and departure performance. This quality service is carving a promising future for Amtrak's new breed of high-speed trains.

In the future, Amtrak plans to resume some of its long distance services and to continuously increase its performance. However, all this depends on how much funding and support the US government and the American people will give to Amtrak.

References:

Welsh, Joe. *The American Railroads*. Wisconsin: MBI Publishing Company, 1999.

Wilner, Frank N. *The Amtrak Story*. Nebraska: Simmons-Boardman, 1994.

Ault, Philip H. *All Aboard: The Story of Passenger Train in America*. New York: Dodd, Mead, 1976.

Alper, Joshua. *American Steam Liner (Video Recording)*. New York: Greystone Communication, 1998.

Chapter-3

Travel Tips for Visitors

Visa and Entry

Documents

Visitors to the United States are required to bring their passport and additional picture ID card such as drivers license for identification. It is advisable to keep a photocopy of all your documents with you, separate from the originals, in case of loss. It is required to show a picture ID every time you purchase alcohol.

Return Tickets

Visitors from countries that participate in a visa waiver program are required to show return tickets; visitors holding B1 and B2 visas are not required to show return tickets upon arrival, however it is wise to have a return ticket as it will help convince the immigration authorities that you have no intention to stay illegally in the US.

Passport

Foreign nationals visiting the United States are required to bring a valid passport (at least six months valid before expiration date) to enter the US, with the exception of citizens of Canada. Canadian citizen are required to show proof of citizenship, such as valid citizenship card, photo ID, or passport.

Visa

US visas can be obtained at US embassies and consulates outside the US (from the US embassy or consulate in your country) and are needed before departure. Visas are B-1 (business) and B2 (pleasure). If your intention in visiting the US is other than B1 or B2, check the US embassy or consulate for information and other visa requirements. Plan your visa application as early as possible. Visit the list of US embassies and consulates worldwide at <<http://www.travel.state.gov/links.html>>.

Visa Waiver Programs

The visa waiver program is for travelers on a participating airline, with round-trip tickets, and a valid passport. A 90-day visitor/business permit will be given to passengers coming from a participating country; passengers should ask for WB status (waiver-business) or WT status (waiver-tourist) at the airport immigration booth upon arrival in the US.

As of this writing the countries included in the Visa Waiver Program are: Andora, Argentina, Australia, Austria, Belgium, Bermuda, Brunei, Canada, Denmark, Finland, France, Germany, Iceland, Ireland, Italy, Japan, Liechtenstein, Luxembourg, Monaco, Netherlands, New Zealand, Norway, Portugal, San Marino, Singapore, Slovenia, Spain, Sweden, Switzerland, United Kingdom, and Uruguay.

Visa Extension

If you need to stay in the US for more than the days stamped on your passport, you may apply for an extension of stay at the INS office. It is advisable that you should apply for an extension prior to the stamp end date in your passport. Call the INS National Customer Service Center toll-free (800) 375-5283, or (800) 767-1833 for information.

Entering the US

Non US nationals should complete an Arrival/Departure Record or Form I-94 while on-board the plane or before reaching the US immigration booth to avoid any delays. Always keep the Arrival/Departure Record or Form I-94 with your passport. The immigration officer has the complete power to grant or deny entry to a visitor. Answer questions properly and try to dress properly; sufficient funds and a return ticket may be requested. A 30-day entry is usually given if everything went well.

Customs

Visitors in the US who are at least 21 years old are allowed to bring 1 liter of alcoholic beverages for personal use; exceeding the 1 liter limitation is subject to duty or internal revenue tax. In addition, visitors are allowed to bring 200 cigarettes (one carton) or 50 cigars or two kilograms (4.4 lbs.) of tobacco; there is no limit on the amount of money you can take in/out of the US.

Crossing the Boarder

The US border to and from Canada and Mexico is well accessible. However, going back to the US visitors should expect to be subjected to various questions and inquiries by the immigration officer, so take your passport, plane tickets, and sufficient funds with you.

US/Mexico Boarder Crossing

Most cities at the US/Mexico border are visa free zone areas (such as Tijuana). Visitors planning to travel further from the border should obtain a visa from the Mexican embassy or consulate. You can obtain your Mexican visa prior to your departure from your country; it is also possible to apply for a Mexican visa in Mexican consulates or embassies in the US. Note that you have to posses a multiple US visa in order to return to the US.

Foreign nationals who wish to obtain a Mexican visa are required to provide the following: valid passport, valid migratory status in the U.S., proof of economic solvency or credit card, round trip airline tickets, and consular fee.

U.S. and Canadian nationals or citizens are required to obtain the Migratory Tourist Form (FMT) also known as "Tourist Card." You can obtain the FMT from any Mexican Consular office, airlines, travel agencies, or any port of entry; a valid passport, birth certificate or naturalization paper is needed. However, if traveling within the border zone (between 15-20 miles into Mexico), you do not need a FMT. Always take with you a photo identification card and proof of citizenship. For more information visit the Mexican embassy website at <<http://www.travelyucatan.com/office-1.htm>>.

US/Canada Boarder Crossing

Amtrak Cascades, Midwest Corridor, Maple Leaf, Adirondack, and Ethan Allen Express offer connection services to and from the US and Canada. Most nationals of western countries do not need a visa to enter Canada. Passengers are subject to inspections by U.S. Customs and Immigration and should provide proof of citizenship (such as Passport or citizenship card). Check if you are holding a proper visa before leaving and entering the US and Canada.

While the train is approaching the US/Canada border you will be given and asked to process a Citizenship and Immigration Canada (CIC) Customs Declaration Card. A CIC officer will collect the Customs Declaration Card once you have arrived in Canada.

If you are coming back to the US, you will be given and asked to process a US Customs Declaration Form when you are boarded on the train. US Customs agents will board the train once it enters the United States to collect your declaration form. Your baggage may be subject to inspection. Please note that the U.S. and Canadian Customs and Immigration regulations and requirements are subject to change, so it is wise to check with respective immigration agencies for any changes.

Some Useful Websites:

U.S. Immigration and Naturalization Service (INS) <<http://www.ins.usdoj.gov>>
U.S. Customs <<http://www.customs.treas.gov>>
Canadian Embassy <<http://www.canadianembassy.org/splash/>>
Canada Customs and Revenue Agency <<http://www.ccra-adrc.gc.ca>>

Work

If you are traveling with a non-immigrant visitor visa (B1/B2), you are not allowed to take any paid work in the US. Failure to comply with the immigration law can be reason for deportation. If you are planning to work in the US you should apply for an H category visa (working visa) or J1 visa (exchange visitors) before leaving your country. H visa allows you to stay and work in the US as a temporary or permanent worker provided that you have an employer that will sponsor your stay and work in the country. J1 visa is usually given to youngsters who wish to take a summer work, to participate as trainees or in student exchange programs. Consult the US embassy or consulate near you for more information.

When to Visit

Proper timing is essential for a nice vacation. It is highly recommended that before planning your visit to the US you ask yourself what you want to do and experience on your trip. Almost all facilities (hotels, transportations, terminals, etc.) in the US are temperature controlled, thus it is generally convenient to travel anywhere in the US. However, outdoor activities are very significant factors for your travel experience, therefore, if you want to have nice, comfortable travel, know where to go, when to go, and what to expect.

If you are planning to go during **summer** (from last Monday of May to the first Monday of September), it is humid and uncomfortably hot in the southern part of the US, hot to warm temperature in the midwest and southwestern part of the country. In addition, during the peak of the traveling season expect long lines, crowds, and a much more expensive price tag in most destinations. On the other hand, it is the best time to enjoy water sports or the sandy beaches.

Autumn (Fall), just like anywhere else, is the best time of the year. The temperature in most parts of the US is pleasant. Mid-September to late November is one of the most beautiful times of the year. The Leap Peeping (when the tree leaves turn from green to dark colors then fall off the trees) is one of the most awaited events, and beautifully observed in the eastern side of the US.

Winter is a magical time of the year as thick snow falls in the northern part of the country (and sometimes in southwestern states and places of high elevation). It is less crowded in most destinations and often there are winter season festivals in many areas. Winter sports are very popular, trees and houses are covered with snow, and taking pictures of towns and cities covered with snow would be a fascinating experience.

Spring is also a pleasant time to visit, with temperate weather in most part of the US. However in some higher places spring comes late or short, therefore, if you are planning to visit at this time don't forget to bring extra warm clothes. The landscape around the US is beautiful, garlanded with colorful flowers. One of the most celebrated events is the Cherry Blossom Festival in Washington DC.

Discount Cards and Privileges

Students Cards

If you are a student you are entitled to various discounts in almost anything you purchase in transportation (trains, buses, airlines, etc.), accommodations, and destinations (museums, monuments, etc.). Bring your student ID (School Identification Card) and if possible apply for ISIC (International Student Identity Card) or the GO 25 (you have to be between 12 to 25 years old) available in most universities, colleges and travel agencies. Also, students are advised to apply for Student Advantage Card at the train station for a 15% discount on almost all Amtrak fares, accommodations, car rentals, museums, and more. Call toll-free: (800) 96-AMTRAK for information.

Hostel Card

Staying in a youth hostel could be a rewarding experience: you could meet new friends and find traveling companions, especially if you are traveling alone. Most hostels in the US are members of Hostelling International/American Youth Hostel (HI/AYH) and affiliated with the International Youth Hostel Federation, therefore if you are planning to stay in a hostel you have to buy the membership card to avail membership discounts each time you use the hostel anywhere around the US, call Tel: (202) 783-6171 for information or visit Hostelling International websites at <<http://www.Hiayh.org>>.

Senior Travelers

Travelers over 50 years of age are entitled to several senior discounts and benefits: ask for transportation, hotel, museum, national park, and other available discounts while traveling.

Bring your picture ID and present it every time you pay. In the US seniors are well facilitated: there are various facilities designed to help and fill the needs of the elder.

Disabled Travelers

Disabled travelers need not worry during their travel in the US as the "Americans with Disabilities Act" (ADA) of 1992, signed by former president George Bush, has made the US the most disabled-friendly place in the world. Buildings and public infrastructures, major transportations (airlines, trains, buses), and most hotels and motels are providing disabled travelers with appropriate disabled-friendly facilities and extra care services. Disabled travelers should also avail discounts and special privileges (free admission, etc.) available in most institutions in the US. There are some organizations and institutions that provide specialized services for disabled travelers:

The Society for Accessible Travel & Hospitality (SATH) established in 1976, offers assistance and support for disabled travelers. SATH 347 Fifth Avenue, Suite 610, New York, NY 10016, Tel: (212) 447-7284.

Safety

Food and Drink

Finding a place to eat is not a problem in the US. As a melting pot of many races and cultures, it is typical to find different world cuisines (from oriental to European, from low cost to the most upscale) almost everywhere. American portions are relatively big compared to what Asian and European are accustomed, thus consider sharing with somebody else if you don't want to waste your food.

A hamburger, soft drink, and fries at fast-food chain restaurants will cost you US $4, or a set combo meal (combination of two dishes) with drinks will cost less than US $10. Most regular restaurants with a decent meal including drinks or wine will cost more or less US $25. Fine dining at upscale restaurants and hotels could cost you almost any price. Water in restaurants or tap water is relatively safe in the US; however bottled water is available almost everywhere for as little as 80 cents to US $1.50, depending on size.

Heath Issue

The US is a relatively safe place to travel and there are many clinics and hospitals with 24-hour emergency service. However, be advised that hospitalization in the US is expensive, so be sure to carry your personal immediate medicine, doctor's prescriptions, and comprehensive travel insurance with you. If possible, before traveling consult your doctor or dentist to make sure that you are fit to travel. Just in case you need to call for an emergency ambulance, **dial 911**.

Insurance

You can purchase your travel insurance to most travel agencies, banks, airlines, etc. Be sure to investigate the policy limitations and the flexibility of the policy (in case you need to make changes while traveling). If possible, choose a policy that will pay the hospitals and doctors directly. If your policy demands you pay for services and are later reimbursed, remember to bring all hospital documents and receipts with you back home for submission to your insurance company.

Travel Safety

The US has high rates of crimes; on the other hand, just like other countries in the world, the US is safe to travel if you know how to avoid risk. It is always advisable to be cautious and avoid isolated places or red districts. If you are alone, always stay in open public places. If you need police help or assistance, **dial 911** or **0** to speak with the operator. Lists of Embassies and Consulates are provided in this book.

Driving in the US

The US has a total 3,885,719 miles (6,370,031 kilometers) of roads and highways that connect all 48 states (not including Alaska and Hawaii) and cities. Freeways in the US are termed in numbers and names: East-west highways have even numbers, and north-south highways have odd numbers. In general, if there are no signs posted on the city streets, the maximum speed is 25 miles per hour and 65 miles per hour on the freeways. You may turn right at most red lights unless specified otherwise. Laws regarding littering and violation of government property are strictly observed and violators could be fined up to thousands of dollars.

Driver's License

Visitors in the US can drive using their national or local driver license from their own country for a period of up to one year. If your country's national or local driver license is written in a language other than English, it is advisable to apply for an International Driver License. Carry your national or local driver license and international license together in case of any traffic violation.

Directions

If you need directions, you can call the Visitor Information Center (listed in most major destinations in this book). Members of AAA (American Automobile Association) can call auto club member services toll-free at (800) 222-4357 for directions and information. There are national and state highway and street maps available for sale in various department stores and bookstores. It is also advisable to monitor radio traffic reports or TV stations for traffic reports.

American Automobile Association (AAA)

Triple A membership gives you free 24-hour emergency roadside assistance, free road maps and travel publications, discounts in insurance, and many tourist destination facilities and accommodations. Triple A annual membership is $52. If you are a member of a motoring association in your own country which is affiliated with Triple A, you should be able to receive Triple A assistance by showing your membership card or documents. For information call toll-free (800) AAA-HELP.

Parking

Parking can be a problem when visiting some busy and popular tourist destinations. Usually there are several parking lots in the city and parking fees vary depending on how near you are to the attraction. In most hotels and restaurants parking and valet service are available, some with nominal fees, but be careful not to leave any important belongings inside the car as there are some theft incidences. Metered street parking spaces are available in most places, and sometimes parking is free. Remember to read signs for parking instructions and notices. There are various curb colors that signify parking rules; green curb means parking for a specified time period, red curb means no parking, white curb is for loading and unloading passengers only. Illegally parked vehicles get tickets or towed away.

Safety Tips

Always use a seatbelt and remember that in the US pedestrians have the right-of-way. It is prohibited to drive under the influence of alcohol or drugs, and violators can be subjected to severe penalties or even imprisonment. It is illegal to carry an open bottle of alcohol in any form inside the car; if you need to carry one, you have to seal it and place it inside the trunk. Call boxes with free phones are placed every few miles along the freeways for emergencies. Be sure to buy insurance (accident insurance) before driving.

Accommodation

Accommodations are varied in almost every place in the US, and travelers will surely find lodging to suit their requirements. The list of the suggested accommodations in each destination in this book was chosen to meet travelers requirements based on the price and location of the establishment. Prices are quoted in the nearest approximate prices: remember that the room rates can be varied seasonally and might change from time to time. Taxes, which vary from place to place, will be added. Address and local numbers were provided and it is highly recommended that you call ahead and make a reservation prior to your arrival in order to get a decent rate. Often in major train depots there are services and lists of recommended local acommodations.

The following is a list of recommended accommodations and their toll-free numbers that are used in this book.

List of US Hotels/Motels	
Best Western Hotel	(800) 5281234
Courtyard by Marriott	(800) 3212211
Days Inn	(800) DAYS INN
Doubletree Hotels	(800) 222 TREE
Embassy Suites	(800) EMBASSY
Meridien Hotels	(800) 2255843
Four Seasons Hotel	(800) 3323442
Hampton Inns	(800)HAMPTON
Hilton Hotels	(800) HILTONS
Holiday Inn	(800) 4654329
Hostelling International	(800) 909 4776
Howard Johnson's	(800) 4464656
Hyatt Hotels	(800) 2331234
Inter Continental Hotels	(800) 3270200
Sheraton Hotels	(800) 3253535
Marriott Hotels & Resorts	(800) 2289290
Omni Hotels	(800) THE OMNI
Radisson Hotels	(800) 3333333
Ramada Hotels	(800) 2RAMADA
The Ritz Carlton Hotel	(800) 2413333
Travel Lodge	(800) 5787878
Westin Hotels & Resorts	(800) 2283000
Wyndham Hotel	(800)WYNDHAM

Public Toilets

Public toilets (commonly called "bathrooms" or "restrooms" in the US) are recently becoming popular in most of US city streets, highway rest stops, and parks; there are mobile toilets, and some newly constructed toilets. Most shopping malls, restaurants, bars, and beaches offer toilets for customer and public use. Toilets are generally clean and well facilitated.

Laundry

Most accommodationss offer self-service laundry facilities or services. In addition, there are self-service coined operated facilities in most towns and cities. Washing a load costs $1 and another $1 for drying. Some facilities have an attendant to do the job for an extra cost. Ask your hotel or hostel for information or look for a telephone directory for the nearest laundry facilities.

Electricity

US voltage is 110 V and plugs have two flat pins or two flat pins with a round one. Plug adaptors are generally available at any hardware or drugstore in the US.

Communications & Post office

Telephone

The telephone system in the US is very large, technologically advanced, and has a multipurpose communications system. On the other hand, visitors often find it very expensive. There are various prepaid telephone cards that will give approximately 100 minutes of world-wide calling time for $10. Prepaid telephone cards can be purchased in souvenir stores, most tourism destinations, telephone companies, malls, and grocery stores.

Dialing Numbers

In the US all phone numbers have a 3-digit area code followed by a 7-digit local number. If you are calling a number with a different area code (usually long distance) you have to dial 1 then the 3-digit area code, then the 7 digit local number. Major US-destination area codes are listed in each destination section of this book.

International Calls

If you want to make a direct international call you have to dial 011 followed by the country code that you are dialing and the phone number. Be aware that dialing international call through the operator can be surprisingly expensive.

Pay Phones

Pay phones are available almost anywhere in the city. You will need nickels, dimes, and quarters for coined pay phones. Local calls usually cost 35 cents to up to 75 cents for the first few minutes, depending on the local area you are calling. There are also modern public phones that accept credit cards or prepaid phone cards.

Hotel Phones

Most five star hotels charge their guest for any local or international phone calls they make, and it can be costly. It is wise to use public pay phones in the lobby if you need to make a call. Most smaller hotels and motels offer free local calls to their customers.

Fax & Telegram

If you need to send a fax you can ask your hotel for any information or services available within the hotel or around the area. There are office service supplies around the city that offer such services where sending fax in the US can cost you up to $1 per page. Telegraph can be sent through Western Union, toll-free (800) 325-6000.

Internet Access

Most hotels, motels, and hostels offer a computer with Internet access. Places like internet cafés and office center offer internet access for $10 an hour or $1 for a few minutes. Some Internet service providers exhibit their services in malls offering free Internet access. Most public libraries in the US allow visitors to use computers and Internet access.

Post Office

US Postal services, or USPS, handles postal services in the US. Postal in the US is inexpensive and reliable. Postcard stamps that are bound within the US cost 21 cents while postcards stamps bound internationally cost 85 cents. First class letter postage to any US destination (up to one ounce) costs 37 cents, plus 23 cents for each additional once.

Money Matters

US Currency

US currency comes in denominations of 1 cent (penny), 5 cent (nickel), 10 cent (dime), 25 cent (quarter), 50 cent (half-dollar) and a dollar (in forms of coin and paper money). Notes come in $1, $2, $5, $10, $20, $50, and $100 denominations.

Cash

It is advisable to carry some small amount of cash with you. 25 cents (quarter), $1, $5, $10, and $20 are the most widely used denominations, so always keep a handful of them with you. You might need cash for bus, metro, tips and other small expenses.

Travelers Checks

The most popular and probably safest way of keeping your money while traveling is to buy travelers checks. A travelers check is as good as cash and is available in several denominations: get them in 20s, 50s and 100. Buy them in US$ to avoid any hassles of going to a bank to change it to US$. You have to sign each check and re-sign them each time you use one. In case of theft or loss, notify the bank or company which issued the checks and make sure to keep a copy of all the check numbers. The most popular travelers checks are American Express and Thomas Cook: both are widely acknowledged and have good policies.

Credit Cards and Debit Cards

Credit cards are widely used in the US and are very useful for emergency purposes. In addition, most credit cards offer a purchase guarantee plan while traveling. Some establishments require credit cards when making reservations (hotels, rent-a-car, etc.); therefore, a couple of credit cards will be useful.

Major Credit Cards Customer Service	
American Express	toll-free (800) 5289135
MasterCard	toll-free (800) 3077309
Visa Card	toll-free (800) 3368472

Taxes

Taxes are varied in each state, and it is almost certain that everything you pay or purchase in the US is being taxed. Sales taxes are different in each state and county, ranging between 4% and 8.5%. There might be other separate taxes (local or city taxes) applied each time you buy or pay for any service in the US, so be sure to ask if tax is included in the price before paying.

Tipping

In the US tipping in restaurants is expected. Normally tips are from 15% to 20% of the total amount of your total receipt. 15% is a standard tip for most services.

Exchange Rates

There are currency exchange counters in most airports and at the border. On the other hand, banks still offer better rates. The following are general exchange rate estimates.

International Exchange Rate		
Country	Units/USD	USD/Units
Australia (Dollar)	1.8552	0.5390
Brazil (Real)	2.3419	0.4270
Canada (Dollar)	1.5728	0.6358
China (Renminbi)	8.2779	0.1208
Denmark (Krone)	8.3704	0.1195
Europe (Euro)*	1.1264	0.8878
Great Britain (Pound)	0.6901	1.4491
Hong Kong (Dollar)	7.7993	0.1282
India (Rupee)	48.905	0.02045
Indonesia (Rupiah)	9361.9	0.0001068
Japan (Yen)	129.951	0.00770
Malaysia (Ringgit)	3.8000	0.2632
Mexico (New Peso)	9.2518	0.1081
Morocco (Dirham)	11.5308	0.0867
New Zealand (Dollar)	2.2395	0.4465
Norway (Krone)	8.5711	0.1167
Philippines (Peso)	50.916	0.01964
Russia (Rouble)	31.182	0.03207
Singapore (Dollar)	1.8153	0.5509
South Africa (Rand)	10.9756	0.0911
South Korea (Won)	1304.15	0.000767
Sri Lanka (Rupee)	96.078	0.01041
Sweden (Krona)	10.3610	0.0965
Switzerland (Franc)	1.6540	0.6046
Taiwan (Dollar)	34.796	0.02874
Thailand (Baht)	43.244	0.02312
Trinidad/Tobago (Dollar)	6.1198	0.1634
Venezuela (Bolivar)	855.71	0.001169

Note: Euro (Austria, Belgium, Finland, France, Germany, Greece, Italy, Ireland, Luxembourg, Netherlands, Portugal, and Spain).

Parks and National Parks

The US is blessed with numerous natural wonders and historical places, and both have become a part of the National Park System which was created in 1916 to promote the preservation of US national treasures. There are more than 360 federal sites in 20 different categories which are designated as national treasures, two of the most well known and visited are the National Parks (established for the preservation of the exceptional natural beauty of America's natural wonders, rich wildlife, and biodiversity) and the National Monuments (designated to protect national historical sites).

Fees

Fees are required in most every park to help finance and contribute to the preservation of the park. Park Fees are paid at the entrance of each National Park. A 7-day entrance fee for vehicles and passengers is $20; 7-day individual fee (in a bus, on foot, bicycle, motorcycle, or horse) is $10; each national park has one year passes for $40.

National Park Pass

The National Parks Pass is an annual pass that provides admission to any US national park that charges an entrance fee. National pass covers the pass holder's vehicle -including the passengers or the pass holder's spouse, children, and parents.

The National Pass costs $50 and is valid for one year based on the date of purchase and it is nontransferable. Visitors can purchase the National Parks Pass at the entrance of any national park or at participating park bookstores. You can purchase the national park pass through mail by sending a $50 check or money order (plus $3.95 for freight) payable to the National Parks Pass, 27540 Avenue Mentry, Valencia, CA 91355; or online at <<http://www.nationalparks.org>>; or call toll-free (888) GO-PARKS. For campground information and reservations call (800) 436-7275 or (800) 365-2267, and (800) 967-2283 for tour reservations.

Golden Eagle

The Golden Eagle hologram may be purchased for an additional $15 and attached to a National Parks Pass to allow travelers to also visit sites managed by the U. S. Fish and Wildlife Service, the U. S. Forest Service, and the Bureau of Land Management. The Golden Eagle holograms are available at National Park Service, Fish and Wildlife Service, and Bureau of Land Management fee stations. The Golden Eagle is nontransferable and is valid until the expiration of the National Parks Pass to which it is attached.

Golden Age Passport and Golden Access Passport

Golden Age Passport is available for senior citizens (62 or older) or permanent residents of the United States while the Golden Access Passport is available for disabled citizens or permanent residents of the United States.

Both passports offer lifetime entrance to US national parks, national wildlife refuges, recreation areas, monuments, and historic sites, and provide various discounts on federal use fees for facilities and services. Both passports are nontransferable and a one-time $10 processing charge for Golden Age Passport application will be charged. You can obtain the passport at any national park.

City Pass

Using CityPass will allow visitors to explore some of the most visited cities of the United States with discounted tickets in a convenient way. CityPass is an actual admission ticket for major attractions of the participating cities. US cities under CityPass are New York, Boston, Philadelphia, Chicago, Seattle, Hollywood (Los Angeles), and San Francisco.

CityPass is valid for nine days after the first day you use it, with exception of Hollywood where it is valid for 30 days from the first day you use it. You can purchase CityPass ticket in any of the participating cities at the first attraction you are visiting. You can also purchase CityPass at your travel agent or online at the CityPass website <<http://www.citypass.com/>>. For information contact City Pass Public Relations and Promotions at Post Office Box 25124, 7635 E. Tail Feather Drive, Scottsdale, AZ 85255. Tel: (480) 513-4746.

US National Parks		
Alabama	**Colorado**	**North Dakota**
-Little River Canyon	-Black Canyon of the Gunnison	-Theodore Roosevelt
Alaska	-Great Sand Dunes	**Ohio**
-Bering Land Bridge	-Mesa Verde	-Cuyahoga Valley
-Denali	-Rocky Mountain	**Oregon**
-Gates of the Arctic	**Florida**	-Crater Lake
-Glacier Bay	-Big Cypress	**South Dakota**
-Katmai	-Biscayne	-Badlands
-Kenai Fjords	-Dry Tortugas	-Wind Cave
-Kobuk Valley	-Everglades	**Tennessee**
-Lake Clark	**Hawaii**	-Great Smoky Mountains
-Noatak	-Haleakala	**Texas**
-Wrangell-St. Elias	-Hawaii Volcanoes	-Big Bend
-Yukon-Charley Rivers	**Kentucky**	-Big Thicket
Arizona	-Mammoth Cave	-Guadalupe Mountains
-Saguaro	**Maine**	**Utah**
-Grand Canyon	-Acadia	-Arches
-Petrified Forest	**Michigan**	-Bryce Canyon
Arkansas	-Isle Royale	-Canyonlands
-Hot Springs	**Minnesota**	-Capitol Reef
California	-Voyageurs	-Zion
-Channel Islands	**Montana**	**Virginia**
-Death Valley	-Glacier	-Prince William Forest
-Joshua Tree	**Nevada**	-Shenandoah
-Kings Canyon & Sequoia	-Great Basin	**Washington**
National Park		-Mount Rainier
-Lassen Volcanic	**New Mexico**	-North Cascades
-Mojave Desert	-Carlsbad Caverns	-Olympic National Park
-Redwood	**North Carolina**	**Wyoming**
-Yosemite National Park	-Great Smoky Mountains	-Grand Teton
		- Yellowstone

Photography

A digital camera gives you flexibility and freedom to shoot and experiment. Before leaving home take time to explore your camera to understand it best. Digital cameras use a lot of batteries, so avoid using your viewfinder if possible as it will save you battery power that you need, especially during a long day trip. Remember to charge the batteries before going to sleep.

Most digital cameras have a delay between pressing the shutter button and the actual picture being taken, therefore hold the camera firmly and wait until the shutter is completely off. Setting your camera at the highest resolution will give you more flexibility in adjusting the picture size before printing it and produce better picture clarity.

Equip your digital camera with a sufficient memory card, an 8 or 16 MB (megabyte) card will give you as little as 30 shots; a 128 MB card will give you more than 300 shots, enough to give you freedom to shoot as many pictures as you wish in each destination. Take time deleting those unwanted shots during your trip; it will give your camera more room for much needed shots later. If you are carrying a laptop computer with you, download stored pictures and then you can reset (empty) your digital camera memory.

Cameras using 35 mm film should use 100 ISO film for sunny or bright conditions, medium speed films (200 ISO) for multi-purpose indoor or outdoor photography with flash, and for low light or flash indoor or outdoor use 400 ISO. Both ISO 200 and 400 are good for all around photography. In addition, 400 ISO speed film is ideal when shooting in soft light or when using flash at distance of more than 10 feet. 800 ISO is faster speed film and provides better color and sharpness for use in low light or when shooting moving objects. Films are available in any grocery store, drug store, and photo store in the US. There are several packages for developing film; prices are from $7 to $15 with a one-hour processing service.

Taking Pictures

If you are taking a portrait picture, try to move closer to fill most of the frame with your subject(s), thus you will avoid taking any undesirable background. On the contrary, if you are taking a picture landscape, try to widen your lens to cover as much view as possible.

The best time for taking pictures (especially landscape photography) is during early morning and late afternoon when the light is softer. Make sure the sun is behind you where it will not to block the camera lens but will shine on the subject. When using a flash indoors, avoid pointing your flash at the glass to avoid unwanted reflections. If taking a shot from the window remember to turn off your flash and place your camera close to the window to avoid reflection, use a polarized filter if you have one.

If you are using a digital camera, take as many pictures as possible: it will give you wider choices of the better and special shots that you like. Then delete unwanted shots later to free your camera's memory. Give yourself time to pick the best view, don't shoot the first thing you see, it is wise to plan your every shot. If you are taking a regular shot, always level your camera with your subject(s) and hold it firm. And remember to avoid posed pictures, try to be more relaxed and natural.

Transportation

Air Travel

The US is well connected by air to the four corners of the world. Major international airlines fly several times each day serving all major cities and destinations in the US.

Domestic Air Travel

If you want to travel by train one way and fly the other way, Amtrak has teamed up with some airlines to provide a cheaper and more convenient passenger travel. Ask your travel agency for information or call Amtrak for combined rail and air information at toll-free (800) 525-0280. The event of the September 11 terrorist attacks in the US have increased airport, baggage, and airline security concerns resulting in somewhat uncomfortable scrutinizing security measures at the airport. More delays in flight schedules and in some bizarre situations, passengers are being forced to evacuate the airport terminal for re-screening.

There are several airlines serving all 50 states and all major destinations in the US. Consult your travel agent, or log on to the Internet and check some travel websites that offer great deals on air tickets. Plan your air travel in advance in order to get the best price. <<http://www.travelocity.com>>,<<http://www.orbiz.com>>, <<http://www.cheaptravel.net>>, and <<http://www.expedia.com>>

List of Major International and Domestic Airlines in the US			
AeroMexico	-(800) 2376639	KLM	-(800) 3747747
Air Canada	-(800) 7763000	Korean Airlines	-(800) 4385000
Air France	-(800) 2372747	Lufthansa	-(800) 6453880
Air Jamaica	-(800) 5235585	Malaysian Airlines	-(800) 5529264
Air New Zealand	-(800) 2621234	Mexicana Airlines	-(800) 5317921
Alaska Airlines	-(800) 4260333	Northwest Airlines	-(800) 2252525
Alitalia	-(800) 2235730	Philippine Airlines	-(800) 4359725
All Nippon	-(800) 2359262	Qantas	-(800) 2274500
America West	-(800) 2359292	Royal Jordanian	-(800) 2230470
American Airlines	-(800) 4337300	Scandinavian Airlines	-(800) 2212350
Austrian Airlines	-(800) 8430002	Singapore Airlines	-(800) 7423333
British Airways	-(800) 2479297	South African Airways	-(800) 7229675
Canadian Airlines	-(800) 4267000	Swissair	-(800) 2214750
Cathay Pacific	-(800) 2332742	TAP Air Portugal	-(800) 2217370
China Airlines	-(800) 2275118	Thai Airways	-(800) 4265204
Continental Air	-(800) 5250280	Transbrazil Airlines	-(800) 8723153
Delta Airlines	-(800) 2211212	TWA (Int'l)	-(800) 8924141
El Al Israel Airline	-(800) 2236700	United Airlines	-(800) 2416522
Finn Air	-(800) 9505000	USAir	-(800) 4284322
Iberia Airlines	-(800) 7724642	Varig Brazilian Airlines	-(800) 4682744
Japan Airlines	-(800) 5253663	Virgin Atlantic	-(800) 8628621

US Airport Codes

ANC	Anchorage International Airport	JFK	New York (Kennedy) International Airport
BHM	Birmingham International Airport	LGA	New York (La Guardia) Airport
ORD	Chicago (O'Hare) International Airport	OAK	Oakland International Airport
DFW	Dallas/Fort Worth International Airport	MCO	Orlando International Airport
DEN	Denver International Airport	PHL	Philadelphia International Airport
DTW	Detroit (Wayne County) Metropolitan Airport	PHX	Phoenix (Sky Harbor) International Airport
ATL	Harts field Atlanta International Airport	PIT	Pittsburgh International Airport
HNL	Honolulu International Airport	SLC	Salt Lake City International Airport
LAS	Las Vegas (McCarran) International Airport	SAN	San Diego International Airport
LAX	Los Angeles International Airport	SFO	San Francisco International Airport
MIA	Miami International Airport	SEA	Seattle/Tacoma Airport
MSP	Minneapolis/ St. Paul International Airport	STL	St. Louis International Airport
MSY	New Orleans International Airport	DC	Washington D.C. (National) Airport
EWR	Newark International Airport	IAD	Washington D.C. (Dulles) International Airport

Railways

The US has 137,707.5 miles (225,750 km) of train routes and 22,000 route-miles are served by commercial train routes. Interstate commercial train services are provided by Amtrak, bringing people to more than 500 destinations around the US with connections to Canada's major cities. Other destinations are connected by motor coaches that are provided by Amtrak. Traveling by train has always been associated with comfort, romance, and pleasure. In addition to these, the advantage of traveling by train is the experience that it has to offer: a chance to see beautiful sceneries and natural wonders, a chance to experience part of the American heritage, and a chance to see the beautiful and elegant train stations located at the heart of cities like Los Angeles, Chicago, New York, Washington D.C, and Boston.

Commuter trains serve short routes in most major cities in the US with multiple schedules each day. They are the fastest and most convenient way of local transportation, but not necessarily the cheapest. Some commuter services are integrated in an Amtrak Rail Pass.

Commuter and Light Rail Transit Services

Many regard commuter rail as an answer to the growing road traffic congestion common in most US big cities. Commuter railways, unlike interstate railways, are designed to move passengers only as far as 100 miles, typically just outside the city or within metropolitan areas. In the US, just like in other countries, commuter trains are commonly financed and managed by a governmental agency.

There are 22 commuter railroad services in the US serving the nation's most populous and industrious cities. Amtrak provides the largest contract-commuter services in the US, serving the states of California, Maryland, Massachusetts, Connecticut, and Virginia. Due to the growing popularity of commuter services, there is continuous on-going development to improve facilities, services, departure frequencies, and to replace old equipment.

Commuter rail is one of the fastest ways to travel within the region, on the other hand, remember that taking commuter trains during morning and evening office rush hours could be uncomfortable. Discounted weekly or monthly multiple ride tickets are available in most cities. The following is a list of commuter train services in the US with address, contact numbers, and websites.

Commuter Railways

Metra Passenger Services (Chicago Commuter Rail Service), 547 West Jackson, Chicago, IL 60661; Tel: (312) 322-6777 or (312) 836-7000; <<http://www.metrarail.com>>.

Tri-County Commuter Rail Authority (South Florida) 800 NW 33rd Street, Suite 100, Pompano Beach, FL 33064; Tel: (800) TRI-RAIL (874-7245) or (305) 836-0986; <<http://www.tri-rail.com>>

Sounder (Seattle), Union Station, 401 S. Jackson St., Seattle, WA 98104; Tel: (206) 398 5000 or (206) 398.5410 (TTY); <<http://www.sounder.org>>

Metrolink (Los Angeles, CA) 700 South Flower Street, Suite 2600, Los Angeles, CA 90017; Tel: (800) 371-LINK (5465) or (213) 347-2800; <<http://www.metrolinktrains.com>>.

ACE (Stockton, CA) P.O. Box 31360, Stockton, CA 95213; Tel: (800)-411-RAIL; <<http://www.acerail.com>>.

Caltrain (San Carlos, CA) 1250 San Carlos Avenue, San Carlos, CA 94070-1306; Tel: (800) 660-4287; <<http://www.caltrain.com/caltrain/index.html>>

North County Transit District (Oceanside, CA) 810 Mission Avenue, Oceanside, CA 92054; Tel: (800)-COMMUTE (266-6883) or (800) COASTER (262-7837). <<http://www.gonctd.com/coaster>>.

Northern Indiana Commuter Transportation District (Chesterton, IN) 33 East U.S. Highway 12, Chesterton, IN 46304; Tel: (800) 356-2079; <<http://www.nictd.com>>.

Rideworks (New Haven, CT) 389 Whitney Avenue, New Haven, CT 06511; Tel: (800) ALL-RIDE (255-7433); <<http://www.rideworks.com/sle>>.

Virginia Railway Express (Alexandria, VA) 1500 King Street, Suite 202, Alexandria, VA 22314; Tel: (703) 684-1001; <<http://www.vre.org>>

Mass Transit Administration of Maryland (MARC) (BWI Airport, MD) BWI Airport, MD; Tel: (800) 325-RAIL (325-7245); <<http://www.mtamaryland.com>>

Massachusetts Bay Transportation Authority (Boston, MA) 10 Park Plaza, Boston, MA 02116; Tel: (617) 222-5000; <<http://www.mbta.com>>.

New Jersey Transit (Newark, NJ) 1 Penn Plaza East, Newark, NJ, 07105-2246; Tel: (800) 772-2222 or (973) 762-5100; <<http://www.njtransit.com>>

OnTrack City Express (Syracuse, NY) P.O. Box 1245, Syracuse, NY 13201; Tel: (800) FOR-TRAIN (367-8724) or (315) 424-1212: <<http://www.syracuseontrack.com>>.

Long Island Rail Road (Jamaica, NY) Jamaica Station, Jamaica, NY 11435; Tel: (718) 558-7400; <<http://www.lirr.org/lirr/>>.

Metro-North Railroad (New York, NY) 347 Madison Avenue, New York, NY 10017; Tel: (800) METRO-INFO (638-7646) or (212) 532-4900; <<http://www.mta.nyc.ny.us/mnr/index.html>>.

Trinity Railway Express (Dallas, TX) P.O. Box 660163, Dallas, TX 75266-0163; Tel: (214) 979-1111 or (877) 657-0146; <<http://www.trinityrailwayexpress.org>>.

Vermont Transportation Authority (Burlington, VT) 1 Main Street Landing, Suite 101 Burlington, VT 05401; Tel: (802) 951-4010; <<http://www.champlainflyer.com>> and <<http://www.vermontrail.org>>.

Sound Transit (Seattle, WA) 401 South Jackson Street, Seattle, WA 98104; Tel: (206) 398-5000 or (888) 889-6368; <<http://www.soundtransit.org>>.

Southeastern Pennsylvania Transportation Authority (Philadelphia, PA) 1234 Market Street, Philadelphia, PA 19107; Tel: (215) 880-7800; <<http://www.septa.org>>.

Light Rail Transits
DART-Dallas Area Rapid Transit (Dallas, TX), 1401 Pacific Avenue, Dallas, Texas 75202; Tel: (214) 979-1111; <<http://www.dart.org/home.htm>>
GCRTA (Cleveland, OH), 315 Euclid Avenue, Cleveland, OH 44114; Tel: (216) 566 5227; <<http://www.gcrta.org>>
Hudson-Bergen (Hudson, NJ), 1 Penn Plaza East, Newark, NJ; Tel: (800) 772-2222 or (973) 762-5100 out of state; <<http://www.njtransit.com>>
Link (Seattle, WA), Union Station, 401 S. Jackson St., Seattle, WA 98104; Tel: (206) 398.5000 or (206) 398 5410 (TTY); <<http://www.linkrail.org>>
MAX (Portland, OR), 4012 SE 17th, Portland 97202; Tel: (503) 962-2444; <<http://www.tri-met.org/max>>
MBTA (Boston, MA), 45 High Street, 9th Floor, Boston, MA 02110 Tel: (617)-222-5000 or (800)-392-6100; <<http://www.mbta.com/Schedmaps/index.cfm>>
Metro-link (St. Louis, MO), call Tel: (314) 982-1406 for information; <<http://www.bi-state.org/index.htm>>
Metro Rail (Los Angeles, CA), One Gateway Plaza, Los Angeles, CA 90012-2952; Tel: (800) COMMUTE; <<http://www.mta.net>>
MTA (Baltimore, MD), Tel: (410) 539-5000 or call toll-free (866) 743-3682; <<http://www.mtamaryland.com/light_rail/light_rail.asp>>
NFTA (Buffalo, NY), 181 Ellicott Street, Buffalo, NY 14203; Tel: (716) 855-7300; <<http://www.nfta.com/metro>>
RTD (Denver, CO), 1600 Blake Street, Denver, Colorado 80202; Tel: (303) 628 9000 or (303) 299 6000; <<http://www.rtd-denver.com>>
San Diego Trolley (San Diego, CA), 1255 Imperial Ave. Ste. 900, San Diego, CA 92101-7490; Tel: (619) 595-4949 <<http://www.sdcommute.com/service/trolleypage.htm>>
Septa (Philadelphia, PA), 1234 Market Street, Philadelphia, Pennsylvania 19107-3780; Tel: (215)-580-7800; <<http://www.septa.com/riding/subways.html>>
SF Muni (San Francisco, CA), 949 Presidio Avenue, #243, San Francisco, CA 94115; Tel: (415) 923-6864; <<http://www.sfmuni.com/>>
BART San Francisco Bay Area Rapid Transit District (San Francisco, CA), serving San Francisco and the Bay area; P.O. Box 12688, Oakland CA 94606-2688; Tel: (510) 465-2278 or (415) 989-2278; <<http://www.bart.gov/index.asp>>
SRTD (Sacramento, CA), 1400 29th Street (at N Street), Sacramento, CA 95816; Tel: (916) 321-2800; <<http://www.sacrt.com>>
The "T" (Pittsburgh, PA), 345 Sixth Avenue, 3rd Floor, Pittsburgh, Pennsylvania 15222-2527; Tel: (412) 442-2000; <<http://www.portauthority.org>>
TRAX (Salt Lake City, UT); Tel: (801) RIDE-UTA (743-3882) or (888) RIDE-UTA (743-3882); <<http://www.utabus.com>>
VTA (San Jose, CA), serving the city of San Jose, Santa Clara, Sunnyvale and Mountain View; 3331 North First Street, San Jose, CA 95134-1906; Tel: (408) 321-2300 or (800) 894-9908; <<http://www.vta.org/light_rail_services.html>>

Bus

Like Amtrak, Greyhound serves the interstate bus routes in the US, including more than 3,700 destinations in North America (excluding Alaska), with connections via local bus in some towns that do not have Greyhound direct services. Interstate bus travel is often agonizing and not necessarily convenient; on the other hand, taking local bus could be one of the cheapest and easiest ways to explore your city destination.

Greyhound's Discovery Pass is designed to make your bus travel easy. It allows travelers to travel in the region of their choice at their convenience on a single pass. For information on fares & schedules call toll-free (800) 229-9424 or Tel: (402) 330-8552. Passengers with disabilities should call toll-free (800) 752-4841 for assistance and additional information. You could also visit Greyhound's website at <<http://www.greyhound.com/>>.

Each major destination in this book has a list and useful information about **local city bus** service. Standard bus fare starts at $1.35 with discounts for seniors and disabled passengers. If you need to transfer buses to reach your destination, you should ask for transfer ticket in order to save money. Bus traveling also offers a chance to meet and interact with the locals and learn.

It is standard that all local buses in the US have basic facilities for disabled passengers, and nearly all buses have wheelchair lifts. In addition there are sometimes bicycle racks, which can hold up to two bicycles on the front of the bus.

Rent-A-Car

There are various car rental companies in the US and prices are varied in each state. Cars are priced based on the type and class of the car that you are renting. An "economy" car is the least that you can rent, expect to pay from $20 to $40 a day, plus tax and optional insurance. It is wise to check and compare prices in larger cities; it is likely that you will find better deals because of increased competition. Ask for discounts, especially if you intend to rent a car for few days. You have to be at least 21 years old with a valid driver's license or international driver's license, and you will need a major credit card to rent a car.

Car Rental Companies	
Alamo	(800) 327-9633
Avis	(800) 831-2847
Budget	(800) 527-0700
Dollar	(800) 800-4000
Enterprise	(800) 325-8007
Hertz	(800) 654-3131
National Car Rentals	(800) 227-7368
Payless	(800) 237-2804
Sears	(800) 527-0770
Thrifty	(800) 367-2277

Be sure to check if the rental contract you are signing includes liability insurance (it is required by law in most states); Americans are covered by their regular car liability insurance policy. If liability insurance is not included on your contract you might want to consider buying it from the car rental company (most car rental companies sell insurance packages). Common optional insurance like Loss Damage Waiver (LDW) and Collision Damage Waiver (CDW) insurance are available at $8. Check with your credit card company for any car insurance liability coverage.

Some rental companies offer unlimited mileage and some will include a certain number of miles, after which you have to pay the exceeding miles. Therefore, you should plan ahead how long you will need a car and how far you are planning to drive. It is wise to consult your travel agency for a fly-drive package while you're still in your home country as they often have better deals and more attractive packages.

There is a list of major rental car companies for every major destination discussed in this book. Major train stations have lists and contacts for rental car companies near the station, and pickup services to/from the station is provided by some rental companies.

Visitors Information Center/Tourist Information Center

Visitor's or Tourist Information Center information is listed for each major destination in this book. These centers provide assistance and information to travelers. Brochures, local information, and promotional materials can be obtained through mail upon request. It is also wise to visit the visitor's information center to gather current events and information; some centers provide free area maps, pamphlets, and local attractions discounts.

Small towns have a **Chamber of Commerce,** run by local businesses that often provide information and lists of attractions, hotels, motels, restaurants, and other local services. The **Convention & Visitors Bureau** promotes the city's facilites and benefits for businesses looking to hold conventions, conferences, and trade expositions. The bureau does not provide assistance and information to walk-in tourists.

US Ten Most Visited Cities

Based on the studies conducted by the US Government Tourism Industry, the most popular cities visited by overseas travelers on year 2000 are: New York City (5.7 million), Los Angeles (3.5 million), Orlando (3.0 million), Miami (2.9 million), San Francisco (2.8 million), Las Vegas (2.3 million), Honolulu (2.2 million), Washington, DC (1.5 million), Chicago (1.4 million), and Boston (1.3 million).

US Ten Most Visited States/Territory					
2000 Rank	State/Territory	2000 Market Share	2000 Visitation (000)	1999 Market Share	1999 Visitation (000)
1	California	24.5%	6,364	25.5%	6,239
2	Florida	23.2%	6,026	23.7%	5,798
3	New York	22.8%	5,922	23.7%	5,798
4	Hawaiian Islands	10.5%	2,727	11.2%	2,740
5	Nevada	9.1%	2,364	9.7%	2,373
6	Massachusetts	5.5%	1,429	5.4%	1,321
7	Illinois	5.3%	1,377	5.4%	1,321
8	Guam	5.1%	1,325	4.2%	1,028
9	Texas	4.5%	1,169	4.3%	1,052
10	New Jersey	3.5%	909	3.7%	905
Sources: US Government Tourism Industry					

Places to see in US

West and Pacific Coast		Midwest	East Coast

West and Pacific Coast

Wyoming
✓ Yellowstone National Park
✓ Grand Teton

Utah
✓ Salt Lake City
✓ Arches
✓ Bryce Canyon
✓ Capitol Reef
✓ Glen Canyon
✓ Rainbow Bridge
✓ Zion

Colorado
✓ Rocky Mountain

Nevada
✓ Las Vegas
✓ Carson City
✓ Lake Tahoe
✓ Lake Mead

New Mexico
✓ Albuquerque
✓ Santa Fe
✓ Carlsbad Caverns National Park
✓ Salinas Pueblo Mission

Arizona
✓ Grand Canyon
✓ Phoenix
✓ Flagstaff

✓ Sunset Crater Volcano

Washington
✓ City of Seattle
✓ Olympic National Park
✓ Mt. Rainer
✓ Mt. Saint Helens

Oregon
✓ City of Portland
✓ City of Salem

California
✓ Redwood National Park
✓ San Francisco
✓ Lake Tahoe
✓ Monterey
✓ Yosemite National Park
✓ Sequoia and King's Canyon National Park
✓ Death Valley
✓ Santa Barbara
✓ Los Angeles
✓ San Diego
✓ Palm Springs

Midwest

South Dakota
✓ Mt. Rushmore

Missouri
✓ St. Louis
✓ Kansas City

Illinois
✓ Chicago
✓ Springfield

Louisiana
✓ New Orleans

Texas
✓ San Antonio
✓ Ft. Worth-Dallas
✓ Houston
✓ Austin
✓ El Paso
✓ Big Bend Natl. Park

East Coast

New York
✓ Niagara Falls
✓ New York City

Massachusetts
✓ Boston

Pennsylvania
✓ Philadelphia

Maryland
✓ Baltimore

District of Columbia
✓ Washington D.C.

Georgia
✓ Atlanta

Florida
✓ Jacksonville
✓ Orlando
✓ Tampa
✓ Miami
✓ Everglades National Park

Chapter-4

Train travel Tips

Train Tickets and Passes

Train tickets are available in coach class, Metroliner and Club/Custom class, Business class, and Sleeping Car accommodation. Coach class is the average Amtrak ticket available on every train route. Metroliner and Club/Custom class tickets are offered mostly in Acela and North Corridor train routes providing travelers first class service and additional facilities. Business Class coach tickets, available in some Northeast and Midwest train routes and the Empire routes, provide travelers with roomier coaches, telephone facilities, changing rooms, personal audio equipment and other added services. Sleeping car accommodations are available only on Amtrak long distance routes and are purchased separately in addition to your tickets.

The cost of your train tickets will be based on the distance traveled and the type of service provided. Remember it is always cheaper to travel during low season, and check any special offers, vacation deals, and seasonal fares for a better deal. A maximum of two children aged 2-15 years old accompanied by a full fare traveler are entitled to half-price fare. Children under 2 years old are free. Seniors and students holding a Student Advantage program card are entitled to up to a 15% discount on most coach fares. There are also special discounts for veterans and disabled passengers. Group travelers are entitled to discounts and other special deals, visit the Amtrak website or call (800) USA-1-GRP for information.

Using Passes is the most economical way of traveling the US by train. There are various type of passes available: the USA Rail Pass designed for international travelers, the North American Rail Pass that allows passengers to travel both the US and Canada under one ticket, and the California Rail Pass that gives you the opportunity to explore California at a reduced fare.

USA Rail Pass

USA Rail Passes are available to non-US residents or foreign travelers. The pass can be purchased outside the US though a travel agency, Amtrak International sales Representative Agency (see Amtrak worldwide sales representatives at "Useful Informaiton and Tips" chapter) or at the Amtrak online ticketing and reservation website <<http://www.Amtrak.com>>. You can also purchase your US rail pass at the Union Station or in most US train depots inside the US.

Make your reservations as early as possible, prepare an itinerary of your train travel, and present it to any Amtrak representative at the ticketing and reservation booth. USA Rail Passes are valid for all Amtrak destinations designated by the type of pass you are holding except Auto Rail and the Canadian section of trains operated jointly by Amtrak and Rail Canada. A valid non-US passport is required when purchasing a US Rail Pass. Always keep a picture ID and your tickets with you for identification. USA Rail Passes are refundable before your travel begins, however Amtrak cancellation policy changes from time to time so check with any Amtrak representative or agency for current policies.

The USA Rail Pass tickets are valid for regular train coach class, and are valid for all Acela Regional and Northeast Direct trains. However, travels on Acela Express, Metroliner train Business class, Club class and Sleeping Car accommodations require additional charges.

There are six different US Rail Passes that cover different regions of the United States: Far West Rail Pass, West Rail Pass, East Rail Pass, North East Rail Pass, Coastal Rail Pass and the National Rail Pass.

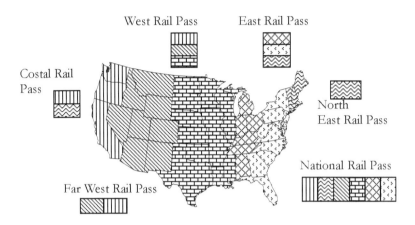

The USA Rail Passes

The **Far West Rail Pass** covers most of the Rocky Mountains to the Pacific Coast (includes the states of Washington, Oregon, California, Idaho, Nevada, Utah, Arizona, and parts of New Mexico, Colorado Wyoming, and Montana).

A 15-Day rail pass costs $190 (Off-Peak Season) and $245 (Peak Season), while a 30-Day rail pass costs $250 (Off Season) and $320 (Peak Season).

The **West Rail Pass** covers US Western and Pacific Coast routes from Chicago across the city of New Orleans (includes the states of Washington, Oregon, California, Idaho, Nevada, Utah, Arizona, New Mexico, Colorado, Wyoming, Montana, Texas, Kansas, Oklahoma, Nebraska, North Dakota, Minneapolis, Iowa, Wisconsin, Illinois, Missouri, Arkansas, part of Mississippi, Tennessee, Louisiana and Kentucky).

A 15-Day rail pass costs $200 (Off-Season) and $325 (Peak Season), while a 30-Day rail pass costs $270 (Off Season) and $405 (Peak Season).

The **East Rail Pass** covers most of the historic sites of the eastern United States, connecting Chicago to the rest of the eastern coast of the United States (includes the states of Illinois, Ohio, Michigan, Pennsylvania, New York, New Jersey, Maryland, Delaware, Connecticut, Rhode Island, Massachusetts, Maine, New Hampshire, West Virginia, Virginia,

Vermont and the District of Columbia; also includes the states of South and North Carolina, Georgia, Florida, Tennessee, Kentucky, Indiana, Alabama, and Mississippi and parts of Louisiana).

A 15-Day rail pass costs $210 (Off Season) and $260 (Peak Season), while a 30-Day rail pass costs $265 (Off Season) and $320 (Peak Season).

The **North East Rail Pass** covers most of the US East border routes with Canada (includes the states of Pennsylvania, New York, Maryland, Delaware, New Jersey, Connecticut, Richmond, Massachusetts, Maine, New Hampshire, Vermont and the District of Columbia). A 15-Day rail pass costs $185 (Off Season) and $205 (Peak Season), while a 30-Day rail pass costs $225 (Off Season) and $240 (Peak Season).

US Rail Pass			
Pass	5 Days	15 Days	30 Days
National			
Peak		$440	$550
Off-Peak		$295	$385
Far West Rail Pass			
Peak		$245	$320
Off-Peak		$190	$250
West Rail Pass			
Peak		$325	$405
Off-Peak		$200	$270
East Rail Pass			
Peak		$260	$320
Off-Peak		$210	$265
North East Rail Pass			
Peak	$149	$205	$240
Off-Peak	$149	$185	$225
Coastal Rail Pass			
Peak			$285
Off-Peak			$235

The **Coastal Rail Pass** covers both the Atlantic and the Pacific coasts of the United States (includes the states of Washington, Oregon and California of the US Pacific Coast and the states of Florida, Georgia, South and North Carolina, Pennsylvania, Maryland, Virginia, New York, Washington D.C, Delaware, New Jersey, Connecticut, Rhode Island, Massachusetts, Maine, New Hampshire, and Vermont in the US Atlantic Coast).

The Costal Rail Pass is only available in the 30-Day duration and costs $235 (Off Season) and $285 (Peak Season).

The **National Rail Pass** covers the whole of mainland United States (not including US territories and states outside the US mainland). A 15-Day rail pass costs $295 (Off Season) and $440 (Peak Season), while a 30-Day rail pass costs $385 (Off Season) and $550 (Peak Season).

Peak fares are in effect from June through August while off-Peak are from September through July. All fares are in US dollars and are subject to change. Check the Amtrak web site for up-to-date fares.

California Rail Pass	
Pass	Fare
Statewide Pass	$159
Northern California Pass	$99
Southern California Pass	$99

California Rail Pass

California Rail Pass allows visitors to travel and explore the state of

California for less. There are three California Rail Pass options: the 7-in-21 Day Statewide Pass, the 5-in-7 Day Northern California Pass, and the 5-in-7 Day Southern California Pass. The Statewide Pass travels to almost one hundred destinations across the state of California including Yosemite Valley and Napa Valley. The Northern California Pass will allows you to explore the northern part of the state of California including San Francisco, San Jose, and Sacramento while the Southern California Pass covers the cities of San Luis Obispo, Santa Barbara, Los Angeles and San Diego. All three passes include all thruway connecting bus service within the state of California. For further information call Amtrak at tool-freel: (800) USA-Rail.

Florida Rail Pass

The Florida Rail Pass is available only to resident of the State of Florida. The Pass allows the traveler for a one year unlimited coach travel and thruway bus connection within the state of Florida from the date of purchase. The pass is subject from several restrictions and it cost US $249.

Explore America Fare

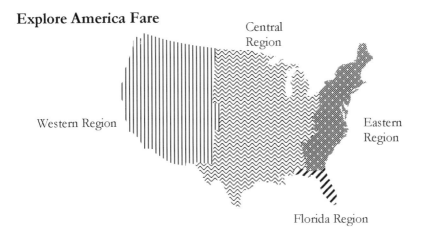

Central
Region

Western Region

Eastern
Region

Florida Region

Explore America Fares are available to both non-US residents and residents. The fares allow passengers to travel in up to four regions (the western region, central region, eastern region and the Florida region) under one special low fare price. Explore America passes are valid for up to 45 days starting from the first day of your travel, with up to three stops along the route. The fare is based on off-peak season prices; ask Amtrak agents for fare travel restrictions.

Passengers traveling under the Explore America Fare are not allowed to travel over the same segment more than once. In addition, the fare is not valid for travel on Acela Express, Metroliner, 7000 series Thruway bus services, VIA Rail Canada, and other non-Amtrak train services. You should make your reservation 7 days prior to your intended departure date.

A one-region pass valid for 45 days costs $279, two regions costs $359, three or four regions costs $429, and the Florida region costs $109.

Explore America Fare by Region	Fares
One Region	$279
Two Regions	$359
Three or Four Regions	$429
Florida Region	$109

North America Rail Pass

North America Rail Pass offered by Amtrak and VIA Rail Canada allows visitors to visit Canada and the United States under one pass with 30 days unlimited train rides across the two countries, serving 900 destinations and more than 28,000 miles of train tracks.

The North American Rail Pass is available to both residents of Canada and the United States and International travelers on the condition that the trip itinerary covers both Canada and the United States. Travelers should be aware of the US/Canada cross-border visa requirements. See under visa requirements.

The North America Rail Pass is valid for coach/economy travel for a period of one year from the date of purchase for US$475 (off peak season) and US$674 (peak season) with a 10% discount available to seniors and students. Additional charge applies in any upgrade to Business Class, Sleeping Car accommodations, Totem Class or Bras d'Or and VIA 1. North American Rail Pass is not valid for travel on Acela Express, Metroliner, Auto Train, on some thruway bus connection services both in US and Canada.

Advance reservation is required, tickets and pass can be obtained by mail or at any Amtrak staffed station in the US, online, or at any travel agency that represents Amtrak. Using the pass during the peak travel period affects the rates of the pass, check other applied restrictions. For further information call Amtrak at toll-free (800) USA-Rail in the US and in Canada call VIA at toll-free (888) 842-7245, international travelers should contact Amtrak international sales representative or visit <<http://www.Amtrak.com>>.

Great American Vacations

Travelers can organize their own travel itineraries, including their prepared accommodations, rent-a-car, attractions, etc., and call Amtrak's Great American Vacations which offers money-saving packages that include accommodations, rent-a-car packages and attraction tickets with the train fare. Call toll-free (800) USA-Rail, toll-free (800) 321-8684, Tel: (404) 881-3060 or visit <<http://www.amtrak.com>> for information.

Air Rail

Air-Rail offered by Amtrak and United Airlines allows travelers to travel via train on one way and fly on the other way to any destination in the US or Canada. In addition, air rail allows passengers up to three stopovers during their train travels. Call toll-free (800) 437-3441.

Rail Sale

Amtrak has recently offered its Rail Sale promo that gives travelers decent discounts on regular coach fares to some Amtrak train destinations. You have to purchase your ticket online through Amtrak Rail Sale program to avail any special promo fare. Visit <<http://www.Amtrak.com>>.

Reservations, Payments and Assigned Seat

If possible, book and reserve your train travels few months before your departure (you can obtain your reservation as much as 11 months in advance through your travel agency, Amtrak international sales agents or on the Amtrak website). Remember to bring with you all needed information regarding your reservation (receipt, reservation number, etc.) for ticket issuance when you arrive in the US.

Amtrak authorizes international travel agencies to set their own policies regarding payment if you are purchasing your train tickets outside the US. If you made your reservation and purchased your tickets online through the Amtrak website, you can pick up your ticket at any Amtrak staffed train station in the US. Or you can use any Quik-Trak Ticket Machine (available in many Amtrak train stations) where you can obtain your train ticket without additional charges and no hassle. You need a major Credit Card or cash to pay for your ticket, and your reservation number. If you are already in the US and decide to travel by train call toll-free (800) USA-Rail or visit any Amtrak staffed station in the US for reservations and to purchase tickets. However, you will always get a better fare if you make your reservation online via the Amtrak website.

Two different valid identifications with picture ID are needed (passport or drivers license), to obtain tickets. You can pay in US Dollar cash, major credit card, personal check, or ATM/Debit Card. Personal checks are not accepted in the State of California except for passengers aged more than 62.

Passengers who have or can provide a permanent mailing address in the US, including the States of Hawaii and Alaska (P.O Boxes, Hotel, and dormitories are not accepted), can obtain their train ticket by mail or express mail delivery. Passengers should allow 10 business days for Amtrak to send the tickets. If there is sufficient time prior to your train departure date, you will receive your ticket by mail or if the departure date is less than 10 days you will receive your ticket through express mail delivery. Reservations made using toll-free (800) USA-Rail are subject to a small handling charge for express mail service.

Tickets are required before boarding for most trains. If one needs to board a train without reservations and tickets, ask any train conductor or representative while you are at the station, you may be allowed to pay your fare in cash or with a major credit card on board on certain trains, although at a much higher fare.

Coach seating assignment in most train routes is based on a first come, first served basis, therefore be sure to arrive early at the station to give yourself a chance to choose a seat. If you are traveling with a companion or group, talk to the train conductor for group seating.

Amtrak's Pacific Northwest Corridor trains serving Seattle, Portland, and Vancouver, BC coach seating are available by reservation only.

Refunds

Most train tickets are refundable, but you have to apply before the designated travel date to receive a refund. There are refund fees of $30 for adults and $15 for children. Partially used one way full fare tickets are eligible for a partial refund without any fee. You can cancel your Sleeping Car accommodation 7 days before your departure date. If you fail to do so, you can apply for the use of Sleeping Car accommodation on your future train travels. Metroliner, Acela Express, First Class accommodation tickets can be refunded and canceled at least an hour prior to the departure.

You can obtain and apply for a refund at any Amtrak ticket office in the US. If you purchase your tickets at a travel agency then you have to return your ticket to the agency. You can also send your tickets to Amtrak via certified mail with return receipt to "Amtrak Customer Refunds, Box 70, 30th St. Station, 30th & Market Sts., Philadelphia, PA 19104-2898" for a refund. Some special promo or discounted tickets may be non-refundable and there are other exceptions and restrictions, therefore ask for cancellation or refund policy before buying your ticket. Tickets are valid for refund only for a period of one year from the date of issue.

Thruway Bus Connections

Thruway buses connect cities and major places that are not served by train. If your destination is not served directly by a train route, thruway bus service will provide coordinated train/bus connections with fares and tickets included in the train fare. In some destinations there is other local transportation situated within or near the train station, so even places that are not served by Amtrak thruway connections are almost as easy accessible.

Train Schedules

Train Schedules are available in all Amtrak train stations. There are individual route lists and complete train schedule booklets free for passengers. If you purchased your ticket on-line and requested ticket mail services, your train schedules are usually attached to your tickets. You can also check the Amtrak website for updated train schedules. Time used on the train schedules are in local time. If you are traveling long distances you should be aware of the US time zone difference and daylight saving time, see "A little about the US" chapter.

Useful Amtrak Telephone Numbers

For general inquiries you can use toll-free number (800) 872-7245 or (800) USA-Rail. For local reservation and ticketing numbers within the US use telephone numbers (212) 582-6875 in New York, (215) 824-1600 in Philadelphia, and (202) 484-7540 in Washington, DC. For Group Travel Information call toll-free number (800)-USA-1GRP. For Disabled Passenger Assistance call toll-free (800) 523-6590. For Shipping Services information call toll-free (800) 368-TRAK; for student discount tickets call toll-free (877) 2JOIN-SA. And for online information visit the Amtrak website at <<http://www.amtrak.com>>.

The Train Fleets

Long Distance Trains:

The Superliner

The Superliner is a bi-level car used on Autotrain, California Zephyr, Cardinal, Capitol Limited, City of New Orleans, Coast Starlight, Empire Builder, Southwest Chief, Sunset Limited, and Texas Eagle services. Manufactured by Pullman-Standard Company it is one of the finest commuter trains in the US. A later generation of Superliner II, designed by Bombardier Company, was added with more roomy compartments and wider windows.

Superliners offer first-class services and have four types of first class Sleeping Car accommodations: the Deluxe Bedroom, the Standard Bedroom, the Family Bedroom, and Accessible Bedroom. All coach seats are spacious and comfortable with overhead baggage storage, reading lights, leg rest, fold down tray table, electrical outlet for your laptop in some seats, and a wide window for superb viewing. There is a Café bar in the lounge car, en-route entertainment, and a dining car with complete meals. On the lower level there are toilets, disabled facilities, and baggage storage racks.

The Viewliner

Viewliners are single-level sleeper cars used on Crescent, Lake Shore Limited, Silver Service, Silver Meteor, Silver Palm, Silver Star and Twilight Shore liner routes. Viewliner has three types of first-class sleeping accommodations: the Deluxe Bedroom, the Standard Bedroom and the Accessible Bedroom. Each room has bigger windows that give better views and folding berth, table, temperature and air controls, video entertainment monitor, earphone outlet, and reading lights.

Short Distance Trains:

The Amfleet

Amfleet travels medium and short distance routes used on the Midwest Corridor, Empire Service, and Northeast Direct routes. Built by the Budd Company of Philadelphia, it provides spacious legroom in coach seats with fold out tray tables, adjustable footrest, individual reading lights, and an overhead luggage rack. The Business class/Club class has added services such as complementary wine, newspaper, food/snacks, and hot towels. There are changing rooms, Railfone, and restrooms on each end of the car and facilities for disabled.

The Cascades

Perhaps one of the most distinctive trains in the US, the European-style trains built by Talgo of Spain and General Motors is used for Cascades routes in the Northern Pacific region serving Seattle, Portland, and Eugene/Springfield. The Cascades has spacious reclining coach seats with overhead luggage racks, individual overhead lights, at-seat video and stereo, and fold down tray tables. Business Class has airy coach seats, outlets for laptop computers, complementary food and beverages, and a newspaper. There are Railfone, toilets, and disabled facilities on board.

The California Cars

The California Cars is used in San Joaquin and other southern California services. It has bi-level coaches with wider windows for a greater viewing experience. Coach seats have electrical outlets for laptops and closed overhead luggage compartments. There are telephone and fax services on board, toilets, and bicycle storage racks. Amtrak and the California Department of Transportation jointly operate the California Cars services.

The Horizon Cars

The Horizon coach has spacious reclining seats with fold out tray tables, individual headlights, and overhead luggage racks. There are two toilets in each car and facilities for disable passengers.

The Metroliner

Metroliner serves the City of New York and Washington D.C. making it one of the busiest in the US. Coach seats are spacious and have comfortable legroom, individual headlights, overhead luggage racks, and fold out tray tables. First class offers much wider seats and added services. Cars have two restrooms on each end and facilities for disabled passengers.

The Acela Express

Acela, running at a top speed of 150 mph (240 km/h) is America's answer to the Japanese bullet train and French TGV, built by Bombardier and Alstson (the same company who built TGV). Acela have multiple train services each day serving passengers commuting between Washington D.C., New York and Boston.

Acela has First class, Business class coach, unreserved coach, café car, and several conference tables. Coach seats are spacious, with electrical outlets for laptop computers, personal audio equipment, and overhead luggage bins; telephones are available in business class, and there is television in the café lounge.

The Auto Train

Auto Train offers non-stop service between Lorton, VA and Sanford, FL, allowing travelers to bring their cars, vans, SUVs or motorbikes with them. Auto Trains use bi-level Superliner cars for passengers and an enclosed car carrier that transports passenger vehicles with them to their destinations. Complementary meals are served, and there is family entertainment. No checked baggage service is available, and only passengers traveling with vehicles can travel Auto Train. Call toll-free (800) USA-Rail.

Train Accommodations and Facilities

Coach Class

Superliner coach seats are comfortable and spacious, and recline to serve as your night accommodation. Each seat has a large window with curtain, wide legroom, adjustable leg rest, fold-down trays, individual reading lamps (not available on some short distance routes), and electrical outlets in some seats. There are overhead baggage racks and additional luggage storage space beside the main door at the lower level of each car.

At the lower level there are restrooms, a changing room, a trash outlet and facilities for disabled passengers. You have a choice of aisle or window seats: seating at the aisle will give you more mobility to move easily away from your seat, while a window seat offers a better view, a little more privacy, and something to lean on especially if you are traveling alone. Seating at the middle of the car eliminates too much noises coming from the car doors at each end and outside noise, and seating at the far end of the car will give you a better view.

Small pillows are provided on board and you can ask for extra pillow or bring your own travel neck pillow. Temperature inside the train can be chilly so consider bringing a blanket; you can also buy an Amtrak souvenir blanket at the Café bar for $8.

Many Northeast routes between Washington D.C. and Boston have "quiet car" sections where mobile phones, pagers, and other electronic devices that create noise, and loud conversation are prohibited. This allows fellow passengers to have a pleasant and comfortable journey. Ask train staff at the station for information. Business class offers deluxe seating with complementary beverages (non-alcoholic), light snacks, seat cup-holders, pillows and blankets.

Sleeper Car

Sleeper cars are mostly available on long distance trains routes. Each priced separately from your train ticket, sleeper rooms include dinning car meals, complementary drinks (coffee, tea, or juices), personal attendants, towels, soap, bed linen, newspaper, and the use of Amtrak Metropolitan lounge. Only passengers with sleeper car tickets are allowed in the sleeper car areas. If you are sensitive to noise, choose a room at the middle of the car.

Each room offers ample daytime seating that converts into comfortable berths at night. There are also fold-down tables, electric outlets, temperature controls, reading lights, a garment rack, and in some routes movies and videos are available. And if you feel lazy you can order your meal delivered to your room.

Super liner Bedroom:

Superliner bi-level sleeper car is used for western and some eastern long distance train routes (the Coast Starlight, Sunset Limited, the Eastern Capital Limited, and Cardinal). Superliner sleeping cars have 5 Deluxe Bedrooms at the upper level, 14 Standard Bedrooms located on both upper and lower levels. One Family Bedroom and one Accessible Bedroom are located at the lower level of the car.

Standard Bedroom

There are ten standard bedrooms on the upper level and four at the lower level. Each accommodates one or two adult passengers and has large window with two reclining seats that convert to upper and lower berths. There are upper and lower headlights, heat and air controls, fold down table, and electrical outlets for shaver, hairdryer, etc. The shower and toilet facilities are located nearby. Room dimensions: 3'6" x 6'6" (1.1 m x 2 m).

Deluxe Bedroom

Deluxe bedrooms are located on the upper level and are designed for two adult passengers. Each room has two reclining seats that convert to upper and lower berths, and a removable divider to join two rooms to accommodate four adult passengers. There is space for a small suitcase, a private sink, and enclosed private shower and toilet. Deluxe room dimensions: 6'6" x 7'6" (2 m x 2.3 m).

Family

The Family bedroom is located at the lower level. Each room has two large windows, an ample room for two adults and two small children. There are sofa and two reclining seats that convert to berths. Each room is equipped with reading lights, heat and air controls, a fold down table, and electrical outlets for shavers, hairdryers, etc. There are shower and restrooms located nearby. Family room dimensions: 5'2" x 9'5" (1.6 m x 2.9 m).

Accessible Bedroom

The Accessible bedroom is located at the lower level; each room has enough space for wheelchair maneuverability and is designed for passengers with special mobility requirements. The lavatory area is located in the room and is separated by a privacy curtain. Each room has two reclining seats that convert to upper and lower berths. Food service in the room is available to passengers upon request. Accessible room dimensions: 6'9" x 9'5" (2 m x 2.9 m).

Viewliner Bedrooms:

Viewliner single level sleeper cars are use in most eastern train routes (except the Sunset Limited, Capital Limited, Cardinal, and Three Rivers). Viewliner sleeping cars were the first single level trains of Amtrak and have mostly replaced the aging Heritage sleeping cars. Viewliner sleeping cars have two Deluxe Bedrooms, twelve Standard Bedrooms, and one Accessible Bedroom. Each room offers similar amenities with Superliner bedrooms, only with much wider windows.

Viewliner Standard

Viewliner standard bedrooms are designed for one or two passengers and feature two chairs that convert to comfortable upper and lower berths, and audio/video equipment. Each room has a private sink and toilet, and nearby shower rooms located at the end of the car. Standard room dimensions: 3'6" x 6'8" (1.1 m x 2 m).

Viewliner Deluxe

Deluxe bedrooms feature a sofa that converts to upper and lower berths for your comfortable nights sleep. Each deluxe room has an enclosed shower, sink and toilet. Two deluxe rooms can be combined into a suite that accommodates up to four adults. There is audio and video equipment in each room. Deluxe room dimensions: 6'8" x 7'1" (2 m x 2.2 m).

Viewliner Accessible

The Viewliner Accessible bedroom is designed for passengers with special mobility requirements and can accommodate up to three passengers. There is a sofa that converts to upper and lower berths. Each room has an enclosed shower, sink, and toilets (easily accessible by wheelchair), a wheelchair storage space, and food room service is available upon request. Accessible room dimensions: 6'8" x 7'1" (2 m x 2.2 m).

Dinning

Dinning onboard the train gives you the opportunity to enjoy a unique train ride experience. In most long distance train routes, there is a complete dining car service with choices of regional cuisine and beverages. Breakfast is served from 6:30 am to 10:30 am, lunch from 11:30 am to 2:30 pm, and dinner is served from 4:30 pm to 8:00 pm.

A standard breakfast menu includes toast, bagel with jam, butter and cream cheese, pancakes, cereal, eggs, and fruit; Lunch: burgers, chicken, sandwiches, salmon, and salad; Dinner: beef, chicken, pasta, seafood, and salad as well as dessert. Vegetarian dishes and children's portions are also available. Kosher and other special food requests are welcome and should be made 72 hours before your departure, call toll-free (800) USA-Rail. On some route you maybe able to order a meal at your seat.

Dining car attendants move through the coaches and take reservations few hours before meals to eliminate waiting in lines. Dining car tables are arranged for four persons, thus you will likely be seating and sharing stories with other guests. The table is setup properly using chinaware, napkins, and nice tablecloths. Meals are reasonably priced: breakfast and lunch entrées range from $10 to $15 for a decent meal while dinner starts at US$15. Wine and other alcohol are a bit pricey.

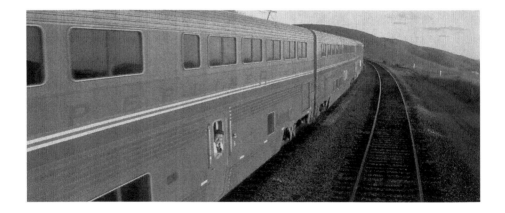

Top: The PacificSurfliner
Bottom Left: Amtrak Lounge Dome
Bottom Right: Dinning Car

Top: Bi-level Car- Amtrak Surf Liner
Bottom Left: Coach Seat   **Bottom Right:** Union Station, Los Angeles, CA.

Lounge or Dome Car

Café bar or snack bar at the lounge car opens at 6:00 am to midnight, with occasional closures for staff breaks. The bar serves snacks, sandwiches, pizza, soup, alcohol, cold and hot beverages, blankets, souvenirs, postcards, etc. There are limited tables at the bar and you can also take your food to the upper lounge car/sightseeing lounge car, or back to your seat. Food prices at the bar are similar to that of convenience stores. Many passengers bring their own snacks, food and drinks on the train with them.

Superliner, Arm fleet, and Heritage Lounge cars are almost similar to each other: they have huge windows that extend to the roof for excellent viewing. Lounge cars feature comfortable and adjustable leather seats, public telephone, electrical outlets, and two TV's that play current popular movies starting in early evenings. In addition, there are reading materials, train routes schedules, magazines, and Amtrak route-specific photographic guides at the center of the lounge.

Summer features a hospitality hour where complementary drinks and snacks are served to everyone and a local tour guide shares some interesting information about route attractions. California car lounge has fax service plug-ins at the lower level lounge added to the above features. More interestingly, lounge cars offer the best opportunities to mingle and meet locals and fellow foreign travelers and win new friends.

First Class Lounge

Passengers traveling on a Sleeping car or with Club or First class tickets are entitled to use the First class lounges departing and arriving in many train stations around the US. In the Northeast the Club Acela lounges are at the main stations in Boston's South Station, New York's Penn Station, Philadelphia's 30th Street Station, and Washington D.C.'s Union Station. On the West First class lounges "formerly known as the Metropolitan Lounges" are located at the main station of Chicago, St. Paul (Minnesota), Portland, New Orleans (the Magnolia Lounge), Miami, and other main major stations around the US.

First class lounges have a staff to attend to first class passengers' needs. There are comfortable seats and conference facilities at the lounges with restrooms, telephones, fax machines, television, internet access, and complementary drinks, snacks, and newspapers. Baggage can be checked for free, ask at reception. Passengers who wish to use the lounges should show their ticket at the lounge counter for admittance.

Entertainment

Passengers will always find something interesting to do while they are on board the train. Aside from endless wondrous scenery, Amtrak offers numerous activities and entertainment for its passengers. There is free PG rated movies and music in every train, in most long distance routes recent popular movies are shown every day in late afternoons. In some coaches there are movie monitors and music available, headphone jacks can be found in the armrest of each seat; you can buy a headset at the Café bar or bring your own.

There are bingo and card games in the lounge car on most trains, and during summer a local tour guide provides a very informative presentation. Amtrak Cascades route between

Bellingham and Portland offers a School on Trains Program for everybody for just $5. Contact any Amtrak staff at the station counter or any train service crew. If you have time and interest, currently Amtrak has the Operation Lifesaver free presentation funded by a federal organization aimed to educate train passengers on how to act safely around trains and railroad crossings; you can send email to bboston@wutc.wa.gov for information.

Baggage and Services

Carry-On Baggage

You can carry some luggage with you on-board the train and there is a luggage rack located near the main door of the train. Each seat has an overhead luggage rack for your carry-on bags and you can also use the space under your seat for your small bags. Passengers are limited to two carry-on bags, a maximum of 50 lb / 23 kg per piece.

Although your belongings are relatively safe inside the train, you should practice extra safety precautions with your valuables. Keep your baggage away from vestibules and aisles, try to follow all safety rules and regulations listed on the back of each seat, and be considerate. Amtrak still encourages passengers to use the check-in baggage facilities if possible to ensure that every passenger's travel experience is comfortable, so try to bring only light luggage.

Sleeping car passengers can carry two or three carry-on baggage of no more than 50 lbs./23 kg. per-piece. Sleeping cars do not have enough space for large baggage, so consider carrying things that you only need during your travel for your convenience. Make sure to tag all your carry-on bags with your name and address. Ask Amtrak staff at station ticket offices or on-board train crew for personal identification tags if you need them.

Checked Baggage

Checking your baggage offers more convenience and safe journey, so consider checking large baggage if possible. Each passenger may check three pieces of baggage (not exceeding 50 pounds each) without any charge. An additional charge of $10 for each extra piece of luggage (up to 3 pieces) is allowed. Overweight luggage (more than 50 pounds) is subject for additional $10 fee per piece. Luggage exceeding 75 pounds won't be accepted.

Baggage checked less than 30 minutes before departure may be delayed. Dangerous, flammable, fragile, valuable, household goods, and animals are prohibited to check in. Passengers with oversized baggage checked in to destinations served by connecting thruway motor coaches should expect delays on their luggage. Normally, checked baggage will be available for claiming within 30 minutes after arrival. You should inspect your baggage for any damage before claiming, and baggage that is not claimed within two days will be subject to a storage fee. Amtrak accepts liability for checked baggage with limitations, call Amtrak for information or visit their website.

Special Items and Bicycle

Amtrak accepts special items such as baby strollers, bicycles, golf bags, skis, musical instruments, etc. to be transported with handling charge. Items must be properly placed in a sturdy container with name and address or identification tags. Passengers could buy bicycle boxes, shipping boxes, and ski bags at stations that accept checked baggage.

Amtrak Shipping Service

Amtrak Mail and Express offer passengers a service to ship their cargo through Amtrak long-haul passenger rail network. Call toll-free customer service Amtrak Express Desk at toll-free (800) 377-6914.

Custom Border Inspections and Checkpoint

Baggage bound for crossing the US/Canada border is subject for regular customs inspection. All carry-on baggage will be x-rayed prior to departure and passengers will be asked to declare their belongings. Remember to place identification tags on all-your luggage: anonymous and unaccompanied baggage is subject to inspections and possible removal by the customs authorities. Amtrak long distance routes in the US (Empire Builder, California Zephyr, Sunset Limited, and Southwest Chief) are subject for midway route security inspections by the local authorities.

At the Train Stations

Complementary "Redcap" service is available at Amtrak's major stations to assist passengers with their bags. There are luggage carts available in some train stations for free (or small fee), and handicapped facilities are available for passengers with mobility problems. Try to arrive as early as possible before your departure, and it is wise to check with the passenger service counter for any changes on your departure time.

In most enclosed stations there are seats for passengers, toilets, vending machines, public phones, a bar or restaurant, and lounge. There is also local information, train information, television, souvenir shops, rent-a-car service, and hotel/motel contacts.

The Train Crew and Services

Just like any airline crew, train crews are trained to serve and to make your train travel comfortable. Amtrak's workforce is divided into Train Crew and Service Crew.

Train crew includes the Conductor, Assistant Conductors, and the people who make sure that the train runs safely. All with few exemptions are Amtrak employees. The conductor is the man in charge on-board the train. In long distance routes train crews change every 6 to 8 hours of work duty.

Throughout the duration of your train trip you will be dealing more with the service crew. Service crew includes the Chief of On-Board Services (many trains operate without a Chief), Car Attendants, Dining Car Chefs, Dining Car Attendants (waiters), Dining Car Steward (head waiter) and Snack Bar Attendant. Tipping is not required, but if you are happy to their services a 10 to 15 % of the total value of your purchase will be enough. Sleeper car passengers usually give $5, or up to $10 each day if very pleased with the service.

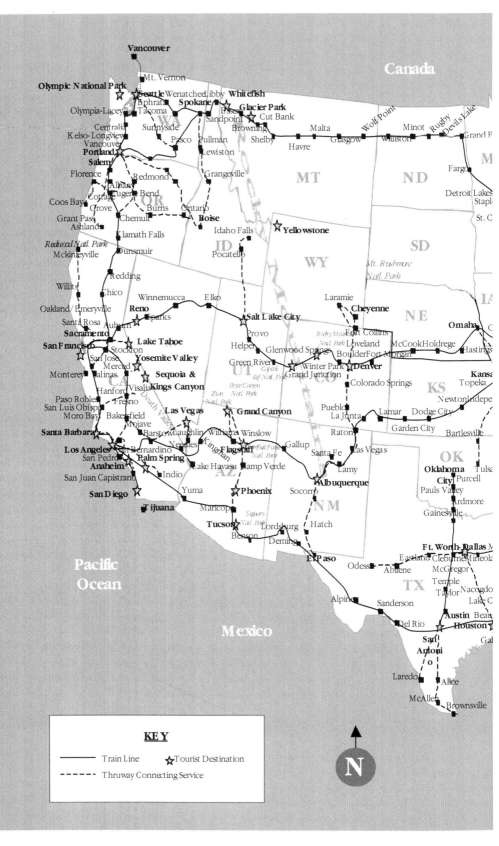

The US Transcontinental Train Routes

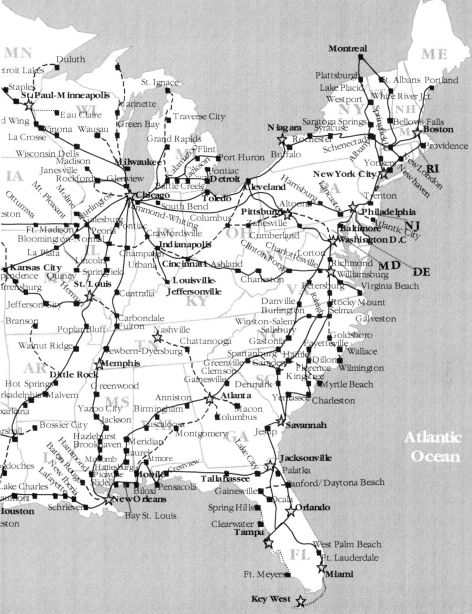

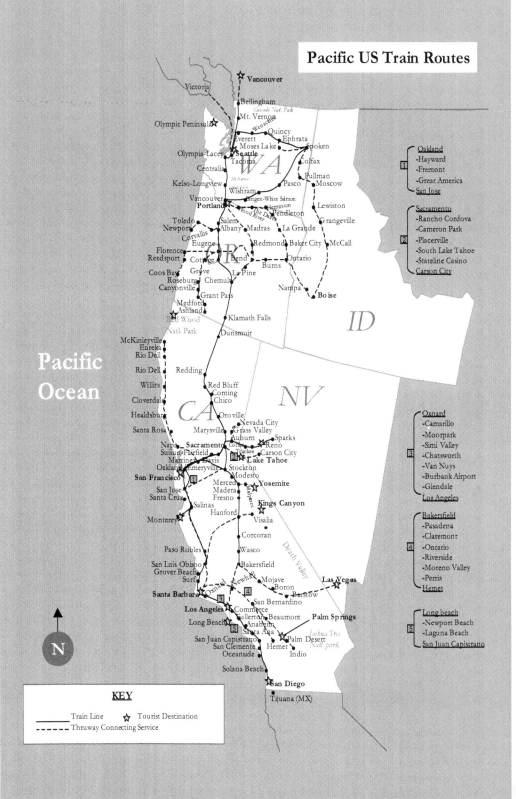

Pacific US Train Routes

WA

OR

ID

CA

NV

Pacific Ocean

Victoria
Vancouver
Bellingham
Olympic Peninsula
Mt. Vernon
Cascade Natl. Park
Quincy
Wenatchee
Everett
Ephrata
Moses Lake
Spokane
Olympia-Lacey
Seattle
Tacoma
Colfax
Centralia
Pullman
Mt Rainer
Kelso-Longview
Pasco
Moscow
Wishram
Vancouver
Bingen-White Salmon
Lewiston
Portland
The Dalles
Hemiston
Hood River
Pendleton
Grangeville
Toledo
Salem
Madras
La Grande
Newport
Albany
Corvallis
Redmond
Baker City
McCall
Eugene
Florence
Ontario
Reedsport
Cottage
Bend
Burns
Grove
Coos Bay
La Pine
Roseburg
Chemult
Nampa
Canyonville
Grant Pass
Boise
Medford
Ashland
Red Wood Natl. Park
Klamath Falls
Dunsmuir
McKinleyville
Eureka
Rio Dell
Rio Dell
Redding
Willits
Red Bluff
Corning
Cloverdale
Chico
Healdsburg
Oroville
Nevada City
Santa Rosa
Marysville
Grass Valley
Auburn
Sparks
Napa
Sacramento
Colfax
Reno
Suisun-Fairfield
Truckee
Carson City
Martinez-Davis
Lake Tahoe
Oakland
Emeryville
Stockton
San Francisco
Modesto
San Jose
Merced
Yosemite
Santa Cruz
Madera
Fresno
Salinas
Kings Canyon
Hanford
Monterey
Visalia
Corcoran
Paso Robles
Wasco
San Luis Obispo
Bakersfield
Grover Beach
Surf
Newhall
Mojave
Las Vegas
Santa Barbara
Oxnard
Boron
Barstow
San Bernardino
Los Angeles
Commerce
Palm Springs
Fullerton
Beaumont
Long Beach
Anaheim
Santa Ana
San Juan Capistrano
Palm Desert
San Clemente
Hemet
Oceanside
Indio
Solana Beach
San Diego
Tijuana (MX)
Death Valley
Joshua Tree Natl. park
Palm Desert Natl. park

1. Oakland
   -Hayward
   -Fremont
   -Great America
   San Jose

2. Sacramento
   -Rancho Cordova
   -Cameron Park
   -Placerville
   -South Lake Tahoe
   -Stateline Casino
   Carson City

3. Oxnard
   -Camarillo
   -Moorpark
   -Simi Valley
   -Chatsworth
   -Van Nuys
   -Burbank Airport
   -Glendale
   Los Angeles

4. Bakersfield
   -Pasadena
   -Claremont
   -Ontario
   -Riverside
   -Moreno Valley
   -Perris
   Hemet

5. Long beach
   -Newport Beach
   -Laguna Beach
   San Juan Capistrano

N

KEY

— Train Line   ☆ Tourist Destination

- - - Thruway Connecting Service

Chapter-5

The US Train Routes and Destinations

The Western Pacific Region Train Routes

The Cascades

One of the most beautiful train routes in the Pacific Northwest region is The Cascades. This line travels some of the most beautiful scenery, towns, and cities of the Northwestern US. It links the states of **Oregon** and **Washington**, and continues north into the Canadian province of **British Columbia**.

Using a European-designed train, The Cascades offers more comfort than standard trains. Passengers enjoy wider seats, more legroom and headroom, priority boarding and disembarking, and complementary newspapers.

Route Destination Highlights

Cascades		
	Canada	
10 20 am-D	Bellingham (WA)	8 00 pm-A
10 46 am	Mount Vernon (WA)	6 56 pm
11 33 am	Everett (WA)	6 20 pm
11 55 am	Edmonds (WA)	5 58 pm
12 45 am-A	**Seattle (WA)**	5 30 pm-D
1 45 pm-D		4 00 pm-A
1 59 pm	Tukwila (WA)	3 32 pm
2 33 pm	Tacoma (WA)	3 02 pm
3 10 pm	Olympia Lacey (WA)	2 22 pm
3 33 pm	Centralia (WA)	2 02 pm
4 12 pm	Kelso Longview (WA)	1 21 pm
4 47 pm	Vancouver (WA)	12 48 pm
5 15 pm-A	**Portland (OR)**	12 30 pm-D

A-Arrival   **D-**Departure
--Multiple Schedules Daily

International Connections

Seattle, WA- Gateway to the magnificent Mt. Rainier, take a day trip to Olympic National Park, visit the Seattle Space needle, take a romantic afternoon walk at the Puget Sound, or tour the famous Klondike Gold Rush Park.

Portland, OR- Visit the Cascade Mountains or explore the Columbia River Gorge, the Multnomah Falls, and what is left of Mt. St. Helens. If you're a book lover, visit the largest independent bookstore in the world, the "Powel's City of Books."

Salem, OR- Visit the AC Gilbert's Discovery Village, Bush House, Jensen Arctic Museum, Marion County Historical Society Museum, Mission Mill Museum, Western Antique Powerland, and the Oregon Electric Railway Historical Society.

Eugene, OR- Experience the original Saturday Market, or visit the oldest weekly open-air crafts festival in the United States. Hendricks Park and Owen Rose Garden present a wonderful display of rhododendrons, azaleas, roses, and other ornamental plants. Visit the Sea Lion Caves and the Pioneer Cemetery, one of the three oldest cemeteries in Eugene and the largest both in acreage and in number of burials. Visit the largest state-supported art museum in Oregon (the University of Oregon Museum of Art), the University of Oregon Museum of Natural History (which holds over 500,000 objects), and the Springfield Museum.

Scenery along the Route

From Vancouver (BC) to Seattle (WA) you'll see magnificent views of the Cascade and other snow-capped mountains, tall pine trees, redwoods, cliffs, rushing rivers, ranches, and small towns.

On your way from Seattle (WA) to Eugene (OR) you will enjoy more snow-covered mountains (most of the year), rich greenery, farms and livestock, rivers, interesting water irrigation systems, and thick forests.

Train Schedules

The Cascades travels daily from Vancouver, British Columbia to Eugene, Oregon. The trip between the two cities takes approximately 12 hours of travel time.

Accommodations

Accommodations are Reserved Coach and Business Class. There is a Bistro Car that serves local cuisine, snacks, soups, sandwiches, and drinks. Restaurant style meals are served in the Dining Car. Other amenities include movies, audio entertainment, rail phones, and electrical outlets. Surfboard racks and bicycle racks are also available.

Additional Information

Your North America Rail Pass is valid at any destination designated by Amtrak or VIA Rail Canada.

Boarder Crossing

If you travel north of Bellingham, Washington, you will cross the border into Canada.

ALL ABOARD!

Vancouver (BC) (Optional destination)

Bellingham (WA)

Bellingham is the last major city at the US-Canadian border. Located in Whatcom County, Bellingham is 90 miles north of Seattle and an hour south of Vancouver, British Columbia. In 1792 the English explorer Captain George Vancouver discovered Bellingham Bay and in 1853 the city of Bellingham was founded.

Bellingham has a total land area of 22 sq. miles (57 sq. kilometers) and a population of approximately 61,240. Bellingham is a harbor city with much of the community relying on the port for their daily activities.

In fact, Bellingham Squalicum Harbor is the second largest in Puget Sound, a port that supports fishing, boat building, shipping, and marina operations. Also, there are passenger ferries that serve the region, and whale watching cruises that boost eco-tourism.

Bellingham's train depot is located at 401 Harris Street Bellingham, WA 98225. The station is staffed and features an enclosed waiting area, restrooms, payphones, Quik-Trak ticket machines, and a snack bar. Transportation options from the station include Greyhound toll-free (800) 231-2222, Whatcom Transportation Authority Tel: (360) 676-6843, and local taxi service.

Bellingham station is served by The Cascades.

Mt Vernon-Burlington (WA)

Mount Vernon is located halfway between Seattle and Canada. It has a total land area of 13 sq. miles (22 sq. kilometers) and a population of some 17,647 people. Mount Vernon was named the county seat of Whatcom County, and then incorporated in 1890. Nearby Burlington has a total land area of 4.85 sq. miles (7.826 sq. kilometers) and population of approximately 4349.

Mt Vernon-Burlington's train depot serves both cities and is located at 725 College Way Mount Vernon, WA 98273. The station is "self-serve" with no attendants. Transportation options from the station include local transit service and local taxi service.

Mt Vernon-Burlington station is served by the Cascades.

Everett (WA)

The city of Everett is located a half-hour north of Seattle. It overlooks the Olympic Mountains to the west, the Cascade Mountain Range to the east, and Mount Rainier to the south.

Everett has a total land area of 30 sq. miles (77 sq. kilometers) and an estimated population of approximately 96,000. Everett is an economic center based on the development of high-technology industries, a deep-water port, naval station, and other industries. Everett has enjoyed a high rate of economic development for many years.

Everett's train depot is located at 2900 Bond St. Everett, WA 98201. The station is staffed and features an enclosed waiting area, restrooms, payphones, and checked baggage service. Transportation options from

Washington (WA)

Capital: Olympia (Population: 5,894,121)
Size: 71,303 sq mi. (184,674 sq km)
Nickname: The Evergreen State, Chinook State
Joined the union on: November 11, 1889 (42nd state)
Motto: By and by
Flower: Coast Rhododendron
Bird: Willow Goldfinch
Song: Washington, My Home
Famous for: Microsoft, Boeing, Space needle.
Major industries: Aerospace, agriculture, and hydroelectric energy.

the station include Greyhound toll-free (800) 231-2222, Everett Transit toll-free (800) 562-1375, and local taxi service.

Trains serving Everett station are the Cascades and Empire Builder.

Edmonds (WA)

The city of Edmonds was founded by George Brackett in 1876 and was incorporated in 1890. The city's downtown area and the adjacent residential areas now occupy the old town site.

The City of Edmonds is located approximately 14 miles north of Seattle, south of Snohomish County, on the shores of Puget Sound. The city's total land area is 7.4 sq. miles (19 sq. kilometers) with a population of approximately 35,500.

Edmonds train depot is located at 211 Railroad Ave. Edmonds, WA 98020. The station is staffed and features an enclosed waiting area, restrooms, payphones, vending machines, and checked baggage service. Transportation options from the station include Greyhound toll-free (800) 231-2222, Community Transit toll-free (800) 562-1375, and local taxi service. Trains serving Edmonds station are The Cascades and Empire Builder.

Seattle (WA)

Seattle, the "Emerald City," is the most well-known and largest city in the state of Washington and in the entire north-western pacific United States. Known for its unique architecture in a romantic setting and its cold winds of the Pacific Northwest, Seattle sits at 14 feet above sea level, located on Puget Sound 113 miles south of the US-Canadian border. Seattle's land area is approximately 84 sq. miles (217.56 sq. kilometers) with water surface of approximately 244.79 sq. miles (394 sq. kilometers) and a total population of roughly 560,000.

Seattle's climate is moderate with mild winters and cool summers. The average temperature is 53.2 degrees F. (13 degrees C.), average high temperature is 75.0 degrees F. (25 degrees C.), average low temperature is 56.4 degrees F (14 degrees C.) and the average rainfall is 3 inches.

Seattle is the oldest city in King County. The area was first settled in 1851 and the city was incorporated in 1865.

The city is a major center for advanced technology: computer software, electronics, medical equipment, and environmental engineering. Seattle is home to some of the biggest companies in the world; among them are Boeing and Microsoft.

Getting Around the City

Airport

Seattle-Tacoma International Airport, or Sea-Tac, is located 13 miles south of Seattle; services to/from the airport and Seattle are by Airport Express Tel: (206) 626-6088 which runs every 15 minutes from 5am to midnight between Sea-Tac and the city's downtown hotels. Metro Transit bus no.174 also serves the airport.

Car Rentals

Rent-a-car services are easily accessible from the train depot: Hertz Car Rental toll-free (800) 654-3131, Budget Rent a Car toll-free (800) 527-0700, and National Car Rental Tel: (206) 448-7368.

Buses and Commuters

Greyhound Tel: (206) 628-5526, Metro Online toll-free (800) 201-4900. Commuter Rail: Sounder toll-free (800) 201-4900. Seattle's Street Cars stop at Main Street a few blocks from King Station. Street Cars will connect you to Seattle's downtown and the city's other main districts.

Train

Seattle's train depot, King Station, is located at 303 South Jackson Street next to the Kingdome in Pioneer Square, Tel: (206) 382-4125. The station is staffed and features an enclosed waiting area, restrooms, checked baggage service, payphones, vending machines, and a Quik-Trak ticket machine. Transportation options from the station include local bus and taxi services.

Trains serving Seattle King station are the Cascades, Coast Starlight, and the Empire Builder.

Visitor Information Center

Seattle's Tourist Information Center is located at 800 Convention Place Tel: (206) 461 5840. Brochures, street maps, bus schedules, and other useful information are also available.

Places to See and Things to Do

Downtown

Seattle Aquarium is located on Pier 59 where visitors can walk to the underwater dome (entrance $9.00, with discount). Just beside the Seattle Aquarium is the 180-degree **Omnidome Film Experience Theater** Tel: (405) 602-DOME. The theater features educational films such as the destructive explosion of Mt. St. Helens. General admission fee is $7.50.

The world known **Seattle Art Museum,** located at 100 University St., displays an impressive 21,000 art exhibits from different parts of the world from old paintings of the masters to some of the best-known art of the modern world. **Ye Olde Curiosity Shop,** located at Pier 54, is not just an ordinary souvenir shop, but it also shows some of the most bizarre relic collections in the region, including mummies.

The **Pike Place Market** hosts some 9 million visitors each year. Visitors enjoy the unique sound and movement of Seattle's downtown public market.

Pioneer Square, the cultural heart of the city, is no doubt admired for its beautiful and colorful historical buildings; it also offers exiting nightlife. **Klodike Gold Rush National Historical Park** has a museum in Seattle commemorating this popular place for miners to begin their journey to Alaska during the Klodike gold rush of 1897-98.

Capitol Hill

Seattle Asian Art Museum is located in three distinct locations in Downtown Seattle at 100 University Street (202) 654-3255, Volunteer Park at 1400 E. Prospect Street (206) 654-3206, and Downtown Waterfront. Known as one of the region's premier art museums, it exhibits art from different corners of the world. General admission is $7.00. **Volunteer Park,** 45 acres of land located at 1247 15th Avenue East, is where Seattle Asian Art Museum and Volunteer Park Conservatory are located. The park is open from 10:00 am to 4:30 pm daily.

Ballard

Golden Gardens Park, located at 8499 Sea View Place Northwest, is 95 acres of land offering breathtaking views of Olympic Mountains and Puget Sound. The park is a great place to stroll the rugged coastline, hike, fish, and take a nice sunbath on the sandy beach. The park is open daily from 4:00 am to 11:30 pm. Admission is free.

Nordic Heritage Museum, located at 3014 NW 67th St., is open from Tuesday to Saturday from 10 am to 4 pm. The museum is the only one of it kind in the US dedicated to honor migrants from the Nordic region (Denmark, Finland, Iceland, Norway, and Sweden). The **Ballard Locks and Ship Canals** located at 3015 NW 54th St. are one of Seattle's favorite attractions. There are many other attractions around the area such as a botanical garden, and Fisherman's Terminal, amongst others.

West Seattle

Alki Beach Park offers extraordinary views of downtown Seattle, Olympic mountain, and Puget Sound. It is a 2½-mile beach located at 1702 Alki Ave SW. These 154 acres of land are favorites for walkers, nature watchers, or even in-line skaters and volleyball fanatics.

Schimitz Park, a 50-acre park, features walking paths, hiking, nature studies, and beautiful scenery of old forest. Park hours are from 4 am to 11:30 pm. The park is located at 5551 SW Admiral Way Seattle. Another park located in the area is the 130-acre **Lincoln Park,** open from 4 am to 11:30 pm.

Fremont

If you are interested in revolutionary art, try the **Artist Republic of Fremont. The Aurora Bridge Troll,** better known as the **Fremont Troll,** is one of the most popular art forms in Seattle and is surprisingly unnoticeable simply because it is located under the north end of Aurora Avenue Bridge. See it for yourself.

University District

Burke Museum of natural history is located at 17th Ave NE and NE 45th St., open daily from 10 am to 5 pm and until 8 pm every Thursday. Entrance fee is $6.50 for Adults, discounts for seniors and students. The nearby **Henry Art Gallery** at 15th Ave. NE and NE 41st St. is open from Tuesday through Sunday from 11 am to 5 pm and on Thursday open until 8 pm. General admission is $6.

Seattle Museum of History and Industry opened in 1952 and is the largest private heritage organization in the state of Washington. The museum exhibits almost everything with historical importance. The museum is located at 2700 24th Avenue East. **Japanese Garden** is 3 1/2 acres of beautifully designed Japanese landscape by well-known designer Juki Iida. The garden is located at 1502 Lake Washington Boulevard. The garden opens only during the months of March through November; general admission fee is $2.50. Another interesting place to visit is the **University of Washington** located at 4014 University Way NE. The University is famous for its architecture and public observatory.

North Seattle

Perhaps one will agree that **Carkeek Park** offers some of the most striking views of Puget and Olympic Mountains, located at 950 NW Carkeek Park Road. These 216 acres of land feature beach access, an environmental education center, trails, and magnificent views.

Green Lake Park located at 7201 East Green Lake Drive is one of Seattle's most loved parks. Hundreds of trees, plants, and animals encompass these 342 acres of both land and small lakes that are naturally preserved. It is an ideal place for recreation and relaxation. Another interesting park is **Magnuson Park** located in northeast Seattle on the Sandpoint Peninsula within a lake. For animal lovers **Woodland Park Zoo** is the place to be. The zoo is located at 5500 Phinney Avenue North of Seattle open daily from 9:30 am to 5 pm, general admission, $8.

Central Seattle

Discovery Park is 534 acres of natural beauty and the largest city park in Seattle. The park is known for its wide space of tranquility and peace, making it one of the most visited places for locals who want to escape the busy and hectic life of the city. The park is located at 3801 W Government Way, open daily. Located on the shore of Lake Washington, just east of downtown Seattle, is **Washington Park Arboretum** known for its spectacular greenery, admission is free.

South Seattle

Perhaps one of the most interesting museums in Seattle is the **Museum of Flight** located at 9404 East Marginal Way S. Seattle. The museum exhibits 54 of the world's most interesting airplanes. General admission is $9, open from 10 am to 5 pm daily. For the tennis enthusiast **Seattle Tennis Center** is the place to be. Operated by Seattle Parks and Recreation, it offers facilities, lessons, and more. Located at 2000 Martin Luther King Jr. Way South, schedules and fees are varied; it is advisable to call for information at (206) 684-4764.

International District

Rich with history and culture, **International District** also known as Chinatown, one of Seattle's oldest neighborhoods. The name International District suggests the wide diversity of experiences you can expect. At the heart of the international district lies the **Wing Luke Museum** that exhibits a unique cultural collection of the Pacific Northwest. The museum was dedicated for the preservation of Asian Pacific American Culture.

Seattle Center

Space Needle perhaps is the most popular destination in the City. Known as the symbol of Seattle, it was constructed for the 1962 Seattle World's Fair. Standing 605 feet tall, it gives the best views of Mt. Rainer, Puget Sound, the Cascade and Olympic Mountains, and the charming city of Seattle. The Space Needle was designed to withstand major earthquakes and a wind velocity of 200 miles per hour. The tower is located at 400 Broad St., open daily from 10 am to 11 pm, general admission $11.

Space Needle

Built in 1962, the first full-scale commercial monorail system in the US the **Seattle Monorail** provides the fastest and most convenient link from downtown to Seattle Center and the Space Needle. The train departs every ten minutes from Westlake Center Mall at 5th Avenue and Pine St. and Seattle Center (beside Space Needle). It operates Monday-Friday from 7:30 am to 11 pm and Saturday-Sunday 9am to 11pm. Roundtrip fare is $2.50. Located at the center of Seattle (near Space Needle) at 305 Harrison St. is the **Seattle Children's Museum** with exhibit galleries and three studio spaces, admission fee $5.50. A few steps away is the **Pacific Science Center** open weekdays from 10 am to 5 pm, weekends and holidays from 10 am to 6 pm, general admission is $8; it's a fun place to visit.

Lake Washington

Located at 5898 Lake Washington Blvd. **Seward Park** is 277 acres of land for picnic and other recreation. The park is open daily from 4 am to 11:30 pm.

Lake Union

Gas Works Park is 20.7 acres of land offering three picnic areas, hills trails (popular for kite enthusiasts), sundial, and spectacular views. Located at 2101 North Northlake Way, open daily from 4 am to 11:30 pm. **Myrtle Edwards Park** is a 3.7 acre park and recreation area with a 1.25-mile bike and pedestrian path along Elliot Bay with breathtaking views of Olympic Mountains, Mount Rainer, and Puget Sound. The park is located at 3130 Alaska Way W.

Around the Area

Mt. Rainier

Perhaps one of the most popular destinations in the state of Washington is Mt. Rainier. Mt. Rainier majestically rises 14,410 feet above sea level and can be seen almost everywhere around the city of Seattle. There are several activities and places to explore in the 235,612 acres of forest reserves at Mt. Rainier National Park such as hiking, camping, car touring, and for the more athletic, mountain climbing.

Mt. Rainier is about 100 miles southeast of Seattle, approximately a three hour drive from Seattle. You can check for available local tours at King Station or any hotel or call Tel: (360) 569-2211 for more information or visit <<http://www.Cityspin.com>>.

Olympic National Park

Olympic National Park is located in northwestern Washington and became a national park in June of 1938. The Park is known for its wilderness, its three different ecosystems (glacier capped mountains, more than 60 miles of rugged Pacific coast, and pleasant rain forest), and for its biological diversity. The national park is home to some unique plants and animals that can be found only at the peninsula.

Getting There

Rent-A-Car

All major car rental companies serve Kings Station, Seattle, and in most Olympic Peninsula towns. Driving directions are provided at most rent-a-car companies.

Ferries

There are Ferry Services for cars and passengers available throughout the year from Port Angeles. Olympic Bus Lines and Tours services are available daily from Seattle Sea-Tac Airport, downtown Seattle, and Port Angeles.

Visitor Information Center

Olympic Park Visitor Center Tel: (360) 452-0330 located at 3002 Mt. Angeles Road in Port Angeles.

Things to Do and Places to Visit.

Olympic National Park is a haven to both leisure and sports visitors. There are various activities that match everyone. Among the popular activities are: backpacking, hiking, camping, horseback riding, fishing, kayaking, nature walk, and whitewater rafting among others.

It is highly recommended to take a wilderness area drive to Hurricane Ridge; turn west for a three-hour drive that will take you to the Hoh Rain Forest. Go further to Rialto or Ruby Beach and view the breathtaking Pacific Coast and Olympic's wilderness beaches.

For information visit the Olympic National Park Visitor Center in Port Angeles.

Fees

A 7-day single vehicle entrance fee of $10, or $5 per individual on foot; Olympic National Park annual pass is $20. There will be an additional fee of $8 to $12 for a camping permit.

Accommodation in Olympic National Park

The **Kalaloch Lodge** is located at 15715 Highway 101, Forks, WA, 98331, **Lake Crescent Lodge** is located at 416 Lake Crescent Road, Port Angeles, WA, 98362, and the **Sol Duc Hot Springs Resort,** write to PO Box 2169, Port Angeles, WA, 98362. It is advisable to check the availability of the lodges.

Accommodation in Seattle

Best Western located at Pioneer Square Hotel 77 Yesler Way, Seattle WA 98104, Tel: (206) 340-1234 toll-free (800) 800-5514; expect to pay $99-$299. **Commodore Motel Hotel** located at 2013 Second Avenue Seattle WA 98121, Tel: (206) 448-8868, expect to pay $60-$80. **Days Inn Downtown Seattle** located at 2205 7th Avenue, Seattle WA 98121, Tel: (206) 448-3434, toll-free (800) 544-8313, expect to pay $70-$160. **The Claremont Hotel** located at 2000 Fourth Avenue at Virginia Seattle WA 98121, Tel: (206) 448-8600 or toll-free (877) 448-8600, expect to pay $120-$230.

International Hostelling located at 84 Union St. Tel: (206) 622-5443, expect to pay $16-$30. **Clarion Hotel Seattle Airport** located at 3000 South 176th Street Seattle WA 98188, Tel: (206) 242-0200, expect to pay $70-$220. **Comfort Suites Downtown Seattle Center** located at 601 Roy Street Seattle WA 98109-3160, Tel: (206) 282-2600, expect to pay $100-$110. **Crowne Plaza Hotel Seattle** located at 1113 Sixth Avenue Seattle WA 98101, Tel: (206) 464-1980, toll-free (800) 521-2762, expect to pay $90-$350.

The Elliot located at 721 Pine Street Seattle WA 98101-1815, Tel: (206) 262-0700, expect to pay $250-$650. **Hampton Inn and Suites Seattle Downtown** located at 700 Fifth Avenue Seattle WA 98109, Tel: (206) 282-7700, expect to pay $80-$230. **Four Seasons Seattle** located at 411 University Street Seattle WA 98101, Tel: (206) 621-1700, expect to pay $340-$400. **Days Inn Seattle International Airport** located at 19015 International Boulevard South Seattle WA 98188, Tel: (206) 244-3600, expect to pay $50-$140.

Holiday Inn Express, Seattle City Center located at 226 Aurora Ave. Seattle WA 98109, Tel: (206) 441-7222, expect to pay $100-$200. **Renaissance Madison Hotel** located at 515 Madison Street Seattle WA 98104, Tel: (206) 583-0300, expect to pay $90-$290. **Holiday Inn, Seattle - Sea Tac** located at 17338 International Blvd. Seattle WA 98188, Tel: (206) 248-1000, toll-free (887) 573-2822, expect to pay $70-$150. **The Mayflower Park Hotel** located at 405 Olive Way Seattle WA 98101, Tel: (206) 623-8700, toll-free (800) 426-5100, expect to pay $110-$245.

The Westin Seattle located at 1900 Fifth Avenue Seattle WA 98101, Tel: (206) 728-1000 expect to pay $100-$430. **Sheraton Seattle Hotel and Towers** located at 1400 Sixth Avenue Seattle WA 98101, Tel: (206) 621-9000, expect to pay $90-$650. **Sorrento Hotel** located at 900 Madison Street Seattle WA 98104-9742, Tel: (206) 622-6400 toll-free (800) 426-1265, expect to pay $150-$600.

Tukwila (WA)

Tukwila is an Indian word meaning "land where the hazelnut grows." The city is located at the center of the Puget Sound region, about 12 miles from Seattle. Tukwila has a land area of 8.6 sq. miles (13 sq. kilometers) and a population of more than 17,000. Tukwila was incorporated in 1908. Tukwila's train depot is located at 7301 S. 158th St. Tukwila, WA 98188. The station is self-serve.

Tacoma (WA)

George Vancouver discovered Tacoma in 1792. The name Tacoma is an Indian name for Mt. Rainier, "Tacobet," meaning "Mother of Waters." Tacoma is located on Commencement Bay in the lower Puget Sound 36 miles south of Seattle, 28 miles north of Olympia (state capital). The size of the city of Tacoma is roughly 49 sq. miles (79 sq kilometers), and its population is 193,556 and continuously growing. Tacoma is Washington's third largest city.

Tacoma was incorporated in 1884 and was called "City of Destiny" when it was designated as the Northern Pacific Railroad's western terminus for its transcontinental railroad in 1873. In 1990 *Money Magazine* named Tacoma as the fourth best place to live in the United States and it became one of the national models for neighborhood protection and enhancement.

A key to Tacoma's economic success is the Port of Tacoma, which ranks as the 6th largest container port in North America (covering over 2,400 acres) and ranks amongst the top 25 for worldwide container trade.

Tacoma's train depot is located at 1001 Puyallup Ave. Tacoma, WA 98421. The station is staffed and features an enclosed waiting area, checked baggage service, restrooms, payphones, a restaurant, and a Quik-Trak ticket machine. Transportation options from the station include Greyhound Tel: (253) 383-4621, Pierce Transit toll-free (800) 562-8109, and local taxi service.

The Cascades and the Coast Starlight trains serve the Tacoma station.

Visitor Information Center

Tacoma-Pierce County Visitor & Convention Bureau is located at 1001 Pacific Ave, Suite #400, Tacoma WA 98402, toll-free (800) 272-2662 or Tel: (253) 627-2836.

Places of Interest

Mount Rainier Scenic Railroad, take the 1 1/2 hour train ride on a steam locomotive; there are three services each day during summer. Write to PO Box 921 Elbe WA 98330 or call Tel: (360) 569-2588 or tree-toll (800) STEAM-11 for information and reservations <<http://www.mrsr.com>>. Visit the **Pettinger-Guiley Observatory,** located at 6103 132 St E Puyallup WA 98373. Tel: (253) 537-2802. **Never Never Land,** exhibiting sculptured figurines of characters from favorite children's stories, is a fun place to visit located at Point Defiance Park 5400 N Pearl Tacoma WA 98407. Tel: (253) 591-5845 (June - Aug) / (253) 305-1000 (Sept - May) <<http://www.tacomaparks.com>>.

Northwest Trek Wildlife Park is a naturalist-guided tram tour with wildlife viewing in animals' natural surroundings. Located at 11610 Trek Dr East Eatonville WA 98328, Tel: (360) 832-6117 or toll-free (800) 433-TREK <<http://www.nwtrek.org>>. **Wolf Haven International** is a sanctuary for nearly 40 wolves, located at 3111 Offut Lake Road Tenino WA 98589. Tel: (360) 264-4695 or toll-free (800) 448-9653 <<http://www.wolfhaven.org>>. **Point Defiance Zoo & Aquarium** 5400 North Pearl St Tacoma WA 98407, Tel: (253) 591-5337 <http://www.pdza.org>.

Port of Tacoma is an international port and economic engine of the City of Tacoma, visit the **Port of Tacoma Observation Tower** located at 1 Sitcum Way, Tacoma WA 98421. Tel: (253) 383-9462 <<http://www.portoftacoma.com>>. Visit the **Tillicum Village & Tours Inc,** a northwest Coast Indian Cultural Center. Attractions include restaurants, cruises, entertainment, and a gift gallery. Located at 2993 SW Avalon Way Seattle WA 98126, Tel: (206) 933-8600 or toll-free (800) 426-1205 <<http://www.tillicumvillage.com>>. **Wild Waves & Enchanted Village** is a 70-acre water and amusement park located at 36201 Enchanted Parkway S Federal Way WA 98003, Tel: (253) 661-8000. <<http://www.wildwaves.com>>.

Museum and Historic Sites

Washington State History Museum is located at 1911 Pacific Ave Tacoma WA 98402, Tel: (253) 272-3500 or toll-free (800) BE-THERE <<http://www.wshs.org>>. **Shanaman Sports Museum** exhibits the evolution of sports in Tacoma-Pierce County through written and visual displays. The Museum is located at 2727 East "D" St Tacoma WA 98421. Tel (253) 848-1360, (253) 627-5857 <<http://www.tacomasports.com/museum.htm>>. The **Asia Pacific Cultural Center** promotes Asian and Pacific Island cultures. Located at 1313 Market St Ste C101 Tacoma WA 98402, Tel: (253) 383-3900. <<http://www.asiapacificcenter.org>>.

The Harold E. LeMay Museum exhibits automobiles and Americana memorabilia. PO Box 44459 Tacoma WA 98444. Tel: (253) 531-8211 <<http://www.lemaymuseum.org>> It is scheduled to open in the Spring of 2005. For vintage motorcycle enthusiasts the **Pioneer Motorcycle Museum** (which will be open Fall 2003) will surely be a place to visit in the future. For information call Tel: (253) 779-4800, or visit their website at <<http://www.pioneercyclemuseum.com>>.

Bremerton Historic Ships Association has a Vietnam-era destroyer open for public display. The museum is located at 300 Washington Beach Ave Bremerton WA 98337. Tel: (360) 792-2457. Exhibiting military aircraft from 1940s through 1980s, the **McChord Air Force Base Museum** is located at Bldg 15 McChord Air Force Base WA 98438, Tel: (253) 984-2485. **Fort Lewis Military Museum** shows off the history of Fort Lewis and the US Army; located at Northwest Bldg 4320 Fort Lewis WA 98433, Tel: (253) 967-7206. <<http://www.lewis.army.mil/DPTMS/POMFI/museum.htm>>.

Commencement Bay Maritime Center museum exhibits Tacoma's maritime heritage, located at 705 Dock St. Tacoma WA 98402, Tel: (253) 272-2750 <<http://home.earthlink.net/~west1943>>. **Children's Museum of Tacoma** is a multiple exhibit, educational hands-on museum both for kids and the whole family. Located at 936 Broadway Tacoma WA 98402, Tel: (253) 627-6031. <<http://www.ohwy.com/wa/c/childrmt.htm>>.

Fort Nisqually Living History Museum exhibits a reconstructed fur trading post. Located at Point Defiance Park, 5400 North Pearl Tacoma WA 98407, Tel: (253) 591-5339 <<http://www.fortnisqually.org>>. **Museum of Glass** serves as an international center for contemporary art. Located at 934 Broadway Ste 204 Tacoma WA 98402. Tel: (253) 396-1768 <<http://www.museumofglass.org>>.

Tacoma Art Museum is located at 12th and Pacific Ave Tacoma WA 98402. Tel: (253) 272-4258 <<http://www.tacomaartmuseum.org>>. Learn about the Washington Pioneers in the late 1800s in buildings on the shores of Puget Sound at the **Steilacoom Historical Museum Association,** located at 1311 Starling St Steilacoom WA 98388. Tel: (253) 584-6547 <<http://www.ohwy.com/wa/s/steilahm.htm>>. The **Washington State History Museum** is located at 1911 Pacific Ave Tacoma WA 98402, Tel: (253) 272-3500, (888) BE-THERE, <<http://www.wshs.org>>. **Steilacoom Tribal Cultural Center and Museum** exhibits the history and culture of the Steilacoom Tribe and other Coast Salish people. The museum is located at 1515 LaFayette St. Steilacoom WA 98388. Tel: (253) 584-6308 <<http://www.ohwy.com/wa/t/tribaccm.htm>>.

Parks

Lake Tapps North Park is an 80-acre park with boating and swimming facilities and trail areas. Located at Pierce County Parks & Recreations 2022 198th Ave E Sumner WA 98390, Tel: (253) 826-9756 <<http://www.co.pierce.wa.us/parks>>. **Brown's Point Lighthouse Park** located at 201 Tulalip St NE Tacoma WA 98422. Tel: (253) 305-1000. The **Gig Harbor Parks and Recreation** located at City of Gig Harbor 3105 Judson St Gig Harbor WA 98335. Tel: (253) 851-8136 <<http://www.ci.gig-harbor.wa.us >>. **Frontier Park** is a 50-acre park that offers meeting rooms, overnight camping, and is the site of the Pierce County Fair. The park is located at 21800 Meridian S Graham WA 98388. Tel: (253) 847-2032 <<http://www.co.pierce.wa.us/parks>>.

Wright Park has hundreds of trees from four continents, located at 6th Ave & "I" St Tacoma WA 98403. Tel: (253) 305-1000 <<http://www.tacomaparks.com>>. **Ruston Way Parks** is a two-mile stretch of waterfront park and beach access located on Ruston Way along Commencement Bay Tacoma WA 98402. Tel: (253) 305-1000 <<http://www.tacomaparks.com>>. **Point Defiance Park** is Tacoma's largest park with beach, trails, forest, gardens, a zoo, marina, historic fort, and logging museum. Located at 5400 North Pearl Tacoma WA 98405. Tel: (253) 305-1000. <<http://www.tacomaparks.com>>.

Accommodations

Bavarian Chalet Motel located at 15007 E Main St-Sumner, WA 98390. Tel: (253) 863-2243. **Best Western Tacoma Inn** located at 8725 S Hosmer-Tacoma, WA 98488. Tel: (253) 535-2880. **Days Inn** located at 3021 Pacific Hwy. E Tacoma, WA 98424. Tel: (253) 922-3500. **Econo Lodge** located at 3518 Pacific Hwy. E-Tacoma, WA 98424. Tel: (253) 922-0550. **Holiday Inn Express** located at 812 S. Hill Pk. Dr.-Puyallup, WA 98373. Tel: (253) 848-4900.

Motel Puyallup located at 1412 Meridian St S-Puyallup, WA 98371. Tel: (253) 845-8825. Chinaberry Hill - An 1889 Victorian Inn & Cottage located at 302 Tacoma Ave North Tacoma, WA 98403. Tel: (206) 272-1282. Northwest Motor Inn located at 1409 S Meridian St-Puyallup, WA 98371. Tel: (253) 841-2600 or toll-free (800) 845-9490. LaQuinta Inn located at 1425 E 27th-Tacoma, WA 98421. Tel: (253) 383-0146. Plum Duff House located at 619 N K Street Tacoma, WA 98403. Tel: (253) 627-6916. The Green Cape Villa Bed & Breakfast located at 705 N. 5th Street Tacoma, WA 98403. Tel: (253) 572-1157 or toll-free (888) 572-1157.

Olympia-Lacey (WA)

Located on the southernmost tip of the Puget Sound, Olympia has a population of 42,514. Olympia's total land area is 41.785 sq. kilometers (25.94 sq. miles) with 4.5 sq. kilometers (3 sq. miles) of water surface. It is the largest city in Thurston County and is one of America's loveliest cities.

Olympia-Lacey's train depot is located at 6600 Yelm Highway S.E. Olympia, WA 98503. The station is unstaffed and features an enclosed waiting area, restrooms, payphones, and vending machines. Transportation options from the station include local taxi and intercity transit toll-free (800) BUS-ME-IT.

Trains serving Olympia-Lacey station are the Cascades and Coast Starlight.

Places of Interest

Built during the 1850's by Daniel R. Bigelow and his wife Ann Elizabeth, The Bigelow House Museum is one of the oldest homes still standing in the Pacific Northwest. The museum is located at 918 Glass Ave. NE, Olympia. Tel: (360) 753-1215. The State Capitol Museum, located in historic Lord Mansion, a few blocks south of the Capitol Campus. The historic Capital Theater is located at 206 Fifth Avenue, SE. If you're coming in April or October take a stroll around the city and experience Art Walk, Olympia's bi-annual art celebration showcasing the quality and diversity of South Puget Sound's artistic and cultural resources.

Olympia Farmers Market is one of the best and busiest farmers markets in the state of Washington, located downtown at the foot of Capitol Way Tel: (360) 352-9096. Designed in the ancient hill and pond style, honoring Olympia's sister city of Yashiro, Japan is the Yashiro Japanese Garden. Thurston County Courthouse, located at 2000 Lakeridge Drive, SW, gives a backdoor look at Olympia and is an interesting place to visit. Stroll through the Madison Scenic Park in late afternoon: it is an excellent place to watch sunsets, located on 10th Avenue East at Lybarger Street.

Accommodations

Comfort Inn Lacey located at 4700 Park Center Avenue. Lacey WA 98516, Tel: (360) 456-6300. Holiday Inn Express Lacey located at 4704 Park Center Avenue NE Lacey WA 98516, Tel: (360) 412-1200. Super 8 Motel Olympia Lacey located at 4615

Martin Way Lacey WA 98503, Tel: (360) 459-8888. **Days Inn Olympia Lacey** located at 120 College Street SE Lacey WA 98503, Tel: (360) 493-1991.

Centralia (WA)

Founded in 1875 by a black man named George Washington, a former slave, Centralia is rich in history; located on Interstate 5 between Seattle and Portland just 22 miles from Washington's state capital. With a total land area of 6 sq. miles (15 sq. kilometers), Centralia has a population of over 12,000.

Centralia is known for its well-preserved town, most of its buildings were built in the late 1800's and at the turn of the century which explains why antique shopping in Centralia has become a popular destination for collectors of fine china, quality furniture, and unusual collectibles.

Some of Centralia's famous architecture is Thompson-Hackney-Williams Home, 1908, at 627 North Pearl Street and the old Elk's Lodge, now the Centralia Antique Mall, at the corner of South Pearl and Locust St. The Olympic Club and Micro Brewery, located at 112 North Tower Ave, is the second oldest saloon in the state of Washington and is listed as a National Historic site. Constructed in 1912, Centralia's train depot, or the Union Depot, is a symbol of Centralia's economic institution.

Mt. St. Helens, a volcano which erupted on May 18th, 1980, is approximately one hour south of Centralia. Visit the U.S. Forest Service Interpretive Center located at Castle Rock which has an extensive display of Mt. St. Helens eruption.

The Nisqually, Cowlitz, and the Chehalis were the first settlers to arrive in the Centralia area. Information on the Indians of the Pacific Northwest is available through the **Centralia Timberland Library** located at 110 South Silver, Centralia, WA 98531.

The Lewis County Historical Museum located in historic Chehalis, is set in the old Northern Pacific Railroad Depot built in 1912. Tel: (360) 748-0831. If you have time take the 12-mile round-trip journey through the picturesque Chehalis River Valley, the **Steam Train Rides** runs from May through September. Tel: (360) 748-9593.

Centralia's train depot is located at 210 Railroad Ave. Centralia, WA 98531. The station is staffed and features an enclosed waiting area, checked baggage services, restrooms, and payphones. Transportation options from the station include Greyhound buses toll-free (800) 231-2222, Twin Transit Tel: (360) 330-2072, and local taxi service Tel: (360) 736-9608.

Trains serving Centralia station are the Cascades and Coast Starlight.

Accommodations

Travelodge located at 1049 Eckerson Road Centralia, WA 98531. Tel: (800) 578-7878. **Travelodge Centralia** located at 1325 Lakeshore Drive Centralia WA 98531, Tel: (360) 736-9344. **Holiday Inn Express Centralia** located at 1233 Alder Street Centralia WA 98531. Tel: (360) 330-9441. **Ferryman's Inn** located at 1003 Eckerson Road Centralia, WA 98531, Tel: (360) 330-2094. **Peppertree Motor Inn** located at 1201 Alder St. Centralia, WA 98531,

Tel: (360) 736-1124. **Park Motel** located at 1011 Belmont Ave. Centralia, WA 98531, Tel: (360) 736-9333. **Centralia Days Inn** located at 702 Harrison Ave. Centralia, WA 98531, Tel: (360) 736-2875.

Kelso-Longview (WA)

Peter Crawford, a surveyor and Scotsman, founded Kelso in 1840. Kelso is located in southwestern Washington on Interstate 5 where the Cowlitz, Coweeman, and Columbia Rivers meet, around 48 miles north of Portland. With a total land area of 7.8 sq. miles (20 sq. kilometers), Kelso has a population of roughly 12,000. A nice and friendly community, Kelso is known as the "City of Friendly People."

Like Centralia, Kelso is a great hub for visiting nearby southwestern Washington State. You can take a day trip or rent a car to travel Mt. St. Helens. Over two million visitors a year visit and view the incredible sight of the aftermath of the Mount St. Helens eruption.

Visitors Information Center

Kelso Volcano and Visitor Center is located off Interstate 5 at Exit 39.

Place of Interest

Visit **Historic Civic Center and Downtown** and appreciate the town's several old buildings, the **Cowlitz County Historical Museum** located at 405 Allen Street, Kelso. Exhibits include historic photos and maps, Tel: (360) 577-3119 for information. The **Port of Longview**, the 3rd largest operating port in the state of Washington, is worth visiting. The **Farmer's Market** is located across the Cowlitz County Exposition Center at 7th & Washington. The market is open from 9 am to 2 pm. Call Tel: (360) 425-1297 for information.

Kelso's train depot is located at 501 S. First St. Kelso, WA 98626. The station is un-staffed and features an enclosed waiting area, Quik-Trak ticket machine, restrooms, and payphones. Transportation options from the station include Greyhound toll-free (800) 231-2222 and local taxi services.

Trains serving Kelso station are the Cascades and Coast Starlight.

Accommodations

Kelso Budget Inn located at 505 N Pacific Kelso WA 98626, Tel: (360) 636-4610. **Motel 6** located at 106 N. Minor Road Kelso, WA 98626, Tel: (360) 425-3229. **Super 8 Motel** located at 250 Kelso Dr Kelso WA 98626, Tel: (360) 423-8880. **Comfort Inn** located at 440 Three Rivers Dr Kelso WA 98626, Tel: (360) 425-4600. **Red Lion Kelso/Longview** located at 510 Kelso Dr Kelso WA 98626, Tel: (360) 636-4400. **Travelodge** located at 838 15th Ave. Longview, WA, Tel: (360) 423-6460. **Town Chalet Motor Hotel** located at 1822 Washington Way Longview, WA, Tel: (360) 423-2020. **Budget Inn Longview** located at 1808 Hemlock St. Longview, WA, Tel: (360) 423-6980. **Holiday Inn** located at 723 Seventh Ave. Longview, WA, Tel: (360) 414-1000.

Vancouver (WA)

Washington State's oldest city, Vancouver was founded in 1824 by fur traders from the Hudson's Bay Company. Located on the north bank of the Columbia River, near the Oregon border, it has a total area of 14.2 sq. miles (36.6 sq. kilometers) and a population of approximately 48,000. Vancouver combines the great interest of a major metropolitan area with small-town charm and abundant recreational opportunities. Designated as "Tree City USA," Vancouver is two-time recipient of the prestigious All America City award.

Here are some of the well known facts about Vancouver: it's home for the oldest living apple tree in the Pacific Northwest which was planted in 1826, it is the oldest permanent non-native settlement in Pacific Northwest, it has the oldest public square in the Pacific Northwest -- Esther Short Park established in 1855, and it has one of the oldest continuously operated airports in the US -- Pearson Field has been in operation since 1925.

Vancouver is a central hub to some of the most popular destinations of the region. The Pacific Coast is less than 90 miles to the west. The Cascade Mountain Range rises on the east. Mount St. Helens National Volcanic Monument and Mt. Hood are less than two hours away, and the spectacular Columbia River Gorge National Scenic Area lies 30 minutes to the east.

Vancouver's train depot is located at Foot of W. 11th St. Vancouver, WA 98660. The station is staffed and features an enclosed waiting area, checked baggage services, restrooms, payphones, and vending machines. There are Car Rental services at the station, Five Star Rent-A-Car Tel: (360) 694-8501 and Enterprise Rent-A-Car Tel: (360) 254-1111. Local transportation options from the station include Greyhound Tel: (360) 696-0186 and Vancouver Cab Tel: (360) 693-1234.

Trains serving Vancouver station are the Cascades, Coast Starlight, and the Empire Builder.

Accommodations

Best Western Inn at Vancouver located at 11506 NE 3rd St. Vancouver, WA 98684, Tel: (360) 254-4000 or toll-free (800) 578-7878. **Comfort Inn** located at 13207 N.E. 20th Ave. Vancouver, WA 98686, Tel: (360) 574-6000, (800) 221-2222. **Holiday Inn Express** located at 9107 N.E. Vancouver Mall Drive, Vancouver, WA 98662 - (360) 253-5000, toll-free (800) 465-4329. **Holiday Inn Express Hotel and Suites** 13101 NE 27th Ave. Vancouver, WA 98686, Tel: (360) 576-1040. **Shilo Inn** - Downtown Vancouver located at 401 E. 13th St. Vancouver, WA 98660-3233, Tel: (360) 696-0411, toll-free (800) 222-2244. **University Inn at Salmon Creek** located at 1500 NE 134th St., Vancouver, WA 98685, toll-free (360) 566-1100.

Portland (OR)

Thruway Motor coach connections to: **Pendleton (OR)** and **Boise (OR); Redmond (OR), Bend (OR)** and **Boise (OR); Grant Pass (OR), Medford (OR), Ashland (OR);** and **Astoria (OR).**

Portland, also known as "The City of Roses," was established in the North West of Oregon where the Columbia and Willamette rivers meet. Portland is about 78 miles from the Pacific Ocean. With a total land area of 130 sq. miles (323 sq. kilometers), it has a total population of more than 2 million. Being designated as the city of roses (Portland's city flower is the Rose), one can surely appreciate the fragrant paths of rose bushes at the International Rose Test Garden where there are more than 500 varieties of roses cultured since 1917.

Asa Lovejoy and Francis Pettygrove founded Portland in 1851. Legend says that Lovejoy, a native of Massachusetts, wanted to name the settlement Boston, and Pettygrove, originally from Maine, wanted to name the settlement Portland. The disagreement was settled with a coin toss. Francis Pettygrove won.

Strolling through downtown Portland is indeed a refreshing experience. Portland is a lovely city of fountains, sculptures, and art.

Portland has a relatively mild climate, with high temperatures in the summer rarely over 80 F (25 degree C) and winter temperatures rarely below 40 F (5 degree C) with average annual rainfall of 37 inches per year.

Getting Around

Airport

Portland International Airport is located at 7000 NE Airport Way Portland, OR 97218, Tel: (503) 460-4234 around 20 minutes from downtown Portland. The airport is served by various modes of transportation; call toll-free (877) 739-4636 for information.

Bus

Local bus services around Portland and the outlying region is served by Tri-County Metropolitan Transportation District of Oregon (Tri-Met) 4012 SE 17th Avenue, Portland, OR 97202, Tel: (503) 238-RIDE. Several Tri-Met bus lines run through the transit mall along 5th and 6th avenues. Passengers ride for free in Portland's "Fareless Square" at the city center.

Oregon (OR)
Capital: Salem (Population: 3,421,399)
Size: 98,386 sq mi. (254,718 sq km)
Nickname: The Beaver State
Joined the union on: February 14, 1859 (33rd state)
Motto: She flies with her own wings
Flower: Oregon grape
Bird: Western meadowlark
Song: Oregon, My Oregon
Famous for: Nike
Major industries: Lumber industry, paper manufacturing industry and transportation equipment.

Taxi

Broadway Cab is located at 1734 N.W. 15th Ave. Portland, OR 97209, toll-free: (800) 248-TAXI. Radio Cab Company is located at 1613 N.W. Kearney St. Portland, OR 97209-2385, Tel: (503) 227-1212. Green Cab and Green Shuttle are located at 10118 E. Burnside Portland, OR 97216, Tel: (503) 234-1414.

Train and Commuter

Portland has a Tri-Met 38-mile light rail system (MAX -Metropolitan Area Express, Tel: (503) 238-RIDE) that connects most parts of the city. Portland Street Car brings visitors along a 4.8-mile loop route around the city serving Portland major tourist destinations. The Vintage

Trolley operates between downtown Portland and Lloyd Center District, free fare. Both MAX and Street Car offer free rides only at the "Fareless Square" district.

Portland's train deport is located at the edge of downtown at 800 N.W. 6th Ave. Portland, OR 97209. The station is staffed and features an enclosed waiting area, checked baggage service, restrooms, payphones, a Quik-Trak ticket machine, and a restaurant. Transportation options from the station include Hertz Car Rental toll-free (800) 654-3131, Greyhound Tel: (503) 243-2357, Tri-County Metropolitan Transportation District of Oregon Tel: (503) 238-RIDE and local taxi services.

The Cascades, Coast Starlight, and Empire Builder serve Portland's train depot.

Visitors Information Center

Portland Oregon Visitors Association, located at 26 S.W. Salmon St. Portland, Tel: (503) 222-2223, toll-free (800) 962-3700.

Portland Oregon Information Center, located at 701 S.W. Sixth Ave. Pioneer Square, downtown Portland; Tel: (503) 275-8355.

Things to Do and Places to See

Visit one of Portland's most popular areas the **Pearl District,** rich in culture and heritage, thousands of visitors visit the District all year round. There are numerous attractions, museum, pubs, art galleries, shopping emporiums, coffee shops, among others. The **Oregon Zoo** is located just five minutes away from downtown Portland on Highway 26, the Sunset Highway. Max Light Rail travels from downtown to the Oregon Zoo. General admission is $6, open from 9am to 4pm during winter and 9am to 6 pm in summer.

Portland Art Museum located at 1219 SW Park Ave. Portland, OR, Tel: (503) 226 2811. The museum was opened in 1892 (one of the oldest in the region) and exhibits some of the most comprehensive art collections from Europe, Asia, and the Pacific Rim -- a must-see.

Oregon Museum of Science and Industry, located at 1945 SE Water Ave., is one of the best science museums in the US. Founded in 1944, it offers 219,000 sq. feet of interactive exhibits and hands-on demonstrations that guarantee to amuse visitors of all ages. Other features included are: one of the biggest planetariums in US, the USS Blueback, and a large screen OMNIMAX Theater. General admission is $7, open from Tuesday to Sunday 9:30 am to 5:30 pm.

Portland Classic Chinese Garden located at NW 3rd & Everett is a local getaway from the hustle and bustle of the city. One will appreciate the tranquility and elegance of the gardens surrounding the area. Designed from the Ming Dynasty era, this Suzhou style garden is well loved for its colors, Chinese buildings and bridges. Open from 10 am to 5 pm during winter and 9 am to 6 pm in summer.

For book lovers, visit the largest independent bookstore in the world, **Powel's City of Books** occupies an entire city block. If you are a beer enthusiast, you should visit Oregon's oldest craft brewery (perhaps not too old) founded in 1984 BridgePort Brewery. Taste and visit Oregon's first brewpub at the **BridgePort Brew Pub** located at 1313 NW Marshall St., also known as Portland's historic "Pearl District."

Accommodations

The Governor Hotel located at 611 S.W. Tenth at Alder Street, Portland, OR 97205. Tel: (503) 224-3400; toll-free (800) 554-3456; expect to pay $170-$500. The **5th Avenue Suites Hotel** located at 506 S.W. Washington, Portland, OR 97204. Tel: (503) 222-0001; toll-free (800) 711-2971; expect to pay $160-$200. **The Benson Hotel,** located at 309 S.W. Broadway, Portland, OR 97205; Tel: (503) 228-2000; toll-free (888) 5-BENSON; expect to pay $180-$200. **Embassy Suites** located downtown at 319 S.W. Pine Street, Portland, OR 97204; Tel: (503) 279-9000; toll-free (800) EMBASSY; expect to pay $150-$500.

Best Western Imperial Hotel located at 400 S.W. Broadway, Portland, OR 97205; Tel: (503) 228-7221; toll-free (800) 453-2323; expect to pay $85 - $110. **Days Inn - City Center** located at 1414 S.W. 6th Avenue, Portland, OR 97201-3404; Tel: (503) 221-1611; toll-free (800) 899-0248; expect to pay $80-$120. **Doubletree Hotel** downtown Portland is located at 301 S.W. Lincoln Street, Portland, OR 97201; Tel: (503) 221-0450; toll-free (800) 222-TREE; expect to pay $90-$150.

Four Points Hotel Sheraton located at 50 S.W. Morrison, Portland, OR 97204; Tel: (503) 227-3312; toll-free (800) 899-0247; expect to pay $90- $150. **Mark Spencer Hotel** located at 409 S.W. 11th, Portland, OR 97205-260; Tel: (503) 224-3293; toll-free (800) 548-3934; expect to pay $70 - $120. **Hilton - Portland** located at 921 S.W. 6th Avenue, Portland, OR 97204; Tel: (503) 226-1611; toll-free (800) HILTONS; expect to pay $150-$250. **Riverplace Hotel** located at 1510 S.W. Harbor Way, Portland, OR 97201; Tel: (503) 228-3233; toll-free (800) 227-1333; expect to pay $145-$250.

Mallory Hotel located at 729 S.W. 15th Avenue, Portland, OR 97205; Tel: (503) 223-6311; toll-free (800) 228-8657; expect to pay $80 - $130. **Rodeway Inn - Convention Center** located at 1506 N.E. 2nd Avenue, Portland, OR 97232; Tel: (503) 231-7665; expect to pay $50-$80. **Thriftlodge Portland Central** located at 949 E. Burnside Street, Portland, OR 97214-1304; Tel: (503) 234-8411; toll-free (800) 525-9055; expect to pay $50-$80.

Salem (OR)

Salem or "Chemeketa," the Indian name for the area which means "meeting or resting place," is located in Willamette Valley, between the Oregon coastline and the Cascade Mountains, 60 miles east of the pacific coast, 50 miles south of Portland, and 64 miles north of Eugene. The Mission of Jason Lee founded the site in 1840, and later it was David Leslie or W.H. Wilson who selected the name "Salem." (Salem comes from the Hebrew word Shalom meaning peace). Salem is the capital of the state of Oregon with a population of more than 120,000. The National Civic League has twice selected Salem as an "All-America City."

Salem is Oregon's third largest and one of Oregon's oldest communities and has a population of approximately 135,000. One of the city's well known landmarks is the capitol building. Built in 1938 mainly of Vermont marble, the building has a Golden Pioneer statue atop its tower.

Salem's train depot is located at 500 13th St. S. E. Salem, OR 97301. The station is staffed and features checked baggage services, payphones, restrooms, and vending machines. Transportation options from the station include Mass Transit District Tel: (503) 588-BUSS, and Yellow Cab Tel: (503) 362-2411 services.

Trains servicing Salem station are the Cascades and Coast Starlight.

Places of Interest

AC Gilbert's Discovery Village located at 116 Marion St. NE Salem, OR 97301, Tel: (503) 371-3631. **Bush House** located at 600 Mission St. SE Salem, OR 97302, Tel: (503) 363-4714. **Jensen Arctic Museum** located at 590 W Church St. Monmouth, OR 97361, Tel: (503) 838-8468. **Marion County Historical Society Museum** located at 260 12th St Salem, OR 97301, Tel: (503) 364-2128. **Mission Mill Museum** located at 1313 Mill St. SE Salem, OR 97301, Tel: (503) 585-7012. **Western Antique Powerland** located at 3995 Brooklake Rd. NE Salem, OR 97303, Tel: (503) 393-2424. **Oregon Electric Railway Historical Society** contact PO Box 308 Lake Oswego, OR 97034, or Tel: (503) 222-2226 for information.

Accommodations

Best Western Mill Creek Inn located at 3125 Ryan Drive Southeast Salem OR 97301; Tel: (503) 585-3332; toll-free (800) 346-9659; expect to pay $50-$90. **Comfort Suites** located at 630 Hawthorne SE Salem OR 97301; Tel: (503) 585-9705; expect to pay $60-$150. **Holiday Inn Express Salem** located at 890 Hawthrone Avenue SE Salem OR 97301; Tel: (503) 391-7000; expect to pay $50-$120. **Rodeway Inn Salem** located at 3195 Portland Road NE Salem OR 97303; Tel: (503) 585-2900; expect to pay $50-$80.

Travelodge Salem located at 1555 State Street Salem OR 97301; Tel: (503) 581-2466; expect to pay $40-$80. **Best Western New Kings Inn** located at 1600 Motor Court NE Salem OR 97301; Tel: (503) 581-1559; toll-free. (877) 594-1110; expect to pay $60-$100. **Super 8 Salem** located at 1288 Hawthorne Northeast Salem OR 97301; Tel: (503) 370-8888; expect to pay $40-$100. **Sleep Inn Salem** located at 3340 Astoria Way NE Salem OR 7303; Tel: (503) 393-6000; expect to pay $50-$100.

Albany (OR)

Albany was founded in 1848 and incorporated in 1864. The city was named Albany, after the state capitol of Albany, New York. Albany is located in the Willamette Valley, 45 miles north of Eugene, 69 miles south of Portland and 24 miles south of Salem. The total land area of Albany is 11.5 sq. miles (29.7 sq. kilometers) and its population is 41,145 making it Oregon's 12th largest city.

Today Albany is an important manufacturing center for rare metals, food processing, timber, and seed industries. Explore Albany's Historic Districts by foot, bicycle, automobile, or organized tours; imagine the slower-paced, quieter days gone by.

Albany's train depot is located at 110 W. 10th St. Albany, OR 97321. The station is staffed and features an enclosed waiting area, checked baggage service, restrooms, payphones, and vending machines. Transportation options from the station include local transit and taxi services.

Trains serving Albany station are the Cascades and Coast Starlight

Places of Interest

Visit the **Albany Regional Museum** located at 136 Lyon St. SW. The museum is open from Monday-Saturday, Noon-4, Tel: (541) 967-7122. Visit Oregon's most restored home, built in 1848, home of Albany founders Thomas and Walter Monteith. **The Monteith House** is located at 518 SW 2nd Ave. Tel: call (541) 926-6829 or (541) 928-0911.

If you're visiting on the 4th of July you should see the **Albany All-Sports Challenge** where loggers from all over the world compete at Timber Linn Memorial Park. See championship logrolling, block chopping, sawing, tree topping, fireworks, and more. Held around the end of July or the first of August, the **Northwest Art & Air Festival** celebrates aviation with Hot Air Balloons, vintage plane displays, and more at the Albany Municipal Airport.

Accommodations

Best Inn & Suites located at 1100 Price Rd. SE, Albany, OR, Tel: (541) 928-5050 or toll-free (800) 626-1900. **Best Western Pony Soldier Inns** located at 315 Airport Rd. SE, Albany, OR, Tel: (541) 928-6322 or toll-free (800) 634-PONY. **La Quinta Inn & Suites** located at 251 Airport Rd. SE, Albany, OR, Tel: (541) 928-0921. **Motel 6** located at 2735 Pacific Blvd. SE, Albany, OR, Tel: (541) 926-4233 or toll-free (800) 4-Motel 6. **Relax Inn** (formerly Motel Orleans) located at 1212 Price Rd. SE, Albany, OR, Tel: (541) 926-0170 or toll-free (800) 321-3352.

Eugene (OR)
Connecting train to **Medford (OR)** and **Ashland (OR); Bend (OR), Eugene (OR)** and **Coos Bay (OR)**

Willamette Valley was first discovered by the Kalapuya Indians who occupied the area for centuries. The City of Eugene was founded in 1852 by Eugene Skinner and it was incorporated in 1862. It is said that in 1853 just after the city was platted and recorded in 1852, the original site of Eugene was relocated to much higher ground after heavy rains flooded the original place.

Eugene is located in western Oregon, 58 miles from the Pacific Ocean, sitting between 400 to 2,000 feet above sea level with total land area of 38 sq. miles (98 sq. kilometers). Eugene is Oregon's second largest city with a population of roughly 137,000.

Eugene is home to well-known universities such as the University of Oregon, Northwest Christian College, Lane Community College, and Eugene Bible College. It explains why a great percentage of Eugene's population are professionals including lawyers, doctors, educators, and architects.

Eugene's train depot is located at 433 Williamette St. Eugene, OR 97401. The station is staffed and features an enclosed waiting area, checked baggage service, restrooms, payphones, and a restaurant. Transportation options from the station include Hertz Car Rental toll-free (800) 654-3131, Lane Transit District, Tel: (541) 687-5555 and VIP Taxi Tel: (541) 484-0920.

Trains Serving Eugene train depot are the Cascades and Coast Starlight.

Places of Interest

Experience the original **Saturday Market,** or the oldest weekly open-air crafts festival in the United States. The first Saturday Market was held on May 9, 1970, and today there are more than 800 participating members and sellers. **Bike Paths:** Eugene is one of the top 10 cities in the US for cycling. The city has more than 53 miles of streets bike lanes. **Hendricks Park & Owen Rose Garden** presents wonderful displays of rhododendrons, azaleas, roses, and other ornamental plants.

Visit the **Sea Lion Caves** located at 91560 Highway 101 Florence OR 97439, Tel: (541) 547-3111, <<http://www.sealioncaves.com>>. If you feel you want to be scared try and visit the **Pioneer Cemetery;** the cemetery is one of the three oldest cemeteries in Eugene and the largest both in acreage and in number of burials.

Visit the largest state supported art museum in Oregon, the **University of Oregon-Museum of Art**. Built in 1932 the museum has 14 galleries and a collection of over 12,500 objects of Asian art, Northwest art, and photography. It is the second largest art museum in the state (currently undergoing a major renovation and expansion to open in 2003). The **University of Oregon-Museum of Natural History,** established in the 1930s, holds over 500,000 objects, of which 30,000 are exhibited. The **Springfield Museum** is located at 590 Main St., Mail: 225 Fifth St., Springfield 97477, Tel: (541) 726-3677.

Other places of interest are: **Criterion Gallery** located at 35 West 8th Avenue Eugene OR 97401, Tel: (541) 683-8474, toll-free (800) 624-4390. The **Lane County Historical Museum** located at 740 West 13th Ave., Eugene 97402, Tel: (541) 687-4239. The **Lane ESD Planetarium** located at 2300 Leo Harris Parkway, Eugene 97402, Tel: (541) 461-8227. The **Oregon Air & Space Museum** located at 90377 Boeing Drive Eugene OR 97402, Tel: (541) 461-1101.

The **Willamette Science and Technology Center (WISTEC)** located at 2300 Leo Harris Parkway, Eugene 97402, Tel: (541) 682-3020. **The Lane Arts Council** located at 44 W. Broadway #304 Eugene, OR 97401. Tel: (541) 485-2278. And the **Maude Kerns Art Center** located at 1910 East 15th Avenue, Eugene 97403, Tel (541) 345-1571.

Accommodations

Ramada Inn Eugene located at 225 Coburg Rd. Eugene OR 97401, Tel: (541) 342-5181. **Quality Inn & Suites Eugene** located at 2121 Franklin Blvd. Eugene OR 97403, Tel: (541) 342-1243. **Phoenix Inn Eugene** located at 850 Franklin Boulevard Eugene OR 97403, Tel: (541) 344-0001; toll-free (800) 344-0131. **Travelodge Eugene** located at 1859 Franklin Blvd. Eugene OR 97403, Tel: (541) 342-6383. **Hampton Inn Eugene** located at 3780 West 11th Avenue Eugene OR 97402, Tel: (541) 431-1225.

Best Western New Oregon Motel located at 1655 Franklin Boulevard Eugene OR 97403, Tel: (541) 683-3669. **Red Lion Hotel Eugene** located at 205 Coburg Road Eugene OR 97401, Tel: (541) 342-5201. **Residence Inn Eugene** located at 25 Country Club Road Eugene OR 97401, Tel: (541) 342-7171. **Hilton Eugene & Conference Center** located at 66 East 6th Avenue Eugene Oregon 97401-2667, Tel: (541) 342-2000. **Hawthorn Inn & Suites Eugene** located at Day Island Road Eugene OR 97401, Tel: (541) 344-8335.

Other Washington and Oregon Train Service

-Seattle to Spokene Service

Washington-Oregon Service

	Seattle-Spokane Service	
2 15 am-D	Spokane (WA)*	12 32 am-A
4 38 am	Ephrata (WA)	9 42 pm
5 43 am	Wenatchee (WA)	8 42 pm
8 43 am	Everett (WA)	5 42 pm
9 08 am	Edmonds (WA)	5 17 pm
10 20 am-A	Seattle (WA)	4 45 pm-D

	Portland-Spokane Service	
2 45 am-D	Spokane (WA)*	12 13 am-A
5 35 am	Pasco (WA)	8 57 pm
7 30 am	Wishram (WA)	6 55 pm
8 04 am	Bingen White Salmon WA)	6 21 pm
9 20 am	Vancouver (WA)	5 07 pm
10 10 am-A	Portland (OR)	4 40 pm-D

D-Departure   **A-** Arrival

*Motorcoach Connection

Boise (ID, Mc Call (ID), Grangeville (ID), Lewiston (ID), Moscow (ID), Pullman (WA), Colfax (WA), Spokane (WA).

Seattle (WA) See Cascade, page 56.

Edmonds (WA) See Cascade, page 54 -56.

Everett (WA) See Cascade, page 54-56.

Wenatchee (WA)

Wenatchee is located at the junction of Wenatchee and Columbia rivers and was first settled in 1870 by ranchers, farmers, and merchants. Wenatchee has a land area of 6.2 sq. miles (16 sq. kilometers) and a population of roughly 22,000. The railroad arrived in the town in 1892 and since then Wenatchee became a significant agricultural trading hub for the region.

Wenatchee is rich in pristine natural beauty. Wenatchee River is one of the most visited sites in the region, and a visit to the Rocky Reach Dam will reward you with the sight of the yearly King Salmon migration. Another favorite attraction is the Wenatchee Valley, rich in breathtaking views and natural wonders.

Wenatchee's train depot is located at Foot of Kittias St. Wenatchee, WA 98801. The station is self-serve and features an enclosed waiting area, restrooms, payphones, and a restaurant. Transportation options from the station include local transit, bus, and taxi services.

Wenatchee is served by the Empire Builder.

Washington (WA)
Capital: Olympia (Population: 5,894,121)
Size: 71,303 sq mi. (184,674 sq km)
Nickname: The Evergreen State, Chinook State
Joined the union on: November 11, 1889 (42nd state)
Motto: By and by
Flower: Coast Rhododendron
Bird: Willow Goldfinch
Song: Washington, My Home
Famous for: Microsoft, Boeing, Space needle.
Major industries: Aerospace, agriculture, and hydroelectric energy.

Ephrata (WA)

Ephrata (named after an orchard in the desert) is located 176 miles east of Seattle. Ephrata has a land area of 6.6 sq. miles (17 sq. kilometers), a population of a little more than 5000, and is the county seat of Grant County. The first known settlement in the area was in 1886 as the result of the Northern Pacific Land Grant Act, Desert Claims Act, and the Homestead Act created to encourage settlement in the region.

Ephrata is known for the mineral waters of Soap Lake which are believed to have a healing power. Other places of interest are the Steamboat Rock State Park, Banks Lake, and the Grand Coulee Dam. Ephrata is just 17 miles from the Grant County International Airport.

Ephrata's train depot is located at 24 Alder St. N. W. Ephrata, WA 98823. The station is unstaffed and features payphones. Transportation available from the station is local bus service.

Ephrata station is served by the Empire Builder.

Spokane (WA)

Spokane is located in the eastern part of Washington State just few miles from the Washington/Idaho border. Spokane has a land area of 56 sq. miles (145 sq. kilometers) and population of around 190,000. Spokane was the first non-Indian settlement in the Pacific Northwest.

The Riverfront Park is one of the most visited places in the area. It is also where the famous Spokane Falls is located. Other places of interest are Manito Park which houses several gardens and a conservatory; the Cheney Cowles Memorial Museum located at 2316 W. First Ave. Spokane, WA 99204, Tel: (509) 456-3931; and the Spokane Opera House.

Spokane's train depot is located at W. 221 First Ave. Spokane, WA 99204. The station is staffed and features an enclosed waiting area, checked baggage service, restrooms, payphones, and vending machines. Transportation options from the station include local transit, bus, and taxi services.

Spokane station is served by the Empire Builder.

- Portland to Spokane Service

Portland (OR) See Cascade, page 70.

Vancouver (WA) See Cascade, page 64-70

BinGen-White Salmon (WA)

BinGen is the sister city of BinGen in Germany, which explains why many of the town's old buildings are of Germanic architecture. The town of BinGen was founded by Theodore Suksdorf in 1892 and was incorporated in 1924.

BinGen's train depot is located at Foot of Walnut St. BinGen, WA 98605. The station is self-serve. Transportation available from the station is taxi service.

BinGen station is served by the Empire Builder.

Wishram (WA)

Wishram's train depot is located at West End of Railroad Ave. Wishram, WA 98673. The station is unstaffed and features an enclosed waiting area and payphones.

Wishram station is served by the Empire Builder.

Pasco (WA)

The city of Pasco is situated at the junction of the Columbia, Yakima, and Snake Rivers and is known as the gateway to the great Columbian Basin. Located 142 miles south of Spokane, Pasco has a land area of 21.8 sq. miles (56 sq. kilometers) and a population of approximately 21,000.

Some of the most visited places in Pasco are the Franklin County Historical Museum; Science and Technology Museum; Sacagawea State Park; Trade, Recreation, and Agricultural Centers; Sporting Complex (the largest in the region); Ice Harbor Dam; the McNary Wildlife Refuge; Palouse Falls; and the Columbia River Exhibition of History.

Pasco's train depot is located at Clark and Tacoma Sts. Pasco, WA 99301. The station is staffed and features an enclosed waiting area, payphones, and vending machines. Transportation options from station include local transit, bus, and taxi services.

Pasco station is served by the Empire Builder.

Spokane (WA) See Seattle to Spokane Route, page 77-78.

The Coast Starlight

One of the most famous train routes in the US, the Coast Starlight, travels three states and some of the major cities and destinations of the western pacific region of the United States. It links the states of **Washington, Oregon,** and **California** and the cities of **Seattle, Portland, Sacramento, San Francisco, Santa Barbara,** and **Los Angeles**.

It began its first service in June 1973. The Coast Starlight route covers 1,389 miles of stunning sceneries of alpine, hills, farms, rock formations, and coastlines. It uses a lightweight aerodynamic locomotive called Genesis that is capable of reaching a speed of 103 miles per hour and double deck Superliner II cars.

Route Destination Highlights

Seattle, WA- Gateway to the magnificent Mt. Rainier, take a day trip to Olympic National Park, visit the Seattle Space needle, take a romantic afternoon walk at the Puget Sound, or tour the famous Klondike Gold Rush Park.

Portland, OR- Visit the Cascade Mountains or explore the Columbia River Gorge, the Multnomah Falls, and what is left of Mt. St. Helens. If you are a book lover, visit the largest independent bookstore in the world, Powel's City of Books.

	Coast Starlight	
9 45 am-D	**Seattle (WA)**	8 25 pm-A
10 43 am	Tacoma (WA)	7 00 pm
11 30 am	Olympia Lacey (WA)	6 12 pm
11 53 am	Centralia (WA)	5 50 pm
12 38 pm	Kelso Longview (WA)	5 04 pm
1 21 pm	Vancouver (WA)	4 23 pm
1 55 pm-A	**Portland (OR)**	4 00 pm-D
2 15 pm-D		3 40 pm-A
3 27 pm	Salem (OR)	2 03 pm
4 00 pm	Albany (OR)	1 30 pm
5 00 pm	Eugene (OR)	12 44 pm
7 55 pm	Chemult (OR)	9 40 am
9 45 pm	Klamath Falls (OR)	8 25 am
12 20 am	Dansmuir (CA)	5 04 am
2 06am	Redding (CA)	3 14 am
3 35 am	Chico (CA)	1 55 am
6 35 am	**Sacramento (CA)**	11 59 pm
6 50 am	Davis (CA)	11 36 pm
7 34 am	Martinez (CA)	10 57 pm
8 10 am-A	Emeryville (CA)	10 15 pm-D
8 20 am-D		10 05 pm-A
8 30 am-A	**Oakland (CA)**	9 50 pm-D
8 45 am-D		9 35 pm-A
9 50 am	San Jose (CA)	8 42 pm-D
10 05 am		8 27 pm-A
11 46 pm	Sallinas (CA)***a**	6 36 pm
1 36 pm	Paso Robles (CA)***b**	4 45 pm
3 10 pm	S. Louis Obispo (CA)	3 43 pm
6 17 pm	**Santa Barbara (CA)**	12 46 pm
7 08 pm	Oxnard (CA)	11 42 am
7 46 pm	Simi Valley (CA)	11 08 am
8 28 pm	Glendale (CA)	10 18 am
9 05 pm-A	**Los Angeles (CA)****	10 00 am-D
*Motorcoach Connection		
--Monterey (CA) a		
--Hearst Castle (CA) b		
** Train Connections		
A-Arrival	D-Departure	

San Francisco, CA- Visit the famous Pier 39, Alcatraz Island or The Rock, the worlds most celebrated bridge the Golden Gate Bridge, the Museum of Modern Art, the exciting Castro, or Union Square. Take the city tram and explore San Francisco's hilly streets or simply walk through the romantic setting of the city by the bays Fisherman's Wharf.

Monterey CA- Take the 17-mile loop at the Monterey Peninsula and discover the rich environment of the Monterey Bay, visit the world famous Monterey Aquarium, or take a few miles drive and explore the rugged mountains and cliffs of Big Sur, that will surely give a great sense of adventure.

Paso Robles- Visit some of California's 48 wineries or just relax and take a bath at several natural hot springs of Paso Robles.

San Luis Obispo, CA- The gateway to the golden coast of California. Explore the magnificent rugged coastline of southern California, visit the famous Hearst Castle, a glance of the peculiar Morro Bay or enjoy surfing in some of the most dangerous coastal waves of the Pacific.

Santa Barbara, CA- See one of the most famous destinations of Southern California and enjoy the sun and surf at the Palm-lined beach, go historic at the Mission Santa Barbara, or simply enjoy shopping in downtown Santa Barbara.

Los Angeles, CA- Known as one of the most controversial cities, Los Angeles is the entertainment capital of the world. See the "walk of fame" on Hollywood Boulevard, visit Universal Studios Hollywood, the world known L.A. County Museum of Art, Beverly Hills, take a dip in some of the most lively beaches in the area: the world famous Malibu Beach, Santa Monica Beach, or Venice Beach, or bring out the child in you and visit Disneyland.

Scenery along the Route

On your way from Seattle (WA) to Portland (OR) you will enjoy the views of the beautiful Puget Sound, snow-covered mountains (most of the year) of the Cascade Range, rich greenery farms and stocks, rivers and water irrigations and thick forests, the splendiferous work of nature.

Hold your camera after passing the Suisun-Fairfield station and look to your left side where US military ships can be seen, and in few minutes the train will be crossing the San Pablo Bay entering Martinez. The route all the way to Emeryville and Oakland are a fresh sight and full of charming bay sceneries.

Prepare your camera or take a drink and snack, relax and sit tight at the lounge car and enjoy the spectacular views of mountains, cliffs, beaches and the Pacific Ocean beginning from Vandenberg Air force Base, Santa Barbara through Ventura.

Train Schedules

Coast Starlight travels daily from Seattle, Washington to Los Angeles, California. The trip between the two cities takes approximately 36 hours (1 1/2 day) of travel time.

Accommodations

Accommodations are Sleeping Car (Standard or Economy, Family, Special and Deluxe), Coach Seat and Disabled facilities. Other service accommodations are Dining Car, Lounge Car, and Pacific Parlor Car.

Complete meals are served in dining car; lounge car offers sandwiches, snacks, and drinks. Movie entertainment is available at the sightseer lounge car in early evening. Metropolitan Lounge is available in Portland for first class passengers.

All Aboard!

For **Seattle (WA)**, **Tacoma (WA)**, **Olympia-Lacey (WA)**, **Centralia (WA)**, **Kelso-Longview (WA)**, **Portland (OR)**, **Salem (OR)**, **Albany (OR)** and **Eugene-Springfield (OR)** see "**The Cascade**"

Chemult (OR) Thruway Motor Coach Connection to **Bend (OR)** and **Redmond (OR)**

Chemult is a small community resort town in the Lake region of southern Oregon just 72 miles north of Klamath Falls and 65 miles south of Bend. The name Chemult means "Wife Dies" in native Indian language.

Some of Chemults popular destinations are the Odell Lake, the Lemolo Lake, Crescent Lake, and the Little Deschutes River. Snowmobile sports and cross-country skiing are Chemults popular winter sports. During summer swimming, boating, fishing, picnicking, water-skiing, camping, hiking, trail biking, and hunting are popular activities.

The Chelmult train depot is located on 2nd St. off Santiam Hwy. Chemult, OR 97731. The station is un-staffed and features payphones, restrooms and a restaurant. Transportation options from the station include local taxi.

Chalmult station is served by the Coast Starlight.

Klamath Falls (OR)

Located in the south central region of Oregon and bordering northern California, the City of Klamath Falls has a land area of 16 sq. miles (42 sq. kilometers) and has a population of around 19,000.

Klamath Falls has an elevation of 4100 feet and is blessed with nature's beauty and wonders. The Upper Klamath Lake, covering 133 square miles, is the largest body of fresh water in the northwest; Mt. Scott with its towering height of 8926 feet is the highest in Klamath County. It is also in Klamath Falls where you can find the largest wintering concentration of Bald Eagles; there are approximately 1000 birds visiting the region during winter.

Klamath train depot is located at 1600 Oak St. / P.O. Box 932 Klamath Falls, OR 97601. The station is staffed and features an enclosed waiting area, checked baggage service, restrooms, payphones, and a restaurant. Transportation options from the station include local taxi service.

Klamath station is served by the Coast Starlight.

Oregon (OR)

Capital: Salem (Population: 3,421,399)
Size: 98,386 sq mi. (254,718 sq km)
Nickname: The Beaver State
Joined the union on: February 14, 1859 (33rd state)
Motto: She flies with her own wings
Flower: Oregon grape
Bird: Western meadowlark
Song: Oregon, My Oregon
Famous for: Nike
Major industries: Lumber industry, paper manufacturing industry and transportation equipment.

Places of Interest

Visit the unspoiled beauty of **Crater Lake National Park** located 60 miles north of Klamath Falls just off Highway 134, Tel: (541) 594-2211. **County Museum** is located at 1451 Main St., Klamath Falls, OR. 97601, Tel: (541) 883-4208. **Native Americans - Klamath Indian Tribes** exhibit artifacts and data on the culture of the Yahooskin, Modoc and Klamath Indians. Tel: (541) 783-2218 or toll-free (800) 524-9787.

Observe more than 500 species of wildlife including the famous Bald Eagle at the **Klamath Wing Watchers Inc,** for information write P.O. Box 251, Klamath Falls, OR 97601, Tel: (541) 883-5732. **Klamath Wildlife Gallery** is located at 2271 Shasta Way, Klamath Falls, OR. 97601, Tel: (541) 884-4230. **Forth Klamath Museum And Park** is a military post established in 1863, Tel: (541) 381-2230. Interested in buying local crafts? Visit the **Crafter Market** located at 3040 Washburn Way, Klamath Falls, OR. 97601, Tel: (541) 882-5270.

Klamath Lake information, contact Meridian Sail Center, 531 SO. 8th St. Klamath Falls, OR.97601, 95410. Tel: (541) 884-7237.

Accommodations

Best Western Klamath Inn located at 4061 S. 6TH ST., Klamath Falls, 97603. Tel: (541) 882-1200. **Crater Hotel** located at 129 North 2nd, Klamath Falls, Oregon 97601. Tel: (541) 882-5055. **Holiday Inn Express Hotel & Suites** located at 2500 South 6th St., Klamath Falls, Oregon 97601. Tel: (541) 884-9999. **Maverick Motel** located at 1220 Main St., Klamath Falls, Oregon 97601. Tel: (541) 882-6688. **Golden West Motel** located at 6402 South 6th St., Klamath Falls, Oregon 97603. Tel: (541) 882-1758.

Cimarron Motel located at 3060 S. 6TH ST., 97603. Tel: (541) 882-4601. **Harriman Spring Resort** located at 26661 Rocky Point Rd., Rocky Point, Oregon. Tel: (541) 356-2331. **MOTEL 6** located at Kane and South 6th St., Klamath Falls, Oregon. Tel: (541) 884-2110. **Quality Inn** located at 100 Main St., Klamath Falls, Oregon 97601. Tel: (541) 882-4666. **Town house Motel** located at 5323 S.6TH ST., KLAMATH FALLS, OR. 97603. Tel: (541) 882-0924. **Travelodge** located at 11 Main St., Klamath Falls, OR. 97601. Tel: (541) 882-4494.

Dunsmuir (CA)

Dunsmuir is located on Interstate 5 north of Redding in northern California, a small-town home to more than 2,000 friendly people. Dunsmuir's land area is 1.8 sq. miles (4.8 sq. kilometers), elevation 2,289 feet above sea level. Dunsmuir was incorporated in 1909.

Dunsmuir train depot is located at 5750 Sacramento Ave. Dunsmuir, CA 96025. The station is un-staffed and features an enclosed waiting area, payphones, and restrooms. Transportation from the station is local taxi service.

Dunsmuir station is served by the Coast Starlight.

Places of Interest

Located on the Sacramento River, North Dunsmuir is known for **Mossbrae Fall,** a graceful and enchanting waterfall, the **Castle Crags State Park**, located six miles south of Dunsmuir, is great for a nice relaxing walk. **Sacramento River** is known for water leisure, sports, and clear fresh water.

Accommodations

Travelodge located at 5400 Dunsmuir Ave, Dunsmuir, CA 96025, Tel: (530) 235-4395. **Dunsmuir Inn** located at 5423 Dunsmuir Ave, Dunsmuir, CA 96025, Tel: (530) 235-4543. **Acorn Inn** located at 4310 Dunsmuir Ave, Dunsmuir, CA 96025, Tel: (530) 235-4805. **Railroad Park Resort** located at 100 Railroad Park Rd, Dunsmuir, CA 96025, Tel: (530) 235-4611. **Bavaria Lodge** located at 4601 Dunsmuir Ave, Dunsmuir, CA 96025, Tel: (530) 235-4707. **Cave Springs-Motel-Resort** located at 4727 Dunsmuir Ave, Dunsmuir, CA 96025, Tel: (530) 235-2721. **Oak Tree Inn** located at 6604 Dunsmuir Ave, Dunsmuir, CA 96025, Tel: (530) 235-2884. **Cedar Lodge Motel** located at 4201 Dunsmuir Ave, Dunsmuir, CA 96025, Tel: (530) 235-4331.

California (CA)
Capital: Sacramento (Population: 33,871,648)
Size: 163,707 sq mi. (424,001 sq km)
Nicknames: The Golden State
Joined the union on: September 9, 1850 (31st state)
Motto: Eureka (I Have Found It)
Flower: Golden Poppy
Bird: California Valley Quail
Song: "I Love You, California"
Famous for: Golden Gate Bridge, Hollywood, Yosemite Valley
Major industries: Manufacturing, Agriculture, Biotechnology, Software and Tourism

Redding (CA)

Redding was founded in 1872, sitting at an elevation of 557 feet above sea level and located at the tip of the California central valley in far northern California. Redding's total land area is 51 sq. miles (132 sq. kilometers) and it has a population of roughly 80,000.

Originally Redding was a mining town that was developed during the California Gold Rush. Today tourism is Redding's primary industry. Some of Redding's tourist spots are Mt. Shasta, the Shasta Lake and Shasta Dam, the Lassen Volcanic National Park and Mt. Lassen (last eruption was 1917).

Redding's train depot is located at 1620 Yuba St. Redding, CA 96001. The station is self-serve, and features restrooms and payphones. Transportation from the station is local taxi service.

Redding station is served by the Coast Starlight.

Places to See and Things to Do

Explore caves and grottos in **Lake Shasta Caverns** toll-free (800) 795-CAVE, or Tel: (530) 238-2341. A 2,000 years old, 1,300 feet long cave **Subway Cave** is located at Hat Creek, near Highway 44 & 89 Junction. **Shasta Dam** at 602 feet high and 3,460 feet long is the second largest and highest concrete structure in the United States. Tel: (530) 275-4463 and Tel: (530) 275-1554. **Shasta Lake** has a total depth of 517 feet; the lake is located 12 miles north of Redding on I-5.

Museums

Carter House Natural Science Museum is located next to the Sacramento River in Redding's Caldwell Park. The museum exhibits 37 species of live animals. The **Fort Crook Museum** exhibits the story of the Indians and early settlers of the area. Other interesting museums are the **J.J. Jackson Memorial Museum,** Tel: (530) 623-5211 and the **Redding Museum of Art & History,** the largest museum institution north of Sacramento, Tel: (530) 243-8801.

Parks

Ide Adobe State Historic Park is a memorial to California's only President, William B. Ide. The park is located 30 miles south of Redding on I-5, 2 miles northeast of Redding. **Ahjumawi Springs State Park** located 80 miles from Redding, Highway 299 East. **Lassen Volcanic National Park** located 48 miles east of Redding, State Highway 44, Tel: (530) 595-4444 and **Shasta State Historic Park** located 6 miles west of Redding on Highway 299 West, Tel: (530) 243-8194.

Accommodations

Americana Lodge located at 1250 Pine Street, Redding, CA Tel: (530) 241-7020. **Best Western Ponderosa Inn** located at 2220 Pine Street, Redding, CA Tel: (530) 241-6300. **Comfort Inn** located at 2059 Hilltop Drive, Redding, CA Tel: (530) 221-6530. **Vagabond Inns** located at 536 Cypress Avenue, Redding, CA Tel: (530) 223-1600.**Grand Manor** located at 850 Mistletoe Lane, Redding, CA Tel: (530) 221-4472. **Doubletree Hotel** Located at 1830 Hilltop Drive, Redding, CA Tel: (530) 221-8700. **Budget Lodge** located at 1055 Market Street, Redding, CA Tel: (530) 243-4231. **Bel Air Motel** located at 540 No. Market Street, Redding, CA Tel: (530) 243-5291. **Holiday Inn** located at 1900 Hilltop Dr., Redding, CA Tel: (530) 221-7500. **Thrift Lodge Casa Blanca** located at 413 No. Market Street, Redding, CA Tel: (530) 241-3010. **Thunderbird Lodge** located at 1350 Pine Street, Redding, CA Tel: (530) 243-5422. **Vagabond Inn** located at 2010 Pine Street, Redding, CA Tel: (530) 243-3336.

Chico (CA)

Chico is located 90 miles north of Sacramento, situated within the northern end of the Sacramento Valley. Chico was founded by General John Bidwell in 1843, and was incorporated in 1872. Chico has a total land area of 22 square miles (58 sq. kilometers) and a population of 64,581.

Chico's train depot is located at the intersection of W. 5th and Orange Sts. Chico, CA 95926. The station is self-serve and features an enclosed waiting area, restrooms, and payphones. Transportation options from the station include local bus, transit, and taxi services.

Chico station is served by the Coast Starlight.

Places of Interest

Chico Museum exhibits the history of the city, located in Carnegie Library building at 141 Salem Street, Tel: (530) 891-4366. Interested to see the world's largest yo-yo? Visit the **National Yo-Yo Museum** located at 320 Broadway Tel: (530) 893-1414. Take a walk in historic downtown Chico and see the city's many fabulous murals at the **Downtown Murals**. Or relax and see **Bidwell Park,** a 3,600 acres park, the third largest municipal park in the United States.

Arts and Theater

Chico Community Theatre (Chico Children's Theatre) is located at 13543 Garner Lane, Tel: (530) 343-4231. **Concert in the Park Series** located in downtown park plaza at 5th & Main Streets, Tel: (530) 345-6500, holds free concerts every Friday 7pm to 8pm.

Gallery

Orient & Flume Art Glass located at 2161 Park Avenue, Tel: (530) 893-0373. Visitors experience the art glass blowing. **Chico Art Center Historic Train Depot** located at 450 Orange Street, Tel: (530) 895-8726.

Accommodations

Budget Hotel located at 2566 Esplanade, Chico CA 95973 Tel: (530) 898-0134. **Holiday Inn** located at 685 Manzanita CT, Chico, CA 95926, Tel: (530) 345-2491. **Best Western Inn** located at 25 Heritage LN, Chico CA 95926, Tel: (530) 894-8600 or toll-free (800) 622-6466. **Chico Days Inn** located at 740 Broadway Chico, CA 95928. **Best Western Heritage Inn** located at 25 Heritage Lane Chico, CA 95926.

Sacramento (CA) See Capitol Corridor, page 136.

Davis (CA)

Davis was named after Jerome C. Davis, a pioneer settler who came to the area and planted 400 acres of wheat, barley, orchards and vineyards. Today Davis is a university-oriented city, home to the world-class University of California at Davis with more than 26,000 students.

Davis is located 13 miles west of Sacramento and 72 miles northeast of San Francisco. Davis' total land area is 8 sq. miles (22 sq. kilometers) and it is home to more than 62,000 residents. Davis has more than 50,000 bicycles and more than 40 miles of bicycle trails.

Davis' train depot is located at 840 2nd St. Davis, CA 95616. The station is staffed and features an enclosed waiting area, checked baggage service, restrooms, payphones, Quik-Trak ticket machine, and a vending machines. Transportation options from the station include local bus, transit, and taxi services.

Trains serving Davis station are California Zephyr, Capitol Corridor and Coast Starlight.

Martinez (CA)

Martinez is one of the oldest Anglo cities in California. Incorporated in 1876, it's a small city with a community of 37,034 residents, living in a land area of 11 square miles (29 sq. kilometers).

Martinez' train depot is located at 601 Marina Vista Drive Martinez, CA 94553-1143. The station is staffed and features an enclosed waiting area, checked baggage service, Quik-Trak ticket machine, restrooms, payphones, and a restaurant. Transportation options from the station include local transit and taxi services.

Trains serving Martinez station are California Zephyr, Capitol Corridor, Coast Starlight and the San Joaquin.

Emeryville (CA) Thruway Motor-coach Connections to Oakland (CA) and San Francisco (CA)

Emeryville was incorporated in 1896, located at the eastern foot of the Bay Bridge on the San Francisco Bay in Oakland CA. Emeryville has a land area of just 1.2 square miles (3 sq. kilometers) and population of roughly 7,000 residents.

A small city with big businesses, Emeryville is home to some of the biggest companies in the world. Also it is said that there are over 250,000 vehicles passing through Emeryville junctions and freeways each day.

Emeryville has a new Amtrak Station located at 5885 Landregan St. Emeryville, CA 94608. The station is expected to accommodate approximately 500,000 passengers each year. Emeryville's train depot is staffed and features an enclosed waiting area, checked baggage service, restrooms, payphones and snack bars.

Transportation options from the station include Hertz Car Rental toll-free (800) 654-3131, city free shuttle service to connect passengers to BART stations, local transit and taxi services.

Trains serving Emeryville station are California Zephyr, Capitol Corridor, Coast Starlight, and the San Joaquin.

Oakland (CA) Thruway Motor-coach Connection to San Francisco (CA)

Oakland is located on the eastern side of San Francisco Bay, across the Oakland-Bay Bridge from San Francisco. Oakland was a former part of a large ranch of 48,000 acres owned by Luis Maria Peralta and later purchased by Horace W. Carpentier. Founded in 1850, Oakland was named after the evergreen oaks that are prominent in the area's landscape. Oakland has a total land area of 56 sq. miles (145 sq. kilometers) and a population of 372,242.

Oakland's train depot is located at 245 Second St. Oakland, CA 94607. The station is staffed and features an enclosed waiting area, checked baggage service, restrooms, payphones, Quik-Trak ticket machine, and vending machines. Transportation options from the station include Hertz Car Rental Tel: (800) 654-3131, local transit, and taxi services.

Trains serving Oakland station are Capitol Corridor, Coast Starlight, and the San Joaquin.

Places of Interest

Chabot Space & Science Center located at 10,000 Skyline Blvd., Oakland, CA, Tel: (510) 530-3480. **Oakland Museum of California** located at 100 Oak St. Oakland CA 94607, Tel: (510) 238-2200 or toll-free: (888) OAK-MUSE. **Western Aerospace Museum** located at 8260 Boeing St. Oakland CA 94614, Tel: (510) 638-7100. **African-American Museum and Library** located at 5606 San Pablo Ave. Oakland CA 94608, Tel: (510) 597-5053. **Pardee Home Museum** located at 672-11th St. Oakland CA 94607-3651, Tel: (510) 444-2187, ext. 201.

Accommodations

Oakland is great alternative to San Francisco's soaring hotel prices.

Hampton Inn Oakland - Airport located at 8465 Enterprise Way Oakland CA 94621; Tel: (510) 632-8900 and toll-free: (800) 426-7866; expect to pay $90-$150. **Comfort Inn** located at 8452 Edes Ave Oakland CA 94621; Tel: (510) 568-1500; expect to pay $80-$150. **Howard Johnson San Francisco Bay Bridge** located at 423 7th St. Oakland CA 29607; Tel: (510) 451-6316; expect to pay $50-$150.

Best Western Inn at the Square Oakland located at 233 Broadway Oakland CA 94607; Tel: (510) 452-4565; expect to pay $90-$150. **Hilton Oakland Airport** located at 1 Hegenberger Road Oakland CA 94621; Tel: (510) 635-5000; expect to pay $70-$300. **Clarion Suites Lake Merritt Hotel** located at 1800 Madison St Oakland CA 94612; Tel: (510) 832-2300 and toll-free: (800) 933-4683; expect to pay $110-$300.

Park Plaza Hotel located at 150 Hegenberger Road Oakland CA 94621; Tel: (510) 635-5300; expect to pay $60-$250. **Holiday Inn Express** located at 66 Airport Access Road Oakland CA 94603; Tel: (510) 569-4400 and toll-free: (800) 651-1883; expect to pay $80-$350. **Marriott Oakland City Center** located at 1001 Broadway Oakland CA 94607; Tel: (510) 451-4000; expect to pay $70-$250. **Ramada Limited Oakland** located at 8471 Enterprise Highway Oakland CA 94621; Tel: (510) 562-4888; expect to pay $70-$130. **Holiday Inn Oakland Metro Airport** located at 500 Hegenberger Rd. Oakland CA 94621; Tel: (510) 562-5311; expect to pay $70-$200.

San Francisco (CA)
Motor-coach connections to **Emeryville (CA)** and **Oakland (CA)**

San Francisco was founded in 1776 and was incorporated as a city on April 15th, 1850. Located at the end of the San Francisco Peninsula on the San Francisco Bay, the city of San Francisco is probably the most popular and the most visited city in the US. There are estimated more than 16 million people visiting the city each year.

San Francisco has a total land area of 47 sq. miles (121 sq. kilometers) and a population of more than 800,000. San Francisco has a moderate, comfortable and relatively cool temperature. Average temperature in spring is 56 F (13 degree C), during summer is 65 F (19 degree C), fall is 61 F (17 degree C), and winter 50 F (10 degree C).

San Francisco is built on a sequence of hills that give breathtaking views of the San Francisco Bay and adjacent islands. There are plenty of things to see and do in San Francisco; shopping, dining, and sightseeing are the most popular activities. Nightlife has always been exciting in San Francisco and one of the city's famous entertainment and hangout destinations is the Castro district. There are more than 3,400 restaurants and drinking establishments and an estimated 30,000 hotel rooms in the city.

The Great Earthquake on April 18, 1906, with a magnitude of 8.25 on the Richter scale is instilled and well remembered, exhibited in many of San Francisco's museums and tourist destinations. The city has more than 40 historical landmarks, including the Golden Gate Bridge, Alcatraz (The Rock), Telegraph Hill and Union Square.

Getting Around

Airport

San Francisco International Airport is located 14 miles south of downtown San Francisco and is one of the busiest airports in the US. There is a shared ride van and bus that operate door-to-door almost anywhere in the Bay Area; fares are between $10 to $25 dollars. A taxi ride from the airport to downtown San Francisco is about 30 minutes journey and costs approximately $35. SamTran Tel: (800) 660-4287 offers bus services between San Francisco International Airport and the surrounding areas. Bus number 292, 193 and Express Route BX, and Express Route KX serve the airport.

Train services are located outside the airport at Millbrae where Caltrain has regular train service from the airport to downtown San Francisco (4th & King Streets). Weekday service operates 5 am to 12 am, 7 am to 12 am Saturday and 8 am to 10 pm Sunday. There are free shuttle bus services that link the airport terminals every hour 5 am to 12 am weekdays, 7 am to 12 am Saturday and 8 am to 10 pm Sunday.

Bus Services

MUNI Buses Tel: (415) 673-MUNI travel the entire city of San Francisco. AC Transit Tel: (415) 817-1717 serves Alameda and Western Contra Costa Counties, and The Golden Gate Transit links SF city to Marin Counties via Golden Gate Bridge. The golden gate transit stops at Van Ness, Lombard, and Geary streets, the Financial District, Civic Center and Trans Bay Terminal in San Francisco.

Rent-A-Car

City Rent-A-Car located at 1748 Folsom/13th St. Tel: (415) 861-1312, Dollar rent a car located at 346 O Farrell/Mason Tel: (415) 771-5301, and Payless rent a car located at 320 O Farrell/Mason Tel: (415) 292-1002.

Commuter, Streetcar and Train

The MUNI Metro Street Cars travels underground through the city, fares are $1 for adults; 35 cent for children and children below five are free, for information call Tel: (415) 673-MUNI.

Cable Cars run on 3 lines (see Places to See and Things to Do-Union Square) from 6 am to 12 am. F Market Historic Street Cars run from 6 am to 12 am, the fleets are historic vintage streetcars acquired by the city from all over the world (only few of its kind still run and operate). Caltrain serving the Peninsula and San Jose area, Caltrain station is located at 4th and Townsend St., toll-free (800) 660-4287.

BART or Bay Area Rapid Transit connects San Francisco to East Bay cities of Oakland, Berkeley, Concord, Richmond, Fremont, and Hayward. BART underground station in SF city is located along Market Street from Civic Center to Embarcadero. Fares range from

$1.10-$4.70 depending on the trip taken (there are ticket machines at the station). Tel: (510) 992-BART, (415) 989-2278 <<http://www.bart.gov>>.

Amtrak's San Francisco Train Pickup Stations are located at the following places, Pier 39, Museum of Modern Art, North Beach, and Union Square.

Visitors Information Center

San Francisco Convention & Visitors Bureau is located at 900 Market Street, Lower Level Hallidie Plaza San Francisco, CA 94102-2804; Tel: (415) 283-0177 and at the Hallidie Plaza; Tel: (415) 283-0177.

Places to See and Things to Do

The most popular areas and attractions in San Francisco: Fisherman's Wharf, Chinatown, the Golden Gate Bridge, Union Square, cable-car rides, and the Golden Gate Park.

Fisherman's Wharf

Fisherman's Wharf is San Francisco's most popular destination. This historic site is home to some of the city's most visited attractions: the **Wax Museum, Ripley's Believe It or Not Museum, Red & White Fleet** and hundreds of shops and restaurants.

Part of the Fisherman's Wharf area is **Pier 39,** located at Beach St. and Embarcadero. Some of the pier's famous attractions are the Underwater World Aquarium, sunning sea lions, numerous stores, restaurants and fleets of bay cruise ships. Visit the **Ghirardelli Store,** the oldest continuous chocolate manufacturer in America, at Ghirardelli Square, located at Anchorage and Cannery St. at the Fisherman's Wharf. **The Cannery,** built in 1907 and once a Del Monte peach cannery, contains numerous shops, galleries, and live entertainment daily.

Take a walk or enjoy a ride on one of San Francisco's many cable cars and explore the **Hyde**

Street Pier where there are several historical ships and a submarine museum open for public viewing. Located at the end of Polk St. is the **Aquatic Park** and the **SF Marine National Historic Park,** a nice place to visit, opens daily.

If you wish to visit San Francisco Bay's nearby islands (including Alcatraz), there are numerous day trips via ferry services around the Wharf. Taking a bay cruise around San Francisco bay offers a breathtaking view of the Golden Gate Bridge, Alcatraz Island, and the city. The bay cruise trip and nearby islands cruise (Alcatraz and Angel Islands) will cost $12-$20. There are other city tours and tours of nearby areas available (Yosemite Valley, Wine Country, Monterey, etc.). Call Blue & Gold Fleet at Tel: (415) 773-1188, Red & White Fleet at Tel: (877) 855-5506 (toll-free), for information.

The Rock (Alcatraz)

Alcatraz or **"The Rock"** was phased out as a federal penitentiary in 1963 and was opened to the public in 1973 as part of the Golden Gate National Recreation Area. Visits to the island are by cruise ship which can be taken at the Fisherman's Wharf. Call Tel: (415) 705-5555 or contact Blue & Gold Fleet at Tel: (415) 773-1188, or Red & White Fleet at Tel: (877) 855-5506 (toll-free).

Chinatown

Explore one of the biggest **China town** areas outside China. Entering through the town's Dragon Gate is highly recommend, located at the streets of Bush and Grant (Grant Avenue is the oldest street in San Francisco), the gate was said to be a gift from Taiwan to San Francisco. There are many shops and restaurants in the 18-city block Chinese district. Visit one of the few buildings that survived the 1906 San Francisco earthquake and fire, among them the **St. Mary's Church** (built in 1852), located between California and Grant St.

Mission District

Mission Dolores, located at 16th and Dolores streets, is the oldest structure in San Francisco. There is a cemetery adjacent to the mission where the city's pioneers are buried.

Golden Gate Bridge

The Golden Gate Bridge

Probably still the most beautiful and popular bridge in the world, the **Golden Gate Bridge**, (Highway 101) completed in 1937, links San Francisco to Marin County. Millions of visitors cross and visit the bridge each year. The Golden Gate Bridge is 1.2 miles long and cost $35 million to built. There is a $3.00 toll collected only when traveling south. Visit Vista Point (the first exit on the Marin side of the bridge) for an outstanding view's of the bridge and the city of San Francisco.

North Beach

Perhaps North Beach could be called the Italian town of San Francisco. Here you'll find the strong presence of the Mediterranean taste. Located at the top of **Telegraph Hill** (on Filbert Street) is **Coit Tower.** From the top of the tower you get a great view of the Bay Bridge, Financial District and Russian Hill. Other places of interest are **Washington Square,** a city block bordered by Filbert, Union, Stockton, and Powel streets. Just beside Washington square is the **Church of St. Peter and Paul**. The **St. Francis of Assisi Church,** dedicated to the city's patron saint, is located at Vallejo St.

Union Square

Union square, bordered by Powel, Geary, Post, and Stockton streets, is the heart of the city. It was dedicated by the city in support of the Union during the civil war. Today Union square is the place to be for shopping: it's the hub of San Francisco's retail district. No matter the size of your budget, you'll find something in Union Square. There are also numerous restaurants, theaters, boutiques, galleries, and professional services around the area. Chinatown is a few blocks away.

The **Maiden Lane** (the city's former red district) is now a place for some of the most expensive shops in the area. Take the **Cable Car** (a must-to-do ride) and explore San Francisco's famous hilly streets. The cable car will take you from Market Street to Fisherman's Wharf. Cable cars operate along three routes: The Powell-Hyde to Victorian Park route (near the Maritime Museum and Aquatic Park); the Powell-Mason to Fisherman's Wharf route and the California Street line to Van Ness Avenue route. Call Tel: (415) 673-MUNI for more information.

Civic Center

Civic Center has some of San Francisco's most beautiful buildings and the city's government seat. You will see the elegant gold decorated dome of the **City Hall**. Visit the historical and famous **Opera House** where the original United Nations charter was signed. The **Main Library**, **Louise M. Davies Symphony Hall**, and the **War Memorial Veterans Building** (where Herbst Theater Performing House and Museum Library are located) are all found within this area.

Financial District

San Francisco's financial district is also a place of tourism interest: the **Embarcadero Center,** a high-rise building (where Hyatt Hotel is located), is home to hotel, theater, and shops. Perhaps the most noticeable building in the city is the **Trans America Pyramid Building**, located at 600 Montgomery at Columbus. The tower is the tallest in the city and has an observatory on the 27th floor. Other places of interest are the historic **Ferry Building** and **Justin Herman Plaza**.

Nob Hill and Russian Hill

San Francisco's rich and famous district, several of the city's upper class citizens built their mansions on the top of Nob Hill and Russian Hill. Climb or descend the famous Lombard Street known as the city's (or the world's?) most **crooked street**. Here you will find some of San Francisco's most famous and luxurious hotels: the Mark Hopkins and Huntington, among others. Located at 1100 California St. (at Jones St.) is the famous **Grace Cathedral** known for its stained glass and concert series.

Union Street and Pacific Heights

Originally called Cow Hollow, Union Street is one of the city's favorite nightlife destinations. There are numerous restaurants and bars in the area Enjoy Victorian architecture in Pacific Heights.

Japan Town

Home of San Francisco's more than 12,000 Japanese residents, the Japan Center is located on Webster and Geary Streets.

San Fracnciso's Skyline

Richmond and Sunset District

Visit the San Francisco Zoo. Some of the zoo's famous attractions are Gorilla World, Koala Crossing, and the Primate Discovery Center. For information call Tel: (415) 753-7083. The University of California San Francisco is located on Sunset Blvd.

Take a nice stroll at San Francisco's **Golden Gate Park.** This 1,000-acre park houses numerous attractions: the **Asian Art Museum**, the **MH de Young Memorial Museum**, the **Japanese Tea Garden**, the **California Academy of Sciences**, **Morrison Planetarium**, **Strybing Arboretum and Botanical Gardens**, different species of plants (including giant Red Woods), and numerous recreational activities.

Stroll **Ocean Beach** and enjoy its sandy shoreline, visit the **Cliff House** located at great Highways and Point Lobos avenues, watch the sea lions that rest at the **Seal Rocks.** The view from **Point Lobos** is worth seeing.

Marina District

The Marina District offers a splendid view of the Golden Gate Bridge. **Marina Green** is a great place to relax. Former military warehouse and pier **Fort Mason Center** now houses museums and theaters, located at Marina Boulevard and Buchanan. Other places of interest are the **Palace of Fine Arts,** located at Marina Blvd and Baker St., and the **Presidio,** a park overlooking the Golden Gate Bridge and the Pacific Ocean.

Castro

Located at the upper end of Market Street, Castro is one of San Francisco's most visited nightlife areas and is home to many of the city's gay residents. The Victorian houses are still prominent in the area. Pubs, clubs, busy night streets, and restaurants are some of the district's most appealing sights. The Castro Theater is worth visiting, located at 429 Castro St., still a well-preserved classic movie house.

The Haight

Haight is known for its famous intersections, **Haight** and **Ashbury** streets, noted for a number of pubs, restaurants, and hippies in the area. Not far away, a visitor can easily recognize the **Sutro Tower** that is adjacent to **Twin Peaks**.

South of Market

The **Yerba Buena Gardens** is located at 701 Mission Street. This 130,000-square-foot garden is dedicated to the youth of the city. There is a children's garden, child-development center, ice-skating rink, Zeum bowling alley, an art and technology center for kids. Nearby is the **Pacific Bell Park**. It is a 41,000-seat baseball stadium. The park is located at 3rd and King Streets.

Places to Eat

American Cuisine, Chinese Cuisine, French Cuisine, Fusion/Californian Cuisine, Healthy Cuisine, Indian Cuisine, Italian Cuisine, Japanese Cuisine, Mexican Cuisine, Middle Eastern Cuisine, Supper Clubs, Thai Cuisine, Vietnamese Cuisine. These are some of the endless list of cuisines that you can find in San Francisco, and the only challenge is which one to choose.

Accommodations

Courtyard Fisherman's Wharf located at 580 Beach Street San Francisco CA 94133; Tel: (415) 775-3800; expect to pay $120-$350. **Days Inn Lombard Street San Francisco** located at 2358 Lombard Street San Francisco CA 94123; Tel: (415) 922-2010; expect to pay $60-$200. **Econo Lodge San Francisco** located at 2505 Lombard St. San Francisco CA 94123; Tel: (415) 921-2505; expect to pay $60-$180.

Crowne Plaza Hotel San Francisco located at 480 Sutter St. San Francisco CA 94108; Tel: (415) 398-8900; expect to pay $140-$370. **Clarion Hotel Bedford Hotel At Union Square** located at 761 Post Street San Francisco CA 94109; Tel: (415) 673-6040; expect to pay $110-$250. **Hilton San Francisco and Towers** located at 333 O' Farrell Street San Francisco CA 94142-0868; Tel: (415) 771-1400; expect to pay $110-$450.

Fairmont Hotel in San Francisco located at 950 Mason Street San Francisco CA 94108; Tel: (415) 772-5000; expect to pay $150-$900. **Grand Hyatt San Francisco** located at 345

Stockton St. San Francisco CA 94108; Tel: (415) 398-1234; expect to pay $150-$450. **Hilton Fisherman's Wharf** located at 2620 Jones Street San Francisco CA 94133; Tel: (415) 885-4700; expect to pay $120-$350. **Holiday Inn Express Fisherman's Wharf** located at 550 North Point Street San Francisco CA 94133; Tel: (415) 409-4600; expect to pay $140 - $300. **Hotel Nikko San Francisco** located at 222 Mason Street San Francisco CA 94102; Tel: (415) 394-1111; expect to pay $150-$550. **Hyatt at Fisherman's Wharf** located at 555 N. Point St. San Francisco CA 94133; Tel: (415) 563-1234; expect to pay $150-$400.

Marriott San Francisco Fisherman's Wharf located at 1250 Columbus Avenue San Francisco CA 94133; Tel: (415) 775-7555; expect to pay $150-$400. **Park Hyatt San Francisco** located at 333 Battery St. San Francisco CA 94111; Tel: (415) 392-1234; expect to pay $180-$600. **Savoy Hotel** located at 580 Geary St. San Francisco CA 94102; Tel: (415) 441-2700; expect to pay: $140-$250. **The Queen Anne Hotel** located at 1590 Sutter St., San Francisco, CA 94109; Tel: (415) 441-2828 or toll-free: (800) 227-3970; expect to pay $90-$190. **Best Western Civic Center Motor Inn** located at 364 9th Street at Harrison San Francisco CA 94103; Tel: (415) 621-2826; expect to pay $80-$150.

Renoir Hotel located at 45 McAllister Street San Francisco CA 94102; Tel: (415) 626-5200 or toll-free: (800) 576-3388; expect to pay $70-$990. **Sheraton Fisherman's Wharf** located at 2500 Mason Street San Francisco CA 94133; Tel: (415) 362-5500; expect to pay $140-$560. **Westin St. Francis** located at 335 Powell Street, San Francisco, CA 94102; Tel: (415) 397-7000; expect to pay $110-$530. **Travelodge San Francisco Airport North** located at 326 South Airport Blvd San Francisco CA 94080; Tel: (650) 583-9600; expect to pay $70-$150. **Travelodge San Francisco Golden Gate** located at 2230 Lombard St. San Francisco CA 94123; Tel: (415) 922-3900; expect to pay $60-$160.

Abigail Hotel located at 246 McAllister San Francisco CA 94102; Tel: (415) 861-9728; expect to pay $90-$160. **Cartwright Hotel** located at 524 Sutter Street at Powell San Francisco CA 94102; Tel: (925) 473-2230; expect to pay $110-$220. **King George Hotel** located at 334 Mason San Francisco CA 94102; Tel: (925) 473-2230 or toll-free: (800) 288-6005; expect to pay $90-$180. **Chancellor Hotel** located at 433 Powell Street San Francisco CA 94102; Tel: (415) 362-2004 or toll-free: (800) 428-4748 expect to pay $60-$150.

Hostelling International (San Francisco Fisherman's Wharf) located at Building 240, Fort Mason, San Francisco, CA 94123-1303; Tel (415) 771-3645; expect to pay $21-$30, international members discount available. **Hostelling International** (San Francisco Downtown) 312 mason St. San Francisco CA 94102-1704; Tel: (415) 788-5604 expect to pay $21-$30, international members discount available.

All Aboard

San Jose (CA)

San Jose or "Pueblo de San Jose de Guadalupe," founded in 1777, was the first civilian settlement in California and was the first city in California to be incorporated (27 March 1850). Part of Santa Clara County, San Jose is the third largest city in California (following Los Angeles and San Diego) and the 11th largest city in the U.S. San Jose is a popular destination to both tourists and business people alike. Located at the southern-most end of

San Francisco Bay, 50 miles south of San Francisco city, San Jose has a land area of 172 sq. miles (443 sq. kilometers) and is home to more than 900,000 residents.

The Capital of Silicon Valley (Center of high-technology industries) San Jose is also home to some of the major fruit packing and canning companies.

San Jose's train depot is located at 65 Cahill St. San Jose, CA 95110. The station is staffed and features an enclosed waiting area, checked baggage service, restrooms and payphones. Transportation options from the station include Hertz Car Rental (800) 654-3131 (toll-free), local transit, and taxi services.

Trains serving San Jose station are the Coast Starlight and the Capitol Corridor.

Places of Interest

There is a large Portuguese population in San Jose, where traditions are still being practiced and strongly felt in some areas. Contact the **Portuguese Heritage Society of California** at P.O. Box 18277 San Jose, California 95158 for more information.

The **Intel Museum and Intel Museum Store,** located at 2200 Mission College Boulevard Santa Clara Tel: (408) 765-0503, is worth visiting. The museum has exhibits which show how computer chips are made and used. **Winchester Mystery House** located at 525 South Winchester Boulevard San Jose Tel: (408) 247-2000, is a 160-room Victorian mansion built by rifle heiress Sarah Winchester with collections of fine craftsmanship and architecture.

Accommodations

Fairmont San Jose located at 170 South Market Street San Jose CA 95113; Tel: (408) 998-1900. **Clarion Inn Silicon Valley** located at 3200 Monterey Road San Jose CA 95111; Tel: (408) 972-2200. **Crowne Plaza San Jose Downtown** located at 282 Almaden Boulevard San Jose CA 95113; Tel: (408) 998-0400. **Days Inn Airport** located at 1280 North 4th Street San Jose CA 95112; Tel: (408) 437-9100. **Hilton San Jose and Towers** located at 300 Almaden Blvd San Jose CA 95110; Tel: (408) 287-2100.

Hyatt San Jose located at 1740 North First Street San Jose CA 95112; Tel: (408) 993-1234. **Extended Stay America** located at 6199 San Ignacio Ave San Jose CA 95119; Tel: (408) 226-4499. **Holiday Inn Express Hotel and Suites** (San Jose International Airport) located at 1350 North Fourth Street San Jose CA 95112; Tel: (408) 467-1789. **Holiday Inn San Jose Silicon Valley** located at 399 Silicon Valley Boulevard San Jose CA 95138; Tel: (408) 972-7800.

Salinas (CA)
Connecting Train to **Carmel (CA)** and motor-coach connection to **Monterey (CA)**

Salinas is located between the Gabilan and Santa Lucia mountain ranges, 20 miles northeast of Monterey, 60 miles south of San Jose, 101 miles south of San Francisco and 325 miles north of Los Angeles. Salinas is named for the Spanish word for "salt marsh" and is also known as the "The Salad Bowl of the World." It is said that Salinas produces 80 percent of the nation's lettuce, 50 percent of its cauliflower and mushrooms, 60 percent of its broccoli, and 90 percent of its artichokes.

Salinas has a total land area of 18 sq. miles (48 sq. kilometers) and has a population of 134,680.

Salinas' train depot is located at 11 Station Place Salinas, CA 93901. The station is staffed and features an enclosed waiting area, checked baggage service, restrooms, vending machines, and payphones. Transportation options from the station include local transit and taxi services.

Salinas' station is served by the Coast Starlight.

Places of Interest

The **Steinbeck Center Foundation** located at One Main Street Salinas, CA 93901, Tel: (831) 796-3833, is worth visiting. **Steinbeck House** is located at 132 Central Ave Salinas, CA, Tel: (831) 424-2735. The **Mission Nuestra Senora de la Soledad** is located at 36641 Fort Romie Road Soledad, CA, Tel: (831) 678-2586. **Pinnacles National Monument** is located 12 miles east of Soledad on Hwy 146 Soledad, CA Tel: (831) 389-4485.

If you are interested in wineries and vineyards, then visit the **Chalone Vineyard** located at Hwy 146 & Stonewall Canyon Road Soledad, CA 93960, Tel: (831) 678-1717. **Cloninger Cellars** located at 1645 River Road Gonzales, CA, Tel: (831) 675-WINE and **Paraiso Springs Vineyards** located at 38060 Paraiso Springs Road Soledad, CA 93960, Tel: (831) 678-0300.

Accommodations

Best Inn located at 109 John St. Salinas, CA 93901, Tel: (831) 424-4801, **Salinas Travel Inn** located at 425 Monterey St. Salinas, CA 93901, Tel: (831) 422-8834. **Travelers Hotel** located at 16 1/2 E. Gabilan St. Salinas, CA 93901, Tel: (831) 758-1198.

Monterey (CA) Thruway Motor coach connection to/from Salinas (CA)

Perhaps one of the most charming cities in the US, Monterey is located on the beautiful Monterey Peninsula, with a population of just about 30,000 residents.

Monterey was originally home to several Native American tribes, the Esselen, Ohlone, and Salinan tribes. Sebastian Vizcaino was the first European to set foot at the area and named it after Count de Monte Rey and later became "Monterey." Monterey has been an important place both historically and politically; it was the capital of Alta California after Mexico declared its independence from Spain in 1822.

After John Drake Sloat of the US Navy captured Monterey in 1846, Monterey became the first capital of the State of California on October 13, 1849. Today, Monterey is one of California's key tourist destinations. Admired by many for its natural beauty and rugged coastline, Monterey has everything to offer. Aside from its historical significance, Monterey also is home to a world known aquarium, jazz festival, famous Fisherman's Wharf, Cannery Row, beaches, parks, entertainment, and recreation.

Getting Around

Airport

Monterey Peninsula Airport is located at Highway 68 and Olmsted Road, Tel: (831) 648-7000. The airport has several local and international connections daily. There are local transportation services at the airport serving the peninsula and nearby places.

Rent-a-Car

Car rental companies serving Monterey are: Avis Car Rentals toll-free (800) 331-1212, Hertz Car Rentals toll-free (800) 654-3131, Budget Car Rentals toll-free (800) 527-0700, Enterprise Car Rentals toll-free (800) 736-8227, National Car Rentals toll-free (800) 227-7368.

Taxi Service

Carmel Taxi Tel: (831) 624-3885 serves the city.

Bus

Monterey/Salinas Transit Tel: (831) 899-2555 serves the Monterey County daily. The Wave Bus serves the waterfront of Monterey Bay area during summer (May-September) fare is $1.

Train

Amtrak thruway motor coach connection from Salinas (CA) serves the following stops along Monterey peninsula: at Transit Plaza located at Tyler and Pearl, Hyatt Regency, Monterey at 1 Old Golf Course Rd., Monterey Bay Aquarium at 886 Cannery Row (93940), Travel Lodge at 675 Munras, and Monterey Marriott Hotel at 350 Calle Principal.

Visitor Information Center

Monterey Visitor Center is located at 401 Camino El Estero, Monterey Tel: (831) 649-1770

Place to See and Things to Do

Monterey Bay Aquarium is located at 886 Cannery Row, Monterey, 93940-1085 <<http://www.montereybayaquarium.org>> Tel: (831) 648-4888. This world-known aquarium exhibits marine animals of the Monterey Bay area. There are more than 300,000 species of marine mammals exhibited at the aquarium, a must-visit site. Admissions are $17.95 (Adult), $7.95 (Child), $14.95 (seniors and students); the aquarium is open from 10 am to 6 pm daily.

The **Cannery Row** is located just beside the Monterey Bay Aquarium at Monterey's historic waterfront. There are unique shops, the first factory outlets of America "the American Tin Cannery," restaurants, entertainment, accommodations and more.

Fisherman's Wharf, one of Monterey's most visited places, is located at Monterey Harbor and offers various seafood, shops, sights, and activities. Visit the **Portraits by Baila** Tel: (831) 336-2419 where visitors can have their own personal portraits for just $5. The Wharf Theatre Tel: (831) 649-2332, has live comedy performances. **Whale Watching** and **Bird Watching** cruises are available at the wharf each day; the cruise will take you to on an approximately 2 hour journey to encounter one of nature's most mysterious mammals: the whales migrating from Alaska to Baja California. Chris's Fishing Trips; Tel: (831) 375-5951, Randy's Fishing Trips; Tel: (831) 372-7440 and Sea Life Tours; Tel: (831) 372-7150, offer daily trips around the Monterey Bay.

An afternoon walk or drive around the **Pacific Grove** area offers a romantic experience. Pacific Grove is known as the heart of the Monterey Peninsula. Victorian architectural buildings, the finest Inns, shops, and restaurants are set at one of Monterey's most beautiful coastal areas. For information call Pacific Grove Chamber of Commerce at Tel: (800) 656-6650.

Take the **17-Mile Drive** and be rewarded with views of the area's breathtaking coastlines and beautiful rock formations. The 17-mile drive is a loop of road that will take you to Pebble Beach and Del Monte Forest. There are various sites, recreation areas, and points of interest along the drive. Allow a half-day for the trip to have a pleasant experience. There is an $8 toll fee (per car) at the entrance (refund of the toll fee upon patronizing the area's establishments is available).

Monterey Bay

Beaches

There are several beaches in the area; some of the most visited are the **Lovers Point Beach** at Ocean View in Pacific Grove, **Marina State Beach** at Reservation Rd. Marina, **Monterey State Beach** at Del Monte, Monterey, **Pfeifer Beach** at Sycamore Canyon off highway 1, **San Carlos Beach Park** at Coast Guard Pier, Monterey, **Carmel Beach** at the end of Ocean Ave. Carmel, and **Asilomar State Beach** at Pacific Grove at highway 68. Be cautious that strong water currents at the bay can be dangerous.

Parks

Andrew Molera State Park located 21 miles south of Carmel Tel: (831) 667-2316, **Pebble Beach** Tel: (831) 625-8416, **Jacks Peak County Park** at scenic highway 68, Monterey Tel: (831) 755-4899, **Monarch Butterfly Sanctuary** at Pacific Grove Tel: (831) 648-5716. Parks nearby Monterey Bay: **Point Sur Light Station** Tel: (831) 625-4419 located 19 miles of Carmel and the **Point Lobos State Park Reserve** Tel: (831) 624-4909 located 3 miles south of Carmel.

Accommodation

Days Inn Fisherman's Monterey located at 1288 Munras Avenue Monterey CA 93940, Tel: (831) 375-2168 or toll-free (800) DAYS-INN Fax. (408) 375-0368, expect to pay $60-$300. **Econo Lodge Monterey** located at 2042 N. Fremont St. Monterey CA 93940, Tel: (831) 372-5851 or toll-free (800) 553-2666 Fax. (831) 372-4228, expect to pay $60-$170. **Holiday Inn Express Monterey** located at 443 Wave St. Monterey CA 93940, Tel: (831) 372-1800 Fax. (831) 372-1969, expect to pay $80-$300. **Comfort Inn Carmel Hill** located at 1252 Munras Ave. Monterey CA 93940, Tel: (831) 372-2908 or toll-free (800) 228-5150 Fax. (831) 372-7608, expect to pay $50-$200.

Doubletree Hotel Monterey located at 2 Portola Plaza, Monterey, CA 93940, Tel: (831) 649-4511, expect to pay $70-$300. **Hyatt Regency Monterey** located at One Old Golf Course Drive Monterey CA 93940-4908, Tel: (831) 372-1234 Fax. (831) 375-6985, expect to pay $100-$350. **Best Western Monterey Beach Hotel** located at 2600 Sand Dunes Drive Monterey CA 93940, Tel: (831) 394-3321 or toll-free (800) 242-8627 Fax. (831) 393-1912, expect to pay $60-$300. **Comfort Inn Munras Avenue** located at 1262 Munras Ave. Monterey CA 93940, Tel: (831) 372-8088 or toll-free (800) 228-5150 Fax. (831) 373-5829, expects to pay $50-$250.

Best Western Monterey Inn located at 2600 Sand Dunes Drive Monterey CA 93940, Tel: (831) 373-5345 or toll-free (877) 373-5345 Fax. (831) 373-3246, expectss to pay $80-$200. **Monterey Marriott** located at 350 Calle Principal Monterey, CA 93940, and Tel: (831) 649-4234 Fax. (831) 372-2968, expectss to pay $100-$300. **Monterey Downtown Travelodge** located at 675 Munras Avenue, Monterey, CA 93940 Tel: (831) 373-1876 or toll-free (800) 578-7878 Fax (831) 373-8693, expect to pay $70-$150. **Casa Munras Garden Hotel** located at 700 Munras Ave. Monterey CA 93940, Tel: (831) 375-2411 or toll-free (800) 222-2558 (National), Fax: (831) 375-1365, expectss to pay $80-$200. **Monterey Hilton** located at 1000 Aguajito Road, Monterey, CA 93940, Tel: (831) 373-6141.

All Aboard!

Paso Robles (CA)

Paso Robles was originally named El Paso de Robles, meaning the pass of the oaks, by Spanish explorers. As with many other towns, the arrival of the Southern Pacific railroad brought prosperity to Paso Robles. Located near the central California coast a few miles from San Luis Obispo, Paso Robles was incorporated in 1889, has a land area of 13 sq. miles (34 sq. kilometers) and today is home to more than 25,000 residents.

Since its beginning, Paso Robles has been known for its hot springs (with curing properties), and many visitors come to visit and relax each year. In addition, winemaking, farming, and ranching also played a key-role in the development of Paso Robles.

Paso Robles' train depot is located at 800 Pine St. Paso Robles, CA 93446. The station is unstaffed and features an enclosed waiting area, restrooms, payphones, and vending machines. Transportation options from the station include local bus, transit and taxi services.

Paso Robles station is served by the Coast Starlight.

Places of Interest

Paso Robles is the gateway to the famous Hearst Castle owned by William Randolph Hearst. Take scenic Highway 46 west through the Santa Lucia Mountains to Highway 1, then head north up the coast to San Simeon. Call toll-free (800) 444-4445 for schedules and information.

California's Rugged Coastline

Accommodations

Sycamore Mineral Springs located at 1215 Avila Beach Dr San Luis Obispo, CA 93401; Tel: (805) 595-7302. **Paso Robles Inn** located at 1103 Spring Street Paso Robles, CA 93446; Tel: (805) 238-2660. **Paso Robles Wine Country Inn** located at 3548 Spring Street Paso Robles, CA 93446; Tel: (805) 238-9616. **Best Western Black Oak Motor Lodge** located at 1135 24th St Paso Robles, CA 93446; Tel: (805) 238-4740. **TraveLodge** located at 2701 Spring Street Paso Robles, CA 93446; Tel: (805) 238-0078. **Best Western Colony Inn** located at 3600 El Camino Real Atascadero, CA 93422; Tel: (805) 466-4449. **Holiday Inn Express Hotel & Suites** located at 2455 Riverside Avenue Paso Robles, CA 93446; Tel: (805) 238-6500.

San Luis Obispo (CA)

Founded by Father Junipero Serra in 1772, San Luis Obispo is one of California's oldest communities. It is located midway between San Francisco (235 miles south) and Los Angeles (200 miles north) at the junction of Highway 101 and Highway 1, north of Santa Barbara. Named after the Bishop of Toulouse (St. Louis of France), San Luis Obispo was incorporated on February 16, 1856.

With a total land area of 9 sq. miles (24 sq. kilometers), San Luis Obispo has population of 44,613. San Luis Obispo serves as the commercial and cultural center of California's Central Coast and is home to California's Cal Poly State University and Cuesta Community College.

San Luis Obispo's train depot is located at 1011 Railroad Ave. San Luis Obispo, CA 93401. The station is staffed and features an enclosed waiting area, checked baggage services, restroom, payphones, and vending machines.

Trains serving San Luis Obispo are the Coast Starlight and Pacific Surfliner.

Places of Interest

Visit the **Charles Paddock Zoo** located at 9100 Morro Road, Highway 41 Atascadero; Tel: (805) 461-5080, see more than 100 animals including the rare Sumatran tigers, red-ruffed birds, and lemurs. **San Luis Obispo Botanical Gardens** El Chorro Regional Park, Hwy. 1 San Luis Obispo, Tel: (805) 546-3501. Made of rocks, shells, cans, and car parts is the **Nit Wit Ridge** located at 881 Hillcrest Drive Cambria, Tel: (805) 927-2690 California Historical Landmark house.

Accommodations

San Luis Obispo Downtown Travelodge located at 345 Marsh Street San Luis Obispo CA 93401; Tel: (805) 543-6443. **Best Western Royal Oak Hotel** located at 214 Madonna Road San Luis Obispo CA 93405; Tel: (805) 544-4410 or toll-free (800) 545-4410. **San Luis Obispo Days Inn** located at 2050 Garfield St. San Luis Obispo CA 93401; Tel: (805) 549-9911. **San Luis Obispo Travelodge** located at 1825 Monterey Street San Luis Obispo CA 93401; Tel: (805) 543-5110. **Garden Street Inn** located at 1212 Garden

Street San Luis Obispo CA 93401; Tel: (805) 545-9802. **Embassy Suites San Luis Obispo** located at 333 Madonna RoadSan Luis Obispo CA 93405; Tel: (805) 549-0800.

Santa Barbara (CA)

Juan Rodriguez Cabrillo, a Portuguese explorer, discovered the Santa Barbara Channel in 1542. But it was the Spanish explorer Vizcaino who first entered and named the channel on December 4, 1602 (St. Barbara's Day). In 1786 Mission de Santa Barbara named the site Santa Barbara.

Known as the "American Riviera," Santa Barbara has a total land area of 11 sq. miles (30 sq. kilometers) and a population of approximately 90,000. Santa Barbara is built on the slopes and coastline of the Santa Ynez Mountains on Hwy 101 on the Pacific Coast, 97 miles (156 km) northwest of Los Angeles.

Santa Barbara enjoys pleasant weather, and for many in nearby cities it's a place for a short-drive vacation, with an average temperature of 63 degrees F. (17 degree C) during spring, 70 degrees F. (22 degree C) during summer, 60 degrees F. (16 degree C) during fall, and 55 degrees F (13 degree C) during winter.

Santa Barbara has 25 miles of beautiful coastline with nine beaches spreading along the towns of Goleta (north of the city) to Carpinteria (south of the city). Santa Barbara offers lots of water activities including swimming, surfing, scuba diving, and fishing. Whale-watching cruises are also a popular activity; a walk at the beach and simply enjoying the sun and sand is one of the popular pastimes.

If you are in the mood for hiking, Santa Barbara offers some of California's best. The surrounding mountains offer hundreds of miles of mountain trails with rewarding views of the Santa Barbara area and the Santa Ynez country. Or if you prefer a less challenging sport,

Santa Barbara Beachside

rent a bike and stroll the city's beautiful surroundings and its historical past such as the old Spanish Mission, built in 1787.

The Santa Barbara train depot is located at 209 State St. Santa Barbara, CA 93101. The station is in the city's center a few blocks from the beaches, historic, and shopping areas. The station is staffed and features an enclosed waiting area, checked baggage service, restrooms, payphones, and a restaurant. Transportation options from the station include Budget Rent a Car (airport with free shuttle) (805) 963-6651, Enterprise Rent-A-Car (1/2 mi) free shuttle (805) 966-3097, and Avis Rent A Car toll-free (800) 230-4898; Yellow cab Tel: (805) 965-5111, SB City Cab Tel: (805) 968-6868, and Greyhound Tel: (805) 965-7551.

Trains serving Santa Barbara Station are Coast Starlight and the Pacific Surfliner.

Places to See and Things to Do

Historical Places

The **Santa Barbara Mission** is located on 2201 Laguna St. Founded in 1786, it was the tenth mission founded by the Spanish missionaries, the "Queen of the Missions," and today is one of the most popular destinations in Santa Barbara. **The Santiago de la Guerra Adobe,** located at 110 East De La Guerra, is one of the city's oldest structures and **The Plaza De La Guerra**, located on De La Guerra St. is where the first city council met in 1850. **El Presidio de Santa Barbara** State Historic Park, located at 123 East Canon Perdidio Street, is one of Santa Barbara's most beautiful historical buildings. The 1929 **Santa Barbara County Courthouse** is located at 1100 Anacapa Street, and it has a magnificent Spanish-Moorish structure and an 80 foot clock tower. Other interesting sites are the **Royal Spanish Presidio of Santa Barbara** located at Santa Barbara and Canyon Perdido Streets and the **Arlington Theatre** located at 1317 State St.

Museums and Galleries

Dedicated to the history of the California region, the **Santa Barbara Historical Museum** is located at 136 E. De La Guerra St, Tel: (805) 966-1601. **The Sea Center,** located at Stearn's Wharf, is open daily from 10 am to 5 pm. The museum offers a look at the areas marine life. The **Santa Barbara Natural History Museum** is located at 2559 Puesta del Sol Road Santa

Barbara CA 93105; Tel (805) 682-4711, open from Monday to Saturday 9am-5pm; Sunday and holidays 10am-5pm.

Santa Barbara Contemporary Arts Forum is located at 653 Paseo Nuevo Santa Barbara, CA 93101, Tel: (805) 966-5373. **Santa Barbara Arts & Crafts Show** located at Chase Palm Park, Cabrillo Blvd. Tel: (805) 962-8956 exhibits original arts & crafts by over 150 local artists. The **Waterhouse Gallery** located at La Arcada, 1114 State St. Tel: (805) 962-8885 exhibits representational and impressionistic works. **Santa Barbara Historical Museum** is located at 136 E. De La Guerra St. Tel: (805) 966-1601 open from Tues-Sat, 10am to 5 pm and Sun from12pm to 5pm. **Santa Barbara Museum of Art** is located at 1130 State St. Tel: (805) 963-4364.

Parks and Zoos

Alameda Park located at Sola and Garden Streets Santa Barbara, CA 93101, Tel: (805) 564-5418. **Hans Christian Andersen Park** located at Atterdag Road (north of Mission Drive) Solvang, CA 93463. **Chase Palm Park** located at 323 East Cabrillo Boulevard Santa Barbara, CA 93101, Tel: (805) 564-5422. **Girsh Park** located at 7050 Phelps Road Goleta, CA 93117, Tel: (805) 968-2773. **Tucker's Grove Park** 805 San Antonio Creek Road Santa Barbara, CA 93111, Tel: (805) 967-1112. **Live Oak Park** located at Highway 154 and Paradise Road Santa Barbara, CA 93105, Tel: (805) 934-6123.

Alpacas

Rocky Nook Park located at 610 Mission Canyon Road Santa Barbara, CA 93105, Tel: (805) 568-2461. **Toro Canyon Park** located at 576 Toro Canyon Road, Montecito Santa Barbara, CA 93108 Tel: (805) 969-3315. **Rincon Beach Park** located at Bates Rd. off Hwy 101 Carpinteria, CA Tel: (805) 568-2460. **Manning Park** is located at 449 San Ysidro Road, Montecito Santa Barbara, CA 93108 Tel: (805) 969-0201.

Carpinteria State Beach Tel: (805) 684-2811 or toll-free (800) 444-7275. **East Beach** located at E. Cabrillo Blvd. and Milpas St. Santa Barbara, CA Tel: (805) 564-5418. **Goleta Beach County Park** located at Sandspit Road Goleta, CA Tel: (805) 967-1300. **Arroyo Burro Beach County Park** located at Cliff Drive Santa Barbara, CA Tel: (805) 687-3714. **Leadbetter Beach** is located at Shoreline and Loma Alta Dr. Santa Barbara, CA Tel: (805) 564-5418. **West Beach** located at E. Cabrillo Blvd. Santa Barbara, CA Tel: (805) 564-5418. **Mesa Beach** located below Shoreline Park Santa Barbara, CA. **Butterfly Beach** located at Channel Drive and Butterfly Lane Santa Barbara, CA.

The **Santa Barbara Botanic Garden** is located at 1212 Mission Canyon Rd. Tel: (805) 682-4726, the garden is open daily. **Andree Clark Bird Refuge** has a wide collections of freshwater birds located at 1400 E. Cabrillo Blvd. Admission is free. The **Channel Islands National Marine Sanctuary** is located at 113 Harbor Way, Suite 150 Santa Barbara, CA 93109, Tel: (805) 966-7107. **The Santa Barbara Zoo** located at 500 Ninos Dr., Tel: (805) 962-5339. Interested to see Llama? The **Flying V Ranch / Llama Memories Gift Shop** located at 6615 East Highway 246 Lompoc, CA 93436, Tel: (805) 735-3577, the farm offers a glimpse of the beautiful animal.

Accommodations

City Center Travelodge Santa Barbara located at 1816 State Street Santa Barbara CA 93101, Tel: (805) 569-2205. **Days Inn Castillo Santa Barbara** located at 116 Castillo Street Santa Barbara CA 93105, Tel: (805) 963-9772 or toll-free (800) DAYS-INN. **Four Seasons Hotel Santa Barbara** located at 1260 Channel Drive Santa Barbara CA 93108, Tel: (805) 969-2261. **Colonial Beach Inn Santa Barbara** located at 206 Castillo St. Santa Barbara CA 93101, Tel: (805) 963-4317 or toll-free (800) 537-8483. **Coast Village Inn Santa Barbara** located at 1188 Coast Village Road Santa Barbara CA 93108, Tel: (805) 969-3266 or toll-free (800) 537-8483.

Sandman Inn Santa Barbara located at 3714 State Street Santa Barbara CA 93105; Tel: (805) 687-2468 or toll-free (800) 556-4638. **Hotel Santa Barbara** located at 533 State St, Santa Barbara CA 93101; Tel: (805) 957-9300. **Inn by the Harbor Santa Barbara** located at 433 W. Montecito St Santa Barbara CA 93101; Tel: (805) 963-7851 or toll-free (800) 537-8483. **Montecito Inn Santa Barbara** located at 1295 Coast Village Road Santa Barbara CA 93108; Tel: (805) 969-7854 or toll-free (800) 556-4638. **The Inn at East Beach** located at 1029 Orilla Del Mar Santa Barbara CA 93103, Tel (805) 965-0546. **Tropicana Inn & Suites Castillo Santa Barbara** located at 223 Castillo St Santa Barbara CA 93101, Tel (805) 966-2219 or toll-free (800) 537-8483.

Doubletree Hotels Fess Parkers Resort located at 633 East Cabrillo Boulevard Santa Barbara CA 93103, Tel: (805) 564-4333 or toll-free (800) 222-TREE. **Montecito del Mar** located at 316 W. Montecito Street Santa Barbara CA 93101, Tel: (805) 962-2006. **Ramada Limited Santa Barbara** located at 4770 Calle Real Santa Barbara CA 93110, Tel: (805) 964-3511 or toll-free (800) 2-RAMADA. **San Ysidro Ranch** located at 900 San Ysidro Lane, Santa Barbara, CA 93108, Tel: (805) 969-5046 or toll-free (800) 368-6788. **Holiday Inn Express Haley Street Santa Barbara** located at 17 W. Haley Street Santa Barbara CA 93101, Tel: (805) 963-9757.

Santa Barbara Beach Travelodge located at 22 Castillo St Santa Barbara CA 93101, Tel: (805) 965-8527 or toll-free (800) 578-7878. **West Beach Inn Santa Barbara** located at 306 W. Cabrillo Blvd. Santa Barbara CA 93101, Tel: (805) 963-4277. **Upham Hotel** located at 1404 De La Vina Street Santa Barbara CA 93103, Tel: (805) 962-0058. **Best Western Beachside Inn** located at 336 West Cabrillo Boulevard, Santa Barbara, CA 93101, Tel: (805) 965-6556 or toll-free (800) 780-7234.

Oxnard is also known as the Sugar town, the Strawberry Capital, the Lima Bean Capital, or the Biggest Little City of the Coast. Visiting it will give you clear reasons for such claims. Oxnard is located on the Pacific Coast in southern California, approximately 35 miles south of Santa Barbara and 62 miles northwest of downtown Los Angeles. Oxnard's land area is 24 Square miles (62 sq. kilometers) and the population is 170,358.

Oxnard is rich in agricultural land and has a variety of business parks and shopping areas. The four Oxnard brothers who made their fortunes in sugar plantations founded Oxnard in 1899.

California (CA)

Capital: Sacramento (Population: 33,871,648)
Size: 163,707 sq mi. (424,001 sq km)
Nicknames: The Golden State
Joined the union on: September 9, 1850 (31st state)
Motto: Eureka (I Have Found It)
Flower: Golden Poppy
Bird: California Valley Quail
Song: "I Love You, California"
Famous for: Golden Gate Bridge, Hollywood, Yosemite Valley
Major industries: Manufacturing, Agriculture, Biotechnology, Software and Tourism

Oxnard's train depot is located at 201 E. 4th St. Oxnard, CA 93030. The station is staffed and features an enclosed waiting area, checked baggage service, restrooms, payphones and a snack bar. Transportation options from the station include Greyhound Tel: (800) 231-2222, Metrolink Commuter Trains Tel: (800) 371-LINK, SCAT Tel (805) 487-4222 and local taxi service.

Trains serving Oxnard station are the Coast Starlight and the Pacific Surfliner.

Places of Interest

Museums

Seabee Museum **is located on** Ventura Road at Sunkist Gate Port Hueneme, CA, Tel: (805) 982-5165. The museum exhibits cultural artifacts from around the globe and a collection of World War II, Korean War, and Vietnam War uniforms and weapons. Gull Wings Children's Museum **is located at** 418 W. Fourth Street Oxnard, California 93030 (805) 483-3005. The museum is dedicated to children; they can explore, experiment, and develop their learning potential and skills while having fun. Carnegie Art Museum **located at** 424 South "C" Street Tel: (805) 385-8179 open Thursday – Saturday from 10am to 5 pm and Sunday from 1 pm to5 pm. The Ventura County Maritime Museum **is** located at 2731 South Victoria Avenue Tel: (805) 984-6260 Open daily from 11:00 am to 5:00 pm.

Visit the restored turn-of-the-century homes at the Heritage Square **located at** 715 South A Street Tel: (805) 483-7960. Channel Islands Harbor is a pleasant place that has more than 2,600 boat slips, 9 marinas, waterside shopping, numerous restaurants, and boat rentals. Tel: (805) 985-4852.

Accommodations

Embassy Suites Mandalay Beach located at 2101 Mandalay Beach Rd, Oxnard, CA 93035, Tel: (805) 984-2500. **Ambassador Motel** located at 1631 S Oxnard Blvd, Oxnard, CA 93030, Tel: (805) 486-8404. **Best Western Oxnard Inn** located at 1156 S Oxnard Blvd, Oxnard,

CA 93030, Tel: (805) 483-9581. **Vagabond Inn** located at 1245 N Oxnard Blvd, Oxnard, CA 93030, Tel: (805) 983-0251. **Flamingo Motel** located at 421 N Oxnard Blvd, Oxnard, CA 93030, Tel: (805) 486-2973.

Casa Sirena Hotel & Marina located at 3605 Peninsula Rd, Oxnard, CA 93035, Tel: (805) 985 6311. **Hilton Financial Plaza** located at 600 Esplanade Dr, Oxnard, CA 93030, Tel: (805) 659-0260. **Viking Motel** located at 421 N Oxnard Blvd, Oxnard, CA 93030, Tel: (805) 486-4973. **Residence Inn** located at 2101 W Vineyard Ave, Oxnard, CA 93030, Tel: (805) 278-2200. **Radisson Hotel** located at 600 Esplanade Dr, Oxnard, CA 93030, Tel: (805) 485-9666. **Wagon Wheel Motel** located at 2751 Wagon Wheel Rd, Oxnard, CA 93030; Tel: (805) 485-3131.

Simi Valley (CA)

It is believed that Simi Valley was first inhabited by the Chumash Indians and was called the "Peaceful Valley." It is also said that the origin of the word "Simi" is the Chumash Indian Village name "Shimiji." The city of Simi Valley was incorporated in 1969. Located west of the San Fernando Valley and less than an hour northwest of Los Angeles, Simi Valley has a total land area of 33 sq. miles (85 sq. kilometers) and a population of more than 110,000 residents.

Simi Valley's train depot is located at 5050 Los Angeles Ave. Simi Valley, CA 93063. The station is unstaffed and features payphones. Transportation options from the station include local transit and taxi services.

Trains serving Simi Valley station are the Coast Starlight and the Pacific Surfliner.

Glendale (CA)

More than 30 sq. miles (79 sq. kilometers) in size, Glendale is the third largest city in Los Angeles County. Located at the eastern end of the San Fernando Valley, at the foot of Verdugo Mountain, Glendale is home to roughly 200,000 residents.

Glendale's 1924 Spanish-Mediterranean train depot (local historic landmark) is located at 400 W. Cerritos Ave. Glendale, CA 91204. The station is unstaffed and features payphones. Transportation options from the station include Glendale Beeline Tel: (818) 548-3960, Los Angeles County Metropolitan Transportation Authority (LAMTA) Tel: 1-800-COMMUTE, and Metrolink Tel: toll-free (800) 371-LINK, and local taxi services.

Trains serving Glendale station are the Coast Starlight and the Pacific Surfliner.

Los Angeles (CA)

On September 4, 1781 El Pueblo de Nuestra Senora La Reina de Los Angeles de Porciuncula, or translated, the Town of Our Lady the Queen of the Angels of Pordiuncula, or in short, Los Angeles was named and founded by then California's governor Felipe de Neve in 1781. It was incorporated on April 4, 1850.

Los Angeles County is one of the largest counties in the US. With a size of 4,081 square miles (10,569 sq. Kilometers), it is larger than a few states in the United States. There are 88 cities and two islands (Santa Catalina and San Clemente) within Los Angeles County.

Los Angeles County has a population of more than 9.9 million residents (approximately 4 million are living in the city of Los Angeles). About 29% of California's residents live in Los Angeles County making it the most populated county in the United States.

The climate of Los Angeles is pleasant and moderate, with an average annual rainfall of 14 inches per year, an average temperature of 64.4 degrees F (18 degree C), 62 degrees F (17 degree C) during spring; 73 degrees F (24 degree C) during summer, 68 degrees F (22 degree C) during fall and 58 degrees F (15 degree C) during winter.

Los Angeles has one of the richest economies in the world. It has become a leading manufacturing, financial, commercial, and transportation center. It has some of the world busiest ports; the port of Los Angeles-Long Beach located in San Pedro Bay is the busiest port on the U.S.'s Pacific Coast.

Los Angeles is the capital of the entertainment industry and home to some of the world's biggest and most modern entertainment production companies. Tourism is one of the city's major industries, and Los Angeles is home to some of the world leading tourist destinations such as **Disneyland** in Anaheim, **Mann's Chinese Theater** in Hollywood, **Hollywood Walk of Fame** on Hollywood Blvd., **Rodeo Drive** in Beverly Hills, **3rd Street Promenade** in Santa Monica, and the many picturesque communities and beaches along the 81 mile-long coast.

Downtown Los Angeles is dominated by its high-rise skyline and artistic architecture. The extensive system of highways, or freeways, accommodate the city's millions of vehicles, and the city's international airport (LAX) still remains one of the best and busiest in the world.

Getting Around

Hollywood Highland

Airport

Los Angeles International Airport (LAX), the third busiest airport in the world, is located 17 miles southwest of downtown Los Angeles. There are shuttle services available at the lower/arrival level islands in front of each of the 9 terminals. The FlyAway Bus Service runs every 30 minutes from 5:30 am to 12:00 am. The Metropolitan Transit free shuttle service at the lower level of the terminals will take you to Metro Green Line Light Rail's Aviation Station that connects to most parts of the city, including downtown LA, toll-free (800) COMMUTE.

City Buses are available at the adjacent Parking Lot 'C' by taking the 'C' Shuttle. Public buses serving LAX are: Santa Monica Big Blue Bus and Torrance Transit, and Culver City Bus Lines. Taxis are available at curbside on the lower level. You should ask the airport information counter for a taxi destination ticket stating the typical fare to major destinations.

Bus

DASH provides services around Los Angeles, including Downtown LA, Hollywood area, the Valleys, Westside, and Venice. For information call Tel: (818) 808-2273. Other buses that serve the city of Los Angles include Metro Transit or MTA toll-free (800) COMMUTE with a wide range of city routes, fares from $1.35 with discount for senior and disabled passengers, and the Santa Monica Big Blue Bus Tel: (310) 451-5444 connecting Santa Monica area to the rest of the city.

Rent-A-Car

Midway Car Rental-Downtown LA located at 519 S. Olive St. Los Angeles, CA 90013, Tel: (213) 627-4449. Fox Rent-A-Car located at 10201 S. La Cienega Blvd. Los Angeles, CA. toll-free (800) 225-4369 and (310) 641-3838. Hertz Car Rental toll-free (800) 654-3131. Afel Rent-A-Car located at 2021 Westwood Blvd. Los Angeles, CA 90025, Tel: (310) 474-3039.

Train

Los Angeles Union Station is located at 800 N. Alameda St. Los Angeles, CA 90012. Los Angeles Union Station is a hub to the city transportation system. Several trans-continental and intercity Amtrak train services serve the station. Commuter Metrolink toll-free (800) 371-LINK and subway Metrorail toll-free (800) COMMUTE link the station to almost all major destinations in the city. Transportation options from the station include MTA bus and downtown DASH shuttles, and call taxis. Los Angeles Union Station is staffed and features an enclosed waiting area, checked baggage services, restrooms, payphones, snack bars, coffee bars, and a restaurant.

Trains serving Los Angeles Union Station are the Coast Starlight, Pacific Surfliner, Southwest Chief, Sunset Limited and the Texas Eagle.

Metro Rail connects the city's major destinations and infrastructure. There are 3 lines that travel north, west, and south of LA. Metro Blue Line connects downtown Los Angeles to Long Beach, Metro Green Line connects Norwalk to Redondo Beach, and the Metro Red Line connects downtown Los Angeles to North Hollywood. The three lines are also inter-connected: the red line joins the blue line downtown at metro center station (7th and Flower streets), while the blue line and green line join at Imperial Highway in Wilmington. Fare is $1.35 and there are ticket machine booths at each station. For information call toll-free (800) COMMUTE.

111

Visitor Information Center

Los Angeles Visitor Information Center – Downtown is located at 685 Figueroa St. (between Wilshire Blvd. and 7th St.) Los Angeles 90017. Open weekdays from 8 am - 5 pm and Saturdays from 8:30 am - 5 pm. Call Tel: (213) 689-8822, fax: (213) 624-1992 for information.

Places to See and Things to Do

Theme Parks and Studios

Disneyland and the California Adventure Parks are located at 1313 Harbor Blvd. Anaheim CA 92803, Tel: (714) 781-4565. Perhaps the most popular family destination in the world, Disneyland offers several attractions including Fantasyland, Tomorrowland, Frontierland, and Adventureland. There are numerous rides and fun things to do inside the two parks. Make sure that you arrive early in the morning and use the "FastPass" to avoid crowds and lines. Disneyland one-day pass includes all rides, at $45 for adult, and $35 for children. Visit online <<http://www.Disneyland.com>> for current information, or Call (714) 781-4565. You should spend at least two days in each park in order to take all the rides and visit all places. Hotels and motels are plentiful in the area. For more information and a list of accommodations see Pacific Surfliner destination Anaheim.

The second most visited attraction in California (after Disneyland) is **Universal Studios Hollywood,** located at 100 Universal City Plaz,a Universal City CA 91608, Tel: (818) 622-3801; just 15 minutes from Hollywood Blvd (You can take the Subway Metrorail at the Hollywood-Highland Station to the Universal City Subway Station, Fare $1.35 each way). See behind the scenes movie and T.V. action and special effects and exciting rides. Tickets are $43 adult, $32.00 senior, and $32 kids. Tel: (818) 508-9600 for current information. **Sony Picture Plaza** is located at 10202 W. Washington Blvd, Culver City, CA 90232. Call Tel: (323) 520-TOUR for studio tour information.

Knott's Berry Farm has more than 150 acres of exciting rides, live entertainment, historic attractions, great dining, and some world-famous attractions. Located at 8039 Beach Blvd. Buena Park CA 90620, Tel: (714) 220-5200, a few minutes from Los Angeles International Airport (LAX) and Disneyland. Tickets are $40-Adult and $30-Child. There are some discounted coupons at the Los Angeles Union Station that will save you up to $30 for ticket purchases (Park Promotion).

Pacific Park located at the Santa Monica Pier, Santa Monica, CA. There are numerous rides, restaurants, and other recreational activities situated beside the ocean. Visit online site at <<http://www.pacpark.com>>, or call (310) 260-8744 for information. **Six Flags Magic Mountain Park** is located at 26101 Magic Mountain, Pkwy Valencia, CA 91355, Tel: (661) 255-4100. Experience the ultimate roller coaster rides! A one-day adult ticket is $42, and a child is $26. Enjoy a nice walk and shop at the **Farmers Market** located at 6333 W. 3rd St., at Fairfax, Tel: (323) 933-9211 where there are more than 110 stalls to shop and 20 restaurants for you to choose from. **Griffith Park** is one of the local favorite destinations for recreational and sports activities.

Historical Site

Visit the mile-long stretch of Hollywood Boulevard sidewalk, the **Hollywood Walk of Fame,** and find the name of your favorite actors. There are more than 2,000 stars stretched along the area. It is said that each actor paid $15,000 for the privilege of being chosen as part of Hollywood Walk of Fame (the price of the Hollywood Blvd. Stars).

Los Angeles Beaches

Visit some of Los Angeles' famous beaches. **Venice Beach** is located a few miles from Santa Monica Pier, take the **Venice Boardwalk,** one of L.A.'s must-see places, where many of the city's lively people gathering each day. There's usually music in the air. **Marina del Rey Beach** located in Marina del Rey, CA 90292, has a marina with many small boats, a romantic setting. **Playa del Rey Beach and Del Rey Lagoon** located in Playa del Rey, CA 90293. **Santa Monica State Beach, Municipal Pier, and Amusement Park** - Pacific Coast Highway at California Incline, Santa Monica, CA 90402. There are lots of things to do and to see, a great place to be. The water is cold, there is a nice bike and skate path, with lots of nice looking people.

Dockweiler State Beach Located at 8255 Vista del Mar, Playa del Rey, CA 90293 is a four-mile sandy beach that has campgrounds, a playground, bike trail, and barbecue pits. **Will Rogers State Beach** is a three-mile long not-so-sandy beach, located at 15100 Pacific Coast Highway at Temescal Canyon Road, Pacific Palisades, CA 90272. Good for surfing.

Museums and Other Places of Interest

The Getty Center has fine collections of art, a must-see museum, located off 405 Freeway at the top of Getty's mountain. Admission is free. **California Science Center** is located at 700 State Drive, LA, CA, 90037. Call Tel: (323) SCIENCE. **California African American Museum** is also located at the California Museum of Science. The museum has a permanent collection of African American arts.

Hollywood Bowl

Los Angeles County Museum of Art is located at 5905 Wilshire Blvd. LA, CA, 90036. Tel: (323) 857-6000, open Monday through Sunday. The **Natural History Museum** is located at 900 Exposition Blvd. LA, CA, 90007. Also in the surrounding area are the Los Angeles Olympic Stadium and other museums. The **Hollywood Entertainment Museum** is located at 7021 Hollywood Blvd. Hollywood, CA, 90028. **Craft & Folk Art Museum** is located at 5814 Wilshire Blvd. Tel (323) 937-4230.

113

Other museums are: the **Autry Museum of Western Heritage** located at 4700 Western Heritage Way, Griffith Park across from the Los Angeles Zoo. General admission is $7, $3 for students; call Tel: (323) 667-2000 for information. The **Museum Of Contemporary Art** is located in three locations: at 250 South Grand Avenue, Los Angeles, CA 90012, at 152 North Central Avenue, Los Angeles, CA 90013, and at 8687 Melrose Avenue, West Hollywood, CA 90069. The **Los Angeles Zoo** is located at 5333 Zoo Drive Los Angeles, California 90027-1498 Open daily from 10 am to 5 pm except December 25.

A very interesting place to see for car enthusiasts is the **Petersen Automotive Museum,** located at 6060 Wilshire Blvd., Los Angeles, CA 90036, (323) 964-6344.It exhibits the history of the development of the automobile and its influence on the culture of Los Angeles. Admissions are: adult - $7; child - $3, and senior - $5. **Ripley's Believe It or Not! Museum** is located at 7850 Beach Blvd., Buena Park, CA 90620, Tel: (714) 522-1155. Open from Mon.-Fri. 11am-5pm; Sat.-Sun. 10am-6pm, admission fees are adult - $8.95, child - $5.25 and senior (55+) - $6.95.

Long Beach Area

The Queen Mary is a WWII-era luxurious ocean liner converted to a museum and a hotel, located at 1126 Queens Highway Long Beach CA 90802-6390, toll-free (800) 437-2934 or (562) 435-3511. Admissions are $19.00 (Adults), $15.00 (Child), $17.00 (Senior), and $16.00 (Groups). If you are coming to Long Beach in mid April you should see the **Toyota Grand Prix of Long Beach**. Also see the Dutch Village setting at the **Queen's Market Place**, situated close to pier J, one of Long Beach's famous nightlife spots. **Pine Ave** is Long Beach's most celebrated street; striking, and full of life and energy, it has numerous restaurants, bars, shops, and entertainment year-round. The **Aquarium of the Pacific** is a world-class aquarium dedicated to Pacific Ocean Marine life, located at 100 Aquarium Way, Long Beach, CA 90802. Tel: (562) 590-3100. Open daily from 10 a.m. to 6 p.m. Admissions are $16.95 (Adult), $9.95 (Child) and $13.95 (Senior).

Queen Mary, Long Beach

Santa Catalina Island

Santa Catalina Island is located about 22 miles off the coast of Long Beach. The Island is worth visiting and is one of LA's most popular tourist destinations. The port town of Avalon in Catalina attracts tourists for its Mediterranean looks. There are casinos, mansions, shops, restaurants, wildlife, and crystal clear water. There are various tours offered to explore the island. A day-trip is possible, but to explore the beauty of the island, a night stay on Catalina Island is highly recommended.

Getting There

The fastest way of getting to Catalina is by Helicopter-Island Express Helicopter Service, Tel: (310) 510-2525 (take the 710 freeway to the Queen Mary (Port of Long Beach or Queen Mary) at the end of the freeway enter the Queen Mary parking lot entrance, follow the signs to "heliport"). The trip is 14 minutes with helicopters departing every hour from 8 am to 5 pm at the San Pedro and Long Beach Boat Terminals. Fares are $68.86 (one way) and $126.98 (round-trip). Make sure that you check in 20 minutes before the departure time. Each passenger is allowed a 25 lb. baggage limit, picture ID is required.

The **Catalina Express Ferry** -Long Beach Downtown Station, is located at 320 Golden Shore Boulevard across the Queensway Channel from the Queen Mary, the ferry departs 3 times daily. Fares are $20.00 one-way and $40.00 round-trip (Adults), $15.25 one-way and $30.50 round-trip (Child) and $18.25 one-way and $36.50 round-trip (Senior). There are also ferry services in San Pedro, toll-free (800) 481-3470.

Accommodations

Holiday Inn Brentwood-Bel Air is located at 170 North Church Lane Los Angeles CA 90049; Tel: (310) 476-6411; expect to pay $70-$270. **Econo Lodge Los Angeles** is located at 11933 Washington Blvd. W. Los Angeles CA 90066; Tel: (310) 398-1651; expect to pay $40-$110. **Doubletree Hotel - Hollywood/Universal Studios** is located at 10740 Wilshire Blvd. Los Angeles CA 90024; Tel: (310) 475-8711; expect to pay $110-$280. **Marriott Downtown Los Angeles** is located at 333 S. Figueroa St. Los Angeles CA 90071; Tel: (213) 617-1133; expect to pay $70-$370.

Carlyle Inn is located at 1119 South Robertson Blvd. Los Angeles CA 90035; Tel: (310) 275-4445 or toll-free (800) 322-7595; expect to pay $100-$180. **Beverly Plaza Hotel** is located at 8384 W. Third Street, West Los Angeles CA 90048; Tel: (323) 658-6600. **The Century Plaza Hotel and Spa** is located at 2025 Avenue of the Stars Los Angeles CA 90067; Tel: (310) 277-2000 or toll-free (800)-228-3000; expect to pay $130-$900. **Holiday Inn Express Century City** is located at 10330 W. Olympic Blvd. Los Angeles CA 90064; Tel: (310) 553-1000 or toll-free (800)-553-1005; expect to pay $100-$180. **Crowne Plaza Hotel International Airport** is located at 5985 W. Century Blvd Los Angeles CA 90045; Tel: (310) 642-7500 or toll-free (888)-315-3700; expect to pay $80-$250.

Holiday Inn Los Angeles Downtown is located at 750 Garland Ave. Los Angeles CA 91423; Tel: (213) 628-9900 or toll-free (800) 628-5240; expect to pay $70-$180. **The New Otani Hotel & Garden** is located at 120 S. Los Angeles St., Los Angeles CA 90012; Tel: (213) 629-1200; expect to pay $80-$280. **Comfort Inn & Suites LAX Airport** is located at 4922 W. Century Blvd Los Angeles CA 90304; Tel: (310) 671-7213; expect to pay $50-$170. **Park Hyatt Los Angeles** is located at Century City 2151 Avenue of the Stars, Los Angeles CA 90067; Tel: (310) 277-1234; expect to pay $170- $950.

Courtyard Century City/Beverly Hills is located at 10320 West Olympic Blvd. Los Angeles CA 90064; Tel: (310) 556-2777; expect to pay $75-$170. **Four Points by Sheraton Los Angeles** is located at 9750 Airport Blvd. Los Angeles CA 90045; Tel: (310) 645-4600; expect to pay $50-$230. **Hilton Los Angeles Airport and Towers** is located at 5711 West Century Blvd. Los Angeles CA 90045; Tel: (310) 410-4000 or toll-free (800) 321-3232; expect to pay $60-$190. **Embassy Suites LAX Intl Airport North** is located at 9801 Airport Boulevard Los Angeles CA 90045; Tel: (310) 215-1000; expect to pay $80-$250. **Comfort Inn Los Angeles** is located at 1710 West 7th Street Los Angeles CA 90017 Tel: (213) 616-3000; expect to pay $60-$100.

Holiday Inn Beverly Hills is located at 1150 S. Beverly Dr. Los Angeles CA 90035; Tel: (310) 553-6561; expect to pay $120-$330. **Hotel Bel-Air** is located at 701 Stone Canyon Blvd. Los Angeles CA 90077; Tel: (310) 472-1211; expect to pay $350-$1170. **Sheraton Gateway Hotel Los Angeles Airport** is located at 6101 W. Century Blvd. Los Angeles CA 90045; Tel: (310) 642-1111 or toll-free (800)-445-7999; expect to pay $80-$550. **Westin Bonaventure Hotel and Suites** is located at 404 South Figueroa St. Los Angeles CA 90071; Tel: (213) 624-1000; expect to pay $80- $450.

Howard Johnson Wilshire Royale Plaza Hotel is located at 2619 Wilshire Blvd. Los Angeles CA 90057; Tel: (213) 387-5311; expect to pay $80-$300. **Wyndham Checkers** is located at 535 South Grand Avenue Los Angeles CA 90071; Tel: (213) 624-0000; expect to pay $100-$300. **Best Western Westwood Pacific Hotel** is located at 11250 Santa Monica Boulevard Los Angeles CA 90025; Tel: (310) 478-1400 or toll-free (800) 780-7234; expect to pay $60-$150. **Hyatt Regency Los Angeles** is located at 711 South Hope Street Los Angeles CA 90017; Tel: (213) 683-1234; expect to pay $100-$380.

The Pacific Surfliner

The Pacific Surfliner serves Southern California routes, stretching along the 232 miles (373 kilometers) of mountains, plains, and magnificent views of the Pacific Ocean. It links the cities of **Paso Robles**, **Santa Barbara**, **Los Angeles**, **Anaheim**, and **San Diego**.

Financed and operated in partnership with the State of California, the Pacific Surfliner uses the new bi-level cars with modern interiors, comfortable seats, much larger windows for viewing, automatic doors, closed overhead compartments, seat tables, electric outlets, and a nice Cafe car.

Route Destination Highlights

San Luis Obispo, CA- Visit the famous Hearst Castle and the magnificent Morro Bay.

Santa Barbara, CA- Enjoy the Beaches of Santa Barbara, explore the Queen of all the Missions - the historic Mission of Santa Barbara, visit some of California's wineries and vineyards, or simply take a mountain hike and take in rewarding views of the Santa Barbara area and the Santa Inez countryside.

Los Angeles, CA- The entertainment capital of the world, Los Angeles has everything to offer. Visit the famous Hollywood Walk of Fame, the Chinese Theater on Hollywood Blvd., Universal Studios, some of the best Museums in the US, Venice Beach, Long Beach, or simply shop at the Farmers Market.

Anaheim, CA- The home of the original Disneyland, take a day or three and indulge the

Pacific Surfliner		
	Passo Robles (CA)	
	Atascadero (CA)	
	San Louis Cal Poly (CA)	
6 35 am	San Louis Obispo (CA)	8 35 pm
6 56 am	Grover Beach (CA)	7 54 pm
	Santa Maria (CA)	
7 12 am	Guadalupe St. Maria (CA)	7 38 pm
7 46 am	Lompoc Surf Sta. (CA)	7 00 pm
	Lompoc (CA)	
	Buellton (CA)	
	Solvang (CA)	
8 54 am	Goleta (CA)	5 42 pm
9 14 am	**Santa Barbara (CA)**	5 28 pm
9 32 am	Carpinteria (CA)	5 04 pm
9 53 am	Ventura (CA)	4 43 pm
10 07 am	Oxnard (CA)	4 29 pm
	Camarillo (CA)	4 14 pm
	Moorpark (CA)	
10 51 am	Simi Valley (CA)	3 05 pm
11 13 am	Chatsworth (CA)	
11 26 am	Van Nuys (CA)	3 28 pm
11 35 am	Burbank Airport (CA)	3 19 pm
11 47 am	Glendale (CA)	3 07 pm
12 10 pm-A 12 25 pm-D	**Los Angeles (CA)**	2 55 pm-D 2 40 pm-A
12 57 pm	Fullerton (CA)	2 08 pm
1 06 pm	**Anaheim (CA)**	1 59 pm
1 15 pm	Santa Ana (CA)	1 50 pm
1 26 pm	Irvine (CA)	1 37 pm
1 40 pm	**San Juan Capistrano (CA)**	1 23 pm
Seasonal	San Clemente Pier (CA)	Seasonal
2 13 pm	Oceanside (CA)	12 49 pm
2 28 pm	Solana Beach (CA)	12 33 pm
3 10 pm	**San Diego (CA)**	12 00 N

A-Arrival
D-Departure
--Multiple Schedules Daily
Thruway Bus Connection

child in you. Visit Disney's California Adventure, Knott's Berry Farm, or the magnificent Crystal Cathedral.

San Juan Capistrano, CA- Take a day-visit and walk to the old Mission San Juan Capistrano, or see and experience the swallows that leave San Juan Capistrano on St. John's day (Oct 23rd) and return each year on St. Joseph's day (March 19th).

San Diego, CA- Home to the world famous San Diego Zoo, San Diego Wild Animal park, and San Diego Sea World. See the magnificent architecture and museums of Balboa Park and the historical Old Town. Extend your visit to the City of Tijuana Mexico, just 30 minutes from San Diego City; Tijuana is a duty free zone.

Beaches- Relax and enjoy some of California's world-renown beaches: Venice Beach, Long Beach, the Beaches of Santa Barbara, Orange County's Huntington Beach and Laguna Beach, San Diego's La Jolla Beach, Pacific Beach, and Mission Beach.

Scenery Along the Routes

The scenery between Paso Robles and San Luis Obispo offers breathtaking views of greenery, mountains, hills, wineries, cattle, horses, and ranches. From Pismo Beach all the way through Ventura are splendid beaches, hillsides, cliffs, and the grand Pacific Ocean. And the views from San Juan Capistrano through San Diego are endless scenes of the region's history and miles of pristine beaches.

Train Schedules

Pacific Surfliner travels daily with multiple departures from Paso Robles to San Diego. The trip between the two cities takes approximately 9-10 hours of travel time.

Accommodations

Accommodations are Unreserved Coach and Reserved Business Class Seats. There is a Cafe car that serves sandwiches, snacks, and drinks. Other amenities include rail phone and electrical outlets; seat audio and video are available in Pacific Business Class. Surfboard racks and bicycle racks are also available.

All Aboard!

For Paso Robles (CA), San Luis Obispo (CA) see "Coast Starlight"

Grover Beach (CA)

The City of Grover was incorporated on the 21st of December, 1959. Grover Beach is located on the central coast of California, 150 miles south of Monterey and 92 miles north of Santa Barbara, with a total land area of 2.3 sq. miles (6 sq. kilometers) and a population of approximately 13,000.

Grover Beach train depot is located at 180 Grand Ave. Grover Beach, CA 93433. The station is self-serve and features an enclosed waiting area and payphones. Transportation from the station is local taxi service.

Grover Beach station is served by the Pacific Surfliner.

Guadalupe- Santa Maria (CA)

Part of Santa Barbara County, the city of Guadalupe Santa Maria is located on the charming central coast of California along the Santa Maria River and within the Santa Maria Valley. The Chumash Indians originally inhabited the area and in 1542 Spanish explorer Juan Rodriguez Cabrillo rediscovered the valley. The original name of the city was "Central City" and in 1885 it was changed to "Santa Maria." The City was incorporated on September 12th, 1905.

Guadalupe Santa Maria is a small agricultural village rich in history. It relied on agriculture for its economic development for many years. At present, the city also enjoys the fruits of other industries such as technology research and development, communications, military operations, other manufacturing industries, and tourism.

California (CA)
Capital: Sacramento (Population: 33,871,648)
Size: 163,707 sq mi. (424,001 sq km)
Nicknames: The Golden State
Joined the union on: September 9, 1850 (31st state)
Motto: Eureka (I Have Found It)
Flower: Golden Poppy
Bird: California Valley Quail
Song: "I Love You, California"
Famous for: Golden Gate Bridge, Hollywood, Yosemite Valley
Major industries: Manufacturing, Agriculture, Biotechnology, Software and Tourism

There are several interesting places in the Guadalupe-Santa Maria area. **Pismo Beach,** just 15 miles northwest of the city, offers great views of the Pacific Ocean. **Point Sal State Beach** is a remote beach known for water sports and recreation. Located west of Guadalupe is **La Purisima Mission State Historic Park,** just take state route 246 south to Lompoc. The town of **Solvang** is a Danish town off Highway 101 just south of Santa Maria.

Guadalupe-Santa Maria train depot is located at 330 Guadalupe St. Guadalupe, CA 93434. The station is unstaffed. Transportation from the station is the Guadalupe Flyer service Tel: (805) 928-5624.

Guadalupe station is served by the Pacific Surfliner.

Lompoc-Surf Sta. (CA)

Just like Santa Maria and Guadalupe, Lompoc's first known settlers were the Chumash Indians. Lompoc (pronounced Lom-Poke) is an Indian word for lake or lagoon. Lompoc was incorporated as a city on August 13, 1888 and become known for its flower seed growing. Lompoc has a land area of 11 sq. miles (29 sq. kilometers) and a population of approximately 46,000 residents. Located on Hwy 1 north of Santa Barbara, Lompoc is also home for the US Vandenberg Air Force Base.

Surf/Lompoc train depot is located at the end of Ocean Ave. West Lompoc, CA 93436, at the Union Pacific Railroad. The station is unstaffed.

Surf/Lompoc station is served by the Pacific Surfliner.

Goleta (CA)

Goleta and Goleta Valley are in Santa Barbara County just eight miles north of Santa Barbara. Located between Los Padres National Forest, Santa Inez Mountains, and the Pacific Ocean, it has a land area of 40,000 acres. The population of Goleta Valley is approximately 77,400. Goleta's residents are proud of their train depot which is listed as one of Santa Barbara County's Historical Landmarks. Goleta Depot was built by the Southern Pacific Railroad Co. in 1901 and was reopened on Oct. 10, 1982.

Goleta's train depot is located at the north end of La Patera Lane Goleta, CA 93117. The station is unstaffed. Transportation from the station is by Santa Barbara Metropolitan Transit District Tel: (805) MTD-3702.

Goleta station is served by the Pacific Surfliner.

Santa Barbara (CA) See Coast Starlight, page 104.

Carpinteria (CA)

Carpinteria (meaning carpentry) was founded by Gaspar de Portola and was incorporated in 1965. Carpinteria is part of Santa Barbara County, located about 12 miles south of Santa Barbara on U.S. 101 and 80 miles from Los Angeles. Carpinteria has a land area of 2.7 sq. miles (7 sq. kilometers) and a population of 15,194 residents.

Carpinteria is a small town appreciated for its beautiful beaches and mountains. Carpinteria's train depot is located at 425 Linden Avenue Carpinteria, CA 93013. The station is unstaffed and features payphones and a restaurant. Transportation from the station is local taxi service.

Carpinteria station is served by the Pacific Surfliner.

Ventura (CA)

Ventura, or the City of San Buenaventura (good fortune), is one of the oldest towns in the state of California, founded in 1782 by the Mission San Buenaventura. The Chumash Indians had a settlement at this site for more than 1,500 years.

Located 63 miles northwest of Los Angeles County, with a land area of 20 sq. miles (53 sq. kilometers), Ventura has a population of more than 105,000 residents. Known for its beaches, Ventura has 43 miles of shoreline for private and public use. The city of Ventura is one of the gateways to the nearby Channel Island National Park (a 250,000-acre sanctuary for marine life and wilderness preserve).

Ventura's train depot is located between Harbor Blvd. and Figueroa St. San Buenaventura, CA 93003. The station is unstaffed and has payphones. Transportation from the station is local taxi service.

Ventura station is served by the Pacific Surfliner.

Oxnard (CA) See Coast Starlight, page 108-109.

Camarillo (CA)

Located just 45 miles northwest of Los Angeles, Camarillo is known for its great climate and friendly community. The total land area of Camarillo is 18 sq. miles (47 sq. kilometers) and the population is roughly 57,000. Camarillo was incorporated in 1964.

Camarillo's train depot is located at Metrolink Sta., 30 Lewis Rd. Camarillo, CA 93010. The station is unstaffed and features payphones. Transportation from the station is local transit service.

Camarillo station is served by the Pacific Surfliner.

Moorpark (CA)

Known as the "Leave it to Beaver Town," Moorpark was named after the apricot that grew throughout its surrounding valley. It was founded in 1887 by Robert W. Poindexter, and was incorporated in July 1983.

Moorpark has a land area of 12 sq. miles (32 sq. kilometers) and a population of 29,727. It is located in the southeastern part of Ventura County, 50 miles northwest of downtown Los Angeles.

Moorpark's train depot is located at 300 High St. Moorpark, CA 93021. The station is self-serve. Transportation from the station is Metrolink toll-free (800) 371-LINK.

Moorpark station is served by the Pacific Surfliner.

Simi Valley (CA) See Coast Starlight, page 108 -109.

Chatsworth (CA)

Chatsworth is located in the San Fernando Valley, part of Los Angeles County. The first known residents of Chatsworth were the Fernandeño and Chumash Indians. In August of 1769 the Franciscan missionary Fray Junipero Serra first recorded the local natives.

Chatsworth train station is a transportation hub for the far west San Fernando Valley train routes. Chatsworth train depot is located at 21510 Devonshire St. Chatsworth, CA 91311. The Station is unstaffed. Transportation options from the station include the Los Angeles County Metropolitan Transportation Authority toll-free (800) COMMUTE and local taxi service.

Chatsworth station is served the Pacific Surfliner.

Van Nuys (CA)

Van Nuys is part of Los Angeles County. The Van Nuys train depot is located at 7724 Van Nuys Blvd. Van Nuys, CA 91405. The station is staffed and features an enclosed waiting area, restrooms, payphones, and vending machines. Transportation options from the station include Hertz Car Rental service toll-free (800) 654-3131, Los Angeles County Metropolitan Transportation Authority toll-free (800) COMMUTE, Metrolink trains and local taxi services.

Van Nuys station is served by the Pacific Surfliner.

Burbank Airport (CA)

Burbank was founded and named after David Burbank (a local rancher) in 1887 and was incorporated in July 1911. Burbank is located 12 miles east of Los Angeles at the end of the San Fernando Valley with a population of around 98,000.

Burbank Airport is one of California's busiest Airports. Thus, aside from regular local travelers, the Burbank train depot also serves airport travelers from different parts of the country.

The Burbank train depot is located at 3750 Empire Ave. Burbank, CA 91505. The station is unstaffed and features payphones and a snack bar. Transportation options from the station include Hertz Car Rental toll-free (800) 654-3131, Metrolink toll-free (800) 371-LINK and local taxi service.

Burbank station is served by the Pacific Surfliner.

Glendale (CA) See Coast Starlight, page 108 -109.

Los Angeles (CA) See Coast Starlight, page 109.

Fullerton (CA)

Founded by George and Edwardamerige (real estate promoters) in 1887, Fullerton was named after George H. Fullerton, also a land agent who routed the Santa Fe railroad through the City. The city was incorporated in 1904.

Located just 22 miles southeast of Los Angeles, with a total land area of 23 square miles (57 sq. kilometers), Fullerton is one of the largest cities in Orange County. Fullerton has a population of about 126,003.

Amtrak's Fullerton station is located in central Fullerton, at 120 East Santa Fe Avenue, Fullerton, CA 92832. The station is staffed and features an enclosed waiting area, checked baggage service, restrooms, payphones, and restaurant. Transportation options from the station include Hertz Car Rental toll-free (800) 654-3131, Orange County Transportation Authority (714) 636-RIDE, Metrolink toll-free (800) 371-LINK, and local taxi service.

Trains serving Fullerton station are the Pacific Surfliner and Southwest Chief.

Anaheim (CA)

Anaheim, assembled from the words "Ana" (from Santa Ana River) and "heim" (from a German word for home meaning "Home by the river"), is originally a German community of farmers and wine merchants. The city was incorporated in 1876 yet grew slowly. The Santa Fe railroad depot was opened in Anaheim in 1887 giving the city better access throughout the region.

Disneyland "The Happiest Place on Earth" was opened in July 1955, which started Anaheim's modern economic changes. Since then, the city has experienced rapid economic growth, an infrastructure facelift, and diversified community.

The city of Anaheim is located 20 miles southeast of Los Angeles in Southern California, and has a land area of 44 sq. miles (114 sq. kilometers) and a population of 306,300 making it the tenth largest city in the State of California. Anaheim enjoys pleasant weather with low humidity and 328 days of sunshine each year. The average annual rainfall is 14 inches with an average temperature of 73 degrees F (22 degree C).

Anaheim's train depot is located at the north end of the Edison Field parking lot or at 2150 E. Katella Ave. Anaheim, CA 92806. The station is staffed and features an enclosed waiting area, checked baggage service, restrooms, payphones, and vending machines. Transportation options from the station include Hertz Car Rental toll-free (800) 654-3131, Metrolink toll-free (800) 371-LINK, and local taxi service.

Anaheim station is served by the Pacific Surfliner.

Tip: If you are traveling from Los Angeles city or other nearby cities to Anaheim it is much cheaper to travel through Metrolink.

Places to See and Things to Do

Children's Museum at La Habra is California's first children's museum, located at the 1923 Union Pacific Depot, 301 S. Euclid St., La Habra, CA 90631, Tel: (562) 905-9793. Open from Mon.-Sat. 10am-5pm; Sun. 1-5pm. Admissions are adult $4.00 and children $4.00 (under 2 free). **Discovery Science Center** exhibits 100 hands-on science displays in eight different themed areas, a 3-D movie and live science demonstrations, the Science of Sports, Gross Me Out, and many more. Located at 2500 N. Main St., Santa Ana, CA 92707, Tel: (714) 542-CUBE, open daily from 10am-5pm. Admissions are adult - $11.50; child (3-17) - $8.50; senior (55+) - $8.50.

Featuring 17 rides and attractions, including a new 3 1/2 story roller coaster, is **Adventure City** located at 1238 S. Beach Blvd., Stanton, CA 92680-4264, Tel: (714) 236-9300. It is a fun place to visit. Admissions for adults & children $11.95, seniors 55+ - $8.95, and children under 1 year are free. Walt Disney's original theme park, **Disneyland,** is located at 1313

Harbor Blvd., Anaheim, CA 92802 Tel: (714) 781-4565. There are eight themed lands with your favorite classic Disney characters, attractions, live entertainment, and parades at downtown Main Street U.S.A. in late afternoons. There are numerous restaurants, gift shops, and shops. Admissions are: adult (10-59 yrs.) - $43.00; senior (60 and over) -$41.00; child (3-9 yrs.) - $33.00. Multi-day tickets (3 days) are adult - $111.00 and child - $87.00. Prices include all theme rides.

Disney's California Adventure is located at 1313 Harbor Blvd., Anaheim, CA 92802 (just in front of Disneyland) Tel: (714) 781-4565. There are three themed lands: Paradise Pier, Hollywood Pictures Backlot, and the Golden State with loop-de-loop. Screaming roller coaster, rapids Grizzly Peak, and the sourdough of Pacific Wharf. Admissions are: adult (10-59) - $43.00; senior (60 and over) - $41.00; child (3-9 yrs.) - $33.00. Multi-day tickets (3 days) are adults - $111.00; child - $87.00.

Said to be "One of the most spectacular religious edifices in the world," is the **Crystal Cathedral** located at 13280 Chapman Ave., Garden Grove, CA 92840, Tel: (714) 971-4069. Designed by Philip Johnson, this 2,890-seat cathedral has 10,000 panes of wall and ceiling glass. Open Mon.-Fri. 9am-3:30pm. Sun. services are 9:30 and 11am

Other places of interest are the **Richard Nixon Library & Birthplace** located at 18001 Yorba Linda Blvd., Yorba Linda, CA 92886, Admissions are: adult - $5.95 and child (8-11) - $2.00. The **Speed Zone** is a race theme park located at 17871 Castleton St. City of Industry CA 91748, toll-free (888) 662-5428, (626) 913-9663 ext. 111.

Accommodations

Park Inn Anaheim located at 1520 S. Harbor Blvd Anaheim CA 92802; Tel: (714) 772-3691 or toll-free (800) 670-7275; expect to pay $40-$150. **Hyatt Regency Alicante Anaheim** located at 100 Plaza Alicante Anaheim CA 92803; Tel: (714) 750-1234 or toll-free (800) 633-7313; expect to pay $80-$400. **Holiday Inn Express-**Main gate Anaheim located at 435 W. Katella Avenue Anaheim CA 92802; Tel: (714) 772-7755 or toll-free (800) 238-5544; expect to pay $80-$150. **Red Roof Inn North Harbor Anaheim** located at 1251 North Harbor

Crystal Cathedral   124

Boulevard Anaheim CA 92801; Tel: (714) 635-6461 or toll-free (800) RED-ROOF; expect to pay $40-$100. **Travelodge Anaheim at the Park** located at 1166 West Katella Avenue Anaheim CA 92802; Tel: (714) 774-7817 or toll-free (800) 578-7878; expect to pay $50-$150.

Ramada Limited Disneyland Area Anaheim located at 800 South Beach Blvd Anaheim CA 92804; Tel: (714) 995-5700 or toll-free (800) 2-RAMADA; expect to pay $50-$100. **Holiday Inn Anaheim at the Park** located at 1221 S. Harbor Blvd. Anaheim CA 92805; Tel: (714) 758-0900 or toll-free (800) 545-7275; expect to pay $60-$200. **Embassy Suites Hotel Anaheim** located at 3100 E. Frontera St. Anaheim CA 92806; Tel: (714) 632-1221 or toll-free (800) EMBASSY; expect to pay $129-$200. **Hilton Anaheim and Towers** located at 777 Convention Way Anaheim CA 92802; Tel: (714) 750-4321 or toll-free (800) 445-8667; expect to pay $50-$400. **Sheraton Anaheim Hotel** located at 900 West Disneyland Drive Anaheim CA 92802; Tel: (714) 778-1700 or toll-free (800) 325-3535; expect to pay $90-$400.

Coachman Inn Anaheim located at 2145 S. Harbor Blvd Anaheim CA 92802; Tel: (714) 971-5556; expect to pay $40-$150. **Comfort Inn Main gate Anaheim** located at 2200 S. Harbor Blvd Anaheim CA 92802; Tel: (714) 750-5211 or toll-free (800) 228-5150; expect to pay $40-$150. **Days Inn Disneyland West Anaheim** located at 1030 West Ball Road Anaheim CA 92802; Tel: (714) 520-0101 or toll-free (800) 331-0055; expect to pay $50-$150. **Econo Lodge Anaheim** located at 1126 Katella Avenue Anaheim CA 92802; Tel: (714) 533-4505; expect to pay $50-$150. **Anaheim Carriage Inn** located at 2125 S. Harbor Blvd Anaheim CA 92802; Tel: (714) 740-1440; expect to pay $70-$150.

Anaheim Marriott Hotel located at 700 W. Convention Wy. Anaheim CA 92802; Tel: (714) 750-8000; expect to pay $70-$400. **Comfort Inn and Suites Katella Way Anaheim** located at 300 East Katella Way Anaheim CA 92802; Tel: (714) 772-8713; expect to pay $70-$150. **Days Inn Disneyland Convention Center Anaheim** located at 1604 S. Harbor Blvd Anaheim CA 92802; Tel: (714) 234-3411 or toll-free (800) DAYS-INN; expect to pay $60-$100. **Comfort Inn and Suites West Anaheim** located at 727 South Beach Boulevard Anaheim CA 92804; Tel: (714) 220-0100; expect to pay $50-$200.

Santa Ana (CA)

Discovered by Gaspár de Portolá, a Spanish expedition leader, in July of 1769, Santa Ana is the capital and the largest city in Orange County. Santa Ana was incorporated as a city in 1886 with a land area of 27 square miles (69 sq. kilometers), Santa Ana has a population of roughly 317,000.

Places of Interest

Bowers Museum located at 2002 N. Main Street Santa Ana, CA 92706 Tel: (714) 567-3600. The museum exhibits art from world cultures. Open from Tuesday - Friday: 10am-4pm, Saturday & Sunday 10am-6pm. Closed on Mondays. The **Discovery Science Center** is located at 2500 North Main Street, Santa Ana, CA Tel: (714) 542-CUBE

Santa Ana's train depot is located at 1000 E. Santa Ana Blvd. Santa Ana, CA 92710. The station is staffed and features an enclosed waiting area, checked baggage service, restrooms, payphones, and snack bar. Transportation options from the station include Greyhound Tel: (714) 542-1311, Orange County Transportation Authority City buses Tel: (714) 636-RIDE, Metrolink Tel: (800) 371-LINK, and local taxi service.

Santa Ana station is served by the Pacific Surfliner.

California (CA)
Capital: Sacramento (Population: 33,871,648)
Size: 163,707 sq mi. (424,001 sq km)
Nicknames: The Golden State
Joined the union on: September 9, 1850 (31st state)
Motto: Eureka (I Have Found It)
Flower: Golden Poppy
Bird: California Valley Quail
Song: "I Love You, California"
Famous for: Golden Gate Bridge, Hollywood, Yosemite Valley
Major industries: Manufacturing, Agriculture, Biotechnology, Software and Tourism

Irvine (CA)

The City of Irvine was incorporated on December 28, 1971, and has a total land area of 46 sq. miles (119 sq. kilometers) and a population of around 143,000.

Scattered evidence of early campsites and rock shelters and other archeological findings proves that prehistoric man was living in the Irvine area 12,000 to 18,000 years ago.

Irvine's train depot is located at 15215 Barranca St. Irvine, CA 92618. The station is staffed and features an enclosed waiting area, snack bar, restrooms, payphones, and Quik-Trak ticket machine. Transportation options from the station include bus service, Orange County Transportation Authority Tel: (714) 636-RIDE, and local taxi service.

Irvine station is served by the Pacific Surfliner.

San Juan Capistrano (CA)

San Juan Capistrano also known as the "Jewel of the Missions," is the oldest settlement in Orange County. It was founded by Father Junipero Serra in November 1776 and incorporated in April 1961.

The seventh of 21 Spanish Missions established in California by Franciscans, Mission San Juan Capistrano is the historic center of Orange County and California's most important cultural and educational center. The Serra chapel is one of the oldest buildings still in use in the state of California.

San Juan Capistrano is known for the swallows that leave on St. John's day (Oct 23) and return each year on St. Joseph's day (March 19). San Juan Capistrano has a total land area of 14 sq. miles (37 sq. kilometers) and a population of 32,100.

Some of the most outstanding architecture of San Juan Capistrano is seen in the town's train depot which was completed in October 1894. San Juan Capistrano's train depot is located at 26701 Verdugo St. San Juan Capistrano, CA 92675. The station is staffed and features an enclosed waiting area, restrooms, payphones, a Quik-Trak ticket machine, and a restaurant. Transportation options from the station include Avis Rent A Car toll-free (800) 230-4898, Dollar Rent A Car toll-free (800) 800-3665 and Enterprise Rent-A-Car Tel: (714) 487-9075; Greyhound (just a block away) toll-free (800) 231-2222, Metrolink toll-free (800) 371-LINK,

Orange County Transportation Authority Tel: (714) 636-RIDE and local taxi service Tel: (714) 951-TAXI.

San Juan Capistrano station is served by the Pacific Surfliner.

Place of Interest

Mission San Juan Capistrano, Take I-5 Hwy. (South) exit at Ortega Hwy turn west; located 2 blocks down on corner of Ortega Hwy and Camino Capistrano. P.O. Box 697, San Juan Capistrano, CA 92693 Tel: (949) 234-1300. Open daily from 8:30am to 5pm. Admissions are adults - $6.00, child (3-12) - $4.00, and seniors (60+) $5.00.

San Clemente (CA)

San Clemente is a product of Seattle's ex-mayor Ole Hanson's dreams of building a Spanish Mediterranean Village. San Clemente has a total land area of 17 sq. miles (44 sq. kilometers) and a population of 49,936 residents.

San Clemente's train depot is located at Municipal Pier San Clemente, CA 92676. The station is self-serve. Transportation options from the station include Metrolink toll-free (800) 371-LINK and the Orange County Transportation Authority Tel: (714) 636-RIDE.

San Clemente station is served by the Pacific Surfliner.

Note: Pacific Surfliner trains only stop at San Clemente station during the summer months. Check with amtrak for any changes in schedules and fares.

Oceanside (CA)

Oceanside is located in the San Luis Rey Valley. The site was populated by Nativeamerican Indians for many years. Father Juan Crespi arrived at the site in July of 1769 and founded the Mission San Luis Rey de Francia (located three-and-a-half miles from the present site of Oceanside) in 1798. The city of Oceanside was incorporated on July 3rd, 1888.

Oceanside has a land area of 42 sq. miles (108 sq. kilometers) and a population of 161,029, and is located 83 miles south of Los Angeles and just 35 miles north of San Diego. Major interstate roads cross and connect the city to most major destinations around the region.

Home to the US Marine Camp Pendleton Marine Corps Base, the city's growth has always been attached to the development of the marine base since it was established in the early 1940's. Oceanside is a lovely place, there's much to see and do in the city. One of the favorite tourist destinations is the Oceanside Small Craft Harbor. The harbor has more than 800 boat slips covering 100 acres of land and water.

Oceanside's train depot is located at 235 S. Tremont Ave. Oceanside, CA 92054. The station is staffed and features an enclosed waiting area, checked baggage service, restrooms, payphones, and snack bar. Transportation options from the station include Hertz Car Rental toll-free (800) 654-3131, North Coast Transit Buses, Metrolink toll-free (800) 371-LINK, local bus and taxi services.

Oceanside station is served by the Pacific Surfliner

Solana Beach (CA)

The city of Solana Beach is a small town located on the northern coast of San Diego County. The first known peoples of Solana Beach are the San Dieguitos Indians and the La Jollans Indians, who came from eastern California and Nevada in 9000 BC.

Solana Beach has a land area of 3.5 sq. miles (9 sq. kilometers) and a population of around 14,000. The city of Solana Beach is mainly a residential community and is well connected to California's major interstate highways.

Solana Beach's train depot is located at 105 Cedros Ave. Solana Beach, CA 92075. The station is staffed and features an enclosed waiting area, checked baggage service, restrooms, payphones, and a restaurant. Transportation options from the station include Avis Rent-A-Car toll-free (800) 230-4898, Orange County Transportation Authority Tel: (714) 636-RIDE, the North Coast Transit and local taxi service.

Solana Beach station is served by the Pacific Surfliner.

San Diego (CA) Gateway to Tijuana (MX)

It was Juan Rodriguez Cabrillo who first landed in San Diego in 1542 and claimed the land for Portugal. Named by Sebastian Vizcaino in 1602, San Diego has a land area of 320 sq. miles (828 sq. kilometers), is the second largest city in California and the seventh largest in the United States. The city of San Diego has a population of approximately 1.3 million residents and more than 2.8 million residents countywide.

The city of San Diego is located in southern California, 120 miles south of Los Angeles and just a few miles north of the US-Mexico border and the city of Tijuana. San Diego has 70 miles of beaches and Pacific Ocean coastline.

San Diego is known for its mild weather with low humidity: the temperature rarely falls below 40 degrees (5 degree C) in the winter with an average annual rainfall of less than 10 inches each year. Most rain falls during months from December through March.

San Diego is known for some world-class tourist attractions: the World-Famous San Diego Zoo and Wild Animal Park, Lego Land California, Sea World San Diego, and various outdoor recreation areas featuring surfing, boating, sailing, and swimming.

San Diego is also known for its economic success and for being one of the major centers of tourism, biotechnology, software, telecommunications, electronics, manufacturing, defense, agriculture, and important scientific research with institutions such as Scripps Institution of Oceanography.

Getting Around

Airport

San Diego International Airport is located 2 miles northwest of San Diego Tel: (619) 686-8065. The airport was recently renovated and has 3 terminals with various state of the art facilities. A courtesy shuttle (Red Bus - equipped with a wheelchair lift) provides free transportation between the 3 terminals. For information, flight arrival/departure details, and car rental inquiries call Tel: (619) 231-2100.

There are buses serving each terminal that take passengers around the city of San Diego. Shuttle Bus and Taxi services to hotels and central San Diego are available from the Transportation Plazas in front of each terminal (taxi fare from San Diego airport to downtown is roughly $10). There are rent-a-car services near the airport; rent-a-car companies can be contacted at the airport Ground Transportation Service Board located at the baggage-claim areas of the terminals Tel: (619) 231-2100.

Bus

San Diego local bus service is run by San Diego Metropolitan Transit System Tel: (619) 233-3004. Fare for most routes is $2, the "Flyer" (which runs between downtown San Diego and the airport) costs more than $2, discount fares are available for seniors. You can ask for a transfer if you wish to make any other bus connections; in addition you can also use bus transfers on San Diego Trolley and the San Diego Coaster Commuter Train. Bus schedules, passes, and permits are available at The Transit Store located at 102 Broadway, downtown San Diego.

Greyhound bus Station is located at 120 W Broadway Tel: (619) 239-9171. It connects San Diego to the rest of the country.

Rent-A-Car

Major rental car companies are **Alamo Rent a Car** located at 2942 Kettner Blvd., Tel: (619) 297-0311. **Hertz Rent a Car** located at 3871 N. Harbor Dr, Tel toll-free (800) 654-3131. **Budget Rent a Car** located at 2535 Pacific Hwy, Tel (619) 235-8313. **Avis Rent a Car** located at 3875 N. Harbor Dr., Tel: toll-free (800) 331-1212. And **Dollar Rent a Car** located at 2499 Pacific Hwy, Tel: (619) 234-3388.

Taxis

San Diego taxi services include American Cab Tel: (619) 292-1111; Orange Cab Tel: (619) 291-3337; Yellow Cab Tel: (619) 234-6161; and Co-op Silver Cabs Tel: (619) 280-5555. Charges are generally $1.50 for the first mile and $1.80 for succeeding miles.

Train

San Diego Trolley is one of San Diego's Landmarks, serving the downtown areas, Old Town, Fashion Valley, Mission Valley, Qualcomm Stadium, the Eastern Part of the City, and the

Mexican border. One-way fares range from $1 to $2.25, with senior and disabled discounts available.

The old San Diego train depot is located at 1050 Kettner Blvd. San Diego, CA 92101. The station is staffed and features an enclosed waiting area, checked baggage service, restrooms, payphones, and a restaurant. Transportation options from the station include Hertz Car Rental toll-free (800) 654-3131, Dollar Rent A Car toll-free (800) 800-3665 and Avis Rent A Car Tool-Free: (800) 230-4898, local transit and taxi service.

San Diego station is served by the Pacific Surfliner.

Special Day Tripper Pass

If you are staying for a few days, a practical way to move around the city is to acquire a Special Day Tripper Pass available at Transit Store located at 120 W Broadway Tel: (619) 239-9171. A one-day pass (cost $5) or a four-day pass (cost $12) will give you an unlimited entrée to Metropolitan Transit System buses and the San Diego Trolley.

Visitors Information Center

San Diego Visitor Information Center is located at 2688 East Mission Bay Dr. San Diego, CA 92109 Phone: (619) 276-8200.

Places to See and Things to Do

Museums, Zoo and Theme Parks

The **San Diego Railroad Museum,** (Main Facility and Train Rides) is located at 31123 1/2 Highway 94 Campo, California 91906, 45 miles east of downtown San Diego, Tel: (619) 478-9937. The Museum exhibits the history of railroads, mainly focused on the San Diego and Arizona Railway area. The Pacific Southwest Railway Museum Association operates the museum.

San Diego Wild Animal Park 15500 San Pasqual Valley Rd., Escondido, CA 92027, Tel: (760) 747-8702. Over 2,000 acres of park land areas with varieties of animals roaming as in their natural habitats. Open daily from 9am until late afternoon. Admission fees are: adults - $25.45, child - $18.45, seniors - $22.90. Visit the world famous **San Diego Zoo** located at 2920 Zoo Dr. San Diego, CA 92103, Tel: (619) 234-3153. There are more than 4,000 animals representing 800 live species of rare birds, mammals, reptiles, and amphibians, and also beautiful botanical gardens. Open daily from 9am until late afternoon. Admissions are: adults - $30.00, child - $17.00, and seniors - $28.95.

Sea World Adventure Park - San Diego is a 150-acres attraction featuring marine life. Located at 500 Sea World Dr., San Diego, CA 92109 Tel: (619) 226-3901 or toll-free (800) SEA- WRLD. Open from 10am-5pm daily, admission fees are: adult - $42.95; child (3-11) - $32.95; and senior (55+) - $39.95. **Lego land** has exciting rides and attractions, located in Carlsbad, 30 minutes north of downtown San Diego Tel: (760) 918-5346. (Car directions: take I-5 and exit to Cannon Road exit then continue to Lego land Drive. Open daily from 9am-6pm, admission fees are adults - $39.95, and child - $33.95.

Balboa Park is located north of downtown San Diego just beside the world famous San Diego Zoo. With 1,400 acres of land area it is the largest urban cultural park in the U.S. The park has museums, theaters, botanical gardens, gardens, and the Globe Theatres.

Historical Sites

Founded on July 1769 the **Mission Basilica San Diego De Alcala** is located in Mission Valley. The mission is open daily from 9am-5pm Tel: (619) 281-8449. The **Old Town**, located just west of Mission Valley, is San Diego's earliest European settlement. There are historic buildings, shops, and restaurants.

A short walk from the San Diego Convention Center is **Seaport Village** where there are more than 50 fine restaurants and shops. In the nearby Gaslamp Quarter (known as the "Historic Heart of San Diego") you'll find clubs, restaurants, galleries, and shops. **North**

Balboa Park

Park is located in central San Diego, a community with fine old buildings, shops, and restaurants.

Beaches

La Jolla, San Diego's "jewel by the sea," offers white beaches, upscale shopping, fine dining, and the Birch Aquarium. **Pacific Beach,** located south of La Jolla & north of Mission beach, offers sun, sand, and surf. **Mission Beach** has a wooden Roller Coaster and Arcade beside the beach. There are restaurants, water sport shops, and gorgeous people. Visit the Coronado home of the historic **Hotel Del Coronado**, fine shops, restaurants, and beaches. Explore **The Boulevard,** one of the best places in San Diego to cruise or hang out with friends.

Visit Mexico

Tijuana is located just thirty minutes north of the US-Mexico border. Take the San Diego Trolley system (light-rail Trolley) from downtown San Diego to the Mexican Border. The trolley station is located just outside the San Diego train depot. You can explore the colorful Mexican culture, enjoy shopping at bargain prices, and try some authentic Mexican cuisine.

Explore the magic of movie making at the Foxploration located on Rosarito, Baja, California, Mexico. It is a 2-4 hour, interactive motion picture attraction. For information write to P.O. Box 439060, 2201, San Diego, CA 92143, or call Tel: (011-52) 661 49412. Located less than a mile from the border is the **Tijuana Culture Center**, the cultural center exhibits Mexico's colorful history and diverse regions. The City of Tijuana is a duty-free zone, which makes the city a shopping paradise. There are lots of bargains on a wide variety of products, such as leather goods, pottery, etc.

Accommodations

Doubletree Hotel San Diego-Del Mar located at 11915 El Camino Real, San Diego, CA 92130-2539; Tel: (858) 481-5900; expect to pay $90-$200. **Hotel Coronado** located at 1500 Orange Avenue Coronado, CA 92118; Tel: (619) 435-6611 or toll-free (800) HOTELDEL; expect to pay $160-$610. **San Diego Yacht & Breakfast** located at 1880 Harbor Island Drive, G Dock San Diego CA; Tel: (619) 297-9484 or toll-free (800) 922-4836; expect to pay $170-$300.

Embassy Suites Hotel San Diego-La Jolla located at 4550 La Jolla Village Drive San Diego, CA 92122; Tel: (858) 453-0400 toll-free (800) EMBASSY; expect to pay $130-$300. **Four Points by Sheraton San Diego** located at 8110 Aero Drive San Diego CA 92123; Tel: (858) 277-8888 or toll-free (800) 992-1441, expect to pay $100-$250. **Hyatt Regency San Diego** located at One Market Place San Diego CA 92101; Tel: (619) 232-1234, expect to pay $160-$350.

Hampton Inn San Diego Downtown located at 1531 Pacific Highway San Diego CA 92101; Tel: (619) 233-8408 or toll-free (800) HAMPTON; expect to pay $80-$150.

Castle Creek Inn Resort & Spa located at Circle R Way San Diego CA 92026; Tel: (760) 751-8800; expect to pay $80-$150. **Holiday Inn San Diego-Harbor View** located at 1617 First Avenue San Diego CA 92101; Tel: (619) 239-9600; expect to pay $90-$200. **Best Inn and Suites San Diego** located at 5399 Adobe Falls Road San Diego CA 92120; Tel: (214) 357-5522 or toll-free (888) 378-2900; expect to pay $40-$100.

Comfort Inn Sea World Area located at Sea World is located 2 miles from the hotel Tel: 4610 De Soto St. San Diego CA 92109 Tel: (858) 483-9800, expect to pay $60-$150. **Clarion Hotel Bayview** located at 660 K Street San Diego CA 92101 Tel: (619) 696-0234 or toll-free (800) 252-7466, expect to pay $70-$310.

Holiday Inn Express San Diego-Sea World Area located at 3950 Jupiter St. San Diego CA 92110; Tel: (619) 226-8000; expect to pay $80-$150. **Comfort Suites Mission Valley** located at 631 Camino Del Rio S. San Diego, CA 92108; toll-free (800) 433-0452 expect to pay $80-$250. **Days Inn And Suites Sea World/Airport** located at 3350 Rosecrans Street San Diego CA 92110; Tel: (619) 224-9800; expect to pay $60-$150.

Hampton Inn San Diego-Airport-Sea World located at 3888 Greenwood San Diego CA 92110, just minutes from the airport, Sea World and San Diego Zoo; Tel: (619) 299-6633; expect to pay $90-$150. **The Westin Horton Plaza San Diego** located at 910 Broadway Circle San Diego CA 92101; Tel: (619) 239-2200; expect to pay $90-$350. **Wyndham Hotel North San Diego** located at 5975 Lusk Boulevard San Diego CA 92121; Tel: (858) 558-1818; expect to pay $100-$240.

Hilton San Diego Airport/Harbor Island located at 1960 Harbor Island Drive San Diego CA 92101; Tel: (619) 291-6700; expect to pay $100-$350. **Marriott San Diego Mission Valley** located at 8757 Rio San Diego Drive San Diego CA 92108; Tel: (619) 692-3800 or toll-free (800)-MARRIOTT; expect to pay $90-$250. **Park Manor Suites Hotel** located at 525 Spruce Street San Diego CA 92103; Tel: (619) 291-0999 or toll-free (800) 874-2649; expect to pay $100-$250.

Balboa Botanical Garden, at the Balboa Park

The Capitol Corridor

Capitol Corridor serves the cities of Sparks (NV), Reno (NV), Sacramento (CA), Berkeley (CA), Oakland (CA), San Francisco (CA), and San Jose (CA), stretching along the 291 miles (468.2 kilometers) of mountains, plains, water, bridges, and the bay area. The Capitol Corridor is financed and operated in partnership with the State of California.

Route Destination Highlights

Sacramento, CA- Visit the Old Sacramento California Railroad Museum, the beautiful and historical Califonia State Capitol, Sacramento State University, Sutter's Fort where gold rush history started, walk and explore the Old Town Sacramento.

Berkeley- Visit the famous University of California Berkeley and explore its museums and fine architecture, spend some romantic time and explore the Berkeley Municipal Rose Garden (considered by many to be the finest Rose Garden in Northern California), take a stroll at Berkeley Marina, Pier, and Cesar E. Chavez Park while enjoying the stunning views of the Golden Gate Bridge and San Francisco skyline.

San Francisco, CA- Visit the famous Pier 39, Alcatraz Island or "The Rock," the world's most celebrated bridge the Golden Gate Bridge, the Museum of Modern Art, the exciting Castro, or Union Square. Take the city tram and explore San Francisco's hilly streets or simply walk through the romantic setting of the city by the bay's Fisherman's Wharf.

	Capitol Corridor	
	Sparks (NV)	
	Reno (NV)	
	Truckee (CA)	
	Soda Spring (CA)	
	Colfax (CA)	
	Auburn (CA)	
	Rocklin (CA)	
	Roseville (CA)	
6 15 am-D	**Sacramento (CA)**	12 55 am-A
6 34 am	Davis (CA)	12 24 am
6 59 am	Suisun Fairfield (CA)	11 58 am
1 20 am	Martinez (CA)	11 39 am
7 48 am	Richmond (CA)	11 09 am
7 56 am	**Berkeley (CA)**	11 01 am
8 00 am	Emeryville (CA)***a**	10 55 am
8 15 am	Oakland (CA)	10 43 am
8 33 am	Hayward (CA)	10 24 am
8 49 am	Fremont Centerville (CA)	10 08 am
9 08 am	Santa Clara (CA)	9 52 am
9 30 am-A	**San Jose (CA)*b**	9 40 am-D

* Thruway Bus Connection
--San Francisco (CA)a
--Santa Barbara (CA)b

A-Arrival   **D-**Departure
--Multiple Schedules Daily

Thruway Bus and Train Connections

San Jose, CA- In the "Heart of Silicon Valley," you can see the Intel Museum and learn how computer chips are made and used. You can also feel the influence of the large Portuguese community.

Scenery Along the Routes

The view when traveling from Sparks, Nevada to Truckee, California is breathtaking. Mountains, lakes, and tall trees manipulate the surrounding area. If you are traveling during winter the surroundings will be covered with snow.

Hold your camera after passing the Suisun-Fairfield station and look to your left side where US military ships can be seen, and in a few minutes the train will be crossing the San Pablo Bay entering Martinez. The route all the way to Emeryville or Oakland is beautiful and full of bay scenery.

Train Schedules

Capitol Corridor travels daily from Sparks, Nevada to San Jose, California. The trip between the two cities takes approximately 9 hours of travel time (a half-day trip).

Accommodations

Accommodation is Unreserved Coach. There is a Cafe car that serves sandwiches, snacks, and drinks. Other amenities are rail phone, electrical outlets, and bicycle racks.

Additional Information

Emeryville and Oakland station offers a service bus to/from San Francisco Airport.

All Aboard!

Auburn (CA)
Motor-Coach connection to/from **Colfax (CA), Soda Spring (CA), Truckee (CA), Reno (NV)** and **Sparks (NV)**

Auburn was founded in 1848 and the city began as a gold mining town. Located 30 miles north east of Sacramento, Auburn is one of the earliest California gold mine settlements. Auburn has a total land area of 5.8 sq. miles (15 sq. kilometers) and a population of 12,386.

The city of Auburn has been restored to its former glory and its gold town flavor can still be seen. Auburn's train depot is located at Nevada and Fulweiler Sts. Auburn, CA 95603. The station is unstaffed. Auburn station is served by the Capitol Corridor.

Rocklin (CA)

Rocklin was founded in 1893, located northeast of Sacramento at the base of the Sierra Foothills just off Interstate 80 in Placer County. Rocklin has a total land area of 12 sq. miles (33 sq. kilometers) and a population of approximately 38,000.

Rocklin's train depot is located at Rocklin Rd. and Railroad St. Rocklin, CA 95677. The station is un-staffed. Rocklin station is served by the Capitol Corridor.

Roseville (CA)

Roseville is located in Placer County just 16 miles northeast of Sacramento, the state capitol, off of Interstate 80. Roseville has a total land area of 30 sq. miles (77 sq. kilometers) and a population of 73,814. Roseville was founded in 1864 and was incorporated on April 10, 1909.

Roseville started as a railroad junction known simply as "Junction." Today Roseville is a thriving city with various business, retail, and industrial economy.

Roseville's train depot is located at 201 Pacific St. Roseville, CA 95661. The station is unstaffed. Transportation options from the station include local bus and taxi services. Trains serving Roseville station are the California Zephyr and the Capitol Corridor.

Sacramento (CA)

Sacramento's history began during the famous California Gold rush; in 1839 John Sutter settled in Sacramento having received a 48,000 acre land grant by the Mexican Governor Alvarado who was then in charge of California. Sacramento was incorporated in 1850 and has been the state capital since 1854. The total land area of Sacramento is 97 sq. miles (250 sq. kilometers) with a population of approximately 400,000. Sacramento is located 90 miles northeast of San Francisco, 383 miles north of Los Angeles, and halfway between San Francisco and the eastern California border with Nevada.

Sacramento has mild temperatures year-round. Summers are dry with little humidity and an abundance of sunshine. Light rain usually falls between December and February. Sacramento's average temperature is: Spring 64 degree F (18 degree C); Summer 75 degree F (25 degree C); Fall 72 degree F (23 degree C) and Winter-51 degree F (12 degree C).

Getting Around

Airport

Sacramento International Airport (SMF) connects the capital to the rest of the world. The airport is located at 6900 Airport Boulevard Sacramento, CA 95837 Tel: (916) 929-5411, just 12 miles northwest of downtown Sacramento, 15 minutes on Interstate 5. Transportation options from the airport include courtesy van service to many local hotels and motels, rent-a-car services, local bus services, and taxi.

Bus

Local bus service around the city is served by Sacramento Regional Transit District, 1400 29th Street (at N Street) Tel: (916) 321-2800. Downtown service center is located at 818 K Street (on the K Street Mall) Tel: (916) 321-BUSS (2877). Other bus services:

California (CA)
Capital: Sacramento (Population: 33,871,648)
Size: 163,707 sq mi. (424,001 sq km)
Nicknames: The Golden State
Joined the union on: September 9, 1850 (31st state)
Motto: Eureka (I Have Found It)
Flower: Golden Poppy
Bird: California Valley Quail
Song: "I Love You, California"
Famous for: Golden Gate Bridge, Hollywood, Yosemite Valley
Major industries: Manufacturing, Agriculture, Biotechnology, Software and Tourism

136

Greyhound Bus Line Tel: (800) 321-2222, Roseville Transit Tel: (800)-COMMUTE and Yolo County Transportation District Tel: (916) 371-2877.

Taxis

Taxi service for the City of Sacramento: Sacramento Cab Company Tel: (916) 331-4141, Checker Cab Tel: (916) 457-2222, Ambassador Taxi Tel: (916) 849-0766, The Cab Co Tel: (916) 372-4939, Associated Cabs Tel: (916) 455-1966, Gold Dust Airport Shuttle Tel: (916) 944-4444, Rainbow Taxi Tel: (916) 446-1817 and Yellow Cab Tel: (916) 444-2222.

Train and Commuter

The Sacramento Regional Transit District (RT) operates 20.6 miles of light rail service around the city using 36 light rail vehicles. Light rail trains operate from 4:30 AM to 1:00 AM daily. Downtown service center is located at 818 K Street (on the K Street Mall) Tel: (916) 321-2800.

Sacramento's train depot is located at 401 "T" St. Sacramento, CA 95814. The station is staffed and features an enclosed waiting area, checked baggage service, a Quik-Trak ticket machine, vending machines, restrooms, and payphones. Transportation options from the station include Hertz Car Rental Tel: (800) 654-3131, local transit, and taxi services.

Trains serving Sacramento station are Coast Starlight, California Zephyr, Capitol Corridor, and San Joaquin.

Visitor Information Center

Sacramento Convention and Visitors Bureau is located at 1303 J St. Suite 600, Sacramento, CA 95814. Tel: (916) 264 7777.

Places to See and Things to Do

Towe Ford Museum located at 2200 Front St, Sacramento, CA, 95814. Tel: (916) 442-6802. Considered as one of California's treasures, **California State Railroad Museum,** Located at 111 I St, Sacramento, CA, 95814. Tel: (916) 552-5252, is open daily from 10:00 AM to 5:00 PM. **California State Indian Museum** located at 2618 K St, Sacramento, CA, Tel: (916) 324-0971. **Crocker Art Museum** is located at 216 O Street, Sacramento, CA, 95814. Tel: (916) 264-5423. Exhibits California's history with a mix of traditional and state-of-the-art technology the **Golden State Museum** located at 1020 O St, Sacramento, CA, 95814. Tel: (916) 653-7524.

The grand **California State Capitol,** located at 10th and Capitol, Sacramento, CA, Tel: (916) 324-0333. The **Governor's Mansion** is located at 1525 H St, Sacramento, CA, Tel: (916) 324-0539. **Sacramento City Zoo** is located at 3930 West Land Park Dr, Sacramento, CA, Tel (916) 264-5885. And those practicing Yoga or simply curious visit the **All Ages Yoga Studio,** located at 3200 Riverside Blvd, Sacramento, CA 95818. Tel: (916) 944-0459. <<http://www.allagesyoga.com>>.

Visit **Foothill Wine Country,** a day trip to the wineries of El Dorado and Amador counties in the Sierra Nevada foothills is well worth your time. Take Highway 50 east to Shenandoah Valley, then turn south on Highway 49. Directions and instruction are available at the Sacramento train depot or the visitor information center.

Accommodations

Doubletree Hotel Sacramento located at 2001 Point West Way Sacramento CA 95815; Tel: (916) 929-8855 and toll-free (800) 222-TREE; expect to pay $70-$250. **Hilton Sacramento Arden West** located at 2200 Harvard Street Sacramento CA 95815-3306; Tel: (916) 922-4700 and toll-free (800) 445-8667; expect to pay $50-$200. **Clarion Hotel Downtown** located at 700 16th St. Sacramento CA 95814; Tel: (916) 444-8000 and toll-free (800) 252-7466; expect to pay $50-$150. **Comfort Suites - Downtown** located at 226 Jibboom St. Sacramento CA 95814; Tel: (916) 446-9400 and toll-free (800) 228-5150; expect to pay $80-$200. **Hawhtorn Suites** located at 321 Bercut Drive Sacramento CA 95814; Tel: (916) 441 1200; expect to pay $50-$180.

Holiday Inn Capitol Plaza located at 300 J St. Sacramento CA 95814; Tel: (916) 446-0100; expect to pay $80-$150. **Hyatt Regency Sacramento** located at 1209 L Street Sacramento CA 95814; Tel: (916) 443-1234; expect to pay $80-$300. **Howard Johnson Plaza-Hotel** located at 3343 Bradshaw Road Sacramento CA 95827; Tel: (916) 366-1266 and toll-free (800) I-GO-HOJO; expect to pay $50-$100. **Quality Inn Sacramento** located at 818 15th Street Sacramento CA 95814; Tel: (916) 444-3980 and toll-free (800) 228-5151; expect to pay $50-$100.

Red Roof Inn Sacramento located at 3796 Northgate Boulevard Sacramento CA 95834; Tel: (916) 927-7117 and toll-free (800) RED-ROOF; expect to pay $50-$100. **Sacramento Travelodge Downtown** located at 1111 H. St. Sacramento CA 95814, Tel: (916) 444-8880 and toll-free (800) 578-7878; expect to pay $70-$150. **Ramada Inn Sacramento** located at 2600 Auburn Boulevard Sacramento CA 95821; Tel: (916) 487-7600 and toll-free (800) 272-6232; expect to pay $70- $150. **Sacramento-Days Inn Downtown/Discovery Park** located at 350 Bercut Drive Sacramento CA 95814; Tel: (916) 442-6971 and toll-free (800) DAYS-INN; expect to pay $50-$100. **Best Western Expo Inn** located at 1413 Howe Ave. Sacramento CA 95825; Tel: (916) 922-9833; expect to pay $50-$100.

Davis (CA) See Coast Starlight, page 82-87.

Suisun-Fairfield (CA)

Suisun (Indian word for West Wind) was an island, linked to its neighboring Fairfield by a causeway. The total land area of Suisun City is 3.7 sq. miles (9 sq. kilometers) its population is around 22,686.

The city of Fairfield was founded in 1856, with a total land area of 57.66 sq. miles (92.86 sq. kilometers) and a population of roughly 96,178. The city was incorporated in 1903.

Place of Interest

Western Railway Museum, located 12 miles east of Fairfield Tel: (707) 374-2978, offers exhibits of streetcars, trains, trams, and a New York "L" Train, among others. Anheuser-Busch Fairfield Brewery Tour is located at 3101 Busch Dr. Fairfield, CA, Tel: (707) 429-7595.

Suisun-Fairfield's train depot is located at 177 Main St. (Under Hwy 12) Suisun-Fairfield, CA 94585. The station is unstaffed and features an enclosed waiting area. Transportation options from the station include local bus and taxi services. Suisun-Fairfield is served by the Capitol Corridor.

Martinez (CA) See Coast Starlight Service, page 82- 87.

Richmond (CA) See San Joaquin Service, page 143 -145.

Berkeley (CA)

The city of Berkeley was named after George Berkeley, an 18th century philosopher, the Bishop of Cloyne. Berkeley is located across the San Francisco Bay from the city of San Francisco (Connected with San Francisco via the Oakland Bay Bridge) and was incorporated in 1878.

Berkeley has a total land area of 10 sq. miles (27 sq. kilometers) and a diverse population of 103,328. Berkeley is home to the University of California Berkeley.

Places of Interest

Berkeley Municipal Rose Garden, located at Euclid Avenue & Eunice Street, is considered by many to be the finest Rose Garden in Northern California. Tilden Regional Park is located at Grizzly Peak Blvd. Berkeley, CA, Tel: (510) 562-PARK. These 2,065 acres of open meadows and forests offer spectacular views of the Bay Area. Lawrence Hall of Science is located at Centennial Drive below Grizzly Peak Blvd. Tel: (510) 642-5132. Nyingma Institute is located at Tibetan Meditation Garden 1815 Highland Place Berkeley, CA 94709, Tel: (510) 843-6812. Berkeley Marina, Pier & Cesar E. Chavez Park, located at the foot of University Avenue, west of 1-80 Tel: (510) 644-8623, offers stunning views of the Golden Gate Bridge and the San Francisco Skyline, there are also restaurants and hotels.

Hall of Health is located at 2230 Shattuck Avenue, lower level, Berkeley, CA 94704, Tel: (510) 549-1564. UC Botanical Garden is located at Centennial Drive above Memorial Stadium, Tel: (510) 642-3343. The garden is one of the world's leading botanical gardens. With special exhibits of redwoods, the old rose section, and the Chinese medicinal herb garden. UC Berkeley Visitor Center is located at 101 University Hall 2200 University Avenue Berkeley, CA 94704, Tel: (510) 642-5215. Visit the picturesque and diverse architecture of the oldest University in California (dates back to 1868) and the second largest of the nine campuses.

Berkeley Art Museum/Pacific Film Archive is located at 2626 Bancroft Way Berkeley, CA 94720, Tel: (510) 642-0808-UAM, (510) 642-1124-PFA. Berkeley Historical Society And Museum is located at 1931 Center Street Berkeley, CA 94701, Tel: (510) 848-0181. Museum of Paleontology is located at 1101 Valley Life Sciences Building UC Berkeley

Campus, Tel: (510) 642-1821. **Habitot Children's Museum** is located at 2065 Kittredge St. Berkeley, CA 94704, Tel: (510) 647-1111. **Phoebe Hearst Museum of Anthropology** is located at 103 Kroeber Hall Bancroft Way at College Avenue Berkeley, CA 94704, Tel: (510) 642-3682.

Berkeley's train depot is located at 3rd St. and University Ave. Berkeley, CA 94710. The station is self-serve. Transportation options from the station include local transit and taxi. Berkeley station is served by the Capitol Corridor.

Emeryville (CA) See Coast Starlight Service, page 82- 87.
Motor-coach connection to **San Francisco (CA)**

Oakland (CA) See Coast Starlight Service, page 82- 87.

Hayward (CA)

William Hayward was the founder of Hayward in 1852 when he purchased 40 acres of land surrounding what is now Downtown Hayward. Hayward was incorporated in 1876. Hayward is located on the east shore of the San Francisco Bay, 25 miles southeast of San Francisco, 14 miles south of Oakland, and 26 miles north of San Jose.

Covering a land area of 43 sq. miles (112 sq. kilometers), Hayward has a population of roughly 123,000. Hayward and its surrounding area flourished due to strategic location, good climate, and rich soil.

Hayward's train depot is located at 22555 Meekland Ave. Hayward, CA 94541. The station is unstaffed. Hayward station is served by the Capitol Corridor.

Fremont-Centerville (CA)

Fremont was founded in 1956; it has a total land area of 78 sq. miles (200 sq. kilometers). Fremont is located on the southeast end of San Francisco Bay, just north of San Jose, and has a population of 203,600 making Fremont the fourth most populated city in the San Francisco Bay Area.

Fremont is a community that is rich in culture and history and has small-town charm, yet is a major high-tech center.

Fremont's train depot, which also serves the town of Centerville, is located at 37260 Fremont Blvd. Fremont, CA 94536. The station is self-serve and features an enclosed waiting area, restrooms, payphones, a Quik-Trak ticket machine, and a snack bar. Transportation options from the station include local transit and taxi services. Fremont station is served by the Capitol Corridor.

Santa Clara (CA)

It was the Ohlone Indians who first inhabited Santa Clara Valley for many centuries, and in 1769 the Spanish explorer Gaspar de Portolá re-discovered the area. Santa Clara was founded in 1777.

Santa Clara is located at the lower end of the San Francisco peninsula near San Jose, with a total land area of 18 sq. miles (47 sq. kilometers) and a population of around 100,000.

Today, Santa Clara is part of the "Silicon Valley," the birthplace and center of the high technology revolution. In addition, the valley is the major employment center in the region.

Santa Clara's train depot is located at Foot of Stars and Stripes Dr. Santa Clara, CA 95110. The station is un-staffed. Transportation available from the station is local transit service. Santa Clara station is served by the Capitol Corridor.

San Jose (CA) See Coast Starlight, page 96- 97.
Connecting train to **Santa Barbara (CA)**

San Joaquin

7 25 am-D	Oakland (CA)	4 05 pm-A
7 35 am	Emeryville (CA)	3 55 pm
7 45 am	Richmond (CA)	3 33 pm
8 18 am	Martinez (CA)	3 06 pm
8 42 am	Antioch Pittsburg (CA)	2 35 pm
	Sacramento (CA)	
	Lodi (CA)	
9 20 am	Stockton (CA)	2 00 pm
9 49 am	Modesto (CA)	1 19 pm
10 03 am	Denair (CA)	1 05 pm
10 28 am	Merced (CA)*a (To **Yosemite**)	12 41pm
10 59 am	Madera (CA)	12 07 am
11 32 am	Fresno (CA)	11 44 am
12 10 pm	Hanford (CA)	11 04 am
12 28 pm	Corcoran (CA)	10 45 am
1 01 pm	Wasco (CA)	10 12 am
1 41 pm-A	Bakersfield (CA)*b (Gateway to **Kings Canyon**)	9 45am-D

*Motorcoach Connection
--Yosemite Valley (CA)a
-- Los Angeles (CA)b
-- Las Vegas (NV)b

A-Arrival
D-Departure
--Multiple Schedules Daily
Thruway Bus

The San Joaquin

San Joaquin travels a 415-mile (667.7 kilometer) route to the heart of California's San Joaquin Valley. It connects the towns and cities of **San Francisco, Oakland, Sacramento, Merced, Fresno,** and **Bakersfield** with throughway bus connections to **Las Vegas**; San Joaquin is also a gateway to three US National Parks: **Yosemite National Park, Kings Canyon,** and **Sequoia National Park.**

San Joaquin's service is financed and operated in partnership between the State of California and Amtrak.

Route Destination Highlights

San Francisco, CA- Visit the famous Pier 39, Alcatraz Island or The Rock, the worlds most celebrated bridge the Golden Gate Bridge, the Museum of Modern Art, the exciting Castro, or Union Square. Take the city tram and explore San Francisco's hilly streets or simply walk through the romantic setting of the city by the bays Fisherman's Wharf.

Yosemite National Park, CA- see the spectacular Yosemite Falls, scenic overlooks and winding trails throughout 1,169 square miles of parkland. Yosemite National Park holds a bit of magic for every traveler.

Kings Canyon and Sequoia National Park, CA- Near Yosemite Valley are Kings Canyon National Park and Sequoia National Park where you can explore the biggest tree in the world, the "Giant Sequoia Tree," which can live to up to 3500 years old. Take a hike and explore the magnificent canyons and forest of Kings Canyon; be sure to bring plenty of film for your camera.

Las Vegas, NV- Take a day or two and have fun exploring the world famous city of Las Vegas! Try your luck and gamble at Las Vegas' many casinos, visit some of the world's most beautiful and biggest hotels, take some breathtaking rides or sit tight and enjoy watching some of Las Vegas' famous live shows, or simply spend the night cruising the city's colorful lights. Las Vegas has something for everyone.

Train Schedules

San Joaquin travels daily from Oakland to Bakersfield, with a throughway bus connection to San Francisco from Oakland. The train trip between the two cities takes approximately 6 hours of travel time (half a day trip).

Accommodations

Accommodations are Reserved Coach. There is a dining car that serves complete meals, and a lounge car that serves sandwiches, snacks, and drinks. Other amenities are electrical outlets and payphones. A bicycle rack is available.

All Aboard!

Oakland (CA) See Coast Starlight Routes, page 82- 87.
Motor-coach connection to **San Francisco (CA)**

Emeryville (CA) See Coast Starlight services, page 82 -87.
Motor-coach connection to **San Francisco (CA)**

Richmond (CA)

Richmond is located 16 miles northeast of San Francisco, between San Pablo Bay and San Francisco Bay. The city of Richmond was incorporated on August 7, 1905. Richmond has a total land area of 56 square miles (145 sq. kilometers) and a population of approximately 100,000.

Richmond has 32 miles of shoreline to which the city's economy and history is deeply attached. The city was home to some of the major shipyards of the Second World War, and one of these, Kaiser Richmond Shipyards, was one of the biggest wartime shipbuilding operations of that time.

Point of Interest

The **East Brother Lighthouse,** constructed in 1873, is known as the oldest of the remaining wood frame beacons on the Pacific Coast. **Point Richmond** is a Victorian style architecture building that has restaurants, shopping, and a recreational area; it is a nice place to visit. Take a walk and relax at **Alvarado Park,** a popular local picnic site.

California (CA)
Capital: Sacramento (Population: 33,871,648)
Size: 163,707 sq mi. (424,001 sq km)
Nicknames: The Golden State
Joined the union on: September 9, 1850 (31st state)
Motto: Eureka (I Have Found It)
Flower: Golden Poppy
Bird: California Valley Quail
Song: "I Love You, California"
Famous for: Golden Gate Bridge, Hollywood, Yosemite Valley
Major industries: Manufacturing, Agriculture, Biotechnology, Software and Tourism

Richmond's train depot is located at 16th St. and Macdonald Ave. Richmond, CA 94802. The station is staffed and features an enclosed waiting area, restrooms, and payphones. Transportation options from the station include local transit and taxi services. Trains serving the Richmond station are the Capitol Corridor and San Joaquin.

Martinez (CA) See Coast Starlight service, page 82- 87.

Antioch-Pittsburg (CA)

The Smith brothers, William and Joseph, founded Antioch in 1849. Located at the San Joaquin and Sacramento Rivers just east of Concord, Antioch has a total land area of 19 sq. miles (50 sq. kilometers) and a population of roughly 91,000.

Antioch's train depot is located at I St. and Santa Fe Tracks Antioch, CA 94509. The station is unstaffed and features restrooms, payphones, and restaurants. Transportation options from the station include local bus or transit and taxi services. Antioch station is served by the San Joaquin.

Sacramento (CA) See Capitol Corridor service, page 136.

Stockton (CA)

Stockton is located in the north central part of California, 60 miles east of California's Bay Area and 40 miles south of Sacramento. Stockton is an inland deep-water port area that has 1,000 miles of waterways.

Stockton was founded by Charles M. Weber in 1849 and was incorporated on July 23, 1850. Stockton is the County seat of San Joaquin County; it has a total land area of 56 sq. miles (145 sq. kilometers) and a population of 243,771.

Just like most other cities and towns of California, Stockton is a product of the California Gold Rush Era when the city served as a staging area for miners. Stockton also became one of the main agricultural centers of the San Joaquin Valley. The city and its community were proud to be chosen to receive the prestigious recognition of All-America City by the National Civic League in 1999.

Stockton's train depot (Stockton – Downtown-Ace Station) is located at 735 S. San Joaquin St. Stockton, CA 95203. The station is staffed and features an enclosed waiting area, checked baggage service, restrooms, payphones, a Quik-Trak ticket machine, and vending machines. Transportation options from the station include local transit and taxi services. Stockton station is served by the San Joaquin.

Modesto (CA)

Modesto, meaning "modesty," was founded in 1870. Located at the heart of San Joaquin Valley in California's Central valley north of Fresno, Modesto was formerly called the "Rose City" and the "Garden City" because of the city's many beautiful rose yards and gardens.

Modesto has a total land area of 30 sq. miles (78 sq. kilometers) and has a population of 191,600, the largest city and the seat of Stanislaus County. Modesto has a Metropolitan Airport that provides several daily flights to and from San Francisco International Airport.

Modesto is proud of its downtown **Modesto arch**, which was built in 1912. The arch is 25 feet high at its center and 75 feet across and has 668 lights. The **Southern Pacific Depot** (present Modesto Transportation Center) is one of Modesto's architectural and historical sites.

Built in 1883 by Robert McHenry, the **McHenry Mansion** is a National Historic Place and a fine example of Victorian and Italian architecture. **McHenry Museum** is located one block from the McHenry Mansion, and exhibits pictures of the early life and culture of Modesto and Stanislaus County. Located downstairs from the McHenry Museum is the **Central California Art League Gallery** which exhibits sculpture and paintings of local artists.

Modesto's train depot is located at 1700 Held Dr. Modesto, CA 95355. The station is staffed and features an enclosed waiting area, restrooms, payphones, and vending machines. Transit and call taxi services are available at the station. Modesto station is served by San Joaquin.

Turlock - Denair (CA)

Turlock is the second largest city in Stanislaus County with a total land area of 9 sq. miles (25 sq. kilometers) and a population of around 57,000. Turlock`is home to California State University Stanislaus (CSUS), located south of Modesto on hwy 99 in central California. The City of Turlock was incorporated in 1908. Nearby Denair has a total land area of 1.9 sq. miles (5 sq. kilometers) and a population of 3,693.

Turlock and Denair's train depot is located at Santa Fe Ave. at Elm St. Denair, CA 95316. The station is unstaffed. Transportation from the station is local taxi service.

Turlock-Denair station is served by San Joaquin.

Merced (CA) Motor-coach connection to Yosemite National Park (CA)

With a size of roughly 2,020 square miles (5,237 sq kilometers), Merced County is known as the world's most productive agricultural area. Located in the heart of the San Joaquin Valley, Merced is known as the "**Gateway to Yosemite National Park**" (it is less than two hours from the Park).

The city of Merced is the seat and the largest city in Merced County, located 110 miles southeast of San Francisco and 310 miles northwest of Los Angeles. The city of Merced has a population of 61,712.

Incorporated in 1889, Merced was traditionally an agricultural economy; today it has more diversified industries of tourism, manufacturing, warehousing and distribution, and packaging.

Merced's train depot is located at 324 W. 24th St. Merced, CA 95340. The station is staffed and features an enclosed waiting area, checked baggage service, restrooms, payphones, and vending machines. Transportation options from the station include local transit and taxi services. Merced station is served by the San Joaquin.

Places to See and Things to Do

Historical Sites and Museums

Built in 1931, **Main Street Theater** is a Spanish colonial style building located on Main Street and Martin Luther King Blvd. **Transpo Center** is a neo-classic railroad station built in 1926 located at 16th and N Streets. Today the building houses the Greater Merced Chamber of Commerce & CVB, the Merced Downtown Association, and the Yosemite Connection and Greyhound bus lines.

Constructed in 1928, **Hotel Tioga,** located on N Street, is a Spanish Renaissance style structure. The hotel is listed on the National Historic Places registry. **Merced Courthouse Museum,** located at 21st & N Streets, Merced, Tel: (209) 723-2401, exhibits Merced County and California State history; free admission. **Merced Agricultural Museum** located at 4498 E. Hwy.140 Merced, Tel: (209) 383-1912. The museum is open from Tuesday through Sunday from 10 am to 4 pm; free admission.

Merced Multicultural Arts Center is located at 645 West Main Street, Merced, Tel: (209) 388-1090. Open weekdays from 9 am to 5 pm. **Applegate Park & Zoo** is located at 26th & R Streets, Merced. A fun place to visit, the park has wild animals, ducks, picnic areas, a rose garden, fountain, and Kiddy land Amusement area. The seasonal **Farmers Market** is open from May through October every Thursday evening from 6 to 9 pm, located on Main Street. There is music, produce, and other recreational activities; a fun place to experience local culture. Call Tel: (209) 383-6908 for information.

Lake Yosemite is located on Lake Road, Merced. Call Tel: (209) 385-7426 for information. It is a great place for various types of water recreation: wind sailing, boating, canoeing, swimming, picnic areas etc. Admission fee is $4 per car. **Grassland Wetlands** located along Highways 140 and 59 Tel: (209) 826-5188. More than 500 species of birds, animals, and plants can be viewed at the area

Accommodations

Comfort Inn Manhattan Beach located at 850 N. Sepulveda Blvd. Merced CA 90266, Tel: (310) 318-1020 toll-free (800) 228-5150. **Marriott Manhattan Beach** located at 1400 Park view Avenue Merced CA 90266 Tel: (310) 546-7511 toll-free (888) MARRIOTT. **Holiday Inn Express** located at 730 Motel Drive Merced CA 95340 Tel: (209) 383-0333.

Merced Yosemite Travelodge is located at 1260 Yosemite Pkwy Merced CA 95340, Tel: (209) 722-6224 toll-free (800) 578-7878. **Ramada Inn** located at 2000 East Childs Avenue Merced CA 95340 Tel: (209) 723-3121 toll-free (800) 2-RAMADA. **Best Western Inn** located at 1033 Motel Drive Merced CA 95035 Tel: (209) 723-2163.

Yosemite National Park

For many years Yosemite Valley has inspired artists and millions of visitors from around the world with its natural beauty, charm, and mysteries. Yosemite Valley became the US's third National Park on October 1st, 1890. One of the best-known examples of a glacier-carved canyon, Yosemite Valley is located in California's Sierra Nevada Mountains reaching a height between 2,000 and 13,000 feet above sea level. The park is rich in wilderness, natural habitats, and countless wonders of nature.

Designated as a World Heritage Site, Yosemite National Park helped change our understanding of man's role in preserving nature, wildlife, and bio-diversity.

Brief History

California's Sierra Nevada was formed by a gradual series of earth upheavals millions of years ago. Later the valley was transformed by a massive glacier that flowed down the canyons forming a hanging valley filled with natural beauty and creating what is today the Yosemite Valley. Yosemite is continuously shaped by climate and erosion today.

In 1864 the park was first protected, and in 1890 Yosemite was established as a national park to preserve its uniqueness and beauty.

Park Fees

Yosemite National Park is open the whole year, 24 hours a day. Entrance fees are required at the gate of the national park.

A 7-day permit for a vehicle and passengers is $20 and for individual persons (on foot, bicycle, motorcycle, etc.) is $10; a one-year Yosemite Pass is available for $40, a one-year Golden Eagle Pass is accepted, and disabled U.S. citizens are free.

Yosemite Valley

Transportation

Amtrak San Joaquin has motor-coach connections from Merced train depot to Yosemite National Park three times daily. The motor-coach driver usually will drop you at your hotel or accommodation. Amtrak full-fare rider has priority boarding.

The Yosemite Area Regional Transportation System, or YARTS, connects the national park with surrounding areas including Merced, Chatey's Valley, Mariposa, and Midpines. Round trip fares (including one time park fee) are from $3 to $20, depending on the origin of the trip. Check with your hotel for ticket information or call toll-free (877) 98-YARTS.

Car rental companies are available in Merced City or Fresno (see Merced section for complete information). The distance between Merced and Yosemite National Park is approximately 80 miles. Vehicles are required to carry tire chains from November through March. Observe speed limits in Yosemite (45 miles per hour and lower in some areas) and stay on designated roads open to the public; vehicles are not permitted off-road.

The park has 196 miles of roads which access several main attractions and destinations, thus it is essential to travel Yosemite by car, shuttle bus, or bike because of its vastness. There is a free shuttle bus system that serves most of the valley.

Bicycles are an efficient way of exploring the park, but remember to remain on designated paved roads or bike paths. Bicycles are not allowed on hiking trails, in meadows, or anywhere off the pavement. Check with your hotel for bike rental information.

When to Visit

Yosemite National Park offers different experiences throughout the year. It is important to plan your visit in order to meet your expectations, maximize your time, and visit Yosemite thoroughly.

Winter (December through March) is magical in Yosemite Valley. Typical weather is snowy and cold with bright sunshine from time to time. Snow covers the landscape, rivers, and mountains. Waterfalls are low but are still flowing. Some roads can be closed, so check the accessibility of roads before traveling. The best time to visit is **spring** (April and May) when the weather ranges from warn, sunny days to occasional snow fall. Rivers and waterfalls are at their high points and the valley is full of life and sound of the roaring water.

During **summer** (June through September) the temperature is warm to hot, with occasional rain. The majority of the park areas are accessible by car. Most flowers are blooming in June, thus the scenery is breathtaking. The falls can be dry or very low during late summer. **Fall** (October and November) is a pleasant time to visit as much of the park areas are open and often there are very few travelers. However, occasional snowfall may close some park areas. Temperatures range from hot to cold, dry to rainy, or snowy. The water level is usually very low and most waterfalls are dry or with low water.

Perhaps the most beautiful time to gaze at Yosemite Valley is at sunset when you will experience the magical effects of the alpenglow on the rock formations of Washburn Point, Glacier Point, Sentinel Dome, El Portal View, and other parts of the valley.

Visiting the valley during full moon is astonishing; the whole valley is illuminated by bright moonlight reflecting on the valley floor, especially if the valley is covered with snow. Also during spring a lunar rainbow can form as the full moon hits Lower Yosemite or Vernal Falls from time to time. The dark sky of Yosemite offers a wide view of the cosmic heaven. Stars and other heavenly bodies are greatly appreciated at Glacier Point.

Places to See and Things to Do

Yosemite Valley

The best time to see waterfalls is during spring (April and May); exploring and trekking the falls are possible and a great experience.

Yosemite Falls, at 2,425 feet, is the world's fifth tallest waterfall. Yosemite Falls is made up

of three separate falls; the upper fall at 1,430 feet, the middle cascades at 675 feet, and the Lower fall at 320 feet. The lower fall is easily accessible with a few minutes walk while the upper fall can be an exhausting hike.

Bridalveil Fall stands at 620 feet and are the first of many waterfalls that can be seen upon entering the park. The best time to see the falls is during spring when the thundering sound and majestic water force is fully on display. The base of the fall is accessible by few minutes walk. Located west of El Capitan is the **Ribbon Fall** standing at 1,612 feet. It is best seen from near the bottom of Bridalveil Fall during spring.

Staircase Falls stand at 1,300 feet and can be best seen during spring from Curry Village or Glacier Point. **Horsetail Fall** stands at 1,000 ft and is famous for its fire-like reflections of the sunset in mid-month of February. The fall can only be seen during winter and early spring, located just east of El Capitan. **Vernal Fall** is a 317-foot fall and is best seen from Glacier Point or by strolling the mist trail. Located just at the top of

Yosemite Falls

149

vernal fall, **Nevada Fall** is a 594-foot fall located at the "giant staircase" area.

At a height of more than 4,000 feet above the valley floor, **Half Dome** is one of the most popular sites of Yosemite. It can be seen throughout eastern Yosemite Valley and Glacier Point. Standing at 3,593 feet, **El Capitan** is the largest granite monolith in the world and is one of the most magnificent sites in the valley. **Cathedral Rocks,** located opposite El Capitan, is another impressive rock formation.

Glacier Point offers an impressive view of Yosemite Valley, Half Dome, and the High Sierra. Located 30 miles from Yosemite Valley, take Highway 41 to Chinquapin junction and turn left onto Glacier Point Road.

Museums

The **Indian Cultural Exhibit** and the **Indian Village** exhibit cultural history of the Miwok and Paiute natives, an interesting place to visit. Inquire at the visitor's center for further information.

Giant Sequoia at Mariposa Grove

Lakes & Rivers

There are a few lakes that are easily accessible in Yosemite National Park. Some of the most visited and accessible lakes are Tenaya, a popular place for picnicking, swimming, and canoeing; Mirror Lake, famous for the mirror image of Half Dome during spring; and Hetch Hetchy Reservoir located just 40 miles from Yosemite Valley (take Highway 120 to Evergreen Road which becomes Hetch Hetchy Road). See the visitor information center in the valley for more information.

Tuolumne Meadows

Tuolumne Meadows sits at 8600 feet and is the largest sub-alpine meadow in the Sierra Nevada. With an elevation ranging from 7000 to 13,000 feet, a visit to the top is rewarding. Tuolumne Meadows is known for its clear blue lakes.

Wilderness and Wildlife

Yosemite National Park has thousands of square miles of scenic wild lands and hundreds of species of wildlife. There are more than 60 species of animals and more than 200 species of birds including California Bighorn Sheep, Bears, Mountain Lions, Coyotes, Mule Deer, Squirrels, Golden Eagles, Great Gray Owls, and Peregrine Falcons, among others.

Yosemite has over 1,300 varieties of plants and 30 kinds of trees. Perhaps one of the most popular is the Giant Sequoia Tree. Giant Sequoia (the largest tree on earth which often lives up to 3200 years) can be seen at Mariposa Grove, Tuolumne Grove, and at the Merced Grove.

Camping inside Yosemite

Camping or sleeping in vehicles is only permitted in designated campsites, read the camping regulations and services inside Yosemite or consult the visitor information center.

Visitors Information Centers

Yosemite Valley Visitor's Center is located in Yosemite Village, west of the post office, Tel: (209) 379-1899. Big Oak Flat Visitor information Center Tel: (209) 375-9501. Wawona Visitor Information Center Tel: (209) 372-0263.

Accommodations

The **Ahwahnee Hotel** (a National Historic Landmark) is a grand hotel with wooden architecture. Ahwahnee Hotel is so popular that you have to book your reservation a few years before your arrival. A favorite destination of world-known figures such as former presidents, millionaires, and famous entertainment stars, the hotel is located in the heart of the park. **Wawona Hotel,** located near the park's south entrance, is a national historic landmark. It is a Victorian building of the 1870s. There is a golf course, a swimming pool, and tennis courts. The hotel is situated just 6 miles from the Mariposa Grove of Giant Sequoias. Other accommodations inside the park are: Yosemite Lodge, Curry Village, Tuolumne Meadow Lodge, White Wolf Lodge, and the High Sierra Camps. For information and reservations call (559) 252-4848 or write to 5410 E. Home Ave., Fresno, CA. <<Http://www.yosemitepark.com>>

Accommodations near/outside the park: **Best Western Yosemite Gateway Inn** located at 40530 Highway 41 Oakhurst CA 93644 (Yosemite National Park is 15 miles away) Tel: (559) 683-2378, toll-free (800) 545-5462. **Yosemite Riverside Inn** Located at 11399 Cherry Lake Road Groveland CA 95321 Tel: (209) 962-7408 or toll-free (800) 626-7408; expect to pay $89-$125. The **Hotel Jeffrey** located near Yosemite National Park, at 1 Main street Coulterville CA 95311, Tel: (209) 878-3471 or toll-free (800) 464-3471. **Groveland Hotel** located at 18767 Main Street Groveland CA 95321, Tel: (209) 962-4000 or toll-free (800) 273-3314, expect to pay $135-$155.

All Aboard!

Madera (CA)

Madera (Spanish for lumber or wood) is located 18 miles north of Fresno, 166 miles southeast of San Francisco, and 240 miles north of Los Angeles on California's Central San Joaquin Valley. The city of Madera covers a total land area of 10 sq. miles (25 sq. kilometers) and is home to approximately 46,000 residents. The city was incorporated in 1907.

Madera is situated near three US national parks: Yosemite National Park, Kings Canyon National Park, and Sequoia National Park.

Madera's train depot is located at Ave. 15 1/2 and 29th Rd. Madera, CA 93637. The station is unstaffed. There is local taxi service at the station. Madera station is served by San Joaquin.

Fresno (CA) Gateway to King's Canyon National Park (CA)

Fresno (Spanish name for ash tree), located in the central San Joaquin Valley of California, is known as the great "Garden of the Sun" because of its agricultural distinction. Fresno was incorporated in 1885, has a total land area of 99 sq. miles (256 sq. kilometers), and a population of approximately 412,000. Fresno is a melting pot of ethnic heritages and cultural diversity: Portuguese, Asian, Indian, Hispanic, Chinese, and Japanese people are among its residents.

Aside from agricultural production, Fresno is also known as the gateway to Kings Canyon and Sequoia National Park via highway 180. The two parks are an hour and a half away from Fresno.

Bellow are Car Rental companies in Fresno that offer services for your travel to Kings Canyon and Sequoia National Park:

- A-U-Save Auto Rental-   Tel: (559)-225-4545
- A Touch of Class   Toll-Free- (888)-575-4667
- Budget Rent-A-Car-   Toll-Free (888)-571-3000
- Avis Car Rental-   Tel: (559)-454-5035
- Dollar Rent-A-Car-   Tel: (559)-252-4000
- Fresno Lincoln Mercury-   Tel: (559)-226-5175
- Enterprise Rent-A-Car-   Tel: (559)-443-4990

Places of Interest

Wild Water Adventures features more than 22 exciting water rides. The park is located at 11413 E. Shaw Ave. Clovis. Tel: (559) 299-Wild. One of the favorites in Fresno, the **Island Water Park** also offers several water rides and other entertainment, located at 6099 W. Barstow, Fresno. Tel: (559) 277-6800.   Other points of interest: the **Forestiere Underground Garden**, 5021 W. Shaw Avenue, Fresno, Tel: (559) 271-0734; **Kearney Mansion Museum**, 7160 W. Kearney Blvd. Fresno. Tel: (559) 441-0862, and the **Legion of Valor Museum**. The museum is dedicated to the recipients of the highest decoration of valor, located at the Veterans Memorial Auditorium 2425 Fresno St. Fresno Tel: (559) 498-0510.

Visitor Information Center

Fresno Convention and Visitors Bureau, 848 M St. 3rd Floor, Fresno 93721 toll-free (800) 788-0836. <<http://www.fresnocvb.org>>

Fresno's train depot is located at 2650 Tulare St. Bldg. B Fresno, CA 93721. The station is staffed and features an enclosed waiting area, restrooms, baggage service, payphones, and vending machines. Transportation options from the station include local bus, transit, and taxis services. Fresno station is served by San Joaquin.

Kings Canyon National Park and Sequoia National Park

Sequoia and King's Canyon National Park is home to the world's largest living thing, the Giant Sequoia tree or the "Sierra Redwood." Located in Eastern California, this area spans from San Joaquin Valley to the summit of Sierra Nevada covering 864,383 acres with an elevation from 1500 feet (in the Ash Mountain region) to 14,494 feet (at the peak of Mount Whitney).

Sequoia National Park was established on September 25, 1890 (the second oldest national park in US second to Yellowstone National Park, WY) and in 1943 the park was merged with the newly created Kings Canyon National Park.

The Giant Sequoia tree grows only on the west slope of California's Sierra Nevada Mountain Range. Sequoia trees grow as high as 311 ft. and weigh as much as 2.7 million pounds. Its bark is about 31 inches thick; its branches grow up to 8 ft. in diameter; and its base measures up to 40 feet in diameter. The oldest Giant Sequoia ever recorded was 3200 years old.

For information visit the park website at <<http://www.nps.gov/seki>>.

Temperature

Temperatures vary by elevation. In winter, December to May, most of the park is covered with snow. Summer can be hot while fall and spring are pleasant with mild temperatures. Be aware that heavy showers or light rain and light snow can happen all year-round, so be prepared and dress in layers.

Travel Directions

If you are traveling from Fresno, Highway 180 takes you directly to Kings Canyon National Park, while Highway 198 takes you to Sequoia National Park if you are coming from the town of Visalia (a few miles from Hanford depot, San Joaquin). The two highways are connected inside the two parks by the General Highway making a loop of curves between the two national parks.

There is a vehicle length limit of 22 feet to enter the park, and check the weather information for the accessibility of the roads.

Transportation

Airport

There are two major airports near Sequoia and Kings Canyon National Park. Visalia Airport is located 35 miles west of Sequoia National Park; shuttle bus at the airport serving the surrounding area is serviced by Status Quo Limousine & Airport Shuttle, toll-free (888) 639-9917, car rental companies are Hertz Car Rental, toll-free (800) 654-3131, and Enterprise Car Rental toll-free (800) 325-8007.

Fresno Air Terminal is located 53 miles west of Kings Canyon National Park. There are Taxi and Bus services at the Fresno Air Terminal, VIA (Yosemite Service) toll-free (800) 369-7275, Fresno Area Express "FAX" (559) 498-1122, and Lemoore NAS Shuttle (559) 997-7000. Rent-a-car services are: Avis toll-free (800) 331-1212, Budget toll-free (800) 527-0700, Hertz toll-free (800) 654-3131, Dollar toll-free (800) 800-4000, and National toll-free (800) 227-7368.

Bus

Greyhound/Trailways has services both in Visalia and Fresno.

Train

Amtrak San Joaquin has services at Hanford (with bus connection in Visalia) and Fresno.

Rental Cars

List of rent-a-car companies are available at San Joaquin destination Fresno.

Area Map

Highway maps and road information outside the two parks are available at the Visitors Information Center in Fresno. National park road map (area map) and park newsletter is available at the park entrance upon paying the park fee.

Shuttles Around the Parks

There are free shuttle services available within Sequoia's Giant Forest during the summer, see the park visitor's information center for information.

Park Entrance Fees

Entrance to the parks is $10 per vehicle (including all passengers) for 7 days, $5 per person if you are traveling on foot, bike, horse, etc. There is a one-year Sequoia/Kings Canyon park pass for $20 and the one-year Golden Eagle Passport available for $50 avails entry to all US national parks.

The Golden Age Passport is available to U.S. residents or citizens 62 years old and over for a one-time $10 fee, and U.S. residents or citizens with disabilities are free of charge through Golden Access Passport.

Hours

The parks are open year-round 24 hours a day except for some areas which might be closed due to snow during winter.

Visitor Information Center

Foothills Visitors Center is located at highway 198 adjacent to Three Rivers, about a mile east of Sequoia Ash Mountain entrance, Tel: (559) 565-3135. Mineral King Ranger Station (closed during winter) is located at Mineral King Road at Sequoia east of highway 198, Tel: (559) 565-3768. Lodgepole Visitors Center (closed during winter) is located 22 miles north of Peak headquarters in Sequoia, Tel: (559) 565-3782. Cedar Grove Ranger Station (closed during winter) is located west of Cedar Grove Village in Kings Canyon, Tel: (559) 565-3793, Grant Grove Visitor Center is located at Grant Grove Village northeast of Kings Canyon park on highway 180, Tel: (559) 565-3341.

Places to See and Things to Do

Sequoia National Park

Giant Forest has a two mile-long trail access route that will take you to the park's beautiful and majestic meadow and giant tree (Sequoia tree). Named by the explorer John Muir in 1875, it houses the second largest tree in the world: the 246.1 foot tall Washington Tree. Also at the giant forest, standing at an elevation of 6725 feet, the **Moro Rock** offers a splendid view of the Great Western Divide and the surrounding canyons. A quarter-mile trail will take you up the 400 steep steps to the top of the rock.

Crescent Meadow, also known as the Gem of the Sierra, is an hour-long trek through beautiful green scenery, located 1½ miles east of Moro Rock parking area. **Tharp's Log** is a cattle ranch built by the Native American settlers in 1860, located in the giant forest area just a mile northeast of Crescent Meadow parking area.

Some facts about Sequoia Tree

- Sequoia tree only grows naturally on the west slope of the Sierra Nevada, California.

- The height of Sequoia tree could reach to up to 311 feet

- The oldest recorded Sequoia tree is approximately 3,200 years old

- Sequoia tree could weigh up to 2.7 million lbs.

- The bark of Sequoia tree could reach to 31 inches thick

- The branches of Sequoia tree could reach 8 feet in diameter

- The base of Sequoia tree could reach 40 feet in diameter

- The chemicals in the wood and bark of Sequoia tree provide resistance to insects and fungi.

- Sequoias have a shallow root system with no taproot

- Sequoia tree don't die of old age, but of falling (toppling)

Sequoia Tree (The largest living thing on earth)

General Sherman Tree, known as the largest living tree in the world, stands at 274.9 feet tall with a circumference of 102.6 feet. The tree weighs approximately 2.7 million pounds and it is more than 2100 years old. The tree is located 2 ½ miles south of Lodgepole visitor center in Sequoia Park on the Congress Trail.

Sequoia and Kings Canyon National Park has the largest cave system in California. The most accessible among these caves is the **Crystal Cave** located south of the Moro Rock turn off. From Generals Highway take the 7-mile road to the cave parking area. Then an hour trek down through the cave. There are streams and small waterfalls on the way.

Kings Canyon National Park

Kings Canyon was formed by the South Split of the Kings River and is known as the deepest in the US with a drop of 8,000 feet at the steepest section of the canyon. These beautiful canyons, comparable to that of Yosemite, are remotely accessible by car. In most cases visitors should take time to trek the 462,000 acres of still unspoiled area of the national park.

Gen. Sherman Tree

General Grant Tree, the third largest tree in the world, is 2000 years old, 267.4 feet tall, and 107.6 feet around. Known as the "Nation's Christmas Tree" there is a yearly Christmas celebration around the snow-covered tree.

Cedar Grove is a small village on flat land next to the Kings River, located near the east end of highway 180, approximately 38 miles from Grant Grove Village. Situated near the river, the canyon has a u-shape glacial characteristic. The village at the deep section of the canyon is near to two spectacular granite stone formations, the Grand Sentinel and the North Dome.

Panoramic Point is located near Grant Grove Village. From the parking area, take the short trail to the 7,520 foot ridge to see splendid views of the Sierra and Kings Canyon. **Boyden Cave,** located just 10 miles west of Cedar Grove, offers daily tours. Tel: (209) 736-2708. There are beautiful waterfalls around the park, and one of the most popular is **Roaring River Falls** found in Cedar Grove.

Big Stump Trail is what remains of the early logging operations in the area. The Mark Twain Stump is the remainder of a 1,700 year-old, 26 foot wide tree cut down in 1891. There is a one mile loop trail located near the entrance to Kings Canyon, 2 ½ miles southwest of Grant Grove Village.

Wildlife

Sequoia and Kings Canyon National Parks are rich in wildlife diversity. It is not uncommon for a visitor to encounter wild animals roaming in the park. Bear warnings are always in effect, and visitors are asked to be responsible in storing their food and to camp only at designated camping areas.

Some animals that live in the park are: Marmots, Mule deer, Mountain Lions, Black Bears, Coyotes, Pikas, Gray Foxes, Bobcats, Raccoons, and Squirrels, amongst others.

Activities

Fishing is allowed in most areas of the parks, but visitors are required to have a California fishing license. Ask at the Sequoia and Kings Canyon National Park Visitor Information Centers for information. **Hiking** is the most popular activity at the two parks. Together the two parks have 140 miles of roads and 800 miles of trails. Other popular activities are horseback riding, camping, exploring the giant sequoias, cross-country skiing, and snowshoe walks.

Accommodations

Best Western Holiday Lodge located at 40105 Sierra Drive, P.O. Box 129, Three Rivers, California, 93271, Tel: (559) 561-4119, toll-free Reservations (888) 523-9909 **Wonder Valley Ranch Resort and Conference Center** located at 6450 Elwood Road Sanger, CA 93657 Tel: (559) 787-2551 toll-free (800) 821-2801. **Johnson's Bed & Breakfast Chalet** located at 64969 Pine Street Hume (Sequoia National Park), CA 93628-9619 Tel: (559) 335-2797.

The **Wuksachi Village** located near Lodgepole Visitor Center at the Sequoia National Park is open year around Tel: (559) 565-4070. **Bearpaw Meadow Camp** located 11.5 miles from Cresent Meadow via the high Sierra trail (inside Sequoia National Park) is open from June to September toll-free (888) 252-5757. **Grant Grove Village** is located inside Kings Canyon National Park 30 miles northwest of Giant Forest and 55 miles east of Fresno via highway 180; open year-round. The **Cedar Grove Lodge** located at the eastern section of Kings Canyon, 31 miles east of Grant Grove Village, is open from May to October. Lodging information inside Kings Canyon National Park is available through Kings Canyon Park Services, PO Box 909, Kings Canyon NP CA 93633.

All Aboard!

Hanford (CA)

Hanford was incorporated on August 8th, 1891. Situated in the San Joaquin Valley directly between of two great cities (215 miles from either San Francisco or Los Angeles), Hanford also serves as a gateway to Sequoia and Kings Canyon National Park. The city of Hanford has a land area of 12 sq. mile (31 sq. kilometers) and a population of 33,897.

Hanford offers a unique blend of old and new, and is a family-orientated community. Hanford is known for its "China Alley," a 100 year-old Chinatown preserved by Chef Winy's family.

Hanford's train depot is located at 200 Santa Fe Ave. #A Hanford, CA 93230. The station is staffed and features an enclosed waiting area, checked baggage service, restrooms, payphones, and a snack bar. Transportation options from the station include local bus, transit, and taxi services. Hanford station is served by the San Joaquin.

Corcoran (CA)

Corcoran is a town with a land area of 5 sq. miles (14 sq. kilometers) and a community of more than 13,000 residents.

Corcoran's train depot is located at Whitley and Otis Ave. Corcoran, CA 93212. The station is self-serve and features payphones and a Quik-Trak ticket machine. Corcoran station is served by the San Joaquin.

Wasco (CA)

Wasco is located in the Bakersfield area; it has a land area of 3 sq. miles (8 sq. kilometers) and a population of approximately 12,412.

Wasco's train depot is located at 700 G St. Wasco, CA 93280. The station is un-staffed and is served by the San Joaquin.

Bakersfield (CA)
Motor-coach connections to: **Los Angeles (CA), Santa Ana (CA), Ocean Side (CA), and San Diego (CA);** and **Las Vegas (NV)**

The first residents of the region were the Yokuts Indians. They were the first settlers of the San Joaquin Valley more than 8000 years ago. It was Father Garces, a Spanish missionary, who rediscovered the place in 1776, and later in 1869 the town was named for one of its first settlers Colonel Thomas Baker.

Bakersfield is located at the southern end of the great San Joaquin Valley. The city of Bakersfield has a total land area of 93 sq. miles (238 sq. kilometers) and a population of approximately 380,000 within metropolitan area and approximately 214,554 in the city of Bakersfield. Bakersfield is the county seat of Kern County.

Kern County is one of the US's top oil producers, and is the third largest agricultural producing county in the nation.

Bakersfield's train depot is located at 601 Truxtun Ave Bakersfield, CA 93301. The station is staffed and features an enclosed waiting area, checked baggage service, restrooms, payphones, and vending machines. Hertz Car Rental Tel: (800) 654-3131 service is available at the station. Other transportation options from the station include local transit and taxi services. Bakersfield station is served by the San Joaquin.

Nevada (NV)
Capital: Carson City (Population: 1,998,257)
Size: 110,567 sq mi. (286,368 sq km)
Nickname: The Sagebrush State, Silver State, and Battle-born State
Joined the union on: October 31, 1864 (36th state)
Motto: All for Our Country
Flower: Sagebrush
Bird: Mountain Bluebird
Song: Home Means Nevada
Famous for: UFO's, Area 51, Las Vegas, and legal prostitution!
Major industries: Agriculture, Tourism, gaming, agricultural products and Wedding and Divorce.

Las Vegas (NV)

Las Vegas is the most exciting and entertaining city in the world. Located in the southwestern corner of Nevada, Las Vegas is the fastest-growing metropolis in the U.S. with a total land area of 83 sq. miles (215 sq. kilometers) and a population of approximately 425,270.

The largest city in Nevada, Las Vegas is a major tourist destination both in the US and in the world. Las Vegas (from a Spanish word for "The Meadows") was first discovered by Mormon settlers in 1855, but it was not until 1905 that Las Vegas was formally founded when the railroad came into the region. In 1911 the city was incorporated by the state legislature.

Sitting at an elevation of 2,020 feet above sea level, Las Vegas' climate is generally dry and comfortable with an average temperature of 66.3 degrees F and an average humidity of 30% all year round.

Today Las Vegas is a spectacular city with luxurious hotels, live entertainment, casinos, fine dining, theme parks, state-of-the art convention facilities, and some of the world most expensive apparel shops.

The world famous Las Vegas Blvd. offers breathtaking architecture (re-creations of the Eiffel Tower of Paris, Venice, ancient Rome, the Sphinx and Pyramid of Egypt, and New York's Manhattan), world known structures and monuments, animatronics shows, water shows, fanfare, and much more. An evening stroll along the boulevard is highly recommended to view the glittering light shows.

Nightlife? Las Vegas has it all, and there's always something to explore and do in the city of never-ending fun.

Climate

Las Vegas is in the middle of the desert. Summer temperatures could reach more than 110 degrees F, and drop as low as 25 degrees F. during winter. With relatively low humidity all year round, be sure to bring your sunscreen and lotion for skin protection.

Getting Around

Airport

McCarran International Airport is located in the heart of the city; most hotels and tourist spots are just a few miles from the airport. Public Transportation is served by Citizens Area Transit, connecting the city and the airport through routes 108 and 109. There are shuttle buses serving the airport, Bell Trans Shuttle Bus Tel: (702) 739-7990, C.L.S. Tel: (702) 740-4050 and Grayline/Coach USA/Express Shuttle Tel: (702) 739-5700. Fares around the city range from $4 to $5.25.

Taxi

Base fare is $2.20 for the first mile and $1.50 each succeeding mile. Taxi services are served by Checker/Yellow/Star Tel: (702) 873-2000, LV/ACE/Union/Vegas-Western Tel: (702) 736-8383, Whittlesea/Henderson Tel: (702) 384-6111, and Desert Cab Company Tel: (702) 386-9102.

Rent-a-Car

There are many rent-a-car companies serving Las Vegas: Avis Tel: (702) 261-5591, Budget Tel: (702) 736-1212, Thrifty (702) 896-7600, National Tel: (702) 261-5391, Dollar Tel: (702) 739-8403, Hertz Tel: (702) 736-4900 and Payless Tel: (702) 736-6147.

Visitor Information Center

Las Vegas Convention Visitors Authority located at 3150 Paradise Rd - Las Vegas, NV 89109-9096, Tel: (702) 892-0711.

Places to See and Things to Do

Caesars Palace

No one would miss the grand architecture of Las Vegas' **Caesars Palace** located at 3570 Las Vegas Blvd. S. Las Vegas, NV 89109, Tel: (702) 731-7110, toll-free (800) 634-6661.

At Caesars Palace's "Caesars Magical Empire" you will experience magical dining and entertainment that will make you feel like an emperor in ancient times. Visit the Forum

The Venetian

161

Shops where you'll find top of the line stores and an animatronics show of lasers, fire, steam, lights, and sound effects. There are also two roller coasters, 3-D simulator thrill rides, submarine, spacecraft, Warren Miller's Ski Ride, and haunted graveyard.

The Venetian

One of Las Vegas' most beautiful and grandest hotels is **The Venetian,** located at 3355 Las Vegas Blvd. S. Las Vegas, NV 89109, Tel: (702) 414-1000, toll-free (888) 283-6423 <<http://www.venetian.com>>. It features some of the city's most romantic places and exciting rides. Visit **Madame Tussaud's Celebrity Encounter** which exhibits more than 100 realistic wax figures of famous celebrities. There are romantic gondola rides, various 3-D motion adventure rides, mystifying Venetian carnival, underwater and outer space adventures. **Guggenheim Las Vegas** has special exhibitions of contemporary painting and sculpture, and other works of art.

The Mirage

One of Las Vegas' most popular sites is **The Volcano** at the Mirage located at 3400 Las Vegas Blvd. S. Las Vegas, NV 89109, Tel: (702) 791-7111, toll-free (800) 627-6667, <<http://www.themirage.com>>. The Volcano erupts every few minutes in the late afternoon, ejecting smoke and fire 100 feet above the water. Also at the Mirage, visit Siegfried & Roy's rare and exotic white tigers (free admission). The **Secret Garden of Siegfried & Roy** exhibits elephants, lions, leopards, panthers, and dolphins. And next door **Treasure Island** features the outdoor show Buccaneer Bay Sea Battle depicting pirates battling the British Navy; there are shows every 90 minutes starting at 4 pm daily.

Circus-Circus Hotel

Visit the mountains of thrills at the **Adventure Dome** and see live circus acts for free at the Circus-Circus Hotel, Casino and Theme Park located at 2880 Las Vegas Blvd. S. Las Vegas, NV 89109, toll-free (800) 634-3450 <<http://www.circuscircus.com>>.

Other Places of Interest on Las Vegas Boulevard

Take a nighttime visit to the **Fountains of Bellagio** at the Bellagio Hotel**.** This magical fountain has a thousand dancing water streams with music, "highly recommended." Bellagio Hotel is located at 3600 Las Vegas Blvd. S. Las Vegas, NV 89109, Tel: (702) 693-7111, toll-free (888) 987-6667, <<http://www.bellagio.com>>. See the **IMAX Theater** with 2-D and 3-D film technology at the Luxor Hotel and Casino located at 3900 Las Vegas Blvd. S. 89119 Las Vegas, NV 89119, Tel (702) 262-4000, toll-free (800) 288-1000, <<http://www.luxor.com>>.

Visit the **Auto Collection** at the Imperial Palace Hotel and Casino located at 3535 Las Vegas Blvd. S. Las Vegas, NV 89109, Tel: (702) 731-3311, toll-free (800) 634-6441 <<http://www.imperialpalace.com>>. There are classic and special automobiles on exhibit. Enjoy the rides at the **Las Vegas Mini Gran Prix** located at 1401 N Rainbow Blvd Las Vegas, NV 89108, Tel: (702) 259-7000 <<http://www.LVMGP.com>>. There are go-kart tracks, amusement rides, 7,000 sq. foot restaurant/party room, and shopping mall.

Experience **Cyber Speedway,** one of Las Vegas' most realistic simulated race car driving experiences at the Sahara Hotel and Casino located at 2535 Las Vegas Blvd. S. Las Vegas, NV 89109, Tel: (702) 737-2111, toll-free (888) 696-2121, <<http://www.saharavegas.com>>.

Sahara Hotel and Casino home of Las Vegas' fastest roller coaster **"SPEED-The Ride"** is located at 2535 Las Vegas Blvd. S. Las Vegas, NV 89109, Tel: (702) 737-2111, toll-free (888) 696-2121, <<http://www.saharavegas.com>>. **MGM Grand Hotel and Casino Lion Habitat** is home to several African lions and cubs, located at 3799 Las Vegas Blvd. S. Las Vegas, NV 89109, Tel: (702) 891-1111, toll-free (800) 929-1111, <<http://www.mgmgrand.com>>. Visit one of France's most known landmarks the "Eiffel Tower" set in the desert of Las Vegas at the **Paris Las Vegas Hotel and Casino** located at 3655 Las Vegas Blvd. South Las Vegas, NV 89109, Tel: (702) 946-7000, toll-free (888) 266-5687 <<http://www.paris-lv.com>. Take the elevator ride to the top of the Eiffel Tower and have a glance of Las Vegas' surrounding desert and the Las Vegas Valley.

Stratosphere Casino Hotel & Tower Stratosphere Tower Hotel & Casino located at 2000 Las Vegas Blvd S Las Vegas, NV 89104, Tel: (702) 380-7777, toll-free (800) 998-6937, <<http://www.stratospherehotel.com>>. There are thrill rides. The hotel that makes you feel like a king, **Excalibur Hotel and Casino** 3850 Las Vegas Blvd. S. Las Vegas, NV 89119, Tel: (702) 597-7777, toll-free (800) 937-7777, <<http://www.excalibur-casino.com>>. **New York-New York Hotel & Casino** located at 3790 Las Vegas Blvd. Las Vegas, NV 89109, Tel: (702) 740-6969, toll-free (800) 693-6763 <<http://www.nynyhotelcasino.com>>, famous for its roller coaster that loops and drops around the hotel's periphery.

M&M'S Academy (Showcase Mall) located at 3785 Las Vegas Blvd S. Las Vegas, NV 89109, Tel: (702) 736-7611, <<http://www.m-ms.com>>, is an interactive shopping and retail complex features M&M's Brand merchandise. Scheduled to open in spring of 2002, **Neonopolis** is located at the corner of Las Vegas Boulevard and Fremont Street. There will be a state-of-the art cinema complex, restaurants, and shops.

Fremont Street Lights

See one of Las Vegas' famous light shows with over two million lights and 540,000 watts of concert-quality sound at the **Fremont Street Experience** at 425 Fremont St. Las Vegas, NV 89101, Tel: (702) 678-5600, toll-free (800) 249-3559, for information <<http://www.vegasexperience.com>>. It's a must see attraction.

Other Places of Interest

The Neon Museum is located at 731 S. 4th Street Downtown Las Vegas. The museum exhibits Las Vegas history. **Guinness World of Records Museum & Gift Shop** is located half a block north of Circus Circus on Las Vegas Blvd., Nevada Tel: (702) 792-0640. The museum exhibits three-dimensional life through color videos, life-size replicas and computerized databanks and more. Open daily from 9am to 10pm. **Nevada State Museum and Historical Society** is located at 700 Twin Lakes Drive Las Vegas, Nevada, Tel: (702)-486-5205. The museum exhibits Las Vegas' 10,000 years of human occupation and the plants and animals of the Mojave Desert.

Las Vegas Natural History Museum is located at 900 Las Vegas Blvd North of Las Vegas, Nevada Tel: (702)-384-DINO. The Museum exhibits dinosaurs, modern-day animals, sharks, and birds. Open daily from 9 am to 4 pm. **Liberace Museum** is located at 1775 E Tropicana Las Vegas, Nevada Tel: (702)-798-5595. There are three exhibit areas on display of Liberace's spectacular cars, costumes, jewelry, photographs, and more. The museum is open Mon to Sat from 10am-5pm, Sun 1 to 5pm, closed during holidays.

Community College of Southern Nevada Planetarium & Observatory located at 3200 E Cheyenne Ave North Las Vegas, NV 89030, Tel: (702) 651-4759 <<http://www.ccsn.nevada.edu/planetarium>>. **Southern Nevada Zoological Botanical Park** is located at 1775 N Rancho Dr Las Vegas, NV 89106, Tel: (702) 647-4685 <<http://www.LASVEGASZOO.ORG>>, open daily from 9 am to 5 pm. One of the largest fitness facilities in Las Vegas is the **Chuck Minker Sports Complex** located at 275 N. Mojave Road, Tel: (702) 229-6563. The **Municipal Swimming Pool** is located at 431 E. Bonanza Road (702) 229-6309. The facility has an Olympic size swimming pool.

Scandia Family Fun Center located at 2900 Sirius Ave. Las Vegas, NV 89102, Tel: (702) 364-0070 has Miniature golf, batting cages, video arcade, bumper boats, go-carts, and a snack bar. **Northwest Leisure Services Center** is a 45,000 sq. foot recreation center with a gymnasium, fitness center, and a dance area, located at 3521 N. Durango Drive, Tel: (702) 240-9622. The **Veterans Memorial Leisure Services Center** is a 45,000 square foot recreation and cultural facility, located at 101 S. Pavilion Center in Summerlin, Tel: (702) 229-2277. It offers gymnasium, fitness and dance areas, classrooms and workshop space. Experience the limit and try to sky dive: it's a 35 second free-fall then a 6 minute parachute ride, **Skydive Las Vegas, Inc.** is located at 1401 Airport Rd, no. 4 Boulder City, NV 89005, Tel: (702) 759-3483, toll-free (800) 875-9348 <<http://www.SkyDiveLasVegas.com>>.

Visit the old Nevada western town of **Bonnie Springs Old Nevada:** there are historic exhibits, a petting zoo, horseback riding, train rides, a restaurant a motel, and more. It's located at Red Rock Canyon Ave. Old Nevada, NV 89004 Tel: (702) 875-4191, <<http://www.bonniesprings.com>>. Open daily from 10:30 am to 5pm. **Ethel M Chocolates Factory & Cactus Garden,** located at 2 Cactus Garden Dr. Henderson, NV 89014, Tel: (702) 433-2500, <<http://www.EthelM.com>>, is an interesting place worth visiting. Completed in 1935, the 726-foot **Hoover Dam** is one of the modern marvels of America. Located 40 miles from Las Vegas, you can tour the dam's interior or walk on top of the structure and appreciate the breathtaking view. Hoover Dam creates the largest man-made lake in the Western Hemisphere, Lake Mead.

Accommodations

Bellagio located at 3600 Las Vegas Boulevard Las Vegas NV 89109, Tel: (702) 693-7111. **Harrahs** located at 3475 Las Vegas Boulevard South Las Vegas NV 89109, toll-free (888) 335-0101. **Circus Circus** located at 2880 Las Vegas Boulevard South Las Vegas NV 89109 Tel: (702) 734-0410, toll-free. (800) 444-CIRCUS, expect to pay $40-$160. **Bally's Las Vegas-A Hilton Casino Resort** located at 3645 Las Vegas Boulevard South Las Vegas NV 89109-4307, Tel: (702) 967-4111, toll-free (800) 644-0777. **Alexis Park Resort and Spa** located at 375 East Harmon Avenue Las Vegas NV 89109, Tel: (702) 796-3300, toll-free (800) 453-8000, expect to pay$50-$260.

The Carriage House located at 105 East Harmon Avenue Las Vegas NV 89109, Tel: (702) 798-1020, expect to pay $50-$200. **Crowne Plaza Hotel** located at 4255 South Paradise Road Las Vegas NV 89109, Tel: (702) 369-4400, expect to pay $80-$200. **Doubletree Club Las Vegas** located at 7250 Pollock Drive Las Vegas NV 89119, Tel: (702) 948-4000, expect to pay $50-$180. **Econo Lodge Central** located at 211 East Flamingo Road Las Vegas NV 89109, Tel: (702) 733-7800, expect to pay $40-$350.

Hawthorn Suites Las Vegas located at 5051 Duke Ellington Way Las Vegas NV 89119, Tel: (702) 739-7000, expect to pay $80-$200. **Travelodge Las Vegas Downtown** located at 2028 East Fremont Street Las Vegas NV 89101, Tel: (702) 384-7540, expect to pay $40-$150. **Hilton Grand Vacations Club at Flamingo Las Vegas** located at 3575 Las Vegas Boulevard Las Vegas NV 89102, Tel: (702) 697-2900. **Flamingo Hilton Las Vegas** located at 3555 Las Vegas Boulevard South Las Vegas NV 89109, Tel: (702) 733-3111, expect to pay $60-$300.

Holiday Inn Las Vegas Boardwalk Casino located at 3750 Las Vegas Boulevard South Las Vegas NV 89109, Tel: (702) 735-2400, toll-free (800) 635-4581, expect to pay $40-$350. **Marriott Suites Las Vegas** located at 325 Convention Center Drive Las Vegas NV 89109 Tel: (702) 650-2000, expect to pay $80-$350. **Caesars Palace Hotel and Casino** located at 3570 Las Vegas Boulevard South Las Vegas NV 89109, Tel: (702) 731-7110, toll-free (800) CAESARS. **MGM Grand Hotel and Casino** located at 3799 Las Vegas Boulevard South Las Vegas NV 89109, Tel: (702) 891-1111 toll-free (800) 929-1111.

Excalibur Hotel and Casino located at 3850 Las Vegas Boulevard South Las Vegas NV 89109-4300, Tel: (702) 597-7777, toll-free. (800) 937-7777. **Tropicana** located at 3801 Las Vegas Boulevard South Las Vegas NV 89109 Tel, (702) 794-2061, expect to pay $60-$200. **New York-New York Hotel and Casino** located at 3790 Las Vegas Boulevard South Las Vegas NV 89109 Tel: (702) 740-6969. **Stratosphere Hotel & Casino** located at 2000 Las Vegas Blvd. S. Las Vegas NV 89104 Tel: (702) 380-7777 toll-free. (800) 99-TOWER. **The Mirage** located at 3400 Las Vegas Boulevard South Las Vegas NV 89109, Tel: (702) 791-7111 toll-free (800) 627-6667.

Empire Builder

One of the most beautiful train routes in the world, the "Empire Builder" connects the cities of Chicago (IL), Seattle (WA), and Portland, (OR). It travels the enchanting 'Land of Lakes' Minnesota, North Dakota, the 'Big Sky' of Montana, and the electrifying beauty of Glacier National Park. Empire Builder crosses the mighty Rocky Mountains and heads to the magnificent Cascade Mountains of Washington State. Empire Builder is a trip that you will never forget!

Route Destination Highlights

Portland, OR- Visit the Cascade Mountains or explore the Columbia River Gorge, the Multnomah Falls, and what is left of Mt. St. Helens. If you are a book lover, visit the largest independent bookstore in the world, Powel's City of Books.

Seattle, WA- Gateway to the magnificent Mt. Rainier, take a day trip to Olympic National Park, visit the Seattle Space needle, take a romantic afternoon walk at the Puget Sound, or tour the famous Klondike Gold Rush Park.

West Glacier, MT- Explore the majestic Glacier National Park. The park covers more than 1,500 sq. miles of rich wilderness and breathtaking beauty. Glacier National Park is home to more than 200 species of birds and 60 species of wildlife.

	Empire Builder	
4 45pm	**Seattle, WA**	10 20 am
5 17 pm	Edmonds, WA	9 08 am
5 42 pm	Everett, WA	8 43 am
12 32 am	Spokane, WA	2 15 am
1 15 am		1 40 am
2 47 am	Sandpoint, ID	11 49 pm
5 41 am	Libby, MT	10 59 pm
7 46 am	Whitefish, MT	9 16 pm
8 16 am	West Glacier, MT	8 26 pm
8 55 am	Essex, MT	7 44 pm
9 54 am	**East Glacier, MT**	6 48 pm
10 10 am	Browning, MT	6 25 pm
10 45 am	Cut Bank, MT	5 52 pm
11 20 am	Shelby, MT	5 22 pm
1 32 pm	Havre, MT	3 43 pm
2 52 pm	Malta, MT	1 25 pm
3 47 pm	Glasgow, MT	12 26 pm
4 33 pm	Wolf Point, MT	11 41 am
7 09 pm	Williston, ND	11 07 am
8 11 pm	Stanley, ND	9 57 am
9 22pm	Minot, ND	9 06 am
9 42 pm		8 46 am
10 38 pm	Rugby, ND	7 19am
11 32 pm	Devils Lake, ND	6 25 am
12 54 am	Grand Forks, ND	5 04 am
2 10 am	Fargo, ND	3 49 am
3 07 am	Detroit Lakes, ND	2 38 am
4 06 am	Staples, ND	1 42 am
5 11 am	St. Cloud, MN	12 40 am
7 05 am	**S.Paul-Minneapolis,**	11 15 pm
8 00 am	**MN**	10 25 pm
9 04 am	Red Wing, MN	8 46 pm
10 09 am	Winona, MN	7 44 pm
11 45 am	La Crosse, WI	7 11 pm
11 26 am	Tomah, WI	6 25 pm
12 07 pm	Wisconsin Dells, WI	5 47 pm
12 25 pm	Portage, WI	5 29 pm
12 58 pm	Columbus, WI	5 00 pm
2 20 pm	**Milwaukee, WI**	3 50 pm
3 27 pm	Glenview, IL	2 34 pm
4 20 pm	**Chicago, IL**	2 10 pm
D-Departure	**A-**Arrival	

St. Paul-Minneapolis, MN- See the fine architecture of Saint Paul City Hall and Courthouse, the impressive Minnesota State Capitol, the Cathedral of St. Paul, the F. Scott Fitzgerald House, and the James J. Hill House.

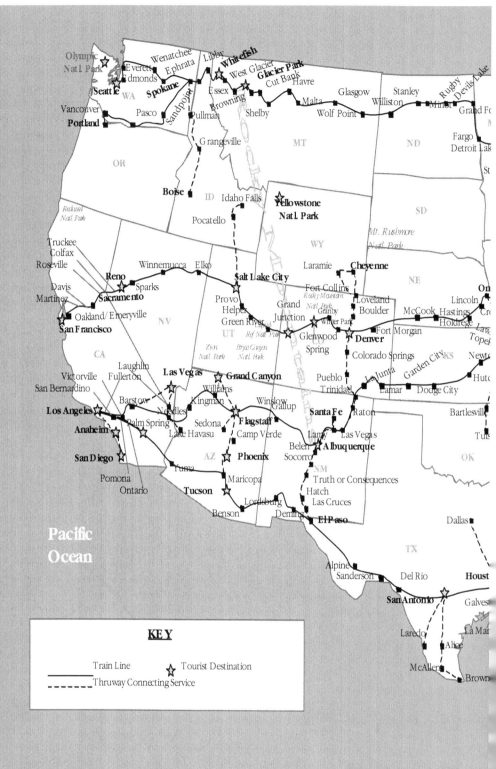

Western US Train Routes

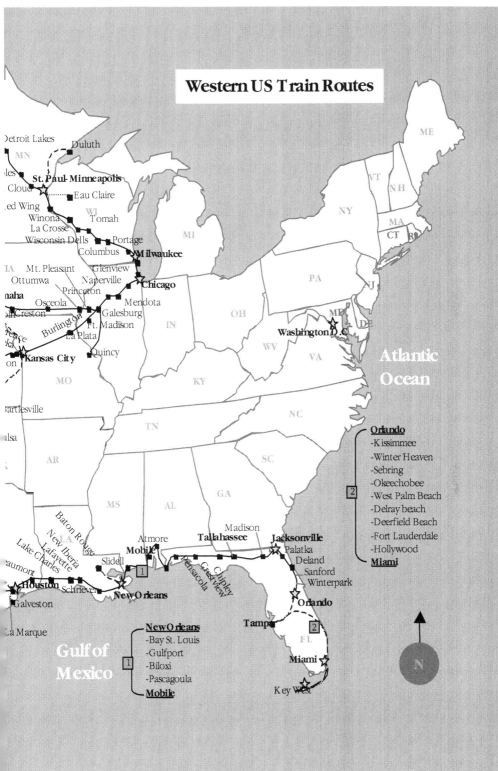

Explore the city of St. Paul through the Capitol City Trolley, and visit the Twin City Model Railroad Club. Visit the Minneapolis Sculpture Garden, Museum of Questionable Medical Devices, and Minnesota Air Guard Museum.

Wisconsin Dells, WI- Watch the world famous Tommy Bartlett Thrill Show, visit the Wax World of the Stars, Beaver Springs Public Aquarium, or explore Wisconsin Dells many geological wonders by taking a Dells Experience Jet Boat ride.

Milwaukee, WI- the city is known for its Summer Fest, the largest and most celebrated music festival in the world. Visit the Historic Pabst Theater one of the city's finest architectural buildings, see the International Clown Hall of Fame, the Circus World Museum, or visit the US official Olympic training center, Pettit National Ice Center.

Chicago, IL- Home to America's tallest building Sears Tower, visit the Museum of Science and Industry and other outstanding museums, admire the charming Centennial Fountain, take a romantic stroll along lake Michigan, and enjoy Chicago's attractive and busy nightlife.

Train Schedules

The Empire Builder travels daily from the city of Chicago, Illinois to the cities of Seattle, Washington and Portland, Oregon. The trip between the three cities takes approximately 2 days and two hours of travel time.

Accommodations

Accommodations are Superliner Reserved Coach and Superliner Sleeping Car. There is a Sightseer Lounge Car serving local cuisine, snacks, sandwiches, soups, and drinks. Restaurant style meals are served in the Dining Car. Other amenities include movies, reading materials, games, and seasonal national park guide presentations.

ALL ABOARD!

Seattle (WA) See Cascade service, page 56.

Edmonds (WA) See Cascade service, page 54- 56.

Everett (WA) See Cascade service, page 54- 56.

Spokane (WA) See Seattle to Spoken service, page 77- 78.

Sandpoint (ID)

Sandpoint is located in northern Idaho, 322 miles from the state capital Boise and 60 miles from the US/Canadian boarder. Sandpoint was first incorporated as a town in 1901, and in 1907 the town of Sandpoint became the city of Sandpoint. Sandpoint has a land area of 3.8 sq. miles (9.9 sq. kilometers) and population of approximately 7,000.

Explore the area via Montana Rockies Rail Tours, 1055 Baldy Park Avenue, Tel: (208) 265-8618; visit the Bonner County Historical Museum located at 905 Ontario St. Sandpoint, ID Tel: (208) 263-2344, Vintage Wheel Museum located at 218 Cedar St. Sandpoint, ID Tel: (208) 263-7173, and the downtown Cedar Street Bridge Public Market.

Sandpoint's train depot is located at Railroad Ave. Sandpoint, ID 83864. The station is un-staffed and features an enclosed waiting area, restrooms, and payphones. Transportation from the station is local taxi service.

Sandpoint station is served by the Empire Builder.

Libby (MT)

Libby is located in northwest of Montana, 210 miles from the state capital Helena, just 35 miles east of Idaho. It has a land area of 1 sq. miles (2.8 sq. kilometers) and population of approximately 3,000. It was the Kootenai Indians who lived in the area for many generations, until the late 1800's when the first white fur traders, miners, and settlers arrived in the area. The site was named after the daughter of the first settlers. The town of Libby was moved to its present location in 1892 when the railroad arrived at the Kootenai River.

Places of interest: the Koocanusa Reservoir known for fishing, water sports, and camping; the Kootenai National Forest and Kootenai Falls located on the Kooteani River. Ski areas: Turner Mountain Ski Area, Big Mountain Ski Area, and Schweitzer Ski Area.

Libby's train depot is located at 100 Mineral Ave. Libby, MT 59923. The station is un-staffed and features an enclosed waiting area, restrooms, and payphones. Transportation from the station is local taxi service.

Libby station is served by the Empire Builder.

Whitefish (MT)

Whitefish was founded when the railroad arrived in the area in 1903. Whitefish is located in northwest Montana, 169 miles from the state capital Helena. Famous as a winter resort, Whitefish has easy access to Big Mountain Ski Area, Glacier National Park, and Whitefish Lake. Whitefish has a land area of 3 sq. miles (7.7 sq. kilometers) and population of more than 5,000.

Whitefish's train depot is located at 500 Depot St. Whitefish, MT 59937. The station is staffed and features an enclosed waiting area, checked baggage service, restrooms, payphones, and vending machines. Transportation options from the station include Hertz Car Rental toll-free (800) 654-3131 and local taxi service.

Whitefish station is served by the Empire Builder.

West Glacier (MT)

Glacier National Park is located in a rugged section of the northern Rockies between the United States and Canada. The American side of Glacier National Park combined with the Canadian Waterton Lakes National Park in Alberta makes up the Waterton-Glacier International Peace Park World Heritage Site.

It covers a land area of more than 1,500 square miles (3,885 sq. kilometers) rich in natural wildlife habitats and sustaining a unique ecosystem. There are 200 species of birds and 60 species of other animals. Wildlife encounter is not uncommon in Glacier National Park: deer, mountain goats, elk, moose, bears, bighorn sheep, and many others are prominent residents of the national park. There are more than 1,000 campsites in the park.

Montana (MT)
Capital: Helena (Population: 902,195)
Size: 147,046 sq mi. (380,849 sq km)
Nickname: The Treasure State, Big Sky Country
Joined the union on: November 8, 1889 (41st state)
Motto: Gold and Silver
Flower: Bitterroot
Bird: Western Meadowlark
Song: Montana
Famous for: big sky, and the birth place of the Missouri River
Major industries: Farm, Agriculture and Tourism

Things to do inside Glacier National Park: Visit the Hungry Horse Dam, the Glacier Maze, or explore the wilderness area. Other recreational activities: horseback riding, boating and canoeing, rafting, fishing, swimming, hiking, and biking. There are Helicopter Tours, Scenic Cruises, and other local tours.

The park is open year-round, see chapter 3 – "Parks and National Parks" section for park fee information. For transportation inside the park contact: Sun Tours at 29 Glacier Avenue, East Glacier park, Montana 59434 toll-free (800) 786-9220. Amtrak station is located parallel to the southern and southwestern borders of the park.

Contact Glacier National Park, P.O Box 128 West Glacier, MT 59936 Tel: (406) 888-7800 for information.

Accommodations

The Viad Corporate Tower, Phoenix, AZ 85077, call Tel: (602) 207-6000 for reservation and hotel information. **The Village Inn Motel** is located on west side of the park on the south shore of Lake McDonald in Apgar village, Tel: (406) 892-2525. **Lake McDonald Lodge** is located on Lake McDonald near the west entrance Tel: (406) 892-2525.

West Glacier's train depot is located on Hwy. #2 West Glacier, MT 59936. The station is un-staffed and features an enclosed waiting area, payphones, and restaurant. Transportation from the station is local taxi service.

West Glacier station is served by the Empire Builder.

Essex (MT)

Essex is located along the banks of the Middle Fork Flathead River near Mount Saint Nicholas. Essex is a popular stop for ski enthusiasts; if you are visiting during the months of June and July there is a great chance that you see mountain goats and other wild animals around the area. One of Essex most popular attractions is the Izaak Walton Inn, a unique inn with train cars converted into a hotel rooms. The inn is listed in the National List of Historic Places.

Essex train depot is located 1/4 Mile E of Izaak Walton Inn Essex, MT 59916. The station is un-staffed and features payphones.

Essex station is served by the Empire Builder.

East Glacier (MT)

East Glacier is located in Glacier County on the east end of Glacier National Park, and is one of the park's major gateways. The Glacier Park International Airport is located nearby. **Hostelling International – Brownie's** is located a few minutes from the train station at 1020 Montana Highway 49 East Glacier park MT 59434 Tel: (406) 226-4426, price $12-up. Call the hostel for pickup service at the train station.

East Glacier's train depot is located at 400 Highway 49 N. East Glacier Park, MT 59434. The station is staffed and features an enclosed waiting area, checked baggage service, restrooms, and a restaurant. Transportation from the station is local transit service.

East glacier station is served by the Empire Builder.

Browning (MT)

Browning is located east of Glacier National Park; it has a land area of 0.2 sq. mile (0.7 sq. kilometer) and population of more than 1,000. Browning is the headquarters of the Blackfeet (Montana's largest tribe) Indian Reservation. Visit the Museum of the Plains Indians located near the intersection of US Highways 2 and 89. The museum exhibits native Indian cultural artifacts and arts.

Browning's train depot is located on Heart Butte Rd. S. Browning, MT 59417. The station is un-staffed and features an enclosed waiting area and restrooms.

Browning station is served by the Empire Builder.

Cut Bank (MT)

Cut Bank is the seat of Glacier County. It is located on the bank of Marinas River, 141 miles north of the city of Helena and just 40 miles south of US/Canadian border. It has a land area of 0.9 sq. miles (2.4 sq. kilometers) and a population of approximately 13,000. Cut Bank was founded when the great railroad arrived in the area.

Cut Bank's train depot is located on US Hwy Number 2 and Central Avenue Cut Bank, MT 59427. The station is un-staffed and features an enclosed waiting area, restrooms, and payphones.

Cut Bank station is served by the Empire Builder.

Shelby (MT)

Shelby is the seat of Toole County and is located in northern Montana, 132 miles north of the state capital Helena. Shelby has a land area of 1.5 sq. miles (4 sq. kilometers) and population of just over 5,000.

Shelby's train depot is located at 198 1/2 St. Railroad Right of Way Shelby, MT 59474. The station is staffed and features an enclosed waiting area, restrooms, payphones, and a restaurant. Transportation options from the station include local bus and taxi services.

Shelby station is served by the Empire Builder.

Havre (MT)

Montana (MT)
Capital: Helena (Population: 902,195)
Size: 147,046 sq mi. (380,849 sq km)
Nickname: The Treasure State, Big Sky Country
Joined the union on: November 8, 1889 (41st state)
Motto: Gold and Silver
Flower: Bitterroot
Bird: Western Meadowlark
Song: Montana
Famous for: big sky, and the birth place of the Missouri River
Major industries: Farm, Agriculture and Tourism

Havre is located in the Great Plains of north central Montana, also popularly known as the "Hi-Line." Havre is approximately 30 miles from the US/Canadian border with a land area of 2.4 sq. miles (6.4 sq. kilometers) and a population of more than 17,000. Havre was founded during the great northern United States railroad expansion; during the early days the town was a transportation hub for shelter, food, and supplies for the train travelers. Today Havre is known for its warm, hospitable people with a diversified economy mainly based on agriculture and outdoor tourism.

Havre's train depot is located at 235 Main St. Havre, MT 59501. The station is staffed and features an enclosed waiting area, checked baggage service, restrooms, payphones, restaurant, and vending machines. Transportation from the station is local taxi service.

Havre station is served by the Empire Builder.

Malta (MT)

Malta is the seat of Philips County located in northeastern Montana. It has a land area of 1 sq. miles (2.7 sq. kilometers) and population of more than 2,000. Malta is still a cowboy town, and a visit at the Bowdoin National Wildlife Refuge Tel: (406) 654-2863 will reward you with a breathtaking wildlife experience. Phillips County Museum, located at 431 Highway 2 E Malta, MT 59538 Tel: (406) 654-1037, exhibits the area's history and dinosaur fossils. Contact the Malta Chamber of Commerce at Tel: (406) 654-1776 for more information.

Malta's train depot is located at 51 S First Street E. Malta, MT 59538. The station is un-staffed and features an enclosed waiting area, restrooms, payphones, and a restaurant.

Malta station is served by the Empire Builder.

Glasgow (MT)

Glasgow was founded in late 1800's as a railroad town located in Montana's Hi-Line region. It has a land area of 1.4 sq. miles (3.6 sq. kilometers) and population of more than 8,000. A few miles south of Glasgow, is one of the world's oldest and largest hydraulic earth-filled dams, the Fort Peck Dam built in 1933.

Glasgow's train depot is located at 424 1st Ave. S. Glasgow, MT 59230. The station is un-staffed and features an enclosed waiting area, restrooms, payphones, and a restaurant.

Glasgow station is served by the Empire Builder.

Wolf Point (MT)

Wolf Point is the county seat of Roosevelt County, located 90 miles west of the Montana/North Dakota border and approximately 75 miles south of the US/Canadian border. Wolf Point has a land area of 0.8 sq. miles (2.2 sq. kilometers) and a population of more than 3,200. Wolf Point was a former wolf hunting ground during the early days of the fur trade in the US, and it was the riverboat liner passengers who marked and called the site Wolf Point.

Wolf Point's train depot is located at 320 Front St. Wolf Point, MT 59201. The station is staffed and features an enclosed waiting area, restrooms, payphones, and a restaurant.

Wolf Point station is served by the Empire Builder.

North Dakota (ND)
Capital: Bismarck (Population: 642,200)
Size: 70,704 sq mi. (183,123 sq km)
Nickname: The Sioux State, Peace Garden State, Flickertail State
Joined the union on: November 2, 1889 (39th state)
Motto: Liberty and union, now and forever: one and inseparable
Flower: Wild prairie rose
Bird: Western meadowlark
Song: North Dakota Hymn
Famous for: the 2063 ft. TV tower, world biggest buffalo statue, large department store.
Major industries: Agriculture, minerals, manufacturing and food processing

Williston (ND)

Williston is located along the banks of the Missouri River in the northwestern corner of North Dakota, 65 miles from the US/Canadian border. It has a land area of 6.9 sq. miles (17.9 sq. kilometers) and population of more than 13,000.

Williston's train depot is located at 1 S. Main St. Williston, ND 58801. The station is staffed and features an enclosed waiting area, checked baggage service, payphones, and vending machines. Transportation from the station is local taxi service.

Williston station is served by the Empire Builder.

Stanley (ND)

Stanley is located in northwestern corner of North Dakota 131 miles from the state capital Bismarck. It has a land are of 1.6 sq. miles (4.3 sq. kilometers) and population of just over a thousand.

Stanley's train depot is located on Main St. and RR Ave. Stanley, ND 58784. The station is un-staffed and features an enclosed waiting area and payphones.

Stanley station is served by the Empire Builder.

Minot (ND)

Minot is located in the north central part of North Dakota, just 55 miles from the US/Canadian border. Minot has a land area of 13 sq. miles (34.3 sq. kilometers) and a population of more than 36,000. Minot's economy is mainly based in agriculture, however finance, education, transportation, and tourism are Minot's other major economic factors.

Places of interest: Scandinavian Heritage Park, located at 1020 South Broadway, ND, features 'Danish Windmill', a 220 year-old house, and other Scandinavian exhibits. The Dakota Territory Air Museum is located at 100 34th Ave NE Minot, ND Tel: (701) 852-8500, Roosevelt Park Zoo is located at 1219 Burdick Expressway East, ND, and the Riverwalk of Minot is a 2.5 mile long trail, the best way to explore Minot.

The Minot Railroad Museum is located at 19 1st Street NE Tel: (701) 852-7091, and Magic City Express located in Roosevelt Park at 1219 Burdick Expressway East has an F8 locomotive. Eastwood Park National Historic District features 18th century houses, a church and synagogue.

Accommodations

Hillcrest Motel located at 1416 S Broadway, Minot, ND 58701 Tel: (701) 852-1214. **Kelly Inn** located at 1510 26th Ave SW, Minot, ND 58701 Tel: (701) 852-4300. **Ho-Hum Motel** located at 2805 Highway 2 and 52 W, Minot, ND 58701 Tel: (701) 852-2191. **Days Inn** located at 2100 4th St SW, Minot, ND 58701 Tel: (701) 852-3646.

Holiday Inn located at 2200 Burdick Expy E, Minot, ND 58701 Tel: (701) 852-2504. **Choice Hotels Intl** located at 1625 20th Ave SE, Minot, ND 58701 Tel: (701) 838-7777. **Pat's Motel & Campground** located at 2025 27th St SE, Minot, ND 58701 Tel: (701) 838-5800. **Fairfield Inn** located at 900 24th Ave SW, Minot, ND 58701 Tel: (701) 838-2424. **Comfort Inn** located at 1515 22nd Ave SW, Minot, ND 58701 Tel: (701) 852-2201. **Best Western Inn** located at 1505 N Broadway, Minot, ND 58703 Tel: (701) 852-3161.

Minot's train depot is located at 400 First Ave. S.W. Minot, ND 58701. The station is staffed and features an enclosed waiting area, checked baggage service, restrooms, and payphones. Transportation options from the station include local transit and taxi services.

Minot station is served by the Empire Builder.

Rugby (ND)

Rugby is located in north-central North Dakota at the Geographical Center of North America. A pyramid shaped monument marks the area the U.S. Geological Survey determined to be the center of North America in 1931. The monument is located on the southeast corner of the intersection of Highway 2 & 3. Other places of interest: the Prairie Village Museum exhibits artifacts from Scandinavian, Russian, and German heritages. Rugby has a land area of 1.8 sq. miles (4.8 sq. kilometers) and population of approximately 3,000.

Rugby's train depot is located at 201 W. Dewey St. Rugby, ND 58368. The station is staffed, and features an enclosed waiting area, checked baggage service, restrooms, payphones, and a restaurant.

Rugby station is served by the Empire Builder.

Devils Lake (ND)

Devils Lake is the county seat of Ramsey County, located in the northeastern portion of the state of North Dakota, 129 miles from the state capital of Bismarck. Devils Lake has a land area of 1.2 sq. miles (3.3 sq. kilometers) and population of more than 8,000.

Devils Lake train depot is located on Railroad Ave. Devils Lake, ND 58301. The station is un-staffed and features an enclosed waiting area and restrooms. Transportation from the station is local taxi service.

Devils Lake station is served by the Empire Builder.

Grand Forks (ND)

Grand Forks is located in east-central North Dakota. Grand Forks was founded in 1870 and was incorporated in 1881. Grand Forks has a land area of 14 sq. miles (37.3 sq. kilometers) and population of roughly 50,000.

Grand Forks' train depot is located at 5555 De Mers Ave. Grand Forks, ND 58201. The station is staffed and features an enclosed waiting area, checked baggage service, restrooms, payphones, and vending machines. Transportation service from the station is local taxi service.

Grand Forks station is served by the Empire Builder.

Fargo (ND)

Fargo is located southeast of the North Dakota/Minnesota state border. Fargo has a land area of 30 sq. miles (77 sq. kilometers) and a population of roughly 90,000. Named after William G. Fargo (one of the partners in Wells-Fargo Express Company), the city of Fargo was first settled by Scandinavian immigrants.

Fargo's average winter temperature is 0 to 18 degrees F. and average summer temperature is 55 to 80 degrees F. with an average annual snowfall of 35 inches.

Fargo's train depot is located at 420 4th St. N. Fargo, ND 58102. The station is staffed and features an enclosed waiting area, checked baggage service, restrooms, payphones, and vending machines. Transportation from the station is local taxi service.

Fargo station is served by the Empire Builder.

Places of Interest

Celebrity Walk of Fame located at Fargo-Moorhead Convention & Visitors Bureau at 44th St. SW, Fargo, ND 58103 Tel: (701) 282-3653. The walk of fame has hundreds of celebrity handprints/footprints and signatures. **Bonanzaville,** located at 1351 West Main Avenue West Fargo, ND 58078 Tel: (701) 282-2822, features historic buildings and museums. **Fargo Dome** located at 1800 University Drive Fargo, ND 58102 Tel: (701) 214-9100 is the largest arena in North Dakota featuring seasonal sports games, shows, and entertainment. **Sports Bubble** located at 2761 12 Ave SW Fargo, ND 58103 Tel: (701) 280-0824 features entertainment facilities such as a mini-golf course, indoor driving range, and more.

Accommodations

Best Western Inn located at 3333 13th Ave S, Fargo, ND 58103 Tel: (701) 235-3333. **Comfort Suites** located at 1415 35th St SW, Fargo, ND 58103 Tel: (701) 237-5911. **Flying J Motel** located at 3150 39th St S, Fargo, ND 58104 Tel: (701) 282-8473. **Microtel Inns & Suites** located at 1101 38th St NW, Fargo, ND 58102 Tel: (701) 281-2109. **C'Mon Inn** located at 4338 20th Ave SW, Fargo, ND 58103 Tel: (701) 277-9944.

Comfort Inn located at 1407 35th St SW, Fargo, ND 58103 Tel: (701) 280-9666. **Econo Lodge** located at 1401 35th St SW, Fargo, ND 58103 Tel: (701) 232-3412. **Comfort Inn** located at 3825 9th Ave SW, Fargo, ND 58103 Tel: (701) 282-9596. **Fairfield Inn** located at 3902 9th Ave SW, Fargo, ND 58103 Tel: (701) 281-0494. **Kelly Inn** located at 4207 13th Ave SW, Fargo, ND 58103 Tel: (701) 277-8821.

Holiday Inn located at 3803 13th Ave S, Fargo, ND 58103 Tel: (701) 282-2700. **Holiday Inn** located at 1040 40th St SW, Fargo, ND 58103 Tel: (701) 282-2000. **Donaldson Hotel** located at 516 1st St N # 2, Fargo, ND 58102 Tel: (701) 235-3193. **Hampton Inn** located at 3431 14th Ave SW, Fargo, ND 58103 Tel: (701) 235-5566. **Quality Inn** located at 301 3rd Ave N, Fargo, ND 58102 Tel: (701) 232-8850. **Days Inn** located at 1507 19th Ave N, Fargo, ND 58102 Tel: (701) 232-0000. **Best Western Inn** located at 3800 Main Ave, Fargo, ND 58103 Tel: (701) 282-2143.

Detroit Lakes (MN)

Detroit Lakes is located in west-central Minnesota, 180 miles northwest of St. Paul the state capital. Detroit Lake has 412 lakes within its area of 4 sq. miles (10.5 sq. kilometers). The City of Detroit Lakes, population 7,000, is the county seat of Becker County, founded by Colonel George Johnston. The City of Detroit Lake was incorporated in 1881.

Detroit Lake's train depot is located at 116 Pioneer St. Detroit Lakes, MN 56501. The station is un-staffed and features an enclosed waiting area and restrooms. Transportation from the station is local taxi service.

Detroit Lake station is served by the Empire Builder

Places of interest: Hamden Slough Nat'l Wildlife Refuge Tel: (218) 439-6319, Tamarac National Wildlife Refuge Tel: (218) 847-2641, Timberline Ranch Tel: (218) 847-3886, and Becker County Museum Tel: (218) 847-2938.

Accommodations

Holiday Haven Motel located at 220 W Lake Dr, Detroit Lakes, MN 56501 Tel: (218) 847-5605. **Holiday Inn** located at Highway 10 E, Detroit Lakes, MN 56501 Tel: (218) 847-2121. **Budget Host Inn** located at 895 Highway 10 E, Detroit Lakes, MN 56501 Tel: (218) 847-4454. **Best Western Inn** located at 615 Highway 10 E, Detroit Lakes, MN 56501 Tel: (218) 847-4483. **59er Motel** located at 19389 Frontage Rd, Detroit Lakes, MN 56501 Tel: (218) 847-3144. **Country Inn & Suites-Carlson** located at 1330 Highway 10 E, Detroit Lakes, MN 56501 Tel: (218) 847-2000.

Minnesota (MN)
Capital: St. Paul (Population: 4,919,479)
Size: 86,943 sq mi. (225,182 sq km)
Nickname: The North Star State, the Land of 10,000 Lakes, Gopher State
Joined the union on: May 11, 1858 (32nd state)
Motto: The North Star
Flower: Showy lady slipper
Bird: Common loon or the Great Northern Diver
Song: Hail Minnesota
Major industries: Farming, agriculture, commerce and tourism

Staples (MN)

Staples is located in central Minnesota, 124 miles northwest of St. Paul. Staples has a land area of 3 sq. miles (8 sq. kilometers) and population of roughly 3,000.

Staples' train depot is located at First Ave. and 4th St. N.E. Staples, MN 56479. The station is un-staffed and features an enclosed waiting area, payphones, and vending machines. Transportation from the station is local taxi service.

Staples station is served by the Empire Builder.

St. Cloud (MN)

St. Cloud is located in central Minnesota, 60 miles northwest of St. Paul-Minneapolis. It has a land area of 14.6 sq. miles (37.6 sq. kilometers) and population of around 200,000.

St Cloud's train depot is located at 555 E. St. Germain St. St. Cloud, MN 56304. The station is un-staffed and features an enclosed waiting area, restrooms, and payphones. Transportation from the station is local taxi service.

St. Cloud station is served by the Empire Builder.

St. Paul – Minneapolis (MN)
Motor-coach connections to **Duluth (MN)** and **Eau Claire (WI)**

St Paul – Minneapolis, also known as the "twin cities," are located in southeastern Minnesota. St. Paul has a land area of 53 sq. miles (136.7 sq. kilometers) while Minneapolis has 59 sq.

miles (153 sq. kilometers), and both cities and their outlying areas have a combined total population of more than 2.7 million.

St. Paul was originally named "Pig's Eye," and later was renamed as St. Paul by Father Galtier. St. Paul has been the state capital since 1847, and is the birthplace and hometown of F. Scott Fitzgerald. The name Minneapolis was taken from the Indian words "Minne" meaning water and "Polis" a Greek word for city. Minneapolis was incorporated as a town in 1856 and as a city in 1867.

St. Paul-Minneapolis has an average annual temperature of 45 degrees F, average annual rainfall of 25 inches per year, and average annual snowfall of 47 inches per year.

Getting Around

Airport

Minneapolis-St. Paul International Airport, 6040 28th Avenue South, Minneapolis, Minnesota 55450 Tel: (612) 726-5555, is located 12 miles south of St. Paul and 16 miles south of Minneapolis. Major car rental company booths are available in the baggage claim area. Local taxi services are available throughout the airport, bus services operated by Metro Transit stop at the Lindbergh Terminal.

Bus

Metro Transit Tel: (612) 349-7000 serves the twin cities. Basic fares are $1.25 and $1.75 during rush hours. Express fares are $1.75 and $2.25 during rush hours. There are special fares for seniors and persons with disabilities. If you need to transfer to another bus in order to reach your destination, you should ask the driver for a transfer ticket. Tourists should buy the $6 Day Pass for one day unlimited bus rides; the pass is available at the transit store, Greater Minneapolis Convention Center, Explore Minnesota, or by calling Tel: (612) 349-7686.

Taxi

Town Taxi Tel: (612) 331-8294, Suburban Taxi/Green and White Taxi Tel: (651) 222-2222.

Rent-A-Car

American Rental System toll-free (800) 886-3733, Sport It Tel: (612) 242-9574.

179

Train and Commuter

St. Paul's train depot is located at 730 Transfer Rd. St. Paul, MN 55114. The station is staffed and features an enclosed waiting area, checked baggage service, restrooms, payphones, and vending machines. Transportation options from the station include Hertz Car Rental toll-free (800) 654-3131 and local taxi service.

St. Paul station is served by the Empire Builder.

Visitor Information Center

The Greater Minneapolis Convention & Visitors Association, 33 South Sixth Street, Suite 4000 Minneapolis, MN 55402 toll-free (888) 676-6757.

Places to See and Things to Do

Alexander Ramsey House, located at 265 S. Exchange St. at Walnut St. St. Paul, MN Tel: (651) 296-8760, this Victorian style house was the home of Minnesota's first governor. The **F. Scott Fitzgerald Birthplace** is located at 481 Laurel Avenue, St. Paul, MN, and the **F. Scott Fitzgerald House** is located at 599 Summit Avenue, St. Paul MN. The **Governor's Residence,** located at 1006 Summit Avenue St. Paul, MN Tel: (651) 297-8177, exhibits memorabilia from the state's many former governors. The **James J. Hill House** is located at 240 Summit Avenue, St. Paul, MN Tel: (651) 297-2555. This historic mansion was the home of James Hill the builder of the transcontinental railroad network the "Empire Builder."

The Cathedral of St. Paul, located at 239 Selby Ave. St. Paul, MN Tel: (651) 228-1766, was patterned after the St. Peter Cathedral of Rome. **The Assumption Church** located in downtown St. Paul at 51 West Ninth Street is a German Romanesque architectural style church admired for its two imposing towers. The church is the oldest in St. Paul.

The **Childrens Museum** located at 1217 Bandana Blvd. N. St. Paul, MN Tel: (651) 644-3818 has several hands-on exhibits. The **Science Museum of Minnesota** located at 30 E. 10th St. St. Paul, MN Tel: (651) 221-9454. **Saint Paul Public Library,** located at 90 W 4th Street, St. Paul, MN Tel: (651) 292-6341, has a wide collection of books and other materials. **The Minnesota Zoo** is located in Apple Valley southwest of downtown Tel: (612) 431-9200; the zoo is home to more than one thousand animals. Looking at St. Paul's skyline you should easily recognize the **First National Bank Building,** at Minnesota and Fifth Streets; it is the tallest building in the city.

Minnesota Brewing Co., located in downtown Saint Paul at 822 W 7th Street, Tel: (651) 290-8209, offers a free brewery tour and beer tasting. **District Del Sol** is home to St. Paul-Minneapolis' Spanish community. There are several Latin restaurants, shops, and arts. The district is located south of Concord St. The historic **Fort Snelling** Tel: (651) 726-1171 is located between the Mississippi River and St. Paul-Minneapolis International Airport.

Lower Town Historic District Surrounding area of E Sixth Street near Sibley Street is the twin city's center of historic buildings and art galleries, restaurants, shops, and more. Also located in Lower Town Historic District is the **Farmer's Market,** located at 290 E 5th Street St. Paul Tel: (651) 227-6856, has various stalls of local produce; the market is open from summer to mid autumn. The beautiful building of **Landmark Center,** located at 75 W Fifth Street, St. Paul, MN Tel: (651) 292-3272, houses the **Minnesota Museum of American Art. Shubert Club Musical Instrument Museum,** located in Landmark Center, 75 West Fifth Street, St Paul MN Tel: (651) 292-3267, has extraordinary collections of musical instruments.

The impressive **Minnesota State Capitol** is located at 75 Constitution Avenue, St. Paul, MN Tel: (651) 297-3521. The huge capitol with magnificent arches and domes is a master piece of architect Cass Gilbert. **Saint Paul City Hall and Courthouse** located at 15 W Kellogg Boulevard, St. Paul, MN Tel: (651) 266-8500. This impressive art deco building is known as one of St. Paul's finest works of architecture. The historic **Saint Paul Hotel** is located downtown on Rice Park at 350 Market Street, St. Paul Tel: (651) 292-9292.

Explore the city of St. Paul in style and visit some of the city's major attractions through the **Capitol City Trolley** in downtown Saint Paul Tel: (651) 223-5600. **Twin City Model Railroad Club** is located at 1021 Bandana Boulevard E, St. Paul Minneapolis Tel: (651) 647-9628, the club exhibits scale trains and the Twin Cities.

Minnesota Vietnam Veteran's Memorial located in downtown Saint Paul at the State Capitol Grounds, Tel: (651) 536-179. **Confederate Air Force Museum** exhibits several aircraft of World War II, located in Hanger 3 on Flemming Field at 310 Airport Road, South of Saint Paul, MN Tel: (651) 455-6942. **Minnesota Air Guard Museum,** located in St. Paul-Minneapolis International Airport Air National Guard Base, MN Tel: (651) 725-5609, exhibits US cold war secret spy planes.

Minneapolis Sculpture Garden is located at Vineland Pl & Lyndale Av. Minneapolis, MN Tel: (612) 375-7577. **Minnesota Zoological Gardens,** home more than 2,000 animals, is located at 13000 Zoo Blvd Apple Valley, MN Tel: (612) 431-9200. **Minneapolis Planetarium** is located in the Minneapolis Library at 300 Nicollet Mall Minneapolis, MN

St. Paul-Minneapolis City Skyline

Tel: (612) 372-6543. **Hennepin History Museum** located at 2303 3rd Ave. S Minneapolis, MN Tel: (612) 870-1329. **Museum of Questionable Medical Devices,** located at 219 Main St. SE Minneapolis, MN Tel: (612) 379-4046, exhibits more than 200 hoax medical devices. **The Guthrie Theater** located at 725 Vineland Pl. Minneapolis, MN Tel: (612) 377-2224. **Walker Art Center,** located at Hennepin Ave. & Vineland Pl. Minneapolis, MN Tel: (612) 375-7600, exhibits American and European 20th century art. **Frederick R. Weisman Art Museum** is located in 333 E River Rd, 200 Minneapolis, MN Tel: (612) 625-9494.

Accommodations

Days Inn Midway St. Paul located at 1964 University Avenue St. Paul MN 55104 Tel: (651) 645-8681 expect to pay $40-$150. **Holiday Inn St. Paul River Centre** located at 175 West 7th Street St. Paul MN 55102 Tel: (651) 225-1515 expect to pay $70-$150. **Radisson City Center Hotel St. Paul** located at 411 Minnesota Street St. Paul MN 55101 Tel: (925) 473-2230 expect to pay $50-$100. **Holiday Inn Express St. Paul** located at 1010 Bandana Blvd. W. St. Paul MN 55108 Tel: (651) 647-1637 expect to pay $70-$150. **Four Points by Sheraton St. Paul Capitol** located at 400 Hamline Avenue St. Paul MN 55104 Tel: (651) 642-1234 expect to pay $80-$200. **St. Paul Hotel** located at 350 Market Street St. Paul MN 55102 Tel: (612) 292-9292 expect to pay $100-$700.

Other accommodations: **Minnesota Bed & Breakfast** located at 305 Roselawn Ave E, St Paul, MN 55117 Tel: (651) 778-2400. **St Paul Hotel** located at 350 Market St, St Paul, MN 55102 Tel: (651) 292-9292. **Radisson Hotel St Paul** located at 11 Kellogg Blvd E, St Paul, MN 55101 Tel: (651) 292-1900. **Travelodge** located at 1870 Old Hudson Rd, St Paul, MN 55119 Tel: (651) 735-2337. **Ramada Inn** located at 1870 Old Hudson Rd, St Paul, MN 55119 Tel: (651) 735-2330. **Midwest Hotel** located at 2144 University Ave W, St Paul, MN 55114 Tel: (651) 646-4770. **Holiday Inn** located at 2201 Burns Ave, St Paul, MN 55119 Tel: (651) 731-2220.

Midway Motel located at 901 Snelling Ave N, St Paul, MN 55104 Tel: (651) 646-4584. **Radisson Inn St Paul** located at 411 Minnesota St, St Paul, MN 55101 Tel: (651) 291-8800. **Vadnais Inn** located at 3364 Rice St, St Paul, MN 55126 Tel: (651) 484-9435. **Red Roof Inns** located at I 494 & Valley Creek Rd, St Paul, MN 55125 Tel: (651) 738-7160. **Staybridge Suites** located at 4675 Rahncliff Rd, St Paul, MN 55122 Tel: (651) 994-7810. **Travel Inn** located at 149 University Ave E, St Paul, MN 55101 Tel: (651) 227-8801. **Mounds View Inn** located at 2149 Program Ave, St Paul, MN 55112 Tel: (763) 786-9151. **Sheraton Hotel** located at 400 Hamline Ave N, St Paul, MN 55104 Tel: (651) 642-1234.

Red Wing (MN)

Red Wing is known for its "Red Wing Shoes" and "Red Wing Stoneware," located just 50 miles southeast of St. Paul-Minneapolis along Lake Pepin. Red Wing is one of the oldest cities in Minnesota, named after a famous Dakota Indian Chief Hoo-poo-hoo-sha, also known as "Wings of Scarlet." The first white missionary settlers arrived in the area in the 1840's, and in 1857 Red Wing was incorporated as a city. Visit Red Wing's historic downtown area restored to its turn of the century beauty. Red Wing has a land area of 35 sq. miles (90 sq. kilometers) and a population of roughly 17,000.

Red Wing's train depot is located on Levee St. Red Wing, MN 55066. The station is un-staffed and features an enclosed waiting area, restrooms, and payphones. Transportation options from the station include local bus and taxi service.

Red Wing station is served by the Empire Builder

Winona (MN)

Winona is located along the Mississippi River in southeast Minnesota. Winona was founded in 1851 and was first named Montezuma by its early European settlers. The name was later changed to Winona, a native Indian word meaning the "eldest" daughter. Winona has a land area of 11.9 sq. miles (30.7 sq. kilometers) and a population of approximately 27,000.

Winona's train depot is located at 65 E. Mark St. Winona, MN 55987. The station is staffed and features an enclosed waiting area, checked baggage service, restrooms, payphones, and a restaurant. Transportation options from the station include local transit and taxi service.

Winona station is served by the Empire Builder

Minnesota (MN)
Capital: St. Paul (Population: 4,919,479)
Size: 86,943 sq mi. (225,182 sq km)
Nickname: The North Star State, the Land of 10,000 Lakes, Gopher State
Joined the union on: May 11, 1858 (32nd state)
Motto: The North Star
Flower: Showy lady slipper
Bird: Common loon or the Great Northern Diver
Song: Hail Minnesota
Major industries: Farming, agriculture, commerce and tourism

La Crosse (WI)

La Crosse is located in western Wisconsin at the junction of the 3 rivers of Mississippi, the Black, and La Crosse rivers. La Crosse is the seat of La Crosse County and it has a land area of 18.5 sq. miles (47.5 sq. kilometers) and a population of more than 51,000.

La Crosse's train depot is located at 601 St. Andrew St. La Crosse, WI 54601. The station is staffed and features an enclosed waiting area, checked baggage service, restrooms, and payphones. Transportation from the station is local taxi service.

La Crosse station is served by the Empire Builder.

Tomah (WI)

Tomah is located in western Wisconsin 86 miles northwest of Madison, the state capital. Tomah was officially founded in 1855 and was incorporated as a city in 1883. Tomah has a land area of 6.4 sq. miles (16.5 sq. kilometers) and a population of approximately 8,000.

Tomah's train depot is located at W. Washington St. Tomah, WI 54660. The station is un-staffed and features an enclosed waiting area. Transportation from the station is local taxi service.

Tomah station is served by the Empire Builder.

Wisconsin Dells (WI)

Wisconsin Dells is located along the banks of Wisconsin River, in central Wisconsin: Just 115 miles west of Milwaukee and 43 miles north of Madison. It has a land area of 18.2 sq. miles (47 sq. kilometers) and population of roughly 3,000. Famous for its many ancient geological wonders and rock formations, Wisconsin Dells is one of the major tourist destinations in the state of Wisconsin.

Places to see and things to do:

Tommy Bartlett Thrill Show, located at 560 Wisconsin Dells Parkway, Wisconsin Dells, WI 53965 Tel: (608) 254-2525, is a world class thrill show featuring water stunts, cultural shows and much more. **Wax World of the Stars,** located at 105 Broadway, Wisconsin Dells, WI 53965 Tel: (608) 254-2184 features more than a hundred wax images of famous personalities. **Ripley's Believe It Or Not Museum** located at 115 Broadway, Wisconsin Dells, WI 53965 Tel: (608) 253-7556. **Beaver Springs Public Aquarium** located at 615 Trout Rd. Wisconsin Dells, Wisconsin Tel: (608) 254-2735. The aquarium is home to thousands of marine animals.

The Dells Experience Jet Boats, located at W 1147 River Bay Rd., Lyndon Station, WI 53944 Tel: (608) 254-8246, offers breathtaking river boat tours. **Noah's Ark-America's Largest Waterpark** located at 1410 Wisconsin Dells Parkway, Wisconsin Dells, WI 53965 Tel: (608) 254-6351 features more than 60 water recreational activities and rides.

Visitor Information Center

Wisconsin Dells Visitor & Convention Bureau 701 Superior Street in downtown Wisconsin Dells, toll-free (800) 223-3557.

Wisconsin Dells train depot is located at Lacrosse St. Wisconsin Dells, WI 53965. The station is un-staffed and features an enclosed waiting area. Transportation from the station is local taxi service.

Wisconsin Dells station is served by the Empire Builder.

Portage (WI)

Portage is located in south central Wisconsin in General Madison Area between the Fox and Wisconsin rivers. It has a land area of 8 sq. miles (21 sq. kilometers) and population of approximately 9,000. Portage is one of the first settlements in Wisconsin. It is believed that the French explorer Nicolet first visited Portage in 1640.

Portage train depot is located at 400 W. Oneida St. Portage, WI 53901. The station is un-staffed and features an enclosed waiting area, restrooms, and payphones. Transportation from the station is local taxi service.

Wisconsin (WI)
Capital: Madison (Population: 5,363,675)
Size: 65,503 sq mi. (169,652 sq km)
Nickname: The Badger State, Dairyland
Joined the union on: May 29, 1848 (30th state)
Motto: Forward
Flower: Wood violet
Bird: Robin
Song: On Wisconsin
Major industries: Farm, paper production, and manufacturing.

Portage station is served by the Empire Builder.

Columbus (WI)

Columbus is located in southern Wisconsin in Columbia County, 25 miles northeast of Madison the state capital. Columbus has a land area of 3.7 sq. miles (9.6 sq. kilometers) and population of approximately 5,000. Columbus was founded in 1839, was incorporated as a village in 1864 and as a city in 1874. Columbus is rich in historical architecture and beauty which is clearly seen in the city's many old and well-maintained buildings. Visit Columbus Main Street Historic District, listed on the National Register and State Register of Historic Places.

Columbus' train depot is located at 359 Ludington St. Columbus, WI 53925. The station is staffed and features an enclosed waiting area, checked baggage service, restrooms, and payphones. Transportation from the station is local taxi service.

Columbus station is served by the Empire Builder

Milwaukee (WI) See Hiawatha service, page 303.

Glenview (IL) See Hiawatha service, page 303.

Chicago (IL) See Illinois and Missouri service, page 268.

California Zephyr

The California Zephyr is one of the most exiting, beautiful, and breathtaking train routes in the US. It connects the cities of San Francisco, Salt Lake City, Denver, and Chicago; it is your gateway to the Great Rocky Mountains and Yellowstone National Park, one of nature's wonders. The California Zephyr uses the historic and earliest transcontinental rail route. Along the way you will be passing some of the most historic and wondrous sites and land in the US. Travelers will see farmland, ranches, prairies, great rivers, lakes, desert, breathtaking mountain views, and beautiful scenery that you can only see traveling by train.

Route Destination Highlights

San Francisco, CA- Visit the famous Pier 39, Alcatraz Island, the world's most celebrated bridge the Golden Gate Bridge, the Museum of Modern Art, the exciting Castro, or Union Square. Take the city tram and explore San Francisco's hilly streets or simply walk through the romantic setting of Fisherman's Wharf.

Sacramento, CA- Visit the Old Sacramento California Railroad Museum, the beautiful and historical California State Capitol, Sacramento State University, Sutter's Fort where gold rush history started, walk and explore the Old Town Sacramento.

Reno, NV- Visit the National Automobile Museum, the historical Reno Arch, and the Nevada Museum of

California Zephyr		
9 35 am	Emeryville, CA	6 10 pm
10 16 am	Martinez, CA	5 26 pm
10 59 am	Davis, CA	4 44 pm
11 35 am	Sacramento, CA	4 15 pm
12 09 pm	Roseville, CA	2 45 pm
12 55 pm	Colfax, CA	1 26 pm
3 11 pm	Truckee, CA	11 26 am
4 16 pm	Reno, NV	10 25 am
4 47 pm	Sparks, NV	10 11 am
4 57 pm		10 01 am
7 27 pm	Winnemucca, NV	6 44 am
9 30 pm	Elko, NV	4 27 am
3 25 am	**Salt Lake City, UT**	1 12 am
3 55 am		12 33 am
5 02 am	Provo, UT	10 48 pm
7 05 am	Helper, UT	846 pm
8 27 am	Green River, UT	7 23 pm
10 45 am	**Grand Junction, CO**	5 35 pm
12 37 pm	Glenwood Springs, CO	3 27 pm
3 52 pm	Granby, CO	12 09 pm
4 22 pm	Fraser Winter Park, CO	11 41 am
730 pm	**Denver, CO**	9 00 am
7 50 pm		8 40 am
9 25 pm	Fort Morgan, CO	6 30 am
12 49 am	Mc Cook, NE	5 08 am
1 54 am	Holdrege, NE	11 59 am
2 42 am	Hastings, NE	3 12 am
4 41 am	Lincoln, NE	1 39 am
4 47 am		1 33 am
5 55 am	Omaha, NE	11 59 pm
6 15 am		11 47 pm
8 03 am	Creston, IA	9 59 pm
8 38 am	Osceola, IA	9 27 pm
10 18 am	Ottumwa, IA	8 11 pm
11 03 am	Mt. Pleasant, IA	7 06 pm
11 35 am	Burlington, IA	6 34 pm
12 23 pm	Galesburg, IL	5 47 pm
1 14 pm	Princeton, IL	4 54 pm
2 26 pm	Naperville, IL	3 44 pm
3 55 pm	**Chicago, IL**	2 45 pm
D-Departure	A-Arrival	

Art. Ski at some of the nearby ski resorts or try your luck at Reno's world-class casinos. Take the tram at Heavenly Ski Resort and see Lake Tahoe's breathtaking scenery from 2,000 feet, or visit the "Tessie" Lake Tahoe Monster Museum.

Salt Lake City, UT- See the Great Salt Lake the 4th largest terminal lake in the world, visit the magnificent Utah State Capitol, the 2002 Winter Olympic Clock, and the Golden Spike

National Historic Site. Spend a nice relaxing afternoon or have your coffee break at the 1910 Rio Grande Depot and visit the International Peace Gardens or Temple Square afterwards.

Yellowstone National Park- The first US national park, Yellowstone is rich with natural wonders and beauty. Visit the park's many geysers and thermal springs. Visit Norris Geyser, Mammoth Hot Springs, Yellowstone Canyon, the Fishing Bridge, Yellowstone Lake, and famous Old Faithful. See and encounter Yellowstone's rich wildlife.

Grand Junction, CO- Visit the Dinosaur Valley Museum and see the region's rich collections of dinosaur fossils. The Colorado National Monument and Colorado Canyons National Conservation Area are both known for their beautiful rock formations, arches, and many other natural wonders.

Denver, CO- Visit the magnificent Colorado State Capitol and admire its beautiful dome covered with gold leaf and the unique Colorado onyx used inside as wainscoting. Take a tour of the second largest gold warehouse in the US, the U.S. Mint, or the factory tours at Coors Brewery. Visit Denver Art Museum; the Museum of Outdoor Art; one of the largest nature and science museums in the US, the Denver Museum of Nature & Science; Colorado's Ocean Journey, home to more than 15,000 marine animals; and the Wings Over the Rockies Air & Space Museum that features historic aircrafts.

Chicago, IL- Home to America's tallest building Sears Tower, visit the Museum of Science and Industry and other outstanding museums, admire the charming Centennial Fountain, take a romantic stroll along Lake Michigan, and enjoy Chicago's attractive and busy nightlife.

Train Schedule

The California Zephyr travels daily from the city of Chicago, Illinois to the cities of Denver, Colorado; Salt Lake City, Utah; Reno, Nevada; and San Francisco, California. The trip between the cities takes approximately 2 days and two hours of travel time.

Accommodations

Accommodations are Superliner Reserved Coach and Superliner Sleeping Car. There is a Sightseer Lounge Car serving local cuisine, snacks, sandwiches, soups, and drinks. Restaurant style meals are served in the Dining Car. Other amenities are movies, reading materials, games, and seasonal national park guide presentations.

All aboard!

Emeryville (CA) See Coast Starlight service, page 82- 87.
Thruway Motor-coach Connections to **Oakland (CA)** and **San Francisco (CA)**

Martinez (CA) See Coast Starlight service, page 82- 87.

Davis (CA) See Coast Starlight service, page 82- 87.

Sacramento (CA) See Capitol Corridor service, page 136.

Roseville (CA) See Capitol Corridor service, page 135

California (CA)

Capital: Sacramento
(Population: 33,871,648)
Size: 163,707 sq mi. (424,001 sq km)
Nicknames: The Golden State
Joined the union on:
September 9, 1850 (31st state)
Motto: Eureka (I Have Found It)
Flower: Golden Poppy
Bird: California Valley Quail
Song: "I Love You, California"
Famous for: Golden Gate Bridge, Hollywood, Yosemite Valley
Major industries:
Manufacturing, Agriculture, Biotechnology, Software and Tourism

Colfax (CA)

Colfax is located in central California 50 miles northeast of Sacramento the state capital. Colfax has a land area of 1.2 sq. miles (3.3 sq. kilometers) and population of more than 1,000.

Colfax train depot is located in Church St. and SP Tracks Colfax, CA 95713. The station is un-staffed.

Colfax station is served by the California Zephyr.

Truckee (CA) Gateway to "Lake Tahoe"

Truckee is located in the Sierra Nevada Mountains just a few miles north of Lake Tahoe. Much of the old west spirit is still visible in today's Truckee. Truckee is famous for its several winter outdoor recreational activities. A number of ski resorts are located around Truckee; other popular activities during summer are camping, water sports, and trekking among others. Truckee is home to approximately 13,000 hospitable people.

Truckee's train depot is located at Railroad St. and Commercial Row Truckee, CA 96160. The station is un-staffed and features an enclosed waiting area and payphones. Transportation options from the station include Hertz Car Rental toll-free (800) 654-3131 and local taxi service.

Truckee station is served by the California Zephyr.

Reno (NV) Gateway to Lake Tahoe

Reno is located in west central Nevada, 4,498 feet above sea level, near the Nevada/California state border, just 27 miles north of Carlson City the state capital. Reno has a land area of 69 sq. miles (178 sq. kilometers) and a population of more than 134,000. Reno was officially founded in 1868 and was named in honor of General Jesse Lee Reno of the Union army. Today Reno is a well-known gambling center housing several world-class casino hotel/resorts and entertainment. Reno is also known as gateway to Lake Tahoe.

Lake Tahoe is located at the westernmost part of central Nevada, just 50 miles from Reno. It is known as one of the most beautiful alpine lakes in the world. The lake is 12 miles wide and 22 miles long situated at the center of the California and Nevada state border. Lake Tahoe is a world-class outdoor activities and sports destination.

188

Getting Around

Airport

Reno/Tahoe International Airport, 2001 East Plumb Lane, Reno, Nevada 89511 Tel: (775) 328-6400 is located 4 miles (6.4 Kilometers) from downtown Reno. Major car rental companies are located on the lower level of the terminal. Local taxi and bus services are also available at the airport.

Bus

Citifare Tel: (775) 348-7433 provides bus services in Reno, Sparks, and outlying areas. Basic fare is $1. Tahoe Area Regional Transit (TART) Tel: (530) 583-8154 provides bus services along northern Lake Tahoe. Fare is $1.25. South Tahoe Area Ground Express (STAGE) Tel: (530) 573-2080 runs bus services in South Lake Tahoe. Tahoe Casino Express, toll-free (800) 446-6128 or Tel: (775) 785-2424 serves the Reno and Lake Tahoe area. Greyhound Bus Lines, toll-free (800) 231-2222, connects Reno to the rest of the country.

Nevada (NV)
Capital: Carson City (Population: 1,998,257)
Size: 110,567 sq mi. (286,368 sq km)
Nickname: The Sagebrush State, Silver State, and Battle-born State
Joined the union on: October 31, 1864 (36th state)
Motto: All for Our Country
Flower: Sagebrush
Bird: Mountain Bluebird
Song: Home Means Nevada
Famous for: UFO's, Area 51, Las Vegas, and legal prostitution!
Major industries: Agriculture, Tourism, gaming, agricultural products and Wedding and Divorce.

Taxi

De Luxe Taxi Service Tel: (775) 355-5555; Capitol Cab Tel: (775) 858-0300; Whittlesea Checker Taxi Tel: (775) 322-2222; Star Taxi Tel: (775) 355-5555; Yellow Cab Tel: (775) 355-5555; Reno-Sparks Cab Tel: (775) 333-3333.

Rent-A-Car

National Car Rental, Tel: (775) 289-3058; Harvey Young, Tel: (775) 289-4473; Enterprise Car Rental toll-free (800) 736-8222; Hertz Car Rental toll-free (800) 654-3131; and Thrifty Car Rental toll-free (800) 367-2277.

Train and Commuter

Reno train depot is located at 135 E. Commercial Row Reno, NV 89501. The station is staffed and features an enclosed waiting area, checked baggage service, restrooms, and payphones. Transportation options from the station include Hertz Car Rental toll-free (800) 654-3131, local transit, and taxi services.

Reno station is served by the California Zephyr.

Visitor Information Center

Reno Chamber of Commerce, 405 Marsh Ave, Reno, NV 89505 Tel: (775) 686-3030.

Reno Visitor Center, 4590 South Virginia Street Reno, NV 89502 toll-free (800) 367-7366.

Places to See and Things to Do

National Automobile Museum located at 10 Lake Street Reno, Nevada Tel: (775) 333-9300 features more than 200 antique automobiles, galleries, shops, and a library. **Nevada Museum of Art** located at 160 W Liberty St Reno, NV 89501 Tel: (702) 329-3333. **The Reno Arch** bordering the Truckee River near the corner of Lake and Mill streets is the city's icon. **Church Fine Arts Building** located in University of Nevada Reno Nevada Tel: (702) 784-6658, has seasonal art exhibits.

Nevada Historical Society Museum located at 1650 N. Virginia St. Reno Nevada Tel: (702) 688-1190 exhibits Indian artifacts, relics, etc. **Nevada Museum of Art/E.L. Weigand Gallery** located at 160 West Liberty Street Tel: (775) 329-3333 exhibits modern, classic, and impressionist arts. **Lake Mansion** located at 4598 S Virginia St Reno, NV 89502 Tel: (702) 829-1868. **Fleischmann Planetarium** located on the edge of the University of Nevada campus, N. Virginia St. Reno Nevada Tel: (702) 784-4811.

Wilbur D. May Center located in Rancho San Rafael Park at 1502 Washington St. Reno Nevada Tel: (702) 785-5961 houses a museum and arboretum. **Wilbur D. May Museum & Arboretum,** located 1 mile north of downtown Reno in Rancho San Rafael Park Tel: (775) 785-4153, exhibits rare art collections and houses a botanical garden and arboretum.

Casinos

Atlantis Casino Resort located at 3800 South Virginia Street Reno, NV Tel: (775) 825-4700. **Peppermill Hotel Casino** located at 2707 S. Virginia St Reno, NV toll-free (800) 282-2444. **Fitzgerald's Hotel Casino** located at 255 North Virginia Street Reno, NV toll-free (800) 535-LUCK. **Sands Regency Hotel Casino** located at 345 North Arlington Reno, NV toll-free (800) 648-3553.

Eldorado Hotel Casino located at 4th and Virginia Streets Reno, NV toll-free (800) 777-5325. **Bonanza Casino** located at 4720 N. Virginia St. Reno, NV Tel: (775) 323-2724. **Circus Circus Hotel Casino** located at 500 North Sierra Street Reno, NV Tel: (775) 329-0711. **Flamingo Reno** located at 55 North Sierra Street Reno, NV Tel: (775) 322-1111.

Ski Resorts

Mt. Rose located at 22222 Mt. Rose Highway, Reno, NV 89511 Tel: (775) 849-0704. **Homewood Mountain Resort** located in Hwy. 89, 6 miles south of Tahoe City, 19 miles north of S. Lake Tahoe at 5145 W. Lake Blvd., PO Box 165, Homewood, CA 96141 Tel: (530) 525-2992. **Alpine Meadows** located 6 miles northwest of Tahoe City, CA, on Hwy 89 Tahoe City, CA 96145 toll-free (800) 441-4423. **Ski Reno Tahoe,** P.O. Box 20935 Reno, NV 89515-0935 toll-free (800) 588-SNOW.

Lake Tahoe Area

Lake Tahoe Historical Society, located next to Chamber of Commerce on Highway 50, South Shore CA Tel: (530) 541-5458, exhibits Native American Indian relics and artifacts. **Tahoe Tessie's Lake Tahoe Monster Museum,** located at 8612 North Lake Boulevard, Kings Beach, CA Tel: (530) 546-8774, exhibits pictures and artifacts from the eyewitness of Tahoe's lake monster. **Lake Tahoe Balloons**, South Lake Tahoe, Tel: (530) 544-1221 or toll-free (800) 872-9294, offers hot air balloon tours around the Tahoe area, call for information.

Take the tram at **Heavenly Ski Resort** and see Lake Tahoe's breathtaking scenery at 2,000 feet. The tram will take you to the Monument Peak Restaurant where you can start the 1 mile Tahoe vista trail. Take Ski Run Blvd. from Highway 50 and follow the signs, call Tel: (775) 586-7000. Take a hike along the 150-mile **Rim Trail** and explore the beauty of Lake Tahoe and its surroundings, contact Tahoe Rim Trail Association Tel: (775) 588-0686. **Woodwind Sailing Cruises** Tel: (775) 588-3000 and **M.S. Dixie II,** Highway 50 at Zephyr Cove Tel: (775) 588-3508 offer cruise services on the lake.

Accommodations

Around Reno

Flamingo Motel located at 520 N Center St, Reno, NV 89501 Tel: (775) 323-3202. **Ramada Vacation Suites** located at 140 Court St, Reno, NV 89501 Tel: (775) 329-4251. **Siena Hotel & Casino** located at 1 S Lake St, Reno, NV 89501 Tel: (775) 337-6260. **Hampton Inn** located at 175 E 2nd St, Reno, NV 89501 Tel: (775) 788-2300. **Travelodge** located at 655 W 4th St, Reno, NV 89503 Tel: (775) 329-3451. **Circus Circus Hotel & Casino** located at 500 N Sierra St, Reno, NV 89503 Tel: (775) 329-0711. **Harrah's Hotel** located at 219 N Center St, Reno, NV 89501 Tel: (775) 786-3232.

Riverboat Hotel & Casino located at 475 S Arlington Ave # 2D, Reno, NV 89501 Tel: (775) 323-8877. **Flamingo Hilton** located at 255 N Sierra St, Reno, NV 89501 Tel: (775) 322-1111. **Hotel Windsor** located at 214 West St, Reno, NV 89501 Tel: (775) 323-6171. **Courtyard Inn Motel** located at 601 W 4th St, Reno, NV 89503 Tel: (775) 786-3356. **Holiday Inn** located at 1000 E 6th St, Reno, NV 89512 Tel: (775) 786-5151. **Hilton Reno** located at 2500 E 2nd St, Reno, NV 89502 Tel: (775) 789-2000.

Atlantis Casino Resort located at 3800 S Virginia St, Reno, NV 89502 Tel: (775) 825-4700. **Donner Inn Motel** located at 720 W 4th St, Reno, NV 89503 Tel: (775) 323-1851. **Best Inn & Suites** located at 1885 S Virginia St, Reno, NV 89502 Tel: (775) 329-1001. **Colonial Casino** located at 250 N Arlington Ave, Reno, NV 89501 Tel: (775) 322-3838. **Midtown Motel** located at 611 W 2nd St, Reno, NV 89503 Tel: (775) 323-7178. **Days Inn** located at 701 E 7th St, Reno, NV 89512 Tel: (775) 786-4070. **Best Value Inn** located at 844 S Virginia St, Reno, NV 89502 Tel: (775) 786-6700.

Around Lake Tahoe

Caesars Tahoe located in Hwy 55 50 Stateline, NV Tel: (775) 588-3515. **Embassy Suites Lake Tahoe Resort** located at 4130 Lake Tahoe Blvd. South Lake Tahoe, CA Tel: (530) 544-5400. **Best Value Inn** located at 954 Park Ave. South Lake Tahoe, CA Tel: (530) 544-4114. **Doug's Mellow Mountain Retreat Youth Hostel** located 1-mile from Heavenly

South Lake Tahoe, CA Tel: (530) 544-8065. **Best Tahoe West Inn** located at 4107 Pine Blvd. South Lake Tahoe, CA Tel: (530) 544-6455 (800) 700-8246.

Inn by the Lake located at 3300 Lake Tahoe Blvd. South Lake Tahoe, CA Tel: (530) 542-0330. **Hansen's Resort** located at 1360 Ski Run Blvd. South Lake Tahoe, CA Tel: (530) 544-3361. **Holiday Inn Express** located at 3961 Lake Tahoe Blvd. South Lake Tahoe, CA Tel: (530) 544-5900. **Harrah's Tahoe** located in Hwy 50 Stateline, NV Tel: (775) 588-6611. **Fantasy Inn** located at 3696 Lake Tahoe Blvd. South Lake Tahoe, CA Tel: (530) 541-4200. **Matterhorn Motel** located at 2187 Lake Tahoe Blvd. South Lake Tahoe, CA Tel: (530) 541-0367.

Sparks (NV)

Sparks is located just a few miles east of Reno, 27 miles north of Carlson city, with an elevation of nearly 4500 feet. Sparks has a land area of 14 sq. miles (36.8 sq. kilometers) and population of approximately 54,000. Sparks is known for its many outstanding recreational activities.

Sparks' train depot is located in Union Pacific Railroad Yard Sparks, NV 89431. The station is un-staffed and features payphones. Transportation for the station is local taxi service.

Sparks station is served by the California Zephyr.

Winnemucca (NV)

Winnemucca is located in north central Nevada sitting at 4,299 feet above sea level. The town of Winnemucca was founded in 1850 and was known by many different names. Winnemucca has a land area of 7.6 sq. miles (19.5 sq. kilometers) and population of approximately 7,000. When visiting Winnemucca visit the Humboldt Historical Museum located at 175 W Jungo Rd & Maple Ave Winnemucca, NV 89445 Tel: (702) 623-2912 and the Buckaroo Hall of Fame located at 30 W. Winnemucca Blvd. Winnemucca NV 89445 Tel: (775) 623-2225.

Winnemucca's train depot is located at 209 Railroad St. Winnemucca, NV 89445. The station is un-staffed.

Winnemucca station is served by the California Zephyr.

Elko (NV)

Elko is located in the northeastern part of Nevada, 230 miles west of Salt Lake City. It has a land area of 9.7 sq. miles (25 sq. kilometers) and population of roughly 15,000.

Elko's train depot is located at 12th and Sharp Sts. Elko, NV 89801. The station is un-staffed and features payphones. Transportation from the station is local taxi service.

Elko station is served by the California Zephyr.

Salt Lake City (UT)

Motor-coach connections to **Pocatello (ID)** and **Idaho Falls (ID),** Gateway to **Yellowstone National Park**

Salt Lake City is the county seat of Salt Lake County and the state capital of Utah. Salt Lake City is located in Northern Utah near the Great Salt Lake, at an elevation of 4,327 feet. With a total land area of 109 sq. miles (282 sq. kilometers) Salt Lake City is home to more than 180,000 residents.

The Mormons lead by Brigham Young founded Salt Lake City in 1847 and originally named the area Deseret. Today Salt Lake City welcomes more than 7 million tourists each year visiting Salt Lake City's many ski resorts and recreation areas. Just less than twenty miles west of Salt Lake City is the one of the world's saltiest lakes, the "Great Salt Lake," said to be twice saltier than the ocean water. Salt Lake City was host to the 2001 Winter Olympic Games, and was named as one of the best places to live in North America several times.

Yellow Stone National Park is located 354 miles north of Salt Lake City. Amtrak has motor-coach connections from Salt Lake City's train station to Idaho Falls, Idaho. The city of Idaho Falls is just situated 117 miles southwest of West Yellowstone via Highway 20.

Salt Lake City has an average temperature of 51.8 degrees F. with an average snowfall of 64 inches per year and an average annual rainfall of 15.7 inches.

Getting Around

Airport

Salt Lake International Airport Tel: (801) 575-2400 is located just 5 miles (8 kilometers) northwest of downtown city center. Major car rental companies are located opposite the ground terminal building. Local bus and taxi are available at the arrival area.

Bus

Utah Transit Authority toll-free (888) RIDE-UTA serves public buses around Salt Lake City.

Taxi

City Cab Company Tel: (801) 363-8400, Ute Cab Co. Tel: (801) 359-7788, Yellow Cab Company Tel: (801) 521-2100.

Rent-A-Car

Superior Limousine Svc. toll-free (800) 234-7408, Sterling Limo & Sedan toll-free (800) 218-5485, Lewis Bros. Stages toll-free (800) 826-5844, Express Shuttle toll-free (800) 321-5554, AA Limo & Motor Coach toll-free (800) 659-7053, Canyon Transportation toll-free (800) 255-1841, S.L.A.S.H. toll-free (800) 359-6826, AAA/ABC Access Limo/Bus toll-free (800) 979-4498, Affordable Apt Shuttle toll-free (801) 561-9805, and A Elegant Intl Limo toll-free (800) 940-6482.

Train and Commuter

Salt Lake City's train depot is located at 340 S. 600 West Salt Lake City, UT 84101. The station is staffed and features an enclosed waiting area, restrooms, payphones, and vending machines. Transportation options from the station include Hertz Car Rental toll-free (800) 654-3131 and local taxi service.
Salt Lake City station is served by the California Zephyr.

Visitor Information Center

Salt Lake City Visitor Information Center, 90 S. West Temple, Salt Lake City, UT Tel: (801) 512-2822.

Utah State Capitol

Places to See and Things to Do

Utah State Capitol, located in Capitol Hill at the northernmost end of State Street, is a grand example of America's fine renaissance buildings. The building was built in 1915 for a cost of $2.7 million. Located just south of the Capitol Building is the **26 Council Hall** which originally housed the city and territorial government offices; today the building is home to the Utah Travel Council. The historic **Cathedral of the Madeleine,** located at 331 East South Temple Tel: (801) 328-8941, is rich Gothic architecture admired for its beautiful stained glass. **Cathedral Church of St. Mark,** located at 231 East 100 South Tel: (801) 322-3400, was built in 1871 and is the oldest non-Mormon church in Utah.

Utah Museum of Fine Arts, located at 410 Campus Center Drive Tel: (801) 581-7332, exhibits more than 17,000 pieces from all over the world. **Utah's Hogle Zoo,** located at 2600 E. Sunnyside Avenue (800 South) Tel: (801) 582-1631, is home to hundreds of animals. The **Children's Museum of Utah** is located at 840 North 300 West Tel: (801) 328-3383. **Utah Museum of Natural History,** located at 1390 E. Presidents Circle (220 South) Tel: (801) 581-4303, exhibits Utah's 200 million years of natural history.

The **Delta Center,** located at 301 W. South Temple, is a 20,700-seat sports and entertainment facility. The **Olympic Clock** is located at South Temple and 300 West near the Delta Center. The bronze arrowhead clock was the official countdown clock of the 2001 Winter Olympic Games. **24 Pioneer Memorial Museum,** located at 300 N. Main Street Tel: (801) 538-1050, is dedicated to the history of Utah. The museum exhibits historic carriages,

Olympic Clock

artifacts, machinery, and engines. **The Golden Spike National Historic Site** is where the final four golden spikes were pounded marking the official completion of the first US transcontinental railroad in May 10 1869. The Historic site is located in Promontory Point, near Brigham City, Utah.

Salt Lake Masonic Temple, located at 650 E. South Temple Tel: (801) 363-2936, features Egyptian, Gothic, and Moorish rooms. The 1910 **Rio Grande Depot,** located at 300 S. Rio Grande Street Tel: (801) 533-3500, formerly housed the train station; today the depot houses a café, shops, historic society, a bookstore, and permanent exhibits. **International Peace Gardens,** located at 1060 S 900 West, features botanical gardens that represent 25 countries. **Trolley Square,** located at 600 South at 700 East Tel: (801) 521-9877, is a national historic site which houses shops, restaurants, and entertainment venues.

Governor's Mansion

Governor's Mansion, located at 603 E. South Temple, is a house of the former senator Thomas Kearns. Today the mansion is home to Utah's governor and is open to public. The **Lion House** located at 63 E. South Temple was the home of Brigham Young, the founder of the city. The **Beehive House** located at 67 E. South Temple is a national historic landmark and was the house of Brigham Young during his terms as the governor of Utah.

Temple Square, located in the middle of downtown Salt Lake City, is one of the most visited sites in the city. It houses the Salt Lake Temple, a dome-shaped Tabernacle home to world acclaimed "Mormon Tabernacle Choir" and the Tabernacle Organ, an assembly hall, and two visitors' centers. The square is rich with outdoor exhibits of sculptures and monuments. Temple Square is admired and popularly visited, especially during the Christmas season when it is lit with small glittering lights.

Just behind the Tabernacle is the **Family History Library** which has the largest genealogical record in the world, more than 2 billion. Opposite the Temple is the **Joseph Smith Memorial Building** which houses the Legacy Theater, family search center, and restaurants. **Eagle Gate and Brigham Young Monument**, located near Temple Square in the heart of Salt Lake City, honors the Mormon pioneers of Salt Lake City.

Great Salt Lake is located 17 miles west of Salt Lake City, on Interstate 80, exit 104 Tel: (801) 250-1898. The Great Salt Lake is the 4th largest terminal lake in the world: it is 28 miles wide, 75 miles long, and 45 feet deep. The lake is part of the ancient lake known as Lake Bonneville. Salt Lake City is situated near numerous national parks: **Arches National Park** is just 232 miles (373 Kilometers), **Bryce Canyon National Park** is 270 miles (434 Kilometers) from Salt

Temple Square

Lake City, and **Dinosaur National Monument** is just 185 miles (298 Kilometers) from Salt Lake City.

Accommodations

Airport Fairfield Inn by Marriott located at 230 North Admiral Byrd Road Salt Lake City, UT 84116 Tel: (801) 355-3331. **Hampton Inn Salt Lake City, Downtown** located at 425 South 300 West Salt Lake City, UT 84101 Tel: (801) 741-1110. **Comfort Suites Airport** located at 172 North 2100 West Salt Lake City, UT 84116 Tel: (801) 715-8688. **Courtyard by Marriott, Downtown** located at 130 West 400 South Salt Lake City, UT 84101 Tel: (801) 531-6000. **Ramada Inn Downtown** located at 230 West 600 South Salt Lake City, UT 84101 Tel: (801) 364-5200.

Best Western Salt Lake Plaza Hotel located at 122 West South Temple Salt Lake City, UT 84101 Tel: (801) 521-0130. **Comfort Inn - Salt Lake City** located at 2055 South Redwood Road Salt Lake City, UT 84104 Tel: (801) 886-0703. **Holiday Inn Downtown** located at 999 South Main Street Salt Lake City, UT 84111 Tel: (801) 359-8600. **Econo Lodge, Downtown** located at 715 West North Temple Salt Lake City, UT 84116 Tel: (801) 363-0062. **Travelodge Temple Square** located at 144 West North Temple Salt Lake City, UT 84103 Tel: (801) 533-8200. **Hilton Salt Lake City Center** located at 255 South West Temple Salt Lake City, UT 84101 Tel: (801) 328-2000.

Amtrak Connecting Motor-coach to Pocatello (ID) and Idaho Falls (ID) - Gateway to "West Yellowstone"

Amtrak Idaho Falls and Pocatello, Idaho motor coach service from Salt Lake City is served by Greyhound bus. Passengers who wish to travel to either Idaho city should notify Amtrak as early as possible. The motor coach connection ticket is in conjunction with the passenger train ticket. The bus leaves Salt Lake City, Utah every morning at 8:30 am and returns at 2:45 pm from Idaho Falls, Idaho. Passengers should be reimbursed for their taxi fare between the Greyhound and Amtrak stations at the counter in the Salt Lake City Amtrak station.

Along the way to Pocatello and Idaho Falls from Salt Lake City you will pass through the Great Salt Lake, the largest lake west of the Mississippi and one of the saltiest body of water in the world; the Golden Spike National Historic Site; Fort Hall in Pocatello, Idaho; the World's Largest Potato Exhibit and the Craters of the Moon National Monument in Blackfoot, Idaho; and Mesa Falls, Idaho.

Pocatello (ID)

Pocatello is located in southeast Idaho in the western foothills of the Rocky Mountains along Interstate highway 15. Pocatello has a land area of 27 sq. miles (71.5 sq. kilometers) and sits at an elevation of 4,365 feet above sea level. Pocatello is home to Idaho State University with more than 12,000 students adding to the city's population of more than 51,000.

Amtrak Station in Pocatello, ID is in Greyhound Station at 215 W Bonneville St. 83204.

Idaho Falls (ID)
Gateway to **Yellowstone National Park**

The City of Idaho Falls is located in the southeastern part of Idaho, 100 miles southwest of West Yellowstone. Idaho Falls has a land area of 14 sq. miles (37.5 sq. kilometers), an elevation of 4,742 feet above sea level, and population of approximately 51,000. Idaho Falls was founded in around 1860 and was named after the famous Idaho Falls located nearby. The city of Idaho Falls is a gateway to West Yellowstone, rental car services are inexpensive but make sure to call as early as possible for reservations. Amtrak Idaho Falls Station is located in Greyhound Station at 850 Denver Rd. 83402.

Rent-a-Car

Avis Rent-A-Car toll-free (888) 897-8448 or Tel: (208) 522-4225; Budget Rent-A-Car toll-free (800) 527-0700 or Tel: (208) 522-8800; Hertz Rent-A-Car toll-free (800) 654-3131 or Tel: (208) 529-3101; National Rent-A-Car toll-free (800) CAR-RENT or Tel: (208) 529-6550.

Visitor Information Center

Eastern Idaho Falls Visitor Center, (EIVC) Tel: 208-523-1010

Places to see: The 1,500 Feet-wide Idaho Falls is located on the Snake River. Tautphaus Park Zoo is located at 2725 Carnival Way Idaho Falls, Idaho 83405 Tel: (208) 528-5552 and the Bonneville Museum is located at 200 N Eastern Ave Idaho Falls, ID 83402 Tel: (208) 522-1400.

West Yellowstone (MT)
Gateway to **Yellowstone National Park**

West Yellowstone, the "Snowmobile Capital of the World," is located in the southwestern corner of Montana, just 1.5 miles from Wyoming and eight miles from Idaho. Gateway to Yellowstone National Park and sitting at 6,666 feet above sea level, West Yellowstone has a land area of 0.7 sq. miles (1.8 sq. kilometers) and population of roughly 1,000 residents. Around the town of West Yellowstone are many small souvenir shops, sports and rental shops, a theater, visitor center, bars, and country restaurants.

West Yellowstone is popularly known as the leading trout fishing and snowmobiling

destination in the US. Visit the **Museum of Yellowstone** located at the historic Union Pacific Depot which exhibits rare native Indian artifacts, photographs, and more. **Grizzly Discovery Center** - A Bear and Wolf Preserve, West Yellowstone, MT 59758 Tel: (406) 646-7001 features exhibits, shops, and films. **Yellowstone Historic Center** located at 121 Madison Avenue, West Yellowstone, MT 59758 Tel: (406) 646-7461. **Playmill Theatre** located at 29 Madison Avenue, West Yellowstone, MT 59758 Tel: (406) 646-7757.

Getting There

Getting to West Yellowstone is via Amtrak thruway bus service to Idaho Falls, Idaho from Salt Lake City train station. All connecting bus fares are included with your train ticket provided that you inform Amtrak well in advance of your itinerary.

Yellowstone Airport is located one mile north of West Yellowstone; the airport is open from June 1 through September 30. The airport is served by Skywest Airlines (Delta Connection). There are car rental services and airport bus pickup services at the airport.

Rental car services are available both in Salt Lake City and Idaho Falls, however it is more convenient to travel via Amtrak thruway bus connection to Idaho Falls, Idaho and pick up your car rental there. From Idaho Falls take highway 20 north to West Yellowstone; take a more relaxed drive to West Yellowstone as there are many places of interest along the way.

There is a Greyhound Bus Line Daily Tour to West Yellowstone from Salt Lake City and it cost approximately $52.00 each way. Call Greyhound for more information Tel: (801) 952-9038.

Getting Around

Bus Tour to Yellowstone National Park

Buffalo Bus Touring Company located at 415 Yellowstone Avenue, West Yellowstone, MT 59758 toll-free: (800) 426-7669. Gray Line Tel: (406) 646-9374.

Yellowstone Adventures located at 131 Dunraven Street, West Yellowstone, MT 59758 Tel: (406) 646-7735.

Snowmobile Rentals

Alpine West located at the corner of Hayden and Gibbon Sts. West Yellowstone toll-free (800) 858-9224. **Yellowstone Rental & Sports** located at 1630 Targhee Pass Highway, West Yellowstone, MT 59758 Tel: (406) 646-9377. **Hi Country Snowmobile Rentals** located in Highway 20 and Hayden Street, West Yellowstone, MT 59758 Tel: (406) 646 7541. **Rendezvous Snowmobile Rentals** located at 415 Yellowstone Avenue, West Yellowstone, MT 59758 toll-free: (800) 426-7669. **Two Top Snowmobile Rental** located at 645 Gibbon Avenue, West Yellowstone, MT 59758 Tel: (406) 646-7802. **High Mark Snowmobile Rentals** located at 123 Hayden Street, West Yellowstone, MT 59758 Tel: (406) 646-7586.

Sled Dog Tours

Klondike Dreams Sled Dog Tours, P.O. Box 268, West Yellowstone, MT 59758 Tel: (406) 646-4988.

Accommodations

Gray Wolf Inn & Suites located at 250 S. Canyon West Yellowstone, MT 59758 Tel: (406) 646-0000 expect to pay $50-$150. **Travelers Lodge** located at 225 Yellowstone Avenue West Yellowstone, MT 59758 Phone: (406) 646-9561 expect to pay $50-$150. **Big Western Pine Motel** located at 234 Firehole Avenue West Yellowstone, MT 59758 Tel: (406) 646-7622 expect to pay $50-$70. **Kelly Inn** located at 104 S. Canyon West Yellowstone, MT 59758 Tel: (406) 646-4544 Seasonal, expect to pay $50-100.

Lazy G Motel located at 123 Hayden Street West Yellowstone, MT 59758. Tel: (406) 646-7586 expect to pay $30-$70. **Alpine Motel** located at 120 W. Madison Avenue West Yellowstone, MT 59758 Tel: 406-646-7544 expect to pay $30-$70. **Pine Shadows Motel** located in West Yellowstone, MT 59758. Tel: (406) 646-7541 expect to pay $50-$70. **Stage Coach Inn** located at 209 Madison Avenue West Yellowstone, MT 59758 Tel: (406) 646-7381 expect to pay $50-$150. **Days Inn** located at 118 Electric Street, West Yellowstone MT 59758 Tel: (406) 646-7656 $42-$149.

Yellowstone National Park (WY)

Established in 1872, Yellowstone was the first national park in the world. It covers 2.2 million acres of natural wonders and beauty stretching throughout the states of Montana, Idaho, and Wyoming. Famous for its beautiful geysers, colorful hot pools, wildlife, alpine lakes, water falls, and bubbling mud caldrons, Yellowstone is one of the most visited national parks in the world, with over three million visitors each year.

Yellowstone is home to varieties of wildlife; a close encounter with wild animals is to be expected while traveling inside the national park. Bison, elk, wolves, bears, and hundreds of different species of birds are the residents of this majestic and mysterious park. Yellowstone National Park is open year-round. Visiting the park during spring and summer visitors will enjoy beautiful scenery of wild flowers, greenery, beautiful lakes, and majestic mountains; winter transforms the park into a majestic wonderland of snow. Yellowstone National Park is located at the center of the Continental Divide.

There are approximately 10,000 thermal features and 300 geysers around Yellowstone National Park. Visitors are advised to take extra caution while visiting the park since there are many accidents and in some cases death each year due to carelessness and accidents.

Park Fees

Park fees are: Seven Day Pass $20 (per vehicle), Annual Pass $40 (per vehicle), National Parks Passport $50 (per vehicle), and the Golden Age Passport $10 (per person). Visitors can purchase their ticket at any Yellowstone Visitor Information Center in West Yellowstone. For more information see chapter 3- Tips for Visitors, Parks and National Parks.

Entrances or Gates

There are five entrances to the national park: West Entrance, West Yellowstone (Montana); North Entrance, Gardiner (Montana); Northeast Entrance, Silver Gate (Montana); East, Cody (Wyoming); and South Entrance, Moran (Wyoming).

Snow Coach Tours and Winter Equipment Rentals

Tours are offered in several areas of the National Park. Daily tours depart from Mammoth Hot Springs, Old Faithful, West Yellowstone, and Flag Ranch outside the south entrance. Snowmobile, ski, and snow gear rental are available in Mammoth Hot Springs Hotel and Old Faithful Snow Lodge.

Geyser

Driving and Snowmobile Inside the Park

Yellowstone has 370 miles of paved roadways that form a large 8 shaped loop, also known as the upper loop, lower loop, and the grand loop. During winter part of these loops are closed so be sure to get road information and a park map at the visitor center and spend time studying them before proceeding to the park.

Exploring the park by snowmobile is one of the fun ways to enjoy the scenery and beauty of Yellowstone. Snowmobiles are rented in West Yellowstone. Cars are allowed inside the park during spring and summer, however the road conditions inside the park are poor. The speed limit is 45 miles per hour in most parts of the park, while in many areas 35 and 25 miles per hour speed limits are imposed. There are road rules to observe when animals are passing along the road, be sure to read the park regulations for safety listed in the Yellowstone National Park map and guide.

Visitor Information Center

West Yellowstone Chamber of Commerce, located at the corner of Yellowstone Avenue and Canyon Street Tel: (406) 646-4403.

Mammoth Hot Springs Albright Visitor Center, located at the park north entrance Tel: (307) 344-2263.

<u>Old Faithful Visitor Center</u>, located in the southern part of the national park Tel: (307) 545-2750.

Places to See and Things to Do

Wildlife

In addition to Yellowstone's pristine mountain ranges, wilderness, and beautiful scenery is a rich open refuge for wildlife. The national park is home to hundreds of protected species, including American bison, elk, moose, bear, wolf, and birds. It is possible that you might encounter wildlife while visiting the park. Visitors are expected to respect and preserve the wildlife while enjoying and experiencing the beauty and richness of Yellowstone National Park.

Madison

The Madison Information Station is located at Madison Junction in the Madison Picnic Area 14 miles from the West Yellowstone Park entrance. The station is a National Historic Landmark, and houses a visitor center, museum, shops, and camping. Turning to your right at the Madison junction from West Yellowstone is **Firehole Canyon Drive**; a beautiful canyon, rock formations, and falls are features in the area.

Norris

Norris is located northwest of Yellowstone 14 miles northeast of Madison off the Grand Loop road. Norris features the beautiful **Norris Geyser Basin**, museum, dining, shopping, and camping. Halfway between Madison and Norris is the Beryl Spring.

Mammoth Hot Springs

Mammoth Hot Springs is located at the north entrance of Yellowstone, 21 miles north of Norris and 5 miles inside of the park north entrance. Mammoth Hot Springs features the magnificent **Mammoth Hot Spring Terraces**, visitor center, shopping, post office, lodging, camping, dining, garage, gasoline station, and a fine museum. There is a theater in the visitor center with seasonal films and video presentations every half hour. **Roaring Mountain** and **Indian Creek** are located along the road from Norris to Mammoth Hot Springs.

Yellowstone Canyon

The spectacular **Yellowstone Grand Canyon** is 1200 feet deep and adorned by the graceful Upper Falls. The canyon is located 12 miles east of Norris. Canyon features a visitor center, post office, lodging, camping, dining, shopping, gasoline station, garage, and showers. Located four miles north of the Canyon junction is the **Washburn Hot Spring Overlook** which offers spectacular views of the park. **North Rim Drive** and **South Rim Drive/Artist Point** are located to the south of the Canyon junction. **Mud Volcano** is located halfway between Canyon and Fishing Bridge.

Fishing Bridge

Fishing Bridge is located in east-central Yellowstone 16 miles south of Canyon. This lovely and romantic bridge is one of the most beautiful sceneries in the park. Yellowstone Lake is located a few meters south of Fishing Bridge. **Yellowstone Lake** is one of the biggest glacier lakes in the world, its shoreline measures 110 miles. Located one mile off the Grand Loop road is the **Fishing Bridge Museum** and **Visitor Information Center.**

West Thumb

West Thumb is located in the south-central area of Yellowstone, 21 miles southwest of Fishing Bridge and 17 miles east of Old Faithful. West Thumb features **West Thumb Geyser Basin, Grant Village**, visitor center, post office, lodging, camping, dining, shopping, garage, showers, and horses.

Old Faithful

Old Faithful is located in southwest Yellowstone 16 miles south of Madison and 17 miles west of West Thumb. Old Faithful is famous for **Old Faithful Geyser,** one of the most popular natural wonders of Yellowstone. Ask the visitor center of the schedules of the geyser's natural thermal water show. Old Faithful features Old Faithful Geyser, visitor center, shopping, camping, lodging, garage, post office, and shower. Located between Madison and Old Faithful are **Firehole Canyon Drive, Fountain Paint Pot, Midway Geyser Basin, Biscuit Basin**, and the **Black Sand Basin.**

Having fun at the steaming river

Accommodations

Old Faithful Snow Lodge and Mammoth Hot Spring Hotel offers Accommodations. Visitors should make their reservations well in advance in order to guarantee space. Call Tel: (307) 344-7901 for reservations. Camping is allowed in designated campsite areas inside the park, permits should be obtained prior to your arrival at the park. Contact the park visitor information center for information.

All Aboard!

Utah (UT)

Capital: Salt Lake City (Population: 2,233,169)
Size: 82,168 sq mi. (212,816 sq km)
Nickname: The Beehive State
Joined the union on: January 4, 1896 (45th state)
Motto: Industry
Flower: Sego lily
Bird: California gull
Song: Utah, We Love Thee
Famous for: Winter Olympics, the Natural Arch, Red Rocks and the Mormons.
Major industries: Agriculture, mining and tourism

Provo (UT)

Provo is located along the Utah Lake just 40 miles south of Salt Lake City at an elevation of 4,549 feet above sea level. Provo has a land area of 39 sq. miles (100 sq. kilometers) and population of more than 100,000. Provo was first sited in 1825 and named after its founded Etienne Provost. The city of Provo is home to Brigham Young University, one of the largest private universities in the world, and the city is a gateway to several national parks located within a few hours of the city.

Provo's train depot is located at 6th South and 3rd West Provo, UT 84601. The station is un-staffed. Transportation from the station is local taxi service.

Provo station is served by the California Zephyr.

Helper (UT)

Helper is located 98 miles southeast of Salt Lake City, with a land area of 1.7 sq. miles (4.6 sq. kilometers) and a population of roughly 5,000. Place of interest: Western Mining & Railroad Museum, located at 296 S. Main in Helper Tel: (801) 472-3009, exhibits railroad equipment, artifacts, archives and more.

Helper's train depot is located at 1 Depot St. Helper, UT 84526. The station is un-staffed and features an enclosed waiting area and restrooms. Transportation from the station is local taxi service.

Helper station is served by the California Zephyr.

Green River (UT)

Green River is located in central-eastern Utah on interstate highway 70. Green River has a land area of 12 sq. miles (32.4 sq. kilometers), an elevation of 4,079 feet above sea level, and a population of just over a thousand. Green River was founded in 1878 and was incorporated in 1906. Green River is surrounded by nature's wonders; the Green River is a world-class destination for rafting, canoeing, and other water sports. The surrounding desert is popular for other nature, leisure, and sports activities. Green River is near Arches National Park, Glen Canyon, and other natural wonders.

Green River's train depot is located at 250 S. Broadway Green River, UT 84525. The station is un-staffed. Transportation form the station is local taxi service.

Green River station is served by the California Zephyr.

Grand Junction (CO)

Grand Junction is located in western central Colorado near the Utah state border, 213 miles west of Denver the state capital. Grand Junction sits at an elevation of 4,583 feet above sea level with a land area of 15 sq. miles (38.4 sq. kilometers) and population of approximately 38,000. Grand Junction is a world-class destination. Known as wine country and well admired for its several historic sites, ski resorts, Rocky Mountains adventures and activities.

Grand Junction's train depot is located at 339 S. First St. Grand Junction, CO 81501. The station is staffed and features an enclosed waiting area, restrooms, payphones, checked baggage service, vending machines, a snack bar and restaurant. Transportation from the station is local taxi service.

Grand Junction station is served by the California Zephyr.

Colorado (CO)

Capital: Denver (Population: 4,301,261)
Size: 103,730 sq mi. (268,660 sq km)
Nickname: The Centennial State
Joined the union on: August 1, 1876 (38th state)
Motto: Nothing Without Providence
Flower: Rocky Mountain Columbine
Bird: Lark Bunting
Song: "Where the Columbines Grow"
Famous for: Skiing, Rocky Mountains
Major industries: Tourism, agriculture, and publication

Places to See and Things to Do

The Grand Junction Valley area is home to wide findings of **Dinosaurs Prehistoric Fossils,** so watch your step and you might find new dinosaur species. Visit the **Dinosaur Valley Museum,** located at 362 Main St., Grand Junction, CO 81506 Tel: (970) 242-0971, exhibits dinosaur fossils from around the region. **Museum of Western Colorado**, located at 248 S. Fourth St, Grand Junction, CO 81506 Tel: (970) 242-0971, exhibits Colorado's natural and social history. The **Cross Orchards Historic Farm,** located at 3073 F Rd., Grand Junction, CO 81506 Tel: (970) 434-9814, exhibits Colorado heritage.

Doo Zoo Children's Museum is located at 248 Colorado Ave., Grand Junction, CO 81506 Tel: (970) 241-5225. **Western Colorado Center for the Arts,** located at 1803 N. 7th St, Grand Junction, CO 81506 Tel: (970) 243-7337, has galleries of modern American Indian culture. **Lincoln Park,** located at 12th and North Avenue, Grand Junction, CO Tel: (970) 244-FUNN, has various recreational activities including a golf course, pools, and more. Shop at **Downtown Grand Junction Shopping District;** there are many shops, galleries, restaurants, and more.

The **Colorado National Monument,** 23,000 acres of canyons, rock formations, arches, and many other natural wonders, is located a few miles west of Grand Junction. Colorado National Monument is popular for hiking, camping, wildlife watching, and other recreational activities. Call the national park visitor center at Tel: (970) 858-3617 for information. Located further west of Colorado National Monument is the **Colorado Canyons National Conservation Area** famous for its many natural arches and nature activities. For information call the Bureau of Land Management at Tel: (970) 244-3000.

Accommodations

Days Inn Grand Junction located at 733 Horizon Drive Grand Junction CO 81506 Tel: (970) 245-7200 expect to pay $30-$150. **Holiday Inn Grand Junction** located at 755 Horizon Drive Grand Junction CO 81506 Tel: (970) 243-6790 expect to pay $70-$130. **Ramada Inn Grand Junction** located at 752 Horizon Drive Grand Junction CO 81506 Tel: (970) 243-5150 expect to pay $40-$150. **Best Western Sandman Motel** located at 708 Horizon Drive Grand Junction CO 81506 Tel: (970) 243-4150 expect to pay $30-$100.

La Quinta Grand Junction located at 2761 Crossroads Blvd. Grand Junction CO 81506 Tel: (970) 241-2929 expect to pay $50-$150. **Grand Vista Hotel** located at 2790 Crossroads Blvd. Grand Junction CO 81506 Tel: (970) 241-8411 expect to pay $100-$130. **Comfort Inn Grand Junction** located at 750 3/4 Horizon Drive Grand Juction CO 81506 Tel: (970) 245-3335 expect to pay $40-$150. **Super 8 Motel** located at 728 Horizon Drive Grand Junction CO 81506 Tel: (970) 248-8080 expect to pay $30-$150. **Best Western Horizon Inn** located at 754 Horizon Drive Grand Junction CO 81506 Tel: (970) 245-1410 expect to pay $40-$100.

Glenwood Springs (CO)

Glenwood Springs is located less than two hours from Grand Junction. Situated along some of the most scenic areas of Colorado, Glenwood Springs is Mecca for outdoor activities enthusiasts. Glenwood Springs is famous for world-class ski resorts, river rafting, kayaking, mountain hiking, and the world re-known Hot Spring. Glenwood Springs is home to roughly 7,000 residents.

Glenwood Springs' train depot is located at 413 7th St. Glenwood Springs, CO 81601. The station is staffed and features an enclosed waiting area, checked baggage service, restrooms, and payphones.

Glenwood Spring station is served by the California Zephyr.

Accommodations

Best Western Antlers located at 171 West 6th Street Glenwood Springs, CO 81601 Tel: (970) 945-8535. **1st Choice Inns** located at 51359 Hwy 6 Glenwood Springs, CO 81601 Tel: (970) 945-8551. **Comfort Inn & Suites** located at 920 Cowen Drive Carbondale, CO 81623 Tel: (970) 963-8880. **Holiday Inn Express - Glenwood Springs** located at 501 West 1st Street Glenwood Springs, CO 81601 Tel: (970) 928-7800. **Ramada Inn** located at 124 West 6th Street Glenwood Springs, CO 81601 Tel: (970) 945-2500. **Best Value Inn & Suites** located at 51871 Hwy 6 Glenwood Springs, CO 81601 Tel: (970) 945-6279.

Homestead Inn located at 52039 Hwy 6 Glenwood Springs, CO 81601 Tel: (970) 945-8817. **Cedar Lodge** located at 2102 Grand Avenue Glenwood Springs, CO 81601 Tel: (970) 945-6579. **Affordable Inns** located at 51823 Hwy 6 Glenwood Springs, CO 81601 Tel: (970) 945-8888. **Budget Host Glenwood** located at 51429 Hwy 6 Glenwood Springs, CO 81601 Tel: (970) 945-5682. **Hampton Inn - Glenwood Springs** located at 401 West 1st Street Glenwood Springs, CO 81601 Tel: (970) 947-9400. **Hotel Denver** located at 402 7th Street Glenwood Springs, CO 81601 Tel: (970) 945-6565. **Caravan Inn** located at 1826 Grand Avenue Glenwood Springs, CO 81601 Tel: (970) 945-7451.

Granby (CO)
Gateway to Rocky Mountain National Park

Located just 75 miles west of Denver, Granby sits at 8,369 feet above sea level in the middle of the Rocky Mountains. Granby is a gateway to Rocky Mountain National Park, several national forests, and large lakes. A popular winter sports destination, Granby is an equally exciting place to explore during summer. Granby is home to roughly 1,000 friendly residents.

Granby's train depot is located at 438 Railroad Ave. Granby, CO 80446. The station is un-staffed and features an enclosed waiting area, restrooms, and payphones. Transportation from the station is local taxi service.

Granby station is served by the California Zephyr.

Places to see and Things to Do

Colorado State Forest State Park, located a few miles north of Granby, is a popular tourist destination. There are hiking, biking, and horseback trails; camping; snowmobile during winter; rich wildlife; and breathtaking scenery. Other national forests and national parks around the area are: the **Arapaho National Forest** Tel: (970) 887-4100 and **Rocky Mountain National Park** Tel: (970) 586-1206. Both are popular places for year around recreation and sports activities. The **Colorado River Headwaters, Williams Fork River,** and **Fraser River** are popular for water sports and river enthusiasts. **Rocky Mountain Repertory Theatre** located at 1025 Grand Avenue Grand Lake, CO Tel: (970) 627-1726 call for information.

Resorts and Sports Shops and Equipments

Berthoud Pass Ski Resort is located near Granby at 43475 Highway 40 Winter Park CO Tel: (970) 726-9287. **Budget Tackle Sporting Goods** located at 255 East Agate Ave. Granby CO Tel: (970) 887-9344. **Fletcher's Sporting Goods** located at 217 West Agate Avenue Granby CO Tel: (970) 887-3747. **Trail Snowmobile Rental** located at 1447 County Road 491 Grand Lake, CO Tel: (970) 627-3215. **Flanagan's Ski Rental** located at 100 East Garnet Granby CO Tel: (970) 887-2554.

Grand Adventures Tours, located at 79303 Highway 40 Winter Park CO Tel: (970) 726-9247, offers snowmobile rides, dog sled rides, and horseback riding. **Sombrero Stables Horseback Riding** located at 304 West Portal Grand Lake, CO Tel: (970) 627-3514. **Mad Adventures** located at 523 Zerex Fraser, CO Tel: (970) 726-5290 offers raft trips and white water trips.

Accommodations

Blue Spruce Motel located at 170 East Agate Ave. Granby, CO Tel: (970) 887-3300. **Broken Arrow Motel** located at 509 West Agate Ave. Granby, CO Tel: (970) 887-3532. **El Monte Motor Inn** located at 425 West Agate Avenue Granby, CO Tel: (970) 887-3348. **Best-Vu Motel** located at 8042 Highway 34 Granby, CO Tel: (970) 887-2034. **Homestead Motel** located at 851 West Agate Avenue Granby, CO Tel: (970) 887-3665. **Daven Haven Lodge** located at 604 Marina Drive Grand Lake, CO Tel: (970) 627-8144. **Mountain Lakes Lodge** located at 10480 US Highway 34 Grand Lake, CO Tel: (970) 627-8448.

Fraser-Winter Park (CO)

Fraser is located just 62 miles west of Denver and is home to approximately 600 residents. Just like Granby, Fraser - Winter Park is a world class and popular year around destination. There are several ski parks in the area, ask your hotel for information.

Fraser-Winter Park's train depot is located at 420 Railroad Ave., Fraser Winter Park, CO 80442. The station is un-staffed and features an enclosed waiting area, restrooms, payphones, and a restaurant. Transportation options from the station include local bus and taxi services.

Fraser-Winter Park station is served by the California Zephyr.

Places to see and Things to Do

Winter Park is located east of **Arapaho National Forest,** a popular destination and recreation area. **Monarch Stables** offer summer and winter horseback rides, hayrides, hot chocolate bonfire rides, sleigh-rides, dinner, lunch, and live entertainment, call Tel: (970) 726-5376. The **Cozens Ranch Museum,** located in Fraser on Highway 40 near Winter Park Tel: (970) 726-5488, is the oldest homestead in Fraser Valley. The historic **Georgetown Loop Railroad** is located between exits 226 and 228 on I-70, just five miles past exit 228.

Ski Rental Shops

Winter Park Sport Shop Tel: (970) 726-5554; **Ski Broker Rental** Tel: (970) 726-8882; **Alpine Sun** Tel: (970) 726-5107; **Ski Exchange Rentals** Tel: (970) 726-9240; **Ski Depot Sports** Tel: (970) 726-8055.

Accommodations

Beaver Village located at 79303 US Highway 40, Winter Park, CO 80482 Tel: (970) 726-5741. **Idlewild Lodge** located at 398 County Road 802, Winter Park, CO 80482 Tel: (970) 726-8352. **Sundowner Motel** located at 78869 US Highway 40, Winter Park, CO 80482 Tel: (970) 726-9451. **Winston's at the Vintage Hotel** located at 100 Winter Park Dr, Winter Park, CO 80482 Tel: (970) 726-8801. **Woodspur Lodge** located at 111 Van Anderson Dr, Winter Park, CO 80482 Tel: (970) 726-8417.

Sitzmark Lodge & Cabins located at 78253 US Highway 40, Winter Park, CO 80482 Tel: (970) 726-5453. **Valley Hi Motel** located at 79025 US Highway 40, Winter Park, CO 80482 Tel: (970) 726-4171. **Winter Park Mountain Lodge** located at 81699 US Highway 40, Winter Park, CO 80482 Tel: (970) 726-4211. **Hideaway Olde World Lodge** located in US Highway 40, Winter Park, CO 80482 Tel: (970) 726-1081. **Snowblaze Condominium Rentals** located at 79114 US Highway 40, Winter Park, CO 80482 Tel: (970) 726-5701.

Viking Lodge located at 78966 Highway 40, Winter Park, CO 80482 Tel: (970) 726-5356. **Viking Lodge & Ski Shop** located at 78966 US Highway 40, Winter Park, CO 80482 Tel: (970) 726-8885. **Gasthaus Eichler Hotel** located at 78786 Highway 40, Winter Park, CO 80482 Tel: (970) 726-5133. **Super 8 Motel** located at 78665 US Highway 40, Winter Park, CO 80482 Tel: (970) 726-8088. **Winter Park Central** located at 79050 US Highway 40, Winter Park, CO 80482 Tel: (970) 726-5587.

Denver (CO)
Motor-coach connections to **Fort Collins (CO), Colorado Springs (CO), Pueblo (CO), Vail (CO), Glenwood Spring (CO)** and **Cheyenne (WY)**

Denver sits at an elevation of 5,280 feet above sea level, located at the foot of the Rocky Mountains in the central part of Colorado. Officially founded in 1858 and incorporated in 1861, Denver has been the state capital since 1876. It has a land area of 154 sq. miles (397 sq. kilometers) and is home to more than 500,000 friendly people.

Many of Denver's historical sites are located within walking distance from the central downtown area. The lower downtown area, the "Lo Do," features some of the most well preserved historical building in the city. Within the central downtown area there are various

211

world-class hotels, museums, arts centers, shops, restaurants, and the city's popular nightspots. Denver hosts nearly 9 million visitors each year.

Denver has a yearly average temperature between 17 to 85 degrees Farenheight, with an average snowfall of 55 inches and average rainfall of 15 inches each year.

Colorado (CO)
Capital: Denver (Population: 4,301,261)
Size: 103,730 sq mi. (268,660 sq km)
Nickname: The Centennial State
Joined the union on: August 1, 1876 (38th state)
Motto: Nothing Without Providence
Flower: Rocky Mountain Columbine
Bird: Lark Bunting
Song: "Where the Columbines Grow"
Famous for: Skiing, Rocky Mountains
Major industries: Tourism, agriculture, and publication

Getting Around

Airport

Denver International Airport, 8500 Peña Boulevard, Denver, Colorado 80249 Tel: (303) 342-2300, is located 23 miles (37 Kilometers) north of central Denver. Major car rental companies are located on level 5 of the terminal building. Skyride buses Tel: (303) 299-6000 ext 121 connect the airport to five different routes including central Denver. Local taxi is available throughout the airport.

Bus

Regional Transportation District (RTD), 1600 Blake Street Denver, CO 80202 toll-free (800) 366-RIDE provides public transit in metropolitan Denver/Boulder. Basic fares are $1.25 peak hours, $0.75 all other times.

Taxi

Denver Yellow Cab, 4500 East 41st Avenue Denver, CO 80216 Tel: (303) 777-7777; Metro Taxi, PO Box 5028 Denver, CO 80217 toll-free (800) USA-TAXI; and Freedom Cabs of Denver, 6030 Smith Road Denver, CO 80216 Tel: (303) 292-8900.

Rent-A-Car

Avis Rent A Car, 1900 Broadway Denver, CO 80202 toll-free (800) 331-1212; Budget Rent A Car, 24050 East 78th Avenue Denver, CO 80249 Tel: (303) 342-7212; Dollar Rent A Car, 23520 East 78th Avenue Denver, CO 80249 Tel: (303) 317-1142; Enterprise Rent-A-Car, 4175 E. Warren Avenue Denver, CO 80222 Tel: (303) 300-2813; National Car Rental, Denver International Airport Denver, CO 80249 toll-free (800) CAR-RENT; and Thrifty Car Rental, 7705 Calawba Ct. Denver, CO 80249 Tel: (303) 342-9400.

Train and Commuter

Ski Train, located at 555 17th Street, 2400 Denver, CO 80202 Tel: (303) 296-4754, takes skiers and sightseers from Denver to the Winter Park Resort on weekends and Fridays from December through April and Saturdays during summer.

Denver's train depot is located at 1701 Wynkoop St. Denver, CO 80202. The station is staffed and features an enclosed waiting area, checked baggage service, restrooms, payphones, a snack bar, and a restaurant. Transportation options from the station include rental car service, local transit, and taxi services.

Denver station is served by the California Zephyr.

Visitors Information Center

Denver Metro Convention & Visitors Bureau's Tourism Department, 1688 Larimer St. Denver, CO 80202 Tel: (303) 892-1112.

Places to See and Things to Do

Visit the magnificent **Colorado State Capitol** located at 200 E. Colfax Ave. Tel: (303) 866-2604. The state capitol is admired for its beautiful dome covered with gold leaf and the unique Colorado onyx used inside as wainscoting. The state capitol is open for visitors. **The U.S. Mint,** located near downtown Denver Tel: (303) 844-3582, is the second largest gold warehouse in the US and each year billions of coins are made here.

Mother Cabrini Shrine, located at 20189 Cabrini Blvd., Golden CO 80401, features a 22-foot statue of Christ situated on the top of the hill overlooking the city of Denver. **The Astor House Museum,** located downtown at 822 12th St., Golden CO 80401 Tel: (303) 278-3557, was the former house of the city's legislator. **The Coors Brewery,** located at 12th & Ford Streets Golden, CO Tel: (303) 277-2337, offers a 40-minute factory tour; guests must be over 21 years old. **Trianon Museum and Art Gallery,** located at 335 14th St., Denver CO 80202 Tel: (303) 623-0739, exhibits 18th century European arts.

Denver Art Museum, located at 13th Street and Acoma Tel: (303) 640-4433, has the largest collection of world arts in the US. **Museum of Outdoor Art,** located at 7600 E. Orchard Rd., 160 N, Englewood CO 80111 Tel: (303) 741-3609, exhibits several magnificent sculpture collections. The **Denver Botanic Gardens** is located at 1005 York Street, Denver, CO, just 10 minutes east of Downtown Denver Tel: (303) 331-4000. The garden exhibits exotic plants and houses a large conservatory. **Leanin' Tree Museum of Western Art,** located at 6055 Longbow Dr., Boulder CO 80301 Tel: (303) 530-1442, exhibits collections of contemporary western arts. **Black American West Museum & Heritage Center,** located at 3901 California St, Denver Tel: (303) 292-2566, dedicated to African American history and heritage.

The Denver Museum of Nature & Science is located at 2001 Colorado Blvd., Denver, CO 80205 Tel: (303) 370-6310. The museum is one of the largest in the US, with extensive collections of dinosaur fossils. The museum houses a planetarium and IMAX theater. **Colorado's Ocean Journey** is located at 700 Water Street, Denver CO 80211 Tel: (303) 561-4450. This aquarium is home to more than 15,000 marine animals. **The Denver Zoo** is located in Denver's City Park, main entrance on 23rd Avenue between Colorado Boulevard and York Street Tel: (303) 376-4800. The zoo is home to more than 3,500 animals and houses the Tropical Discovery, the Northern Shores, and the Primate Panorama.

Six Flags Elitch Gardens Theme Park is located at 2000 Elitch Circle Denver, Co 80204 Tel: (303) 595-4386 and features thrill rides, restaurants, and other entertainments. **Wings over the Rockies Air & Space Museum** is located in Hanger No. 1, Bldg. 401 of Old Lowery Air Force Base at 711 E. Academy Blvd., Denver CO 80220 Tel: (303) 360-5360. The museum features historic aircrafts.

Accommodations

Cambridge Hotel Denver located at 1560 Sherman Street Denver CO 80203 Tel: (303) 831-1252 expect to pay $70-$200. **Fairfield Inn Denver Cherry Creek** located at 1680 South Colorado Boulevard Denver CO 80222 Tel: (303) 691-2223 expect to pay $50-$100. **Days Inn Business Place Denver** located at 7030 Tower Road Denver CO 80249 Tel: (303) 373-1500 expect to pay $40-$100. **Mark I Guest Suites** located at 1190 Birch Street Denver CO 80220 Tel: (303) 331-7000 expect to pay $40-$150.

Hawthorn Suites - Denver Tech located at 5001 South Ulster Denver CO 80237 Tel: (303) 804-9900 expect to pay $40-$150. **Extended Stay Denver Lakewood So** located at 7393 West Jefferson Avenue Lakewood CO 80235 Tel: (303) 986-8300 expect to pay $30-$70. **Courtyard Denver Downtown** located at 934 16th Street Denver CO 80202 Tel: (303) 571-1114 expect to pay $70-$300. **Rodeway Inn Denver** located at 12033 East 38th Ave Denver CO 80239 Tel: (303) 371-0740 expect to pay $30-$70. **Holiday Inn** located at 5150 South Quebec Denver CO 80111 Tel: (303) 689-9696 expect to pay $50-$150. **Towne Place Suites Denver Southeast** located at 3699 South Monaco Street Parkway Denver CO 82037 Toll Free: (303) 759-9393 expect to pay $50-$100.

Holiday Inn Downtown Denver located at 1450 Glenarm Place Denver CO 80202 Tel: (303) 573-1450 expect to pay $80-$200. **Four Points by Sheraton Denver Cherry Creek** located at 600 South Colorado Boulevard Denver CO 80246 Tel: (303) 757-3341 expect to pay $50-$180. **Homestead Denver Cherry Creek** located at 4444 Leetsdale Drive Glendale CO 80246 Tel: (303) 388-3880 expect to pay $40-$100. **Best Western Executive Hotel Denver** located at 4411 Peoria Street Denver CO 80239 Tel: (303) 373-5730 expect to pay $60-$150.

Fort Morgan (CO)

Fort Morgan is located in northeast Colorado just 81 miles from the city of Denver. Farms and ranches dominate today's Fort Morgan.

Fort Morgan's train depot is located on S. Ensign St. Fort Morgan, CO 80701. The station is un-staffed and features an enclosed waiting area, restrooms, and payphones. Transportation from the station is local taxi service.

Fort Morgan station is served by the California Zephyr.

McCook (NE)

McCook is the county seat of Red Willow County located in southwest Nebraska, nearly 14 miles north of the Kansas border. McCook has a land area of 5.3 sq. miles (13.6 sq. kilometers) and population of approximately 8,500.

McCook's train depot is located at 101 Norris Ave. McCook, NE 69001. The station is un-staffed and features an enclosed waiting area, restrooms, payphones, and a vending machine.

McCook station is served by the California Zephyr.

Holdrege (NE)

Holdrege is located in south central Nebraska, near the Kansas state border. Holdrege has a land area of 3.5 sq. miles (9 sq. kilometers) and population of roughly 6,000. Founded in 1883, Holdrege still retains its Swedish heritage. While visiting Holdrege see the "Promise of the Prairie" statue dedicated to the city by the internationally acclaimed sculptor George W. Lundeen. The sculpture is located in Holdrege North Park.

Holdrege's train depot is located at 100 West Ave. Holdrege, NE 68949. The station is un-staffed and features an enclosed waiting area, restrooms, and payphones. Holdrege station is served by the California Zephyr.

Nebraska (NE)
Capital: Lincoln (Population: 1,711,263)
Size: 77,358sq mi. (200,357 sq km)
Nickname: The Tree Planter State, Cornhusker State, Beef State
Joined the union on: March 1, 1867 (37th state)
Motto: Equality Before the Law
Flower: Goldenrod
Bird: Western Meadowlark
Song: Beautiful Nebraska
Famous for: Chimney Rock
Major industries: Farm, agriculture, chemicals, and transportation equipment

Hasting (NE)

Hasting is located in the agricultural heartland of south-central Nebraska. Hasting is home to more than 24,000 friendly people and is known for its annual Cottonwood Festival, Hastings College, and the annual migration of cranes and waterfowl -- a spectacle for bird enthusiasts.

Hasting's train depot is located at 501w. First St. Hasting, NE 68901. The station is staffed and features an enclosed waiting area, check baggage service, restrooms, and payphones. Transportation from the station is local taxi service.

Hasting station is served by the California Zephyr.

Lincoln (NE)

Lincoln, also known as the "star city," is the state capital, located in the southeastern part of the state of Nebraska. Lincoln has a land area of 63 sq. miles (163 sq. kilometers) and a population of approximately 225,000.

Lincoln's train depot is located at 201 N. 7th St. Lincoln, NE 68508. The station is staffed and features an enclosed waiting area, checked baggage service, restrooms, payphones, and vending machines. Transportation options from the station include local transit and taxi services.

Lincoln station is served by the California Zephyr.

Visitor Information Center

<u>Lincoln Visitors Center</u>, 201 N 7th St # 101 Lincoln, NE 68508 Tel: (402) 434-5348.

Places to See and Things to Do

Established in 1867, the **Historic Haymarket** has interesting shops, galleries, bookshops, and restaurants. **Museum of Nebraska History,** located at 131 Centennial Mall N Lincoln, NE 68508 Tel: (402) 471-4754, exhibits Nebraska's 10,000 years of natural history. **National Museum of Roller Skating** is located at 4730 South St Lincoln, NE 68506 Tel: (402) 483-7551 and features the history of roller-skating.

The grand **Nebraska State Capitol,** located at the beginning of 14th to 16th and H to K Streets Lincoln, NE Tel: (402) 471-4764, stands at 400 feet and houses courtyards and an observation deck. The **Frank H Woods Telephone Museum** is located at 2047 M St Lincoln, NE 68510-1029 Tel: (402) 436-4640. **Great Plains Art Collection** is located at N 13th St. R St Lincoln, NE 68508 Tel: (402) 472-6220. **Lincoln Children's Museum** located at 1420 P Street Lincoln NE 68508 Tel: (402) 477-4000.

Accommodations

Comfort Suites located at 4231 Industrial Ave, Lincoln, NE 68504 Tel: (402) 476-8080. **Econo Lodge** located at 2410 NW 12th St, Lincoln, NE 68521 Tel: (402) 474-1311. **Ramada Inn** located at 1101 W Bond St, Lincoln, NE 68521 Tel: (402) 475-4971. **Embassy Suites Hotel** located at 1040 P St, Lincoln, NE 68508 Tel: (402) 474-1111. **Holiday Inn** located at 141 N 9th St, Lincoln, NE 68508 Tel: (402) 475-4011. **Ramada Limited** located at 4433 N 27th St, Lincoln, NE 68521 Tel: (402) 476-2222. **Traveodge** located at 2801 W O St # 6, Lincoln, NE 68528 Tel: (402) 475-4921. **Best Western Airport Inn** located at 3200 NW 12th St, Lincoln, NE 68521 Tel: (402) 475-9541.

Days Inn located at 2920 NW 12th St, Lincoln, NE 68521 Tel: (402) 475-3616. **Hampton Inn** located at 1301 W Bond Cir, Lincoln, NE 68521 Tel: (402) 474-2080. **Fairfield Inn** located at 4221 Industrial Ave, Lincoln, NE 68504 Tel: (402) 476-6000. **Holiday Inn** located at 1133 Belmont Ave, Lincoln, NE 68521 Tel: (402) 435-0200. **Red Roof Inn** located at 6501 N 28 St, Lincoln, NE 68504 Tel: (402) 438-4700. **Hawthorn Suites Hotel** 2 located at 16 N 48th St, Lincoln, NE 68504 Tel: (402) 464-4400.

Omaha (NE)
Motor-coach connection to **Kansas City (KS)**

Omaha is located in the far eastern central part of Nebraska along the western bank of the Missouri River, 47 miles northeast of the city of Lincoln, the state capital. Omaha has a land area of 101 sq. miles (260 sq. kilometers) and population of approximately 340,000. Omaha was an important railroad transportation center since the beginning of the city. Omaha was also one of the major gateway cities to the west and became one of the most important commercial centers in the region.

Places to See and Things to Do

The General Crook House is located at 30th and fort Street Tel: (402) 455-9990, the Henry Doorly Zoo located at 3701 South 10th Street Tel: (402) 733-8400, and the Omaha Botanical Gardens located at 5th & Cedar Street Tel: (402) 333-2359. The Fremont Dinner Train is located at 1835 N Somers Fremont toll-free (800) 942-7245 and the Historic Old Marketplace features antique shops and more, a fun place to visit.

Omaha's train depot is located at 1003 S. 9th St. Omaha, NE 68108. The station is staffed and features an enclosed waiting area, checked baggage service, restrooms, payphones, and vending machines. Transportation from the station is local taxi service.

Omaha station is served by the California Zephyr.

Accommodations

Best Western Inn located at 1504 Harney St, Omaha, NE 68102 Tel: (402) 342-1500. **Economy Inn** located at 2211 Douglas St, Omaha, NE 68102 Tel: (402) 345-9565. **Clarion Hotel** located at 10909 M St, Omaha, NE 68137 Tel: (402) 331-8220. **Courtyard by Marriott** located at 113 S 10th St, Omaha, NE 68102 Tel: (402) 346-2200. **Wyndham Garden Hotel** located at 11515 Miracle Hills Dr, Omaha, NE 68154 Tel: (402) 496-7500. **Marriott Hotels & Resorts** located at 10220 Regency Cir, Omaha, NE 68114 Tel: (402) 399-9000.

> *Iowa (IA)*
> **Capital:** Des Moines
> (Population: 2,929,324)
> **Size:** 56,276 sq mi. (145,754 sq km)
> **Nickname:** The Hawkeye State
> **Joined the union on:** December 28, 1846 (29th state)
> **Motto:** Our liberties we prize and our rights we will maintain
> **Flower:** Wild Rose
> **Bird:** Eastern Goldfinch
> **Song:** Song of Iowa
> **Famous for:** American Gothic, corn
> **Major industries:** Agriculture and farming

Comfort Inn located at 10919 J St, Omaha, NE 68137 Tel: (402) 592-2882. **Econo Lodge** located at 7833 Dodge St, Omaha, NE 68114 Tel: (402) 391-7100. **Days Inn** located at 10560 Sapp Brothers Dr, Omaha, NE 68138 Tel: (402) 896-6868. **Hampton Inn** located at 9720 W Dodge Rd, Omaha, NE 68114 Tel: (402) 391-5300. **Sheraton Omaha Hotel** located at 1615 Howard St, Omaha, NE 68102 Tel: (402) 342-2222. **Best Western Inn** located at 4706 S 108th St, Omaha, NE 68137 Tel: (402) 339-7400.

Creston (IA)

Creston is located in southwestern Iowa. Founded in 1868, it is the seat of Union County. Creston has a land area of 5 sq. miles (13 sq. kilometers) and population of approximately 8,000. Places to see: Creston Restored Depot, located at 116 W. Adams, Creston, IA Tel: (515) 782-7021, exhibits railroad artifacts; and the Union County Historical Village and Museum located in McKinley Park, Creston Tel: (641) 782-4405.

Creston's train depot is located on Pine and Adams Sts. Creston, IA 50801. The station is un-staffed and features an enclosed waiting area and payphones. Transportation from the station is local taxi service.

Creston station is served by the California Zephyr.

Osceola (IA)
Gateway to Iowa's capital city of **Des Moines**

Osceola is located 37 miles south of the city of Des Moines. Osceola has a land area of 5 sq. miles (12.9 sq. kilometers) and population of approximately 4,500. Places to see: The Clarke County Historical Museum, located at 1030 S. Main, Osceola Tel: (641) 342-4246, exhibits regional historical artifacts.

Osceola's train depot is located on Main and E. Clay Sts. Osceola, IA 50213. The station is un-staffed and features an enclosed waiting area, restrooms, payphones, and vending machines. Transportation from the station is local taxi service.

Osceola station is served by the California Zephyr.

Ottumwa (IA)

Ottumwa, also known as "City of Bridges," is located in southeastern Iowa in the Des Moines River Valley. The foundation of Ottumwa started in the early 1840's. Ottumwa is well appreciated for its fascinating bridges, one of the most famous being the Jefferson Street Viaduct, listed on the National Register of Historic Places. Ottumwa has a land area of 15.8 sq. miles (40.6 sq. kilometers) and population of more than 25,000.

Places to see: the Ottumwa Depot Museum exhibits railroad memorabilia and steam engines. The Court Hill Historic District between 6th and Court Streets features historic houses from the mid 1800's to early 1900's.

Ottumwa's train depot is located at 210 W. Main St. Ottumwa, IA 52501. The station is staffed and features an enclosed waiting area, checked baggage service, restrooms, and payphones. Transportation options from the station include local bus and taxi services.

Ottumwa station is served by the California Zephyr.

Mt. Pleasant (IA) Gateway to **Iowa City, IA**

Mount Pleasant is located in southeastern Iowa, about 50 miles south of Iowa City. Mount Pleasant has a land area of 7.2 sq. miles (18.5 sq. kilometers) and a population of more than 9,000.

Places to see: the Midwest Old Threshers Heritage Museum is located at 1887 Threshers Rd. Mount Pleasant, IA Tel: (319) 385-8937; the Midwest Central Railway, Mt. Pleasant, IA 52641 Tel: (319) 385-2912 operates seasonal steam trains tours.

Mount Pleasant's train depot is located at 418 N. Adams St. Mount Pleasant, IA 52641. The station is staffed and features an enclosed waiting area, restrooms, payphones, and vending machines. Transportation from the station is local taxi service.

Mouth Pleasant station is served by the California Zephyr.

Burlington (IA)

Burlington is located in the south easternmost part of Iowa at the bank of Mississippi River, 142 miles from Des Moines the state capital. Burlington has a land area of 13 sq. miles (34 sq. kilometers) and population of approximately 28,000. Burlington was Iowa's first territorial capital.

Burlington's train depot is located at 300 S. Main St. Burlington, IA 52601. The station is un-staffed and features an enclosed waiting area, restrooms, payphones, and vending machines. Transportation options from the station include local transit and taxi services.

Burlington station is served by the California Zephyr.

Places to See: The Snake Alley, located on Sixth Street Burlington, IA Tel: (319) 752-6365, is according to Ripley's Believe It or Not the world most crooked street. Port of Burlington, Welcome Center, and Historic Building is located at 400 Front Street on the Mississippi River Tel: (319) 752-8731 and features historical exhibits, shops, and an information center. The Burlington City Park has railroad exhibits.

Accommodations

Villager Lodge located at 2731 Mount Pleasant St, Burlington, IA 52601 Tel: (319) 752-7777. **Arrowhead Motel** located at 2520 Mount Pleasant St, Burlington, IA 52601 Tel: (319) 752-6353. **Best Western Inn** located at 3001 Winegard Dr, Burlington, IA 52601 Tel: (319) 753-2223. **Fairfield Inn** located at 1213 N Roosevelt Ave, Burlington, IA 52601 Tel: (319) 754-0000. **Holiday Inn** located at 1601 N Roosevelt Ave, Burlington, IA 52601 Tel: (319) 752-0000. **Comfort Inn** located at 3051 Kirkwood St, Burlington, IA 52601 Tel: (319) 753-0000. **Ramada Inn** located at 2759 Mount Pleasant St, Burlington, IA 52601 Tel: (319) 754-5781.

Galesburg (IL) See Illinois Zephyr service, page 295- 297.

Princeton (IL) See Illinois Zephyr service, page 295- 297.

Naperville (IL) See Illinois Zephyr service, page 295- 297.

Chicago (IL) See Illinois and Missouri service, page 268

Southwest Chief

Southwest Chief takes passengers to some of the most enchanting land of the western United States. The Southwest Chief is your gateway to the exciting city of Los Angeles, the mighty and Beautiful Grand Canyon, the enchanting land of New Mexico, Colorado, and the windy city of Chicago. Along the way you will see endless beautiful desert, mountains, the beginning of the Rocky Mountains, tunnels, fields, ranches, historical sites, wildlife, and natural wonders. **Don't forget to send your postcard!**

Route Destination Highlights

Los Angeles, CA- The ntertainment capital of the world, Los Angeles has everything to offer. Visit the famous Hollywood Walk of Fame, the Chinese Theater on Hollywood Blvd., Universal Studios, some of the best Museums in the US, explore Venice Beach, Long Beach, or simply shop at the Farmers Market.

Grand Canyon, AZ- Visit one of the most popular and beautiful Natural Wonders of the World. Trek the mighty canyon and test your stamina, explore the hidden beauty of the Grand Canyon.

Albuquerque, NM- See the Telephone Pioneers of America Museum, the Indian Pueblo Cultural Center, the LodeStar Astronomy

	Southwest Chief	
6 45 pm-D	**Los Angeles, CA**	8 40 am-A
7 45 pm	Fullerton, CA	6 42 am
8 46 pm	San Bernardino, CA	5 46 am
9 58 pm	Victorville, CA	4 30 am
10 54 pm	Barsow, CA	3 54 am
1 18 pm	Needles, CA	1 22 am
3 21 am	Kingman, AZ	1 27 am
5 31 am	**Williams Jct., AZ**	11 16 pm
606 am-A	Flagstaff, AZ	10 38 pm-D
6 11 am-D		10 33 pm-A
7 07 am	Winslow, AZ	9 36 pm
8 51 am	Gallup, NM	7 55 pm
12 25 pm-A	**Albuquerque, NM**	5 32 pm-D
12 55 pm-D		4 59 pm-A
2 03 pm	Lamy, NM	3 09 pm
3 50 pm	Las Vegas, NM	1 20 pm
5 36 pm	Raton, NM	11 40 am
6 34 pm	Trinidad, CO	10 39 am
8 23 pm-A	La Junta, CO	925 qm -D
8 33 pm-D		915 am-A
9 21 pm	Lamar, CO	7 15 am
11 41 pm	Garden City, KS	657 am
12 28 am	Dodge City, KS	6 13 am
2 10 am	Hutchison, KS	4 34 am
2 48 am	Newton, KS	3 56 am
2 57 am	Topeka, KS	1 54 am
5 12 am	Lawrence, KS	1 23 am
8 11 am-A	**Kansas City, MO**	10 36 pm-D
8 21 am-D		10 31 pm-A
10 31 am	La Plata, MO	8 25 pm
11 35 am	Forth Madison, IA	7 22 pm
12 29 pm-A	Galesburg, IL	6 21 pm-D
12 31 pm-D		6 19 pm-a
1 22 pm	Princeton, IL	5 29 pm
1 44 pm	Mendota, IL	5 06 pm
2 34 pm	Naperville, IL	4 16 pm
4 36 pm-A	**Chicago, IL**	3 15 pm-D
D-Departure		A-Arrival

Center, and the National Atomic Museum. Be amazed and visit the American International Rattlesnake Museum, the Turquoise Museum, or take Scenic Train Rides. Relax at the spas or explore the beauty of the land of Enchantment by air in one of Albuquerque's exiting hot air balloons.

Kansas City, MO- Visit the city of fountains and explore the American Jazz Museum, the Negro Leagues Baseball Museum, the gorgeous Kansas City Union Station, the famous

Kansas Speedway, and the Harvey-Davidson Assembly Plant. Try the city's famous Barbeque while enjoying jazz music.

Chicago, IL- Home to America's tallest building Sears Tower, visit the Museum of Science and Industry and other outstanding museums; admire the charming Centennial Fountain and take a romantic stroll along lake Michigan; and enjoy Chicago's attractive and busy nightlife.

Train Schedules

The Southwest Chief travels daily from Los Angeles, California to Chicago, Illinois. The trip between the two cities takes approximately 2 days of travel time.

Accommodations

Accommodations are Superliner Reserved Coach and Sleeping Car. There is a Sightseer Lounge Car serving local cuisine, snacks, sandwiches, soups, and drinks. Restaurant style meals are served in the Dining Car. Other amenities are movies, reading materials, games, travelogues hospitality hour, and seasonal national park guide presentations.

All Aboard!

California (CA)

Capital: Sacramento (Population: 33,871,648)
Size: 163,707 sq mi. (424,001 sq km)
Nicknames: The Golden State
Joined the union on: September 9, 1850 (31st state)
Motto: Eureka (I Have Found It)
Flower: Golden Poppy
Bird: California Valley Quail
Song: "I Love You, California"
Famous for: Golden Gate Bridge, Hollywood, Yosemite Valley
Major industries: Manufacturing, Agriculture, Biotechnology, Software and Tourism

Los Angeles (CA) See Coast Starlight service, page 109.

Fullerton (CA) See Pacific Surf Liner service, page 120- 122.

San Bernardino (CA)

San Bernardino is the seat of San Bernardino County located in southern California just 59 miles east of Los Angeles. It has a land area of 55.3 sq. miles (142 sq. kilometers) and population of approximately 200,000. San Bernardino was founded in the early 1800's by the missionaries of the San Gabriel Mission and was named after St. Bernardino de Sienna. The city of San Bernardino was incorporated in 1854. The famous "Route 66 Rendezvous" is held in San Bernardino every third week of September each year.

San Bernardino's train depot is located at 1170 W. 3rd St. San Bernardino, CA 92410. The station is staffed and features checked baggage service and payphones.

San Bernardino station is served by the Southwest Chief.

Victorville (CA)

Victorville is located in the Mojave Desert east of San Bernardino, 97 miles northeast of Los Angeles. Victorville was founded in the late 1800's and was incorporated in 1962. Home of the former George Air Force Base, Victorville has a land area of 42 sq. miles (108 sq. kilometers) and a population of more than 60,000. California Route 66 Museum, located at 16849 Route 66 "D" St. Victorville, CA Tel: (760) 261-US66, exhibits pictures and has a library and gallery dedicated to the historic Route 66. The museum also houses a gift shop.

Victorville's train depot is located at 16858 D St. Victorville, CA 92392. The station is un-staffed and features payphones. Transportation options from the station include local bus and taxi services.

Victorville station is served by the Southwest Chief.

Barstow (CA)

Barstow is located in the heart of the high desert of San Bernardino County at the junction of Interstate Highway 15 and 40. Barstow has a land area of 23 sq. miles (59 sq. kilometers) and population of approximately 22,000. Near Barstow is the famous Ghost Town of Calico, take the Ghost Town Road exit I-15. Calico is a California Historical Landmark; a journey to the town of Calico will take you back in time. Call toll-free (800) TO-CALICO for information.

Barstow's train depot is located at 685 N. 1st Ave. Barstow, CA 92311. The station is un-staffed and features an enclosed waiting area and payphones. Transportation options from the station include local transit, bus, and taxi services.

Barstow station is served by the Southwest Chief.

Needles (CA)

Needles is located in southeastern California just 15 miles from the state border of Arizona. Needles was founded in 1882 as a way station for the Santa Fe Railroad. Needles has a land area of 30 sq. miles (77 sq. kilometers) and population of more than 5,000.

Needles' train depot is located at 900 Front St. Needles, CA 92363. The station is un-staffed and features payphones. Transportation options from the station include local bus and taxi services.

Needles station is served by the Southwest Chief.

Kingman (AZ)

Kingman is located in the northwest corner of Arizona 145 miles west of the Grand Canyon and 35 miles east of the Colorado River. Kingman's elevation is 3,334 feet above sea level and it is home to approximately 35,000 residents. The town of Kingman was founded in 1881 and was a famous stop on Route 66. Kingman is situated near several ghost towns. Two of these towns are Oatman and Chloride. Another place of interest is the Museum of

History & Arts located at 400 W Beale St Kingman, AZ 86401-5708 Tel: (928) 753-3195. View the beautiful natural rock formations around the Kingman area.

Kingman's train depot is located at 4th and Andy Devine Sts. Kingman, AZ 86401. The station is un-staffed and features an enclosed waiting area, restrooms, and payphones. Transportation from the station is local taxi service.

Kingman station is served by the Southwest Chief.

Arizona (AZ)
Capital: Phoenix (Population: 5,130,632)
Size: 113,642 sq mi. (296,400 sq km)
Nickname: The Grand Canyon State
Joined the union on: February 14, 1912 (48th state)
Motto: Ditat Deus (God Enriches)
Flower: Flower of the saguaro cactus
Bird: Cactus Wren
Song: "Arizona March Song"
Famous for: The Grand Canyon
Major industries: Tourism, Agriculture, Copper, Manufacturing

Williams (AZ)
Gateway to **Grand Canyon National Park**

Williams is located along the Ponderosa pines or the Kaibab National Forest (along historic Route 66). First settled in 1874, Williams is a small city with a population of 2900. The city of Williams has been welcoming tourists to the Grand Canyon for more than a century.

Other attractions and points of interest: The Native American Tipi reserve, nearby ghost towns, and the Sedona (Oak Creek area). One can also spend a nice afternoon and evening shopping, dining, or strolling along the old brick sidewalks of the historic district of Williams.

For those who want to experience the old west the vintage steam train restored to its former might, "the Grand Canyon Railway," will surely give you a glimpse of the Old Wild West. The Grand Canyon Railway takes visitors straight to the South Rim of the Grand Canyon.

The Grand Canyon Railway is a 1900 restored locomotive. The trip from the city of Williams to the South Rim of the Canyon will start at the old 1908 Williams Depot and end at the only remaining log depot in the US, the historic Grand Canyon Depot built in 1910.

Train travel on the Grand Canyon Railway is not just an experience of the old west train transportation; during the trip you will be entertained by old west musical performances, deluxe food choices, plus the superb hospitality services from the railway's friendly staff. Truly it's a grand experience.

Travel time from Williams to the South Rim of the Canyon will take about 2½ hours. Fares are approximately $50 for adults and $20 for children under 16 for a coach, with additional $12 and $50 for any upgrade of Club Class and Chief Class. Prices are subject to change; call Grand Canyon Railway for information. For schedules, ticket reservations, and other information call toll-free (800) THE-TRAIN <<http://www.thetrain.com>>.

If you decided to rent a car in Flagstaff or Williams to travel to the Grand Canyon (south rim), the following directions could be helpful: Grand Canyon South Rim is about 60 miles north of Interstate 40 from Williams via highway 64, 80 miles northwest of Flagstaff via highway 180, while the North Rim is 44 miles south of Jacob Lake, AZ, via highway 67.

There are several bus services between Grand Canyon National Park and Flagstaff that could help you for your connecting bus to the Grand Canyon: Nava-Hopi Tours toll-free (800) 892-8687, and South Rim Travel Tel: (928) 638-2748. But certainly the most fashionable way and probably the ultimate experience of getting to the Grand Canyon is by taking the famous "Grand Canyon Railroad."

Amtrak provides a connection to the Grand Canyon via the Grand Canyon Railroad, call Amtrak for information, toll-free (800) USA-Rail. Williams' train depot is located at the Fray Marcos Hotel 235 N. Grand Canyon Blvd. Williams Junction, AZ 86046. The station is un-staffed.

Williams station is served by the Southwest Chief.

Grand Canyon National Park (AZ)

The Grand Canyon, with over 5 million visitors each year, is the most popular and visited US National Park. Sitting at a height of more than 7,000 feet above see level (South Rim), the Grand Canyon offers a breathtaking and magical experience. The Grand Canyon is located in the northwest part of Arizona.

Considered the most impressive example of erosion in grand scale anywhere in the world, Grand Canyon is beyond compare in its landscape. Known as one of the natural wonders of the world, Grand Canyon National Park became a national monument in 1908, a national park in 1919, and a World Heritage Site in 1979.

Grand Canyon National Park covers more than 1.2 million acres. The vast majority of the park is inaccessible due to the predominance of the cliffs. At the heart of the canyon lies the majestic Colorado River that divides the south and north of the Grand Canyon. Grand Canyon Park covers 277 miles of the Colorado River and the adjacent uplands.

It is possible to cross the river that divided the canyon through the Phantom Ranch. However, be advised that the high altitude of both South and North Rims may cause difficulty for visitors with respiratory or heart problems. Hikers are advised to take all necessary precautions in planning your Grand Canyon trekking.

Visitors will have to deal with great differential elevation of more than 10,000 feet from start to your final destination. Thus, trekking at this elevation can be demanding. Also, try to consider a two or more day trek, especially during summer where temperatures along the Colorado River at the bottom of the canyon can reach as high as 120° F.

South Rim is more than 7,000 feet above sea level, thus you have to expect snowfall during winter and cool nights even in summer. While the North Rim is at 8,000 feet above sea level, you should prepare for possible light snow year round. In addition, weather is particularly unpredictable during spring and fall. Therefore be prepared for a variety of conditions.

If you wish to camp anywhere in the park outside the developed campgrounds on the rims, you must acquire a permit from the Backcountry Information Center. (Consult the park information center for more information or see Chapter 3- Tips for Visitors, Parks and National Parks).

Park Fees

Each visitor coming to the national park pays $10 for a seven-day entry permit. While a private, non-commercial vehicle of any type regardless of the number of passengers will pay $20 for a seven-day entry permit. See chapter 3, Tips for Visitor- Parks and National Park for more information.

Getting Around

Bus

Concessioner Tours offers tours around the South Rim, call Tel: (303) 297-2757 or Tel: (928) 638-2631. Trans Canyon Shuttle Tel: (928) 638-2820 provides seasonal shuttle service between the south and north rims of the Grand Canyon. Grand Canyon Coaches operates Eco-Shuttle between hotels and businesses in Grand Canyon Village, call for information Tel: (928) 638-0821.

Air Tour

The following air tour operators are located at Grand Canyon Airport, just south of Tusayan, and offer air tours around the Grand Canyon area.

Airplane Tour: Airstar, P.O. Box 3379 Grand Canyon, Arizona 86023 Tel: (928) 638-2622; Air Grand Canyon / Sky Eye Air Tours, P.O. Box 3399 Grand Canyon, Arizona 86023 Tel: (928) 638-2686; Grand Canyon Airlines, P.O. Box 3038 Grand Canyon, Arizona 86023 Tel: (928) 638-2407.

Helicopter Tour: Papillon Grand Canyon Helicopters P.O. Box 455 Grand Canyon, Arizona 86023 Tel: (928) 638-2419; Airstar Helicopters P.O. Box 3379 Grand Canyon, Arizona 86023 Tel: (928) 638-2622; Kenai Helicopters P.O. Box 1429 Grand Canyon, Arizona 86023 Tel: (928) 638-2764.

Taxi

Taxi service is available to the Grand Canyon Airport, trailheads, and other destinations. Call Tel: (928) 638-2822 or (928) 638-2631, ext. 6563.

Visitor Information Center

Grand Canyon View Information Plaza (South Rim) is open from 9am to 7pm and is located at Mather Point.

The Desert View Information Center (South Rim) is open from 9am to 7pm and is located at the park's east entrance on the South Rim.

North Rim Visitor Center is open from 8am to 6pm and is located at the Bright Angel Peninsula.

Places to See and Things to Do

Trekking the Grand Canyon

Backpacking, camping, and trekking are the most popular outdoor recreation activities in the Grand Canyon. Popular outdoor sites and destinations in the park are: Desert View Campground, Mather Campground, Trailer Village in South Rim, and North Rim Campground located on the North Rim of Grand Canyon. There are several museums and theaters located inside and near the park. For more information about the parks, seasonal activities, and facilities contact the Grand Canyon National Park Visitor Information Center.

Accommodations

Inside Grand Canyon National Park

AMFAC Parks & Resorts handles the majority of hotel bookings inside the Grand Canyon, call Tel: (928) 638-2631 or Tel: (303) 297-2757. Visitors should book well in advance, especially during the summer months.

Outside Grand Canyon National Park

Grand Canyon Holiday Inn Express located in Highway 64, Grand Canyon, AZ 86023 Tel: (520) 638-3000. **Grand Canyon Quality Inn** located in Highway 64, Grand Canyon, AZ 86023 Tel: (520) 638-2673. **Best Western Grand Canyon Squire Inn** located in US 180 & Az 64, Grand Canyon, AZ 86023, Tel: (520) 638-2681. **Grand Hotel** located in State Highway 64, Grand Canyon, AZ 86023 Tel: (520) 638-3333. **Moqui Lodge-South Rim** located in Highway 64, Grand Canyon, AZ 86023 Tel: (520) 638-2424. **Roadway Inn** located in Highway 64, Grand Canyon, AZ 86023 Tel: (520) 638-2414.

All Aboard!

Flagstaff (AZ)

Flagstaff is located in north central Arizona, 116 miles north of Phoenix the state capital. Flagstaff has a land area of 63.5 sq. miles (163 sq. kilometers) and population of more than 45,000. Flagstaff was founded on July 4, 1876 as a post for travelers. In 1891 Flagstaff became the county seat of Coconino County and was incorporated as a city in 1928.

Places of interest: Flagstaff is one of the two gateways to the south rim of the Grand Canyon. The city is home to various transportation services serving the national park; Coconino National Forest is well accessible from Flagstaff. Other sites include the Museum of Northern Arizona, Lowell Observatory located in downtown Flagstaff, the Sunset Crater Volcano National Monument located 15 miles north of Flagstaff off Highway 89, and the Meteor Crater located just 35 miles east of Flagstaff off I-40.

Flagstaff's train depot is located at 1 E. Santa Fe Ave. Flagstaff, AZ 86001. The station is staffed and features an enclosed waiting area, checked baggage service, restrooms, payphones, and vending machines. Transportation options from the station include rental car service and local taxi service.

Flagstaff station is served by the Southwest Chief.

Winslow (AZ)

Winslow is located along the famous Route 66 (Interstate 40). Sitting at 4,856 feet above sea level, Winslow has a land area of 11.7 sq. miles (30 sq. kilometers) and population of approximately 12,000. Visit the Old Trails Historical Museum Tel: (928) 289-5861 located in downtown Winslow's business district which exhibits Route 66 memorabilia.

Winslow's train depot is located at E. 2nd St. Winslow, AZ 86047. The station is un-staffed and features an enclosed waiting area, restrooms, and payphones.

Winslow station is served by the Southwest Chief.

New Mexico (NM)

Capital: Santa Fe (Population: 1,819,046)
Size: 121,365 sq mi. (314,334 sq km)
Nickname: The Land of Enchantment
Joined the union on: January 6, 1912 (47th state)
Motto: It Grows As It Goes
Flower: Yucca
Bird: Roadrunner
Song: O Fair New Mexico and Asi es Nuevo Mexico
Famous for: Ancient Pueblo, Santa Fe, the first Atomic Bomb
Major industries: Research and development (energy, nuclear, solar and geothermal), chemicals, food products, equipments, livestock, agriculture and tourism.

Gallup (NM)

Gallup is located in northwestern New Mexico, just 25 miles from the Arizona state border and 173 miles west of Albuquerque. Sitting at 6,515 feet above sea level, it has a land area of 11 sq. miles (28.5 sq. kilometers) and a population of more than 19,000.

Gallup's train depot is located at 210 East Hwy. 66 Gallup, NM 87301. The station is un-staffed and features an enclosed waiting area, restrooms, and payphones. Transportation from the station is local taxi service.

Gallup station is served by the Southwest Chief.

Albuquerque (NM)

Albuquerque is located in north-central New Mexico 54 miles southwest of Santa Fe, the state capital. Albuquerque has a land area of 133 sq. miles (342 sq. kilometers) and population of approximately 385,000. Native American Indians first inhabited Albuquerque thousands of years ago.

The Spanish arrived in the area in the mid 1500's; years later the first flocks of Spanish settlers arrived and inhabited the area. The site was first named Bosque Grande de San Francisco Xavier. Until in 1706, a permanent settlement was established and the site was named Albuquerque after the Duke of Albuquerque. In 1885 Albuquerque was incorporated as a town and again as a city in 1889. Albuquerque is on the famous "Route 66."

Getting Around

Airport

Albuquerque International Sunport, PO Box 9948, Albuquerque, New Mexico 87119 Tel: (505) 244-7700, is located 4 miles (6.5 kilometers) southeast of central Albuquerque. Major car rental companies serve the airport; there is a shuttle van that picks-up and brings customers to the car rental company outside but near the airport. The shuttle is located on the first level of the terminal building. Local taxi and bus services are also available at the airport.

Bus

City of Albuquerque Transit Department, 100 1st Street, SW Albuquerque, NM 87102 Tel: (505) 843-9200, serves the city of Albuquerque and the outlying areas. Basic fare is $1, ask for passes and discount fare information.

Taxi

Yellow-Checker Cab, 500 Kinley NE, Albuquerque, NM 87102 Tel: (505) 842-5292. Albuquerque Cab Company, 3223 Los Arboles NE Albuquerque, NM 87107 Tel: (505) 883-4888.

Rent-A-Car

Alamo Rent A Car, toll-free (800) 462-5266 or Tel: (505) 842-4057; Avis Rent A Car, Tel: (505) 842-4080; Budget Car & Truck Rental, Tel: (505) 344-7196.

Train and Commuter

Albuquerque's train depot is located at 214 First St. S.W. Albuquerque, NM 87102. The station is staffed and features an enclosed waiting area, checked baggage service, restrooms, payphones, and vending machines. Transportation options from the station include rental car service, local transit, bus, and taxi services.

Albuquerque station is served by the Southwest Chief.

Visitors Information Center

Albuquerque Visitor Information Center, located in Downtown in Albuquerque Convention Center's East Complex, Lower Level at 401 2nd St NW 87102 toll-free (800) 284-2282.

Albuquerque Visitor Information Center, Old Town Information Center, located on Plaza Don Luis on Romero NW, across from the San Felipe de Neri church.

Places to See and Things to Do

If you are visiting Albuquerque during the month of October you might have a chance of seeing the **Kodak International Balloon Fiesta.**

Telephone Pioneers of America Museum is located at 201 Third St., rm. 710 Albuquerque, New Mexico Tel: (505) 245-5883. **NM Museum of Natural History & Science,** located at 1801 Mountain Rd NW, Albuquerque 87104 Tel: (505) 841-2800, exhibits dinosaur fossils and more. **Science Center and Children's Museum of Albuquerque** is located at 2100 Louisiana NE #98, Albuquerque 87110 Tel: (505) 842-1537.

Indian Pueblo Cultural Center, located at 2401 12th St NW, Albuquerque 87104 Tel: (505) 843-7270, houses a museum and shops, and on weekends there are native Indian dances and craft demonstrations. **National Hispanic Cultural Center,** located at 1701 4th Street SW, Albuquerque 87102 Tel: (505) 246-2261, exhibits art and houses a library and genealogy center. **Doll Museum & Shoppe** located at 5201 Constitution Ave NE, Albuquerque 87110 Tel: (505) 255-8555 exhibits antique & modern dolls.

LodeStar Astronomy Center, located at 1801 Mountain Rd NW, Albuquerque 87104 Tel: (505) 841-5985, features a motion simulator, observatory, and more. **Museum of Archaeology & Biblical History** located at 10110 Constitution NE, Albuquerque 87112 Tel: (505) 332-4253. **National Atomic Museum** of Albuquerque Tel: (505) 284-3243 exhibits aircraft, weaponry, and houses a science museum. **New Mexico Holocaust & Intolerance Museum & Study Center** is located at 415 Central Ave NW, Albuquerque 87102 Tel: (505) 247-0606. **Tinkertown Museum,** 121 Sandia Crest Road, Sandia Park 87047 Tel: (505) 281-5233 features works of New Mexico's Ross Ward. **Albuquerque Museum of Art & History** located at 2000 Mountain Rd NW, Albuquerque 87104 Tel: (505) 243-7255. **American International Rattlesnake Museum** located in Old Town at 202 San Felipe NW Ste A, Albuquerque 87104 Tel: (505) 242-6569.

Turquoise Museum, located at 2107 Central NW, Albuquerque 87104 Tel: (505) 247-8650, exhibits rare turquoise from different parts of the world. **Albuquerque Aquarium** is located at 2601 Central Ave NW, Albuquerque 87104 Tel: (505) 764-6200. The aquarium is home to hundreds of marine creatures, it features a water tunnel, coral reef, shark tank, and many more. **Rio Grande Zoo,** located at 903 Tenth St SW, Albuquerque 87102 Tel: (505) 764-6200, is home to more than 1,000 exotic animals.

Sandia Lakes Recreation Area, located at 11143 Hwy 85 NW, Alb 87114 Tel: (505) 897-3971, offers outdoor recreation facilities and activities. **Rio Grande Nature Center,** located

View from the train, New Mexico

at 2901 Candelaria NW, Albuquerque 87107 Tel: (505) 344-7240, has 2 miles of trails. **Rio Grande Botanic Garden** is located at 2601 Central Ave. NW, Albuquerque 87104 Tel: (505) 764-6200.

Ballooning

Albuquerque Sweet Escape Balloon Rides, Tel: (505) 891-7634, offers balloon rides.

Amusement Park

Beach Water Park, located at 1600 Desert Surf Lp, Albuquerque 87107 Tel: (505) 345-6066, features water slides, pools, a lazy river, and more. **Clift's Amusement Park,** located at 4800 Osuna NE, Albuquerque 87109 Tel: (505) 881-9373, features rides and water attractions.

Native American Centers

Pueblo of Jemez-Dept of Tourism located at 7413 Highway 4, Jemez Pueblo 87024 Tel: (505) 834-7235 features gift shops, a museum, and native Indian arts.

Spas

Cascade Gardens Spa & Wellness Center, located at 3107 Eubank NE Suite 1, Albuquerque 87111 Tel: (505) 332-0848.

Train Rides

Cumbres & Toltec Scenic Railroad, 500 Terrace Ave, NM 17, Chama 87520 Tel: (505) 756-2151 offers an exiting 64-mile steam locomotive train tour around the scenic railroad of northern New Mexico, highly recommended! **Santa Fe Southern Railway**, 410 S Guadalupe, Santa Fe 87501 Tel: (505) 989-8600 offers old west train trips around the region. **Durango & Silverton Narrow Gauge RR & Museum**, 479 Main Ave, Durango 81301 Tel: (970) 247-2733 offers scenic mountain tours.

Wineries/Vineyards

Gruet Winery, located at 8400 Pan American Frwy NE, Albuquerque 87113 Tel: (505) 821-0055, is known as one of the best white wine producers in the world.

Accommodations:

Holiday Inn Express Airport located at 2331 Centre SE, Albuquerque 87106 Tel: (505) 247-1500. **Comfort Inn** located at Albuquerque Airport, 2300 Yale SE, Albuquerque 87106 Tel: (505) 243-2244. **Wyndham Albuquerque Hotel** located at 2910 Yale SE, Albuquerque 87106 Tel: (505) 843-7000. **Hampton Inn** – Airport located at 2231 Yale SE, Albuquerque 87106 Tel: (505) 246-2255.

Courtyard by Marriott located at Airport, 1920 Yale Blvd SE, Albuquerque 87106 Tel: (505) 843-6600. **Route 66 Hostel** located at 1012 Central SW, Albuquerque 87102 Tel: (505) 247-1813. **Radisson Hotel** – Airport located at 1901 University SE, Albuquerque 87106 Tel: (505) 247-0512. **Best Western Airport Inn** located at 2400 Yale SE, Albuquerque 87106 Tel: (505) 242-7022.

Downtown Area

Downtown Inn located at 1213 Central Ave NW, Albuquerque 87102 Tel: (505) 247-1061. **Double Tree Hotel** – Albuquerque located at 201 Marquette NW, Albuquerque 87102 Tel: (505) 247-3344. **Hyatt Regency Albuquerque** located at 330 Tijeras NW, Albuquerque 87102 Tel: (505) 842-1234. **Econo Lodge Downtown** located at 817 Central NE, Albuquerque 87102 Tel: (505) 243-1321.

Old Town Area

El Vado Motel located at 2500 Central SW, Albuquerque 87104 Tel: (505) 243-4594. **Econo Lodge Old Town** located at 2321 Central NW, Albuquerque 87104 Tel: (505) 243-8475. **Sheraton Old Town** located at 800 Rio Grande Blvd NW, Albuquerque 87104 Tel: (505) 843-6300. **Monterey Non-Smokers Motel** located at 2402 Central SW, Albuquerque 87104 Tel: (505) 243-3554.

New Mexico (NM)

Capital: Santa Fe (Population: 1,819,046)
Size: 121,365 sq mi. (314,334 sq km)
Nickname: The Land of Enchantment
Joined the union on: January 6, 1912 (47th state)
Motto: It Grows As It Goes
Flower: Yucca
Bird: Roadrunner
Song: O Fair New Mexico and Asi es Nuevo Mexico
Famous for: Ancient Pueblo, Santa Fe, the first Atomic Bomb
Major industries: Research and development (energy, nuclear, solar and geothermal), chemicals, food products, equipments, livestock, agriculture and tourism.

Lamy (NM)

Lamy's train depot is located on County Rd. 41-ctr of Town Lamy, NM 87540. The station is staffed and features an enclosed waiting area, restrooms, and payphones. Transportation from the station is local taxi service.

Lamy station is served by the Southwest Chief.

Las Vegas (NM)

Part of Santa Fe Train, Las Vegas is located at the foot of the Sangre de Cristo Mountains 132 miles east of Albuquerque the state capital. Originally named Our Lady of the Sorrows of the Great Meadows (not to be mistaken as the famous city of Las Vegas, Nevada), Las Vegas has a land area of 7.4 sq. miles (19 sq. kilometers) and population of approximately 17,000. The Las Vegas City Museum and Rough Riders Memorial Collection located at 725 Grand Avenue Las Vegas, New Mexico 87701 and the Fort Union National Monument located 25 miles north of Las Vegas off I-25.

Las Vegas' train depot is located on Railroad and Lincoln Sts. Las Vegas, NM 87701. The station is un-staffed and features an enclosed waiting area, restrooms, and payphones. Transportation from the station is local taxi service.

Las Vegas station is served by the Southwest Chief.

Raton (NM)

Raton is located in the northeastern region of New Mexico, near the state border of Colorado. Known as New Mexico's northern gateway, Raton sits at 6,920 feet above sea level. It has a land area of 7 sq. miles (18 sq. kilometers) and population of roughly 8,000. Places of interest: Raton Museum located at 216 S 1st St Raton, NM 87740 Tel: (505) 445-8979, and the Raton Pass at the Historic Santa Fe Trail. The train will pass through the thrilling Raton Pass Tunnel.

Raton's train depot is located at 201 S. 1st St. Raton, NM 87740. The station is un-staffed and features an enclosed waiting area, restrooms, payphones, and vending machines. Transportation from the station is local taxi service.

Raton station is served by the Southwest Chief.

Colorado (CO)
Capital: Denver (Population: 4,301,261)
Size: 103,730 sq mi. (268,660 sq km)
Nickname: The Centennial State
Joined the union on: August 1, 1876 (38th state)
Motto: Nothing Without Providence
Flower: Rocky Mountain Columbine
Bird: Lark Bunting
Song: "Where the Columbines Grow"
Famous for: Skiing, Rocky Mountains
Major industries: Tourism, agriculture, and publication

Trinidad (CO)

Trinidad is located in southern Colorado near the New Mexico state border just 23 miles north of Raton. Trinidad has a land area of 4.2 sq. miles (11 sq. kilometers) and population of approximately 9,000.

Trinidad's train depot is located on Pine St. Trinidad, CO 81082. The station is un-staffed and features an enclosed waiting area, restrooms, payphones, and a restaurant. Transportation from the station is local taxi service.

Trinidad station is served by the Southwest Chief.

La Junta (CO)

La Junta (Spanish word meaning "junction") is located in Southeast Colorado and was founded in 1875 as a stop on the Santa Fe Railroad. The city was incorporated in 1881 with a land area of 2.6 sq. miles (6.7 sq. kilometers). Today's population is approximately 12,000.

La Junta's train depot is located at 1st and Colorado Sts. La Junta, CO 81050. The station is staffed and features an enclosed waiting area, checked baggage service, restrooms, payphones, and vending machines.

La Junta station is served by the Southwest Chief.

233

Lamar (CO)

Lamar is located in southeast Colorado along the Arkansas River. Lamar has a land area of 4.1 sq. miles (10.7 sq. kilometers) and population of roughly 9,000.

Lamar's train depot is located at Main and Beech Sts. Lamar, CO 81052. The station is unstaffed and features an enclosed waiting area, restrooms, and payphones.

Lamar station is served by the Southwest Chief.

Garden City (KS)

Garden City is located southwest of Kansas; it has a land area of 7.4 sq. miles (19 sq. kilometers) and population of more than 24,000.

Visit the "Big Pool," Garden city's prime local and tourist attraction. The Big Pool is about half a city block in size and holds 2.5 million gallons of water. Also located in the area is the Lee Richardson Zoo.

Garden City's train depot is located at South 7th St. Garden City, KS 67846. The station is staffed and features an enclosed waiting area, checked baggage service, restrooms, payphones, and vending machines. Transportation from the station is local taxi service.

Garden City station is served by the Southwest Chief.

Dodge City (KS)

Dodge City is located in southwest Kansas and was founded in 1872. Dodge City was known by many nicknames since the city's foundation: it was called Cowboy Capital, Beautiful Bibulous Babylon of the Frontier, Wickedest Little City in America, and Buffalo Capital of the World. Dodge City has a land area of 12 sq. miles (31 sq. kilometers) and population of approximately 22,000.

Places of interest: Take the **Dodge City Trolley,** departing from Third and W Wyatt Earp Blvd; **Marchel Ranch** features live buffalo and more, located at Western Entertainment Facility, for Reservations Tel: (620) 227-7307; and the **Boot Hill Museum and Front Street** located at Front Street & Fifth Street Tel: (620) 227-8188. The **Home of Stone,** located at 112 E Vine Tel: (620) 225-8186, one of the best examples of the 1800's Dodge City.

Santa Fe Trail Tracks, located 9 miles West of Dodge on HWY 50, is listed on the National Register of Historic Sites and features the largest continuous wagon trail tracks of the pioneers still visible along the entire route of the trail. **Carnegie Center for the Arts,** located at 701 Second Tel: (620) 225-6388, is listed on the National Register of Historic Sites. **Kansas Teachers' Hall of Fame** located at 603 Fifth Tel: (620) 225-7311, the hall also houses the **Gunfighters Wax Museum.**

Dodge City's train depot is located at Central and Wyatt Earp Sts. Dodge City, KS 67801. The station is un-staffed and features an enclosed waiting area, restrooms, and payphones. Transportation from the station is local transit.

Dodge City station is served by the Southwest Chief.

Hutchison (KS)

Hutchinson is located in south central Kansas southwest of Wichita. Hutchison has a land area of 21 sq. miles (53 sq. kilometers) and population of approximately 40,000.

Places of interest: the Dillon Nature Center, 3002 East 30th Hutchinson, Kansas Tel: (316) 663-7411, is a national nature sanctuary. The Hutchinson Art Center is located at 405 North Washington Hutchinson, Kansas 67501 Tel: (316) 663-1081, the Kansas Cosmosphere and Space Center is located at 1100 N. Plum Hutchinson, KS 67501 Tel: (316) 662-2305, and the Hutchinson Zoo is located at 600 East Blanchard at Carey Park Tel: (316) 694-2693.

Hutchison's train depot is located at 3rd and Walnut Sts. Hutchinson, KS 67501. The station is un-staffed and features an enclosed waiting area and restrooms. Transportation from the station is local taxi service.

Hutchison station is served by the Southwest Chief.

Kansas (KS)

Capital: Topeka (Population: 2,688,418)
Size: 81,823 sq mi. (211,922 sq km)
Nickname: Sunflower State, the Breadbasket of America
Joined the union on: January 29, 1861 (34th state)
Motto: To the stars through difficulties
Flower: Sunflower
Bird: Western Meadowlark
Song: Home on the Range
Famous for: Turkey Red Wheat, Walter Chrysler
Major industries: Agriculture, farming, Aircraft Manufacturing

Newton (KS)

Newton is located in south central Kansas north of Wichita. The city was named after the town of Newton Massachusetts in 1871. Newton has a land area of 7.8 sq. miles (20 sq. kilometers) and population of more than 17,000.

Newton's train depot is located at 414 North Main St. Newton, KS 67114. The station is staffed and features an enclosed waiting area, checked baggage service, restrooms, payphones, and vending machines. Transportation from the station is local taxi service.

Newton station is served by the Southwest Chief.

Topeka (KS)

Topeka is located in northeast Kansas near the geographic center of the United States. Topeka is the state capital of Kansas; it has a land area of 55 sq. miles (142 sq. kilometers) and population of approximately 127,000. Topeka was home to vice president Charles Curtis, the only Native American vice president. Settlers from Lawrence and New England founded Topeka in 1854.

Getting Around

Bus

Topeka Metropolitan Transit Authority, 201 North Kansas Avenue Topeka, KS 66603 Tel: (913) 233-2011, serves the city and the outlying areas.

Train and Commuter

Topeka's train depot is located at 5th and Holliday Sts. Topeka, KS 66607. The station is staffed and features an enclosed waiting area, checked baggage service, restrooms, and payphones. Transportation from the station is local taxi service.

Topeka station is served by the Southwest Chief.

Visitor Information Center

Topeka Convention & Visitors Bureau, 1275 SW Topeka Boulevard Topeka, Kansas 66612 Tel: (785) 234-1030 or toll-free (800) 235-1030.

Places to See and Things to Do

The **Kansas State Capitol** is located in downtown at 10th and Jackson Topeka, KS 66612 Tel: (785) 296-3966. The 1908 **Carousel in the Park/Mini-Train** is located at 635 SW Gage Blvd. Parks & Recreation of Topeka Topeka, KS 66603 Tel: (785) 273-1191. **Historic Ward-Meade Park,** located at 124 N.W. Fillmore Topeka, Kansas Tel: (785) 368-3888, is the best example of the early days of Kansas. The park houses a Victorian mansion, botanical gardens, and more. The man-made **Lake Shawnee Recreational Area** located at 3137 SE 29th Topeka, KS Tel: (785) 267-1156 is famous for water recreation, walking trails, and other outdoor activities.

The Topeka Symphony, located at 727 S. Kansas Ave. Topeka, Kansas Tel: (785) 232-2032, features various performances each seasons. **Metropolitan Ballet of Topeka** located at 4013 SW 21st Topeka, Kansas Tel: (785) 271-0190.

Listed on the National Register of Historic Places, **Cedar Crest,** located at One Cedar Crest Rd. (I-70 & Fairlawn Rd.) Topeka, KS 66601 Tel: (785) 296-3636, is residence to the governor of Kansas. **Curtis House,** located at 11th and Topeka Blvd. Topeka, KS 66612 Tel: (785) 357-1371, is home of the only Native American vice president. **Kansas Center for Historical Research** located at 6425 SW 6th Topeka, KS 66615 Tel: (785) 272-8681, ext. 116 or 117 features one of the largest collections of research materials of different disciplines in the US.

Combat Air Museum, located in Forbes Field P.O. Box 19142 Topeka, KS 66619 Tel: (785) 862-3303, exhibits aviation memorabilia, weaponry, military vehicles, and aircraft. **Kansas National Guard Museum** is located in Forbes Field, 6700 SW Topeka Blvd, Building 301 Topeka, KS Tel: (785) 862-1020; the museum also features a library, an archives, and shops.

Kansas Museum of History, located at 6425 SW 6ᵗʰ Topeka, KS 66615-1099 Tel: (785) 272-8681, features the history of Kansas presented in various media. **Mulvane Art Museum,** located on the campus of Washburn University at 17th and Jewell Topeka, KS 66621 Tel: (785) 231-1124, exhibits an extensive collection of arts and written works from the region. **Topeka Zoological Park** located at 635 SW Gage Blvd. Topeka, KS 66606 Tel: (785) 272-5821 is home to 400 animals.

Accommodations

Comfort Inn located at 1518 SW Wanamaker Rd. Topeka, KS 66604 toll-free (800) 228-5150. **Courtyard by Marriott** located at 2033 SW Wanamaker Rd. Topeka, KS 66604 toll-free (800) 228-2800. **Best Western Candlelight Inn** located at 2831 SW Fairlawn Topeka, KS 66614 toll-free (800) 223-8892. **Fairfield Inn by Marriott,** 1530 SW Westport Rd. Topeka, KS 66604 toll-free (800) 228-2800. **Regency Inn by Marriott** located at 3802 SW Topeka Blvd. Topeka, KS 66609 Tel: (785) 266-5525. **Best Western Topeka Inn & Suites** located at 700 SW Fairlawn Rd. Topeka, KS 66606 toll-free (800) 877-9TOPEKA. **Holiday Inn Express & Suites** located at 901 SW Robinson Topeka, KS 66606 toll-free (800) HOLIDAY.

Lawrence (KS)

Missouri (MO)
Capital: Jefferson City (Population: 5,595,211)
Size: 69,709 sq mi. (180,546 sq km)
Nickname: The Show-me State
Joined the union on: August 10, 1821 (24th state)
Motto: The welfare of the people shall be the supreme law
Flower: Hawthorn
Bird: Bluebird
Song: Missouri Waltz
Famous for: The Arc of St. Louis, the beer (Budweiser) and the cynicism ("show me")
Major industries: Automobile and parts manufacturing, beer, and defense and aerospace technology research and development

Lawrence is located in northeastern Kansas, halfway between Topeka and Kansas City. Lawrence has a land area of 21 sq. miles (59.4 sq. kilometers) and population of approximately 80,000. Lawrence was founded in 1854 and is home to Kansas University which was founded in 1864.

Lawrence's train depot is located at 413 E. 7th St. Lawrence, KS 66044. The station is un-staffed and features payphones and vending machines. Transportation from the station is local taxi service.

Lawrence station is served by the Southwest Chief.

Kansas City (KS) (MO) See Illinois and Missouri service, page 290.

Connecting train to **Jefferson City (MO)**, **St. Louis (MO)** and **Chicago (IL)** through Illinois and Missouri Routes

La Plata (MO)

La Plata is located in northeastern Missouri near the Iowa state border. La Plata has a land area of 1.1 sq. miles (3 sq. kilometers) and population of roughly 2,000.

La Plata's train depot is located on Rural Rte. 1 La Plata, MO 63549. The station is un-staffed and features an enclosed waiting area, restrooms, and payphones.

La Plata station is served by the Southwest Chief.

Fort Madison (IA)

Fort Madison is located in southeast Iowa at the bank of the Mississippi River. Fort Madison has a land area of 9.3 sq. miles (24 sq. kilometers) and population of more than 12,000.

Places of interest: Fort Madison Art Center 613 Ave. G Tel: (319) 372-3996, and the historic Old Fort Madison located in River View Park Tel: (319) 372-6318. The North Lee County Historical Center located at 814 10th St. Tel: (319) 372-7661 exhibits civil war memorabilia, arrowhead displays, and much more. The Western Railroad, located off Highway 2 between Fort Madison and Donnellson, IA Tel: (319) 837-6689, and the 1909 Old Santa Fe Depot Tel: (319) 372-6318 are listed on the National Register of Historic Places and feature train memorabilia.

Fort Madison's train depot is located at 1601 20th St. Fort Madison, IA 52627. The station is staffed and features an enclosed waiting area, restrooms, payphones, and vending machines.

Fort Madison station is served by the Southwest Chief.

Galesburg (IL)

Galesburg is linked to the **Texas Eagle routes** through Motor coach Throughway Connections.

Historic Galesburg, also known as "America's Small Town and Rail City," is located in prairie land of west-central Illinois. Founded by George W. Gale in 1837, Galesburg became the first anti-slavery town in the state of Illinois. In addition, Galesburg was part of the "underground railroad" network that saved hundreds of Black Americans from slavery.

Galesburg has a land area of 17 sq. miles (44 sq. kilometers) and a population of more than 35,000. Galesburg is a lovely city full of history; visitors should visit Seminary Street Historic Commercial District, a restored historical downtown area which takes visitors back to the old Midwest era. Also in Galesburg's Downtown District there are many shops, restaurants, and entertainment sites.

Local Transportation

Local Bus

Burlington Trailways Tel: (309) 342-6715, and City Bus Co, Tel: (309) 342-4242.

Taxi

Courtesy Cab, Tel: (309) 341-1077 and City Cab, Tel: (309) 341-6161.

Rent-a-Car

Louis Lakis Ford Car Rental, Tel: (309) 342-1121, Avis Rent A Car, toll-free (800) 230-4898, and Enterprise Rent-A-Car, toll-free (800) RENT-A-CAR.

Train

Galesburg's train depot is located at 225 S. Seminary St. Galesburg, IL 61401. The train station is staffed and features an enclosed waiting area, restrooms, payphones, and vending machines. Trains serving Galesburg station are the California Zephyr, Midwest Corridor, and the Southwest Chief.

Priceton (IL) See Illinois Zephyr service, page 295-297

Mendota (IL) See Illinois Zephyr service, page 295-297

Chicago (IL) See Illinois and Missouri service, page 268

	Sunset Limited	
10 30 pm-D	**Los Angeles, CA**	8 05 am-A
11 22 pm	Pomona, CA	4 18 am
11 37 pm	Ontario, CA	4 08 am
1 04 am	**Palm Springs, CA**	2 38 am
4 19 am	Yuma, AZ	1 25 am
6 57 am	Maricopa, AZ	10 50 pm
9 10 am	Tuczon, AZ	9 29 pm
10 07 am	Benson, AZ	7 35 pm
12 50 pm	Lordsburg, NM	5 31pm
12 57 pm	Deming, NM	4 37 pm
3 01 pm-A 3 21 pm-D	El Passo, TX	3 07 pm-D 2 20 pm-A
8 06 pm	Alpine, TX	11 03 am
9 57 pm	Sanderson, TX	9 10 am
12 23 am	Del Rio, TX	6 35 am
4 11 am-A 5 25 am-D	**San Antonio, TX**	3 40 am-D 2 50 am-A
10 10 am-A 10 28 am-D	**Houston, TX**	10 00 pm-D 9 38 pm-A
12 13 pm	Beaumont, TX	7 08 pm
1 37 pm	Lake Charles, LA	5 43 pm
3 08 pm	Lafayette, LA	4 12 pm
3 34 pm	New Iberia, LA	3 45 pm
4 55 pm	Schriever, LA	2 19 pm
7 25 pm-A 10 30 pm-D	**New Orleans, LA**	12 45 pm-D 9 20 am-A
11 55 pm	Bay St. Louis, MS	6 28 am
12 23 am	Gulfport, MS	5 56 am
12 46 am	Biloxi, MS	5 33 am
1 21 am	Pascagoula, MS	5 03 am
2 20 am	Mobile, AL	4 10 am
3 26 am	Atmore, AL	300 am
6 15 am-A 6 30 am-D	Pensacola, FL	1 20 am-D 1 05 am-A
7 40 am	Crestview, FL	11 17 pm
9 10 am	Chipley, FL	9 51 pm
12 32 pm	**Tallahassee, FL**	8 46 pm
1 59 pm	Madison, FL	7 03 pm
3 00 pm	Lake City, FL	6 04 pm
4 40 pm-A 5 00 pm-D	**Jacksonville, FL**	5 00 pm-D 4 45 pm-A
6 24 pm	Palatka, FL	3 12 pm
7 11 pm	De Land, FL	2 24 pm
7 36 pm	Sanford, FL	2 00 pm
8 05 pm	Winter Park, FL	1 33 pm
8 45 pm-A	**Orlando, FL**	1 15 pm-D

D-Departure   **A**-Arrival

Sunset Limited

The Sunset Limited is the longest intercontinental train route in the US. At more than 2,700 miles, it connects the cities of Los Angeles, San Antonio, Houston, New Orleans, Tallahassee, Jacksonville, and Orlando. This line travels some of the most beautiful scenery and natural wonder of the southern United States.

Routes Destination Highlights

Los Angeles, CA- The entertainment capital of the world, Los Angeles has everything to offer. Visit the famous Hollywood Walk of Fame, the Chinese Theater on Hollywood Blvd., Universal Studios, some of the best Museums in the US, explore Venice Beach, Long Beach, or simply shop at the Farmers Market.

Palm Springs, CA- Take the Palm Springs Aerial Tramway, the largest revolving aerial tramcars in the world, up 8,516-feet to the top of Mt. San Jacinto, or take the Celebrity Tours and see homes of many famous celebrities. Visit the Indian Canyons with large collections of natural fan palm, and the Living Desert, home for various exotic animals.

El Paso, TX- Take the Wyler Aerial Tramway, at 5,632-feet above sea level it offers breathtaking views of the surrounding areas and Mexico, see the beautiful Tiffany glass dome in Hilton Camino Real, the El Paso Holocaust Museum and Study, and the Border Patrol Museum features the history of US border Patrol.

San Antonio, TX- Visit the historical Alamo or take a romantic boat ride at the River walk. Take a short steam locomotive ride at the Railroad Miniature Railway, or take a stroll through the historic San Antonio Mission National Park. See a breathtaking view of San Antonio from the 750-foot Tower of America or visit "Shamu" at San Antonio's very own Sea World.

Houston, TX- Visit NASA's Johnson Space Center, or downtown Houston and explore many of the city's historical buildings and sites, Texas Avenue and the Tranquility Park, or visit the observation deck on the Chase Tower that offers a breathtaking view of the City of Houston, Houston Zoo, and Houston Museum of Natural Science. Visit nearby Galveston, one of Texas' prime coastal destinations.

New Orleans, LA- Visit the famous French Quarter, the French Market, the Mardi Gras Fountains, the Louisiana Superdome, and the Old U.S. Mint. Explore art galleries, antique shops, and restaurants on Magazine Street; see the famous Louisiana white alligator at the Audubon Zoological Gardens, the Aquarium of the Americas known as one of the best in the US, or be amazed at the New Orleans Historic Voodoo Museum. Take a fun and educational Cajun cooking lesson at Bayou Country's "Cookin' on the River," explore Mardi Gras World located near Algiers, or try your luck at the casinos.

Jacksonville, FL- Visit Jacksonville Historical Center and learn about the history of Jacksonville, see the Treaty Oak, the oldest living thing in Jacksonville and one of the oldest in the state of Florida, take a relaxing walk at the Riverwalk and visit the Friendship Park and Fountain, one of the largest in the world. Enjoy a romantic dinner with entertainment by taking a River Cruise, explore Big Talbot Island, and see the Mayport Lighthouse, American Lighthouse and Maritime Museum, or explore the historic St. Augustine district.

Orlando, FL- Explore some of the world's greatest theme parks, Walt Disney World, Universal Studios Florida, Sea World, Skull Kingdom, and Discovery Island, the world largest aviary, amongst others. See the Mennello Museum of American Folk Art, the Central Florida Railroad Museum, and the Kennedy Space Center, or sit and relax and be amazed by the world's most enchanting and artistic circus, the Cirque du Soleil.

Train Schedule

The Sunset Limited travels three times each week from Los Angeles, California to Orlando, Florida. The trip between the two cities takes approximately three and a half days of travel time.

Accommodations

Accommodations are Superliner Reserved Coach and Superliner Sleeping Car. There is a Sightseer Lounge Car serving local cuisine, snacks, sandwiches, soups, and drinks. Restaurant style meals are served in the Dining Car. Other amenities are movies, reading materials, games, and seasonal national park guide presentations.

All Aboard!

Los Angeles (CA) See Coast Starlight service, page 109.

241

Pomona (CA)

Pomona is located in the center of the Greater Los Angeles Basin, on the eastern-most border of Los Angeles County. Named after the Roman goddess of fruit, Pomona was incorporated in 1888. Pomona is the fifth largest city in the Los Angeles County, it has a land area of 14 square miles (36.7 sq. kilometers) and a population of 147,000.

Pomona's train depot is located at 156 W. Commercial St. Pomona, CA 91768. The station is un-staffed and features payphones. Transportation options from the station include local transit and taxi services.

Pomona station is served by the Sunset Limited and the Texas Eagle.

Ontario (CA)

Ontario is located in Western San Bernardino County, 40 miles east of Los Angeles and 20 miles west of San Bernardino. Ontario has a land area of 31.2 square miles (80 sq. kilometers) and population of 151,488.

Ontario's train depot is located at 228 S. Plum St. Ontario, CA 91764. The station is un-staffed and features payphones. Transportation from the station is local taxi service.

Trains serving Ontario station are the Sunset Limited and the Texas Eagle.

Palm Springs (CA)

Palm Springs is located at the western edge of the Coachella Valley, within the Colorado Desert, 120 miles southeast of Los Angeles and 120 miles northeast of San Diego. It has a land area of 51.8 square miles (133 sq. kilometers) and population of 45,000. Palm Springs is a popular winter destination mainly for the upper class vacationer and the Hollywood stars.

The site of what is now Palm Springs was first inhabited 10,000 years ago and the present descendant of the Agua Caliente Band of Cahuilla Indians are believed to have lived in the area for 2,000 years. The Spaniards arrived in the area in 1774, and the city of Palm Springs was incorporated in 1938.

Palm Springs enjoys 354 days of sunshine with less than 5.2 inches of rain, winter temperatures average in the 70s with nights in the mid-40s. The dry desert heat of summer pushes daytime temperatures into triple digits.

California (CA)
Capital: Sacramento (Population: 33,871,648)
Size: 163,707 sq mi. (424,001 sq km)
Nicknames: The Golden State
Joined the union on: September 9, 1850 (31st state)
Motto: Eureka (I Have Found It)
Flower: Golden Poppy
Bird: California Valley Quail
Song: "I Love You, California"
Famous for: Golden Gate Bridge, Hollywood, Yosemite Valley
Major industries: Manufacturing, Agriculture, Biotechnology, Software and Tourism

Getting Around

Airport

Palm Springs International Airport is located at 3400 East Tahquitz Canyon Way Palm Springs CA 92262 Tel: (760) 318-3800; it connects the city of Palm Springs to the rest of North America and the Pacific region.

Bus

Sun Bus serves downtown Palm Springs and valley Tel: (760) 343-3451 and Greyhound Tel: (760) 325-2053 connects Palm Springs to the rest of the country.

Taxi

VIP Express Taxi Tel: (760) 322-2264, Ace Taxi Tel: (760) 321-6008, Classic Cab Tel: (760) 322-3111, Mirage Taxi Tel: (760) 322-2008, Yellow Cab of the Desert Tel: (760) 345-8398.

Rent-A-Car

Rent-A-Wreck Tel: (760) 773-0755, Alamo Tel: (760) 778-6271, Dollar Airport Tel: (760) 325-7333, Eagle Rider Motorcycle Rentals Tel: (760) 251-5990, Budget Airport Tel: (760) 778-1960, Aztec Rent-a Car & Truck Tel: (760) 325-2294, Avis Tel: (760) 778-6300, National Airport Tel: (760) 327-1438, Hertz Airport Tel: (760) 778-5100 and Foxy Wheels Car Rental Tel: (760) 321-1234.

Train and Commuter

Palm Springs' train depot is located at Indian Canyon Dr and I-10 Palm Springs, CA 92262. The station is un-staffed and features restrooms and payphones.

Palm Springs station is served by the Sunset Limited.

Visitor Information Center

Palm Springs Desert Resorts Convention and Visitors Bureau, 69-930 Highway 111 Rancho Mirage, CA 92270 Tel: (760) 770-9000 or toll-free (800) 967-3767.

Official Palm Springs Visitors Information Center, 2781 North Palm Canyon Drive, Palm Springs, CA 92262 toll-free (800) 347-7746.

Places to See and Things to Do

Palm Springs Aerial Tramway takes passengers from the Valley Station to Mountain Station in Mt. San Jacinto State Park and Wilderness. The tram features the largest revolving aerial tramcars in the world transporting visitors up to 8,516-feet at the top of Mt. San Jacinto. The state park is popular for hiking, cross-country skiing, and other outdoor activities. Tramway fee is $20, call Tel: (760) 325-4227 for information. **Celebrity Tours,**

Palm Springs is home to many famous celebrities; for celebrity tour maps and information consult the Visitors Information Center or call Tel: (760) 770-2700.

Agua Caliente Cultural Museum is located at 960 E. Tahquitz Canyon Way 101 Palm Springs CA 92262 Tel: (760) 778-1079. **Palm Springs Desert Museum**, located at 101 Museum Drive Palm Springs CA 92262 Tel: (760) 325-7186, exhibits permanent collections of western American arts. **General Patton Memorial Museum** is located at 62510 Chiriaco Road Chiriaco Summit CA 92201 Tel: (760) 227-3483.

Indian Canyons is located at Agua Caliente Band at the end of South Palm Canyon Drive Tel: (760) 325-3400. The canyon features the largest natural fan palm oases, popular outdoor destinations. **The Living Desert** is located at 47-900 Portola Avenue Palm Desert CA 92260 Tel: (760) 346-5694. The park houses a botanical garden, zoo, and offers interpretive tours. **Palm Springs Air Museum** located at 745 N. Gene Autry Trail, Palm Springs CA 92262 Tel: (760) 778-6262, exhibits WWII fighter planes. **Children's Discovery Museum** is located at 71-701 Gerald Ford Drive Rancho Mirage CA 92270 Tel: (760) 321-0602.

Accommodations

Oasis Villa Resort Hotel located at 4190 E. Palm Canyon Dr. Palm Springs, CA 92264-5200 Tel: (760) 328-1499. **Orbit Inn** located at 562 W. Arenas Palm Springs, CA 92262 Tel: (760) 323-3585. **Andalusian Court** located at 458 West Arenas Palm Springs, CA 92262 toll-free (888) 947-6667. **Casa Cody B & B Country Inn** located at 175 South Cahuilla Road Palm Springs, California 92262 toll-free (800) 231-2639. **Terra Cotta Inn Resort & Spa** located at 2388 East Racquet Club Road Palm Springs, California 92262 toll-free (800) 786-6938.

Alpine Gardens Hotel (Gay Friendly) located at 1586 East Palm Canyon Drive Palm Springs CA, 92264 Tel: (760) 323-2231 or toll-free (888) 299-7455. **Casitas Laquita** (Lesbian Friendly) located at 450 East Palm Canyon Drive Palm Springs, California 92264 Tel: (760) 416-9999. **Palm Court Inn** located at 1983 North Palm Canyon Drive Palm Springs, CA 92264 toll-free (800) 667-7918.

A Place in the Sun located at 754 San Lorenzo Road Palm Springs, California 92264 toll-free (800) 779-2254. **Palm Court Inn** located at 1983 N. Palm Canyon Dr. Palm Springs, CA 92264-2919 Tel: (760) 416-2333. **The Nurturing Nest** located at 11149 Sunset Ave. Desert Hot Springs, CA 92240 Tel: (760) 251-2583.

The Willows Historic Palm Springs Inn located at 412 West Tahquitz Canyon Way Palm Springs, CA 92262 toll-free (800) 966-9597. **The Palms at Palm Springs** located at 572 N. Indian Canyon Palm Springs, CA 92262-6030 Tel: (760) 325-1111 **Palm Garden Resort** located at 950 N. Indian Canyon Dr. Palm Springs, CA 92262-2919 Tel: (760) 323-1328. **Ocotillo Lodge** located at 1111 E. Palm Canyon Dr. Palm Springs, CA 92264 Tel: (760) 416-0678.

Arizona (AZ)
Capital: Phoenix (Population: 5,130,632)
Size: 113,642 sq mi. (296,400 sq km)
Nickname: The Grand Canyon State
Joined the union on: February 14, 1912 (48th state)
Motto: Ditat Deus (God Enriches)
Flower: Flower of the saguaro cactus
Bird: Cactus Wren
Song: "Arizona March Song"
Famous for: The Grand Canyon
Major industries: Tourism, Agriculture, Copper, Manufacturing

Yuma (AZ)

Yuma is located in the southwestern corner of Arizona near the borders of California and Mexico. Famous for the Sand Dunes located in west Yuma, it is a popular destination for desert outdoor enthusiasts and movie productions. The dune is visible from the train after crossing the Colorado River from California. Yuma was known by a few other names such as Colorado City and Arizona City; it wasn't until 1873 that the site got its present name Yuma, named after the Yuma Indians who lived in the area for many years. Yuma is home to approximately 77,500 residents.

Getting Around

Airport

Yuma International Airport is located 5 miles south of the train station.

Bus

Greyhound is located at 170 East 17th Place Yuma Tel: (520) 783-4403.

Taxi

City Taxi Cab (520) 343-1131, Dial A Ride (520) 782-0043, Yellow Cab (520) 783-4444.

Train and Commuter

Yuma's train depot is located at 281 Gila St. Yuma, AZ 86364. The station is un-staffed and features an enclosed waiting area, restrooms, and payphones. Transportation from the station is local taxi service.

Yuma station is served by the Sunset Limited.

Maricopa (AZ) Gateway to Phoenix (AZ)

Maricopa is located in south-central Arizona just 58 miles south of Phoenix, the state capital. Maricopa is home to approximately 9,000 residents. Visit the Ak-Chin Indian Community located in Maricopa, Arizona 85239 Tel: (928) 568-2227.

Maricopa's train depot is located at 19427 N. John Wayne Parkway Maricopa, AZ 85239. The station is staffed and features an enclosed waiting area.

Maricopa station is served by the Sunset Limited.

Tucson (AZ)

Tucson, or the "Old Pueblo," is the second largest city in the state of Arizona and was founded in 1776 as a Spanish supply station; it was originally settled by the Native American Indians. Located in southeastern Arizona, Tucson is home to more than 300,000 people.

Getting Around

Airport

Tucson International Airport is located 10 miles from the center of downtown Tucson. Tel: (520) 889-1000.

Bus

Sun Tran Bus Tel: (520) 792-9222 serves the city of Tucson. Greyhound, located at 2 S 4th Ave. Tucson Tel: (520) 792-3475, connects the city to the rest of the country.

Taxis

Yellow Cab Tel: (520) 624-6611, Checker Cab Tel: (520) 623-1133, Allstate Cab Tel: (520) 881-2227, Stage Coach Tel: (520) 889-1000.

Rent-A-Car

Avis Rent-a-Car Tel: (520) 294-1495 and Budget Car & Truck Rental toll-free (800) 279-3734.

Train and Commuter

Tucson's train depot is located at 400 E. Toole St. Tucson, AZ 85701. The station is un-staffed and features an enclosed waiting area, restrooms, payphones, and vending machines. Transportation from the station is local taxi service.

Tucson station is served by the Sunset Limited.

Visitor Information Center

Tucson Visitor Information Center is located in La Placita Village near Tucson Convention Center at 100 S. Church Ave., Tucson, Arizona 85701 toll-free (800) 638-8350.

Places to See and Things to Do

Old Town Artisans/La Cocina Restaurant & Catering, located at 201 N. Court Ave. Tucson, AZ 85701 toll-free (800) 782-8072, exhibits Native American arts, food, and costumes. **Old Tucson Studios,** located at 201 S. Kinney Road Tucson, AZ 85735 Tel: (520) 883-0100, features live shows, entertainment, a saloon, and more. **Tohono Chul Park** is

246

located at 7366 N. Paseo del Norte Tucson, AZ 85704 Tel: (520) 742-6455. **Tucson Botanical Gardens** is located at 2150 N. Alvernon Way Tucson, AZ 85712 Tel: (520) 326-9686. **Reid Park Zoo,** located at 1100 S. Randolph Way Tucson, AZ 85716 Tel: (520) 791-3204, is home to hundreds of exotic animals.

Accommodations

Copper Cactus Inn located at 225 W Drachman St, Tucson, AZ Tel: (520) 622-7411. **Dream House Motel** located at 1365 W Miracle Mile Tucson AZ Tel: (520) 791-7531. **Ghost Ranch Lodge and Restaurant** located at 801 W Miracle Mile Tucson AZ Tel: (520) 791-7565. **Radisson Suite Hotel Tucson** located at 6555 E Speedway Blvd. Tucson, AZ Tel: (520) 721-7100. **Inn at the Airport** located at 7060 S Tucson Blvd Tucson AZ Tel: (520) 746-0271. **Mansion** located at 106 W Mabel St, Tucson AZ Tel: (520) 882-9710. **Arizonan Motel** located at 437 W Miracle Mile Tucson, AZ Tel: (520) 623-8702.

El Camino Motel located at 297 E Benson Hwy Tucson AZ Tel: (520) 624-3619. **Flamingo Hotel** located at 1300 N Stone Ave, Tucson AZ Tel: (520) 770-1910. **Desert Edge Motel** located at 3562 E Benson Hwy Tucson, AZ Tel: (520) 294-0748. **Budget Inn Motel** located at 3033 S 6th Ave. Tucson, AZ Tel: (520) 884-1470. **Candlelight Suites** located at 1440 S Craycroft RD, Tucson AZ, Tel: (520) 747-1440. **Paradise Inn Motel** located at 1701 S 6th Ave, Tucson AZ Tel: (520) 623-9501.

New Mexico (NM)

Capital: Santa Fe (Population: 1,819,046)

Size: 121,365 sq mi. (314,334 sq km)

Nickname: The Land of Enchantment

Joined the union on: January 6, 1912 (47th state)

Motto: It Grows As It Goes

Flower: Yucca

Bird: Roadrunner

Song: O Fair New Mexico and Asi es Nuevo Mexico

Famous for: Ancient Pueblo, Santa Fe, the first Atomic Bomb

Major industries: Research and development (energy, nuclear, solar and geothermal), chemicals, food products, equipments, livestock, agriculture and tourism.

Benson (AZ)

Benson is located in Cochise County southeast of Tucson; it has a population of approximately 4,500. Benson was founded in 1880 and was named after Judge William B. Benson, a friend of the president of the Southern Pacific Railroad. Kartchner Cavern State Park is located nine miles outside of Benson Tel: (520) 586-2283. The caves feature large stalagmites, columns and houses, an amphitheater, and Discovery Center.

Benson's train depot is located at 4th and San Pedro Sts. Benson, AZ 85602. The station is un-staffed and features payphones. Transportation from the station is local taxi service.

Benson station is served by the Sunset Limited.

Lordsburg (NM)

Lordsburg is located in southwest New Mexico between the Burro Mountains and the Pyramid Mountains. Lordsburg is the county seat of Hidalgo County, has a land area of 8.4 sq. miles (21.6 sq. kilometers), and has a population of approximately 3,000. Lordsburg is known as gateway to some of New Mexico's "ghost towns."

Places of interest: **Shakespeare Ghost Town**, located two and a half miles south of Lordsburg, N.M. 88045 Tel: (505) 542-9034 and listed on the national Historic Register, is the remains of the area's pioneers. Another ghost town in the area is the **Steins Railroad Ghost Town** is located 16 miles west of Lordsburg.

Getting Around

Airport

Lordsburg Municipal Airport, 1000 E. Airport Road Tel: (505) 542-9863.

Bus

Greyhound station is located at 112 Wabash St. Tel: (505) 542-3412.

Train

Lordsburg's train depot is located at E. Railroad Ave. and SP Tracks Lordsburg, NM 88045. The station is un-staffed and features payphones and a restaurant.

Lordsburg station is served by the Sunset Limited.

Accommodations

Holiday Inn Express located at 1408 South Main Street Tel: (505) 542-3666. **Budget Motel** located at 816 E. Motel Drive Tel: (505) 542-3567. **Holiday Motel** located at 512 East Motel Drive Tel: (505) 542-3535. **Days Inn** located at 816 E. Motel Drive Tel: (505) 542-3600.

Deming (NM)

Deming is located in southwest New Mexico near the Mexico border. Deming is home to the only known "Duck Races" in the world held each August. Deming has a land area of 5.8 sq. miles (14.9 sq. kilometers) and a population of more than 10,000.

Deming's train depot is located at 301 E. Railroad Ave. Deming, NM 88030. The station is un-staffed and features an enclosed waiting area and restrooms. Transportation from the station is local taxi service.

Deming station is served by the Sunset Limited.

El Paso (TX)

El Paso is located at the westernmost tip of the state, along the Rio Bravo Del Norte, bordering Mexico on the southwest and state of New Mexico on the on the northwest. El Paso has a land area of 247 sq. miles (635 sq. kilometers) and population of more than 563,000.

Getting Around

Airport

El Paso International Airport, 6701 Convair Drive, El Paso, Texas 79925 Tel: (915) 772-4271, is located 5 miles (8 kilometers) northeast of El Paso. Major car rental companies are located at the airport arrival area; local taxi and bus operate at the airport.

Bus

Sun Metro Bus Lines Tel: (915) 533-3333 serves the city of El Paso and the outlying areas. Greyhound is located at 200 W San Antonio St. Tel: (915) 532-2365.

Taxi

Yellow Cab Tel: (915) 533-3433, Texas Cab Tel: (915) 562-0022, and Checker Cab Tel: (915) 532-2626.

Rent-A-Car

Advantage Car Rental, Tel: (915) 772-857, Avis Tel: (915) 779-2700, Budget Rent-A-Car Tel: (915) 778-5287, Hertz Car Rental toll-free (800) 654-3131, and the Alamo Rent-A-Car toll-free (800) 327-9633.

Train

El Paso's train depot is listed in the National Registry of Historic Places and it is located at 700 San Francisco St. El Paso, TX 79901. The station is un-staffed and features an enclosed waiting area, restrooms, payphones, and vending machines. Transportation options from the station include rental car, local transit, and taxi services.

El Paso station is served by the Sunset Limited.

Visitor Information Center

El Paso Convention & Visitors Bureau, One Civic Center Plaza El Paso, TX 79901 Tel: (915) 534-0600 or toll-free (800) 351-6024.

Places to See and Things to Do

Wyler Aerial Tramway 1700 McKinley El Paso, Texas 79930 Tel: (915) 566-6622. Located at 5,632-feet above sea level, the view at the top offers a birds-eye view of the surrounding area and Mexico. Listed on the National Historical Register the **Hilton Camino Real,** located at 101 S. El Paso St. El Paso, TX Tel: (915) 534-3000, is admired for its beautiful

Tiffany glass dome. **McKelligon Canyon** located on the north side of El Paso on McKelligon Canyon Rd. Tel: (915) 564-9138. The 1856 **Concordia Cemetery** is located at 3800 Yandell Dr. El Paso, TX. Take El Paso's **Scenic Drive**; from downtown El Paso take Stanton St. north, then go right on Rim Road. The scenic drive offers the best view of the city of El Paso. **El Paso Zoo,** located at 4001 E. Paisano El Paso, TX 79905 Tel: (915) 544-1928, is home to hundreds of animals, from America and Asia.

Chamizal National Memorial, located at 800 S. San Marcial El Paso, TX Tel: (915) 534-6668, houses a museum. **The Bridge Center for Contemporary Arts,** located at 127 Pioneer Plaza El Paso, TX Tel: (915) 532-6707, exhibits contemporary and experimental art. **El Paso Holocaust Museum and Study Center,** located at 401 Wallenberg Drive El Paso, TX 79912 Tel: (915) 833-5656, is dedicated to educating about the events of the Holocaust. **Insights - El Paso Science Museum,** located at 505 N Santa Fe St. El Paso, TX 79901 Tel: (915) 542-2990, has hands-on exhibits. **Border Patrol Museum,** located at 4315 Transmountain Rd. El Paso, TX Tel: (915) 759-6060, features the history of US border Patrol.

El Paso Museum of History, located at 12901 Gateway West El Paso, TX 79927 Tel: (915) 858-1928, features history of American Native Indians, the early Spanish conquest of the region, and the old west. **Natural History Museum** is located in North Park Mall at 9348 Dyer, Suite J El Paso, TX 79924. **Wilderness Park Museum** located at 4301 Trans-Mountain Rd. El Paso, TX 79924 Tel: (915) 755-4332. **El Paso Museum of Art** located at 1 Arts Festival Plaza El Paso, TX Tel: (915) 532-1707. The museum features permanent and seasonal arts exhibits.

McKelligon Canyon

Accommodations

Best Western Inn located at 7144 Gateway Blvd E, El Paso, TX 79915 Tel: (915) 779-7700.
Americana Inn located at 14387 Gateway Blvd W, El Paso, TX 79928 Tel: (915) 852-3025.
Comfort Inn located at 900 N Yarbrough Dr, El Paso, TX 79915 Tel: (915) 594-9111.
Holiday Inn located at 6655 Gateway Blvd W, El Paso, TX 79925 Tel: (915) 778-6411.
Marriott Hotels & Resorts located at 1600 Airway Blvd, El Paso, TX 79925 Tel: (915) 779-3300. **Ramada Inn** located at 6099 Montana Ave, El Paso, TX 79925 Tel: (915) 772-3300.
Westin Paso Del Norte Hotel located at 101 S El Paso St, El Paso, TX 79901 Tel: (915) 534-3000.

Hampton Inn located at 6635 Gateway Blvd W, El Paso, TX 79925 Tel: (915) 771-6644.
Hilton located at 2027 Airway Blvd, El Paso, TX 79925 Tel: (915) 778-4241. **La Quinta Inn** located at 9125 Gateway Blvd W, El Paso, TX 79925 Tel: (915) 593-8400. **Red Roof Inn** located at 7530 Remcon Cir, El Paso, TX 79912 Tel: (915) 587-9977. **Travelodge** located at 409 E Missouri Ave, El Paso, TX 79901 Tel: (915) 544-3333.

Travelodge located at 7815 N Mesa St, El Paso, TX 79932 Tel: (915) 833-2613. **Radisson Suites** located at 1770 Airway Blvd, El Paso, TX 79925 Tel: (915) 772-3333. **Holiday Inn** located at 900 Sunland Park Dr, El Paso, TX 79922 Tel: (915) 833-2900. **Embassy Suites Hotel** located at 6100 Gateway Blvd E, El Paso, TX 79905 Tel: (915) 779-6222. **Days Inn** located at 5035 S Desert Blvd, El Paso, TX 79932 Tel: (915) 845-3500. **Best Value Inn** located at 7840 N Mesa St, El Paso, TX 79932 Tel: (915) 584-4030.

Alpine (TX)

Alpine is located in southwestern Texas and it is the gateway to Big Ben National Park. Alpine has a land area of 4 sq. miles (10.3 sq. kilometers) and a population of approximately 6,000. Big Bend National Park is located south of Alpine and spans some 800,000 acres rich in wildlife and wilderness.

Alpine's train depot is located at 102 W. Holland St. Alpine, TX 79830. The station is un-staffed and features an enclosed waiting area and payphones.

Alpine station is served by the Sunset Limited.

Sanderson (TX)

Sanderson is known as the Cactus Capital of Texas. Sanderson has a land area of 4.2 sq. miles (10.8 sq. kilometers) and population of more than 1,000. The scenery between Sanderson and Del Rio is an endless beauty of rock formations and breathtaking desert. A few miles northwest of Del Rio you will pass through Amistad National Recreation Area, also known as the Grand Canyon of Texas, located near the Mexico border. The train will cross the river canyon and it offers an astonishing view of the Canyon.

Sanderson's train depot is located at 201 Downey St. Sanderson, TX 79848. The station is un-staffed and features an enclosed waiting area, restrooms, and payphones.

Sanderson station is served by the Sunset Limited.

Del Rio (TX)

Del Rio, known for San Felipe Springs, is located in southwest Texas a few miles from the Mexico border. Del Rio has a land area of 14.8 sq. miles (38 sq. kilometers) and a population of more than 30,000.

Del Rio's train depot is located at 100 N. Main St. Del Rio, TX 78840. The station is unstaffed and features an enclosed waiting area, restrooms, and payphones. Transportation options from the station include rental car, local bus, and taxi services.

Del Rio station is served by the Sunset Limited.

San Antonio (TX) See Texas Eagle service, page 327.
Connecting train to **St. Louis, Missouri**, and **Chicago, Illinois** via **Texas Eagle**, and to **Oklahoma City, Oklahoma** via **Heartland Flyer**. Motor-coach connections to **Laredo (TX) and Brownsville (TX)**

Houston (TX)

Houston is the largest city in Texas and the fourth largest city in the United States. It has a land area of 545 sq. miles (1,398 sq. kilometers) and a population of approximately 2 million residents within the city and an estimated 4.5 million people within the metropolitan area. Houston is located in southeastern Texas just 50 miles from the Gulf of Mexico. The Allen brothers founded Houston in 1836.

Houston is home to the world's largest rodeo the "Houston Livestock Show and Rodeo" which attracts almost 2 million visitors each year. Home to 18 Fortune 500 companies and the largest medical center in the world (the Texas Medical Center), Houston is host to almost 40 million travelers each year visiting or passing through the city. Houston's economy is based on oil and gas exploration, technology, medical, and tourism.

Houston enjoys a pleasant and mild sunny and tropical climate, although it can be much hotter if the humidity is high. Houston has an average annual rainfall of 50 inches.

Getting Around

Airport

George Bush Intercontinental Airport, 2800 North Terminal Road, Houston, Texas Tel: (281) 230-3100 is located 22 miles (35 kilometers) north of Houston. Major rental car representatives are available at the airport. Local taxis are available at the south side of terminals A, B, and C and at the west end of Terminal D. Bus services throughout the region are available at the airport. Call Coach USA/Express Shuttle USA Tel: (713) 523-8888 for information. The Houston Metropolitan Transit Authority provides local bus services to the airport and the rest of the city.

Bus

METRO transit system offers local bus services around Huston and the outlying areas Tel: (713) 635-4000. There are free Downtown Trolleys that bring passengers around the downtown Houston area. Greyhound Bus Lines toll-free (800) 231-2222 connects Houston to the rest of the country.

Taxi

Square Deal Cab Company Tel: (713) 659-7236, Fiesta Cab Company Tel: (713) 225-2666, Liberty Cab Company Tel: (713) 695-6700, Yellow Cab Company Tel: (713) 236-1111, and United Cab Company Tel: (713) 699-0000.

Rent-A-Car

Budget Rent-A-Car toll-free (800) 527-0700, Alamo Rent-A-Car toll-free (800) GO-ALAMO, Avis Rent-a-Car toll-free (800) 230-4898, Dollar Rent-a-Car toll-free (800) 800-3665, Thrifty Car Rental toll-free (800) THRIFTY, National Car Rental toll-free (800) CAR-RENT.

Train and Commuter

Houston's train depot is located at 902 Washington Ave. Houston, TX 77002. The station is staffed and features an enclosed waiting area, checked baggage service, restrooms, payphones, and vending machines. Transportation options from the station include local transit and taxi services.

Houston station is served by the Sunset Limited.

Visitor Information Center

Greater Houston Convention and Visitors Bureau, 901 Bagby, Suite 100 Houston, Texas 77002 Tel: (713) 437-5200.

Places to See and Things to Do

Visit NASA's Johnson Space Center at Space Center Houston located 21 miles south of the City of Houston at 1601 NASA Road Houston TX 77058 Tel: (281) 244-2105. The center features educational exhibits in space exploration, information about the Space Shuttle, and more. See the 1939 **City Hall** located just northwest of Tranquility Park, **Downtown Houston** has recently been revitalized; many of the city's historical buildings and sites were renovated to their former glory. Other places of interest inside the city of Houston are **Texas Avenue** and **Tranquility Park**, dedicated to the first landing on the moon by the Apollo 11 mission. The observation deck at the 60th floor of **Chase Tower,** Tel: (713) 223-0441 located at 600 Travis Street, offers a breathtaking view of the City of Houston.

Museum of Fine Arts located at 1001 Bissonnet (at Main) Houston TX 77005 Tel: (713) 639-7300. The museum exhibits art from antiquity and modern eras. **Contemporary Arts Museum,** located at 5216 Montrose Boulevard, Houston Tel: (713) 284-8250, exhibits both national and international contemporary art. **Museum of Health and Medical Science,** located at 1515 Hermann Drive Houston TX 77004 Tel: (713) 521-1515, exhibits medical exploration of internal human body. **Houston Museum of Natural Science,** One Hermann Circle Drive Houston, TX 77030 (713) 639-4629, houses the Planetarium, Observatory, Butterfly Center, and an IMAX Theatre.

Aventure Bay Water Theme Park located at 13602 Beechnut Houston TX 77083 Tel: (281) 530-5979. **Houston Zoo** located in Hermann Park is home to more than 5,000 animals from seven hundred different species. **Six Flags Astro World & Water World,** located at 9001 Kirby Drive Houston TX 77054 Tel: (713) 799-8404, features rides, games, shops, and restaurants. **The Reef,** located at 4800 Schurmier Rd. Houston TX 77048 Tel: (713) 991-3483, features water recreation and entertainment. Visit **Galveston,** located just 50 miles southeast of Houston, one of Texas' prime coastal destinations. Galveston is popularly known for its beachfront, historical district, and its many resorts and hotels.

Accommodations

Doubletree Hotel at Allen Center located at 400 Dallas at Bagby, Houston, TX 77002 Tel: (713) 759-0202. **Hyatt Regency Houston** located at 1200 Louisiana, Houston, TX 77002 Tel: (713) 654-1234. **Embassy Suites Hotel Near The Galleria** located at 2911 Sage Rd., Houston, TX 77056 Tel: (713) 626-5444. **Quality Inn and Suites Galleria** located at 9041 Westheimer Rd., Houston, TX 77063 Tel: (713) 783-1400. **The Westin Oaks Hotel** located at 5011 Westheimer, Houston, TX 77056 Tel: (713) 960-8100. **Doubletree Post Oak** located at 2001 Post Oak Blvd., Houston, TX 77056 Tel: (713) 961-9300. **J.W. Marriott on Westheimer by the Galleria** located at 5150 Westheimer, Houston, TX 77056 Tel: (713) 961-1500.

Sheraton Suites Houston located at 2400 West Loop South, Houston, TX 77027 Tel: (713) 586-2444 **Inter-Continental Houston** located at 2222 West Loop South, Houston, TX 77027 Tel: (713) 627-7600. **The Houstonian Hotel, Club & Spa** located at 111 N. Post Oak Ln., Houston, TX 77024 Tel: (713) 680-2626. **Holiday Inn** located at 7787 Katy Fwy., Houston, TX 77024 Tel: (713) 681-5000. **Howard Johnson Express** located at 4602 Katy Fwy, Houston, TX 77007 Tel: (713) 861-9000. **Four Seasons Hotel** located at 1300 Lamar, Houston, TX 77010 Tel: (713) 650-1300. **Hotel Derek** located at 2525 West Loop South, Houston, TX 77027 Tel: (713) 961-3000.

Beaumont (TX)

Beaumont is located in eastern Texas near the Gulf of Mexico and Louisiana State border just 82 miles east of Houston. Beaumont has a land area of 80.7 sq. miles (207 sq. kilometers) and a population of 109,000. Beaumont was founded in 1824 and was incorporated in 1838.

Beaumont's train depot is located at 2555 W. Cedar St. Beaumont, TX 77704. The station is un-staffed and features an enclosed waiting area, restrooms, and payphones. Transportation from the station is local taxi service.

Beaumont station is served by the Sunset Limited.

Visitor Information Center

Babe Didrikson Zaharias Museum & Visitors Center, 1750 IH 10 East Beaumont, TX 77703 (409) 833-4622.

Places to See and Things to Do

Texas Energy Museum, located at 600 Main St. Beaumont, Texas Tel: (409) 833-5100, exhibits the history of the petroleum industry. **Telephone Pioneer Museum** located at 555 Main Street Beaumont, TX 77701 Tel: (409) 839-6072. **Edison Plaza Museum,** located at 350 Pine St. Beaumont, Texas Tel: (409) 839-3089, exhibits history of electrical industry.

Oaks Historic District bordered by Laurel Street, Interstate 10 East, Second Street, and 11th Street, features some of the earliest buildings in the city. The 1845 Greek Revival house **John Jay French Historic House,** located at 2995 French Road Tel: (409) 898-0348 or 898-3267, is one of the oldest in the city. **St. Anthony Cathedral,** located at 700 Jefferson Drive Beaumont, TX Tel: (409) 833-6433, is modeled after the St. Paul Basilica of Rome. **Art Museum Of Southeast Texas,** located at 500 Main St Beaumont, TX 77701 Tel: (409) 832-3432, features an outdoor sculpture garden.

Accommodations

Comfort Inn located at 1590 I-10 S, Beaumont, TX 77707 Tel: (409) 840-2099. **Crown Motel** located at 8685 College St, Beaumont, TX 77707 Tel: (409) 866-2324. **Holiday Inn** located at 3950 Interstate 10 S, Beaumont, TX 77705 Tel: (409) 842-5995. **Hampton Inn** located at 3795 I-10 S, Beaumont, TX 77705 Tel: (409) 840-9922. **La Quinta Inn** located at 220 Interstate 10 N, Beaumont, TX 77702 Tel: (409) 838-9991. **Travel Inn** located at 2690 Interstate 10 E, Beaumont, TX 77703 Tel: (409) 892-8111. **Courtyard By Marriott** located at 2275 I-10 S, Beaumont, TX 77705 Tel: (409) 840-5750. **Holiday Inn** located at 2095 N 11th St, Beaumont, TX 77703 Tel: (409) 892-2222.

 Spindletop Motel located at 6015 S M L King Jr Pkwy, Beaumont, TX 77705 Tel: (409) 835-1230. **Ramada Inn** located at 1295 N 11th St, Beaumont, TX 77702 Tel: (409) 892-7722. **Fairfield Inn** located at 2265 I-10 S, Beaumont, TX 77705 Tel: (409) 840-5751. **Days Inn** located at 30 Interstate 10 N, Beaumont, TX 77702 Tel: (409) 838-0581. **Best Western Inn** located at 1610 Interstate 10 S, Beaumont, TX 77707 Tel: (409) 842-0037. **Ramada Inn** located at 4085 Interstate 10 S, Beaumont, TX 77705 Tel: (409) 842-1111. **Best Western Inn** located at 2155 N 11th St, Beaumont, TX 77703 Tel: (409) 898-8150. **Hilton** located at 2355 Interstate 10 S, Beaumont, TX 77705 Tel: (409) 842-3600.

Lake Charles (LA)

Lake Charles is located in the southwestern part of Louisiana near the Texas State border. Lake Charles has a land area of 32 sq. miles (83 sq. kilometers) and a population of more than 70,000. Lake Charles is known for its white-sand freshwater lake.

Lake Charles' train depot is located at 433 Railroad Ave. Lake Charles, LA 70601. The station is un-staffed. Transportation from the station is local taxi service.

Lake Charles station is served by the Sunset Limited.

Places to Visit and Things to Do

Mardi Gras Museum of Imperial Calcasieu located at 809 Kirby, 2nd floor Lake Charles, LA 70601, Tel: (337) 430-0043. **Artisans Gallery** located at 204 W. Sallier Lake Charles, LA 70601 Tel: (337) 439-3793. **Imperial Calcasieu Museum** located at 204 W. Sallier St. Lake Charles, LA 70601 Tel: (337) 439-3797 features the history of Lake Charles and Southwest Louisiana. **DeQuincy Railroad Museum & City Park** located at 400 Lake Charles Ave. DeQuincy, LA 70633 Tel: (337) 786-2823. **Children's Museum** located at 925 Enterprise Blvd. Lake Charles, LA 70601 Tel: (337) 433-9420.

North Beach/Interstate 10 - Lake Charles located in N. Lakeshore Dr. Lake Charles, LA 70601. Call Tel: (800) 456-SWLA for information. **I-210 South Beach/LaFleur Beach** situated along the Interstate 210 Lake Charles, LA. Call toll-free (800) 456-SWLA for information.

Accommodations

Chateau Motor Inn located at 2022 Ruth Street Sulphur, LA 70663 Tel: (337) 527-8146. **Best Western Richmond Suites** located at 2600 Moeling St. Lake Charles, LA 70615 Tel: (337) 433-5213. **Comfort Inn of Lake Charles** located at 921 N. Martin Luther King Lake Charles, LA Tel: (337) 491-1000. **Holiday Inn Express** located at 402 N. Martin Luther King Lake Charles, LA 70601 Tel: (337) 491-6600. **Holiday Inn Express** located at 102 Mallard Road Sulphur, LA 70665 Tel: (337) 625-2500. **Best Western Delta Downs** located at 2267 Old Highway 90 Vinton, LA 70668 Tel: (337) 589-7492.

Lafayette (LA)

Lafayette is situated in south central Louisiana 52 miles west of Baton Rouge, the state capital. Lafayette was first settled in 1763 by the Acadian settlers from Canada, officially founded in 1821 and incorporated in 1836. Home to approximately 95,000 residents, it has a land area of 41.3 sq. miles (106 sq. kilometers). Lafayette's economy is mainly based on the oil and gas industry.

Lafayette's train depot is located at 133 E. Grant St. Lafayette, LA 70501. The station is un-staffed and features an enclosed waiting area, restrooms, payphones, and vending machines. Transportation from the station is local taxi service.

Lafayette station is served by the Sunset Limited.

Places to See and Things to Do

The 1821 Dutch Romanesque architecture **St. John**

Louisiana (LA)
Capital: Baton Rouge (Population: 4,468,976)
Size: 51,843 sq mi. (134273 sq km)
Nickname: The Pelican State, the Sugar State, Creole State
Joined the union on: April 30, 1812 (18th state)
Motto: Union, Justice, and Confidence
Flower: Magnolia
Bird: Pelican
Song: Give Me Louisiana and You Are My Sunshine
Famous for: Creole and Cajun Cuisine, Mardi Gras, French Quarters
Major industries: Tourism, manufacturing, minerals, petroleum products, marine

Cathedral, Oak Tree & Museum is located at 914 St John Street Lafayette LA 70501. The 1800 **Alexandre Mouton House** 1122 Lafayette St Lafayette LA 70501 built by the founder of Lafayette, Jean Mouton. **Angels of Louisiana,** located at 1507-C Kaliste Saloom Lafayette LA 70508, features a gallery of angels. **Lafayette Natural History Museum and Planetarium** located at 637 Girard Park Drive Lafayette LA 70503. **Vermilionville,** located at 1600 Surrey Street Lafayette LA 70508 Tel: (318) 233-4077, features historical museum.

Accommodations

Best Western Inn located at 1801 W Pinhook Rd, Lafayette, LA 70508 Tel: (337) 233-8120. **Holiday Inn** located at 2032 NE Evangeline Thruway, Lafayette, LA 70501 Tel: (337) 233-6815. **Fairfield Inn** located at 2225 NW Evangeline Thruway, Lafayette, LA 70501 Tel: (337) 235-9898. **Courtyard by Marriott** located at 214 E Kaliste Saloom Rd, Lafayette, LA 70508 Tel: (337) 232-5005. **Best Suites of America** located at 125 E Kaliste Saloom Rd, Lafayette, LA 70508 Tel: (337) 235-1367. **Days Inn** located at 1620 N University Ave, Lafayette, LA 70506 Tel: (337) 237-8880. **Holiday Inn Express** located at 2503 SE Evangeline Thruway, Lafayette, LA 70508 Tel: (337) 234-2000. **Hilton** located at 1521 W Pinhook Rd, Lafayette, LA 70503 Tel: (337) 235-6111. **Comfort Inn** located at 1421 SE Evangeline Thruway, Lafayette, LA 70501 Tel: (337) 232-9000. **LA Quinta Inn** located at 2100 NE Evangeline Thruway, Lafayette, LA 70501 Tel: (337) 233-5610.

Travelodge located at 1101 W Pinhook Rd, Lafayette, LA 70503 Tel: (337) 234-7402. **Rodeway Inn** located at 1801 NW Evangeline Thruway, Lafayette, LA 70501 Tel: (337) 233-5500. **Quality Inn** located at 1605 N University Ave, Lafayette, LA 70506 Tel: (337) 232-6131. **Red Roof Inn** located at 1718 N University Ave, Lafayette, LA 70507 Tel: (337) 233-3339.

New Iberia (LA)

New Iberia is located 18 miles southeast of Lafayette and 127 miles west of New Orleans. New Iberia was founded in 1779 by the Spanish and was named after the old name of Spain "Iberia." New Iberia was incorporated in 1836; it has a land area of 10 sq. miles (26 sq. kilometers) and population of approximately 32,000.

New Iberia's train depot is located in Washington St. and Railroad Tracks New Iberia, LA 70560. The station is un-staffed and features an enclosed waiting area, restrooms, and payphones.

New Iberia station is served by the Sunset Limited.

Schriever (LA)

Schriever is located in Terrebonne Parish south of Baton Rouge in south-central Louisiana. Schriever has a land area of 13.5 sq. miles (34.8 sq. kilometers) and population of approximately 5,000.

Schriever's train depot is located at S. Rte. 20 and 26 Rte. 24 Schriever, LA 70395. The station is un-staffed and features an enclosed waiting area and restrooms.

Schriever station is served by the Sunset Limited.

New Orleans (LA) See "The City of New Orleans" service, page 384.
Connecting train to **Chicago (IL)** via the City of New Orleans, Motor-coach connection to **Baton Rouge (LA)**

Bay St. Louis (MS)

Bay St. Louis is located west of Gulfport and Biloxi on the Gulf of Mexico 57 miles east of New Orleans. Bay of St. Louis has a land area of 5.7 sq. miles (14.8 sq. kilometers) and population of more than 8,000.

Bay St. Louis' train depot is located at 303 S. Railroad Ave. Bay St. Louis, MS 39520. The station is un-staffed and features payphones. Transportation from the station is local taxi service.

Bay St. Louis station is served by the Sunset Limited.

Gulfport (MS)

Gulfport is located in southernmost point of Mississippi, along the Gulf of Mexico Mississippi coast. Part of the Biloxi Indian's homeland, Gulfport was first claimed and settled by the French in 1699 under the leadership of Pierre LeMoyne d'Iberville. Gulfport is has a land area of 22.8 sq. miles (58.5 sq. kilometers) and is home to more than 40,000 residents.

Gulfport's train depot is located at 1419 27th Ave. Gulfport, MS 39501. The station is un-staffed and features an enclosed waiting area and payphones. Transportation from the station is local taxi service.

Gulfport station is served by the Sunset Limited.

Places to See and Things Do

United States Naval Home, located at 1800 Beach Drive Gulfport MS 39507 Tel: (228) 897-4016, exhibits Second World War memorabilia. **The Lynn Meadows Discovery Center,** located at 246 Dolan Ave Gulfport MS 39507 Tel: (228) 897-6039, is an interactive children's museum. **Wet Willy's,** located at 1200 Beach Blvd Gulfport MS 39507 Tel: (228) 896-6592, features water activities and entertainment. **Gulfport Centennial Museum,** located at 1419 27th Ave Gulfport MS 39502 Tel: (228) 868-5849, features the history of Gulfport. The **CEC/Seabee Memorial Museum,** located at 5200 CBC 2nd St Gulfport MS 39501 Tel: (228) 871-3164, depicts the history of the U.S. Navy's Civil Engineer Corps.

Accommodations

Casino Beach Resort located at 4410 West Beach Blvd Gulfport MS 39501 Tel: (228) 868-4969. **Best Western- Beach View Inn** located at 2922 West Beach Blvd Gulfport MS

39501 Tel: (228) 864-4650. **Days Inn Gulfport** located at 15250 Poole St Gulfport MS 39503 Tel: (228) 864-5135. **Fairfield Inn** located at 15151 Turkey Creek Dr Gulfport MS 39503 Tel: (228) 822-9000. **Holiday Inn Airport** located at 9415 Highway 49 North Gulfport MS 39503 Tel: (228) 868-8200.

Days Inn & Suites located at 4128 West Beach Blvd Gulfport MS 39501 Tel: (228) 865-7878. **Comfort Inn Gulfport** located at 9343 Highway 49 Gulfport MS 39503 Tel: (228) 863-5500. **Caravelle Beach Front Inn & Suites** located at 802 Beach Dr Gulfport MS 39507 Tel: (228) 896-9444. **Best Western-Seaway Inn** located at 9475 Highway 49 Gulfport MS 39503 Tel: (228) 864-0050. **Alamo Plaza Motel** located at 2230 Beach Blvd Gulfport MS 39507 Tel: (228) 896-4422.

Biloxi (MS)

Biloxi is located at the southernmost tip of Mississippi Gulf Coast, 151 miles southeast of Jackson, the state capital. Biloxi has a land area of 19.8 sq. miles (50.8 sq. kilometers) and a population of more than 54,000. Biloxi is an emerging premier tourism destination; its economy is thriving mainly on tourism-related industries. Biloxi has nine casinos and more than 8,500 hotel and motel rooms easy accessible to Biloxi Gulf Coast Beach.

Biloxi's train depot is located at 860 Esters Blvd. Biloxi, MS 39530. The station is un-staffed and features payphones. Transportation options from the station include local transit and taxi services.

Mississippi (MS)
Capital: Jackson (Population: 2,844,658)
Size: 48,434 sq mi. (125,444 sq km)
Nickname: The Magnolia State
Joined the union on: December 10, 1817 (20th state)
Motto: By valor and arms
Flower: Magnolia
Bird: Mockingbird
Song: Go, Mississippi
Famous for: Blues, Elvis Presley, and Kermit the Frog!
Major industries: Agriculture, Fisheries, and Manufacturing

Biloxi station is served by the Sunset Limited.

Places to See and Things to Do

Beauvoir, Jefferson Davis Home & Presidential Library located at 2244 Beach Blvd Biloxi MS 39531 Tel: (228) 388-9074. **Father Ryan House Bed & Breakfast,** located at 1196 Beach Blvd Biloxi MS 39530 Tel: (228) 435-1189. **The Redding House,** located at 770 Jackson St Biloxi MS 39532 Tel: (228) 436-9700, is one of the oldest Greek revival homes in Biloxi. The 1848 **Biloxi Lighthouse,** call Tel: (228) 435-6308 for information. **The Ohr-O'Keefe Museum of Art** located at 136 G. E. Ohr St Biloxi MS 39530 Tel: (228) 374-5547. **Biloxi Mardi Gras Museum** located at 119 Rue Magnolia Biloxi MS 39530 Tel: (228) 435-6245.

Accommodations

Econo Lodge of Biloxi located at 1776 Beach Blvd Biloxi MS 39531 Tel: (228) 374-7644. **Hampton Inn-Biloxi** located at 13921 Big Ridge Rd Biloxi MS 39532 Tel: (228) 872-6370. **Isle of Capri Casino Resort** located at 151 Beach Blvd Biloxi MS 39530 Tel: (228) 435-5400. **Ramada Limited Biloxi Beach** located at 1768 Beach Blvd Biloxi MS 39531 Tel: (228) 432-1997. **Balmoral Inn** located at 120 Balmoral Ave Biloxi MS 39531 Tel: (228) 388-

6776. **Best Inn & Suites-Biloxi** located at 1686 Beach Blvd Biloxi MS 39531 Tel: (228) 436-0201.

Flamingo Beach located at 1746 Beach Blvd Biloxi MS 39531 Tel: (228) 436-4327. **Cabana Motel** located at 2766 Beach Blvd Biloxi MS 39531 Tel: (228) 388-2181. **Beach Manor Inn** located at 662 Beach Blvd Biloxi MS 39530 Tel: (228) 436-4361. **Broadway Inn Express** located at 2688 Beach Blvd Biloxi MS 39531 Tel: (228) 388-1185. **La Linda Inn** located at 1836 Beach Blvd Biloxi MS 39531 Tel: (228) 388-4621. **Holiday Inn Biloxi Beachfront** located at 2400 Beach Blvd Biloxi MS 39531 Tel: (228) 388-3551. **Best Western-Swan Motel** located at 1726 Beach Blvd Biloxi MS 39531 Tel: (228) 432-0487.

Pascagoula (MS)

Pascagoula is located on the Gulf of Mexico a few miles from the Alabama State border. Pascagoula has a land area of 15 sq. miles (39 sq. kilometers) and a population of over 25,000. A famous destination for water sports and related activities, it features an international deep-water port and is home to the U.S Naval Station Pascagoula.

Pascagoula's train depot is located at 505 Railroad Ave. Pascagoula, MS 39567. The station is un-staffed and features payphones. Transportation from the station is local taxi service.

Pascagoula station is served by the Sunset Limited.

Mobile (AL)

Mobile is located in the south-westernmost tip of Alabama, at the Alabama Gulf Coastal area. Mobile has a land area of 119 sq. miles (305.7 sq. kilometers) and population of more than 211,000. An all American City, Mobile is famous for its hospitable and friendly residents. Surrounding Mobile is rich flora and fauna and the area is a well-known destination for outdoor activity enthusiasts.

Mobile's train depot is located at 11 Government St. Mobile, AL 36601. The station is staffed and features an enclosed waiting area. Transportation options from the station include local transit and taxi services.

Mobile station is served by the Sunset Limited.

Atmore (AL)

Alabama (AL)
Capital: Montgomery (Population: 4,447,100)
Size: 57,919 sq mi. (150,010 sq km)
Nickname: The Heart of Dixie, The Cotton State, the Camellia State
Joined the union on: December 14, 1819 (22nd state)
Motto: We Dare Defend Our Rights
Flower: Camellia
Bird: Yellowhammer
Song: "Alabama"
Famous for: Nat King Cole, Lionel Ritchie and Joe Lewis
Major industries: Paper, Chemicals, and Rubber and Plastics

Atmore is located in southwestern Alabama, a few miles from the Florida State border. Atmore is home to more than 8,000 residents and has a land area of 8 sq. miles (21 sq. kilometers).

Atmore's train depot is located at 107 E. Louisville St. Atmore, AL 36502. The station is un-staffed and features an enclosed waiting area and payphones.

Atmore station is served by the Sunset Limited.

Pensacola (FL)

Pensacola is situated in far west of Florida near the Alabama State Border, 174 miles west of Tallahassee. Pensacola is one of the oldest cities in Florida; many of its old buildings and structures are still well preserved. Also known as the city of five flags, today's Pensacola is a prime tourist destination. Visit downtown Pensacola, it reflects the atmosphere of the old Pensacola. The Seville Historic District is one of the most visited areas in the city. Other places to see are the National Museum of Naval Aviation, the 1832 St. Michael's Cemetery, and the Pensacola Historical Museum located on Zaragosa Street. Pensacola is home to approximately 59,000 residents and it has a land area of 22.8 sq. miles (58.6 sq. kilometers).

Pensacola's train depot is located at 980 E. Heinburg St. Pensacola, FL 32501. The station is staffed and features an enclosed waiting area, checked baggage service, restrooms, payphones, and vending machines. Transportation from the station is local taxi service.

Pensacola station is served by the Sunset Limited.

Crestview (FL)

Crestview is located 49 miles east of Pensacola and 153 miles west of Tallahassee, the state capital. Crestview has a land area of 10.4 sq. miles (26.8 sq. kilometers) and a population of approximately 10,000.

Crestview's train depot is located at 101 N. Main St. Crestview, FL 32536. The station is un-staffed and features payphones. Transportation from the station is local taxi service.

Crestview station is served by the Sunset Limited.

Chipley (FL)

Chipley is situated just 86 miles west of Tallahassee. It has a land area of 3.9 sq. miles (10 sq. kilometers) and a population of roughly 4,000.

Chipley's train depot is located at 101 S. Seventh St. Chipley, FL 32428. The station is un-staffed and features an enclosed waiting area and payphones.

Chipley station is served by the Sunset Limited.

Tallahassee (FL)

Tallahassee is the state capital of Florida and is located in northern Florida. Tallahassee has a land area of 63.5 sq. miles (163.8 sq. kilometers) and a population of approximately 148,000. First founded in 1539-1540 by the Spanish explorer Hernando de Soto, Tallahassee was incorporated in 1825.

Getting Around

Airport

Tallahassee Regional Airport Tel: (850) 891-7800 is located 7 miles from downtown Tallahassee. Rental car companies, local taxi, transit, shuttles, and hotel services are available at the airport terminal.

Bus

Taltran City Bus Tel: (850) 891-5200 operates city bus routes around the Tallahassee area; call the bus company for information. Old Town Trolley Tel: (850) 891-5200 or Tel: (850) 413-9200 offers free downtown commuter services.

Taxi

Yellow Cab Tel: (850) 580-8080, Red Cab Tel: (850) 425-4606, Ace Taxi Tel: (850) 521-0100, and City Taxi Tel: (850) 562-4222.

Rent-A-Car

Enterprise Rent-A-Car Tel: (850) 878-1500 and Thrifty Car Rental Tel: (850) 576-RENT or toll-free (800) FOR-CARS.

Florida (FL)

Capital: Tallahassee (Population: 15,982,378)
Size: 65,758 sq mi. (170,313 sq km)
Nickname: The Sunshine State
Joined the Union On: March 3, 1845 (27th state)
Motto: In God we trust
Flower: Orange Blossom
Bird: Mockingbird
Song: The Suwanee River
Major industries: Tourism, agriculture, manufacturing, mining, marine

---

Train and Commuter

Tallahassee's train depot is located at 918 1/2 Railroad Ave. Tallahassee, FL 32310. The station is staffed and features an enclosed waiting area, checked baggage service, restrooms, and payphones. Transportation options from the station include local transit and taxi services.

Tallahassee station is served by the Sunset Limited.

Visitor Information Center

Tallahassee Area Visitor Information Center, Downtown Tallahassee at 106 East Jefferson Street Tel: (850) 413-9200 or toll-free (800) 628-2866.

Places to See and Things to Do

Downtown Marketplace, located in downtown/Ponce de Leon Park at Park Ave. (850) 980-8727, features local artists, performers, and farmer's market. **The Capitol** is located downtown at S. Duval St. (850) 488-6167. **Old Capitol Museum** is located in downtown S. Monroe St. (850) 487-1902. **Park Avenue Historic District** located at 106 E. Jefferson St.

850-413-9200 is Tallahassee's oldest green space. The Georgian-style **Governors Mansion** is located at 700 N. Adams St. (850) 488-4661.

Listed on the National Register of Historic Places, the **Lemoyne Art Foundation,** located at 125 N. Gadsden St. (850) 222-8800, houses a gallery, sculpture garden, and more. **Florida Vietnam Veterans Memorial,** located in downtown across from Old Capitol Museum, features 40-foot American flag. The 1841 **Union Bank Museum,** located in downtown, Apalachee Pkwy. Tel: (850) 487-3803, is the oldest surviving bank in Florida. **Mission San Luis,** located at 2020 W. Mission Rd. (850) 487-3711, is an archeological site of Tallahassee's long history of settlements.

Museum of Florida History, located at 500 S. Bronough St. (850) 245-6400, exhibits civil war memorabilia, Spanish Galleon Treasures, and more. **Riley Museum Center of African American History and Culture** located at 419 E. Jefferson St. (850) 681-7881. **Tallahassee Museum of History and Natural Science,** located at 3945 Museum Dr. (850) 576-1636, has hands-on exhibits, nature trails, a zoo, and more. **Mary Brogan Museum of Art and Science,** located in downtown at Kleman Plaza, 350 S. Duval St. (850) 513-0700, features hand-on exhibits, educational programs, and more.

Maclay State Gardens located at 3540 Thomasville Rd. (850) 487-4556 is a beautiful garden featuring various outdoor recreational activities. **The Kirk Collection,** located in Public Broadcast Center at 1600 Red Barber Plaza (850) 487-3086, exhibits antique collections of radios, TVs, and other sound equipment. **Tallahassee Antique Car Museum** is located at 3550-A Mahan Dr. (850) 942-0137. **621 Gallery,** located at 621 Industrial Dr., Railroad Square (850) 224-6163, exhibits various form of art. **Museum of Florida History Gallery,** located at 500 S. Bronough St. (850) 488-1484, has permanent art exhibits. **Old Capitol Gallery,** located in Old Capitol Museum, Downtown, S. Monroe St. (850) 487-2980, has seasonal arts exhibits.

Accommodations

Courtyard Tallahassee North located at 1972 Raymond Diehl Road Tallahassee FL 32308 Tel: (850) 422-0600 expect to pay $50-$150. **Econo Lodge North** located at 2681 North Monroe Street Tallahassee FL 32303 Tel: (850) 385-6155 expect to pay $50-$100. **La Quinta Tallahassee South** located at 2850 Apalachee Parkway Tallahassee FL 32301 Tel: (850) 878-5099 expect to pay $40-$100. **Red Roof Inn Tallahassee** located at 2930 Hospitality Street Tallahassee FL 32303 Tel: (850) 385-7884 expect to pay $40-$100. **Holiday Inn Select Tallahassee Downtown Capitol** located at 316 West Tennessee Street Tallahassee FL 32301 Tel: (850) 222-9555 expect to pay $50-$250.

Fairfield Inn Tallahassee located at 3211 North Monroe Street Tallahassee FL 32303 Tel: (850) 562-8766 expect to pay $50-$100. **Doubletree Hotel Tallahassee** located at 101 South Adams Street Tallahassee FL 32301 Tel: (850) 224-5000 expect to pay $50-$150. **Days Inn Tallahassee North** located at 2800 North Monroe Street Tallahassee FL 32303 Tel: (850) 385-0136 expect to pay $30-$100. **Courtyard Tallahassee** located at 1018 Appalachee Parkway Tallahassee FL 32301 Tel: (850) 222-8822 expect to pay $50-$190. **Quality Inn and Suites Tallahassee** located at 2020 Apalachee Parkway Tallahassee FL 32301 Tel: (850) 877-4437 expect to pay $50-$500.

Comfort Suites Tallahassee located at 1026 Apalachee Parkway Tallahassee FL 32301 Tel: (850) 224-3200 expect to pay $50-$170. Comfort Inn Tallahassee located at 2727 Graves Road Tallahassee FL 32303 Tel: (850) 562-7200 expect to pay $50-$100. Best Western Pride Inn and Suites located at 2016 Apalachee Parkway Tallahassee FL 32301 Tel: (850) 656-6312 expect to pay $50-$70.

Madison (FL)

Madison is located 51 miles east of Tallahassee in central north Florida. Madison has a land area of 2.3 sq. miles (6 sq. kilometers) and a population of roughly 3,500. The Cotton planters founded Madison in 1838. Downtown Madison has been preserved showing the city's many historical sites and structures. Visit the Four Freedoms Park located at the center of downtown Madison.

Madison's train depot is located at 1000 S. Range St. Madison, FL 32340. The station is un-staffed. Transportation from the station is local taxi service.

Madison station is served by the Sunset Limited.

Lake City (FL)

Lake City is the seat of Columbia County located 60 miles west of Jacksonville in northeastern Florida. Lake City has a land area of 10.5 sq. miles (27 sq. kilometers) and a population of more than 12,000. The Battle of Olustee is re-enacted in Lake City every February and celebrated with many activities and entertainment.

Lake City's train depot is located at 1200 Lake Jeffery Rd. Lake City, FL 32055. The station is un-staffed and features payphones. Transportation from the station is local taxi service.

Lake City station is served by the Sunset Limited.

Jacksonville (FL) See Silver Meteor/Silver Star/Silver Palm service, page 547.

DeLand (FL) See Silver Meteor/Silver Star/Silver Palm service- Jacksonville to Miami service, page 552- 553.

Sanford (FL) See Silver Meteor/Silver Star/Silver Palm service- Jacksonville to Miami service, page 552- 553.

Winter Park (FL) See Silver Meteor/Silver Star/Silver Palm service- Jacksonville to Miami service, page 552- 553.

Orlando (FL) See Silver Meteor/Silver Star/Silver Palm service- Jacksonville to Miami service, page 553.
Motor-coach connection to **St. Petersburg (FL)** Train Connection via **Silver Service** to **Miami (FL)**

Midwestern US Train Routes

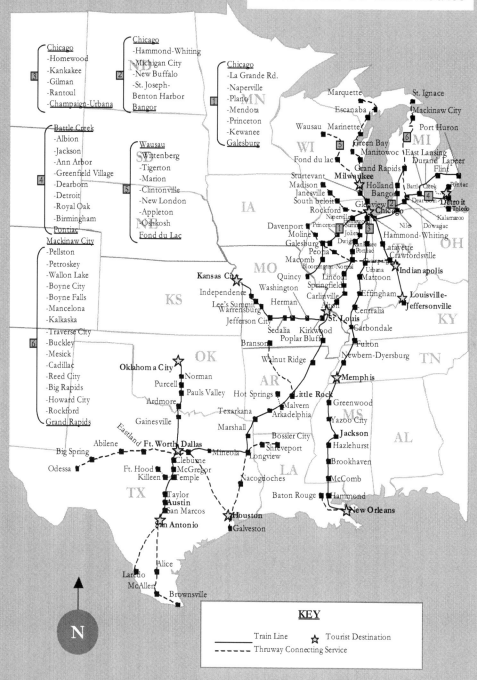

Chicago [3]
-Homewood
-Kankakee
-Gilman
-Rantoul
-Champaign-Urbana

Chicago [2]
-Hammond-Whiting
-Michigan City
-New Buffalo
-St. Joseph-
 Benton Harbor
-Bangor

Chicago [1]
-La Grande Rd.
-Naperville
-Plano
-Mendota
-Princeton
-Kewanee
-Galesburg

Battle Creek [4]
-Albion
-Jackson
-Ann Arbor
-Greenfield Village
-Dearborn
-Detroit
-Royal Oak
-Birmingham
-Pontiac

Wausau [5]
-Wittenberg
-Tigerton
-Marion
-Clintonville
-New London
-Appleton
-Oshkosh
-Fond du Lac

Mackinaw City [6]
-Pellston
-Petroskey
-Wallon Lake
-Boyne City
-Boyne Falls
-Mancelona
-Kalkaska
-Traverse City
-Buckley
-Mesick
-Cadillac
-Reed City
-Big Rapids
-Howard City
-Rockford
-Grand Rapids

KEY

Train Line — ☆ Tourist Destination

Thruway Connecting Service - - - - -

N

The US Midwest Region Train Routes

The Midwest Corridor Services
(Illinois and Missouri Service, Illinois Zephyr Service, Illini Service, and Hiawatha Service)

The Midwest Corridor is one of the key train systems in the Central United States. It links the states of Illinois, Wisconsin, Michigan, Indiana, Missouri, and the province of Ontario Canada through its several train services: the Illinois and Missouri, Illini, Hiawatha, and the Michigan Services. It connects the cities of Chicago, Milwaukee, Indianapolis, Detroit, St. Louis, Kansas City, and Louisville. Midwest Corridor also serves the city of Toronto, ON, Canada.

The Midwest Corridor is jointly financed and operated by Amtrak and the States of Illinois, Michigan, Missouri, and Wisconsin.

Route Destination Highlights

Chicago, IL- Home to America's tallest building the Sears Tower, visit the Museum of Science and Industry and other outstanding museums, admire the charming Centennial Fountain, take a romantic stroll along lake Michigan, and enjoy Chicago's busy nightlife.

Milwaukee, WI- The city is known for its Summer Fest, the largest and most celebrated music festival in the world. Visit the historic Pabst Theater which is one of the finest architectural buildings in the city, see the International Clown Hall of Fame and the Circus World Museum, or visit the US official Olympic training center the Pettit National Ice Center.

Springfield, IL- Visit Abraham Lincoln's hometown and the city's historical places.

St. Louis, MO- Famous for its "Arc of St. Louis" located along the bank of the Mississippi River, visitors can visit the top of the arch to have bird-eye view of the lovely city of St. Louis. Visit the popular Busch Stadium, the zoo, or the exciting St. Louis Fair during the month of July.

Kirkwood, MO- Explore the old lovely city of Kirkwood and visit the Transportation Museum, the Magic House, and some of the town's antique shops, restaurants, and local specialty shops.

Jefferson City- Known for its beautiful architecture, visit Missouri State Capitol and the Governor's Mansion.

Kansas City, MO- Visit the City of Fountains and explore the American Jazz Museum, the Negro Leagues Baseball Museum, the gorgeous Kansas City Union Station, the famous Kansas Speedway, and the Harvey-Davidson Assembly Plant. Try the city's famous Barbeque while enjoying jazz music.

Train Schedules

The Midwest Corridor travels daily from Chicago to major cities in the states of Illinois, Indiana, Michigan, Missouri, and Wisconsin.

Accommodations and Services

Accommodations are Reserved Coach Class and Business Class. There is a Cafe car that serves local cuisine, snacks, soups, sandwiches, and drinks and a Dining Car that serves complete meals in most trains. There are a few spaces for unpacked bicycles which you should reserve in advance.

Additional Information

Advance coach seat reservation is needed and there are rental car companies in bigger cities.

Boarder Crossing

International connecting routes through Via Rail Canada from Port Huron, Michigan to Toronto, Ontario, Canada.

Illinois and Missouri Service

The Illinois and Missouri route is served directly by Amtrak's "Ann Rutledge." There are other train services (the Kansas City Mule and St. Louis Mule) which offer connecting services daily between the two states. The Illinois and Missouri route brings passengers to some of the most alluring scenery of the states of Illinois and Missouri. It connects the cities of Chicago, Springfield (the birth place of Abraham Lincoln), St. Louis, and Kansas City.

Amtrak, in cooperation with the National Park Service, offers an onboard interpretive guide who relates tales as well as other valuable information along the historic railroad routes of the two states.

Scenery along the Route

From Chicago (IL) to St. Louis (MO) you'll see old towns and cities with charming Western-

Illinois and Missouri Routes
Chicago (IL)
Summit (IL)
Joliet (IL)
La Grande Road (IL)
Naperville (IL)
Plano (IL)
Mendota (IL)
Priceton (IL)
Kawanee (IL)
Galesburg (IL)
Macomb (IL)
Quincy (IL)
Dwight (IL)
Pontiac (IL)
Bloomington (IL)
Lincoln (IL)
Springfield (IL)
Carlingville (IL)
Alton (IL)
St. Louis (MO)
Kirkwood (MO)
Washington (MO)
Hermann (MO)
Jefferson City (MO)
Sedalia (MO)
Warrensburg (MO)
Lee's Summit (MO)
Independence (MO)
Kansas City (MO)

Multiple Train Departure Daily (left side)

Multiple Train Departure Daily (right side)

American architecture and endless colorful fields. Prepare yourself and your camera while the train is approaching the City of St. Louis for its magnificent Arch. The route from St. Louis and Kansas City is full of nature and greenery.

All Aboard!

Chicago (IL)

It was Jean Baptiste Point DuSable, a person of French-African decent, who found and first settled in the site which is now Chicago (Indian word meaning "strong" or "great") in 1779, and in 1833 the town of Chicago was established and later incorporated as a city in 1837. Located at the southwestern shore of Lake Michigan, the city of Chicago covers 225 sq. miles (588 sq. kilometers) and is traditionally divided into three areas: the north, west, and south sides. The central part of the city is known as the "loop," named for the city's elevated train route's round design.

Chicago has an average temperature of 49.9 degrees F, average low temperature of 21.0 degrees F, and an average high temperature of 73.2 degrees F. As of 2001, Chicago has approximately 2,896,016 residents who come from different backgrounds, races, and cultures.

Chicago is one of the most historical cities of the US; it played a significant role in the history of east and west United States and functioned as a transportation and commercial hub between the two regions. Chicago's first railroad track was completed in 1848. Since then the railroad continuously extended and connected the city throughout the region. In the same year the Illinois and Michigan Canal was also opened connecting Chicago with the Mississippi River, making the city more accessFible both to commercial vehicles and travelers. The Illinois and Michigan Canal is a 60-mile canal route which runs from Chicago's Navy Pier on Lake Michigan to Starved Rock Illinois, spreading to 41 districts across the region. In 1865, the Union Stockyards were opened and the city's economy had become one of the most important in the US.

Illinois (IL)
Capital: Springfield (Population: 12,419,293)
Size: 55,593 sq mi. (143,987 sq km)
Nicknames: The Land of Lincoln
Entered the union: December 3, 1818 (21st state)
Motto: State sovereignty, national union
Flower: Violet
Bird: Cardinal
Song: Illinois
Famous for: Sears Towers
Major industries: Coal, agriculture, and oil

Chicago also has had some dark moments in its history: in 1871 the city of Chicago was leveled to the ground by fire. The fire caused 300 deaths, left more than 90,000 local residents homeless, and caused an estimated $200 million loss of property. Monuments and other structures were erected to commemorate the sad events. The people of Chicago also took the opportunity to rebuild and modernize the city. In the years to follow, Chicago became the city of innovators.

The Home Insurance Building, a nine-story building built in 1885, was the world's first "skyscraper," and in 1892 Chicago operated the first elevated trains which formed the downtown "loop." It became one of the major attractions during the World Columbian Exposition of 1893 in Chicago. Since then Chicago has held many other international expositions, sports events, conventions, academic and business seminars and forums.

In 1955 Chicago's O'Hare International Airport began its service connecting the city to the rest of the US and the world. Today O'Hare International Airport is one of the busiest airports in the world. Chicago is home to many great museums of contemporary and modern art and it also has the world's largest public library with an extensive collection of rare and valuable books.

Perhaps one of Chicago's greatest assets is its multicultural people, almost three million people of diverse origin and culture. This is also the very reason why Chicago is one of the world's greatest cities. Chicago is one of the most visited cities in the world; each year there are more than 30 million visitors to the city making tourism one of the city's major industries. There are almost 30,000 hotel rooms in the city, hundreds of restaurants, and many tourist destinations that will meet traveler's expectations.

Amongst the city's many tourism spots, the most popular and visited are: Navy Pier with more than 9 million visitors each year, the Lincoln Park Zoo with 3 million visitors each year, and the Field Museum of Natural History with more than 2 million visitors each year. Other popular destinations: the Museum of Science and Industry, John G. Shedd Aquarium, Art Institute of Chicago, Sears Tower Skydeck, Hancock Observatory, Adler Planetarium & Astronomy Museum, Museum of Contemporary Art, DuSable Museum of African American History, and the Museum of Broadcast Communication.

Summer and winter can be extreme in Chicago, so consider visiting the city during spring or autumn. And hold tight to your umbrella or hat while visiting the "windy city."

Getting Around

Chicago has a very convenient and developed local transportation system. If you need train or bus route information throughout the Chicago Metro area call the Illinois Department of Transportation at Tel: (312) 836-7000 or (708) 836-7000.

Chicago has an underground system of pedestrian walkways (the Pedways) making the city easy to navigate especially during harsh weather. The walkways are connected to the city's major transportation system, the loop shops, and commercial buildings. Information and maps of the walkways are available in hotels and at the visitor information center.

Airport

Chicago is served by two major airports, O' Hare International Airport and Midway Airport. O' Hare International Airport is located at 10000 West O' Hare Chicago, IL 60666, Tel: (773) 686-3700, about 17 miles northeast of downtown Chicago. The airport is accessible from downtown Chicago and surrounding areas through local mass transit lines, regional trains, and buses (located at the main entrance of each terminal).

Midway Airport is located at 5700 South Cicero Chicago, IL 60638 Tel: (773) 838-0600 just ten miles from downtown Chicago. Midway airport is accessible through Chicago Transit Authority (CTA) via Orange Line. The trip from the airport to downtown Chicago is approximately 20-30 minutes; there are regional buses and shuttles serving downtown and suburban destinations.

The transportation department encourages the "Shared-Ride" program where 2-4 passengers can share a taxicab from O'Hare or Midway airport to any downtown location between 22nd St. and Fullerton Ave., Lake Michigan and Ashland Ave. On the other hand, passengers should be extra cautious.

Bus

CTA operates bus services around the city for information call CTA Toll-Free: (888) YOUR-CTA or (888) 968-7282; <<http://www.yourcta.com/>>

Pace offers suburban bus service. Pace Headquarters is located at 550 West Algonquin Road, Arlington Heights Tel: (312) 836-7000 or (708) 836-7000. Round-trip tickets are $7.50 (exact fare is required) and can be purchased at Pace Headquarters in Arlington Heights.

Taxis

Just like any other city in the US, Chicago has a large network of taxicabs and it is easy to get one almost anywhere in the city. Fares vary from $1.90 to $4.00 upon entry, $1.60 for each additional mile, and there is a 50-cent surcharge for each extra passenger. American-United Taxi Tel: (773) 248-7600, Checker Cab Tel: (312) 243-2537, Flash Cab Tel: (773) 561-1444 and Yellow Cab Tel: (312) 829-4222 are amongst Chicago's major taxi companies.

Rent-A-Car

Victory Rent-A-Car located at 1352 W. Lake St., Chicago, IL, Tel: (312) 666-7728. Delaware Cars and Limousines located at 1325 West Lake Chicago IL 60607, Tel: (312) 337-2800. Cloud 9 Specialty Car Rentals located at Chicago Suburbs, Chicago IL, Tel: (630) 707-7368. Avis Rent-a-Car Toll-Free: (800) 331-1212, and Budget Rent-a-Car Tel: (630) 968-6661.

Commuter Lines and Trains

Metra has 495-mile Metra system serving 230 stations connecting Chicago to the rest of the region. For Information call Tel: (312) 322-6777 or TTY (312) 322-6774, website << http://www.metrarail.com>>.

Chicago Transit Authority (CTA) operates "the Loop," an elevated train / subway service that circles downtown Chicago. For information call CTA at Tel: (312) 836-7000 or visit <<http://www.yourcta.com/>>.

Chicago's Free Trolley is provided by the City of Chicago to aid visitors. The trolley has daily service bringing visitors to Chicago's most popular museums, shopping destinations, attractions, and the city's major transportation services. Passengers can just catch a trolley at any stop marked by a "Free Trolley" sign. Call Toll-Free: (877) 244-2246.

Amtrak stops at the Chicago Union Station located at 225 S. Canal St. Chicago, IL 60661. Chicago Union Station is a historical landmark and one of the most beautiful and grandest train stations in the US. The station a staffed and features an enclosed waiting area, checked baggage service, restrooms, payphones, shops, a restaurant, and snack bars. Transportation options from the station include Hertz Car Rental Toll-Free: (800) 654-3131 Budget Rent A Car Toll-Free: (800) 527-0700, and Enterprise Rent A Car Toll-Free: (800) RENT-A-CAR; Greyhound Toll-Free: (312) 408-5980, Chicago Transit Authority (CTA) Tel: (312) 836-7000 which runs local buses and commuter services, and local taxi service.

Trains serving Chicago Station are: California Zephyr, Capitol Limited, Cardinal, City of New Orleans, Empire Builder, Hiawatha, Illinois Service, Kentucky Cardinal, Lake Shore Limited, Michigan Services, Missouri Routes, Pennsylvanian, Southwest Chief, Texas Eagle and the Three Rivers.

Visitors Information Center

There are several visitor information centers in Chicago. Chicago Water Works Visitor Center is located at 163 E. Pearson at Michigan, Chicago, IL and Chicago Cultural Center Visitor Information Center is located at 77 East Randolph Street at Michigan Avenue, Chicago, IL. Call the Chicago Office of Tourism at toll-free (877) CHICAGO; (866) 710-0294 (TTY) for information.

Places to See and Things to Do

The **Buckingham Fountain** is located in Grant Park, Congress Parkway and Columbus Drive; call Tel: (312) 742-7529 for information. One of the most popular sites in the city is the Buckingham Fountain which opens only during summer when visitors will experience the magnificent light and water show with music. **Centennial Fountain** is located at 300 N. McClurg Ct., at Chicago River; call Tel: (312) 751-6635 for information. The huge, magnificent fountain is open only during the months of May through October.

John Hancock Observatory is situated at 875 N. Michigan Ave. on the 94th floor (at the height of 1,127 feet) of the John Hancock Center. Tel: (312) 751-3681 or toll-free (888) 875-VIEW. The observatory features an open-air Skywalk, Sky Tours, Sound scope 3-D "talking" telescopes, a Chicago history wall, and much more.

Navy Pier is one of Chicago's famous landmarks. The pier has more than 50 acres of parks, gardens, shops, restaurants, and attractions such as a Ferris wheel and carousel. The pier is located at 600 E. Grand Ave. Tel: (312) 595-PIER, or toll-free (800) 595-PIER. **River walk Gateway** has the city's largest public work of art: a 336 foot-long wall installation which consists of sixteen narrative panels and twelve decorative panels. River walk is located at 400 E Wacker Dr., Tel: (312) 744-6630.

Sears Tower is America's tallest building. The Sky deck Observatory on the 103rd floor offers a spectacular view of Chicago. Admissions are Adults $9.50, Senior Citizens $7.75, Children 3-11 $6.75, Children under 3 free. Sears Tower is located at 233 S. Wacker Dr., Tel: (312) 875-9696.

Wicker Park is one of the oldest and most established neighborhoods in Chicago, famous for its Victorian architecture building and some of Chicago's most entertaining nightlife. Wicker Park 1500 N. Wicker Park Ave., Chicago, IL 60622 Tel: (773) 276-1723.

Chicago Public Library is the world's largest public library. The library has more than two million shelved volumes accessible to the public. The museum is located at Harold Washington Center 400 South State Street, Chicago; <<http://www.chipublib.org>> The **Newberry Library** is a self-directed research library with an extensive collection of rare books, maps, and manuscripts. The library is located at 60 West Walton Street, Tel: (312) 943-9090. <<http://www.newberry.org>>.

Lincoln Park Zoo is located at Cannon Dr. at Fullerton Parkway (2400 north), Tel: (312) 742-2000. The zoo is one of the oldest in the US. There are many activities and things to see for the whole family. Free Admission. **Brookfield Zoo** is home to more than 400 species of animals. The zoo is located at 8400 W. 31st St., Brookfield, Tel: (708) 485-2200.

Architecture

Clarke House Museum is the oldest house building in Chicago. The museum gives visitors a glimpse of a middle class family in 1830's Chicago. The museum is located at 1827 S. Indiana Avenue, Chicago 60616, Tel: (312) 326-1480. **Smith Museum of Stained Glass Windows**, located at the Navy Pier, 700 E. Grand Ave. Tel: (312) 791-6049, showcases religious windows of Chicago's European immigrants and has some of the most diverse collections anywhere. **Robie House** is known for its spectacular 174 exquisite art glass windows and doors; located at 5757 S. Woodlawn St., Chicago 60637, Tel: (773) 834-1847. **Glessner House Museum**, built in 1887, is a National Historic Landmark and is located at 1800 S. Prairie Avenue, Chicago 60616, Tel: (312) 326-1480.

Museums and Aquariums

A. Philip Randolph Pullman Porter National Museum and Gallery is dedicated to A. Philip Randolph, the Brotherhood of the Sleeping Car Porters, and the African American Railroad attendants. The museum exhibits a collection of vintage historical photos preserving and presenting moments in time. The museum is located at 10403 S. Maryland Ave., Tel: (773) 928-3935.

Adler Planetarium and Astronomy Museum was the first planetarium in western hemisphere. The museum has hands-on exhibits and sky shows; located at 1300 South Lake Shore Drive; Tel: (312) 922-7827 <<http://www.adlerplanetarium.org>>. **John G. Shedd Aquarium** is the world's largest indoor aquarium, displaying 8,000 aquatic animals from around the world. Located at 1200 South Lake Shore Drive; Tel: (312) 939-2438 <<http://www.sheddnet.org>> .

Field Museum exhibits more than 20 million specimens and cultural objects. The museum is located on Roosevelt Road at Lake Shore Drive; Tel: (312) 922-9410; <<http://www.fmnh.org>>. **Chicago Athenaeum Museum** is an international museum of art, architecture, and design. The museum is located at 6 North Michigan Avenue, Tel: (312) 281-0175. The **Ernest Hemingway Birthplace & Museum** is located at 339 North Oak Park Avenue; Tel: (708) 848-2222 or toll-free (877) HEMINGWAY; <<http://www.hemingway.org/tour>>.

The **Art Institute of Chicago** located at 111 South Michigan Avenue Tel: (312) 443-3600; <<http://www.artic.edu>>. The museum has the biggest collection of Impressionist Art, it exhibits more than 300,000 works of art, including "A Sunday Afternoon on La Grand Jatte" by Georges Seurat, "American Gothic" by Grant Wood, "Nighthawks" by Edward Hopper, and some of the finest work of Claude Monet.

Balzeka's Museum of Lithuanian Culture is dedicated to the preservation of Lithuanian culture. Located at 6500 South Pulaski Road Tel: (312) 582-6500. The **DuSable Museum of African-American History** is dedicated to the collection, preservation, and interpretation of the history and culture of Africans and Americans of African descent. Located at 740 East 56th Place Tel: (312) 947-0600 <<http://www.dusablemuseum.org>>. **Mexican Fine Arts Center** has the largest Latino cultural institution in the US. Located at 1852 West 19th Street; Tel: (312) 738-1503 <<http://www.mfacmchicago.org>>. **Swedish American Museum Center** is located at 5211 North Clark Street Chicago 60640 Tel: (312) 728-8111. The museum is dedicated to preserving the Midwest's rich Swedish heritage; it exhibits materials related to Swedish-American history <<http://www.samac.org>>.

Chicago Children's Museum is located on Navy Pier at 700 E. Grand Avenue, Chicago 60611. The museum has lots of activities to encourage children to explore their senses. <http://www.chichildrensmuseum.org>> Tel: (312) 527-1000. **Kohl Children's Museum** encourages children to touch and explore the exhibits and participate in planned daily activities. The museum is located at 165 Green Bay Road, Wilmette. Toll-free (888) 564-5543 <<http://www.kohlchildrensmuseum.org>>.

The **Museum of Contemporary Art** exhibits painting, sculpture, photography, video and film, and has performances; Located at 220 East Chicago Avenue Tel: (312) 280-2660 <<http://www.mcachicago.org>>. **The Museum of Contemporary Photography** is located at Columbia College, 600 South Michigan Avenue Tel: (312) 663-5554; free admission. **Center for Intuitive and Outsider Art** exhibits art by untrained artists, made by African-Americans, eccentrics, isolates, compulsive visionaries, and mentally ill artists. Located at 756 North Milwaukee Avenue; Tel: (312) 243-9088 <<http://outsider.art.org>>.

Museum of Broadcast Communications exhibits hands-on displays, broadcasting memorabilia, and more than 60,000 public archives of radio and television programs and commercials. Located at the Chicago Cultural Center, Michigan Avenue at Washington Street; Tel: (312) 629-6000 <<http://www.mbcnet.org>>, free admission. The **National Vietnam Veterans Art Museum** is located at 1801 South Indiana Avenue, Tel: (312) 326-0270. The museum exhibits works of art by 115 artists who served in Vietnam.

Museum of Science and Industry is located at 57th Street and Lake Shore Drive, Tel: (312) 684-1414. The museum displays more than 800 exhibits and 2,000 interactive units, and an Omnimax movie dome facility <<http://www.msichicago.org>>. The **Museum of Surgical Science** has 7,000 surgery-related objects, manuscripts, and artworks in its collections that illustrate the history and development of modern medical practice. The museum is located at 1524 North Lake Shore Drive, Tel: (312) 642-6502 <<http://www.imss.org>>. **Peggy Notebaert Nature Museum** is located in Lincoln Park at 2430 North Cannon Drive, Tel: (312) 755-5100. Peggy Notebaert Nature Museum is Chicago's first and only museum to specialize in the ecology and natural history of the Midwest <<http://www.chias.org>>.

The Art Institute of Chicago is one of the world's leading museums. It exhibits paintings, sculptures, prints, drawings, photographs, textiles, decorative arts, architectural fragments, and includes art of Asia, Africa, Oceania, and the Americas. The Museum is located at 111 S. Michigan Avenue, Chicago 60603-6110, Tel: (312) 443-3600. The Peace Museum is one of a kind in the US. The museum is dedicated to promoting peace. Visitors will find John Lennon's guitar, manuscripts from Bono of the band U2, and other collections and memorabilia. The museum is located at 314 W. Institute Place, Tel: (312) 440-1860.

The Terra Museum of American Art exhibits and interprets American art, promoting understanding and appreciation of the region's artistic heritage. The museum is located at 664 N. Michigan, Chicago 60611 Tel: (312) 664-3939. The Chicago Historical Society is a major museum and research center and has seasonal exhibits of Chicago and American history. The museum is located at Clark Street and North Avenue, Chicago 60614 Tel: (312) 642-4600. Oriental Institute Museum exhibits the history, art, and archeology of the ancient Middle East Asia. The museum is located at 1155 E. 58th Street, Chicago 60637, Tel: (773) 702-1062.

Accommodation

Claridge Casino & Hotel located at 1244 N Dearborn Pkwy Chicago IL 60610; Tel: (312) 787-4980 Toll-Free: (800) 245-1258; expect to pay $160-$300. Hilton Chicago and Towers located at 720 South Michigan Avenue Chicago IL 60605; Tel: (312) 922-4400; expect to pay $110-$450. The Fairmont Chicago located at 200 North Columbus Drive Chicago IL 60601; Tel: (312) 565 8000 Toll-Free: (800) 441-1414; expect to pay $140-$500. Cass Hotel located at 640 N Wabash Ave Chicago IL 60611; Tel: (312) 787-4030 Toll-Free: (800) 227-7850; expect to pay $80-$100. Best Western Hawthorne Terrace located at 3434 North Broadway Chicago, Il 60657; Tel: (773) 244-3434 Toll-Free: (888) 675-2378; expect to pay $130-$160.

The Drake Hotel located at 140 East Walton Place Chicago IL 60611; Tel: (312) 787-2200; expect to pay $120-$1000. Clarion Hotel Barcelo Hotel located at 5615 North Cumberland Avenue Chicago IL 60631; Tel: (773) 693-5800; expect to pay $70-$150. Days Inn Gold Coast Hotel located at 1816 N Clark Street Chicago IL 60614; Tel: (312) 664-3040 Toll-Free: (800) DAYS-INN; expect to pay $80-$150. Crowne Plaza Hotel located at 701 North Michigan Avenue Chicago IL 60611; Tel: (312) 440-1500; expect to pay $130-$490. Ameri Suites Chicago O'Hare located at 8101 Higgins Road Chicago IL 60631; Tel: (773) 867-0000; expect to pay $80-$150. Belden Stratford Hotel located at 2300 North Lincoln Park West Chicago IL 60614; Tel: (773) 281-2900; expect to pay $100-$200.

Comfort Inn and Suites Downtown located at 15 East Ohio Chicago IL 60611, Tel: (312) 494-1515 Toll-Free: (888) 775-4111; expect to pay $139-$250. Doubletree Hotels Chicago Downtown located at 198 East Delaware Place Chicago IL 60611, Tel: (312) 664-1100 Toll-Free: (800) 222-TREE; expect to pay $130-$350. Embassy Suites Hotel Chicago located at 600 North State Street Chicago IL 60610; Tel: (312) 943-3800; expect to pay $150-$350.

Marriott Chicago Downtown located at 540 North Michigan Avenue Chicago IL 60611; Tel: (312) 836-0100; expect to pay $150-$450. Hilton Garden Inn Chicago Downtown located at 10 East Grand Avenue Chicago IL 60611; Tel: (312) 595-0000; expect to pay

$130-$350. **Holiday Inn Downtown Sears Tower** located at 506 West Harrison Street Chicago IL 60607; Tel: (312) 957-9100; expect to pay $100-$250. **Quality Inn Downtown** located at 1 Mid-city Plaza Chicago IL 60661; Tel: (312) 829-5000; expect to pay $80-$150. **Travel lodge Downtown** located at 65 East Harrison Chicago IL 60605; Tel: (312) 427-8000 Toll-Free: (800) 578-7878; expect to pay $80-$150.

Hyatt Regency Chicago located at 151 East Wacker Drive Chicago IL 60601; Tel: (312) 565-1234 Toll-Free: (800) 233-1234; expect to pay $140-$390. **Holiday Inn Chicago O'Hare Kennedy** located at 8201 West Higgins Road Chicago IL 60631; Tel: (773) 693-2323; expect to pay $90-$190. **Hotel Inter-Continental Chicago** located at 505 North Michigan avenue Chicago IL 60611; Tel: (312) 944-4100; expect to pay $120-$450.

Omni Ambassador East located at 1301 North State Parkway Chicago IL 60610; Tel: (312) 787-7200; expect to pay $120-$330. **Palwaukee Inn** located at 1090 South Milwaukee Avenue Chicago IL 60090; Tel: (925) 473-2230; expect to pay $90-$130. **Marriott Chicago O'Hare** located at 8535 West Higgins Road Chicago IL 60631; Tel: (773) 693-4444 Toll-Free: (800) MARRIOTT; expect to pay $90-$250.

Summit (IL)

The city of Summit is located just two miles from Chicago's Midway airport. Summit has a total land area of 2.1 sq. miles (5.5 sq. kilometers) and a population of almost 10,000.

Summit's train depot is located at Archer and Center Ave. Summit, IL 60501. The station is not staffed and has payphones. There are local transit and taxi services at the station; Summit station is served by the Midwest Corridor.

Joliet (IL)

The city of Joliet is located 44 miles southwest of Chicago. This beautiful city is situated along the Des Plaines River and the Illinois & Michigan Canal, and is home to almost 95,000 residents. Joliet has a total land area of 28 sq. miles (72 sq. kilometers).

Joliet is known for its section of historic Illinois & Michigan Canal Corridor (I&M Canal National), which runs from Chicago's Navy Pier on lake Michigan to Starved Rock Illinois passing through the center of Joliet. There are riverboat casinos and other attractions on the river.

Joliet's train depot is located at 50 E. Jefferson St. Joliet, IL 60431. The station is staffed and features an enclosed waiting area, restrooms, payphones, vending machines, and checked baggage services. There is transit service at the station; trains serving Joliet station are the Midwest Corridor and Texas Eagle.

Dwight (IL)

Dwight is a small town home for some 4,300 residents. This lovely town is located near three major highways and is served by a local airport, Dwight Aero Service. Dwight's train depot is located at 119 W. Main St. Dwight, IL 60420. The station is not staffed and features an enclosed waiting area. There is local taxi service available at the station. Dwight station is served by the Midwest Corridor.

Pontiac (IL)

Pontiac is located 100 miles southwest of Chicago and 200 miles northeast of St. Louis. The city of Pontiac was established in 1838 and is the seat of Livingston County. Pontiac has a total land area of 4 sq. miles (11 sq kilometers) and a population of about 12,000. The city has a thriving retail and light manufacturing business and is known for its restored historic buildings, brick streets, swinging bridges, and parks. One of the best examples is the Yost House Museum located at 298 W Water St. Pontiac, IL 61764-1757, Tel: (815) 844-7401.

Pontiac's train depot is located at 721 W. Washington St. Pontiac, IL 61764. The station is not staffed and features an enclosed waiting area. There is taxi service at the station; trains serving Pontiac station are the Midwest Corridor and Texas Eagle.

Bloomington-Norman (IL)

Bloomington-Norman is known as the twin city, the train station is located in Norman. Norman is home to more than 45,000 residents and is home to Illinois State University. It is also in Norman where President Lincoln delivered his last speech.

Bloomington has a total land area of 16 sq. miles (43 sq. kilometers) and a population of approximately 64,000. Bloomington is the seat of McLean County located in the heart of Central Illinois, just 125 miles southwest of Chicago, 155 miles northeast of St. Louis, and 64 miles northeast of the state capital, Springfield. Bloomington also has an important figure to share; the city was George Pullman's home. Pullman was a visionary, entrepreneur, and a great social reformer. He introduced the first deluxe class passenger cars and founded and built the town of Pullman.

If you are planning to visit Bloomington, see Prairie Aviation Museum located at RR 1, Bloomington, IL 61704-9801, Tel: (309) 663-7632, or see some of Bloomington's cultural and entertainment shows. And if you are curious where Beer Nuts come from, Bloomington has the answer.

Bloomington-Norman's train depot is located at 100 E. Parkinson St. Norman, IL 61761. The station is staffed and features an enclosed waiting area, restrooms, payphones, vending machines, and checked baggage service. Transportation options from the station include rent a car service: A-1 Rent-A-Car Tel: (309) 454-6747, Avis Rent A Car toll-free (800) 230-4898; and local taxi service: Circle City Cab Tel: (309) 829-5342, American City Cab Tel: (309) 828-5656.

Trains serving Bloomington-Norman station are the Midwest Corridor and Texas Eagle.

Lincoln (IL)

Lincoln has a total land are of 5.4 sq. miles (14 sq. kilometers) and a population of 15,369, it is the only town named after president Abraham Lincoln with the Lincoln's blessing. Lincoln is located just 30 miles from Illinois' capital, Springfield. Lincoln is known for its many historical sites and museums. The Postville Courthouse State Historic Site, New Salem State Historic Site, and Lincoln College Museum are worth visiting; other interesting places include the Watermelon Christening Site, the site where Lincoln christened the town of Lincoln using the juice of a watermelon in 1853.

Lincoln's train depot is located at Broadway and Chicago St. Lincoln, IL 62656. The station is not staffed. Trains serving the Lincoln station are the Midwest Corridor and Texas Eagle.

Springfield (IL)

Springfield is the state capital of Illinois (since 1837) and the seat of Sangamon County government. Springfield is located in the center of the state of Illinois about 200 miles southwest of Chicago and 100 miles north of St. Louis, with a total land area of 42 sq. miles (110 sq. kilometers) and a population of more than 113,000 people.

Springfield has always been associated with Abraham Lincoln, as written and seen in the city's history and many historical landmarks. Today, Springfield has a very diverse economy amongst the city's top industries are insurance, health, tourism, productions, and exporting. There are over a million visitors to the city each year, paying respect to one of America's greatest leaders, Abraham Lincoln, and visiting the city's other historical sites.

Springfield's train depot is located at Washington and 3rd Sts. Springfield, IL 62701. The station is staffed and features an enclosed waiting area, restrooms, payphones, vending machines, and checked baggage service. Transportation options from the station include local transit service and local taxi service.

Trains serving Springfield station are Midwest Corridor and Texas Eagle.

Visitors Information Center

Springfield Convention & Visitors Bureau is located at 109 North 7th Street, Springfield, IL 62701. Tel: (217) 789-2360 toll-free (800) 545-7300, ext. 30.

Lincoln Visitor Center is located at 426 South 7th Street, Tel: (217) 492-4150.

Places to See and Things to Do

Lincoln Tomb is located at Oak Ridge Cemetery, Tel: (217) 782-1717. One of the most visited cemeteries in the US, this is where the remains of Abraham Lincoln and several of his family members were laid to rest.

The city of Springfield is full of President Lincoln's monuments, museums, and memorabilia; some of them are **Lincoln's New Salem,** a place where Abraham Lincoln grew up and worked, **Lincoln Home,** a national historic landmark, and **Lincoln-Herndon Law Offices** where the president once worked.

Serving as the Illinois statehouse from 1839 to 1876, the **Old State Capitol Historical Site** is one of Springfield's best-known landmarks Tel: (217) 785-7960. The **Illinois State Museum** is located at Spring and Edwards, Springfield, IL, Tel: (217) 782-7386. Exhibits include the Ice Age Mastodons (one of the largest animals in the world) and a Children's Discovery room, amongst others. **Springfield Children's Museum** located in downtown Springfield at 619 East Washington Street, Springfield, IL, Tel: (217) 789-0679. The museum has many exhibits and interactive displays.

Washington Park Botanical Gardens is located at Washington Park, Springfield, IL. Tel: (217) 753-6228. The **Henson Robinson Zoo** is located at 1100 East Lake Drive, Springfield, IL, Tel: (217) 753-6217. The zoo is home to more than 33 species of exotic and local animals. **Lake Springfield** has 57 miles of shoreline with 4,235 acres of water. The lake is famous for leisure and recreational activities.

Carlinville (IL)

Carlinville, the only town in the world with that name, was founded in 1828. Situated near Springfield, the town is rich in history that is still preserved in the town's many old streets and buildings. A visit to Carlinville's downtown historic district offers visitors a glimpse of the town and the region's past.

Carlinville's train depot is located at 128 Alton St. Carlinville, IL 62626. The station is not staffed. The station is served by the Midwest Corridor.

Alton (IL)

Alton is one of the most historic river cities in America; part of Piasa county, Alton is located at the junction of three great rivers: the Mississippi, the Illinois, and the Missouri. Alton has a population of around 33,000 living in an area of just 12 sq. miles (33 sq. kilometers). The city of Alton is filled with great stories and history. It was founded by Rufus Easton in 1818, and most of the city's historical buildings and landmarks are still well preserved.

During the 1800's, crossing the Mississippi River to Alton was viewed by many African slaves living in Missouri as salvation: the gate to freedom from slavery. The state of Illinois, unlike Missouri, was a slave-free state. It was said that more than 75,000 slaves escaped and traveled through the "underground railroad" system on their way to Canada.

It is also in Alton where the famous Civil War Penitentiary, also known as the Confederate Prison, is located. Alton's rich history can be viewed from today's many antique merchants selling part of Alton's memorabilia. Perhaps the most popular personality of Alton was the 8' 11" tall man named Robert Wadlow. Robert was born in 1918 and became the tallest man in history. Today, Robert's life-size statue stands in the city of Alton.

There are various things to see and do in Alton. The city has many shops, restaurants, entertainment places, historical places, and nightlife spots. Two of the city's main river attractions include the Clark Bridge, spanning the Mississippi river connecting the states of Missouri and Illinois, and the Melvin Price Locks and Dam.

Alton is also known as the center for viewing the great American Bald Eagle. Every winter the eagle's seasonal migration from northern America to River Bend areas bring around 2,000 eagles, and with them a major tourism and scientific event.

Alton's train depot is located at 3400 College Ave. Alton, IL 62002. The station is staffed and features payphones and vending machines. Transportation options from the station include rent a car service: Enterprise Rent-A-Car toll-free (800) RENT-A-CAR and Roberts Ford Car Rental Tel: (816) 466-7220; taxi service: Piasa Cab Tel: (618) 462-4488 and Alton American Tel: (618) 465-5559; and Madison Country Transit.

Trains serving Alton station are the Midwest Corridor and Texas Eagle.

Saint Louis (MO)
Connecting train to **San Antonio, Texas** via the **Texas Eagle**

St. Louis is located 250 miles east of Kansas City and 300 miles southwest of Chicago in east-central Missouri on the west bank of the Mississippi River. The population of St. Louis is about 400,000, with a total land area of 62 sq. miles (160 sq. kilometers). The city of St. Louis is the center of 12 other counties with an overall size of approximately 7,000 sq. miles and a population of more than 2.7 million.

Missouri (MO)

Capital: Jefferson City (Population: 5,595,211)
Size: 69,709 sq mi. (180,546 sq km)
Nickname: The Show-me State
Joined the union on: August 10, 1821 (24th state)
Motto: The welfare of the people shall be the supreme law
Flower: Hawthorn
Bird: Bluebird
Song: Missouri Waltz
Famous for: The Arc of St. Louis, the beer (Budweiser) and the cynicism ("show me")
Major industries: Automobile and parts manufacturing, beer, and defense and aerospace technology research and development

St. Louis has an annual 38 inches of rainfall and an annual snowfall of 19.8 inches. The average winter temperature is below 0°F to 55 degrees F and an average summer temperature of 57°F to 90 degrees F. Stormy and severe weather can occur year-round.

Laclede and Chouteau, French fur traders from New Orleans, founded St. Louis in 1764 and named the site after the French King Louis IX. The Spanish acquired St. Louis from the French in 1770, but later it was given back to France and became part of United States in 1803. The city of St. Louis was incorporated in 1823 and grew to be an important center for trade and the US western expansion. The population grew tremendously and other immigrants from different parts of Europe and eastern America settled there.

St. Louis' strategic location (with regard to waterways and railroads) gave the city a great advantage as a trade route hub between the east, south, and western parts of the country. During the 1900's, St. Louis became a major economic center and an important link in transcontinental train travel. In 1904 the city hosted the World's Fair and the Summer Olympic Games brining millions of people to the city.

Between the two World Wars the population of St. Louis soared to more than 800,000 due to the massive migration of mainly African Americans from different areas of the US. The migration created many problems for the city and many people gradually moved to suburban areas; by the 1980's the city's population had fallen to less than half a million.

During the 60s, 70s, and 80s city re-development was introduced in an effort to revitalize the former glory of the city. It was also during this period when many of the city's historical sites were restored and protected. The Gateway Arch was opened in 1965, dedicated to the city's role in America's westward expansion, followed by the constructions of Busch Memorial Stadium, the renovation of the Union Station, and more.

The Great Mississippi River flood of 1993 devastated many parts of the city and some would say it was one of the darkest times in the history of the city and the region. Today St. Louis is a major industrial center, home to major American corporations and major manufacturing industries. The city of St. Louis is second to Detroit in car production, headquarters of Anheuser-Busch, home of Barnes-Jewish and St. Louis University Hospitals, Emerson Electric, Boeing, Bank of America, May Department Stores, Monsanto, Ralston Purina, and Trans World Airlines.

Getting Around

Airport

Lambert-St. Louis International Airport is one of the major airports in the United States. Lambert is one of the fastest growing airports in the world, and it continuously expands its terminals and services. There is a free passenger shuttle which runs continuously between the Main and East Terminals of the airport. For airport information call (314) 426-8000.

Greyhound and Bi-State (local bus service) are located at the entrance to the intermediate lot, south of the main terminal, while Metro link terminal is located on the upper level of the main and east terminals through the parking garage on all levels. There are hotel courtesy vehicle services at the main terminal. Share Van services to downtown St. Louis are also available for $11 each way: passengers should purchase their tickets at main terminal exit MT12. Call (314) 427-3311. Rent-a-car counters are located at the main entrance of the lower level, between exits MT17 and MT12

Rent A Car

Rent-a-Wreck is located at 582 St. Peters Road, St. Charles / St. Peters, MO, Tel: (636) 928-3848 and Toll-Free: (800) 242-4088. Enterprise Rent-a-Car is located at 14374 Manchester Road, St. Louis, MO 63109, Tel: (636) 519-9080. Budget Rent-a-Car of St. Louis is located at 801 Sprit of St. Louis Blvd, Chesterfield MO 63005, Tel: (636) 532-0234.

Other rent-a-car companies are: Alamo Toll-Free:: (800) 327-9633, Avis Toll-Free:: (800) 831-2847, Dollar Toll-Free:: (800) 800-4000, Hertz Toll-Free:: (800) 654-3131, National Toll-Free:: (800) 227-7368 and Thrifty Toll-Free:: (800) 367-2277.

Bus

MetroLink Shuttles and Garden Express offer tourist services around the city. It brings visitors to St. Louis' major tourist attractions. A one-way adult fare costs only $1.25. MetroBus 707 N 1st St Stop 1 St. Louis, MO 63102, Tel: (314) 231-2345 serves most areas of St. Louis and St. Louis County. Fare is $1.25, one-day pass is $4 valid on all MetroBus and MetroLink light rail routes, and buses generally run from 4:00 a.m. until 2:00 a.m.

<<http://www.bi-state.org>> Greyhound Bus Lines 1450 N. 13th Street Tel: (314) 231-4485 or Toll-Free: (800) 231-2222 connects St. Louis to the rest of the US.

Taxi

County Cab Company 9930 Meeks Boulevard, St. Louis, MO 63132, Tel: (314) 991-5300 Taxicab transportation service provided by safe, courteous drivers. Harris & Eagle Cab Company 3740 Enright Ave, St Louis, MO 63108, Tel: (314) 535-5087. Laclede Cab Company 600 S Vandeventer Ave, St Louis, MO 63110, Tel: (314) 652-3456.

Commuter and Train

St. Louis Metro links light rail system has 34 miles of rails stretching along Missouri and Illinois. The train begins at Lambert-St. Louis International Airport and ends in suburban Belleville, Illinois making it one of the most convenient and economical ways of exploring St. Louis and its suburban areas.

Tickets are available at each station: a one-way fare costs $1.25 and the fare from the airport to downtown St. Louis costs as little as $3. Daily passes that can be used both for Metro link and local buses are available for $4. Trains run every 15 minutes. Designated free ride zone areas allow passengers to board without any charge. Metro link Tel: (314) 982-1406 for information; <<http://www.bi-state.org/index.htm>>.

Amtrak St. Louis' train depot is located at 550 S. 16th St. St. Louis, MO 63103. The station is staffed and features an enclosed waiting area, restrooms, payphones, vending machines, and checked baggage service. Transportation options from the station include Hertz Car Rental Toll-Free: (800) 654-3131, and local taxi service. Trains serving St. Louis are the Midwest Corridor and Texas Eagle.

Visitors Information Center

St. Louis Visitors Centers is located at 7th & Washington Ave., Lambert Airport and Kiener Plaza, Toll-Free: (800) 916-0092.

St. Louis Convention & Visitors Commission is located at One Metropolitan Square, Ste. 1100, St. Louis, MO 63102, Tel: (314) 421-1023 or Toll-Free: (800) 916-0092.

Places to See and Things to Do

St. Louis Gateway Arch was designed by architect Eero Saarinen. The stainless steel arch rises 630 feet high and spans 630 feet. Construction began in 1961 and the Arch was officially opened in 1966. There is an underground circular gallery under the monument where visitors can take the $7 dollar elevator ride to the top of the arch. The gallery also houses the Visitors Information Center which exhibits 100 years of westward expansion. The arch is located beside of the Mississippi River where it enters the city of St. Louis. Wild Canid Survival & Research Center is a captive breeding facility for endangered wolves from different part of the world. There are daytime and evening educational tours. The research center is located at I-44 & Antire Rd Eureka, MO 63025; Tel: (636) 938-5900 <<http://www.wolfsanctuary.org>>.

Unlike the Hollywood Walk of Fame in Hollywood Blvd. honoring known movie personalities of the entertainment industry, the **St. Louis Walk of Fame** honors famous St. Louisians (including Tina Turner). The one hundred plaques are located at the Loop, at 6504 Delmar Blvd. St. Louis, MO 63130; Tel: (314) 727-STAR <<http://www.stlouiswalkoffame.org>>.

Saint Louis Zoo is a home for more than 6,600 animals and is one of the best zoos in the US. The zoo is located at 1 Government Drive St. Louis, MO 63110; Tel: (314) 781-0900 <<http://www.stlzoo.org>>.

St. Louis Union Station was once the largest train station in the US. Today the station houses a hotel, mall, and restaurants. The station is located at 1820 Market Street St. Louis, MO 63103. Tel: (314) 421-6655 <<http://www.stlouisunionstation.com>>. **Museum of Transportation** exhibits more than 300 samples of different modes of transportation such as locomotives, cars, buses, streetcars, and aircraft. The museum is located at 3015 Barrett Station Rd. St. Louis, MO 63122; Tel: (314) 965-7998 <<http://www.museumoftransport.org>>. **St. Louis Fire Dept. Museum** exhibits historical equipment and memorabilia. The museum is located at 1421 N. Jefferson Ave. St. Louis, MO 63106; Tel: (314) 289-1933

Saint Louis University is located at 221 N. Grand Blvd. St. Louis, MO 63103; Tel: (314) 977-8886. The university is the oldest institution of higher education west of the Mississippi <<http://www.slu.edu>>. **Dental Health Theatre** is the only one of its kind in the world;

St. Louis Gateway

the theatre exhibits 16 three-foot-high fiberglass teeth. The theater is located at 727 N. First St., Ste. 103 St. Louis, MO 63102; Tel: (314) 241-7391. **First Missouri State Capitol** was Missouri's state capitol from 1821 to 1826, listed as a Missouri State Historic Site. The old capitol is located at 200-216 South Main St. St. Charles, MO 63301. Tel: (636) 940-3322.

The **Old Courthouse** has a gallery that tells the history of St. Louis. The courthouse is located at 11 N. Fourth St. St. Louis, MO 63102. Tel: (314) 655-1700. <<http://www.nps.gov/jeff>>

American Kennel Club Museum of the Dog is located at 1721 S. Mason Rd., St. Louis, MO 63131, Tel: (314) 821-3647. This unique museum is dedicated to man's best friend, exhibiting dog paintings and artifacts <<http://www.akc.org>>. The **Anheuser-Busch Brewery** offers tours to visitors which include the historic Brew house, Budweiser Clydesdale stables, and much more, a great experience for a beer enthusiast. The Brewery is located at 12th & Lynch Streets St. Louis, MO 63118. Tel: (314) 577-2626 <<http://www.budweisertours.com>>.

Holocaust Museum & Learning Center is located at 12 Millstone Campus Dr. St. Louis, MO 63146; Tel: (314) 432-0020, ext. 3711. The museum exhibits memorabilia of the Holocaust <<http://www.hmlc.org>>. **St. Louis Science Center** exhibits more than 700 displays related to technology, the environment, archaeology, and it has an Imax Theater. The science center is located at 5050 Oakland Ave. St. Louis, MO 63110 Toll-Free: (800) 456-7572 <<http://www.slsc.org>>.

Meramec Caverns, located near St. Louis at Highway W 44 & Exit 230 Stanton, MO 63079 Toll-Free: (800) 676-6105, offers exiting adventures and leisure activities <<http://www.AmericasCave.com>>. **Mastodon State Historic Site** is an ancient site of Missouri's Ice Age animals and the Native Americans who inhabited the area more than 10,000 years ago. 1050 Museum Dr. Imperial, MO 63052. Tel: (636) 464-2976 <<http://www.mostateparks.com/mastodon.htm>>. **Calvary Cemetery** is a gravesite of some well-known figures: playwright Tennessee Williams and General William Sherman among others. Visitors will also be interested by the architectural beauty of the tombs and memorials. The cemetery is located at 5239 West Florissant Ave. St. Louis, MO 63115. Tel: (314) 381-1313.

Laclede's Landing Wax Museum, located at 720 N. Second St. St Louis, MO 63102, Tel: (314) 241-1155, exhibits almost 200 costumed wax figures originally from London. **Laumeier Sculpture Park & Museum** is one of the major sculpture parks in the US. The museum is located at 12580 Rott Rd. St. Louis, MO 63127, Tel: (314) 821-1209 <<http://www.laumeier.com>>. The **City Museum** is located in downtown St. Louis at 701 N. 15th St., St. Louis, MO 63103, Tel: (314) 231-2489. The museum has art, science, and history exhibits <<http://www.citymuseum.org>>.

Miniature Museum of Greater St. Louis exhibits rotating shows of dolls, dollhouses, room boxes and vignettes, furniture, and other scale models. The museum is located at 4746 Gravois St Louis, MO 63116, Tel: (314) 832-7790 <<http://www.miniaturemuseum.org>>. **World Ways Children's Museum** is a fun travel adventure and educational museum located at 15479 Clayton Rd. St. Louis, MO 63131, Tel: (636) 207-7405 <<http://www.worldways.org>>. **Missouri History Museum** is located at 5700 Lindell Blvd. St. Louis, MO 63112-0040, Tel: (314) 746-4599 <<http://www.mohistory.org>>. **Deutschheim State Historic Site and Museum** is dedicated to the 19th century German American immigrant. The museum exhibits German culture and heritage. The museum is located at 109 W. Second St. Hermann, MO 65041. Tel: (573) 486-2200 <<http://www.mobot.org/Stateparks/deutsch_s.html>>.

The **Saint Louis Art Museum**, located at 1 Fine Arts Dr St. Louis, MO 63110; Tel: (314) 721-0072, exhibits collections of ancient to contemporary art <<http://www.slam.org>>. **Soldiers Memorial Military Museum** is dedicated to St. Louis' war veterans and heroes and exhibits war memorabilia; located at 1315 Chestnut St. Louis, MO 63103; Tel: (314) 622-4550. **The Black World History Museum** exhibits images and memorabilia of St. Louis' famous black Americans. The museum is located at 2505 St. Louis Ave. St. Louis, MO 63106; Tel: (314) 241-7057.

International Bowling Museum and Hall of Fame is home for the St. Louis Cardinals Hall of Fame Museum, located at 111 Stadium Plaza St. Louis, MO 63102; Tel: (314) 231-6340 <<http://www.bowlingmuseum.com>>. **The Magic House- St. Louis Children's Museum** has more than 100 hands-on educational exhibits for children, one of the best children museums in the US. The museum is located at 516 S. Kirkwood Rd. St. Louis, MO 63122. Tel: (314) 822-8900 <<http://www.magichouse.org>>.

Missouri Botanical Garden houses the largest traditional Japanese garden in North America. The garden is located at 4344 Shaw Blvd. St. Louis, MO 63166; Tel: (314) 577-9400 <<http://www.mobot.org>>. At 1,293 acres, **Forest Park** is one of the largest urban parks in the US. The park houses the Art Museum, History Museum, Science Center, Zoo, The Muny Theater, Jewel Box Greenhouse, and recreation area. The park is located at 5600 Clayton Ave. St. Louis, MO 63110. Tel: (314) 289-5300 <<http://www.stlouis.missouri.org/citygov/parks>>. **The Butterfly House** exhibits thousands of butterflies in free flight; visitors can also observe the natural process of butterfly life cycle. The Butterfly House is located at 15193 Olive Blvd. Chesterfield, MO 63017. Tel: (636) 530-0076 <<http://www.butterflyhouse.org>>.

The **Museum of Contemporary Religious Art** is the first museum of interfaith contemporary art, located at 3700 W. Pine Pedestrian Mall St. Louis, MO 63103; Tel: (314) 977-7170 <<http://www.mocra.slu.edu>>. The **Old Cathedral (Basilica of Saint Louis, King of France)** located at 209 Walnut St. St. Louis, MO 63102; Tel: (314) 231-3250, is one of St. Louis' earliest churches. The basilica is a national monument and famous for its breathtaking collection of mosaics <<http://www.catholic-forum.com/stlouisking>>. **Shrine of St. Joseph** is a 1840's Baroque-style church with a beautiful altar and the largest handmade Pfeffer tracker organ, located at 1220 N. 11th St St. Louis, MO 63106; Tel: (314)

St. Louis City Skyline

231-9407. **Historic Trinity Lutheran Church** is the oldest Lutheran church west of the Mississippi River. The Church is located at 1805 S. 8th St. St. Louis, MO 63104; Tel: (314) 231-4092 <<http://www.historictrinitystlouis.com>>.

The **National Shrine of Our Lady of the Snows** is the largest outdoor shrine in North America. The shrine is located at 442 S. DeMazenod Dr. Belleville, IL 62223; Tel: (314) 241-3400 <<http://www.snows.org>>. **St. Francis de Sales Parish,** or the Cathedral of South St. Louis, is a national historic site and famous for its gothic architecture, stained glass, statues, and altar. It is located at 2653 Ohio Ave. St Louis, MO 63118; Tel: (314) 771-3100 <<http://www.archstl.org/parishes/archstl/0267.html>>. **Black Madonna Shrine** has many sacred multi-colored rock grottos. The shrine is located at 100 Saint Josephs Hill Rd Pacific, MO 63069. Tel: (636) 938-5361 <<http://www.blackmadonnashrine.org>>.

Visit the **Soulard Farmers Market** located at 730 Carroll St St. Louis, MO 63104; Tel: (314) 622-4180. The market was founded in 1779 and today there are more than 150 stalls with fresh local produce; open throughout the year. **Six Flags St. Louis** is a theme park and water park with various rides and entertainment. The theme park is located at I-44 W at Allenton 6 Flags Rd. Pacific, MO 63069; Tel: (636) 938-4800 <<http://www.sixflags.com>>. **Raging Rivers Water Park,** located just 40 minutes from St Louis, has huge wave pools, rivers, and other entertainment. Located at 100 Palisades Pkwy Grafton, IL 62037; Tel: (618) 786-2345 <<http://www.ragingrivers.com>>.

Accommodations

Courtyard St Louis Downtown is located at 2340 Market Street at Jefferson St. Louis, MO 63103; Toll-Free: (800) 932-2198; expect to pay $80-$200. **Days Inn St. Louis Downtown** is located just 8 blocks from the St. Louis Arch at 1133 Washington Avenue St. Louis, MO 63101; Tel: (314) 231-4070; expect to pay $50-$100. **Embassy Suites St. Louis-Downtown** is located at 901 North 1st Street St. Louis, MO 63102; Toll-Free: (800) EMBASSY; expect to pay $100-$250. **Econo Lodge St. Louis** is located close to downtown St. Louis at 1351 Dunn Road St. Louis, MO 63138-2065; Toll-Free: (800) 553-2666; expect to pay $50-$100.

Hyatt Regency St. Louis is located at 1 St. Louis Union Station St. Louis, MO 63103; Toll-Free: (800) 400-5400; expect to pay $100-$300. **Hampton Inn St. Louis - Union Station** is located at downtown St. Louis at 2211 Market Street St. Louis, MO 63103; Toll-Free: (800) HAMPTON; expect to pay $70-$150. **Doubletree Hotel and Conference Center St. Louis** is located at 16625 Swingley Ridge Road St. Louis, MO 63017-1798; Tel: (636) 532-5000; expect to pay $60-$150.

Four Points by Sheraton St. Louis West is located 6 miles from Lambert International Airport at 3400 Rider Trail South St. Louis MO 63045; Toll-Free: (888) 625-5144; expect to pay $50-$150. **Hilton St. Louis Airport** is located at 10330 Natural Bridge Road St. Louis, MO 63134-3303; Tel: (314) 426-5500; expect to pay $70-$150. **Best Western Airport Inn** is located less than a mile from Lambert International Airport at 10232 Natural Bridge Road St. Louis, MO 63134-3302; Toll-Free: (800) 872-0070; expect to pay $50-$100.

Doubletree Club St. Louis Airport is located at 9600 Natural Bridge Road St. Louis, MO 63134; Tel: (925) 473-2230; expect to pay $60-$150. **Days Inn Airport St. Louis**

is located at 4545 Woodson Road St. Louis, MO 63134; Tel: (314) 423-6770; expect to pay $40-$100. **Courtyard Airport/Earth City** is located at 3101 Rider Trail South St. Louis, MO 63044; Tel: (314) 209-1000; expect to pay $60-$150.

Millennium Hotel St. Louis is located across the Gateway Arch at 200 South 4th Street St. Louis, MO 63109; Toll-Free: (800) 465-6486; expect to pay $70-$230. **Holiday Inn Express St. Louis** is located 3 miles from downtown St. Louis at 2625 Lafayette St. Louis, MO 63104; Toll-Free: (800) 465-4329; expect to pay $60-$150. **Holiday Inn Select St. Louis Downtown Convention Center** is located at 811 North 9th Street St. Louis, MO 63101; Toll-Free: (800) 465-4329; expect to pay $50-$180. **The Ritz-Carlton St Louis** is located nine miles west of downtown St Louis at 100 Carondelet Plaza St. Louis, MO 63105; Toll-Free: (800) 241-3333; expect to pay $150-$600. **The Westin St. Louis** is located at 811 Spruce Street St. Louis MO 63102; Toll-Free: (800) WESTIN-1; expect to pay $80-$400.

Holiday Inn Forest Park is located at 5915 Wilson Avenue St. Louis, MO 63110; Toll-Free: (800) 465-4329; expect to pay $100-$150. **Omni Majestic Hotel** is a listed at National Register of Historic Buildings is located at 1019 Pine Street St. Louis, MO 63101; Toll-Free: (800) THE-OMNI; expect to pay $60- 150. **Sheraton Clayton Plaza Hotel St. Louis** is located in the heart of the Clayton financial and business district at 7730 Bonhomme Avenue St. Louis, MO 63105; Toll-Free: (888) 625-5144; expect to pay $80-$370.

Chase Park Plaza Hotel is located at 212 North Kings highway St. Louis, MO 63108; Tel: (314) 633-3000; expect to pay expect to pay $100-$250. **Comfort Inn Southwest** is located at 3730 South Lindbergh Boulevard St. Louis, MO 63127-1397; Toll-Free: (800) 228-5150; expect to pay $40-$100. **Best Western Kirkwood Inn** is just 15 minutes from downtown located at 1200 South Kirkwood Road St. Louis MO 63122; Tel: (314) 821-3950 and Toll-Free: (800) 435-4656; expect to pay $80 - $110.

Kirkwood (MO)

Kirkwood was founded in 1853 with a total land area is 8.9 sq. miles (23 sq. kilometers) and a population of approximately 29,000 residents. Kirkwood is located just 15 minutes from Lambert-St. Louis International Airport and Interstate 270. This beautiful town is known for its historic and lovely architecture and friendly community. There are many small and local business establishments in the town centers or downtown. It is common for the locals of Kirkwood to describe their town in many superlative words such as "marvelous" or "wonderful," therefore if you visit the fabulous town of Kirkwood, don't be surprised!

Point of Interest

Magic House/St Louis Children's Museum has educational hands-on exhibits for children; the museum is one of the most visited in the US. The museum is located at 516 S. Kirkwood Rd Kirkwood MO. **Powder Valley Nature Conservation Center** located at 11715 Cragwold Rd Kirkwood MO, near Interstate 44 & Interstate 270. The center exhibits educational information on local wildlife.

The **Historic Kirkwood Train Depot** was built in 1893 and is located at 110 W. Argonne Rd. Kirkwood, MO 63122. The station is staffed and features an enclosed waiting area, restrooms, and payphones. Transportation options from the station include local transit, bus, and taxi services.

Kirkwood station is served by the Midwest Corridor.

Washington (MO)

Washington was one of the first American cities west of the Mississippi, located 50 miles west of St. Louis and 66 miles from the state's capital, Jefferson City. Officially founded in 1839, today's Washington has a total land area of 6.6 sq. miles (17 sq. kilometers) and a population of 13,243 friendly residents.

Many German descendants migrated to the site during the early 1800's and are still living in Washington. The city has one of the busiest recreational riverfronts in the region and is a regional center for medical care and commerce.

Washington's train depot is located at Front and Elm Sts. Washington, MO 63090. The station is "self serve;" transportation from the station is taxi service. Washington station is served by the Midwest Corridor.

Hermann (MO)

German settlers who wanted to build a city where German culture could flourish in the US established the town of Hermann in 1836. Testimony to the early German pioneers is well preserved in the city's museums. Today Hermann is home to about 3,000 residents living in a total land area of 1.9 sq. miles (5 sq. kilometers). Hermann is known for its wineries and heritage. There are many restaurants, antique shops, boutiques, and accommodations in the area.

Hermann's train depot is located at Wharf and Gutenburg Sts. Hermann, MO 65041. The station is "self-serve" and features payphones and a visitors parking area. Hermann station is served by the Midwest Corridor.

Jefferson City (MO)

The capital city of the "Show Me" State, Jefferson City is located on the banks of the Missouri river at the center of the state of Missouri. The city was established in December 1831 and was named after Thomas Jefferson, the third president of the United States. Jefferson City is the center of Missouri's state government and political world, with a total

287

area of 26.8 sq. miles (68.8 sq. kilometers). Jefferson City is home to more than 36,000 residents.

Jefferson City's train depot is located at 101 Jefferson St. Jefferson City, MO 65101. The station is staffed and features payphones, vending machines, and restrooms. Transportation from the station is local taxi service. Jefferson City station is served by the Midwest Corridor.

Visitor Information Center

Jefferson City Convention & Visitors Bureau 213 Adams Street PO Box 2227, Jefferson City MO 65102-2227; Tel: (573) 632-2820 or Toll-Free: (800) 769-4183.

Places to See

The Missouri Capitol is known for its magnificent dome that dominates the skyline of downtown Jefferson City. The dome is 238 feet above the ground and topped by a bronze statue of Ceres (the goddess of vegetation). Admission is free; call Tel: (573) 751-4127 for information. Located northeast of the capitol building is the **All Missouri Veterans Memorial** which was dedicated in November 1991 and has a limestone colonnade, waterfall, and eight black marble posts forming a path called the "Veterans Walk."

Other places of interest are the **Harry S. Truman State Office Building** Tel: (573) 751-2624), the **Museum of Missouri Military History** located 6 miles from Jefferson City on Hwy 50 Tel: (573) 638-9603 and the **Cole County Historical Museum** 109 Madison Street Jefferson City, MO 65101, Tel: (573) 635-1850 which exhibits the history of Missouri's political and government developments.

Governor's Mansion and Garden has been home for 32 governors of Missouri and the beautiful mansion and garden is open to visitors. Contact the Missouri Mansion Preservation offices at (573) 751-7929 for information. **Missouri Veterinary Museum** is the only museum in the US dedicated to veterinary medicine. Exhibits include artifacts and medical instruments and old veterinary practice memorabilia. The museum is one-of-a-kind and worth a visit; located at 2500 Country Club Drive Jefferson City, MO 65109, Tel: (573) 636-8737.

Accommodations

Best Western Inn located at 1937 Christy Dr, Jefferson City, MO 65101, Tel: (573) 635-4175. **Capitol Plaza Hotel** located at 415 W McCarty St, Jefferson City, MO 65101, Tel: (573) 635-1234. **Hampton Inn** located at 4800 Country Club Dr, Jefferson City, MO 65109, Tel: (573) 634-7440. **Lakeside Motel** located at 5629 Highway 50 W, Jefferson City, MO 65109, Tel: (573) 893-2512. **Ramada Inn** located at 1510 Jefferson St, Jefferson City, MO 65109, Tel: (573) 635-7171. **Hampton Inn** located at 1800 Christy Dr, Jefferson City, MO 65101, Tel: (573) 893-8000.

Hotel De Ville located at 319 W Miller St, Jefferson City, MO 65101, Tel: (573) 636-5231. **Monroe Plaza Hotel** located at 422 Monroe St, Jefferson City, MO 65101, Tel: (573) 636-5101. **Holiday Inn Express** located at 1716 Jefferson St, Jefferson City, MO 65109, Tel: (573) 634-4040. **Fairfield Inn** located at 3621 W Truman Blvd, Jefferson City, MO 65109,

Tel: (573) 761-0400. **Budget Inn** located at 1309 Jefferson St, Jefferson City, MO 65109, Tel: (573) 636-6167. **Comfort Inn** located at 1926 Jefferson St, Jefferson City, MO 65109, Tel: (573) 636-2797. **Super 8 Motel** located at 1710 Jefferson St, Jefferson City, MO 65109, Tel: (573) 636-5456.

Sedalia (MO)

The charming city Sedalia was founded in 1860 and still preserves its rich history and heritage. Known as the "Queen City of the Prairies" to many, Sedalia's economic success was closely identified with the west railroad expansion. Today Sedalia is a home to more than 20,000 warm-hearted people; a trip to downtown Sedalia is just like a journey back in time.

Sedalia's train depot is located at Pacific and Osage Sts. Sedalia, MO 65301. The station is self-serve and features an enclosed waiting area, restrooms, and payphones. Transportation from the station is local taxi service. Sedalia station is served by the Midwest Corridor.

Warrensburg (MO)

Named after Martin Warren, a blacksmith pioneer of the area, Warrensburg was founded in 1833. Located just 50 miles east of Kansas City, Warrensburg has a total land area of 8 sq. miles (21 sq. kilometers) and a population of more than 15,000. The city of Warrensburg has a very diverse economy based on manufacturing, commercial, and retail enterprises. Warrensburg is also home for Hawker Energy Products, Whiteman Air Force Base, Harmon Electronics, and Western Missouri Medical Center among others.

Warrensburg's train depot is located at 100 S. Holden St. Warrensburg, MO 64093. The station is self-serve and features an enclosed waiting area, restrooms, and free parking area. Transportation from the station is local taxi service. Warrensburg station is served by the Midwest Corridor.

Lee's Summit (MO)

Located east of Kansas City, Lee's Summit was founded in 1865 by William B. Howard. The city of Lee's Summit has a population of more than 45,000. Many have argued the origin of the city's name "Lee" and "Summit." Some claimed that the name Lee was given in honor of the Confederate General Robert Lee, while others have argued that the name was actually misspelled as "Lee" instead of "Lea" in honor of one of the city's respected citizens Dr. Lea. The word "summit" refers to the fact that the city is the highest point of the train line between Kansas City and St. Louis. Lee's Summit is a beautiful community rich with warm people and nature's beauty.

Lee's Summit train depot is located at 220 S. Main St. Lee's Summit, MO 64063. The station is self-serve and features an enclosed waiting area, restrooms, and payphones. Transportation from the station is local taxi service. Lee's Summit Station is served by the Midwest Corridor.

Independence (MO)

The city of Independence was founded in 1827 and was incorporated in May of 1832 and again in 1849. The city of Independence is known for Harry S. Truman, the 33rd president of the United State who grew up and died in the city. The remains of Harry S. Truman and his wife were buried in the courtyard of the "Harry S. Truman Library" in Independence. The city of Independence is located a few miles east of Kansas City at the south shore of the Missouri River. It has a land area of 49 sq. miles (126 sq. kilometers) and a population of more than 120,000.

Places of Interest

Harry S. Truman library located at 500 W. US Hwy. 24 Independence, MO 64050, toll-free (800) 833-1225. This is where the remains of the late president were buried, and there you'll also find a replica of President Truman's Oval Office -- one of the favorite attractions in the library. Other attractions include: the **Harry S. Truman Home** is located at 219 N. Delaware St. Independence; the **Jail Museum-1859** located at 217 N. Main St Independence, MO 64050-2804, Tel: (816) 252-1892 and the **National Frontier Trails Center** located at 318 W Pacific Ave Independence, MO 64050-4372, Tel: (816) 325-7575.

Independence's train depot is located at 600 S. Grand Ave. Independence, MO 64050. The station is self-serve and transportation from the station is local taxi service. Independence station is served by the Midwest Corridor.

Kansas City (MO, KS)
Kansas City has a connecting train to **Denver (CO)**, **Albuquerque (NM),** and **Los Angeles (CA)** via the **Southwest Chief**.

Kansas City is known as the "Heart of America." With an area of 198 sq. miles (510 sq. Kilometers), it is the eighth largest city in the US. Kansas City has a total population of 443,400. Kansas City is also known for its fountains, steaks, barbeque, and Jazz; it is home to Hallmark Cards, Farmland Industries, Russell Stover Candies, Hoechst Marion Roussel Pharmaceuticals, the Nazarene Church, Unity School of Christianity, American Century, and many more.

Francois Chouteau, a trader from St. Louis, founded the site in the early 1820's. Other settlers followed in the following years; John Calvin McCoy founded his trading post and called it Westport in 1833 and in 1845 it replaced the town of Independence as a transportation hub for trading to west. In 1838 McCoy and "Town Company" purchased a 271-acre farmland for $4,220 which later became the city of Kansas named after the early settlers of the region, the Kanza Indians. And in 1853 Kansas was incorporated by the state of Missouri as the City of Kansas.

Transportation

Airport

Kansas City International Airport is located at 601 Brasilia Avenue, Kansas City, Missouri 64153, Tel: (816) 243-3000. There are various ground transportation options at the airport bringing passengers around the region. The "On-Airport Shuttle Service" takes passengers between the airports parking lots and terminals. Transportation options from the airport include shuttle services, taxi, Metro bus, limousine service, and rent-a-car.

Rent-a-Car

Avis Rent A Car, 936 Tel Aviv, K.C., MO, Tel: (816) 243-5763 or (800) 331-1212. Enterprise Rent-A-Car, 13010 South U.S. Interstate 71, Grandview, MO, Tel: (816) 966-8188 or (800) 736-8222. Dollar Rent-A-Car, 962 Tel Aviv, Kansas City, MO, Tel: (816) 243-5600 or (800) 800-4000. Budget Rent A Car, 901 Tel Aviv, Kansas City, MO, Tel: (816) 243-5757 or (800) 677-3681.

Local Bus Service

K.C.A.T.A. (The Metro) offers services around the City of Kansas, 1200 E. 18th, K.C., MO. Tel: (816) 221-0660.

Trolley Tours

Kansas City Trolley offers an all-day pass giving passengers multiple rides to trolley around the city. Tel: (816) 221-3399 and toll-free (888) 471-6050.

Taxi

Yellow Cab has services around the city of Kansas; Tel: (816) 471-6050 or toll-free (888) 471-6050; <<http://www.mtsi-kc.com>>.

Train

Kansas City's train depot is located at 2200 Main St. Kansas City, MO 64108. The station is staffed and features an enclosed waiting area, restrooms, payphones, and a snack bar. Transportation options from the station include Hertz Car Rental, toll-free (800) 654-3131, local transit, and taxi services. Trains serving Kansas City station are the Midwest Corridor and the Southwest Chief.

Kansas (KS)
Capital: Topeka (Population: 2,688,418)
Size: 81,823 sq mi. (211,922 sq km)
Nickname: Sunflower State, the Breadbasket of America
Joined the union on: January 29, 1861 (34th state)
Motto: To the stars through difficulties
Flower: Sunflower
Bird: Western Meadowlark
Song: Home on the Range
Famous for: Turkey Red Wheat, Walter Chrysler
Major industries: Agriculture, farming, Aircraft Manufacturing

Visitor Information Center

Convention and Visitors Bureau of Greater Kansas City is located at 1100 Main Street, Suite 2550, Kansas City, MO 64105; Tel: (816) 221-5242

Places to See and Things to Do

Fort Leavenworth is the oldest fort west of the Mississippi, located in Fort Leavenworth, K.S., MO, toll-free (800) 844-4114. The fort includes Frontier Army Museum, Buffalo Soldier Monument, Oregon & Santa Fe Trail wagon ruts, and much more. **Liberty**

Memorial Tel: (816) 221-1918 is located in Penn Valley Park, south of Union Station. The memorial and museum complex were dedicated to World War I. **Vietnam Veterans Memorial** is dedicated to Vietnam war veterans, located at 43rd and Broadway, K.C., MO.

City Hall Observation Deck is located at 414 E. 12th St., K.C., MO. Tel: (816) 513-3143. The observation deck is on the 30th floor and offers a breathtaking view of Kansas City. Admission is free <<http://www.kcmo.org>>. **H&R Block Art space Kansas City Art Institute** is dedicated to the education of contemporary and visual arts. The museum is located at 16 E 43rd K.C., MO, Tel: (816) 802-3426. **Kansas City Convention and Entertainment Centers** are located at 13th & Broadway, K.C., MO, toll-free (800) 821-7060.

39th Street is a colorful neighborhood district with various restaurants, bookstores, and shops. Tel: (816) 561-5411 for information. **Westport** is Kansas City's oldest historic district; there are shops, restaurants, galleries, and bars in the area located at Westport Road and Broadway, K.C., MO. Tel: (816) 756-2789. Visit the **City Market** located at 20 E. 5th Suite 201 K.C., MO; Tel: (816) 842-1271. The city market is the largest open market in the Midwest <<http://www.kc-citymarket.com>>.

Kansas City Museum is located at 3218 Gladstone, K.C., MO, Tel: (816) 483-8300. The museum displays hands-on science and history exhibits. **Toy and Miniature Museum** exhibits antique toys, dolls houses, and scale miniatures. The museum is located at 5235 Oak, K.C., MO, Tel: (816) 333-2055.

Cathedral of the Immaculate Conception is located at 416 W. 12th, K.C., MO. The cathedral was built in 1882 with neo-classical architecture. **Grace and Holy Trinity Cathedral,** located in downtown Kansas City at 415 West 13th Street, Kansas City, MO, the cathedral is a Norman-Gothic architecture style. **Pilgrim Chapel,** a national historic place, is a Gothic stone chapel located in Hyde Park at 3801 Gill ham Road, Kansas City, Mo.

Harley-Davidson Final Assembly Plant has a museum and tour center, exhibiting production of the famous motorbikes. The museum is located at 11401 N. Congress, K.C., MO, toll-free (888) 875-2883. **Kansas City Zoological Park** is located at 6700 Zoo Drive, Swope Park, K.C., MO; Tel: (816) 513-5700. The zoo is home to hundreds of animals and a Sprint IMAX Theatre <<http://www.kansascityzoo.org>>. **Union Station Kansas City** is located at 30 W. Pershing Road, K.C., MO; Tel: (816) 460-2222. The museum is one of the most beautiful Union Stations in the US and inside the station there is a science center, theaters, shops, and restaurants.

Hallmark Visitors Center exhibits the 90-year history of Hallmark Cards, located at Crown Center, Level 3, K.C., MO. Tel: (816) 274-3613. **Kansas City Public Library** is located at 311 E.12th, K.C., MO; Tel: (816) 701-3510. **Columbian Theatre, Museum & Art Center** is a century old historical building known for its six murals, located at 521 Lincoln Ave., Wamego, K.S, MO, toll-free (800) 899-1893. **Kemper Museum of Contemporary Art** is located at 4420 Warwick, K.C., MO, Tel: (816) 561-3737.

Airline History Museum is located at 201 N.W. Lou Holland Dr. (downtown airport), K.C., MO, toll-free (800) 513-9484. The museum demonstrates the history of air travel.

Belton, Grandview & Kansas City Railroad Co. located at 502 Walnut Belton, MO. Tel: (816) 331-2632, has a 45-minute train trip .

Kansas City Blues & Jazz Festival is held in Kansas City every July for 3 full weeks, toll-free (800) 530-5266. **Spirit Festival,** held during the weekend of Labor Day, is the largest festival of its kind in the US. There are jazz, blues, rock, reggae, country, and gospel music performances by regional and local artists. For information call Tel: (816) 221-4444. **American Jazz Museum** located at 1616 E. 18th St., K.C., MO, Tel: (816) 474-VINE. The museum is dedicated to one of the greatest cultural contributions of African Americans: Jazz. **18th and Vine Authority** complex houses the American Jazz Museum, Blue Room Jazz Club, Horace M. Peterson III Visitors Center, and the Negro Leagues Baseball Museum. The Complex is located at 1616 E. 18th St., K.C., MO, Tel: (816) 474-8463. **Black Archives of Mid-America,** located at 2033 Vine, K.C., MO, Tel: (816) 483-1300, houses one of the largest collections of African American memorabilia, artifacts, and research material in the central United States.

Benjamin Ranch West offers horseback riding along 230 acres of wooded trails. The ranch is located at 5308 E. 87th St. (Inter state 435 & E. 87th.), K.C., MO. Tel: (816) 765-1100. **American Royal Livestock, Horse Show & Rodeo** has traditional shows and entertainment, 1701 American Royal Court, K.C., MO. toll-free (800) 821-5857 <<http://www.americanroyal.com>>. **Oceans of Fun** located off I-435, Exit 54 (Parvin Road), K.C., MO; toll-free (800) 877-4386. The water park features more than 60 acres of water playgrounds.

Harrah's North Kansas City Casino located at Hwy. 210 & Chouteau Traffic way, North K.C., MO, toll-free (800) HARRAHS; one of the most visited casinos in Kansas City <<http://www.harrahs.com>>. **Isle of Capri Casino** also offers fine dining with jazz entertainment. The casino is located at 1800 E. Front St., K.C., MO, Tel: (816) 855-7777 <<http://www.isleofcapricasino.com>>. **Argosy Riverside Casino** located at 777 N.W. Argosy Parkway, Riverside, MO. toll-free (800) 270-7711, is a riverboat casino <<http://argosykc.casinocity.com>>.

Accommodations

Airport Hampton Inn located at 11212 N. Newark Circle K.C., MO 64153; toll-free (800) HAMPTON or Tel: (816) 464-5454; expect to pay $70-$100. **American Inn East** located at 4141 S. Noland Rd Independence, MO 64055; toll-free (800) 905-6343; expect to pay $50-$100. **Americ Inn Motel & Suites** located at 2512 N.W. Prairie View Rd. Platte City, MO 64079; toll-free (800) 634-3444; expect to pay $74-$130. **Ameri star Casino** located at I-435 N. at 210 Hwy. K.C., MO 4120; toll-free (800) 499-4961; expect to pay $100-$150. **Ameri Suites KCI** located at 7600 NW 97th Terrace K. C., MO 64153; toll-free (800) 74-SUITE; expect to pay $80-100.

Comfort Inn Merriam/Kansas City located at 6401 E. Frontage Road Merriam, KS 66202; toll-free (800) 228-5150; expect to pay $60-80. **Comfort Suites Airport** located at 11951 N.W. Ambassador Dr. K.C., MO 64153; toll-free (800) 834-8535; expect to pay $70-$100. **Courtyard by Marriott – East** located at 1500 N.E. Coronado Dr. Blue Springs, MO; toll-free (800) 321-2211; expect to pay $89-$100. **Doubletree Hotel at Corporate Woods** located at Kansas City Corporate Woods 10100 College Boulevard Overland Park, KS 66210;

toll-free (800) 222-TREE; expect to pay $80-$350. **Embassy Suites - Country Club Plaza** located at 220 W. 43rd St. K.C., MO 64111; toll-free (800) EMBASSY; expect to pay $130-$200. **Harrah's Hotel & Casino** located at I-35 N. at 210 East North K.C., MO 64116; toll-free (888) HARRAHS; expect to pay $100-$150. **Hilton-Kansas City Airport** located at 8801 N.W. 112th St. K.C., MO 64153; toll-free (800) 525-6322; expect to pay $70-$200.

Holiday Inn Citicentre located at 1215 Wyandotte K.C., MO 64105; toll-free (800) 354-0986; expect to pay $100-$120. **Hyatt Regency Crown Center** located at 2345 McGee K.C., MO 64108; toll-free (800) 233-1234; expect to pay $120-$200. **Marriott Kansas City-Downtown** located at 200 W. 12th Street K.C., MO 64105; toll-free (800) 228-9290; expect to pay $100-$2000. **Sheraton Suites Country Club Plaza** located at 770 W. 47th K.C., MO 64112; toll-free (800) 325-3535; expect to pay $100-180. **The Westin Crown Center** located at One Pershing Road K.C., MO 64108; toll-free (800) 228-3000; expect to pay $220-$1,000. **Wyndham Garden Hotel - Overland Park** located at 7000 W 108th St. Overland Park, KS 66211; toll-free (800) WYNDHAM; expect to pay $80-$130.

Illinois Zephyr Service

All Aboard !

Chicago (IL) See Illinois and Missouri service, page 268.

Summit (IL) See Illinois and Missouri service, page 275- 276.

Joliet (IL) See Illinois and Missouri service, page 275- 276.

La Grange (IL)

La Grange is located 14 miles west of Chicago and 170 miles north of Springfield. La Grange has a total

	Illinois Zephyr	
5:55 pm-D	**Chicago (IL)**	10 :35 am-**A**
	Summit (IL)	
	Joliet (IL)	
6 :14 pm	La Grande Road (IL)	9 :54 am
6 :30 pm	Naperville (IL)	9 :38 am
6:53 pm	Plano (IL)	9:16 am
7:20 pm	Mendota (IL)	8:49 am
7 :40 pm	Priceton (IL)	8 :30 am
8 :03 pm	Kawanee (IL)	8 :06 am
8 :34 pm	Galesburg (IL)	7 :38 am
9 :12 pm	Macomb (IL)	7 :00 am
10 :18 pm-**A**	Quincy (IL)	6 :12 am-**D**

D-Departure   **A**-Arrival

land area of 2.3 sq. miles (6 sq. kilometers) and a population of more than 15,000. La Grange's train depot is located at 25 W. Burlington Av, La Grange, IL 60525. The station is self-serve and features an enclosed waiting area and payphones. Transportation options from the station include local transit and taxi services.

La Grange station is served by the Midwest Corridor.

Naperville (IL)

Naperville is one of the fastest growing communities in the region with a population of 130,000 and a total land area of 28 sq. miles (72 sq. kilometers); it is one of the largest cities in the state of Illinois.

Naperville's train depot is located at E. 4th and Ellsworth Ave. Naperville, IL 60540. The train station is staffed and features an enclosed waiting area, restrooms, and payphones. Transportation options from the station include local transit and taxi services. Trains serving Naperville station are the California Zephyr, Midwest Corridor, and Southwest Chief.

Plano (IL)

Illinois (IL)
Capital: Springfield (Population: 12,419,293)
Size: 55,593 sq mi. (143,987 sq km)
Nicknames: The Land of Lincoln
Entered the union: December 3, 1818 (21st state)
Motto: State sovereignty, national union
Flower: Violet
Bird: Cardinal
Song: Illinois
Famous for: Sears Towers
Major industries: Coal, agriculture, and oil

Located just 52 miles west of Chicago, Plano has a total land area of 1.9 sq. miles (5 sq. kilometers) and a population of approximately 5,500. Plano was founded in 1854 when the railroad extended westward from the city of Chicago. Plano's train depot is located in Downtown Plano, Plano, IL 60545. The station is not staffed. Plano station is served by the Midwest Corridor.

Mendota (IL)

Mendota is located 83 miles west of Chicago and 125 miles north of Springfield. Mendota has a population of just 7,000 and a land area of 3 sq. miles (8 sq. kilometers). The newly remodeled cultural museum housed in Mendota's Hume-Carnegie Museum is a popular attraction. The Union Depot Railroad Museum exhibits railroad memorabilia and a large operating model train.

Mendota's train depot is located on 8th St. Mendota, IL 61342. The station is self-serve and features an enclosed waiting area, restrooms, and payphones. Trains serving Mendota station are the Midwest Corridor and the Southwest Chief.

Princeton (IL)

Situated in the heartland of north-central Illinois, Princeton is a proud community of more than 7,000 in a small town with a land area of just 3.9 sq. miles (9.8 sq. kilometers).

Princeton's train depot is located at 107 Bicentennial Dr. Princeton, IL 61356. The station is not staffed and features an enclosed waiting area, restrooms, and payphones. Trains serving Princeton station are the California Zephyr, Midwest Corridor, and the Southwest Chief.

Kewanee (IL)

Having led the world in hog production in 1948, Kewanee was officially called the "Hog Capital of the World" by order of the Illinois Legislature. Kewanee has a population of 12,969 and a land area of 5.8 sq. miles (15 sq. kilometers).

Kewanee's train depot is located at 3rd and Depot St. Kewanee, IL 61443. The station is self-serve and features an enclosed waiting area and payphones. Transportation from the station is local taxi service. Kewanee station is served by the Midwest Corridor.

Galesburg (IL)

Galesburg is linked to the Texas Eagle routes through Motor coach Throughway Connections.

Historic Galesburg, also known as "America's Small Town and Rail City," is located in prairie land of west-central Illinois. Founded by George W. Gale in 1837 Galesburg became the first anti-slavery town in the state of Illinois. In addition, Galesburg was part of the "underground railroad" network that saved hundreds of Black Americans from slavery.

Galesburg has a land area of 17 sq. miles (44 sq. kilometers) and a population of more than 35,000. Galesburg is a lovely city full of history; visitors should visit Seminary Street Historic Commercial District, a restored historical downtown area which takes visitors back to the old Midwest era. Also in Galesburg's Downtown District there are many shops, restaurants, and entertainment sites.

Local Transportation

Local Bus

Burlington Trail ways, Tel: (309) 342-6715 and City Bus Co, Tel: (309) 342-4242.

Taxi

Courtesy Cab, Tel: (309) 341-1077 and City Cab, Tel: (309) 341-6161.

Rent-a-Car

Louis Lakis Ford Car Rental, Tel: (309) 342-1121, Avis Rent A Car, toll-free (800) 230-4898, and Enterprise Rent-A-Car, toll-free (800) RENT-A-CAR.

Train

Galesburg's train depot is located at 225 S. Seminary St. Galesburg, IL 61401. The train station is staffed and features an enclosed waiting area, restrooms, payphones, and vending machines. Trainsserving Galesburg station are the California Zephyr, Midwest Corridor, and the Southwest Chief.

Macomb (IL)

Macomb is the seat of McDonough County and is located along the "Burlington Trail." The city was named after General Alexander Macomb. Macomb has a land area of 9.3 sq. miles (24 sq. kilometers) and a population of almost 20,000.

Some of Macomb's places of interest are the **Blandin House Museum,** located at 215 S. Chestnut St. Blandinsville, IL 61420, Tel: (309) 652-3673. The **McDonough County Courthouse** located at Courthouse Square, Macomb, IL 61455. **Museum of Geology** located at Tillman Hall Western Illinois University Macomb, IL 61455, Tel: (309) 298-1368.

The **Pineapple Gallery**, located at 204 W. Jefferson Macomb, IL 61455, Tel: (309) 837-1914, exhibits pottery and lamps from well-known artists. The **University Art Gallery/Museum** located just north of Sherman Hall at Western Illinois University, Macomb, IL 61455. Tel: (309) 298-1587. The museum exhibits various visual arts.

Macomb's train depot is located at 120 E. Calhoun St. Macomb, IL 61455. The station is not staffed and features an enclosed waiting area, restrooms, and payphones. Transportation from the station is local taxi service. Macomb station is served by the Midwest Corridor.

Quincy (IL)

Quincy is named after President John Quincy Adams and is located at the bank of the Mississippi river. Quincy has a population of 40,366 and a land area of 12.8 sq. miles (33 sq. kilometers). Just like Galesburg, Quincy was an important stop of the "underground railroad" that saved many Black slaves fleeing the US to Canada. In addition, many Mormons fleeing persecution in Missouri used the city for temporary stops and shelter.

Some of Quincy's attractions are the **Gardner Museum of Architecture** located at 332 Maine St. Quincy, IL 62301-3929, Tel: (217) 224-6873, and the **Historic Quincy Business District** situated at 300 Civic Center Plaza #209 Quincy, IL 62301-4139, Tel: (217) 228-8696.

Quincy's train depot is located at 30th St. and Wismann Lane Quincy, IL 62301. The station is self serve and features an enclosed waiting area. Transportation from the station is local taxi service. Quincy station is served by the Midwest Corridor.

Illini Service

All Aboard!

Chicago (IL) See Illinois and Missouri service, page 268.

Homewood (IL)

Homewood, located 25 miles south of Chicago, was founded by early European settlers in 1830. In 1853 James Hart named the town Hartford. Also that year the railroad came to the town which continued to grow becoming known for its train station, "Thornton Station." Finally, in 1869, the town was listed and recognized by the United States Post Office Department as Homewood and later, in 1893, the town was incorporated. Today Homewood has a population of 19,278 and a land area of 5 sq. miles (13 sq. kilometers).

Illini		
4:00 pm D	**Chicago (IL)**	9:35 pm-A
4:40 pm	Homewood (IL)	8:32 pm
5:10 pm	Kankakee (IL)	7:59 pm
5:32 pm	Gilman (IL)	7:35 pm
6:01 pm	Rantoul (IL)	7:09 pm
6:25 pm	Champaign Urbana (IL)	6:55 pm
7:07 pm	Matoon (IL)	6:08 pm
7:33 pm	Effingham (IL)	5:42 pm
8:21 pm	Centralia (IL)	4:58 pm
8:50 pm	Du Quoin (IL)	4:19 pm
9:30 pm-A	Carbondale (IL)	4:05 pm-D
D-Departure	**A**- Arrival	

Homewood's train depot is located at 181 First St. and Park Ave. Homewood, IL 60430. The station is staffed and features an enclosed waiting area, restrooms, and payphones. Transportation from the station is local transit service.

Trains serving Homewood station are the City of New Orleans and Midwest Corridor.

Kankakee (IL)

The historical region of what is now the Kankakee was originally occupied by the Illini and Miami Indians, the Kickapoo and Mascouten Indians, and the Potawatomi Indians who hunted along the Kankakee River in the early years of the 1760s. By the 1770s the Indian tribes known as the "Three Fires" (the Potawatomi, Ottawa, and Chippewa) dominated the area.

Noel Le Vasseur, better known as the father of Kankakee, in 1838 initiated the first European settlement of the area. Today Kankakee has a land area of 10 sq. miles (26 sq. kilometers) and a population of 27,575.

Some of Kankakee's most visited places are: The Kankakee County Historical Society Art Museum which exhibits a collection of the works of famed sculptor George Gray Barnard, Indian artifacts, and local history. Riverview Historic District is known for the Victorian homes and gardens along the river. The Kankakee County Courthouse, built in 1909, is a beautiful architectural centerpiece of Kankakee. The Kankakee River is nine miles of leisure activities.

Kankakee's train depot is located at 199 S. East Ave. Kankakee, IL 60901. The station is self-serve and features an enclosed waiting area and payphones.

Trains serving Kankakee station are the City of New Orleans and Midwest Corridor.

Gilman (IL)

Gilman is a small town located 82 miles south of Chicago. The town has a land area of 1.9 sq. miles (5 sq. kilometers) and just 1,816 residents. Gilman's train depot is located at the Intersection of US 24 and US 45 Gilman, IL 60938. The station is not staffed. Gilman station is served by the Midwest Corridor.

Illinois (IL)
Capital: Springfield (Population: 12,419,293)
Size: 55,593 sq mi. (143,987 sq km)
Nicknames: The Land of Lincoln
Entered the union: December 3, 1818 (21st state)
Motto: State sovereignty, national union
Flower: Violet
Bird: Cardinal
Song: Illinois
Famous for: Sears Towers
Major industries: Coal, agriculture, and oil

Rantoul (IL)

Rantoul is located within the Champaign/Urbana general area of east-central Illinois. Rantoul is home for Chanute Air Force Base and the 2000 Hot Air Balloon National Championships. Rantoul has a population of 17,212 and a land area of 6.6 sq. miles (17 sq. kilometers).

Rantoul's train depot is located on N. Kentucky St. Rantoul, IL 61866. The station is self-serve and features an enclosed waiting area, restrooms, and payphones. Transportation from the station is local taxi service.

Rantoul station is served by the Midwest Corridor.

Champaign-Urbana (IL)

Situated 129 miles south of Chicago, Champaign-Urbana is home to more than 63,000 residents. Champaign-Urbana is known as a world class hi-tech city much appreciated for its small city atmosphere with the convenience of the latest technological facilities. Some of Champaign-Urbana's most popular destinations are the city's University Library, the third largest academic library in the US. The World Heritage Museum, Museum of Natural History, Krannert Art Museum, and John Philip Sousa Museum, all located at the city's University. And the Krannert Center for the Performing Arts is said to be one of best in the US.

Champaign-Urbana's train depot is located at 45 E. University Ave. Champaign, IL 61820. The station is staffed and features an enclosed waiting area, checked baggage service, restrooms, payphones, and vending machines. Transportation options from the station include local transit, bus, and taxi services.

Trains serving Champaign-Urbana station are the Midwest Corridor and City of New Orleans.

Mattoon (IL)

Mattoon is also a product of the old railroad expansion; located in the heart of Central Illinois the city has a land area of 6.6 sq. miles (17 sq. kilometers). The town was named after William B. Mattoon and the town was incorporated in 1855. Today, Mattoon has a population of roughly 20,000, of which more than half were originally from Kentucky and Tennessee.

Mattoon's train depot is located at 1718 Broadway Mattoon, IL 61938. The station is not staffed and features an enclosed waiting area, restrooms, and payphones. Transportation from the station is local taxi service.

Trains serving Mattoon station are the Midwest Corridor and the City of New Orleans.

Effingham (IL)

It was in 1814 when the first settlers came along the Little Wabash River, but development only came when the railroad arrived in the area in 1850. Since then the area experienced unprecedented growth, businesses and tourism flourished. The original name of the town was Broughton, changed in 1859 to Effingham in honor of a British Lord who refused to fight the colonists during the Revolutionary War.

Today, Effingham is home to more than 12,500 residents and has a thriving economy based on trade, industrial, and transportation industries.

Effingham's train depot is located on S. Bankers St. Effingham, IL 62401. The station is self-serve and features an enclosed waiting area, restrooms, and payphones. Transportation options from the station include local transit and taxi services.

Trains serving Effingham station are the Midwest Corridor and City of New Orleans.

Centralia (IL)

Centralia is located in south-central Illinois just 70 miles east of St. Louis. Founded in 1852, Centralia has a land area of 6.6 sq. miles (17 sq. kilometers) and a population of approximately 18,000. Centralia has been a major transportation and service center since the city's foundation, and it remains so today.

Centralia's economy is based on transportation and manufacturing. Interesting attractions are the 165-foot tall Carillon filled with bells, and the "Centralia Hot Air Balloon Fest." Centralia's train depot is located at 103 E. Broadway Centralia, IL 62801. The station is self-serve.

Trains serving Centralia station are the City of New Orleans and Midwest Corridor.

Du Quoin (IL)

Du Quoin is located 289 miles south of Chicago and 124 miles southeast of Springfield. Du Quoin has a land area of 5.8 sq. miles (15 sq. kilometers) and a population of 6,697.

Du Quoin's train depot is located at 20 N. Chestnut St. Du Quoin, IL 62832. The station is un-staffed and features an enclosed waiting area and payphones. Transportation from the station is local taxi service.

De Quoin station is served by the Midwest Corridor.

Carbondale (IL)

Home of the Southern Illinois University and founded in 1869, Carbondale is located in Jackson County southwest of Mt. Vernon between Murphysboro and Marion about 100 miles southeast of St. Louis, Missouri. The city began as a railroad town that greatly depended on the Illinois Central Railroad. Carbondale has a population of 26,454 and a land area of 10 sq. miles (26 sq. kilometers).

Carbondale's train depot is located at 401 S. Illinois St. Carbondale, IL 62901. The station is self-serve and features an enclosed waiting area, checked baggage service, payphones, restrooms, and vending machines. Transportation options from the station include local transit, bus, and taxi service.

Trains serving Carbondale station are the Midwest Corridor and the City of New Orleans.

Hiawatha Service

All Aboard!

Hiawatha Service		
D-Departure **A**- Arrival		
8:25 am-D	**Chicago (IL)**	7:57 am-**A**
8:47 am	Glenview (IL)	7:25 am
9:24 am	Sturtevant (WI)	6:44 am
9:54 am-**A**	**Milwaukee (WI)**	6:20 am-**D**
-Multiple Trains Service Daily		

Traveling between Chicago and Milwaukee, a distance of only 86 miles, the Hiawatha is Amtrak's shortest intercity passenger train route.

Chicago (IL) See Illinois and Missouri service, page 268.

Glenview (IL)

Glenview is located 18 miles north of Chicago. It has a population of 37,093 and a land area of 12 sq. miles (31 sq. Kilometers), founded in 1673 by Pere Marquette and Joliet.

Glenview's train depot is located at 1116 Depot St. Glenview, IL 60025. The train station is staffed and features an enclosed waiting area, checked baggage service, restrooms, and payphones. Transportation options from the station include local transit and taxi services.

Trains serving Glenview station are the Midwest Corridor and the Empire Builder.

Wisconsin (WI)
Capital: Madison (Population: 5,363,675)
Size: 65,503 sq mi. (169,652 sq km)
Nickname: The Badger State, Dairyland
Joined the union on: May 29, 1848 (30th state)
Motto: Forward
Flower: Wood violet
Bird: Robin
Song: On Wisconsin
Famous for: The first state to legislate Gay Rights
Major industries: Farm, paper production, and manufacturing.

Sturtevant (WI)

Sturtevant is located 62 miles north of Chicago and 24 miles south of Milwaukee. Sturtevant has a population of just 3,803 and land area of 2.3 sq. miles (6 sq. Kilometers).

Sturtevant's train depot is located at 2904 Wisconsin St. Sturtevant, WI 53177. The station is self-serve and features an enclosed waiting area, restrooms, and payphones. Transportation options from the station include local transit and taxi services. Sturtevant station is served by the Midwest Corridor.

Milwaukee (WI)
Motor-coach connection to Fond du Lac (WI) and Wausau (WI)

Milwaukee is called the "Genuine American City" or to some, the "Beer Capital of the Nation." The name Milwaukee comes from the Indian name, Milliocki, meaning
"gathering place by the waters." Geographically, Milwaukee is located on the western shore of Lake Michigan at the junction of the three rivers, the Kinnickinnic, Menomonee, and Milwaukee.

The first settlers of Milwaukee were the French traders and trappers in the 1830s. With a land area of 97 sq. miles (249 sq. kilometers), Milwaukee is the largest city in state of Wisconsin with a diverse community of roughly 630,000.

Milwaukee is one of the most vibrant cites of the Midwest known for its numerous architectural wonders, rich culture, world class events, and true American personality. Milwaukee is home to the world-known Harley-Davidson Motorcycles and the Miller Brewing Company. Milwaukee is also known for world-class festivals and events; one of the most anticipated is the yearly Summer Fest, the largest and most celebrated music festival in the US. Noted city attractions are the Milwaukee Public Museum, the Milwaukee Art Museum, the Humphrey I-Max Theater, Discovery World, and the Miller Park baseball stadium.

Getting Around

Airport

General Mitchell International Airport connects the city of Milwaukee to the rest of the United States and major cities of the world. The airport is located at 5300 S. Howell Avenue Milwaukee, WI 53207; toll-free (888) 458-8653 or Tel: (414) 747-5300 <<http://www.mitchellairport.com>>.

Car rental services from the airport: Alamo toll-free (800) 327-9633, Avis toll-free (800) 831-2847, Budget toll-free (800) 527-0700, Hertz toll-free (800) 654-3131 and National toll-free (800) 328-4567. The Airport Connection, 5140 S. 3rd Street Milwaukee, WI 53237-0497, toll-free (800) 236-5450 offers a shuttle service from the airport to Milwaukee's major hotels and other business locations <<http://www.mkelimo.com>>.

Bus services from the airport: Badger Coaches Tel: (414) 276-7490 offer services to and from Lake Mills and Madison; Greyhound Lines Tel: (414) 272-2158 or toll-free (888) 287-6359 offers services to and from Appleton, Fond du Lac, Green Bay, Manitowoc, Oshkosh, and Sheboygan; Public Transit Tel: (414) 344-6711 offers services to and from Milwaukee County via MTS Route 80, and Wisconsin Coach Lines Tel: (262) 542-8861 offer services to and from Milwaukee, Waukesha, Racine, and Kenosha Counties.

Bus

Milwaukee County Transit System 1942 N. 17th Street Milwaukee, WI 53205, Tel: (414) 344-6711, provides public transportation throughout Milwaukee County <<http://www.ridemcts.com>>. Coach USA Milwaukee/Wisconsin Coach Lines, 1520 Arcadian Avenue Waukesha, WI, 53186, toll-free (800) 236-2015 offers tours around the area and the rest of the country <<http://www.wisconsincoach.com>>. Greyhound Lines Inc., 606 N. James Lovell Street Milwaukee, WI 53233, Tel: (414) 272-9949, connects Milwaukee to the rest of the country with over 2,900 destinations <<http://www.greyhound.com>>.

Taxi

American United Taxicab Service, Inc., 646 S. 2nd Street Milwaukee, WI 53204; Tel: (414) 220-5000. Yellow Cab Co-Op, 1840 N. Martin Luther King Drive Milwaukee, WI 53212; Tel: (414) 271-1800.

Rent-A-Car

Avis Rent A Car, Park East Hotel 916 E. State Street Milwaukee, WI 53202; Toll-Free: (800) 331-1212. Budget Rent A Car 550 W. Grange Avenue Milwaukee, WI 53207; Toll-Free: (800) 527-0700. Enterprise Rent-A-Car, 1560 E. Moreland Boulevard Waukesha, WI 53186; Toll-Free: (800) 736-8222. Mayfair Rent-A-Car 4747 S. Howell Avenue Waukesha, WI 53207; Tel: (414) 489-6600. Thrifty Car Rental 6039 S. Howell Avenue Milwaukee, WI 53207; Tel: (414) 483-5870. Hertz Rent-A-Car 501 W. Edgerton Avenue Milwaukee, WI 53207; Toll-Free: (800) 654-3131.

Commuter and Train

East Troy Electric Railroad Museum 2002 Church Street East Troy, WI 53120, Tel: (262) 642-3263, located 35 miles southwest of Milwaukee, operates ten-mile trolley trips through the southern Wisconsin countryside. The Trolley of Lake Geneva 1050 Carey Street Lake Geneva, WI 53147 Toll-Free: (800) 537-6819, operates fully enclosed trolleys around the city of Milwaukee.

Milwaukee's train depot is located at 433 W. St. Paul Ave. Milwaukee, WI 53203. The station is staffed and features an enclosed waiting area, checked baggage services, restrooms, payphones, and a restaurant. Transportation options from the station include Hertz Car Rental Toll-Free: (800) 654-3131, local transit, and taxi services.

Trains serving Milwaukee station are the Midwest Corridor and Empire Builder.

Visitor Information Center

Historic Cedarburg - Visitors Center at the Corner of Washington & Spring Street, P. O. Box 104 Cedarburg, WI 53012; Toll-Free: (800) CDR-BURG (237-2874) or Tel: (262) 377-9620 <<http://www.cedarburg.org>>.

GMCVB Corporate Office located at 101 W. Wisconsin Avenue Suite 425 Milwaukee, WI 53203; Toll-Free: (800) 231-0903 or Tel: (414) 273-3950.

Midwest Express Center located at 400 W. Wisconsin Avenue Milwaukee, WI 53203; Tel: (414) 908-6205.

Places to See and Things to Do

Cathedral of St. John the Evangelist located at 802 N. Jackson Street Milwaukee, WI 53202; Tel: (414) 276-9814. A historic landmark, the cathedral built in 1853 is the seat of the Catholic Archdiocese of Milwaukee. **St. Josaphat Basilica Foundation** located at 569 W.

Lincoln Avenue Milwaukee, WI 53207; Tel: (414) 645-5623. Built in 1901 the basilica's design was modeled after St. Peter's in Rome, a historical landmark.

Discovery World Museum located at 815 N. James Lovell Street Milwaukee, WI 53233; Tel: (414) 765-9966. The museum features hands-on exhibits, live performances, educational workshops, laboratories, Discovery world, and more. **Charles Allis Art Museum** located at 1801 N. Prospect Avenue Milwaukee, WI 53202; Tel: (414) 278-8295. The museum exhibits an art collection, English garden, and much more. **Milwaukee Art Museum** located at 750 N. Lincoln Memorial Drive Milwaukee, WI 53202; Tel: (414) 224-3200. The museum has 20,000 pieces of art.

Milwaukee Public Museum located at 800 W. Wells Street Milwaukee, WI 53233-1478; Tel: (414) 278-2722. The museum exhibits dinosaurs, tropical gardens, and live butterflies. **America's Black Holocaust Museum,** located downtown at 2233 N. 4th Street Milwaukee, WI 53212; Tel: (414) 264-2500, is dedicated to the injustices suffered by people of African heritage. **Betty Brinn Children's Museum,** located at 929 E. Wisconsin Avenue Milwaukee, WI 53202; Tel: (414) 291-0888, features hands-on exhibits and interactive programs for young children.

Humphrey IMAX Dome Theater located at 800 W. Wells Street Milwaukee, WI 53233; Tel: (414) 319-4629. The theater has a six-story screen showing educational films. A national historic landmark, the **Irish Cultural and Heritage Center of Wisconsin** was built in 1887 specializing in Irish genealogy, located at 2133 W. Wisconsin Avenue Milwaukee, WI 53233-1910; Tel: (414) 345-8800. **Milwaukee Public Library,** located at 814 W. Wisconsin Avenue Milwaukee, WI 53233; Tel: (414) 286-3032, is a historic landmark admired for its mosaic floors. Visitors are welcome to use library facilities and services.

Pabst Theater located at 144 E. Wells Street Milwaukee, WI 53202; Tel: (414) 286-3663. This baroque architecture building is one of the most admired in Milwaukee; the Pabst Theater was built in 1895 and is a national historic landmark. **The Marcus Amphitheater** located downtown at 200 N. Harbor Drive Milwaukee, WI 53202; Tel: (414) 273-2680 or toll-free (800) 938-4510. The amphitheater offers a spectacular view of Milwaukee's skyline. **Villa Terrace Decorative Arts Museum** located at 2220 N. Terrace Avenue Milwaukee, WI 53202; Tel: (414) 271-3656. The museum is an Old Italian Renaissance architectural villa with gardens set along Lake Michigan.

International Clown Hall of Fame located at 161 W. Wisconsin Avenue Suite LL700 Milwaukee, WI 53203; Tel: (414) 319-0848. The hall exhibits memorabilia of world-known clowns and there are art galleries that feature historical artifacts. **Lakefront Brewery, Inc.** located at 1872 N. Commerce Street Milwaukee, WI 53212-3701; Tel: (414) 372-8800. Visitors are invited to take a tour and learn something about the city's old beer making tradition.

Around Milwaukee

Circus World Museum located at 550 Water Street, Baraboo, WI 53913; Tel: (608) 356-8341 or Toll-Free: (866) 693-1500. The museum features live circus performances and also holds the world's largest collections of circus wagons. **East Troy Electric Railroad Museum** located 35 miles southwest of Milwaukee at 2002 Church Street in East

Troy, WI 53210; Tel: (262) 642-3263. The museum offers a short train rides around Milwaukee countryside.

Harley-Davidson Tour Center located at Northwest 11700 W. Capitol Drive Wauwatosa, WI 53222; Tel: (414) 535-3666. Visitors will experience the actual assembly process of the Harley-Davidson's engines. **Cedar Creek Winery** located at N70 W6340 Bridge Road, Cedarburg, Wisconsin 53012; Tel: (262) 377-8020 or Toll-Free: (800) 827-8020 and the **Mason Creek Winery** located at W322 N7942 Petersen Road Hartland, WI 53029; Tel: (262) 646-5766. Both offer tours in their wineries where visitors will have the chance to learn from a wine expert and the opportunity to try some of the best wine of the region.

Genesee Woolen Mill located at S40 W28178 Highway 59 Waukesha, WI 53188; Tel: (262) 521-2121. A visit to the mill offers visitors an opportunity to experience the actual processing of wool freshly taken from sheep. The **Milwaukee County Zoo,** located at 10001 West Blue Mound Road, Milwaukee, Wisconsin, 53226; Tel: (414) 771-3040, is home to more than 350 species of animals.

Old World Wisconsin located at S103 W37890 Highway 67 Eagle, WI 53119; Tel: (262) 594-6300. This open-air museum exhibits the 19th and early 20th century lifestyle of the early immigrants of Wisconsin. **Schlitz Audubon Nature Center** located at Northeast 1111 E. Brown Deer Road Milwaukee, WI 53217; Tel: (414) 352-2880 and **Wehr Nature Center** located at Southwest 9701 W. College Avenue Franklin, WI 53132; Tel: (414) 425-8550, both offer recreation activities and nature awareness.

Mitchell Gallery of Flight located at General Mitchell International Airport, 5300 S. Howell Avenue Milwaukee, WI 53207-6189; Tel: (414) 747-4503. Admission is free. **Old Falls Village Museum** located at Northwest N96 W15791 County Line Road Menomonee Falls, WI 53051; Tel: (262) 250-5096 or Toll-Free: (800) 801-6565. The village is one of the oldest settlements in the region, known for its historic houses and buildings. **Wisconsin Maritime Museum** located at 75 Maritime Drive Manitowoc, WI 54220; Tel: (920) 684-0218. The museum is the largest maritime museum in the Midwest. It exhibits the USS COBIA, a WWII submarine, and much more.

Pettit National Ice Center located at 500 S. 84th Street Milwaukee, WI 53214; Tel: (414) 266-0100. The ice center is the official US Olympic Training Center, the only one of its kind in the US. Milwaukee's top winter resorts: **Old Highlander Ski Hill** located at Olympia Resort & Spa 1350 Royale Mile Road, Oconomowoc, WI 53066; Tel: (262) 567-0311 or Toll-Free: (800) 558-9573; and **The Mountain Top Ski Hill** located at Grand Geneva Resort & Spa 7036 Grand Geneva Way, Lake Geneva, WI 53147; Tel: (262) 248-8811. Visitors who want to experience skydiving should visit the **Sky Knights Sport Parachute Club** located at W1341 Hwy L East Troy, WI 53120; Tel: (262) 642-9494, the club offers skydiving services.

Accommodations

Days Inn located at 1673 S 108th St, Milwaukee, WI 53214; Tel: (414) 771-3399. **Hampton Inn Milwaukee Airport** located at 1200 West College Avenue Milwaukee WI 53221; Tel: (414) 762-4240. **Clarion Hotel** located at 5311 S Howell Ave, Milwaukee, WI 53207; Tel: (414) 481-2400. **Econo Lodge** located at 6541 S 13th St, Milwaukee, WI 53221; Tel: (414)

764-2510. **Four Points by Sheraton Milwaukee Airport** located at 4747 South Howell avenue Milwaukee WI 53207; Tel: (414) 488-000. **Hilton Milwaukee City Center** located at 509 West Wisconsin avenue Milwaukee WI 53202; Tel: (414) 271-7250.

Courtyard by Marriott located at 300 W Michigan St, Milwaukee, WI 53203; Tel: (414) 291-4122. **Best Western Inn** located at 710 N Old World 3rd St, Milwaukee, WI 53203; Tel: (414) 224-8400. **Holiday Inn Milwaukee** located in downtown Milwaukee at 611 West Wisconsin Avenue Milwaukee WI 53203; Tel: (414) 273-2950. **Best Western Inn** located at 251 N Mayfair Rd, Milwaukee, WI 53226; Tel: (414) 774-3600. **Capitol Manor Motel** located at 7012 W Appleton Ave, Milwaukee, WI 53216; Tel: (414) 461-8050. **Days Inn** located at 11811 W Blue Mound Rd, Milwaukee, WI 53226; Tel: (414) 771-4500. **Four Points Hotel Milwaukee** located at 4747 S Howell Ave, Milwaukee, WI 53207; Tel: (414) 481-9130.

Hotel Wisconsin located at 720 North Old World Third street Milwaukee WI 53203; Tel: (414) 271-4900. **Astor Hotel** located at 924 E Juneau Ave, Milwaukee, WI 53202; Tel: (414) 271-4220. **Bay Mont Inns & Suites** located at 250 E Wisconsin Ave #1150, Milwaukee, WI 53202; Tel: (414) 905-2000. **Parkay Hotel** located at 1570 W National Ave, Milwaukee, WI 53204; Tel: (414) 645-4410. **Sheraton** located at 8900 N Kideer Ct, Milwaukee, WI 53209; Tel: (414) 355-8585. **Sheraton Four Points** located at 4747 S Howell Ave, Milwaukee, WI 53207; Tel: (414) 488000. **Ambassador Hotel** located at 2308 W Wisconsin Ave, Milwaukee, WI 53233; Tel: (414) 342-8400. **Hampton Inn** located at 1200 W College Ave, Milwaukee, WI 53221; Tel: (414) 762-4240.

Hilton located at 11600 W Park Pl, Milwaukee, WI 53224; Tel: (414) 359-9823. **Holiday Inn** located at 545 W Layton Ave, Milwaukee, WI 53207; Tel: (414) 482-4444. **Hyatt Hotels & Resorts** located at 333 W Kilbourn Ave, Milwaukee, WI 53203; (414) 276-1234. **Radisson Hotel Mayfair** located at 2303 N Mayfair Rd, Milwaukee, WI 53226; Tel: (414) 257-3400. **Westwood Hotel & Suites** located at 201 N Mayfair Rd, Milwaukee, WI 53226; Tel: (414) 771-4400. **Wyndham Milwaukee Ctr.** located at 139 E Kilbourn Ave, Milwaukee, WI 53202; Tel: (414) 276-8686. **The Pfister Hotel** located at 424 East Wisconsin Avenue Milwaukee WI 53202; Tel: (414) 273-8222. **Hampton Inn** located at 5601 N Lovers Lane Rd, Milwaukee, WI 53225, Tel: (414) 466-8881.

10 30 pm-D	**Los Angeles, CA**	8 05 am
11 22 pm	Pomona, CA	4 18 am
11 37 pm	Ontario, CA	4 08 am
1 04 am	**Palm Springs, CA**	2 38 am
4 19 am	Yuma, AZ	1 25 am
6 57 am	Maricopa, AZ	10 50 pm
9 10 am	Tuczon, AZ	9 29 pm
10 07 am	Benson, AZ	7 35 pm
12 50 pm	Lordsburg, NM	5 31pm
12 57 pm	Deming, NM	4 37 pm
3 01 pm	El Passo, TX	3 07 pm
3 21 pm		2 20 pm
8 06 pm	Alpine, TX	11 03 am
9 57 pm	Sanderson, TX	9 10 am
12 23 am	Del Rio, TX	6 35 am
4 11 am-A	**San Antonio, TX**	3 40 am-D
7 00 am-D		11 15 pm-A
8 32 am	San Marcos. TX	7 25 am
9 31 am	**Austin, TX**	6 43 pm
10 22 am	Taylor, TX	5 49 pm
11 25 am	Temple, TX	4 56 pm
11 51 am	McGregor, TX	4 13 pm
1 00 pm	Cleburne, TX	3 05 pm
1 58 pm	Fort Worth, TX	2 23 pm-D
2 28 pm		1 48 pm-A
3 28 pm-A	**Dallas, TX**	12 35 pm-D
3 38 pm-D		12 15 pm-A
5 23 pm	Mineola, TX	9 35 am
6 15 pm	Longview, TX	8 38 am
648 pm	Marshal, TX	8 03 am
8 11pm	Texarkana, AR/TX	6 43 am
925 pm	Arkadelphia, AR	5 18 am
949 pm	Malvern/Hot Spring, AR	4 57 am
10 59 pm	**Little Rock, AR**	4 12 am
1 01am	Walnut Ridge, AR	1 57 am
204 am	Poplar Bluff, MO	1 02 am
6 22 am-A	**St. Louis, MO**	9 10 pm-D
7 00 am-D		9 00 pm-A
7 41 am	Alton, IL	8 01 pm
8 50 am	Springfield, IL	6 55 pm
9 20 am	Lincoln, IL	6 20 pm
10 01 am	Bloomington/ Normal, IL	5 47 pm
10 32 am	Pontiac, IL	5 12 pm
11 39 am	Joliet, IL	4 25 pm
12 40 pm-A	**Chicago, IL**	3 30 pm-D

D-Departure   A-Arrival
Train Connections

Texas Eagle

Texas Eagle connects some of the most exciting cities of the Midwest; it links the cities of Chicago, Springfield, St. Louis, Little Rock, Dallas, Fort Worth, Austin, and San Antonio, traveling through the states of Illinois, Missouri, Arkansas, and Texas. In addition, Texas Eagle has thruway motor-coach connections to Branson (MO), Hot Springs (AR), Bossier City / Shreveport (LA), Houston, Galveston (TX), and Fort Hood (TX) and train connections to Kansas City (MO) via Ann Rutledge, Oklahoma City (OK) via the Heartland Flyer, and Los Angeles (CA) via the Sunset Limited. Journey from Chicago, Illinois to San Antonio, Texas or vise-versa and you'll traverse 1,306 miles (2,102 kilometers) using the Superliner Coaches.

Route Destination Highlights

Chicago, IL- Home to America's tallest building the Sears Tower, visit the Museum of Science and Industry and other outstanding museums, admire the charming Centennial Fountain, take a romantic stroll along lake Michigan, and enjoy Chicago's busy nightlife.

Springfield, IL- Visit Abraham Lincoln's hometown and the city's historical places.

St. Louis, MO- Famous for its "Arc of St. Louis" located along the bank of the Mississippi River, visitors can visit the top of the arch to have bird-eye view of the lovely city of St. Louis. Visit the popular Busch Stadium, the zoo, or the exciting St. Louis Fair during the month of July.

Little Rock, AR- Visit Arkansas' State Capital, the oldest west of the Mississippi River. Experience Broadway in Little Rock at the Celebrity Attractions. Stroll

309

at the city's charming areas: the Governors Mansion, Riverfront, and Little Rock Historic District.

Longview, TX- Home to the largest hot air balloon race in the US the "Great Texas Balloon Race" held in July, see the AlleyFest or visit Longview's historic train depot.

Dallas, TX- See Dealey Plaza and the Sixth Floor Museum that exhibits memorabilia of President JF Kennedy's assassination; or see the Conspiracy Museum and learn stories of US President assassinations and political controversy. See the grand "Reunion Tower," Fair Park, the lovely houses at the Old City Park, Texas Motor Speedway, and Medieval Times Castle.

Fort Worth, TX- Explore the famous Fort Worth Stockyards District and watch an actual rodeo. See the rich architectural heritage of old Fort Worth at Sundance Square, the beautiful depiction of a 19th century cattle drive at the Chisholm Trail Mural, or take a wild roller-coaster ride at Six Flags.

Austin, TX- Witness the nightly exodus of millions of Mexican free-tailed bats at Congress Avenue Park. Enjoy Austin's nightlife on East Sixth Street, and explore the city's best bars and entertainment spots.

San Antonio, TX- Visit the historic Alamo or take a romantic boat ride at the River Walk. Take a short steam locomotive ride at the Railroad Miniature Railway, or take a stroll at the historic San Antonio Mission National Park. See the breathtaking view of San Antonio from the 750-foot Tower of Americas, or visit "Shamu" at San Antonio's very own Sea World.

Scenery along the Route

From Chicago (IL) to St. Louis (MO) you'll see old towns and cities of charming western-American architecture and endless colorful fields. Prepare yourself and your camera while the train is approaching the City of St. Louis for its magnificent Arch. The Ozark Mountains, pine forest, lakes, and ranches dominate the views down to San Antonio (TX).

Train Schedules

Texas Eagle travels daily between the cities of Chicago, Illinois and San Antonio, Texas.

Accommodations and Services

Accommodations are Reserved Coach and Sleeping Car. There is a Cafe car that serves local cuisine, snacks, soups, sandwiches, and drinks and a Dining Car that serves complete meals. There is en-route entertainment and a seasonal "Trails & Rails" national park guide presentation.

All Aboard!

Chicago (IL) See Illinois and Missouri service, page 268.

Joliet (IL) See Illinois and Missouri service, page 275- 276.

Pontiac (IL) See Illinois and Missouri service, page 275- 276.

Bloomington-Normal (IL) See Illinois and Missouri service, page 275- 276.

Lincoln (IL) See Illinois and Missouri service, page 275- 276.

Springfield (IL) See Illinois and Missouri service, page 277.

Alton (IL) See Illinois and Missouri service, page 278.

St. Louis (MO) See Illinois and Missouri service, page 279.

Poplar Bluff (MO)

Poplar Bluff is located southeast of Missouri 150 miles from St. Louis. Poplar Bluff has a land area of 17 sq. miles (27 sq. kilometers) and is home to more than 18,000 residents. Poplar Bluff is a hub city for the region, and it continuously growing. The city has historical museums, art museums, a convention center, a national forest, and other natural wonders. The Moark Regional Railroad Museum located at 303 Moran Street, Poplar Bluff, MO 63901 Tel: (573) 785-4539 exhibits model trains and railroading memorabilia.

Poplar Bluff's train depot is located at 400 S. Main St. Poplar Bluff, MO 63901. The station is self-serve and features an enclosed waiting area, restrooms, and payphones. Transportation from the station is local taxi service.

Poplar Bluff station is served by the Texas Eagle.

Walnut Ridge (AR)

Walnut Ridge is part of Lawrence County located on the banks of the Cache River near the Missouri and Arkansas state border. Walnut Ridge has a land area of 2.3 sq. miles (6 sq. kilometers) and residents of roughly 5000. The surrounding areas of the region are spotted with ranches, farms, country homes, and resorts.

Walnut Ridge's train depot is located at Hwy. 67 and Main St. Walnut Ridge, AR 72476. The station is unstaffed and features an enclosed waiting area, restrooms, and vending machines. Transportation from the station is local taxi service.

Walnut Ridge station is served by the Texas Eagle.

Little Rock (AR)
Motor-coach connection to **Branson (MO)**

Little Rock is the state capital and the largest city of Arkansas, known for its beautiful architecture and charming setting. Located in the center of Arkansas and the United States,

Little Rock has a land area of 103 sq. miles (266 sq. kilometers) and a population of more than 180,000.

Little Rock has an average annual temperature of 61.7 degrees F (18 degree C) with an average snowfall of 5.2 inches.

Getting Around

Airport

Little Rock National Airport is located at One Airport Drive Little Rock AR 72202-4402, Tel: (501) 372-3439. Local taxis and rent-a-car services are available at the arrival terminal. R & R Transport Tel: (501) 362-2724, Hot Springs Shuttle Tel: (501) 376-4422, Bette Bus toll-free (800) 752-8745 and the Inter Shuttle Tel: (501) 376-7433 all offer services from the airport and around the region. Central Arkansas Transit Tel: (501) 375-6717 connects the airport to the rest of the city.

Bus

The Central Arkansas Transit Authority 901 Maple Street North Little Rock AR 72114 Tel: (501) 375-6717 provides regular bus service around the city of Little Rock.

Arkansas (AR)
Capital: Little Rock (Population: 2,673,400)
Size: 52,075 sq mi. (134,874 sq km)
Nickname: The Natural State, The Land of Opportunity
Joined the union on: June 15, 1836 (25th state)
Motto: The People Rule
Flower: Apple Blossom
Bird: Mockingbird
Song: "Arkansas"
Famous for: Douglas Macarthur, Bill Clinton
Major industries: Agriculture, Lumber, and Cotton

Taxis

Taxi services include Capitol Cab Tel: (501) 568-0462, Black and White/Yellow Cabs Tel: (501) 374-0333, Veterans Cab Tel: (501) 374-0333, and Worthey Cab Tel: (501) 680-0678.

Rent-a-Car

Budget Rent-A-Car toll-free (800) 527-0700.

Train and Commuter

Little Rock's train depot is located at Union Station Sq. Little Rock, AR 72201. The station is staffed and features an enclosed waiting area, checked baggage service, restrooms, payphones, and vending machines. Transportation from the station is local taxi service.

Little Rock station is served by the Texas Eagle.

Visitors Information Center

Little Rock Convention and Visitors Bureau is located at Robinson Center Markham and

Broadway, Little Rock, AR 72201. Mailing Address: P. O. Box 3232, Little Rock, AR 72203 toll-free (800) 844-4781.

Places to See and Things to Do

Arkansas Arts Center is located at 501 East 9th Street Little Rock, AR 72202, Tel: (501) 372-4000. The art center has nine galleries, museums, a research center, and theaters <<http://www.arkarts.com>>. **Clinton Library,** visit the Cox Building at 120 Commerce St. Little Rock, AR Tel: (501) 918-3032 for the library information and exhibits. **Arkansas State Capitol** located at 1 Capitol Mall, Capitol Avenue and Woodlane Little Rock, AR 72201 Tel: (501) 682-5080 is an 1899 neo-classical design building. **Celebrity Attractions (Broadway Series)** features Broadway shows and many famous personalities, located at 300 S. Spring St., Ste. 100 Little Rock, AR 72201 Tel: (501) 244-8800 <<http://www.celebrityattractions.com>>.

Children's Museum of Arkansas is located in the historic Union Station in downtown Little Rock at 1400 West Markham Little Rock, AR 72201 Tel: (501) 374-6655. The museum has hands-on exhibits for every family member <<http://www.cmuseum.org>>. Little Rock **IMAX Theatre** is located at the Aerospace Education Center at 3301 East Roosevelt Road Little Rock, AR 72206, Tel: (501) 376-IMAX. There are exhibits, arts, shops, and other entertainment within the center <<http://www.aerospaced.org>>. **Central High Museum** is a known civil rights landmark in Little Rock which also houses a visitor information center. The museum is located at 2125 Daisy L. Gatson Bates Drive Little Rock, AR 72202, Tel: (501) 374-1957 <http://home.swbell.net/chmuseum>>.

EMOBA - The Museum of Black Arkansans is located at 1208 Louisiana Street Little Rock, AR 72202, Tel: (501) 372-0018. The museum is dedicated to the history of Arkansas' African Americans. **Arkansas Children's Theatre**, located at 501 E. 9th St. Little Rock, AR 72202, Tel: (501) 372-4000, has a live classic and contemporary stage show for children <<http://www.arkarts.com >>. **Historic Arkansas Museum** located at 200 East 3rd Street Little Rock, AR 72201, Tel: (501) 324-9351 is the former Arkansas Territorial Restoration; the museum has live historical performances. <<http://www.arkansashistory.org>>.

Governor's Mansion Historic District is a late 19th and early 20th century neighborhood that has been restored. Located within the old downtown Little Rock, a walk in the district offers a glimpse of the city's beautiful architecture. **Little Rock Zoo** is home to 600 species of animals, birds, reptiles, and amphibians from around the world. The zoo is located at 1 Jonesboro Drive Little Rock, AR 72205, Tel: (501) 663-4733. <<http://www.littlerockzoo.com>>.

Listed as one of Arkansas National Historic Places, **McArthur Park Historic District** is Little Rock's oldest districts. It houses the 36-acre McArthur Park and some of the city's most beautiful houses. Also within the district is the **Villa Marre,** located at 1321 South Scott Street Little Rock, AR Tel: (501) 371-0075, which was built in 1881 and is one of the most famous houses in the area. **McArthur Museum of Arkansas Military History** exhibits the military history of Arkansas and was dedicated to General Douglas McArthur. The museum is located at 503 East 9th Street Little Rock AR 72202, Tel: (501) 376-4602.

Museum of Discovery is a fun place to visit; there are several scientific and futuristic exhibits. The museum is located at 500 East Markham, Suite 150 Little Rock, AR 72201 toll-free (800) 880-6475 <<http://www.amod.org >>. **Arkansas Museum of Science and History** is located at 503 East 9th Street Little Rock, AR 72201 Tel: (501) 396-7050. The museum building is one of the oldest in Little Rock. **The Old State House Museum** located at 300 West Markham Little Rock, AR 72201 Tel: (501) 324-9685, is the former state capitol and is the oldest capitol building still standing west of the Mississippi River <<http://www.oldstatehouse.com>>.

Accommodations

Ramada Inn located at 120 West Pershing North Little Rock, AR 72114, Tel: (501) 758-1851. **Baymont** located at 4311 Warden Road North Little Rock, AR 72116, Tel: (501) 758-8888. **Days Inn** located at 5800 Pritchard Drive North Little Rock, AR 72117, Tel: (501) 945-4100. **Residence Inn** located at 4110 Health Care Drive North Little Rock, AR 72117, Tel: (501) 945-7777. **Travelodge** located at 3100 North Main Street North Little Rock, AR 72116, Tel: (501) 758-8110. **Holiday Inn Express & Suites** located at 4306 McCain Blvd. North Little Rock, AR 72117, Tel: (501) 945-4800. **Hampton Inn** located at 500 West 29th Street North Little Rock, AR 72114, Tel: (501) 771-2090.

Arkansas Excelsior Hotel located at 3 Statehouse Plaza, Little Rock AR 72201, Tel: (501) 375-5000. **Best Western Inn & Suites** located at 5710 Pritchard Drive North Little Rock, AR 72117, Tel: (501) 955-9453. **Country Inn & Suites** located at 110 East Pershing North Little Rock, AR 72114, Tel: (501) 758-2002. **Doubletree Hotel Little Rock** located at 424 West Markham Little Rock AR 72201, Tel: (501) 372-4371. **Red Roof Inn Little Rock** located at 7900 Scott Hamilton Dr. Little Rock AR 72209, Tel: (501) 562-2694. **Holiday Inn Arpt East Little Rock** located at 3201 Bankhead Dr. Little Rock AR 72295, Tel: (501) 490-1000. **Hilton Inn Little Rock** located at 925 South University Little Rock AR 72204-1601, Tel: (501) 664-5020.

Malvern (AR)

Malvern was founded in 1870 and is the seat of Hot Spring County. Malvern has a land area of 7.4 sq. miles (19 sq. kilometers) and a population of 9,256. Malvern is gateway to Hot Springs National Park. Malvern is known as the "Brick Capitol of the World" and the city celebrates through its annual Brickfest.

Malvern's train depot is located at 200 E. 1st St. Malvern, AR 72104. The station is unstaffed and features payphones. Transportation from the station is local taxi service.

Malvern station is served by the Texas Eagle.

Arkadelphia (AR)

Arkadelphia is located 60 miles southwest of Little Rock. It has a land area of 7 sq. miles (18 sq. kilometers) and a population of 10,912. Arkadelphia is home to Ouachita Baptist University and Henderson State University.

Arkadelphia's train depot is located at 798 S. 5th St. Arkadelphia, AR 71923. The station is unstaffed. Transportation options from the station include Rent and Go Auto Rental Tel: (870) 246-5991 and Arkadelphia Taxi Company Tel: (870) 230-3012.

Arkadelphia station is served by the Texas Eagle.

Texarkana (AR/TX)

Texarkana is a city between the two states (Arkansas and Texas). The city's train depot is located just in the middle of the boundary of the two states. Therefore if you are on the west side of station you are in Texas while if you are on the east you are in the state of Arkansas. Two mayors and local governments serve the city of Texarkana; it has a land area of 16 sq. miles (43 sq. kilometers) and a population of more than 22,000.

Texarkana's train depot is located at 100 E. Front St. Texarkana, AR 75502. The station is staffed and features an enclosed waiting area, checked baggage service, payphones, and vending machines. Transportation from the station is local taxi service.

Texarkana station is served by the Texas Eagle.

Marshal (TX)

The city of Marshal is one of the most celebrated in the state of Texas. Marshall was one of Texas' richest cities during the 1860's. It was the western capital of the Confederate army during the American Revolution. Marshall has a land area of 24 sq. miles (62 sq. kilometers) and a population of 23,682.

Marshall's beautiful brick train depot built in 1912 is one of the city's attractions; right in front of the station is the old hotel Ginocchio built in 1896 and known to be haunted.

Marshal's train depot is located at Foot of N. Washington St. Marshall, TX 75670. The station is unstaffed and features an enclosed waiting area, restrooms, payphones, and vending machines. Transportation from the station is local taxi service.

Marshal station is served by the Texas Eagle.

Longview (TX)
Motor-coach connection to **Houston (TX), Galveston (TX)** and **Bossier City (LA)**

Longview was founded in 1870. The discovery of oil in the area in 1930's increased the city's population dramatically and also helped the economy of western Texas to revitalize after the Great Depression. Longview has a land area of 52.6 sq. miles (135 sq. kilometers) and population of 70,300.

Interesting places to visit in Longview include the

Texas (TX)
Capital: Austin (Population: 20,851,820)
Size: 268,601 sq mi. (695,676 sq km)
Nickname: The Lone Star State
Joined the union on: Dec. 29, 1845 (28th state)
Motto: Friendship
Flower: Bluebonnet
Bird: Mockingbird
Song: Texas, Our Texas
Famous for: The Alamo, Steaks, and Nice People
Major industries: Commerce, Real Estate, Oil and Gas, and Tourism

315

Longview train depot which is regarded as one of the city's most noted landmarks, the AlleyFest arts and crafts festival in June, and the Great Texas Balloon Race held in July is one of the largest in hot air balloon festivals in the US.

Longview's train depot is located at 905 Pacific Ave. Longview, TX 75602. The station is staffed and features an enclosed waiting area, checked baggage service, restrooms, payphones, and vending machines. Transportation from the station is local taxi service.

Longview station is served by the Texas Eagle.

Mineola (TX)

Mineola was founded in the 1840's and since that time it has played an important role in the development of railroads and trade in the region. Mineola has a land area of 5 sq. miles (13 sq. kilometers) and a population of less than 5000. The historical city of Mineola was designated as "Texas Main Street City" in 1989 and since then the state of Texas has spent millions of dollars for the restoration of the city's many historical treasures including the Mineola train station.

A visit to historic downtown Mineola is rewarding: there are several restaurants, antique shops, and specialty shops, among others. Visit the craft malls which have several shops with merchandise made by Mineola's local artists. The Select Theater is said to be the one of the oldest in the State of Texas. Mineola is also known for its "Iron Horse Heritage Festival" which celebrates the significance of the railroad to Mineola's early development.

Mineola's train depot is located at 115 E. Front Street Mineola, TX 75773. The station is unstaffed and features an enclosed waiting area, payphones, and vending machines. Transportation options from the station include local bus and taxi service.

Mineola station is served by the Texas Eagle.

Dallas (TX)
Motor-coach connection to Odesa (TX)

Dallas is located east of Fort Worth and 181 miles northeast of Austin. Founded in 1841 as a trading post, just like other prosperous cities in the US, the expansion of the railroad made Dallas an important transportation and business hub in the region. Dallas has a land area of 345 sq. miles (887 sq. kilometers) and a population of 1,052,300.

Dallas is the US Southwest's financial and business center holding several international and world conventions and forums. Dallas is the most visited city in the state of Texas making tourism one of the major industries of the city. It is said that Dallas has more shopping centers and restaurants than any other city in the United States.

Dallas' skyline gives an imposing view while the train is approaching the city. The city's tallest building, Bank of America Plaza, dominates the Dallas skyline. Beside the Dallas union station is the 560-foot Reunion Tower giving an impressive view of the city.

Getting Around

Airport

Dallas/Fort Worth International Airport is located 15 miles (24 kilometers) northwest of Dallas, P.O. Drawer 619428, DFW Airport, TX 75261-9428 Tel: (972) 574-8888. Airporter bus Tel: (817) 334-0092 serves the airport for $10 each way; the Super Shuttle toll-free (800) 648-7051 has a shared ride service for $16.00. Taxis are available at the arrival hall. There are several rent-a-car services at the airport arrival area. Trinity Railway Express connects the airport to Dallas medical district.

Bus

Dallas Area Rapid Transit (DART) Tel: (214) 979-1111 operates Dallas local bus, light rail, and commuter rail systems. Bus fare is $1 and a one-day pass costs $2. Greyhound is located at 205 S Lamar Dallas Tel: (214) 655-7082.

The DART electric trolley bus service serves most downtown routes, rides cost $0.50 each way. McKinney Avenue Transit Authority Tel: (214) 855-0006 operates 20th century trolley buses that connect uptown and downtown Dallas.

Taxi

Dallas local taxis are served by: Cowboy Cab Tel: (214) 428-0202 and Yellow Cab Tel: (214) 426-6262.

Rent-a-car

Alamo Tel: (800) 327-9633, Hertz Car Rental toll-free (800) 654-3131 and Enterprise Rent-A-Car toll-free (800) RENT-A-CAR, Avis Tel: (800) 331-1212 and Dollar Tel: (800) 800-4000. Exotic Car Rental of Texas Tel: (972) 633-8183 and Rent-a-Wreck of Dallas Tel: (214) 398-7368 have some interesting collections of cars.

Train and Commuter

DART operates Dallas Light Rail; the Red and Blue lines stop at the Union Station. The fare is $1 and a one-day pass costs $2. Passes and tickets are sold at the station vending machines, while tickets can also be obtain in most grocery stores around Dallas. Trinity Railway Express commuter rail service serves Dallas' medical district, Dallas/Fort Worth International Airport, and downtown Fort Worth. McKinney Avenue Transit Authority Tel: (214) 855-0006 has restored streetcars that operate along McKinney Avenue through Dallas' Uptown area.

Dallas' train depot is located at 400 S. Houston St. Dallas, TX 75202. The station is staffed and features an enclosed waiting area, checked baggage service, restrooms, payphones, and vending machines. Transportation options from the station include McKinney Avenue Transit Authority Tel: (214) 855-0006, Dallas Area Rapid Transit Tel: (214) 979-1111,

Greyhound Tel: (214) 655-7082, Cowboy Cab Tel: (214) 428-0202 and Yellow Cab Tel: (214) 426-6262.

Dallas station is served by the Texas Eagle.

Visitors Information Center

Dallas Convention and Visitors Bureau 1201 Elm Street (Suite 2000) Dallas, TX 75270, Tel: (214) 572-1000 or toll-free (800) C-DALLAS.

Places to See and Things to Do

Dealey Plaza and the Sixth Floor Museum exhibits memorabilia of the infamous day of November 22nd 1963 when President J.F. Kennedy was assassinated. The museum also displays a detailed life story of the late President. The museum is the most visited in Dallas, located at 411 Elm Street, Dallas Tel: (214) 747 6660. Admission is $6. Other places of interest are: **JFK Memorial** located downtown on Main Street and Market Street at the Dallas County Historical Plaza, and the **Conspiracy Museum** located at 110 South Market Street Tel: (214) 741-3040 which exhibits other stories of US Presidential assassinations and political controversy.

Fountain Place is known for its charming setting of fountains, trees, and streams. A night visit to the square will be a fascinating experience. Fountain Place is located at 1445 Ross Avenue, at North Field Street Tel: (214) 855-7766. **Old City Park: The Historical Village of Dallas** has many Victorian era buildings and farms. The park is located at 1717 Gano, Dallas Tel: (214) 421-5141. **West End Historic District** is an old warehouse area developed and converted to house restaurants, shops, and museums. Located at the West End Historic District is the **American Museum of the Miniature Arts**, 2001 Lamar, Dallas Tel: (214) 969-5502. The museum exhibits rare antique toys, dollhouses, and scale models amongst others.

Wilson Block Historic District has the oldest and most well-preserved houses in the city of Dallas. Along the historic district of Swiss Avenue is the famous Arnold House and Frederick Wilson house. The historic district is located at 2922 Swiss Avenue, Dallas Tel: (214) 821-3290 <<http://www.preservationdallas.org>>. The **Dallas Museum of Art** is located at 1717 North Harwood Street Tel: (214) 922-1200. The museum exhibits ancient and modern arts from different parts of the world. Admission is $6 <<http://www.dm-art.org >>. **Reunion Tower,** located at 300 Reunion Blvd, is one of the most popular landmarks of Dallas. The 560 foot tall observation Tower was constructed as part of Hyatt Hotel Dallas.

Created for the 1936 Texas Centennial Exposition, **Fair Park** is 277 acres of entertainment venues, shops, restaurants, museums, a concert hall, and theaters. It is advisable to plan your visit to the park in order to maximize your time. The park is located at 1300 Robert B McCullum Street, Dallas Tel: (214) 670-8400 <<http://www.fairparkdallas.com>>.

Inside the Fair Park

Age of Steam Railroad Museum exhibits steam trains and old railroad memorabilia, a fun place to visit. The museum is located in Fair Park at 1105 Washington St, Dallas Tel: (214) 428-0101. Admission is: $5.00 adults, $2.50 children. Also located in Fair Park is the **African American Museum** located at 3635 Grand Ave. Dallas Tel: (214) 565-9026, and the **Music Hall** located at 909 1st Ave, Dallas Tel: (214) 565-1116.

The **Museum of Natural History** is located at 3535 Grand Avenue Tel: (214) 421-3466; the **Science Place** located at 1318 Second Avenue Tel: (214) 428-5555 has more than 350 hands-on exhibits and houses an IMAX Theater; and the recently opened **Women's Museum** is located at 3800 Parry Avenue Tel: (214) 915-0860.

Other places of interest are: **Dallas City Hall** located at 1500 Marilla Street, Dallas Tel: (214) 670-5111, **Thanks-Giving Square** located at 1627 Pacific Ave, Dallas Tel: (214) 969-1977 and the **Morton H Meyerson Symphony Center** located at 2301 Flora Street Tel: (214) 670-3600. **Dallas Arboretum** located at 8525 Garland Road, Dallas Tel: (214) 327-8263 has 66 acres of trees, gardens and lawns and two mansions. The **Dallas World Aquarium and Zoological Garden** is the world's largest freshwater aquarium. The aquarium also has 85,000 gallons of saltwater and a tropical rainforest. It is located at 1801 N Griffin St, Dallas Tel: (214) 720-2224.

Accommodations

Le Meridien located at 650 N. Pearl, Dallas TX Tel: (214) 979-9000. **Adams Mark** located at 400 Olive, Dallas TX Tel (214) 922-8000 or toll-free (800) 444-ADAM. **Hotel Adolphus** located at 1321 Commerce St., Dallas TX; Tel: (214) 742-8200. **Sheraton Hotel** located at 2101 N Stemmons Fwy, Dallas TX Tel: (214) 747-3000 or toll-free (800) 325-3535. **Hotel Lawrence** located at 302 S. Houston, Dallas TX, Tel: (214) 761-9090.

Wyndham Hotel, located at 2201 N Stemmons Fwy, Dallas TX Tel: (214) 748-1200 or toll-free (800) WYNDHAM. **Hyatt Hotel** located at 300 Reunion Blvd, Dallas TX Tel: (214) 651-1234 or toll-free (800) 233-1234. **Wilson World Hotel** located at 2325 N. Stemmons Fwy, Dallas TX Tel: (214) 630-3330. **Holiday Inn** located at 1933 Main St. Dallas TX Tel: (214) 741-1100 or toll-free (800) HOLIDAY. **American Suites** located at 1907 N. Lamar, Dallas TX Tel: (214) 999-0500 or toll-free (800) 833-1516.

Fort Worth (TX)
Connecting train to **Oklahoma (OK) (Heartland Flyer)**

Fort Worth is located 170 miles north of Austin. Forth Worth has a land area of 283 sq. miles (728 sq. kilometers) and a population of approximately 490,000. Forth Worth was first settled in 1849 as an Army Post. It was in 1876 when the first train arrived in Fort Worth and established the city as an economic hub.

Forth Worth is known for its unique and diverse museum, beautiful old-town architecture, rodeos, and warm friendly people. The Fort Worth train station is the original Santa Fe station built in 1899. A new Fort Worth station is being built just beside the historic Santa Fe station.

Getting Around

Airport

Dallas/Fort Worth International Airport is located 18 miles (29kilometers) northeast of Fort Worth, P.O. Drawer 619428, DFW Airport, TX 75261-9428 Tel: (972) 574-8888. Airporter bus Tel: (817) 334-0092 serves the airport for $10 each way; the Super Shuttle toll-free (800) 648-7051 has a shared ride service for $16.00. Taxis are available at the arrival hall, the fare from the airport to downtown Fort Worth is approximately $32. There are several rent-a-car services at the airport arrival area. Trinity Railway Express connects the airport to downtown Fort Worth.

Bus

Fort Worth Transportation Authority, "the T" Tel: (817) 215-6200, serves the city of Fort Worth. Fare is $1 each way and riding within downtown Fort Worth is free. Bus no. 2 operates among the city's many tourist attractions. Greyhound located at 901 Commerce, Fort Worth Tel: (817) 429-3089 connects the city to most of the country.

Taxi

Fort Worth's local taxi service is by Yellow Cab Tel: (817) 535-5555.

Rent-a-car

Avis Rent A Car toll-free (800) 230-4898, Hertz Car Rental toll-free (800) 654-3131 and Advantage Rent-A-Car toll-free (800) 777-5500.

Train and Commuter

Trinity Railway Express commuter rail service serves Dallas medical district, Dallas/Fort Worth International Airport, and downtown Fort Worth.

Fort Worth's train depot is located at 1501 Jones St. Fort Worth, TX 76102. The station is staffed and features an enclosed waiting area, checked baggage service, restrooms, payphones, and vending machines. Transportation options from the station include Fort Worth Transportation Authority, Greyhound, and local taxi service.

Trains serving Fort Worth station are the Heartland Flyer and Texas Eagle.

Visitors Information Center

Fort Worth Convention and Visitors Bureau 415 Throckmorton Fort Worth, TX 76102 Tel: (817) 336-8791 or toll-free (800) 433-5747.

Places to See and Things to Do

Fort Worth Stockyards District is one of the most visited areas of Fort Worth. The district had preserved its western heritage. There are several restaurants, events, and outlets as well as the popular rodeos. Also located at the Stockyards is the **1896 locomotive Tarantula Train** toll-free (800) 952-5717; the train offers a ride around the Stockyard from Eighth Avenue. The district is located around N.W. 28th St., N.W. 23rd St., Ellis Ave., and Packers Ave. Fort Worth Tel: (817) 624-4741. **Sundance Square** located in downtown Fort Worth is a rich heritage of restored and preserved architecture of the old Fort Worth. Sundance Square has several restaurants, shops, theaters, museums, halls, and entertainment venues.

Chisholm Trail Mural depicts cattle drives of the 19th century Fort Worth. The murals can be seen in downtown Fort Worth at 400 Main Street, Fort Worth Tel: (817) 390-8711. **Fort Worth Water Gardens** has several sculptures and fountains popular amongst locals; the gardens are located in downtown Fort Worth at Commerce and Houston Streets, Tel: (817) 871-7698. The **Fire Station No. 1** is the city's first firehouse, located at second and Commerce Street Tel: (817) 732-1631. **Fort Worth Museum of Science and History** located at 1501 Montgomery St. toll-free (888) 255-9300 exhibits many natural wonders and houses a theater and planetarium. **Imagisphere Children's Museum** has hands-on exhibits, like the tropical rain forest and many more. The museum is located at North Hills Mall 7624 Grapevine TX 76180 Tel: (817) 589-9000.

Fort Worth Botanic Garden has 114 acres of land with more than 2,500 exotic and native plant species. The garden is located at 3220 Botanic Garden Blvd. Fort Worth, Tel: (817) 871-7686. **Fort Worth Nature Center and Refuge** has 3,500 acres of sanctuary and 25 miles of trails perfect for hiking or urban retreats. The refuge is located at 9601 Fossil Ridge Rd. Fort Worth, TX 76135 Tel: (817) 237-1111. **Fort Worth Zoo** is located at 1989 Colonial Pkwy Fort Worth, TX Tel: (817) 871-7050. The zoo has more than 5000 rare and exotic animals. Admission is: adults $8.50, children $6.00, and seniors $5.00. **Fossil Rim Wildlife Center** Tel: (254) 897-2960 is an African Safari-style scenic drive located in Glen Rose. There are various endangered animals along the 3000 acres of wildlife preserve.

Log Cabin Village, located at 2100 Log Cabin Village Lane Fort Worth, TX 76119 Tel: (817) 926-5881, exhibits the life of the old days of Texas and is an interesting place to visit. **NRH2O-Family Water Park** has water slides and a wave pool. The park is located at 9001 Grapevine Hwy. North Richland Hills, TX 76180 Tel: (817) 427-6500. Located just 10 miles from Fort Worth are **Six Flags Over Texas** and **Six Flags Hurricane Harbor** Tel: (817) 640-8900; they are amongst the most popular parks in Texas with roller coasters and many rides, a huge wave pool, and a 62-foot water slide. Both parks are located in Arlington, TX 76006.

Other places of interest are: the 1895 red granite **Tarrant County Courthouse**, a national historic place located at 100 W. Weatherford Street Fort Worth Tel: (817) 884-1111. The **Modern Art Museum of Fort Worth** located at 1309 Montgomery St, Fort Worth Tel: (817) 738-9215. **Fort Worth Outlet Square** located at 3rd at Throckmorton Tel: (817) 415-3720. The **National Cowgirl Hall of Fame** located in Sundance Square at 111 W 4th Fort Worth Tel: (817) 336-4475 and the **Cowtown Coliseum** located in Stockyards at 121 E. Exchange Tel: (817) 625-1025, is the indoor rodeo built in 1908.

Accommodations

Radisson Plaza Hotel located at 815 Main St. FT. TX 76102; Tel: (817) 870-2100, or toll-free (800) 333-3333; **Ramada Plaza Hotel Fort Worth Convention Center** located at 1701 Commerce St. FT. TX 76102; Tel: (817) 335-7000, or (800) 2-RAMADA. **Renaissance Worthington Hotel** is located at 200 Main St. FT. TX 76102; Tel: (817) 870-1000 or toll-free (800) 433-5677. **Hilton Garden Inn Fort Worth North** is located at 4400 N Freeway FT. TX 76137, Tel: (817) 222-0222 or toll-free (800) HILTONS. **Holiday Inn North Fossil Creek** located at 2540 Meacham Blvd. FT. TX 76106; Tel: (817) 625-9911 or (800) HOLIDAY. **Holiday Inn South & Conference Center** located at 100 Alta Mesa Blvd. East FT. TX 76134, Tel: (817) 293-3088 or toll-free (800) HOLIDAY.

Cleburne (TX)

Cleburne was founded in 1854, originally called Camp Henderson and later renamed Cleburne after General Pat Cleburne of the Confederate army in 1867. Cleburne has a land area of 19.5 sq. miles (50 sq. kilometers) and residents of around 23,000. The Layland Museum is an interesting place to visit.

Cleburne's train depot is located at 206 Border Street Cleburne, TX 76031. The station is unstaffed. Transportation options from the station are car rental: Forrest Chevrolet Car Rental Tel: (817) 645-4351 and Enterprise Rent-A-Car toll-free (800) RENT-A-CAR; Central Texas Trailways Tel: (817) 645-6636, and Yellow Cab Tel: (817) 318-8088.

Cleburne station is served by the Texas Eagle.

McGregor (TX)

McGregor was founded in 1882. It has a land area of 5.4sq. miles (14 sq. kilometers) and a population of roughly 5000. McGregor's economy is based on agriculture, technology, and research.

McGregor's train depot is located at One Amtrak Blvd. McGregor, TX 76657. The station is unstaffed and features an enclosed waiting area, restrooms, payphones, and vending machines. Transportation from the station is local taxi service.

McGregor station is served by the Texas Eagle.

Temple (TX)
Motor-coach connection to **Killen (TX)** and **Fort Hood (TX)**

Temple is located 60 miles north of Austin in Central Texas. Temple was a product of Santa Fe's 19th century railroad expansion. Temple was originally called Mudville, Tanglefoot, and Ratsville, indicating the town's image in the early days.

Temple has a land area of 43 sq. miles (111 sq. kilometers) and a population of approximately 55,000. Places of interest include the historic downtown district, the Railroad and Pioneer Museum at 710 Jack Baskin Street, Tel: (254) 298-5172, and the restored historic Santa Fe depot.

Temple's train depot is located at 315 W. Ave. B Temple, TX 76501. The station is staffed and features an enclosed waiting area, checked baggage service, restrooms, payphones, and vending machines. Transportation options from the station are local transit, bus, and taxi services.

Temple station is served by the Texas Eagle.

Taylor (TX)

Taylor is located in southwest Williamson County, 35 miles northeast of Austin. Taylor was founded in 1876 and was incorporated in 1882. Taylor's original name was Taylorsville; it was changed into Taylor in 1892. Taylor has a land area of 10.8 sq. miles (27.8 sq. kilometers) and a population of approximately 13,000.

Taylor's train depot is located at 118 E. Front St. Taylor, TX 76574. The station is self-serve.

Taylor station is served by the Texas Eagle.

Austin (TX)

Austin, founded in 1838, is located in the center of Texas 125 miles (322 kilometers) from San Antonio, Dallas, and Houston. The capital of the state of Texas, Austin has a land area of 349 sq. miles (564 sq. kilometers) and a population of more than 1 million including the metropolitan area making Austin the 16th largest city in the US.

Austin was founded in 1838 and back then site was called Waterloo. The capital was moved to Austin during the 1830's and the site was renamed after the "Father of Texas" Stephen F. Austin. Today Austin is one of the "Best Places for Business" according to Forbes, one of the most visited cities in Texas, and amongst the cleanest cities in the US.

Austin has moderate temperatures, sunny most of the time with an average temperature of 68 degrees F. (22 degrees C.) and an average annual rainfall of 32 inches. Visitors should observe the largest nightly urban bat movements of Mexican free-tailed bats at the Congress Avenue Bridge: it's a unique experience. Austin claims to be the "Live Music Capital of the World" having hundreds of live music performance venues around the city.

Getting Around

Airport

Austin-Bergstrom International Airport is located at 3600 Presidential Boulevard Austin, Texas Tel: (512) 530-ABIA, just 9 miles from downtown Austin. There are several rent-a-car services located at the airport baggage claim area: Alamo Tel: (512) 474-2922, Avis Tel: (512) 476-6137, Advantage Tel: (512) 388-3377, Budget Tel: (512) 478-9945, National Tel: (512) 476-6180 and Hertz Tel: (512) 478-9321. Public taxis area available at the arrival terminal, Super Shuttle Tel: (512) 258-3826 located at the baggage claim area has taxi minibus service from the airport to Austin. Capital Metro Buses Tel: (512) 474 1200 numbers 100 and 350 connect the airport to the rest of the city.

Bus

Capital Metropolitan Transportation Authority Tel: (512) 474-1200 operates around the city and the outlying areas. Other bus services are the River City Flyer serving downtown Austin located at 116 E 6th St. Austin; Hill Country Flyer and Twilight Flyer operating from Cedar Park located at 401 E Whitestone Blvd. Austin Tel: (512) 477-8468. Greyhound is located at 916 E Koenig Tel: (512) 458-3823.

Taxis

Taxi services around Austin are served by: Yellow American Tel: (512) 452-9999, Austin Cab Tel: (512) 478-2222 and Roy's Cab Tel: (512) 482-0000.

Rent-a-car

Hertz Rent-A-Car toll-free (800) 654-3131, Avis Rent-A-Car toll-free (800) 230-4898 and Budget Rent-A-Car toll-free (800) 527-0700.

Train and Commuter

The Austin & Texas Central Railroad Tel: (512) 477-8468 operates an excursion steam train from Austin and around Texas Hill Country.

Austin's train depot is located at 250 N. Lamar Blvd. Austin, TX 78703. The station is staffed and features an enclosed waiting area, checked baggage service, restrooms, payphones, and vending machines. Transportation options from the station include rent-a-car services, local transit, Greyhound, and taxis.

Austin station is served by the Texas Eagle.

Visitors Information Center

Austin Visitor Information Center is located at 201 E. 2nd St. Austin, TX 78701, Tel: (512) 583-7235 <<http://www.austintexas.org>>.

Capitol Visitors Center is located at 1857 General Land Office Building Austin, TX 78711 Tel: (512) 305-8400.

Places to See and Things to Do

Visit the lively and historic district of **East Sixth Street** which has numerous restaurants, bars, shops, and live music; a great place for entertainment. If you are visiting Austin during summer, see the Symphony's Summer Music Festival at **Symphony Square** located at 1101 Red River Austin, TX 78701, toll-free (888) 462-3787. **Old Bakery and Emporium** accommodate shops and a visitor information desk, located at 1006 Congress Avenue Austin, TX 78701 Tel: (512) 477-5961. **Texas State Cemetery** is designated as one of Austin's landmarks; many famous Texans were burried here. The cemetery is located at 909 Navasota St. Austin, TX 78702, Tel: (512) 463-0605. Witness the nightly exodus of more than a million Mexican free-tailed bats from spring to late summer, referred to as the **Congress Avenue Bats,** located at Austin's Congress Avenue Bridge Tel: (512) 478-0098.

The **Texas Governor's Mansion** is located at 1010 Colorado Austin, TX 78701 Tel: (512) 463-5516. The **Texas State Capitol** is located at 11th and Congress Austin, TX 78711, Tel: (512) 463-0063. Said to be one of the most romantic and scenic places in Austin, **Mt. Bonnell** rewards visitors who climb the nearly one hundred steps with views of lake Austin and West Lake Hills. Mt. Bonnell is located at 3800 Mt. Bonnell Rd. Austin.

Zilker Botanical Gardens is located at 2220 Barton Springs Road Austin TX 78746, Tel: (512) 478-6875 and **Zilker Park/Barton Springs Pool** is located at 2100 Barton Springs Road Austin, TX 78746, Tel: (512) 476-9044. The park is a popular water recreation spot for locals. **Umlauf Sculpture Garden & Museum,** located at 605 Robert E. Lee Road Austin TX 78704 Tel: (512) 445-5582, exhibits more than a hundred sculptures of Charles Umlauf. **Lady Bird Johnson Wildflower Center** located at 4801 La Crosse Avenue Austin, TX 78739 Tel: (512) 292-4200. This botanical garden houses several courtyards, terraces and meadows, and is popular for its beautiful architecture.

Lyndon B. Johnson Presidential Library and Museum located at 2313 Red River Austin, TX 78705 Tel: (512) 916-5136. One of the most popular presidential libraries in the US, the library houses a museum and millions of historical papers. **Texas State Library & Archives** houses the Texas state archives and other historical documents. The library is located at 1201 Brazos Austin, TX 78701 Tel: (512) 463-5514.

The Bob Bullock Texas State History Museum located at the corner of Martin Luther King, Jr. Blvd. and N. Congress Ave. Austin, TX 78711, Tel: (512) 936-8746. The museum exhibits the history of the Lone Star State, Texas. The museum also houses the only IMAX Theater in Austin <<http://www.thestoryoftexas.com>>. **Austin Children's Museum** is located at 201 Colorado Street Austin, TX 78701 Tel: (512) 472-2499. The museum features educational, hands-on programs. The **Mexico-Arte Museum** is dedicated to the Latin culture. The museum exhibits Latin contemporary and historical arts and is located at 419 Congress Avenue Austin, TX 78701 Tel: (512) 480-9373.

Texas Military Forces Museum and All-Faiths Chapel exhibits the development of Texas military forces; the museum is located at Camp Mabry at 2200 W. 35th Street Austin, TX 78703 Tel: (512) 465-5659. **Republic of Texas Museum** is located at 510 East Anderson Lane Austin TX 78752 Tel: (512) 339-1997, the museum is dedicated to the historical development of Texas.

The **Austin Museum of Art** located in downtown Austin at 823 Congress Ave. Austin TX 78701, Tel: (512) 495-9224 exhibits world modern and contemporary art. **Austin History Center** located at 810 Guadalupe Austin, TX 78701 Tel: (512) 499-7480. The historical center is a research library that focuses on the history of Austin and Travis County. The **Austin Nature & Science Center** is located at 301 Nature Center Drive Austin, TX 78746 Tel: (512) 327-8180. The science center houses the Discovery Lab, Nature of Austin, and the Small Wonders, highlighting the surrounding natural habitats of Austin.

Center for American History located at the University of Texas at Austin at Sid Richardson Hall, Unit 2 Austin, TX 78712, Tel: (512) 495-4515. The museum is dedicated to the history of the development of the United States. The museum exhibits Texas and its natural history. The **Jack S. Blanton Museum of Art** located at the University of Texas at the Harry Ransom Center Austin TX 78712, Tel: (512) 471-7324 is one of the leading art museums in Texas; the museum has thousands of permanent collections dedicated to the history of western civilization. **Texas Memorial Museum** located at the University of Texas Campus at 2400 Trinity Street Austin, TX 78705 Tel: (512) 471-1604.

George Washington Carver Museum located at 1165 Angelina Street Austin, TX 78702 Tel: (512) 472-4809. The museum is dedicated to African-American history and culture. **Center for Women & Their Work** located at 1710 Lavaca Austin, TX 78701 Tel: (512) 477-1064, the museum has seasonal visual arts exhibitions of popular American artists. **Harry Ransom Humanities Research Center** located at the University of Texas Campus at 21st and Guadalupe Austin TX 78713-7219 Tel: (512) 471-8944; the museum has a wide collection of 20th century British, American, and French literary materials including visual arts, film, photography, and theatre arts.

Accommodations

Clarion Inn & Suites located at 2200 Interstate 35 South Austin TX 78704, toll-free (800) 434-7378; expect to pay $50-$150. **Doubletree Austin** located at 6505 I-35 North Austin TX 78752-4346, Tel: (512) 454-3737; expect to pay $60-$250. **Doubletree Hotels Club University Area Austin** located at 1617 IH-35 North Austin TX 78702, Tel: (512) 479-4000; expect to pay $70-$150. **Econo Lodge Austin** located at 6201 US 290 E Austin TX 78723; toll-free (800) 553-2666; expect to pay $35-$100. **Embassy Suites Austin Airport** located at 5901 North Interstate 35 Austin TX 78723, toll-free (800) 362-2779; expect to pay $70-$150. **Comfort Inn Delmar Austin** located at 700 Delmar Ave Austin TX 78752; toll-free (800) 228-5150; expect to pay $50-$100.

Courtyard Austin South located at 4533 South IH-35 Austin TX 78744, Tel: (512) 912-1122; expect to pay $60-$150. **Days Inn North Austin** located at 820 E Anderson

Lane Austin TX 78752, Tel: (512) 835-4311; expect to pay $50-$100. **Holiday Inn Express** located at 7622 I-35 North Austin TX, Tel: (512) 467-1701; expect to pay $50-$100. **La Quinta Inn Capitol** located at 300 E 11th St Austin TX 78701-2412, Tel: (512) 476-1166 toll-free (800) 531-5900; expect to pay $50-$150.

The Driskill Hotel located at 604 Brazos St, Austin TX 78701-3247, toll-free (800) 252-9367; expect to pay $200-$300. **Hyatt Regency Austin on Town Lake** located at 208 Barton Springs Rd Austin TX 78704-1211, Tel: (512) 477-1234 or toll-free (800) 233-1234; expect to pay $90-$250. **Marriott at Capitol Austin** located at 701 E 11th St Austin TX 78701-2622 Tel: (512) 478-1111 or toll-free (800) 228-9290; expect to pay $75-$250. **Renaissance Austin Hotel** located at 9721 Arboretum Boulevard Austin TX 78759, Tel: (512) 343-2626; expect to pay $50-$300.

Omni Austin Hotel Downtown located at 700 San Jacinto Blvd Austin TX 78701-3231, Tel: (512) 476-3700 or toll-free (800) 843-6664; expect to pay $50-$350. **Hilton and Towers North Austin** located at 6000 Middle Fiskville Road Austin TX 78752-4315, toll-free (800) 347-0330; expect to pay $60-$250. **Inter-Continental Stephen F. Austin** located at 701 Congress Avenue Austin TX 78701, Tel: (512) 457-8800; expect to pay $75-$700.

San Marcos (TX)

San Marcos was founded in 1808 and later abandoned due to constant native Indians attacks. In 1851 the first permanent settlers arrived in the area and later the town was incorporated in 1877. San Marcos is located just 31 miles southwest of Austin; it has a land area of 17.5 sq. miles (45 sq. kilometers) and a population of around 38,500.

San Marcos is known for the annual Republic of Texas Chilympiad (chili cooking contest), Wonder Caves, and Southwest Texas State University.

San Marcos' train depot is located at 338 South Guadalupe Street San Marcos, TX 78666. The station is unstaffed. Transportation from the station is local taxi service.

San Marcos station is served by the Texas Eagle.

San Antonio (TX)
Connecting train to **Los Angeles (CA), New Orleans (LA), Orlando (FL)** via Sunset Limited; Motor-coach connections to **Laredo (TX) and Brownsville (TX)**

San Antonio is one of the most popular and charming cities in the US; it is located 74 miles southeast of Austin in south central Texas. The early Indians called the area "Yanaguana," meaning "clear water," and on June 13, 1691 the early Spanish explorers founded San Antonio and it was named after the Italian martyr Saint Anthony.

San Antonio has a rich historical heritage; it was here in 1836 where the battle that inspired the Texan people to rise for freedom took place in the Mission San Antonio de Valero, also known as the "Alamo." San Antonio celebrated its 250th anniversary in 1968 with HemisFair.

Strategically located in the center of Texas, San Antonio was a hub for several major railroad routes. Today San Antonio is a thriving metropolis; it is America's ninth largest city and has a land area of 336 sq. miles (862 sq. kilometers) and a population of roughly 1.2 million.

San Antonio has an average temperature of 69.9 degrees F (23 degrees C) and an average annual rainfall of 27 inches.

Getting Around

Airport

San Antonio International Airport is located 8.6 miles North of San Antonio, at 9800 Airport Blvd San Antonio, Texas 78216. The bus going to the airport stops in downtown at 1100 E. Commerce, San Antonio Tel: (210) 207-3450. Taxi to the airport will cost around $15 for approximately 20 minutes of travel time.

Transportation options from the airport include rent a car, city bus service by Metropolitan Transit Tel: (210) 362-2020 fare from the airport to downtown or vise-versa is $0.75, and share-a-ride shuttle offered by SATRANS (210) 281-9900 fare is $9.00 to downtown district or $16 round trip; other destinations by zone charge. Courtesy vehicle service is available for passengers from the airport to and from designated hotels around San Antonio.

Bus

Metropolitan Transit (VIA) serves San Antonio and the rest of the Bexar County, 800 West Myrtle St., San Antonio, Tel: (210) 362-2020. The standard bus fare is 80 cents (one way) with several discounts and reduced fares for elderly and disabled. Metropolitan Transit (VIA) also offers special passes. Greyhound Bus is located at 500 N St. Mary's, San Antonio Tel: (210) 270-5824; it connects San Antonio to the rest of the country. Metropolitan Transit "streetcar buses" serve the city.

Taxi

Taxis serving San Antonio: Yellow Cab Tel: (210) 226-4242, AAA Taxi Tel: (210) 558-8888, Checker Cab Tel: (214) 222-2151.

Rent-A-Car

Advantage Rent-A-Car toll-free (800) 777-5500, Alamo Rent-A-Car toll-free (800) 327-9633, Budget toll-free (800) 527-0700, Dollar Rent A Car toll-free (800) 800-4000, Avis Rent-A-Car toll-free (800) 831-2847, The Hertz Corporation toll-free (800) 654-3131, Thrifty toll-free (800) 367-2277 and Enterprise toll-free (800) 736-8222.

Train and Commuter

San Antonio's train depot is located in St. Paul Square, between the Sunset Station complex and the Alamo Dome at 1174 E. Commerce St. San Antonio, TX 78205. The station is staffed and features an enclosed waiting area, checked baggage service, restrooms, payphones, and vending machines. Transportation options from the station include Hertz Car Rental toll-free (800) 654-3131 and local taxi service.

Trains serving San Antonio station are the Texas Eagle and the Sunset Limited.

Visitor Information Center

San Antonio Convention & Visitors Bureau is located at 203 S. St. Mary's St., 2nd floor San Antonio, Texas 78205; Tel: (210) 207-6700 or toll-free (800) 447-3372.

Places to See and Things to Do

The Alamo is located at 300 Alamo Plaza Tel: (210) 225-1391. The Alamo was established in 1718 as the first mission of San Antonio, this historical site is one of the most visited in Texas. The Alamo is the site where 189 defenders of the city fell after a constant attack of the Mexican army on March 6, 1836 during the American/Mexican War <<http://www.thealamo.org>>.

Perhaps the most romantic part of the old city of San Antonio is the **River Walk** or **Paseo Del Rio** located in the heart of downtown at 454 Soledad, River Ste. 2. San Antonio, TX. Tel: (210) 227-4262. There are restaurants, shops, nightclubs, and hotels complemented by gardens, a lovely stream, and the tall cypress, oak, and willow trees. Visitors can take the romantic three-mile river cruise or simply stroll along the walkway by the river. Also located near the River Walk is San Antonio's oldest surviving neighborhood, **La Villita**, dating back to the mid 1700's.

Casa Navarro State Historical Park is located at 228 S. Laredo St. San Antonio, TX Tel: (210) 226-4801. The historical park was the residence of the prominent Texas Mexican legislator Jose Antonio Navarro. The park shows examples of Texas' rich Mexican heritage.

The Alamo

Admission is: adults $2, children $1 (children under 6 free). **Market Square- El Mercado** is located at 514 W. Commerce San Antonio, TX. Tel: (210) 207-8600. Market Square is rich in Mexican atmosphere with music and many shops; it's a fun place to visit.

The most elegant residential area of San Antonio during the late 1800's was the **King William Historic Area,** located just 25 blocks from downtown at the bank of the San Antonio River. The area was Texas first historic district. A State and National Historic Landmark, the **Majestic Theater** located at 224 E. Houston, San Antonio TX. Tel: (210) 226-5700 is a fine example of an old vaudeville theater. Built in 1860 by Carl Hilmar Guenther is the historic **Guenther House** located at the foot of the King William at 205 E. Guenther, San Antonio TX, toll-free (800) 235-8186. The house museum has memorabilia of the old community <<http://www.guentherhouse.com>>.

IMAX Theater at River Center is located at 849 E. Commerce, River Center Mall, street level, on the Crocket Street Entrance toll-free (800) 354-4629. The theater features the 45-minute story of the siege and fall of the Alamo, titled the "Alamo - The Price of Freedom," admission is: adults $8.95; children; $4.75 and seniors $7.95 <<http://www.IMAX-sa.com>>. **Plaza Wax Museum & Ripley's Believe It or Not!** located at 301 Alamo Plaza Tel: (210) 224-9299 exhibits 250 lifelike wax figures of famous people and old artifacts <<http://www.plazawaxmusuem.com>>.

San Antonio Mission National Historical Park, park headquarters are located at 2202 Roosevelt Ave. San Antonio, Tel: (210) 534-8833. The historic park has several missions and historical sites that were established during the long history of San Antonio. **Mission**

River Walk /Paseo Del Rio

Concepcion, San Jose, and San Juan Capistrano; Espada Dam and Aqueduct, Acequia irrigation systems; and the Rancho de las Cabras are among the most significant architectural sites in the park <<http://www.nps.gov/saan>>. **Buckhorn Saloon and Museum** located at 318 E. Houston, San Antonio TX Tel: (210) 247-4000. Situated near the Alamo, the museum exhibits artifacts of Texas history and wildlife from different parts of the world. Admission is: adults $8.99, children $6.50; available discounts for seniors and military personnel.

San Antonio Botanical Gardens and Conservatory, located at 555 Funston Pl. San Antonio, TX Tel: (210) 207-3255, covers 33 acres of different kinds of gardens and a climatically controlled conservatory with various halls and various exotic gardens. Admission is: adults $4, children $1, and seniors $2 <<http://www.sabot.org>>. **San Antonio Zoological Garden and Aquarium** located at 3903 N. St. Mary's San Antonio, TX. Tel: (210) 734-7183. One of the best in the US, the zoo has 35 acres of land housing more than 3,500 animals. Admission is: adults $7, children and seniors $5. **Japanese Tea Garden** is located at 3800 North St. Mary's St. (at the northwestern edge of Brackenridge Park).

Railroad Miniature Railway is a miniature replica of an 1863 Central Pacific Huntington steam locomotive; it travels 2 ½ miles of track. For information and tickets visit 3910 N. St. Mary's, San Antonio TX.

Considered the most beautiful building in San Antonio, the **Spanish Governor's Palace** is located at 105 Plaza De Armas San Antonio, TX. Tel: (210) 224-0601. The Governor's Palace is a national historic landmark which housed many officials of the Spanish province of Texas. **Sunset Station** is located at 1174 E. Commerce, San Antonio TX. Tel: (210) 222-9481. The station was built in 1902 and has world-class entertainment, restaurants, and shops set up in an early Texan atmosphere.

Visitors can easily recognize the grandeur of San Antonio's **Tower of the Americas** located at 600 HemisFair Park, San Antonio,

The Tower of the Americas

TX Tel: (210) 207-8615. The 750 ft. tall tower was the symbol edifice of the 1968 HemisFair. The view from the observation deck offers breathtaking views of the city of San Antonio and the surrounding areas. Admission is: adults $3, children $1 and seniors $2. Other interesting places are the **Vietnam War Memorial** located at Veterans Memorial Plaza; **San Antonio Children's Museum** Tel: (210) 212-4453 ext. 1306; and the **McNay Art Museum** Tel: (210) 824-5368.

Six Flags is located just 15 minutes from downtown San Antonio; take Interstate 10 West at La Cantera Parkway, then exit north loop 1604. The park has 22 rides and games including a classic wooden roller coaster and much more; toll-free (800) 473-4378 <<http://www.sixflags.com>>. **Splashtown** is a family water park that features exiting water rides located at 3600 IH. 35 North, San Antonio, TX Tel: (210) 227-1400 <<http://www.splashtownsa.com>>. San Antonio's **Sea World** is located just 16 miles northeast of downtown San Antonio at Ellison Drive and Westover Hills Boulevard, Tel: (210) 523-3606. Visit San Antonio's famous killer whale "Shamu" and prepare to get wet. There are rides and other entertainment at the park <<http://www.seaworld.com>>.

Accommodations

Marriott, Riverwalk is located at 711 E Roverwalk St. San Antonio, TX. Tel: (210) 224-4555. **Hyatt Regency San Antonio, Riverwalk** is located at 123 Losoya St. San Antonio, TX. Tel: (210) 222-1234. **Westin Riverwalk** is located at 420 Market St. San Antonio, TX. Tel: (210) 224-6500. **San Antonio Riverwalk Plaza Resort Hotel** is located at 100 Villita St. San Antonio, TX. Tel: (210) 225-1234. **Hawthorn Suites, Riverwalk** is located at 830 North Saint Mary's St. San Antonio, TX. Tel: (210) 527-1900.

Homewood Suites, Riverwalk is located at 432 W. Market St. San Antonio, TX. Tel: (210) 222-1515. **Holiday Inn, Riverwalk** is located at 217 North Saint Mary's St. San Antonio, TX. Tel: (210) 224-2500. **Four Points Sheraton, North Riverwalk** is located at 110 Lexington San Antonio, TX. Tel: (210) 223-9461. **Adam's Mark Hotel San Antonio, Riverwalk** is located at 111 East Pecan St. San Antonio, TX. Tel: (210) 354-2800.

Comfort Suites, Downtown is located at 1002 South Laredo San Antonio, TX. Tel: (210) 472-1002. **Days Inn, Downtown** is located at 1500 Laredo St. San Antonio, TX. Tel: (210) 271-3334. **Courtyard by Marriott, Downtown Market Square** is located at 600 Santa Rosa South San Antonio, TX. Tel: (210) 229-9449. **Holiday Inn, Downtown/Market Square** is located at 318 West Durango Blvd. San Antonio, TX. Tel: (210) 225-3211.

Holiday Inn Express Hotel, Downtown is located at 524 South Saint Mary's St. San Antonio, TX. Tel: (210) 354-1333. **Ramada, Downtown** is located at 1122 S Laredo St. San Antonio, TX. Tel: (210) 229-1133. **Rodeway Inn, Downtown** is located at 900 N Main Ave. San Antonio, TX. Tel: (210) 223-2951.

Fairfield Inn by Marriott is located at 620 South Santa Rosa Ave. San Antonio, TX. Tel: (210) 299-1000. **Holiday Inn, Alamo** is located at 320 Bonham San Antonio, TX. Tel: (210) 225-6500. **La Quinta Inn and Convention Center** is located at 1001 E. Commerce St. San Antonio, TX. Tel: (210) 222-9181. **Residence Inn - Alamo Plaza** is located at 425 Bonham St. San Antonio, TX. Tel: (210) 212-5555. **Saint Anthony Hotel (Wyndham Grand Heritage Hotel)** is located at 300 E Travis San Antonio, TX. Tel: (210) 227-4392.

Heartland Flyer

Heartland Flyer		
5 25 pm-D	Forth Worth, TX	12 55 pm-A
6 45 pm	Gainesville, TX	11 14 am
7 31 pm	Ardmore, OK	10 30 am
8 26 pm	Pauls Valley, OK	9 34 am
8 51 pm	Purcell, OK	9 09 am
9 11 pm	Norman, OK	8 50 am
9 55 pm-A	Oklahoma City, OK	8 25 am-D
D-Departure	**A-**Arrival	

The Heartland Flyer travels a more than 200 mile-long (322 kilometers) route to the heart of the state of Oklahoma. It connects the towns and cities of Fort Worth (TX), Gainesville (TX), Norman (OK), and Oklahoma City (OK) with a connecting train to Chicago (IL) and San Antonio (TX) via the Texas Eagle, and to Los Angeles (CA) via the Sunset Limited.

Heartland Flyer service is financed and operated in partnership with the state of Oklahoma.

Route Destination Highlights

Fort Worth, TX- Explore the famous Fort Worth Stockyards District and watch an actual rodeo. See the rich architectural heritage of the old Fort Worth at Sundance Square, see the beautiful 19th century cattle drive of Ft. Worth depicted in the Chisholm Trail Mural, or take a wild roller-coaster ride at Six Flags.

Gainesville, TX- Visit and shop at the Prime Outlets, see the newly restored Downtown State Theater, or taste Gainesville's famous fried pies at the Gainesville Fried Pie Co.

Norman, OK: See the graceful Spanish Gothic architecture of the Sooner Theater, the historic Santa Fe Depot, the University of Oklahoma's museums, and the Cleveland County Historical House and get a glimpse of Oklahoma's rich heritage.

Oklahoma City, OK- Visit the site of the infamous Alfred P. Murrah Federal Building bombing of May 19, 1995 and pay respect to the victims at the Oklahoma City National Memorial and Museum. See the only state capitol in the US with a working oil well or visit the **Paseo District** and enjoy some of the city's best nightly entertainment and restaurants.

Train Schedules

The Heartland Flyer travels daily from Fort Worth, Texas to Oklahoma City, Oklahoma and vise-versa. The travel time between the two cities is approximately 5 hours.

Accommodations

Accommodation is Reserved Coach. There is a Cafe car that serves snacks, soups, sandwiches, and drinks. There are few spaces for unpacked bicycles which you should reserve in advance.

All Aboard!

Forth Worth (TX) See Texas Eagle service, page 319.

Gainesville (TX)

Gainesville is located 65 miles north of Ft. Worth. It has a land area of 13.6 sq. miles (35 sq. kilometers) and residents of roughly 15,000. Gainesville is the seat of the county and a transportation hub between the various outlying areas. Gainesville has an estimated 12 million visitors annually making tourism one of Gainesville's major industries.

The city has recently restored several of its landmarks such as the historic Gainesville Santa Fe Depot and the Downtown State Theater. Other places of interest are the Frank Buck Zoo, Lake Murray, the Butterfield Stage, Gainesville Prime Outlets, and the Gainesville Fried Pie Co. which is famous for is local fried pies.

Gainesville's train depot is located at 605 E. California St. Gainesville, TX 76240. The station is self-serve.

Gainesville station is served by the Heartland Flyer.

Texas (TX)
Capital: Austin (Population: 20,851,820)
Size: 268,601 sq mi. (695,676 sq km)
Nickname: The Lone Star State
Joined the union on: Dec. 29, 1845 (28th state)
Motto: Friendship
Flower: Bluebonnet
Bird: Mockingbird
Song: Texas, Our Texas
Famous for: The Alamo, Steaks, and Nice People
Major industries: Commerce, Real Estate, Oil and Gas, and Tourism

Ardmore (OK)

Ardmore is located in south-central Oklahoma a few miles from the Oklahoma/Texas state border and 90 miles from Oklahoma City. Ardmore is the county seat of Carter County with a land area of 34 sq. miles (88 sq. kilometers) and a population of around 29,000. The native Chickasaw Indians originally occupied the surrounding areas of the present city of Ardmore.

Ardmore was also a product of the railroad expansion of the west. The Santa Fe Railroad arrived here in 1887, and the same year the first settlers arrived and the city emerged. The city was chartered in 1898 and was incorporated in 1959. Ardmore was twice named an All-American City.

Place of Interest

The Greater SW Historical Museum, located at 35 Sunset Dr. SW Ardmore OK 73401-2852 Tel: (580) 226-3857, exhibits memorabilia of Ardmore's long history. Also visit the **Eliza Cruce Hall Doll Museum** located at Ardmore Public Library 320 E St. NW Ardmore Tel: (580) 223-8290.

Ardmore's train depot is located at 210 E. Main St. Ardmore, OK 73401. The station is un-staffed. Transportation options from the station include McCulloh Motor Car Rental Tel: (580) 223-1500, Enterprise Rent-A-Car toll-free (800) RENT-A-CAR, and Ardmore Taxi Tel: (580) 223-6867.

Ardmore station is served by the Heartland Flyer.

Pauls Valley (OK)

Pauls Valley is located at the Washita river basin in south central Oklahoma just 53 miles south of Oklahoma City. Pauls Valley has a land area of 7.4 sq. miles (19 sq. kilometers) and a population of more than 6,000.

Pauls Valley's train depot is located at 1 Santa Fe Plaza Pauls Valley, OK 73075. The station is un-staffed.

Pauls Valley station is served by the Heartland Flyer.

Purcell (OK)

Purcell is located in the center of the state of Oklahoma just 32 miles from Oklahoma City. Purcell is the birthplace of the state of Oklahoma; it was here that the founding fathers of Oklahoma came to discuss statehood before presentation to the congress in 1893. Oklahoma became the 46th state in November 16, 1907.

Purcell has a land area of 7.8 sq. miles (20 sq. kilometers) and a population of around 6,000. Places of interest in Purcell include the historic Love Hotel, listed as a National Historic Site, which now houses an antique shop and a Butlers Home.

Purcell's train depot is located on East Main St. Purcell, OK 73080. The station is self-serve.

Purcell station is served by the Heartland Flyer.

Norman (OK)

Norman is located 17 miles south of Oklahoma City, founded in 1889 and incorporated in May 1891. The city of Norman was named after its surveyor Abner E. Norman and has a land area of 178 sq. miles (458 sq. kilometers) and a population of approximately 93,000. Just like most cities in the west, Norman emerged through the development of the railroad system.

Today Norman is the third largest city in Oklahoma and home to the first higher education institution in the state, the University of Oklahoma. It is famous for its historical monuments and sites.

Getting Around

Local bus

Norman Metro Transit Tel: (405) 325-2278 serves the city of Norman and the rest of the area with daily services.

Capital: Oklahoma City
(Population: 3,450,654)
Size: 68,679 sq mi. (177,877 sq km)
Nickname: The Sooner State
Joined the union on:
November 16, 1907 (46th state)
Motto: Labor conquers all things
Flower: Mistletoe
Bird: Scissor-tailed flycatcher
Song: Oklahoma
Famous for: 1995 Oklahoma City Bombing
Major industries: Food processing, machinery and petroleum.

Taxi

Norman Checker Cab Tel: (405) 329-3333 and Norman Yellow Cab Co. Tel: (405) 329-3335.

Train

Norman's train depot is located at 200 S. Jones Ave. Norman, OK 73069. The station is un-staffed.

Norman Station is served by the Heartland Flyer.

Visitor Information Center

Norman Tourist Information Office 224 W Gray St (Suite 100) Tel: (405) 366-8095 or toll-free (800) 767 7260.

Places of Interest

The Sooner Theater is located at 101 E. Main Norman, OK; the theater stages various yearly performances. Set in graceful Spanish Gothic architecture, it is one of the most popular buildings in the region. The Theater is listed on the Oklahoma List of Historic sites and the National Register of Historic Places. **The Santa Fe Depot,** located at the "Legacy Trail Park" 200 S. Jones Ave. Norman Tel: (405) 366-5472, houses the Norman Arts and Humanities Council and Amtrak Norman stops.

The **Fred Jones Jr. Museum of Art** is located at the University of Oklahoma, 410 W. Boyd Street, Norman Tel: (405) 325-3272 and exhibits some of Oklahoma's best art collections. The museum has Indian and modern American art. **The Sam Noble Oklahoma Museum of Natural History** is located at 2401 Chautauqua Ave. Norman, OK 73072 Tel: (405) 325-4712. The museum is the largest university-based museum in the US and exhibits galleries that are dedicated to Oklahoma's 300 million years of natural history.

The Jacobson House Native American Cultural Center located at 609 Chautauqua Norman Tel: (405) 366-1667. Known for its architectural style and historical importance, the center has libraries and art collections of local and international art. **Western History Collections,** located at the University of Oklahoma's Monnet Hall, 630 Parrington Oval Tel: (405) 325-2904, houses more than 65,000 books, manuscripts, and more. The Western History Collection is the largest in Western United States. **The Cleveland County Historical House,** located at 508 N. Peters Ave. Norman, Tel: (405) 321-0156, is of 1900 Queen Anne Architecture and a registered national historic site. A visit to the house offers a glimpse of a middle-class residence of early Oklahoma.

Accommodations

Econolodge located at 100 26th Dr. Norman, OK 73069 Tel: (405) 364-5554. **Holiday Inn** located at 1000 Interstate Drive Norman, OK 73072 Tel: (405) 364-2882. **La Quinta Inns**

& Suites located at 930 Ed Noble Norman, OK 73072 toll-free (800) NU-ROOMS. **Hampton Inn** located at 309 Norman Court Center, Norman, OK 73072 Tel: (405) 366-2100.

Travelodge located at 225 N. Interstate Drive Norman, OK 73069 Tel: (405) 329-7194. **Thunderbird Lodge** located at 1430 24th Avenue, SW Norman, OK 73069 Tel: (405) 329-6990. **Villager Lodge** located at 1200 24th Avenue Southwest, Norman, OK 73072 toll-free (800) 500-9869. **Residence Inn** located at 2681 Jefferson Norman, OK 73072 toll-free (800) 331-3131.

Oklahoma City (OK)

Oklahoma is located in the central part of the state of Oklahoma and is the state capital. Founded on April 22, 1889, the site was part of the grasslands opened by government for settlement; Oklahoma became the state capital in 1910, with a total land area of 614 sq. miles (1,575 sq. kilometers) and population of nearly half a million.

The city of Oklahoma sits on oil fields that were discovered during the early 20th century. The discovery triggered a mass migration to the city and contributed to the progress of the city's economy. Some of the oil wells are still visible in some part of the city; one of the most famous is the "Petunia" located in the southern vicinity of the State Capitol.

Oklahoma City is the site of the infamous Alfred P. Murrah Federal Building bombing of May 19, 1995. The Oklahoma City National Memorial and Museum was dedicated to the victims of the horrendous act of terrorism.

Oklahoma City has mild weather with an average nine inches of snowfall during winter. Summer is hot and humid with relatively mild winds to cool you down.

Getting Around

Airport

Oklahoma City is served by Will Rogers World Airport Tel: (405) 680-3200 located 5 miles from Oklahoma City Center at 7100 Terminal Drive, Box 937, Oklahoma City, Oklahoma 73159-0937.

There are shuttle services that take passengers to and from airport/Oklahoma City: Airlink Shuttle Vans Tel: (405) 632-3442, Metro Express Tel: (405) 681-3311, and Airport Express Tel: (405) 681-3311. Taxis and rent-a-car are available at the central lower level of the terminal. Jefferson Bus Company Tel: (405) 235-6425, bus numbers 1030, 1620, and 2215 connect the airport and the Union Bus Station in Oklahoma City.

Bus

METRO Transit operates local bus service around the city. City Bus Terminal is located at 20 W. Reno OKC OK Tel: (405) 235-7433. Greyhound, located at 427 W Sheridan OKC OK Tel: (405) 235-6425, provided intercity bus service. Oklahoma Spirit Trolley serves most of downtown Oklahoma City and Amtrak train station.

Taxi

Yellow Cab (405) 232-6161, ABC Cab (405) 235-1431, and Metro Taxi (405) 525-5526.

Train and Commuter

Oklahoma City's train depot is located at 100 South E. K. Gaylord Blvd. Oklahoma City, OK 73102. The station is un-staffed and features an enclosed waiting area, payphones, and vending machines.

Oklahoma City station is served by the Heartland Flyer.

Visitor Information Center

Oklahoma City Convention and Visitors Bureau is located at 189 W Sheridan, Oklahoma City Tel: (405) 297-8912 or toll-free (800) 225-5652.

Places to See and Things to Do

Dedicated to the victims of the Alfred P. Murrah Federal Building bombing of May 19, 1995, the **Oklahoma City National Memorial and Museum** is located at 620 North Harvey OKC OK Tel: (405) 235-3313. **Oklahoma Heritage Center** located at 201 NW 14th OKC, OK Tel: (405) 235-4458. The 1917 mansion houses classic furniture, library, galleries, and memorabilia of the old Oklahoma. A visit to the **Paseo District** offers entertainment,

Oklahoma City Skyline

338

restaurants, and shops; the district is located at NW 30th and Shartel OKC, OK.

State Museum of History is located beside the capitol at 2100 N. Lincoln Blvd. OKC, OK Tel: (405) 521-2491. The Museum of History is dedicated to Oklahoma's long natural history; there are galleries, artifacts, and entertainment. The first mansion in Oklahoma City, built in late 19th century, the **Overholser Mansion** is located at 405 NW 15th OKC, OK Tel: (405) 528-8485. The mansion is still has its original furnishings. **Oklahoma Firefighters Museum** located at 2716 NE 50th OKC, OK Tel: (405) 424-3440. The museum is the first fire station in Oklahoma and exhibits Oklahoma's old fire engines.

Omniplex located at 2100 NE 52nd OKC, OK toll-free (800) 532-7652 houses a planetarium, galleries, gardens, a greenhouse, the Red Earth Indian Center, Kirkpatrick Science and Air Space Museum, the International Photography Hall of Fame and Museum, and more. The **World Organization of China Painters Museum** is dedicated to Chinese arts; there are exhibits of rare hand-made china, a research room, and Chinese art study room. The museum is located at 2641 NW 10th OKC, OK Tel: (405) 521-1234.

For a sporty and thrilling experience visit the **OKC Rock Climbing Center,** located next to the south end of the Bricktown Canal. Tel: (405) 319-1400. It offers up to 145 feet of rock climbing with classes, shops, and facilities. The city's famous country music show, the **Oklahoma Opry,** located at 404 W. Commerce, OKC, OK 73109 Tel: (405) 632-8322 has a regular Saturday night musical show.

Visit the only state capitol in the US with a working oil well south of the capitol. The Oklahoma **State Capitol** is located at NE 23rd & Lincoln Blvd. OKC, OK Tel: (405) 521-3356. One of the most popular sites in the city is the **World of Wings Pigeon Center**

Oklahoma City National Memorial and Museum

located at 2300 NE 63rd OKC, OK Tel: (405) 478-5155. Dedicated to honoring the bird of peace, the Pigeon Center has a museum and library.

State Fair Park located at 500 Land Rush Street OKC, OK Tel: (405) 948-6700 has various yearly events; there are rodeos, concerts, horse shows, and the annual State Fair of Oklahoma. It's a great place to meet the locals. **Will Rogers Park** has a beautiful rose garden, fresh water ponds, an arboretum, Olympic-size swimming pool, golf course, and recreation facilities. The park is located at 36th Street and N. Portland OKC, OK.

A spirit of the old west still exist in **Read Ranch** Tel: (405) 258-2999 which offers trail rides, meal rides, and an experience to come close-up to long horn cattle and buffalo. The ranch is located at Route 1, West of Chandler on Route 66, OK, just 35 minutes from Oklahoma City. See the actual live working cowboys at **Stockyards City,** the largest beef market in the world. At Cowtown there are shops, jewelry, and a delicious beef restaurant. Take the Agnew exit South off I-40 to Exchange Ave call Tel: (405) 235-8675 for information.

Oklahoma City entertainment district the **Bricktown** has restaurants, shops, a canal, and ballpark. Bricktown is located at Sheridan Avenue at Mickey Mantle Drive OKC, OK Tel: (405) 236-INFO. Less attractive than the San Antonio Riverwalk, the **Water Taxi of Oklahoma** operates in Oklahoma's manmade Bricktown canal located in Bricktown Tel: (405) 234-TAXI.

White Water Bay has 30 water rides, slides, pools, and water activities; a fun place to break the heat of summer. The water park is located at 3908 W. Reno OKC, OK Tel: (405) 943-9687. Admission is: $16.99 Adults, $12.99 Senior Citizens and children under 48" tall.

Bricktown, Oklahoma City

Other places of interest are: the **International Gymnastics Hall of Fame** located at 120 N Robinson OKC OK Tel: (405) 235-5600. **National Cowboy and Western Heritage Museum** located at 1700 NE 63rd St OKC OK Tel: (405) 478-2250. The **Myriad Botanical Gardens,** a 17-acre park west of the Amtrak station, houses the 7-story Crystal Bridge Tropical Conservatory located at 100 Myriad Gardens OKC OK Tel: (405) 297-3995. **Remington Park** has horse racing located at One Remington Place OKC OK toll-free (800) 456-9000; and one of the biggest zoos in the US, the **Oklahoma City Zoological Park** is located at 2101 NE 50th OKC OK Tel: (405) 424-3344.

Myriad Botanical Garden, Oklahoma City

Accommodations

Days Inn Airport located at 4712 W. I-40, OK 73128 Tel: (405) 947-8721. **Comfort Inn Historic Route 66** located at 4017 NW 39th Expwy, OK 73112 Tel: (405) 947-0038. **Courtesy Inn** located at 6600 NW Expwy, OK 73132 Tel: (405) 722-8694. **Embassy Suites Hotel** located at 1815 S. Meridian, OK 73108 Tel: (405) 682-6000. **Microtel Inn & Suites** located at 624 S. MacArthur, OK 73128 Tel: (405) 942-0011.

Catalina Motel located at 4801 S. Shields, OK 73129 Tel: (405) 634-2432. **Quality Inn Southwest** located at 7800 C.A. Henderson Blvd., OK 73139 Tel: (405) 632-6666. **Ramada Inn and Conference Centers** located at 4345 N. Lincoln Blvd, OK 73105 Tel: (405) 528-2741. **Plaza Inn** located at 3200 S. Prospect, OK 73170 Tel: (405) 672-2341. **Grandison**

Inn at Maney Park located at 1200 N. Shartel, OK 73103 Tel: (405) 232-8778. **Quality Suites** located at 3850 S. Prospect Avenue (I-35 & Grand) OK Tel: (405) 670-5800.

Days Inn located at 12013 N. I-35 Service Rd, OK 73131 Tel: (405) 478-2554. **Marriott Oklahoma City** located at 3233 N.W. Expwy, OK 73112 Tel: (405) 842-6633. **Hilton Oklahoma City Northwest** located at 2945 N.W. Expwy, OK 73112 Tel: (405) 848-4811. **Courtyard by Marriott** located at 1515 NW Expressway, OK 73118 Tel: (405) 848-0808. **Best Western Trade Winds Inn** located at 1800 E. Reno, OK 73117 Tel: (405) 235-4531.

Hampton Inn located at 13500 Plaza Terrace, OK 73120 Tel: (405) 752-7070. **Governors Suites Hotel** located at 2308 S. Meridian, OK 73108 Tel: (405) 682-5299. **Econolodge West** located at 8200 W. I-40, OK 73128 Tel: (405) 787-7051. **Four Points Hotel by Sheraton** located at 6300 E. Terminal Dr., OK 73159 Tel: (405) 681-3500. **Economy Inn** located at 501 N.W. 5th, OK 73102 Tel: (405) 235-7455. **Nu-Homa Motel** located at 3528 N.W. 39th, OK 73112 Tel: (405) 943-0966. **Hampton Inn Airport** located at 1905 S. Meridian, OK 73108 Tel: (405) 682-2080. **Holiday Inn Airport** located at 2101 S. Meridian, OK 73108 Tel: (405) 685-4000. **Hilton Garden Inn-OKC Airport** located at 801 S. Meridian, OK 79108 Tel: (405) 942-1400.

Michigan Services

(The Pere Marquette, Twilight Limited, Lake Cities, International, and Wolverine services)

The Michigan service takes passengers to the beautiful state of Michigan. It connects Chicago and Illinois to Michigan's major cities and destinations. The Michigan Service also connects the state of Michigan and the province of Ontario, Canada through joint services of Amtrak and VIA Rail Canada.

The Michigan Services are: the Twilight Limited which travels between Chicago, Illinois and Pontiac, Michigan; the Wolverine which travels between Chicago, Illinois and Pontiac, Michigan; the Lake Cities which travels between Chicago, Illinois and Detroit, Michigan; the Pere Marquette which travels between Chicago, Illinois and Grand Rapids, Michigan; and the International which travels between Chicago, Illinois and Toronto, Ontario Canada. The Pere Marquette is jointly funded by the state of Michigan and Amtrak while the International is jointly operated by Amtrak and VIA Rail Canada.

Route Destination Highlights

Chicago, IL- Home to America's tallest building, Sears Tower, visit the Museum of Science and Industry and other outstanding museums; admire the charming Centennial Fountain; take a romantic stroll along Lake Michigan; and enjoy Chicago's attractive and busy nightlife.

Detroit, MI- See the Detroit Auto Show, Motown Historical Museum, Greenfield Village, and Henry Ford Museum.

Scenery along the Route

Visit the winter water wonderland of Michigan. If you are in the mood for the great outdoors, Michigan is the place. With over 95 state parks, you can easily enjoy boating, camping, hiking, and any other outdoor activities that might interest you. If you enjoy indoor activities, Michigan has hundreds of museums, thousands of restaurants, and plenty for you to enjoy indoors. Relax and enjoy the scenery aboard an Amtrak train with several trains daily to many cities in Michigan.

Michigan Services

Multiple Train Departure Daily

| Chicago (IL) |
| Hammond Whiting (IN) |
| Michigan City (IN) |
| Niles (MI) |
| Dowagiac (MI) |
| Kalamazoo (MI) |
| Battle Creek (MI) |
| East Lansing (MI) |
| Durand (MI) |
| Flint (MI) |
| Lapeer (MI) |
| Port Huron (MI) |
| Albion (MI) |
| Jackson (MI) |
| Ann Arbor (MI) |
| Greenfield Village (MI) |
| Dearborn (MI) |
| **Detroit (MI)** |
| Royal Oak (MI) |
| Birmingham (MI) |
| Pontiac (MI) |

| --Chicago (IL) |
| --New Buffalo (MI) |
| --St. Joseph-Benton Harbor (MI) |
| --Bangor (MI) |
| --Holland (MI) |
| --Grand Rapids (MI) |
| **Canada** |

Schedules

The Michigan Service has multiple departures daily from Chicago, Illinois to Detroit and other major cites and destinations of the state of Michigan. The Michigan Service also connects passengers to Ontario, Canada through VIA Rail Canada.

Accommodation

Accommodations are Reserved Coach and Business Class. There is a Cafe Car that serves snacks, soups, sandwiches, and drinks.

Boarder Crossing

The International has connecting routes through Via Rail Canada from Port Huron, Michigan to Toronto, Ontario, Canada.

International Service

All Aboard!

Chicago (IL) See Illinois and Missouri service, page 268

Hammond- Whiting (IN)

Hammond's train station serves both the cities of Hammond and Whiting, located just 16 miles southeast of Chicago. Hammond has a land area of 23 sq. miles (59 sq. kilometers) and a population of approximately 85,000.

Hammond-Whiting's train depot is located at 1135 Calumet Ave. Hammond, IN 46320. The station is staffed and features an enclosed waiting area, checked baggage service, restrooms, payphones, and vending machines. Transportation from the station is local taxi service.

Trains serving Hammond-Whiting station are Lake Shore Limited, International Service, Pennsylvanian, and Three Rivers.

Indiana (IN)

Capital: Indianapolis (Population: 6,080,485)
Size: 36,420 sq mi. (94,327 sq km)
Nickname: The Hoosier State
Joined the union on: December 11, 1816 (19th state)
Motto: The Crossroads of America
Flower: Peony
Bird: Cardinal
Song: On the Banks of the Wabash
Famous for: Racing Car, David Letterman
Major industries: Minerals, Oil

Michigan City (IN)

Michigan City is located 60 miles east of Chicago, Illinois on the southern shore of Lake Michigan at the border of the states Indiana and Michigan. Michigan City has a land area of 19 sq. miles (51 sq. kilometers) and a population of approximately 14,000.

Michigan City was planed and designed to be a harbor city to serve as Indiana's trading post in Lake Michigan. The city was incorporated in 1836. Michigan City's economic development was based on its natural waterways (flowing waters from Trail Creek), currently used for lumber and gristmills. The arrival of railroad industry in the city opened a new potential for the development of the city's economy and social growth. A train factory was setup and by the 1850's Michigan City was home to one of the nation's largest train car manufacturers. Michigan pioneers came from the states of New York, Michigan, Europe, and Syria to work as factory workers. Traces of the city's rich history are still visible in downtown Michigan City.

Places of interest: The Barker Mansion, located at 631 Washington Street Michigan City, IN 46360 Tel: (219) 873-1520, offers a glimpse of the city's rich history; the Washington Park Zoo is located at the Michigan City Lake Front; the Hesston Steam Museum is located at 1201 E. 1000 N La Porte, IN 46350 Tel: (219) 778-2783; and the Main Street Farmers Market, located on 8th & Washington Streets, opens every Saturday during summer.

Michigan City's train depot is located at 100 Washington St. Michigan City, IN 46360. The station is self-serve and features payphones. Transportation from the station is local taxi service.

Michigan City station is served by the International Service.

Niles (MI)

The City of Niles is located on the southern edge of the state of Michigan, about 90 miles east of Chicago. It has a population of roughly 13,000 and a land area of 5.8 sq. miles (15 sq. kilometers). Niles has more than 300 years of history, making it the oldest settlement in the state of Michigan. The downtown Niles area still possesses the rich culture and history of Niles; the city hall, Carnegie Library (present home to the Chamber of Commerce), and the city's many museums still hold the legacy of the city's long history.

Niles is also known as the "City of Four Flags," having been under siege by the Spanish, French, English, and American forces. This made the city one of the most diverse in the region. The city of Niles was once a trading hub and a gateway to the western US; today its unique old Midwestern atmosphere has made the city one of the most filmed in the movie industry.

Michigan (MI)

Capital: Lansing (Population: 9,938,444)
Size: 96,810 sq mi. (250, 737 sq km)
Nickname: The Wolverine State
Joined the union on: Jan. 26, 1837 (26th state)
Motto: If you seek a pleasant peninsula, look around you
Flower: Apple blossom
Bird: Robin
Song: None
Famous for: Tulips, cars, cornflakes
Major industries: Car manufacturing, minerals, farming, agriculture and tulips

Places of Interest: Known for its stained glass window, the Victorian Chapin Mansion is the present City Hall built in 1884. City hall is located at 5th and Main streets. Fort St. Joseph Museum exhibits Native American, English, and French artifacts, located just behind the city hall. Four Flags Hotel, located on the corner of 4th and Main streets, was built in 1925 and hosted many famous and infamous Americans like Eleanor Roosevelt and Al Capone. Niles

345

Rail Depot, located just north of 5th Street, is Neo-Romanesque architecture and one of the most admired buildings in Niles.

Niles' train depot is located at 598 Day St. Niles, MI 49120. The station is staffed and features an enclosed waiting area, checked baggage service, restrooms, payphones, and vending machines. Transportation from the station is local taxi service.

Niles station is served by the International Service.

Dowagiac (MI)

Dowagiac, a native Indian word meaning "foraging ground," is located in southwestern Michigan. It has a land area of 3.9 sq. miles (10 sq. kilometers) and about 6,500 residents. The first permanent settlers of the city arrived in 1824 and in 1877 the city was incorporated.

Dowagiac's train depot is located at 100 Railroad Dr. Dowagiac, MI 49047. The station is un-staffed and features an enclosed waiting area, restrooms, and payphones.

Dowagiac station is served by the International Service.

Kalamazoo (MI)

Kalamazoo, a native Indian word meaning "the rapids at the river crossing," is the city's second name. Kalamazoo was first called Bronson, for its pioneer Titan Bronson in 1831. After Titan Bronson was accused and later convicted of stealing a cherry tree, the name of the town was change to Kalamazoo. Today Kalamazoo has a land area of 24.9 sq. miles (64 sq. kilometers) and is home to more than 80,000 residents.

Places of interest: The **Historic Districts of Stuart Avenue, South and Vine Streets** has a number of restored historical buildings arranged in a line depicting the rich history of the city of Kalamazoo. The **Kalamazoo Mall,** established in 1959, was the first outdoor mall in the US. The four-block mall is located between Lovell Street and Eleanor Street. The art deco architecture of the 1931 **Kalamazoo City Hall,** located at 241 W. South Street, is one of the finest examples of Kalamazoo's great architectural treasure. Part of the black slave underground railway network the **Underground Railway Home,** located on Cass Street east of Highway 131 in Schoolcraft Tel: (616) 679-4689, was built in 1835 by Dr. Nathan Thomas. **Bronson Park,** dedicated to Titan Bronson the founder of Kalamazoo, is where President Lincoln made his only speech in State of Michigan.

Kalamazoo's train depot is located at 459 N. Burdick St. Kalamazoo, MI 49006. The station is staffed and features an enclosed waiting area, checked baggage service, restrooms, payphones, and a snack bar. Transportation options from the station include local bus and taxi services.

Kalamazoo station is served by the International Service.

Battle Creek (MI)

Battle Creek is located just 121 miles (196 kilometers) west of the city of Detroit. Battle Creek, one of the largest cities in Michigan, has a land area of 43 sq. miles (111 sq. kilometers) and a population of more than 54,000. Battle Creek is one of the major stops of the Black Slaves who used the Underground Railroad to seek freedom in Canada.

Kellogg's Cereal City, USA is located at 171 West Michigan Avenue Battle Creek, Michigan 49017 Tel: (616) 962-6230. It has family attractions and entertainment dedicated to the cereal industry. The W.K. Kellogg Bird Sanctuary is located at 12685 East C Avenue Augusta, MI 49012 Tel: (616) 671-2510. The Binder Park Zoo is one of Battle Creek's most visited attractions and houses the "Safari to Wild Africa" where visitors can view a large collection of African wildlife. If you are coming in the first week of July, the Battle Creek Hot Air Balloon Festival is celebrated. Also during summer, Battle Creek celebrates its yearly Cereal Festival.

Battle Creek's train depot is located at 104 Capitol Ave. S.W. Battle Creek, MI 49017. The station is staffed and features an enclosed waiting area, checked baggage service, restrooms, payphones, and vending machines. Transportation options from the station include local transit, bus, and taxi services.

Battle Creek station is served by the International Service.

East Lansing (MI)

East Lansing is located just 4 miles northeast of Lansing, the state capital. East Lansing has a land area of 9.3 sq. miles (24 sq. kilometers) and population of 50,677 hospitable residents. East Lansing is home to Michigan State University, one of the largest universities in the US.

East Lansing's train depot is located at 1240 S. Harrison St. East Lansing, MI 48823. The station is staffed and features an enclosed waiting area, checked baggage service, restrooms, payphones, and a snack bar. Transportation options from the station include local transit and taxi services.

East Lansing station is served by the International Service.

Durand (MI)

Durand was incorporated in 1932 and was named after US Congressman George H. Durand in 1976. It has a land area of 1.7 sq. miles (4.4 sq. kilometers) and a population of just 4,300. Durand is located in the Lansing metro area at the junction of highway 71 and Interstate 69. The growth of Durand was attributed to the arrival and development of the railroad system in the city in early 1900's.

Durand was one of Michigan's railroad hubs and the city's railroading legacy is still visible in its museums and historical treasures. The Michigan Railroad History Museum is located at 200 Railroad Street Durand, MI Tel: (517) 288-3561 and exhibits Michigan's history of railroading, train cars, trolleys, and scale trains.

Durand's train depot is located at 200 Railroad Ave. Durand, MI 48429. The station is un-staffed and features an enclosed waiting area, restrooms, and payphones. Transportation from the station is local taxi service.

Durand station is served by International Service.

Flint (MI)

Flint is located just 52 miles (84 kilometers) southeast of the state capital Lansing. Flint has a land area of 34 sq. miles (88 sq. kilometers) and a population of 140,761. Flint's major economic generator is based on car manufacturing; there are 22 General Motors plants in the city.

Flint's train depot is located at 1407 S. Dorr Hwy. Flint, MI 48503. The station is staffed and features an enclosed waiting area, restrooms, payphones, and vending machines. Transportation options from the station include local transit and taxi services.

Flint station is served by the International Service.

Places to See

The world's largest Christmas store, **Brunner's Christmas Wonderland** located at 25 Christmas Lane, Frankenmuth, 48734 Tel: (517) 652-9931 is visited by more than 2 million visitors each year. **The Genesee Belle** offers a scenic cruise on Mott Lake departing from Crossroads Village & Stepping Stone Falls Tel: (810) 736-7100. **Stepping Stone Falls** is a man-made cascade of waterfalls. The falls is lighted at night creating magical colors. The falls is located at the foot of Mott Lake at 5161 Branch Rd., Flint, 48506 Tel: (810) 736-7100.

One of the largest farmers markets in Michigan, the **City of Flint Farmers Market,** is located northeast of downtown Flint near the main Post Office at 420 E. Boulevard Flint 48502 Tel: (810) 766-7449. **Crossroad Village and Huckleberry Railroad** offers train tours using a steam locomotive narrow gauge railroad. The village is located at 6140 Bray Rd., Flint 48505 Tel: (810) 736-7100. The **Steam Railroading Institute** houses a railroad history complex and heads the restoration of a 1941 locomotive, Project 1225; the institute also has railroading programs. It is located in Owosso, MI 48867 Tel: (517) 725-9464.

Buick Gallery and Research Center exhibits vintage Buick and other automobile memorabilia. The center is located at 303 Walnut Street, Flint 48503 Tel: (810) 760-1415. **Alfred P. Sloan Museum** exhibits artifacts, photographs, unique cars, and the history of General Motors; the museum is located at 1221 E. Kearsley St., Flint, 48503 Tel: (810) 237-3450. **The Longway Planetarium** at 60 feet is the biggest in Michigan, the planetarium host a laser light shows. The planetarium is located at 1310 E. Kearsley St., Flint 48503 Tel: (810) 237-3400.

Flint Institute of Arts, located at 1120 E. Kearsley St., Flint 48503 Tel: (810) 234-1695, exhibits more than 6,500 works of art. **Whaley Historical House,** former home of local banker Robert Whaley, is a late 1800's Victorian architecture. The house museum is located at 624 E. Kearsley St., Flint 48503 Tel: (810) 235-6841.

Accommodations

Red Roof Inn Flint located at G-3219 Miller Road Flint MI 48507 toll-free (800) RED-ROOF. **Days Inn Flint** located at 2207 West Bristol Road Flint MI 48507 Tel: (810) 239-4681. **Comfort Inn** located at 2361 Austin Parkway Flint MI 48507 Tel: (810) 232-4222. **Sleep Inn Flint** located at 2325 Austin Parkway Flint MI 48507 Tel: (810) 232-7777. **Ramada Inn and Conference Center Flint** located at G-4300 West Pierson Road Flint MI 48504, toll-free (888) 298-2054. **Courtyard by Marriott** located at 5205 Gateway Center Flint MI 48507 Tel: (810) 232-3500.

Lapeer (MI)

Lapeer is located 69 miles (111 kilometers) east of Lansing and has a land area of 5.4 sq. miles (14 sq. kilometers) and a population of roughly 10,000. Lapeer was founded in 1831 and was incorporated in 1869. The Lapeer County Courthouse built in 1846 is the oldest in Michigan and is still in use.

Lapeer's train depot is located at 73 Howard St. Lapeer, MI 48446. The station is un-staffed and features an enclosed waiting area, restrooms, and payphones. Transportation from the station is local taxi service.

Lapeer station is served by International Service.

Port Huron (MI)
Connecting train to **Toronto, Ontario (Canada)**

Port Huron is located on the eastern end of Michigan, 114 miles east of Lansing. Port Huron has a land area of 8 sq. miles (21 sq. kilometers) and a population of about 34,000. The first settlers in Port Huron were in 1790 along the Black River area. Port Huron is one of Michigan's gateways to Ontario, Canada.

Water sports and recreation are Port Huron's popular activities. The city hosts the Macinach Island Sailboat Race each summer. It was in Port Huron where Thomas Edison spent his boyhood and there is a museum dedicated to the scientist located on Thomas Edison Drive.

Port Huron's train depot is located at 2223 16th St. Port Huron, MI 48060. The station is staffed and features an enclosed waiting area, restrooms, and payphones. Transportation from the station is local taxi service.

Port Huron is served by the International Service.

Twilight Limited, Lake Cities and Wolverine Services

All Aboard!

Chicago (IL) See Illinois and Missouri service, page 268.

Hammond-Whiting (IN) See Michigan International service, page 344- 347.

Michigan City (IN) See Michigan- International service, page 344- 347.

Niles (MI) See Michigan- International service, page 344- 347.

Dowagiac (MI) See Michigan- International service, page 344- 347.

Kalamazoo (MI) See Michigan- International service, page 344- 347.

Battle Creek (MI) See Michigan- International service, page 344- 347.

Albion (MI)

Albion is located in south-central Michigan at the "Forks" of the Kalamazoo River 33 miles south of the city of Lansing. Albion has a land area of 4.2 sq. miles (11 sq. kilometers) and a population of just over 10,000. The city was named after the town of Albion, New York in 1835. Being situated at the forks of the Kalamazoo River many mills and industries have flourished in Albion.

Albion's train depot is located at 300 N. Eaton St. Albion, MI 49224. The station is un-staffed and features an enclosed waiting area and payphones.

Albion station is served by Twilight Limited, Lake Cities and Wolverine Services

Michigan (MI)
Capital: Lansing (Population: 9,938,444)
Size: 96,810 sq mi. (250, 737 sq km)
Nickname: The Wolverine State
Joined the union on: Jan. 26, 1837 (26th state)
Motto: If you seek a pleasant peninsula, look around you
Flower: Apple blossom
Bird: Robin
Song: None
Famous for: Tulips, cars, cornflakes
Major industries: Car manufacturing, minerals, farming, agriculture and tulips

Jackson (MI)

Jackson, named after President Andrew Jackson, is situated 33 miles south of the state capital of Lansing at the far southern part of central Michigan. Jackson has a land area of 11.1 sq. miles (28.6 sq. kilometers) and population of 37,446. The first setters of the area were the Native Indians; in the early 1820's the first settlers from New York arrived.

The arrival of the railroad system in Jackson in 1841 triggered the economic progress of the county. Coal production and agricultural production are amongst Jackson's prime economic generators. It was here in Jackson were the first Republican Party was organized and held its first convention in July, 1854. Many of the city's historical landmarks and structures are still visible and well preserved. Jackson's countryside has one of the most beautiful landscapes in the state of Michigan; streams, wood forest, meadows, and wildlife dominate the landscape.

Point of interest: the Ella W. Sharp Park Tel: (517) 787-2320 is the largest park in Jackson with over 500 acres of recreational activities and a museum. The Kate Palmer Wildlife Sanctuary, Tel: (517) 783-3661 located along Sandstone Creek, Jackson is a wildlife sanctuary that features birds and exotic flowers. Indian Brooks Farm, Tel: (517) 750-2743 is an educational farm that has something for the whole family featuring agricultural and aquaculture exhibits.

Jackson's train depot is located at 501 E. Michigan Ave. Jackson, MI 49201. The station is staffed and features an enclosed waiting area, checked baggage service, restrooms, and payphones. Transportation options from the station include local transit and taxi services.

Jackson station is served by Twilight Limited, Lake Cities and Wolverine Services

Ann Arbor (MI)

Ann Arbor is located in southeastern Michigan, just 45 miles west of Detroit and 52 miles southeast of the city of Lansing with a land area of 26 sq. miles (67 sq. kilometers) and a population of approximately 111,000. Ann Arbor was officially founded in 1824 and incorporated in 1851; it's home to the University of Michigan and hosts the annual Ann Arbor Blues & Jazz Festival during the month of September.

Ann Arbor's train depot is located at 325 Depot St. Ann Arbor, MI 48104. The station is staffed and features an enclosed waiting area, checked baggage service, restrooms, payphones, and vending machines. Transportation options from the station include Hertz Car Rental toll-free (800) 654-3131 and local taxi service.

Ann Arbor station is served by Twilight Limited, Lake Cities and Wolverine Services.

Places of Interest

Exhibit Museum of Natural History, located at 1109 Geddes Ave., Ann Arbor (734) 764-0478, exhibits dinosaurs and prehistoric life. Admission is free. **Gerald R. Ford Presidential Archives** exhibits President Ford's original files from his Presidency. The Presidential archive is located at 1000 Beal Ave., Ann Arbor (734) 741-2218. The 1853 Greek house, the **Kempt House Center** exhibits the long history of Ann Arbor. The house museum is located at 312 S. Division, Ann Arbor Tel: (734) 994-4898. The 1885 Queen Anne **Historic Hack House Museum** exhibits artifacts of the 19th and early 20th century America. The house museum is located at 775 County St., Milan Tel: (734) 439-7522; by appointment only.

Ann Arbor Sunday Artisans Market (Kerrytown), held from May through November, features local crafts and entertainment. The market is located between Fourth Ave and Fifth Ave. Tel: (734) 973-0064. **Old Road Dinner Train** located at 424 W. Adrian Street, Blissfield Tel: (517) 486-2141.

U of M Kelsey Museum of Archeology exhibits almost 100,000 artifacts from ancient civilizations. The museum is located at the University of Michigan at 434 S. State, Ann Arbor Tel: (734) 764-9304. **U of M Stearns Musical Collection** exhibits more than 2,000 musical instruments, one of the largest collections in the world, located at 1100 Bates Dr., Ann Arbor Tel: (734) 763-4389. **U of M Museum of Art** has one of the largest art exhibits in Michigan; the museum is located at 525 S. State, Ann Arbor Tel: (734) 764-0395. **U of M Nichols Arboretum** located at Geddes Rd., east of Observatory. **U of M Matthew Botanical Gardens** is located at 1800 N. Dixboro Rd., Ann Arbor Tel: (734) 998-7061.

The **Ypsilanti Automotive Heritage Museum** is located at 112 E. Cross St., Ypsilanti Tel: (734) 482-5200. **Ypsilanti Antique Auto, Truck & Fire Museum** houses the largest collection of vintage cars in the midwest. The museum is located at 110 W. Cross Street, Ypsilanti Tel: (734) 483-0042, admission is free, call for appointment. The 1860 Victorian mansion **Ypsilanti Historical Museum** exhibits the early 19th century Ypsilanti mansion. The mansion is located at 220 N. Huron, Ypsilanti Tel: (734) 482-4990.

Accommodation

Courtyard by Marriott located at 3205 Boardwalk St, Ann Arbor, MI 48108 Tel: (734) 995-5900. **Hampton Inn** located at 2300 Green Rd, Ann Arbor, MI 48105 Tel: (734) 996-4444. **Lost Beach Resort** located at 616 Church St, Ann Arbor, MI 48104 Tel: (734) 761-7444. **Clarion Hotel** located at 2900 Jackson Ave, Ann Arbor, MI 48103 Tel: (734) 665-4444.

Hawthorn Suites Hotel located at 3601 Green Ct, Ann Arbor, MI 48105 Tel: (734) 327-0011. **Comfort Inn** located at 2455 Carpenter Rd, Ann Arbor, MI 48108 Tel: (734) 973-6100. **Red Roof Inn** located at 3505 S State St, Ann Arbor, MI 48108 Tel: (734) 665-3500. **Residence Inn** located at 800 Victors Way, Ann Arbor, MI 48108 Tel: (734) 996-5666. **Embassy Suites Hotel** located at 200 E Huron St, Ann Arbor, MI 48104 Tel: (734) 662-7100.

Crown Plaza located at 610 Hilton Blvd, Ann Arbor, MI 48108 Tel: (734) 761-2929. **Sheraton Hotel** located at 3200 Boardwalk St, Ann Arbor, MI 48108 Tel: (734) 996-0600. **Days Inn** located at 2380 Carpenter Rd, Ann Arbor, MI 48108 Tel: (734) 971-0700. **Holiday Inn Crown Plaza** located at 610 Hilton Blvd, Ann Arbor, MI 48108 Tel: (734) 761-7800. **Ramada Inn** located at 3750 Washtenaw Ave, Ann Arbor, MI 48104 Tel: (734) 971-2000.

Dearborn (MI)

Dearborn is located about 8 miles west of Detroit with a land area of 39 sq. miles (63 sq. kilometers), a population of roughly 98,000, and a motto of "Be Nice to People." Dearborn was named after Major Gen. Henry Dearborn who first settled in 1786; the city was incorporated in 1929.

The city of Dearborn is the hometown of Henry Ford and home to one of the most successful car corporations in the world, the Ford Motor Company. The Henry Ford Estate, Tel: (313) 593-5590 and the Henry Ford Museum & Greenfield Village located at 20900 Oakwood Blvd. Dearborn, Michigan 48124 Tel: (313) 271-1620. The Henry Ford Museum, the Automotive Hall of Fame, and the new Spirit of Ford are amongst Dearborn's famous tourist attractions.

Dearborn's train depot is located at 16121 Michigan Ave. Dearborn, MI 48126. The station is staffed and features an enclosed waiting area, checked baggage service, restrooms, payphones, and vending machines. Transportation options from the station include Hertz Car Rental toll-free (800) 654-3131 and local taxi service.

Dearborn station is served by Twilight Limited, Lake Cities and Wolverine Services.

Places of Interest

Henry Ford Museum & Greenfield Village exhibits the 350 years of cultural and social development of America. The museum is located at 20900 Oakwood Blvd, Dearborn Tel: (313) 271-1620.

Dearborn Historical Museum is dedicated to the preservation of Dearborn history; this 1833 building is said to be one of Michigan's oldest and is the oldest surviving building in Dearborn. Tel: (313) 565-3000, admission is free.

Detroit (MI)

Detroit is located 80 miles southeast of the city of Lansing and 275 miles east of Chicago, Illinois. It has a land area of 139 sq. miles (360 sq. kilometers) and a population of almost 1 million. Detroit was founded on July 24, 1701 by the French explorer Antoine de la Moth Cadillac. Detroit has been under three rulers: French, British, and the Americans. It was in 1760 when the British acquired the city and later ceded to the American as the result of Jay's Treaty in 1796. The city of Detroit was incorporated in 1815.

Henry Ford, a local of Dearborn and son of a farmer, made the city of Detroit into what it is today, "the automobile capital of the world." It was here in 1896 that Henry Ford built his first car and the famous Henry Ford car mass production method (assembly line) was born.

Detroit is home to some of the biggest corporations in the world: General Motors Corporation, Chrysler Corporation, Blue Cross Blue Shield, and MCN Corporation are just the few. Detroit is also home to Motown record company.

Getting Around

Airport

Detroit Metro Airport, Tel: (734) 247-7678 is located 20 miles (32 kilometers) southwest of Detroit. There are major car rental companies available outside the arrival area. Local taxis are easily accessible at the airport; cabs and limousine services are offered by Metro Cars toll-free (800) 456-1701. The Smart Bus Company offers local bus services connecting the airport to the rest of the region. The bus stops at the Smith Terminal near the ground transportation offices.

Bus

Smart Bus, 660 Woodward Ave., First National Building, 9th Fl Detroit, MI 48226 Tel: (313) 962-5515 serves the city of Detroit and the rest of the region. General bus fare is $1.50 each way, discounted fare for seniors and disabled passengesr. Exact fare is required.

Taxi

Victor Cab, 7116 S. Wayne Road Romulus, MI 48174 Tel: (734) 467-7026 serves the entire city of Detroit.

Rent-A-Car

National Car Rental Detroit Metro Airport, Building 338, Lucas Drive Detroit, MI 48242 Tel: (734) 941-7000. Enterprise Rent-A-Car, 11375 S. Middle belt Romulus, MI 48174 Tel: (734) 784-2119. Thrifty Car Rental, 29111 Wick Road Romulus, MI 48174 Tel: (734) 946-7830 and Budget Rental Car, 8715 Wick ham Road Romulus, MI 48174 Tel: (734) 641-7038

Commuter and Train

The Detroit Trolley, Jefferson Ave. and Washington Blvd. Detroit, MI 48226 Tel: (313) 933-1300 operates around downtown Detroit serving Grand Circus Park, Michigan Ave. Lafayette Blvd., Fort Street, Cobo Hall, and Mariner's Church. The Detroit Transportation Corporation, Julian C. Madison Building 1420 Washington Blvd., 3rd Fl Detroit, MI 48226 Tel: (313) 224-2160 operates an Automated Light Rail System in the Detroit Central Business District.

Detroit's train depot is located at 11 W. Baltimore Ave. Detroit, MI 48202. The station is staffed and features an enclosed waiting area, checked baggage service, restrooms, and payphones. Transportation option from the station includes Hertz Car Rental toll-free (800) 654-3131, local transit, and taxi services.

Detroit station is served by Twilight Limited, Lake Cities and Wolverine Services.

Visitor Information Center

Detroit Visitors Bureau, 211 W. Fort St. Ste 1000, Detroit, MI 48226 Tel: (313) 202-1800 or toll-free (800) 338-7648.

Detroit Michigan Convention & Visitors Bureau, 100 Renaissance Center Suite 1900 Detroit, MI 48243 Tel : (313) 259-4333.

Places to See and Things to Do

Detroit Science Museum located at 5020 John R Street Detroit MI 48202 Tel: (313) 577-8400. The museum also houses an IMAX Theater and a Digital Dome Planetarium. **The Detroit Institute of Arts** located at 5200 Woodward Avenue Detroit, Michigan 48202 Tel: (313) 833-7900. **Detroit Historical Museum** located at 5401 Woodward Avenue Detroit, Michigan 48202 Tel: (313) 833-1805. Admission is: adults $4.50, students and seniors $2.25. **The Charles H. Wright Museum of African American History** is located at 315 E. Warren Ave. Detroit, Michigan 48201 Tel: (313) 494-5800. The museum is dedicated to the life and history of African Americans.

Dossin Great Lakes Museum located on Belle Isle at 100 Strand Drive Belle Isle Detroit, Michigan 48207 Tel: (313) 852-4051. Admission is: adults $2.00, students and seniors $1.00, and children under 12 are free. **The Michigan Transit Museum** located at Michigan Transit Museum Depot 200 Grand, Mt. Clemens, MI 48043. The museum is dedicated to the preservation of the history of mass transportation. **North America International Auto Show** located at Cobo Center One Washington Boulevard Detroit, MI 48226. Admission is: adult $10, senior $5, and children under 12 are free with accompanying adult.

Lionel Trains, located at 26750 23 Mile Road Chesterfield, MI, 48051 Tel: (810) 949-4100, ext 1211, offers tours at their corporate headquarters. **Historic Fort Wayne** located at 6325 West Jefferson Avenue Detroit, Michigan 48209 Tel: (313) 833-1800. **Holocaust Memorial Center** located at 6602 West Maple Road West Bloomfield, MI 48322 Tel: (248) 661-0840. **Detroit Zoological Park** located at the northwest corner of the intersection of Woodward Avenue and Ten Mile Road (I-696) Royal Oak. Admission is: adults $8, children $6, and senior $6. **Belle Isle Aquarium** is located on Belle Isle on E. Jefferson at E. Grand Blvd.

Accommodations

Omni Detroit Hotel River Place located in the center of Detroit 1000 River Place Detroit MI 48207 expects to pay $60-$200. **Holiday Inn Livonia/Detroit West** 17123 N. Laurel Park Drive Livonia MI 48152 toll-free (800) HOLIDAY expects to pay $150-$250. **Residence Inn Dearborn** 5777 Southfield Service Drive Detroit MI 48228 Tel: (313) 441-1700 expects to pay $80-$200. **Atheneum Suite Hotel & Conference Center** 1000 Bush Avenue Detroit MI Tel: 313 962-2323 expects to pay $170-$300. **Marriott Detroit Metro Airport** Detroit Metropolitan Airport Detroit MI 48282 Tel: (734) 941-9400 expects to pay $80-$230. **Comfort Inn Detroit** located only three miles from Detroit City Airport at 1999 East Jefferson Avenue Detroit MI 48207 Tel: (313) 567-8888 expects to pay $70-$150.

Best Western Inn located at 1020 Washington Blvd, Detroit, MI 48226 Tel: (313) 887-7000. **Courtyard by Marriott** located at 333 E Jefferson Ave, Detroit, MI 48226 Tel: (313) 222-7404. **Detroit Marriott Renaissance** located at 400 Renaissance Ctr, Detroit, MI 48243 Tel: (313) 568-8000. **Huntington Hotels** located at 109 W Alexandrine St, Detroit, MI 48201 Tel: (313) 833-9410. **Econ Lodge** located at 17729 Telegraph Rd, Detroit, MI 48219 Tel: (313) 531-2550.

Packard Motel located at 1500 E Grand Blvd, Detroit, MI 48211 Tel: (313) 923-6228. **Wright Hotel** located at 118 W Columbia St, Detroit, MI 48201 Tel: (313) 961-4114. **Omni Detroit Hotel-The River** located at 1000 River Place Dr, Detroit, MI 48207 Tel: (313) 259-9500. **Days Inn** located at 3250 E Jefferson Ave, Detroit, MI 48207 Tel: (313) 568-2000. **Hilton Windsor** located at 277 Riverside Dr, Detroit, MI 48215 Tel: (313) 962-3834. **Holiday Inn** located at 5801 Southfield Hwy, Detroit MI 48228 Tel: (313) 336-3340. **Residence Inn** located at 5777 Southfield Hwy, Detroit MI 48228 Tel: (313) 441-1700.

Royal Oak (MI)

Royal Oak is located 11 miles north of Detroit; it has a land area of 12 sq. miles (31 sq. kilometers) and population of 65,410. The city of Royal Oak was incorporated in 1921.

The Orson Starr House is listed in Michigan's State Register of Historic Sites as one of Royal Oak's most visited attractions. Other places of interest are the Royal Oak Farmers Market which has local produce and other products and the Detroit Zoo, home to more than 1,500 animals, located at the intersection of Interstate 696 and Woodward Avenue.

Royal Oak's train depot is located at 201 S. Sherman Dr. Royal Oak, MI 48067. The station is un-staffed and features an enclosed waiting area, payphones, and vending machines. Transportation options from the station include local transit, bus, and taxi services.

Royal Oak station is served by Twilight Limited, Lake Cities and Wolverine Services.

Birmingham (MI)

Birmingham is located just 15 miles north of Detroit. It has a land area of 4.6 sq. miles (12 sq. kilometers) and population of 20,147. The city was named after Birmingham, England.

Birmingham's train depot is located at 449 South Eaton St. Birmingham, MI 48009. The station is un-staffed and features payphones. Transportation options from the station include local transit and taxi services.

Birmingham station is served by Twilight Limited, Lake Cities and Wolverine Services.

Pontiac (MI)

Pontiac is named after the famous Indian Chief of the local native tribes. Pontiac has a land area of 19.8 sq. miles (51 sq. kilometers) and population of 71,166. The first settlers arrived at the site in 1818 and the town was incorporated in 1861. Like most other towns and cities of Michigan, Pontiac's growth was attributed to the arrival and development of the railroad system. The **Lawrence Street Gallery,** located at 6 N. Saginaw Street Tel: (248) 334-6716, is the oldest in the city of Pontiac. The gallery exhibits various types of arts and crafts.

Michigan (MI)
Capital: Lansing (Population: 9,938,444)
Size: 96,810 sq mi. (250, 737 sq km)
Nickname: The Wolverine State
Joined the union on: Jan. 26, 1837 (26th state)
Motto: If you seek a pleasant peninsula, look around you
Flower: Apple blossom
Bird: Robin
Song: None
Famous for: Tulips, cars, cornflakes
Major industries: Car manufacturing, minerals, farming, agriculture and tulips

Pontiac's train depot is located at 1600 Wide Track Dr. Pontiac, MI 48342. The station is un-staffed and features an enclosed waiting area, payphones, and vending machines. Transportation options from the station include local transit, bus, and taxi services.

Pontiac station is served by Twilight Limited, Lake Cities and Wolverine Services.

Pere Marquette Service
All Aboard!

Chicago (IL) See Illinois and Missouri service, page 268.

Hammond- Whiting (IN) See Michigan- International service, page 344- 347.

New Buffalo (MI)

New Buffalo is located 132 miles southwest of the city of Lansing. It has a land area of 2 sq. miles (5.5 sq. kilometers) and population of just 2,317.

It was the Native American Indians who were the first settlers of the site before Captain Wessel Whittaker rediscovered the place while taking shelter from a violent Lake Michigan storm in November 1834. The next year Captain Whittaker came back at the site setting up the first permanent settlement. In 1836 the town was incorporated and named New Buffalo after Buffalo, New York.

The arrival of the railways in New Buffalo in the late 1840's triggered the development of a tourism industry in the town: many hotels, restaurants, and bars were established. New Buffalo prospered and its population dramatically increased.

The N.B Railroad Museum is located at 530 S. Whittake :, New Buffalo MI 49117 Tel: (616) 469-3166 and the Wilkinson Heritage Museum is located at 15300 Red Arrow Highway Lake Side MI 49116 Tel: (616) 469-2090.

New Buffalo's train depot is located at Whitaker and Railroad Tracks New Buffalo, MI 49117. The station is un-staffed and features payphones and a snack bar.

New Buffalo station is served by Pere Marquette Service.

Michigan (MI)
Capital: Lansing (Population: 9,938,444)
Size: 96,810 sq mi. (250, 737 sq km)
Nickname: The Wolverine State
Joined the union on: Jan. 26, 1837 (26th state)
Motto: If you seek a pleasant peninsula, look around you
Flower: Apple blossom
Bird: Robin
Song: None
Famous for: Tulips, cars, cornflakes
Major industries: Car manufacturing, minerals, farming, agriculture and tulips

St. Joseph-Benton Harbor (MI)

St. Joseph was founded in 1675 and was incorporated as a town in 1834. It has a land area of 3.4 sq. miles (8.8 sq. kilometers) and population of almost 10,000.

St. Joseph-Benton Harbor's train depot is located at 410 1/2 Vine St. St. Joseph, MI 49085. The station is un-staffed and features an enclosed waiting area, a quik-trak ticket machine, payphones, and restaurants. Transportation from the station is local taxi service.

St. Joseph-Benton Harbor is served by the Pere Marquette Service.

Bangor (MI)

Bangor is at the heart of Van Buren County; it has a land area of 1.8 sq. miles (4.7 sq. kilometers) and population of approximately 2,000. Bangor was named after the town of Bangor in Maine, where the first settlers of Bangor Michigan came from and settled the area in 1837. It was not until 1877 when the town was finally incorporated.

Bangor is appreciated for its beautiful landscape, thus tourism is the town's prime industry followed by other small manufacturing related industries, wineries, and fruit productions.

Bangor's train depot is located at 541 Railroad St. Bangor, MI 49013. The station is un-staffed and features an enclosed waiting area and payphones. Wine-county train tour is available at the Bangor train depot.

Bangor station is served by Pere Marquette Service.

Holland (MI)

Holland is located just 82 miles west of Lansing and 151 miles northeast of Chicago. It has a land area of 14.2 sq. miles (36.6 sq. kilometers) and population of more than 40,000. Holland has the largest Dutch population in Michigan: more than 90 percent of the city's population is from the Netherlands. Holland was incorporated in 1847; the town was burned and leveled in 1871 then successfully rebuilt.

Holland's train depot is located at 250 E. 7th St. Holland, MI 49423. The station is un-staffed and features an enclosed waiting area, a quik-trak ticket machine, payphones, and vending machines. Transportation options from the station include local bus and taxi services.

Holland station is served by Pere Marquette Service.

Places of Interest

Visit the only blue and white delftware factory in the US at **Deklomp Wooden Shoe & Delft Factory** located at 12755 Quincy Avenue Holland, MI 49424-8285 Tel: (616) 399-1900. Admission is free. **Windmill Island** features the only 278 year-old authentic Dutch windmills in the US, 7th Street at Lincoln Ave. Holland, MI 49423-2990. Tel: (616) 355-1030. Admissions are: adult $6 children $3. **Tulip City Antique Mall** located at 3500 US 31 Holland, MI 49424 Tel: (616) 786-4424.

Veldheer Tulip Gardens is open starting in April (depending on the Tulip blooming season), 12755 Quincy Holland, MI 49424-8285 Tel: (616) 399-1900. Admissions are: adults $5, and children $3. **Holland Museum** located at 31 West 10th Street Holland, MI 49423-3101 toll-free (888) 200-9123. **Saugatuck Boat Cruises** located at 716 Water Street Saugatuck, MI 49453 Tel: (616) 857-4261. Admissions are: adults $10, children $6. **Dutch Village Theme Park** located at 12350 James Street Holland, MI 49424-8613 Tel: (616) 396-1475 or toll-free (800) 285-7177. Admissions are: adults $7, children $5.

Accommodations

Blue Mill Inn located at 409 US Highway 31, Holland MI 49423 Tel: (616) 392-7073. **Haworth Inn & Conference Center** located at 225 College Ave, Holland, MI 49423 Tel: (616) 395-7200. **Lake Shore Motel Resort** located at 1645 S Shore Dr, Holland, MI 49423 Tel: (616) 335-5355. **Webster's Inn** located at 5941 Washington Rd, Holland, MI 49423 Tel: (616) 393-6315. **Sunset Harbor Cottages** located at 327 Lakeshore Dr S, Holland, MI 49424 Tel: (616) 399-9626.

Comfort Inn located at 422 E 32nd St, Holland, MI 49423 Tel: (616) 392-1000. **Budget Host Wooden Shoe Motel** located at 465 US Highway 31, Holland MI 49423 Tel: (616) 392-8521. **Hampton Inn** located at 12427 Felch St, Holland, MI 49424 Tel: (616) 399-8500. **Lake Ranch Resort Condos** located at 2226 Ottawa Beach Rd, Holland, MI 49424 Tel: (616) 399-9380. **Fairfield Inn** located at 2854 W Shore Dr, Holland, MI 49424 Tel: (616) 786-9700.

Rosewood Pointe Retreat House located at 806 N Shore Dr, Holland, MI 49424 Tel: (616) 396-1502. **Super 8 Motel** located at 680 E 24th St, Holland, MI 49423 Tel: (616) 396-8822. **Country Inn by Carlson** located at 12260 James St, Holland, MI 49424 Tel: (616) 396-6677. **Days Inn** located at 717 Hastings Ave, Holland, MI 49423 Tel: (616) 392-7001. **Holland Inn** located at 482 E 32nd St, Holland, MI 49423 Tel: (616) 396-1424. **Holiday Inn** located at 650 E 24th St, Holland, MI 49423 Tel: (616) 394-0111.

Grand Rapids (MI)
Motor-coach Connections to **Mackinaw City (MI)** and **St. Grace (WI)**

Grand Rapids is located 61 miles west of the city of Lansing. It has a land area of 44.8 sq. miles (115 sq. kilometers) and population of almost 200,000. Native American Indians first occupied the area for thousands of years. It was Issac McCoy who founded Grand Rapids in 1825, and in 1826 Louis Campau, a French trader, established the first trading post in the area. Grand Rapids was incorporated on April 2, 1850.

Getting Around

Airport

Gerald R. Ford International Airport serves the city of Grand Rapids and the western Michigan region. The airport is located at 44th Street and Patterson Avenue SE. Grand Rapids Tel: (616) 233-6000.

Bus

Rapid Bus serves the Grand Rapids and surrounding areas; the bus terminal is located at the downtown transit center on Ionia Av. and Lyon St. Tel: (616) 776-1100. Greyhound serves the intercity bus services. The Bus Terminal is located on Wealthy Street and Grandville Avenue. Tel: (616) 456-1709 or toll-free (800) 231-2222.

Rent-A-Car

Enterprise Rent A Car, 187 Monroe Avenue NW, Suite 190 Grand Rapids, MI 49503 Tel: (616) 776-7665 or toll-free (800) RENT A CAR and Thrifty Car Rental, 5091 Broadmoor SE Grand Rapids, MI 49512 Tel: (616) 940-3333 or toll-free (800) 367-2277.

Commuter and Train

The Grand Rapids Trolley Co., LLC located at 332 Kingswood Dr. SE Grand Rapids, MI 49506 Tel: (616) 954-7000 provides services in west Michigan.

Grand Rapids' train depot is located at Market and Wealthy Sts. Grand Rapids, MI 49503. The station is self-serve and features an enclosed waiting area, restrooms, and payphones. Transportation options from the station include local transit and taxi services.

Grand Rapids is served by Pere Marquette Service.

Visitor Information Center

The Grand Rapids/Kent County Convention & Visitors Bureau, located at 140 Monroe Center NW Grand Rapids, MI 49506 Tel: (616) 459-8287 or toll-free (800) 678-9859.

Woodland Shopping Center located at 3915 28th Street SE Grand Rapids, MI 49512 toll-free (800) 678-9859.

Places to See and Things to Do

Frederic Meyer Gardens & Sculpture Park houses the largest tropical conservatory in Michigan and exhibits numerous gardens and sculptures. The park is located at 1000 East Beltline Ave. NE Grand Rapids, MI 49525 Tel: (616) 957-1580. The **John Ball Zoological Garden** houses more than 1,000 animals; the museum is located at 1300 W. Fulton St. Grand Rapids, MI 49504 Tel: (616) 336-4301.

Grand Rapids Art Museum exhibits renaissance and modern arts. The museum is located in downtown Grand Rapids at 155 N. Division Ave. at Pearl St. Grand Rapids, MI 49503 Tel: (616) 831-1001. **Grand Rapids Children's Museum** located at 11 Sheldon Ave. NE Grand Rapids, MI 49503 Tel: (616) 235-4726. The museum has educational, hands-on exhibits. **Gerald R. Ford Museum** located at 303 Pearl St. NW Grand Rapids, MI 49504 Tel: (616) 451-9263.

Public Museum of Grand Rapids (Van Andel Museum Center) exhibits history, culture, science, and features a 1928 Carousel. The museum is located at 272 Pearl St. NW Grand Rapids, MI 49504 Tel: (616) 456-3977. The 1908 **Meyer May House** is one of the few Frank Lloyd Wright house still in existence. The house is located at 450 Madison Ave. SE Grand Rapids, MI 49503 Tel: (616) 246-4821. **Roger B. Chaffee Planetarium at Van Andel Museum Center** is located at 272 Pearl St. NW Grand Rapids, MI 49504 Tel: (616) 456-DOME.

The **Common Gentry Carriage** offers tours around downtown Grand Rapids and Heritage Hill Historic District. Contact PO Box 32 Sand Lake, MI 49343 Tel: (616) 636-4398. **The**

Grand Lady Riverboat offers lunch, brunch, and dinner sightseeing cruises with entertainment. The riverboat is located at 4243 Indian Mounds Dr. SW Grandville, MI 49418 Tel: (616) 457-4837.

Heritage Hill Historic District is one of Grand Rapids national historic districts; the districts covers five blocks east of downtown located at 126 College Ave. SE, Grand Rapids, MI 49503 Tel: (616) 459-8950. **Fruit Ridge Country Markets** has greenhouses, farm markets, historical sites, and many other shops. The country market is located at MSU Extension Office: 836 Fuller Ave. NE Grand Rapids, MI 49503 Tel: (616) 336-3265.

Accommodations

Amway Grand Plaza Hotel located at 187 Monroe Ave NW, Grand Rapids, MI 49503 Tel: (616) 774-2000. **Days Inn** located at 5500 28th St SE, Grand Rapids, MI 49512 Tel: (616) 949-8400. **Crown Plaza** located at 5700 28th St SE, Grand Rapids, MI 49546 Tel: (616) 957-1770. **Courtyard by Marriott** located at 11 Monroe Ave NW, Grand Rapids, MI 49503 Tel: (616) 242-6000. **Residence Inn** located at 2701 E Beltline Ave SE, Grand Rapids, MI 49546 Tel: (616) 957-8111.

Hampton Inn located at 4981 28th St SE, Grand Rapids, MI 49512 Tel: (616) 956-9304. **Comfort Inn** located at 4155 28th St SE, Grand Rapids, MI 49512 Tel: (616) 957-2080. **Days Inn** located at 310 Pearl St NW, Grand Rapids, MI 49504 Tel: (616) 235-7611. **Grand Rapids Inn** located at 250 28th St SW, Grand Rapids, MI 49548 Tel: (616) 452-2131. **Hampton Inn** located at 500 N Center Dr NW, Grand Rapids, MI 49544 Tel: (616) 647-1000.

Holiday Inn located at 3333 28th St SE, Grand Rapids, MI 49512 Tel: (616) 949-9222. **Ramada Inn** located at 65 28th St SW, Grand Rapids, MI 49548 Tel: (616) 452-1461. **Best Western Inn** located at 4101 28th St SE, Grand Rapids, MI 49512 Tel: (616) 942-2550. **Econ Lodge** located at 5175 28th St SE, Grand Rapids, MI 49512 Tel: (616) 956-6601. **Holiday Inn** located at 255 28th St SW, Grand Rapids, MI 49548 Tel: (616) 241-6444. **Red Roof Inn** located at 5131 28th St SE, Grand Rapids, MI 49512 Tel: (616) 942-0800.

Kentucky Cardinal

The Kentucky Cardinal links the states of Illinois, Indiana, and Kentucky and the cities of Chicago (IL), Indianapolis (IN), and Louisville (KY), logging more than 300 miles (480 kilometers) of train travel. The Kentucky Cardinal uses Superliner Cars where passengers enjoy wider seats, more legroom and headroom, and comfortable sleeping car rooms.

Route Destination Highlights

Chicago, IL- Home to America's tallest building Sears Tower, visit the Museum of Science and Industry and other outstanding museums, admire the charming Centennial Fountain, and take a romantic stroll along Lake Michigan. Also enjoy Chicago's attractive and busy nightlife.

	Kentucky Cardinal	
7:55 pm-D	Chicago (IL)	8:37 am-A
9:07 pm	Dyer (IN)	6:49 am
9:56 pm	Rensselaer (IN)	6:49 am
11:03 pm	Lafayette (IN)	6:05 am
11:35 pm	Crawfordsville (IN)	4:32 am
12:55 pm	Indianapolis (IN)	2:50 am
1:35 pm		1:30 am
6:55 pm	Louisville (KY)	10:10 am
7:40 pm-A	Jeffersonville (IN)	9:20 am-D
D-Departure		**A**- Arrival

Indianapolis, IN- Visit the Indianapolis Motor Speedway, it has the largest collection of racing cars, vintage cars, and racing memorabilia in the US; the National Art Museum of Sport exhibits the largest collection of sports art in the US; Hoosier Park and Indianapolis Raceway Park are some of the best multi-purpose motor sports facilities in the world. Visit the Indiana Basketball Hall of Fame, the Historic State Capitol, Medal of Honor Memorial, and Indiana War Memorial, or relax and enjoy performances by the Indianapolis Jazz Orchestra and the Indianapolis Symphony Orchestra, recognized as one of the best in the US.

Louisville, KY- See the famous Kentucky Derby, take a river cruise on the Belle of Louisville, see the amazing Glassworks and experience the art of glass blowing, visit the Kentucky Shakespeare Festival held during the months of June and July, the Thomas Edison House, and the Museum of Faiths.

Scenery along the Route

Travelers will see many Midwestern mansions and farms in the state of Indiana.

Train Schedules

The Kentucky Cardinal travels daily from Chicago, Illinois to Louisville, Kentucky. The trip between the two cities takes approximately 12 hours.

Accommodation

Accommodations are Reserved Coach and Sleeping Car. There is a Cafe car that serves local cuisine, snacks, soups, sandwiches, and drinks and a Dining Car that serves complete meals.

362

All Aboard!

Chicago (IL) See Illinois and Missouri service, page 268.

Dyer (IN)

Dyer is located just 30 miles southeast of Chicago, 15 miles south of Lake Michigan along the Illinois/Indiana state border. The town of Dyer covers 3.7 sq. miles (9.7 sq. kilometers) of land area and has a population of roughly 11,000. It was the Pottawatoomie Indians who lived in the site for many years until the first white settlement came in 1830.

It was in 1857 when the first trains stopped in Dyer, mainly for commerce, and during the civil war the town served as an overnight shelter for the Union soldiers. The town of Dyer was incorporated in 1910.

Dyer's train depot is located on Sheffield Rd. Dyer, IN 46311. The station is self-serve and features an enclosed waiting area and payphones.

Dyer station is served by the Kentucky Cardinal.

Rensselaer (IN)

Rensselaer is located 80 miles southeast of Chicago and 105 miles north of Indianapolis. Rensselaer has land area of 1.8 sq. miles (4.8 sq. kilometers) and a population of 5,294.

Rensselaer's train depot is located at 619 N. Cullen St. Rensselaer, IN 47978. The station is un-staffed and features payphones.

Rensselaer station is served by the Kentucky Cardinal.

Indiana (IN)

Capital: Indianapolis (Population: 6,080,485)
Size: 36,420 sq mi. (94,327 sq km)
Nickname: The Hoosier State
Joined the union on: December 11, 1816 (19th state)
Motto: The Crossroads of America
Flower: Peony
Bird: Cardinal
Song: On the Banks of the Wabash
Famous for: Racing Car, David Letterman
Major industries: Minerals, Oil

Lafayette (IN)

Lafayette is located just 59 miles northwest of Indianapolis and is the seat of Tippecanoe County. It has a population of approximately 45,000 and a land area of 13.4 sq. miles (34.6 sq. kilometers). It was here in Lafayette where the famous Battle of Tippecanoe was fought in 1811.

Lafayette is home to Purdue University, Aluminum Company of America (ALCOA), Siemens, Subaru-Isuzu automobile plant, and Fairfield Manufacturing Company.

Lafayette's train depot is located at 5th and Main streets, Lafayette, IN 47901. The station is un-staffed and features an enclosed waiting area, payphones, restrooms, and vending machines. Transportation

363

options from the station include local transit, bus, and taxi services.

Lafayette station is served by the Kentucky Cardinal.

Crawfordsville (IN)

Crawfordsville is the seat of Montgomery County located just 47 miles northwest of Indianapolis. Crawfordsville has a land area of 76 sq. miles (19.5 sq. kilometers) and a population of just over 14,000.

The Old Jail Museum located at 225 N Washington St. Crawfordsville, IN 47933-1737 Tel: (765) 362-5222 is a restored 1882 county jail which exhibits Indian artifacts, arts, and a revolving prison cell.

Crawfordville's train depot is located at Spring and Green streets, Crawfordsville, IN 47933. The station is self-serve and features payphones. Transportation options from the station include local bus and taxi services.

Crawfordsville station is served by the Kentucky Cardinal.

Indianapolis (IN)

Indianapolis is located in the center of the state of Indiana. With a land area of 362 sq. miles (936.7 sq. kilometers) and a population of 731,327, it is one of the largest cities in the US. Indianapolis became the state capital in 1820 and the city's design was laid out by the same architect who designed Washington D.C., Alexander Ralston.

Known as the racing capital of the world and the amateur sports capital of the world, Indianapolis has hosted more than 400 national and international sporting events including the Brickyard 400 (NASCAR), Indianapolis 500, and the Formula 1 U.S. Grand Prix. The city also invested millions of dollars in building and maintaining the city's many state-of-the-art sports facilities; sports events are a major source of economic activity in the city.

Indianapolis hosted the nation's first union station in 1888 and today has many known museums, gardens, wineries, entertainment establishments, theatres, and orchestras.

Getting Around

Airport

Indianapolis International Airport is located at 2500 S. High School Road, Suite 100, Indianapolis, Indiana 46241 Tel: (317) 487-7243, seven miles (11 kilometers) from central Indianapolis. There are several ground transportation services that connect the airport to the rest of the region. Hotel courtesy shuttles and airport limousines are available at the ground transportation center located at the lower level of the parking garage. Also, there are share-ride limousine services by Affinity Limousine & Tours Tel: (317) 870-5466 and Hoosier Limousine Tel: (317) 248-8879. Call taxis are located at lower terminal drive, local bus services are served by Carey Indiana toll-free (800) 888-4639 and IndyGo Tel: (317) 635-3344.

Bus

Indianapolis local bus services are served by IndyGo Tel: (317) 635-3344. Intercity bus services are served by Greyhound toll-free (800) 231-2222. The bus station is located at 350 S. Illinois Street Indianapolis.

Taxi

Indianapolis Yellow Cab, 3801 W. Morris St. Indianapolis, IN 46241 Tel: (317) 247-6233 or toll-free (800) TAXICAB.

Carriages

Yellow Rose Carriages, 1327 N. Capitol Ave. Indianapolis, IN 46202 Tel: (317) 634-3400 and Circle City Carriages, 324 S. College Ave. Indianapolis, IN 46202 Tel: (317) 387-1516 operate romantic carriage tours around Indianapolis area.

Rent-A-Car

Dollar Rent-A-Car located at 6175 W. Minnesota St. Indianapolis, IN 46241 Tel: (317) 227-0418, Budget Rent-A-Car located at 8225 W. Washington St. Indianapolis, IN 46231 toll-free (800) 527-0700, Avis Rent-A-Car located at 6050 W. Raymond St. Indianapolis, IN 46241 Tel: (317) 248-4860, Love Inc. Rent-A-Bent Car located at 2302 E. Washington St. Indianapolis, IN 46201 Tel: (317) 637-LOVE, National Car Rental located at 7111 W. Washington St. Indianapolis, IN 46241 Tel: (317) 243-1150 and Enterprise Rent-A-Car located at 1729 S. U.S. 31, Ste. A Greenwood, IN 46142 Tel: (317) 887-0131.

Train and Commuter

Indianapolis' train depot is located at 350 S. Illinois St. Indianapolis, IN 46225. The station is staffed and features an enclosed waiting area, payphones, and a restaurant. Transportation options from the station include local taxi and bus services.

Indianapolis station is served by the Kentucky Cardinal.

Visitor Information Center

Indianapolis Visitor Information Center, One North Capitol   Ste 700 Indianapolis   IN 46204 Tel: (317) 233-6761.

Places to See and Things to Do

Admired for its lovely stained glass windows and architecture, **Scottish Rite Cathedral** also houses a pipe organ. The cathedral is located at 650 N. Meridian St. Indianapolis Tel: (317) 262-3100. The **Historic State Capitol** is located at the Corner of Capitol Ave. & Washington St. Indianapolis Tel: (317) 233-5293. **Indianapolis Arts Garden** has musical, dance, and theater performances open to the public. It is located at the intersection of Washington and Illinois streets, Indianapolis Tel: (317) 631-3301.

Medal of Honor Memorial is dedicated to the recipients of the US's highest military honor. The memorial is located on the north side of downtown Indianapolis at Central Canal in White River State Park. **Indiana War Memorial** is dedicated to the war heroes of World War I, World War II, Korean, and Vietnam Wars. The museum exhibits war memorabilia and weaponries and is located at 431 N. Meridian St. Indianapolis Tel: (317) 232-7615.

Museums

The Children's Museum of Indianapolis is located at 3000 N. Meridian St. Indianapolis, IN 46208-4716 Tel: (317) 334-3222. The museum houses ten galleries, a theater, and planetarium. The **Indiana Medical History Museum** has the oldest pathology laboratory in the US and exhibits several medical facilities. The museum is located at 450 W. Vermont St. Indianapolis, IN 46222 Tel: (317) 635-7329.

Indiana Transportation Museum is located in Forest Park, Noblesville, Indiana, about 20 miles north of downtown Indianapolis Tel: (317) 773-6000. The museum is dedicated to the preservation of Indiana's railroad history and demonstrating to visitors the history and experience of railroad travel. **President Benjamin Harrison Home** is the three-story Victorian mansion home of the 23rd US President. The Harrison home is located at 1230 N. Delaware St. Indianapolis, IN 46202 Tel: (317) 631-1888.

Indiana State Museum exhibits Indianapolis Hoosier history; the museum is located at 202 N. Alabama St. Indianapolis, IN 46204 Tel: (317) 232-1637. **Eiteljorg Museum of American Indians and Western Art** exhibits western and native Indian arts and artifacts. The museum is located at 500 W. Washington St. Indianapolis, IN 46204 Tel: (317) 636-9378. **Indianapolis Museum of Art** houses gardens, pavilions, theater, halls, and a greenhouse. The museum exhibits African, Asian, American, and European contemporary art. The museum is located at 1200 W. 38th St. Indianapolis, IN 46208-4196 Tel: (317) 920-2650. **Museum of Miniature Houses** has collections of dollhouses; the museum is located at 111 E. Main St. Carmel, IN 46032 Tel: (317) 575-9466.

Indianapolis Motor Speedway has the largest collection of racing cars, vintage cars, and racing memorabilia. The speedway museum is located at 4790 W. 16th St. Indianapolis, IN 46222 Tel: (317) 484-6747. **Morris-Butler House**, designated in the National Register of Historic Places, is a Victorian-architecture house museum which exhibits life in Indiana in old times. The museum is located at 1204 Park Ave. Indianapolis, IN 46202 Tel: (317) 636-5409. **American Cabaret Theatre** has regular musical shows; the theater is located at 401 E. Michigan St. Indianapolis, IN 46204 Tel: (317) 631-0334.

Broadway In Indianapolis has Broadway entertainment in its Murat Centre and Clowes Memorial Hall, 200 Medical Dr. Carmel, IN 46032 Tel: (317) 818-3960. The **National Art Museum of Sport** is a unique and interesting place to see, it exhibits the largest collection of sports art in the US. The museum is located at University Place - IUPUI at 850 West Michigan Street Indianapolis, IN 46202-5198 Tel: (317) 274-3627.

The **Flower Barn** has Everlasting Flower farm tour located at 2865 Elizaville Rd. Lebanon, IN 46052 Tel: (317) 846-1059. **Freetown Village** demonstrates the life of the African American after the civil war. The village is located at 25 Indiana Ave., Ste. 200 Indianapolis, IN 46202 Tel: (317) 631-1870. **Indianapolis Zoo** is home to more than 3,000 animals set in their natural habitats, and the **White River Gardens** houses a botanical garden and exotic plants. The zoo and gardens are located at 1200 W. Washington St. Indianapolis, IN 46222 Tel: (317) 630-2001.

Block Party has various adult entertainments, games, and restaurants. Block Party is located at 4102 Claire Dr., 82nd St. & Dean Rd. Indianapolis, IN 46240 Tel: (317) 578-7941. **Hoosier Park** is Indiana's only pari-mutuel racetrack and features live racing. The park is located at 4500 Dan Patch Circle Anderson, IN 46013 toll-free (800) 526-RACE. **Indianapolis Raceway Park** is one of the best multi-purpose motor sports facilities in the world. The raceway has yearly scheduled race track events Tel: (317) 291-4090. **Racers Indoor Karting at Union Station** has adult racing entertainment. The indoor karting track is located at 302 S. Meridian St. Indianapolis, IN 46225 Tel: (317) 972-6666.

Easley Winery located at 205 N. College Ave. Indianapolis, IN 46202 Tel: (317) 636-4516 and **Chateau Thomas Winery** located at 6291 Cambridge Way Plainfield, IN 46168 Tel: (317) 837-9463 has wine tasting, wine shops, and field tours for visitors. **Historic Landmarks Foundation of Indiana** offers walking tours of historic downtown Indianapolis. The foundation is located at 340 W. Michigan St. Indianapolis, IN 46202-3204 toll-free (800) 450-4534.

Indiana Historical Society houses a research library and music room. The society has seasonal exhibitions, educational programs, gift shops, and a café bar. The society is located at 450 W. Ohio St. Indianapolis, IN 46202-3269 Tel: (317) 232-1882. **Noël Studio** exhibits art works of Nancy Noël, located at 618 W. 73rd St. Indianapolis, IN 46278 Tel: (317) 297-1117. **Indiana Basketball Hall of Fame** exhibits videos and artifacts of Indiana's basketball heritage. The hall is located at One Hall of Fame Ct. New Castle, IN 47362 Tel: (765) 529-1891. **IMAX Theater** is located at 650 W. Washington St. Indianapolis, IN 46204 Tel: (317) 233-4629.

Arts

Indianapolis Jazz Orchestra has a 16-piece jazz ensemble in a cabaret setting. The orchestra plays at the Indiana Roof Ballroom at 10535 E. Washington St., PMB 305 Indianapolis, IN 46229 toll-free (866) 696-7545. **Indianapolis Chamber Orchestra** has annual performances of classical masters. The chamber is located at Clowes Memorial Hall, 4600 Sunset Ave. Indianapolis, IN 46208 Tel: (317) 940-9607. **Indianapolis Symphony Orchestra**, recognized as one of the best in the US, has year-round performances. The symphony is located at 45 Monument Circle Indianapolis, IN 46204 Tel: (317) 262-1100.

Accommodations

Crowne Plaza Indianapolis, located at the downtown Union Station, 123 West Louisiana Street Indianapolis IN 46225 Tel: (317) 631-2221. **Canterbury Hotel,** a Registered Historic Landmark, located at 123 South Illinois Street Indianapolis IN 46225 Tel: (317) 634-3000. **The Westin Indianapolis** located at 50 South Capitol Avenue Indianapolis IN 46204 Tel:

(317) 262-8100. **Sheraton Indianapolis Hotel and Suites** located at 8787 Keystone Crossing Indianapolis IN 46240 Tel: (317) 846-2700. **Amerisuites Indianapolis** located in the Northside Business district at 9104 Keystone Crossing Indianapolis IN 46240 Tel: (317) 843-0064.

Doubletree Hotels (University Place Conference Center) located at 850 West Michigan Street Indianapolis IN 46202 Tel: (317) 269-9000. **Omni Indianapolis** located at 8181 North Shadeland Avenue Indianapolis IN 46250 Tel: (317) 849-6668. **Comfort Inn** located at 3880 West 92nd Street Indianapolis IN 46268-3101 Tel: (317) 872-3100. **Country Hearth Inn Indianapolis** 3851 Shore Drive Indianapolis IN 46254 Tel: (317) 297-1848.

Marriott Indianapolis in downtown located at 350 West Maryland Indianapolis IN 46225 Tel: (317) 822-3500. **Hawthorn Suites** located in east Indianapolis just five miles from downtown Indianapolis at 7035 Western Select Drive Indianapolis IN 46219 Tel: (317) 322-0011. **Hyatt Regency Indianapolis** located across from the Indiana State Capitol at One South Capitol Avenue Indianapolis IN 46204 Tel: (317) 632-1234. **Embassy Suites Indianapolis** in downtown located at 110 West Washington Indianapolis IN 46204 Tel: (317) 236-1800.

Holiday Inn located in east Indianapolis near downtown at 6990 East 21st Street Indianapolis IN 46219 Tel: (317) 359-5341. **Best Western Inn** located at 4450 Southport Crossings Dr, Indianapolis, IN 46237 Tel: (317) 888-5588. **Clarion Inn & Suites** located at 7001 Corporate Dr, Indianapolis, IN 46278 Tel: (317) 298-3700. **Days Inn** located at 401 E Washington St, Indianapolis, IN 46204 Tel: (317) 637-6464. **Comfort Inn** located at 530 S Capitol Ave, Indianapolis, IN 46225 Tel: (317) 631-9000. **YMCA** located at 860 W 10th St, Indianapolis, IN 46202 Tel: (317) 634-2478.

Jeffersonville (IN) and Louisville (KY)

Jeffersonville (IN)

Jeffersonville is located 104 miles southeast of Indianapolis on the state line between Indiana and Kentucky. It has a land area of 9.5 sq. miles (24.6 sq. kilometers) and a population of more than 22,000.

The first settlement of the site was around 1786 with the construction of a military post. There are no clear records of why the site was named Jeffersonville, but many believe that the place was named Jeffersonville in 1801 in honor of President Thomas Jefferson who became president that year. The following year Jeffersonville became the county seat.

The early economic growth of the city can be attributed to the development of the steamboat industry in the region, which is still visible today if you travel along the banks of Ohio River. Today Jeffersonville's economy is also based on industrial, transportation, tourism, and services.

Places of interest: the **Old Jeffersonville National Register of Historic Places District** in Jeffersonville's downtown area including the business district, riverfront, and residential blocks. A visit to downtown Jeffersonville will reward you with a glimpse of the town's rich history still preserved in the city's many national historic registered places.

Howard Steamboat Museum & Mansion has guided tours set in a Victorian Mansion with antique furnishings and steamboat memorabilia. The museum is located at 1101 E. Market St. Jeffersonville, IN 47131 toll-free (888) 472-0606.

Louisville (KY)

Louisville is located on the banks of the Ohio River at the border of the states of Indiana and Kentucky. Louisville is comprised of seven counties and has a population of almost a million. Louisville is home to some of the most recognized personalities, it's the home town of the actor Tom Cruise (Tom Mapother), the 12th president of the United States Zachary Taylor, and Patty and Mildred Hill, the sisters who wrote one of the most celebrated songs in the world: "Happy Birthday to You."

Louisville was founded in 1778 and named after the King of France Louis XVI. It was chartered in 1780 and has a very rich history. A visit to downtown Main Street will reward visitors with sights of the city's many cast-iron storefront facades, second only to the city of New York. Louisville is known for the Kentucky Derby Festival, celebrated with the US's largest fireworks display. The city also has the busiest canal system in the world.

Getting Around

Airport

Louisville International Airport, 700 Administration Drive, PO Box 9129, Louisville, Kentucky 40209, Tel: (502) 367-4636 is located 6 miles (9.7 kilometers) from downtown Louisville. There are local bus and taxi services serving the airport, R & R Limousine Service Tel: (502) 957-4254 and Watkins Limousine Service Tel: (812) 218-8122 also serve the airport.

Bus

Transit Authority of River City, 1000 W. Broadway Louisville, KY 40203 Tel: (502) 585-1234 operates local bus services around the region.

Water transit

Waterway River Transit, 4127 Chapel Lane New Albany, IN 47150 Tel: (812) 981-7060 operates water taxi services in Louisville on the Ohio River and the surrounding areas.

Taxi

Ready Cab Company, P.O. Box 19168 Louisville, KY 40259 Tel: (502) 417-4406 and Yellow Cab, 1601 S. Preston St. Louisville, KY 40217 Tel: (502) 637-6511.

Kentucky (KY)
Capital: Frankfort (Population: 4,041,769)
Size: 39,732 sq mi. (102,907 sq km)
Nickname: The Bluegrass State
Joined the union on: June 1, 1792 (15th state)
Motto: United We Stand, Divided We Fall
Flower: Goldenrod
Bird: Kentucky cardinal
Song: My Old Kentucky Home
Famous for: Abraham Lincoln, Muhammad Ali, and the Louisville Slugger
Major industries: Machinery, tourism, minerals

Rent-A-Car

Avis Rent A Car, 711 W. Jefferson St. Louisville, KY 40202 Tel: (502) 561-0768, Enterprise Rent-a-Car, 3718 Bardstown Road Louisville, KY 40218 toll-free (800) RENT-A-CAR, Budget Car/Truck Rental, 4330 Crittenden Drive Louisville, KY 40209 toll-free (800) 527-7000, and Thrifty Car & Truck Rental, 3700 Crittenden Drive Louisville, KY 40209 Tel: (502) 367-2277.

Train and Commuter

Louisville-Jeffersonville's train depot is located at Louisville Union Station 1000 West Broadway Louisville, KY 40203. The station is un-staffed and features an enclosed waiting area, restrooms, and vending machines.

Louisville-Jeffersonville station is served by the Kentucky Cardinal.

Visitor Information Center

Louisville Convention and Visitors Bureau, 400 South First Street Louisville, KY 40202 Tel: (502) 584-2121 or toll-free: (800) 626-5646.

Places to See and Things to Do

Kentucky Derby Museum located at Churchill Downs in Louisville also hosts the famous 126 year-old horseracing event, the Kentucky Derby. **The Belle of Louisville** offers river cruises on board the historic Belle and Charming Spirits, located in downtown at 401 W. River Road Louisville, KY 40202 Tel: (502) 574-2992. Experience the art of glass blowing at **Glassworks**, featuring world-known artists, located at 815 W. Market St. Louisville, KY 40202 Tel: (502) 584-4510. **The Louisville Science Center** located at 727 West Main Street Louisville, KY 40202 Tel: (502) 561-6100. **Kentucky Shakespeare Festival** is held during the months of June and July in Louisville Central Park, 1114 South Third Street Louisville, KY 40203 Tel: (502) 583-8738.

Brennan House Historic Home, of Victorian architecture, is the only historic residential home in downtown Louisville, located at 631 S. Fifth Street Louisville, KY 40202 Tel: (502) 540-5145. **The Portland Museum** located 2308 Portland Avenue, Louisville, Kentucky Tel: (502) 776-7678. **Conrad/Caldwell House Museum** is of Victorian Romanesque architecture, located at 1402 St. James Court Louisville, KY Tel: (502) 636-5023.

Thomas Edison House exhibits Edison's memorabilia, artifacts, and scientific inventions. The house is located at 729-31 E. Washington Street Louisville, KY 40202 Tel: (502) 585-5247. **Museum of Faiths** is a unique museum dedicated to Louisville historical faith. The museum is located at 429 W. Muhammad Ali Blvd. 100 Louisville, KY 40202 Tel: (502) 583-3100. **Farmington Historical House Museum** was designed by Thomas Jefferson, built in 1810, located at 3033 Bardstown Road Louisville, KY 40205 Tel: (502) 452-9920.

Actors Theater of Louisville located at 316 W. Main Street Louisville, KY 40202 toll-free (800) 428-5849 has theatrical performances, a gallery, and restaurant. The **W.L. Lyons Brown Theater** is an elegant 1,400-seat theatre and conference center located at 315 W.

Broadway Louisville, KY 40202 Tel: (502) 562-0188. **Kentucky Art and Craft Gallery** located at 609 W. Main St. Louisville, KY 40202 toll-free (800) 446-0102 exhibits modern art made by Kentucky's talented local artists.

Accommodation

Courtyard by Marriott located at 9608 Blairwood Rd. Louisville, KY 40222 Tel: (502) 429-0006. **Days Inn Suites** located at 4051 Cane Run Road Louisville, KY 40216 Tel: (502) 447-3700. **Economy Inn** located at 3304 Bardstown Road Louisville, KY 40218 Tel: (502) 456-2861. **Best Western Ashton Inn Suites** located at 653 Phillips Lane Louisville, KY 40209 Tel: (502) 375-2233. **Hampton Inn Brooks** located at 180 Willabrook Dr. Brooks, KY 40109 Tel: (502) 957-5050. **Holiday Inn Express Hotel & Suites** located at 1620 Alliant Ave Louisville, KY 40299 Tel: (502) 240-0035.

Best Western Westport Inn & Suites located at 3711 Chamberlain Ln. Louisville, KY 40241 Tel: (502) 814-0004. **Ramada Inn Riverfront** located at 700 W. Riverside Dr. Jeffersonville, IN 47130 toll-free (800) 537-3612. **Hyatt Regency Louisville** located at 320 W. Jefferson Street Louisville, KY 40202 Tel: (502) 587-3434. **Red Roof Inn Southeast** located at 3322 Red Roof Inn Place Louisville, KY 40218 Tel: (502) 456-2993. **SpringHill Suites by Marriott** located at 10101 Forest Green Blvd. Louisville, KY 40241 Tel: (502) 326-3895.

Courtyard by Marriott Downtown located at 100 South Second Street Louisville, KY 40202 Tel: (502) 562-0200. **Louisville Marriott East** located at 1903 Embassy Square Blvd Louisville, KY 40299 Tel: (502) 499-6220. **Red Roof Inn & Suites** located at 2009 N. Mulberry Elizabethtown, KY 42701 Tel: (270) 765-4166. **University Plaza Hotel** located at 1021 Wilkinson Trace Bowling Green, KY 42103 Tel: (270) 745-0088. **Hilton Garden Inn** located at 1530 Alliant Avenue Louisville, KY 40299 Tel: (502) 297-8066.

DoubleTree Club located at 101 E. Jefferson Street Louisville, KY 40202 Tel: (502) 585-2200. **Seelbach Hilton Hotel** located at 500 S Fourth Avenue Louisville, KY 40202 Tel: (502) 585-3200. **Executive West Hotel** located at 830 Phillips Lane Louisville, KY 40209 Tel: (502) 367-2251. **Travelodge** located at 3315 Bardstown Road Louisville, KY 40218 Tel: (502) 452-1501. **Residence Inn by Marriott** located at 120 N. Hurstbourne Lane Louisville, KY 40222 Tel: (502) 425-1821.

Microtel Inn located at 1221 Kentucky Mills Drive Louisville, KY 40299 Tel: (502) 266-6590. **Galt House Hotel** located at 140 N Fourth Avenue Louisville, KY 40202 Tel: (502) 589-5200. **Days Inn Jeffersonville** located at 350 Eastern Blvd. Jeffersonville, IN 47130 Tel: (812) 288-9331. **Best Western - Brownsboro Inn** located at 4805 Brownsboro Road Louisville, KY 40207 Tel: (502) 893-2551. **Holiday Inn Southwest** located at 4110 Dixie Highway Louisville, KY 40216 Tel: (502) 448-2020.

Ramada Limited Inn & Suites located at 2912 Crittenden Drive Louisville, KY 40209 Tel: (502) 637-6336. **Hawthorn Suites** located at 751 Cypress Station Drive Louisville, KY 40207 Tel: (502) 899-5959. **Embassy Suites** located at 9940 Corporate Campus Dr. Louisville, KY 40223 Tel: (502) 426-9191. **Days Inn Central** located at 1620 Arthur Street Louisville, KY 40208 Tel: (502) 636-3781. **Breckinridge Inn** located at 2800 Breckinridge Lane Louisville, KY 40220 Tel: (502) 456-5050.

City Of New Orleans

8:00 pm-D	Chicago (IL)	9:00 am-A
8:45 pm	Homewood (IL)	7:44 am
9:23 pm	Kankakee (IL)	7:13 am
10 :34 pm	Champaigne-Urbana	6 :10 am
11 :13 pm	Matoon (IL)	5 :23 am
11 :37 pm	Effingham (IL)	4 :57 am
12 :25 am	Centralia (IL)	4 :10 am
1 :21 am-A	Carbondale (IL)	3 :16 am D
1 :26 am -D		3 :11 am-A
3 :14 am	Fulton (KY)	12 :59 am
3:56 am	Newbern (TN)	12:17 am
6:32 am-A	Memphis (TN)	10:35 pm D
6:55 am-D		10:05 pm-A
9:05 am	Greenwood (MS)	7:27 pm
9:56 am	Yazoo City (MS)	6:32 pm
11:12 am	Jackson (MS)	5:34 pm
11:48 am	Hazlehurst (MS)	4:39 pm
12:10 am	Brookhaven (MS)	4:19 pm
12:37 am	McComb (MS)	3:53 pm
1:35 pm	Hammond (LA)	3 :00 pm
3:40 pm-A	New Orleans (LA)	1:55 pm-D

D-Departure
A- Arrival

The City of New Orleans

The City of New Orleans connects America's most musical cities. It travels more than 900 miles (1,444 kilometers) from north to south in the central United States, connecting the windy city of Chicago, Memphis (the birth place of Blues), and the heart of Jazz and Mardi Gras, New Orleans. The City of New Orleans serves the states of Illinois, Kentucky, Tennessee, Mississippi, and Louisiana.

The City of New Orleans has Thruway motor-coach connections to Mobile (LA), Baton Rouge (LA), St. Louis (MO), and Kansas City (MO); and connecting trains to Los Angeles, Jacksonville (FL), and Orlando (FL) via Sunset Limited.

Route Destination Highlights

Chicago, IL- Home to America's tallest building Sears Tower, visit the Museum of Science and Industry and other outstanding museums, admire the charming Centennial Fountain, and take a romantic stroll along Lake Michigan. Also enjoy Chicago's attractive and busy nightlife.

Memphis, TN- Visit Graceland the home of the famous king of rock n' roll, Elvis Presley, the Sun Studio where many music legends were born, or the Beale St. Historic District known as the heart of Memphis where you can relax and enjoy the district's many bars, restaurants, and shops with plenty of music. Take a walk to the 150 year-old Historic Elmwood Cemetery it offers a glimpse of Memphis history, visit the Davies Manor Plantation it is the oldest log house in Shelby County, the Chucalissa Museum it exhibit Native-American artifacts and a pre-Columbian village, tour the Gibson Guitar Memphis, see the the National Civil Rights Museum, Memphis Transportation Museum, or take the Main Street Trolley and enjoy the city atmosphere of Memphis.

Jackson, MS- Visit the Alamo Theater one of the few remaining dual-use theaters in the United States, the 1846 City Hall which houses a Masonic Hall and survived the devastation of the civil war, and the Mississippi State Capitol one of the best examples of Beaux Arts. See the Jackson Zoo, it houses the famous Discovery Zoo, which is regarded as one of the best in the region, the Oaks House Museum the oldest house in Jackson City built in 1853 and the Mississippi Sports Hall of Fame and Museum it exhibits history and archives of Mississippi's great athletes.

New Orleans, LA- Visit the famous French Quarters, the French Market, the Mardi- Gras Fountains, the Louisiana Superdome, and the Old U.S. Mint. Explore art galleries, antique shops and restaurants in Magazine Street; see the famous Louisiana white alligator at the Audubon Zoological Gardens, the Aquarium of the Americas known as one of the best in the US, or be amaze at the New Orleans Historic Voodoo Museum. Take the fun and educational Cajun cooking lesson at Bayou Country's "Cookin' on the River," explore the Mardi Gras World located near Algiers, or try your luck at the casinos.

Scenery along the Route

From Chicago (IL) to New Orleans (IL) you'll see charming towns, great Midwestern cities, farms, plantations, and prairies. Arriving in the city of Chicago gives a spectacular view of one of America's most spectacular towering skylines. Amtrak's New Orleans train depot is located just beside the world famous Louisiana Superdome.

Train Schedules

The City of New Orleans travels daily from Chicago to New Orleans, connecting major cities of the states of Illinois, Kentucky, Tennessee, Mississippi, and Louisiana.

Accommodations and Services

Accommodations are Superliner Sleeping Car and Reserved Coach. There is a Sightseer Lounge Car that serves local cuisine, snacks, soups, sandwiches, and drinks and a Dining Car that serves complete meals in most trains. There is en-route entertainment and a seasonal Trails & Rails national park guide presentation.

All Aboard!

Chicago (IL) See Illinois and Missouri service, page 268

Homewood (IL) See Illini service, page 299- 302.

Kankakee (IL) See Illini service, page 299- 302.

Champaign-Urbana (IL) See Illini service, page 299- 302.

Mattoon (IL) See Illini service, page 299- 302.

Effingham (IL) See Illini service, page 299- 302.

Centralia (IL) See Illini service, page 299- 302.

Carbondale (IL) See Illini service, page 299- 302.

Kentucky (KY)
Capital: Frankfort (Population: 4,041,769)
Size: 39,732 sq mi. (102,907 sq km)
Nickname: The Bluegrass State
Joined the union on: June 1, 1792 (15th state)
Motto: United We Stand, Divided We Fall
Flower: Goldenrod
Bird: Kentucky cardinal
Song: My Old Kentucky Home
Famous for: Abraham Lincoln, Muhammad Ali, and the Louisville Slugger
Major industries: Machinery, tourism, minerals

Fulton (KY)

Fulton is known as the Banana Capital of the US since it was the center of the banana industry for throughout the town's long history. The yearly Banana Festival in mid-September is one of the town's attractions. Fulton is located at the border of the states of Kentucky and Illinois, 255 miles northwest of Nashville; it has a land area of 2.6 sq. miles (6.8 sq. kilometers) and a population of a little more than 3,000.

Fulton's train depot is located at Hwy 51 North, 1/4 mi. N. of Purchase Pkwy Fulton, KY 42041. The station is un-staffed and features an enclosed waiting area.

Fulton station is served by the City of New Orleans.

Newbern-Dyersburg (TN)

Newbern is situated 140 miles west of Nashville and 78 miles north of Memphis. Newbern has a population of 2,515 and a land area of 3.7 sq. miles (9.6 sq. kilometers). Newbern station also served the town of Dyersburg.

Newbern's train depot is located at 108 Jefferson St., Newbern, TN 38059. The station is self-serve and features an enclosed waiting area, restrooms, and payphones.

Newbern station is served by the City of New Orleans.

Memphis (TN)

Memphis is the birthplace of Rock n' Roll and the Blues; it is hard to separate the city from its most famous resident Elvis Presley. Located on the banks of the mighty Mississippi River near the boarder of the states of Tennessee and Mississippi, the city of Memphis has a land area of 256 sq. miles (663 sq. kilometers) and a population of more than 660,000. Memphis is part of Shelby County.

Memphis is known as the prime hardwood lumber center in the world and the third largest railroad hub in the United States. The city is home to some of Fortune 500 companies such as FedEx, AutoZone, International Paper, and other major US companies. Memphis has produced several music legends among them are B.B. King, Jerry Lee Lewis, Al Green, and Elvis Presley.

Some of the city's most visited places are: Graceland, the home of the King of Rock n' Roll Elvis Presley, is said to be the second most visited house in the US, second only to the White House; historic Beale Street has several restaurants, shops, cafes, and clubs; or see some of Memphis' Jazz, Blues, and Rock music festivals.

Getting around

Airport

Memphis International Airport, Memphis-Shelby County Airport Authority, is located 8 miles (12 km) south of Memphis city center, 2491 Winchester Road, Suite 113, Memphis, TN 38116-3856. Tel: (901) 922-8000.

The Memphis Area Transit Authority (MATA) Tel: (901) 274-MATA offers public bus services to and from the airport and surrounding areas. The bus stop is located at the lower outer drive near Terminal C. There are complementary Hotel/Motel Shuttle buses serving the airport, telephone for airport pick-up in the baggage claims A, B, and C.

Major car rental companies: Avis, Alamo, Budget, Dollar, Hertz, Enterprise, and National have pick-up services from the airport; the direct telephone station board is located at baggage claims A, B, or C.

Local taxis are available on the ground floor in front of the terminal outside the Northwest Airline baggage claim. There is a Taxi Service Booth that assists passengers. Minimum fare is $8.00 plus airport surcharge of .75 cents.

Local Bus

Memphis Area Transit Authority (MATA) Tel: (901) 274-6282 provides public transport from 4:30 am until 11:15 pm throughout the city of Memphis. MATA also provides Trolley 2 services around Memphis downtown area

Tennessee (TN)
Capital: Nashville (Population: 5,689,283)
Size: 42,146 sq mi. (109,158 sq km)
Nickname: The Volunteer State
Joined the union on: June 1, 1796 (16th state)
Motto: Agriculture and Commerce
Flower: Iris
Bird: Mockingbird
Song: Tennessee Waltz
Famous for: The Tennessee Waltz and Walking Horses (you have to see it!)
Major industries: Chemical and related products, processed foods, and garments.

Taxi

Checker Cab Company Tel: (901) 577-7777, Advantage Cab Company Tel: (901) 844-9999, Metro Cab Company Tel: (901) 323-3333, Yellow Cab Company Tel: (901) 577-7777 and City Wide Cab Company Tel: (901) 324-4202.

Rent-A-Car

Alamo rent-a-car Tel: (901) 332-8412, Avis rent-a-car Tel: (901) 345-3514, Hertz rent-a-car Tel: (901) 345-5680, Thrifty rent-a-car Tel: (901) 345-0170, Budget rent-a-car Tel: (901) 398-8888, Enterprise rent-a-car Tel: (901) 345-8588, Dollar rent-a-car Tel: (901) 396-2495, and National rent-a-car Tel: (901) 345-0070.

Commuter and Train

MATA Tel: (901) 274-6282 operates antique trolleys that run down Main Street and a Riverfront Loop which brings passengers to the banks of the Mississippi River, the Pyramid, and Mud Island.

Memphis' train depot is located at 545 S. Main St. Memphis, TN 38103. The station is staffed and features an enclosed waiting area, checked baggage service, restrooms, payphones, and vending machines. Transportation options from the station include local transit, taxi, and rent-a-car services.

Memphis station is served by the City of New Orleans.

Visitor Information Center

Memphis Visitor Information Center, 340 Beale Street Memphis, TN 38103 Tel: (901) 543-5333.

Places to See and Things to Do

Graceland is the home of the famous king of rock n' roll, Elvis Presley. The museum exhibits Elvis artifacts and memorabilia and houses the Jungle Room, Elvis' private jets, an automobile museum, and the 'Sincerely Elvis' museum. Graceland is located at 3734 Elvis Presley Blvd. Memphis, TN 38116 Tel: (901) 332-3322. Visit the birthplace of rock n' roll, **Sun Studio** where many music legends were born; a guided tour is advisable, the studio is located at 706 Union Ave. Memphis, TN 38103 Tel: (901) 521-0664. **Beale St. Historic District** is the heart of Memphis. There are several bars, restaurants, and shops with plenty of music. The district is located at 203 Beale St. Memphis, TN 38103 Tel: (901) 526-0110.

Mud Island River Park has galleries, a museum, and monorail to take visitors around the park; it also houses the Memphis Belle pavilion. The park is located at 125 N Front St. Memphis, TN 38103 Tel: (901) 576-7241. **Memphis Belle Pavilion** houses the famous WWII Memphis Belle Plane, located in Mud Island River Park Tel: (901) 576-7241. **The Woodruff Fontaine House** is an 1870 restored French Victorian Mansion located at 680 Adams Ave. Memphis, TN 38105 Tel: (901) 526-1469. The **WONDERS: The Memphis International Cultural Series** exhibits the wonders of Russian Royalty; there are jewelries, ceremonial customs, weaponry, and galleries. The museum is located at 119 S Main St., C-180 Memphis, TN 38103 Tel: (901) 521-2642. **Cooper-Young Entertainment District** has several shops, restaurants, and galleries; the district is located at S Cooper St. & Young Ave. Memphis, TN 38104.

Many agree that a walk to the 150 year-old **Historic Elmwood Cemetery** offers a glimpse of Memphis history. The cemetery is located at 824 S Dudley St. Memphis, TN 38104 Tel: (901) 774-3212. **Davies Manor Plantation** is designated as a National Historic Place; the house is the oldest log house in Shelby County, the plantation is located at 9336 Davies Plantation Rd. Memphis, TN 38133 Tel: (901) 386-0715.

Memphis Botanic Garden has 96 acres of land, houses a Japanese garden, rose garden and more. The garden is located at 750 Cherry Rd. Memphis, TN 38117-4699 Tel: (901) 685-1566. **Memphis Motorsports Park** features drag strip and dirt track races every week, located at 5500 Taylor Forge Rd. Millington, TN 38053 Tel: (901) 358-7223. The **Race-On**

Driving Experience located at 525 North Main Street Memphis, TN 38105 toll-free (866) 4-RACEON.

The **Art Museum of the University of Memphis** exhibits contemporary art, Egyptian antiquities, and western African artifacts. The museum is located at the Communication & Fine Arts Building at 3750 Norriswood Memphis, TN 38152-6540 Tel: (901) 678-2224. **National Ornamental Metal Museum** is the only museum in the US dedicated to the art of metalwork. The museum has actual artists creating at the museum. The museum is located at 374 Metal Museum Dr. Memphis, TN 38106 Tel: (901) 774-6380. The **Childrens Museum of Memphis** has hands-on exhibits for the whole family, located at 2525 Central Ave. Memphis, TN 38104 Tel: (901) 320-3170.

Chucalissa Museum has Native-American artifacts and a pre-Columbian village. The museum is located at 1987 Indian Village Dr. Memphis, TN 38109 Tel: (901) 785-3160. The **Memphis Pink Palace Museum & Planetarium** is the most visited art museum in Tennessee; it houses a planetarium and IMAX theater. The museum is located at 3050 Central Ave. Memphis, TN 38111 Tel: (901) 763-IMAX. **Union Planters IMAX Theater** is located at the Memphis Pink Palace Museum at 3050 Central Ave. Memphis, TN 38111 Tel: (901) 320-6362. **Fire Museum of Memphis** exhibits the facts and memorabilia of Memphis' fire history and also offers educational fire safety instruction. The museum is located at 118 Adams Ave. Memphis, TN 38103 Tel: (901) 320-5650.

The Dyersburg Army Air Base Memorial Association, Inc. and Veteran's Museum houses exhibits from WWI, WWII, Korean War, Vietnam War, and Desert Storm Wars. The museum is located at 719 West Main Halls, TN 38040 Tel: (901) 836-7400. **Alex Haley House Museum** is the home of Pulitzer award winner Alex Haley, located at 200 South Church St Henning, TN 38041 Tel: (901) 738-2240. Admission is: adults $2.50 and students $1. **Memphis Brooks Museum of Art** is the oldest and largest fine arts museum in the state of Tennessee, located at Overton Park at 1934 Poplar Ave. Memphis, TN 38104 Tel: (901) 544-6200.

The National Civil Rights Museum located at the Lorraine Motel at 450 Mulberry St. Memphis, TN 38103 Tel: (901) 521-9699. The museum is one-of-a-kind in the US and is dedicated to educate and inspire visitors about the struggle and importance of the respect of human rights. **W.C. Handy House Museum** is the house of the father of the Blues, W.C. Handy. The museum exhibits artifacts and memorabilia, located at 352 Beale St. Memphis, TN 38103 Tel: (901) 522-1556. **Slavehaven/Burkle Estate Museum** exhibits slave routes and hiding places of the slave underground railroad for freedom. The museum is located at 826 N Second St. Memphis, TN 38107 Tel: (901) 527-3427.

Peabody Place Museum & Gallery exhibits extensive collections of Asian art. The museum is located at Pembroke Square, Concourse Level 119 S Main St. Tel: (901) 523-ARTS. **Viking Culinary Arts Center** located at 119 S Main St., 6th Floor at the Peabody Place-Pembroke Square Memphis, TN 38103 Tel: (901) 578-5822. The **Center for Southern Folklore** is a great place to see art, blues, jazz, and other music performances. The center is located at 119 South Main Memphis, TN 38101 Tel: (901) 525-3655. **Gibson Guitar Memphis** features a factory tour of the famous guitar company, a museum, café, and entertainment, located at 145 Lt. George W. Lee Ave. Memphis, TN 38103 toll-free (800) 4-GIBSON.

Other places of interest are: **Coors Brewing Company** located at 5151 E Raines Rd. Memphis, TN 38118 Tel: (901) 375-2100; **Cordova Cellars Winery & Vineyards** located at 9050 Macon Rd. Cordova, TN 38018 Tel: (901) 754-3442; **Jack Daniels Distillery** located 4 1/2 hours drive from Memphis at Lynchburg, TN 37352 Tel: (931) 759-6180.

The Memphis Zoo located at 2000 Galloway Memphis, TN 38112 Tel: (901) 276-WILD. **Memphis Transportation Museum** is located at 125 N Rowlett St. Collierville, TN 38117 Tel: (901) 362-0602. The **Main Street Trolley** located at 547 N Main St. Memphis, TN 38105 Tel: (901) 274-6282. **Memphis Queen Line Riverboats** located at 45 Riverside Dr. Memphis, TN 38103 Tel: (901) 527-BOAT. **Overton Square Entertainment District** is located at Madison at Cooper Memphis, TN 38104 Tel: (901) 278-6300.

Peabody Place Retail and Entertainment Center located on Second St., downtown Tel: (901) 260-7314. **The Peabody Ducks** are located at 149 Union Ave. Memphis, TN 38103 Tel: (901) 529-4000. **Southland Greyhound Park** located at 1550 Ingram Blvd. West Memphis, AR 72301 toll-free (800) 467-6182 and the **Pinch Historic District** located on North Main St. from the Cook Convention Center to the North Parkway Entertainment area in downtown Memphis.

Arts and Theater

Memphis Symphony Orchestra has seasonal classical performances, 3100 Walnut Grove Rd., #501 Memphis, TN 38111 Tel: (901) 324-3627, call for information. **Lindenwood Concerts** has seasonal performances, 2400 Union Ave. at E Pkwy Memphis, TN 38112 Tel: (901) 458-1652. **Ballet Memphis** is an international acclaimed Ballet featuring seasonal performances, 7950 Trinity Rd. Cordova, TN 38088-3675 Tel: (901) 737-7322. **NARAS** Memphis chapter of the Recording Academy (GRAMMY) is located at 168 Beale St., 2nd Floor Memphis, TN 38103 Tel: (901) 525-1340.

Accommodations

Drury Inn and Suites Northeast located a few minutes from downtown at 1556 Sycamore View Memphis TN 38134 toll-free (800) 378-7946 expect to pay $60-$80. **Hampton Inn & Suites Peabody Place Memphis** located at 175 Peabody Place Memphis TN 38103 Tel: (901) 260-4000 expect to pay $90-$300. **Comfort Inn Airport Graceland Memphis** located at 1581 Brooks Rd. Memphis TN 38116 toll-free (800) 228-5150 expect to pay $50-$110. **Days Inn at Graceland Memphis** located near Memphis International Airport at 3839 Elvis Presley Boulevard Memphis TN 38116 Tel: (901) 346-5500 expect to pay $40-$110.

Hilton East Memphis located in Memphis' upscale district at 5069 East Sanderlin Avenue Memphis TN 38117 toll-free (800) 445-8667. **Holiday Inn Mt. Moriah Memphis** located at 2490 Mt. Moriah Memphis TN 38115 Tel: (901) 362-8010. **Wyndham Second Street Memphis** located at 300 North 2nd Street Memphis TN 38105 Tel: (901) 525-1800. **Elvis Presley Boulevard Inn** located at 2300 Elvis Presley Blvd, Memphis, TN 38106, Tel: (901) 948-1522. **French Quarter Suites** located at 2144 Madison Ave, Memphis, TN 38104, Tel: (901) 728-4000. **Iris Motel** located at 1950 Elvis Presley Blvd, Memphis, TN 38106, Tel: (901) 774-5906.

Howard Johnson Inn Downtown Memphis located at 22 North Third Street Memphis TN 38103 Tel: (901) 543-0507. **Memphis Marriott Downtown Memphis** overlooking the Mississippi River located at 250 North Main Street Memphis TN 38103 Tel: (901) 527-7300. **The Peabody Memphis,** listed in the National Register of Historic Places, is located at 149 Union Avenue Memphis TN 38103 toll-free (800) 323-7500. **Travelodge Springbrook Memphis** located at 1360 Springbrook Ave. Memphis TN 38116 toll-free (800) 578-7878. **Days Inn** located at 3839 Elvis Presley Blvd, Memphis, TN 38116, Tel: (901) 346-5500.

Embassy Suites Hotel located at 1022 S Shady Grove Rd, Memphis, TN 38120, Tel: (901) 684-1777. **Crown Inn** located at 4046 Lamar Ave, Memphis, TN 38118, Tel: (901) 366-5440. **Executive Lodging** located at 6135 Mount Moriah Rd Ext # 102, Memphis, TN 38115, Tel: (901) 363-8894. **Fairfield Inn** located at 4760 Showcase Blvd, Memphis, TN 38118, Tel: (901) 795-1900. **Hampton Inn** located at 2979 Millbranch Rd, Memphis, TN 38116, Tel: (901) 396-2200. **Hilton Hotels Corp** located at 755 Crossover Ln, Memphis, TN 38117, Tel: (901) 374-5000. **Holiday Inn** located at 1837 Union Ave, Memphis, TN 38104, Tel: (901) 278-4100.

Intown Suites Rooms located at 3533 Hickory Hill Rd, Memphis, TN 38115, Tel: (901) 547-6051. **Guest House Inns Hotel & Suite** located at 4300 American Way, Memphis, TN 38118, Tel: (901) 366-9333. **Hawthorn Suites Hotel** located at 1070 Ridge Lake Blvd, Memphis, TN 38120, Tel: (901) 682-1722. **Marriott Hotels & Resorts** located at 2625 Thousand Oaks Blvd, Memphis, TN 38118, Tel: (901) 362-6200. **Holiday Inn** located at 6101 Shelby Oaks Dr, Memphis, TN 38134, Tel: (901) 388-7050. **Holiday Inn** located at 2240 Democrat Rd, Memphis, TN 38132, Tel: (901) 332-1130. **Lamplighter Motor Inn** located at 667 S Bellevue Blvd, Memphis, TN 38104, Tel: (901) 726-1000.

Greenwood (MS)

Greenwood is situated 82 miles north of Jackson City; it has a land area of 9.3 sq. miles (23.9 sq. kilometers) and a population of more than 18,000.

Greenwood's train depot is located at 506 Carrollton Ave. Greenwood, MS 38930. The station is un-staffed and features an enclosed waiting area and restrooms. Transportation options from the station include local taxi service.

Greenwood station is served by the City of New Orleans.

Yazoo City (MS)

Mississippi (MS)

Capital: Jackson (Population: 2,844,658)
Size: 48,434 sq mi. (125,444 sq km)
Nickname: The Magnolia State
Joined the union on: December 10, 1817 (20th state)
Motto: By valor and arms
Flower: Magnolia
Bird: Mockingbird
Song: Go, Mississippi
Famous for: Blues, Elvis Presley, and Kermit the Frog!
Major industries: Agriculture, Fisheries, and Manufacturing

Yazoo City is located just 44 miles north of Jackson City and is the county seat of Yazoo County. It has a land area of 9.7 sq. miles (25 sq. kilometers) and a population of 12,427. The city of Yazoo was immortalized in the Willie Morris book "Good Old Boy" based on the legend the Witch of Yazoo.

Yazoo's train depot is located at 222 W. Broadway Yazoo City, MS 39194. The station is un-staffed and feature payphones. Transportation from the station is local taxi service.

Yazoo station is served by the City of New Orleans.

Jackson (MS)

The town of LeFleur's Bluff was renamed Jackson and became the capital of the state of Mississippi in honor of the late Major General and President Andrew Jackson in November 28, 1821. The city has a very rich history and was a constant victim of war destructions. During the civil war the town was destroyed several times by the Union Army. The town's historical City Hall is the only surviving original building.

Being strategically located in the center of the state of Mississippi, Jackson is a major distribution center served by several international and regional airlines, an efficient rail system, and trailer freight services. Jackson is home to the University of Mississippi Medical Center and some of the nation's major telecommunication industries.

Jackson has land area 109 sq. miles (282 sq. kilometers) and a population of more than 202,000. It has an average summer temperature of 81 degrees F (28 degrees C) and average winter temperature of 48 degrees F (8 degrees C).

Jackson City has a series of great parades and festivals: the Dixie National Rodeo & Livestock Show and Western Festival is celebrated during the month of February, the Mississippi Championship Hot Air Balloon Race is held every July, the Mississippi State Fair held during October, and Christmas in Jackson. Call Jackson Convention and Tourist Bureau for information (see below).

Getting Around

Airport

Jackson International Airport, 100 International Drive, Box 7 Jackson, MS 39208; is located 5 miles east of Jackson City. There are local taxis, rent-a-car services, and shuttles available at the airport.

Bus

The City of Jackson Transit System, 200 South President Street P.O. Box 17 Jackson, MS 39205 Tel: (601) 960-1084, offers local bus services throughout Jackson City and the surrounding areas. Greyhound - Trailways Bus Lines is located at 201 S. Jefferson Street Jackson, MS 39201 Tel: (601) 353-6342; it connects the city to the rest of the country.

Taxi

Veterans Cab Tel: (601) 977 1000, Citicab Co. Tel: (601) 355-8319, Deluxe Cab Co. Tel: (601) 948-4761 and Yellow Cab Co. Inc. Tel: (601) 922-3782.

Rent-A-Car

Enterprise Rent-A-Car Tel: (601) 664-0106, Avis Rent A Car Tel: (601) 939-5853, Hertz Rent A Car Tel: (601) 939-5312, Budget Car Rental Tel: (601) 932-2126 and National Car Rental Tel: (601) 939-5713.

Commuter and Train

Jackson's train depot is located at 300 W. Capitol St. Jackson, MS 39201. The station is staffed and features an enclosed waiting area, checked baggage service, restrooms, payphones, and vending machines. Transportation options from the station include local transit and taxi services.

Jackson station is served by the City of New Orleans.

Visitor Information Center

Jackson Convention and Tourist Bureau 921 North President Street Jackson, MS 39202 Tel: (601) 960-1891 or toll-free (800) 354-7695.

Places to See and Things to Do

Alamo Theater is one of the few remaining dual-use theaters in the United States. Built in the 1940's, it is designated as a National Historic Landmark and features Western and Black American films, Vaudeville acts, stage bands, etc. The theater is located at 333 North Farish Street, Jackson, MS 39202 Tel: (601) 352-3365. The **War Memorial Building** houses a military museum, located at 120 S. State Street, Jackson, MS Tel: (601) 354-7207.

Built in 1846, **City Hall,** which houses a Masonic Hall, survived the devastation of the civil war and is still standing. It was rumored that Gen. Sherman spared the building because he himself was a Mason. City Hall is located at 219 S. President Street, Jackson, MS Tel: (601) 960-1084. **Mississippi State Capitol** is one of the best examples of Beaux Arts Classical architecture. Built in 1903, it is the seat of the state government, located at 400 High Street, Jackson, MS Tel: (601) 359-3114. **The Old Capitol Museum of Mississippi History** is located on State Street at Capitol Jackson, MS 39205-0571 Tel: (601) 359-6920. It exhibits Mississippi's prehistoric era; the Old Capitol was built in 1839 and is designated a National Historic Landmark.

Jackson Zoo houses the famous Discovery Zoo, which is regarded as one of the best in the region. It is home to some of the most exotic animals of the world, located at 2918 W. Capitol Street, Jackson, MS Tel: (601) 352-2580. Admission is: adults $4, children & seniors $2. **LeFleur's Bluff State Park** features a public golf course, swimming pools, boating, fishing, camping, and other recreation activities. The park is located at 2140 Riverside Drive, Jackson, MS Tel: (601) 987-3985.

Mississippi Museum of Natural Science exhibits natural history of the Mississippi region. The museum houses a 100,000-gallon aquarium with more than 200 species of marine animals and a 1,700 sq. foot green house called the "Swamp" which exhibits alligators, turtles, and fish. The museum is located at LeFleur's Bluff State Park at 2148 Riverside Drive, Jackson, MS Tel: (601) 354-7303. Admission is: adults $4, seniors $3, and children $2. **Mississippi Museum of Art** has more than 3000 pieces in its collection, mainly dedicated to the great Mississippian. Admission is: adults $5, seniors $4, and students $2. The museum is located at 201 E. Pascagoula Street, Jackson, MS Tel: (601) 960-1515. The **Oaks House Museum** is the oldest house in Jackson City built in 1853 by James Boyd. The museum is located at 823 N. Jefferson St., Jackson, MS Tel: (601) 353-9339. Admission is: adults $2 and children $1.

Mississippi Agriculture and Forestry Museum is a 40,000 square foot center that exhibits Mississippi's rich agricultural and lumber history, an interesting and educational museum. The museum is located at 1150 Lakeland Drive, Jackson, MS toll-free (800) 844-8687. Admission is: adults $4, children $2, and seniors $3. **Mynelle Gardens** is known as Mississippi's Botanical Wonderland. The botanical garden is located at 4736 Clinton Blvd., Jackson, MS Tel: (601) 960-1894. Admission is: adults $2 and children $.50.

Mississippi Sports Hall of Fame and Museum exhibits history and archives of Mississippi's great athletes. The museum is located at 1152 Lakeland Jackson, MS 39236-6021 toll-free (800) 280-FAME. Admission is: adults $5, students and seniors $3.50. **Smith Robertson Museum and Cultural Center** exhibits the history of Mississippi's African-American community. The center and the museum are located at 528 Bloom Street, Jackson, MS Tel: (601) 960-1457. One of the best entertainment facilities in Jackson City is the **Russell C. Davis Planetarium/Ronald E. McNair Space Theater** which houses a planetarium, one of the regions best theaters, and entertainment (laser show, star show, etc.). The planetarium and the theater are located at 201 E. Pascagoula Street, Jackson, MS Tel: (601) 960-1550.

Accommodations

Jameson Inn Jackson located at 585 Beasley Road Jackson MS 39206 Tel: (601) 206-8623. **Hilton Jackson and Conference Center** located at 1001 East County Line Road Jackson MS 39211 Tel: (601) 957-2800. **Clarion Hotel** located at 400 Greymont Ave, Jackson, MS 39202 Tel: (601) 969-2141. **Holiday Inn Express and Suites** located at 310 Greymont Avenue Jackson MS 39202 Tel: (601) 948-4466. **Best Suites Of America** located at 5411 I 55 N, Jackson, MS 39206 Tel: (601) 899-9000.

Comfort Inn located at 2800 Greenway Dr, Jackson, MS 39204 Tel: (601) 922-5600. **Dollar Save Inn** located at 3740 I 55 S, Jackson, MS 39212 Tel: (601) 373-1040. **Days Inn** located at 1035 Highway 49 S, Jackson, MS 39218 Tel: (601) 932-5553. **Courtyard by Marriott** located at 6280 Ridgewood Court Dr, Jackson, MS 39211 Tel: (601) 956-9991. **Crowne Plaza Downtown** located at 200 E Amite St, Jackson, MS 39201 Tel: (601) 969-5100. **Days Inn** located at 2616 Highway 80 W, Jackson, MS 39204 Tel: (601) 969-5511.

Fairfield Inn located at 5723 I 55 N, Jackson, MS 39206 Tel: (601) 957-8557. **Econo Lodge** located at 3880 I 55 S, Jackson, MS 39212 Tel: (601) 373-1244. **Fairview Inn Bed & Breakfast** located at 734 Fairview St, Jackson, MS 39202 Tel: (601) 948-3429. **Huntingtons Grille** located at 1001 E County Line Rd, Jackson, MS 39211 Tel: (601) 957-1515. **Microtel Inns & Suites** located at 614 Monroe St, Jackson, MS 39202 Tel: (601) 352-8282. **Quality**

Inn located at 400 Greymont Ave, Jackson, MS 39202 Tel: (601) 969-2230. **Old Capitol Inn** located at 226 N State St, Jackson, MS 39201 Tel: (601) 359-9000.

Scottish Inn located at 2263 Highway 80 W, Jackson, MS 39204 Tel: (601) 969-1144. **Edison Walthall Hotel** located at 225 E Capitol St, Jackson, MS 39201 Tel: (601) 948-6161. **Residence Inn** located at 881 E River Pl, Jackson, MS 39202 Tel: (601) 355-3599. **Parkside Inn** located at 3720 I 55 N, Jackson, MS 39211 Tel: (601) 982-1122. **Regency Inn** located at 1714 Highway 80 W, Jackson, MS 39204 Tel: (601) 354-4931. **Southern Comfort Motel** located at 4508 Methodist Farm Rd, Jackson, MS 39213 Tel: (601) 366-2071. **Travelodge** located at 5925 I 55 N, Jackson, MS 39213 Tel: (601) 957-5500. **Vieux Carre Apartment Homes** located at 3975 I 55 N, Jackson, MS 39216 Tel: (601) 982-3182.

Hampton Inn located at 320 Greymont Ave, Jackson, MS 39202 Tel: (601) 352-1700. **Red Roof Inn** located at 700 Larson St, Jackson, MS 39202 Tel: (601) 969-5006. **Ramada Inn** located at 1525 Ellis Ave, Jackson, MS 39204 Tel: (601) 944-1150. **Super 8 Motel** located at 2655 I 55 S, Jackson, MS 39204 Tel: (601) 372-1006. **La Quinta Inn** located at 150 Angle Dr, Jackson, MS 39204 Tel: (601) 373-6110. **Tarrymore Motel** located at 1651 Terry Rd, Jackson, MS 39204 Tel: (601) 355-0753. **Rodeway Inn** located at 3880 I 55 S, Jackson, MS 39212 Tel: (601) 373-1244. **Holiday Inn** located at 2649 Highway 80 W, Jackson, MS 39204 Tel: (601) 355-3472.

Hazlehurst (MS)

Hazlehurst is the county seat of Copiah (the calling panther) County located just 30 miles south of Jackson City. It has a population of 5000 and land area of 4 sq. miles (11 sq. kilometers). The city of Hazlehurst was chartered in 1865.

Hazlehurst's train depot is located at N. Ragsdale St. Hazlehurst, MS 39083. The station is self-serve and feature payphones.

Hazlehurst station is served by the City of New Orleans.

Brookhaven (MS)

Samuel Jayne, who came from New York in search of new opportunities, founded Brookhaven in 1818. Located 129 miles north of New Orleans, it has a land area of 7.4 sq. miles (19 sq. kilometers) and population of approximately 12,000 residents. Brookhaven's economy includes manufacturing, distribution, technology, oil, farming, and services.

Brookhaven's train depot is located at Railroad Ave. Brookhaven, MS 39601. The station is un-staffed and feature payphones. Transportation from the station is local taxi service.

Brookhaven station is served by the City of New Orleans.

McComb (MS)

McComb was named after its founder Colonel Henry McComb and was originally called Elizabethtown. The city of McComb is located 60 miles south of Jackson City and 80 miles north of New Orleans. McComb hospitality is known throughout the region and was selected as the Hospitality City of the state of Mississippi. McComb has a land area of 7.4 sq. miles (19 sq. kilometers) and a population of just around 14,000.

McComb's train depot is located at 114 N.W. Railroad Blvd. McComb, MS 39648. The station is un-staffed and features an enclosed waiting area, restrooms, payphones, and vending machines. Transportation from the station is local taxi service.

McComb station is served by the City of New Orleans.

Hammond (LA)

The city of Hammond was named after Peter Hammond, the first settler of the area. Hammond was America's first strawberry capital and was the center for shoe production during the US civil war. Hammond is located just 40 miles from Baton Rouge and has a land area of 11 sq. miles (29 sq. kilometers) and population of around 17,000.

Hammond's train depot is located at N.W. Railroad Ave. Hammond, LA 70401. The station is staffed and features an enclosed waiting area, checked baggage service, restrooms, and payphones. Transportation from the station is local taxi service.

Hammond station is served by the City of New Orleans.

New Orleans (LA)

New Orleans is one of the most festive, mysterious, and highly visited cities in the US. Located in southeast Louisiana on the Mississippi River and 110 miles from the Gulf of Mexico, New Orleans has a land area of 182 sq. miles (467 sq. kilometers) and a population of almost half a million.

Robert Cavelier, a French explorer, first rediscovered the site of the present New Orleans in 1682; native Indians were living at the area at that time. A second French expedition reached the area in 1699 lead by Jean Baptiste Le Moyne and Sieur de Bienville who later pioneered the site settlements and named it Nouvelle Orleans (New Orleans) in 1718. In 1722 New Orleans became the capital of the Louisiana Colony and it was incorporated as a city in 1805.

The city became part of the Spanish colony as a result of the Treaty of Paris in 1763, and later it became the capital of Spanish Louisiana. A secret transaction between the US and France took place in 1800 where New Orleans was returned to France and later the United States purchased Louisiana and it became the 18th US state.

Louisiana (LA)	
Capital: Baton Rouge (Population: 4,468,976)	
Size: 51,843 sq mi. (134273 sq km)	
Nickname: The Pelican State, the Sugar State, Creole State	
Joined the union on: April 30, 1812 (18th state)	
Motto: Union, Justice, and Confidence	
Flower: Magnolia	
Bird: Pelican	
Song: Give Me Louisiana and You Are My Sunshine	
Famous for: Creole and Cajun Cuisine, Mardi Gras, French Quarters	
Major industries: Tourism, manufacturing, minerals, petroleum products, marine	

In 1827 the first Mardi Gras celebration was held in New Orleans and in 1835 the United States Mint was established in the city. The port of New Orleans became one of the busiest ports in the US ranking fourth busiest in the world in 1840. New Orleans also had some low moments in its long history: in 1853 a yellow fever epidemic killed more than 8,000 people in the city, and during the civil war the city played an important marine strategic role for both the Confederacy and the Union.

New Orleans has a moderate-tropical climate with mild winter and longer pleasant summer. It has an average temperature of 59.8 degree F with an average humidity of 76 percent. New Orleans has an average yearly rainfall of 62 inches.

Mardi Gras (Fat Tuesday) is New Orlean's most celebrated annual festival. It was in 1699 that the first recorded Mardi Gras celebration by native Indians was observed by the French explorers. Mardi Gras is celebrated before the Lenten period of the Christian tradition. The event is celebrated with colorful costumes, spectacular floats, dances, and music. For many, it is the time where people allow themselves a day of madness.

Getting Around

Airport

New Orleans International Airport is located 22 miles from the New Orleans central business district at 900 Airline Highway, Kenner, LA 70062 Tel: (504) 464-0831. The airport shuttle service is by Airport Shuttle, 4220 Howard Ave., New Orleans, LA 70125 Tel: (504) 522-3500. It connects the airport to New Orleans' major hotels and tourist destinations; the fare is around $20.

Taxis are available at the airport's lower level outside the baggage claim area; fare from the airport to New Orleans business district cost approximately $25. Jefferson Public Transit Tel: (504) 367-7433 offers bus services to/from the airport and the rest of the city; the bus pick-up station is located at the airport upper level entrance no. 7, fare $1.50.

Bus

New Orleans Regional Transit Authority Tel: (504) 242-2600 operates public bus services in New Orleans; basic fare is $1.50. Greyhound bus terminal toll-free (800) 229-9424 is located near the Fairmont New Orleans. The Magazine streetcar (or Street bus) and the Vieux Carre also serve New Orleans downtown district and French Quarter.

Taxi

United Cabs, Inc. toll-free (800) 323-3303 operates taxi services around New Orleans.

Rent-A-Car

Alamo, toll-free (800) 327-9633; National, toll-free (800) 227-7368; Hertz, toll-free (800) 654-3131; AVIS, toll-free (800) 331-1212; Enterprise, Tel: (504) 464-6171.

Horse Carriage

Perhaps one of the most romantic and memorable ways of exploring New Orleans is by Carriage. Carriages are part of the old New Orleans tradition, part of the city's way of life since its birth. Visitors are recommended to take the Carriage ride starting at St. Louis Street (between Chartres and Royal) or at Decatur Street (beside Jackson Square). There are several tours and carriage services around the area, finding one is easy.

Train and Commuter

New Orleans St. Charles streetcars are a moving heritage, perhaps one of the most famous in the US. The street cars are one of the most convenient and popular ways of exploring the French Quarter, it brings passengers to Bourbon Street's popular bars and nightclubs. Fares are $1.25 (exact fare) and a day pass is $5 (recommended). The Riverfront Street Car Line uses the Melbourne W-2 Streetcars. The streetcars run through ten stops, from Esplanade Ave. at the riverfront to Thalia St.; fares are $1.25 one way, additional 10 cents for transfer.

New Orleans' train depot is located at 1001 Loyola Ave. New Orleans, LA 70113. The station is staffed and features an enclosed waiting area, checked baggage service, restrooms, payphones, and a snack bar. Transportation options from the station include local transit, bus, and taxi services. Other transportation options include Hertz Car Rental toll-free (800) 654-3131.

Trains serving New Orleans station are the City of New Orleans, the Crescent, and the Sunset Limited.

Visitor Information Center

New Orleans Visitors Information Center 7450 Paris Rd., New Orleans, LA 70128 Tel: (504) 246-5511.

New Orleans Metropolitan Convention & Visitors Bureau 1520 Sugar Bowl Dr., New Orleans, LA 70112 Tel: (504) 566-5005.

Greater New Orleans Black Tourism Network 1520 Sugar Bowl Dr., New Orleans, LA 70112 toll-free (800) 725-5652.

Places to See and Things to Do

Old U.S. Mint is an 1800's landmark that houses Jazz and Mardi Gras exhibits, located near the French Quarter at 400 Esplanade Ave., New Orleans, LA 70116 Tel: (504) 586-6968. **Riverwalk Marketplace** has several restaurants and shops located just beside the Mississippi river, also near the French Quarter, at No. 1 Poydras, New Orleans, LA 70130 Tel: (504) 522-1555. **Magazine Street** Tel: (504) 891-4191 has several blocks of art galleries, antique shops, and restaurants.

The French Quarter, the site of New Orleans' first settlement, contains the lovely Jackson Square, located along the Mississippi River; visitors should also visit the Quarter's famous entertainment venues, restaurants, and bars on Bourbon Street. **French Market** is New Orleans' visitors' shopping center; it's five blocks of entertainment, dining, and shopping: a must-visit place. The market begins with Cafe Du Monde, 1008 N. Peters, New Orleans, LA

70116 Tel: (504) 522-2621. **Mardi Gras Fountains** has colorful waterworks located at Lakeshore Dr, New Orleans, LA, 70130. The 87,500-seat **Louisiana Superdome** is located in front of New Orleans' train depot, at 1500 Poydras St., New Orleans, LA 70112, Tel: (504) 587-3808 is considered the most beautiful in the world. The dome hosted New Orleans' most celebrated fairs, conventions, entertainment and sports events.

The seat of New Orleans Spanish colonial government, the **Cabildo,** is located at 701 Chartres St., New Orleans, LA 70116 Tel: (504) 568-6968. The site exhibits Louisiana's history. **Merrill B. Domas** exhibits American Indian Arts and jewelry. The museum is located at 824 Chartres St., French Quarter, New Orleans, LA 70116, Tel: (504) 586-0479. **Hermann-Grima Historic House** is a national historical landmark; the historic house portrays the French Quarter of the 1800's and the lifestyle of Creole People. The historic house is located at 820 St. Louis St., New Orleans, LA 70112 Tel: (504) 525-5661.

Museums

The **Musee Conti Historical Wax Museum** exhibits New Orleans known historical and

popular figures and houses the Haunted Dungeon. The museum is located at 917 Conti St., New Orleans, LA 70112 Tel: (504) 525-2605. **New Orleans Museum of Art** exhibits world arts from Asia, Africa, and the West, located at 1 Collins Diboll Circle, City Park, New Orleans, LA 70124 Tel: (504) 488-2631. **Louisiana State Museum** is located in the French Quarter, New Orleans, LA 70116, Tel: (504) 568-6968, one of the most visited tourist destinations in the city. **Louisiana Children's Museum** is located at 420 Julia St., New Orleans, LA 70130, Tel: (504) 523-1357. The museum has hands-on exhibits for every member of the family; there is also live entertainment.

New Orleans Historic Voodoo Museum offers guided tours and exhibits artifacts and sacred voodoo objects. The museum is located at 724 Dumaine St., New Orleans, LA 70116 Tel: (504) 523-7685. The **Confederate Museum** is the oldest in Louisiana; it exhibits memorabilia of the Civil War. The museum is located at

At the French Quarter

387

929 Camp St., New Orleans, LA 70130 Tel: (504) 523-4522. **Jackson Barracks Military Museum** exhibits weaponry, tanks, and memorabilia of the revolution. The museum is located at 6400 St. Claude Ave., New Orleans, LA 70146 Tel: (504) 278-6242.

1850 House is a row of historical houses of the antebellum period. Many houses are open to the public. The houses depict the 19th century New Orleans lifestyle, located at 523 St. Ann St., New Orleans, LA 70116 Tel: (504) 568-6968. Another place of historical interest is the well admired **Gallier House Museum,** the residence of the famous architect James Gallier, located at 1118-1132 Royal St, New Orleans, LA, 70116 Tel: (504) 523 6722.

Parks

New Orleans Botanical Garden is located at Victory Ave., New Orleans, LA 70124. Tel: (504) 483-9386. The garden has beautiful sculptures, fountains, and ponds; it also houses the famous Pavilion of the Two Sisters. **New Orleans Fair Grounds** hosts various events throughout the year and is also home to the New Orleans Jazz Festival. The Fair Grounds are located near the French Quarter at 1751 Gentilly Blvd., New Orleans, LA 70119 Tel: (504) 944-5515.

The **City Park,** Tel: (504) 488-2896 and located at No. 1 Palm Dr., New Orleans, LA 70124, is an old local recreational favorite. The historic 1500-acre park houses gardens, live oaks, and recreational facilities. Also in City Park is the historical wooden carousel, at **Carousel**

Gardens located on Victory Ave., New Orleans, LA 70124 Tel: (504) 488-2896. Mini train rides, boating and fishing, a tennis center, and Storyland are also popular attractions in the park.

The **Aquarium of the Americas** is one of the best in the US, home to more than 7500 aquatic animals and the world largest collection of sharks. The aquarium is located at 1 Canal St., New Orleans, LA 70130 Tel: (504) 861-2537. Also at the aquarium is the **Entergy IMAX Theatre,** a five-story screen theater, call Tel: (504) 581-IMAX for information.

One of the most visited zoos in the region is **Audubon Zoological Gardens** Tel: (504) 861-2537 located at 6500 Magazine St., New Orleans, LA 70118. The zoo has more than a

Bourbon Street, French Quarters

thousand animal residents including the famous Louisiana white alligator. There is a one hour riverboat cruise service between Aquarium of America and the Audubon Zoo, served by **John James Audubon Aquarium/Zoo Riverboat Cruise** toll-free (800) 233-2628.

Culture

Bayou Country's "Cookin' on the River" offers educational and fun Cajun cooking lessons, a great taste of the local culture; Bayou Country 600 Decatur St., 3rd Level, Jackson Brewery Millhouse, New Orleans, LA 70130 toll-free (800) 850-3008. Visit **Mardi Gras World** and you will see the elaborate festive colors of Mardi Gras floats, costumes, and carnival ornaments. It's a fun place to see, located near Algiers at 233 Newton Street New Orleans, LA, 70114 Tel: (504) 361-7821.

Entertainment and Casinos

Maxwell's Toulouse Cabaret, located in the French Quarter at 615 Toulouse St., New Orleans, LA 70130 Tel: (504) 523-4207, features New Orleans' finest Jazz music performed by popular artists. New Orleans top casinos: **Bally's Casino Lakeshore Resort** toll-free (800) 57-BALLY located at One Stars and Stripes Blvd., New Orleans, LA 70126; **Harrah's New Orleans Casino** located near French Quarter at 1201 St. Peter, New Orleans, LA 70116 Tel: (504) 533-6000 and the **Flamingo Casino** located downtown at River-walk Tel: (504) 587-7777.

River Cruises

Steamboat Natchez offers lunch or dinner Jazz Harbor Cruises using steam powered sternwheeler vessels. The steamboat cruise is located at Toulouse St. Wharf at JAX Brewery, New Orleans, LA, 70130, toll-free (800) 233-2628. Other river cruises are: **Creole Queen** Tel: (504) 524 0814 and **Cajun Queen** Tel: (504) 524 0814.

Place to Eat

Cafe Du Monde, located at 800 Decatur St., New Orleans, LA 70116, Tel: (504) 581-2914, is a French coffee house serving nice hot French doughnuts. **Broussard's Restaurant,** located at 819 Rue Conti, New Orleans, LA 70112 Tel: (504) 581-3866, is a nice stylish restaurant serving French and Creole cuisines. **Chart House** located on Jackson Square at 801 Chartres St., New Orleans, LA 70116 Tel: (504) 523-2015 has great steaks, prime rib and seafood.

Brennan's Restaurant, located at 417 Royal St., New Orleans, LA 70130, Tel: (504) 525-9711, specializes in French and Creole cuisines. **Copeland's of New Orleans** located at 4338 St. Charles Ave., New Orleans, LA 70130, Tel: (504) 830-1000. Informal dining and popularly known for its pastas, seafood, fish, chicken, and beef selections. **House of Blues** located at 225 Decatur St., New Orleans, LA 70130 Tel: (504) 529-3480, with live entertainment and a gospel brunch Sundays. **French Quarter Candy Market** located at 600 Decatur St. #320, Jax Brewery, New Orleans, LA 70130 Tel: (504) 522-6224. Try its famous Creole praline candies.

Accommodations

Avenue Garden Hotel located at 1509 St. Charles Ave, New Orleans LA 70130 toll-free (800) 379-5322 expect to pay $50-$300. **Dauphine Orleans Hotel** located at 415 Dauphine St, New Orleans LA USA 70116 Tel: (504) 586-1800 expect to pay $80-$350. **Alexa on Royal** located at 100 Royal Street New Orleans LA 70130 Tel: (504) 962-0600 expect to pay $70-$280. **Ambassador Hotel** located at 535 Tchoupitoulas Street New Orleans LA 70130 Tel: (504) 527-5271 expect to pay $60-$250. **Andrew Jackson Hotel** located in the French Quarter, at 919 Royal St, New Orleans, LA 70116 Tel: (504) 561-5881 expect to pay $80-$150.

Clarion Hotel Grand Boutique located at 2001 St. Charles Ave New Orleans LA 70130 Tel: (504) 558-9966 expect to pay $100-$300. **Days Inn Canal Street/Historic District New Orleans** located at 1630 Canal St, New Orleans LA 70112 expect to pay $40-$150. **Econo Lodge New Orleans** located at 4940 Chef Menteur Highway New Orleans LA 70126 Tel: (504) 940-5550 expect to pay $40-$150. **Comfort Suites Downtown** located at 346 Baronne St. New Orleans LA 70112 Tel: (504) 524-1140 expect to pay $70-$400. **Courtyard New Orleans Downtown Convention Center** located at 300 Julia Street New Orleans LA 70130 Tel: (504) 598-9898 expect to pay $70-$250. **French Quarter Courtyard Hotel** located at 1101 North Rampart New Orleans LA 70116 Tel: (504) 522-7333 expect to pay $50-$200.

Hilton Garden Inn New Orleans Downtown located at 1001 South Peters Street New Orleans LA 70130 expect to pay $90-$250. **Holiday Inn New Orleans-French Quarter** located at 124 Royal St. New Orleans LA 70130 Tel: (504) 529-7211 expect to pay $70-$250. **Hyatt Regency New Orleans** located at 500 Poydras Plaza New Orleans LA 70113-1805 Tel: (504) 561-1234 expect to pay $100-$300.

Holiday Inn New Orleans-Downtown located at 330 Loyola Avenue New Orleans LA 70112 Tel: (504) 581-1600 expect to pay $70-$200. **Quality Inn Midtown** located at 3900 Tulane Ave. New Orleans LA 70119 Tel: (504) 486-5541 expect to pay $50-$190. **Travelodge Baronne Plaza Hotel** located at 201 Baronne St, New Orleans LA 70112 Tel: (504) 522-0083 expect to pay $50-$130. **St. Pierre Hotel** located at 911 Burgundy St, New Orleans LA 70116 toll-free (800) 225-4040 expect to pay $80-$150.

Brent House Hotel located at 1512 Jefferson Hwy New Orleans LA 70121 Tel: (504) 835-5411 expect to pay $70-$1200. **Olde Town Inn** located at 1001 Marigny St, New Orleans 70117 Tel: (504) 949-5815 expect to pay $50-$350. **Ramada Inn French Quarter - New Orleans** located at 131 Rue Decatur, New Orleans LA 70130 Tel: (504) 569-0600 expect to pay $80-$350. **Marriott New Orleans** near French Quarter at 555 Canal Street New Orleans LA 70130-2300 Tel: (504) 581-1000 expect to pay $90-$380. **Ramada Plaza Hotel - The Inn on Bourbon** located at 541 Bourbon St, New Orleans LA 70130 Tel: (504) 524-7611 expect to pay $70-$300. **Best Western French Quarter Landmark Hotel** located 3 blocks from Bourbon Street, at 920 North Rampart St, New Orleans LA 70116 Tel: (504) 524-3333 or toll-free (800) 535-7862 expect to pay $90-$250.

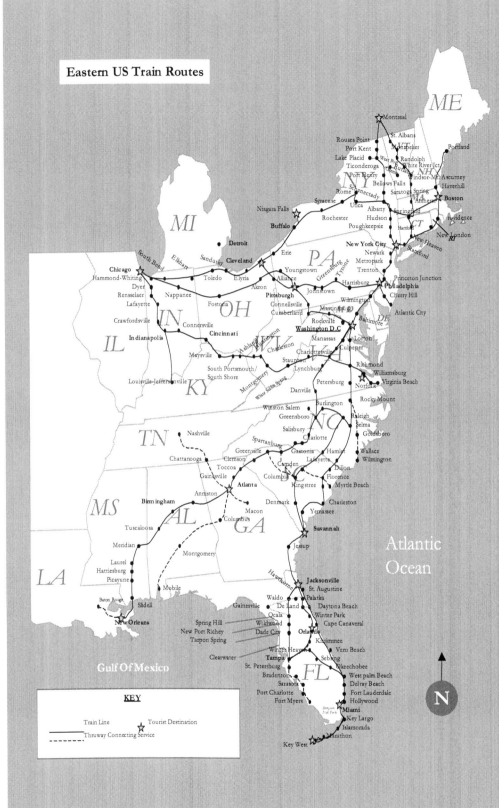

Eastern US Train Routes

KEY

Train Line ☆ Tourist Destination

Thruway Connecting Service

The US Eastern Region Train Routes

Lake Shore Limited

The Lake Shore Limited brings passengers to some of the most scenic lakes, grand rivers, and canals in the US. It will take you to some of the most historical places in eastern United States. Lake Shore limited links the states of Illinois, Indiana, Ohio, Pennsylvania, New York, and Massachusetts.

Lakeshore Limited		
7:45 pm-**D**	**Chicago (IL)**	10:45 am-**A**
8:35 pm	Hammond Whiting (IN)	9:27 am
9:37 pm	South Bend (IN)	8:24 am
9:58 pm	Elkhart (IN)	8:03 am
10:51 pm	Waterloo (IN)-EST	7:14 am
12:16 am	Bryan (OH)ET	7:46 am
1:08 am-**A**	**Toledo (OH)**	6;55 am-**D**
1:25 am-**D**		6:34 am-**A**
2:15 am	Sandusky (OH)	5:43 am
2:50 am	Elyria (OH)	5:10 am
3:53 am	**Cleveland (OH)**	4:40 am
5:19 am	Erie (PA)	2:36 am
6:48 am-**A**	**Buffalo Depew (NY)**	12:55 am-**D**
6:56 am-**D**		12:44 am-**A**
8:10 am	Rochester (NY)	11:44 pm
9:30 am	Syracuse (NY)	10:26 pm
10:26 am	Utica (NY)	9:27 pm
11:48 am	Schenectady (NY)	8:10 pm
12:30 pm-**A**	Albany (NY)*	7:45 pm D
12:55 pm-**D**		7:05 pm-**A**
3:33 pm	Croton Harmon (NY)	5:18 pm
3:20 pm-**A**	**New York (NY)**	4:35 pm-**D**

EST-Eastern Standard, Time ET-Eastern Time
D-Departure **A**-Arrival

*Connecting Train to Poughkeepsie (NY)
--Albany (NY)
--Hudson (NY)
--Rhinecliff-Kingston (NY)
--Poughkeepsie

Route Destination Highlights

Chicago, IL- Home to America's tallest building, Sears Tower; visit the Museum of Science and Industry and other outstanding museums; admire the charming Centennial Fountain and take a romantic stroll along Lake Michigan; and enjoy Chicago's attractive and busy nightlife.

Buffalo, NY- Visit the site of Buffalo's Undergroun Railroad at the Michigan Street Baptist Church, see part of the Erie Canal recognized as one of the great engineering marvels of the 19th Century, the Lower Lakes Marine Historical Society Museum that features artifacts relating to the creation of the Erie Canal. Visit the Mark Twain Room and the Buffalo and Erie County Naval and Military Park exhibits a destroyer, WWII submarine, and missile cruiser.

Rochester, NY- See the International Museum of Photography and Film; the 1822 Charlotte/Genesee Lighthouse, one of the oldest in the great lakes area; the Genesee River waterfalls; or enjoy water sports at Lake Ontario.

Albany, NY- Visit the oldest Neo-Gothic Cathedral structure in the US, the Cathedral of The Immaculate Conception or the Shrine of North American Martyrs, the birthplace of blessed Kateri Tekakwitha. See the 1761 Georgian architecture Schuyler Mansion, the home of the American revolutionary general Philip Schuyler. The Empire State Aerosciences Museum exhibits aviation models and houses galleries and an airpark.

New York, NY- See and admire the most popular statue in the world, the Statue of Liberty; explore the Ellis Island Immigration Museum, Central Park, Times Square, the United Nations, and some of the tallest buildings in the world. Visit the 1913 Beaux architecture Grand Central Terminal, the Museum of Sex, and the Museum of Modern Art.

Boston, MA- Take a walk and explore the Freedom Trail, visit the Massachusetts State House built in 1798. The Boston Irish Famine Memorial, beautiful Beacon Street, the Old State House, Museum of Fine Arts Boston, Museum of Transportation, and the Museum of Bad Art. Climb the Skywalk Observation Deck or meet the locals at Harvard Square, visitors should also visit Harvard University and the Massachusetts Institute of Technology.

Scenery along the Routes

The Lake Shore Limited takes passengers through some of the loveliest scenery of eastern United States. It travels along the Mohawk River where passengers see the famous Native American Highway and later catch a glimpse of Lake Erie when you reach Indiana. When the train reaches the state of New York you will pass through the beautiful Finger Lakes region, the Erie Canal, historical monuments, and majestic bridges.

Train Schedules

The Lake Shore Limited travels daily from Chicago, Illinois to New York City, New York. The trip between the two cities takes approximately 20 hours of travel time.

Accommodations

Accommodations are Reserved Coach and Viewliner Sleeping Car. There is a Lounge and Cafe car that serves local cuisine, snacks, soups, sandwiches, and drinks. Audio/video entertainment is available in sleeping cars. The Dining Car serves complete meals.

All Aboard!

Chicago (IL) See Illinois and Missouri service, page 268.

Hammond-Whiting (IN) See Michigan- International service, page 344- 347.

South Bend (IN) See Capitol Limited service, page 431

Elkhart (IN)

Elkhart is located in northern Indiana a few miles from the Michigan/Indiana border. It has a land area of 17 sq. miles (44.3 sq. kilometers) and a population of approximately 45,000. Elkhart was founded in 1832 and was incorporated in 1858.

Elkhart's train depot is located at 131 Tyler Ave. Elkhart, IN 46515. The station is staffed and features an enclosed waiting area, checked baggage service, restrooms, payphones, and vending machines. Transportation options from the station include local taxi service.

Trains serving Elkhart station are the Lake Shore Limited and Pennsylvanian.

Waterloo (IN)

Waterloo's train depot is located at Lincoln and Center Sts. Waterloo, IN 46793. The station is un-staffed and features payphones.

Trains serving Waterloo station are the Capitol Limited, Lake Shore Limited, and the Pennsylvanian.

Bryan (OH)

Bryan is located 54 miles west of Toledo; it has land area of 3.9 sq. miles (10 sq. kilometers) and a population of approximately 9,000.

Bryan's train depot is located at Page and Lynn St. Bryan, OH 43506. The station is un-staffed and features payphones. Transportation from the station is local taxi service.

The Lake Shore Limited serves Bryan station.

Toledo (OH) See Capitol limited service, page 432.

Sandusky (OH)

Sandusky is located along the shore of Lake Erie, 60 miles west of Cleveland. Sandusky has a land area of 9.7 sq. miles (25.9 sq. kilometers) and a population of roughly 30,000. Founded in 1818, Sandusky is admired for its several 1800's Victorian buildings but is better known as home of the amusement park Cedar Point. Places of interest: Visit the Sandusky Underground Railroad Terminals toll-free (800) 255-ERIE, the Maritime Museum of Sandusky is located at 125 Meigs Street near Battery Park, Sandusky Tel: (419) 624-0274, and the Eleutheros Cooke House (built in 1843-44) located at 1415 Columbus Avenue in Sandusky toll-free (800) 940-9478.

Sandusky's train depot is located at Depot St. and Hayes Ave. Sandusky, OH 44870. The station is un-staffed and features payphones. Transportation from the station is local taxi service.

Trains serving Sandusky station are the Lake Shore Limited and the Pennsylvanian.

Elyria (OH) See Capitol Limited service, page 433.

Cleveland (OH) See Capitol Limited service, page 434

Erie (PA)

The name Erie means "Raccoon" and the city of Erie is located in the far northwest of the state of Pennsylvania, the only port city in the state. The city was founded in 1795 but it was in 1615 when Rev. Joseph Le Caron first sighted the area. Erie has a land area of 22 sq. miles (56.9 sq. kilometers) and a population of more than 100,000.

Erie's early industry was based on lumber milling and later the city became more industrialized as it remains today. In addition, Erie is a popular tourist destination as each year millions of visitors gather and visit the city's long span of fresh-water beach sand.

Places of interest: The Discovery Square Inc. is located at 400 French St 20 Erie, PA 16507 Tel: (814) 452-1942, the Erie Historical Museum is located at 356 W 6th St Erie, PA 16507 Tel: (814) 871-5790, and the Niagara US Brig located at 150 E Front St Erie, PA 16507 Tel: (814) 871-4596.

Erie's train depot is located at 14th and Peach Sts. Erie, PA 16501. The station is un-staffed and features an enclosed waiting area, restrooms, and payphones. Transportation options from the station include local transit and taxi services.

Erie station is served by the Lake Shore Limited.

Buffalo-Depew (NY)

Buffalo is located on the coast of Lake Erie, just 25 miles south of Niagara Falls. Buffalo is the second largest city in the state of New York having a land area of 40.9 sq. miles (105 sq. kilometers) and a population of approximately 330,000. Buffalo was founded in 1803 and incorporated as a city in 1832. Buffalo was a major railroad hub in the early 1900's; it became a center for the steel industry and the largest trade center of grain and livestock in the world. Buffalo was home of U.S. President Millard Fillmore. Buffalo is a gateway city for Niagara Falls.

Getting Around

Airport

Buffalo Niagara International Airport, 4200 Genesee Street, Buffalo, New York 14225 Tel: (716) 630-6000, is located 9 miles (14 kilometers) east of Buffalo. Major rental car service is available at the airport. The NFTA-Metro operates bus services around Buffalo; local bus no. 24 serves the airport, Amtrak station, and Buffalo while bus no. 30 serves the airport and Niagara. The Independent Taxi Association Tel: (716) 633 8294 serves the airport and the rest of the city and nearby towns.

Bus

Metro Bus, 181 Ellicott St. Buffalo, NY 14203 Tel: (716) 855-7211, handles the local bus services around Buffalo. The Niagara Falls International Transportation Center, Fourth and Niagara Sts. Niagara Falls, NY Tel: (716) 285-9319, serves the Niagara area. Greyhound, 181 Ellicott St. Buffalo, NY 14203 Tel: (716) 855-7531, connects Buffalo to the rest of the country.

Taxi

South Buffalo Cab Tel: (716) 822-6300, Taxi Ltd. Tel: (716) 827-0200, City Service Taxi Buffalo Tel: (716) 852-4000, Broadway Taxi Tel: (716) 896-4600, Niagara Air Bus Tel: (716) 625-6222, Radio Taxi Service Tel: (716) 633-4200, Liberty Taxi toll-free (800) 455-TAXI, and Dependable Taxi Tel: (716) 876-5555.

Rent-A-Car

Budget Car and Truck Rental, Downtown Buffalo Tel: (716) 882-7045, Budget Car and Truck Rental, Buffalo Niagara International Airport -Cheektowaga Tel: (716) 632-4662, Enterprise Rent-a-Car Tel: (716) 884-6666, Avis Rent-a-Car, Buffalo Niagara International Airport toll-free (800) 331-1212, Hertz Rent-a-Car, Cheektowaga, NY Tel: (716) 632-4772.

New York (NY)
Capital: Albany (Population: 18,976,457)
Size: 54,475 sq mi. (141,090 sq km)
Nickname: The Empire State
Joined the union on: July 26, 1788 (11th state)
Motto: Excelsior
Flower: Rose
Bird: Bluebird
Song: I Love New York
Famous for: Statue of Liberty, Niagara Falls, Manhattan
Major industries: Tourism, foreign trade, publishing, entertainment, farm and agriculture.

Train and Commuter

Buffalo/Depew train depot is located at 55 Dick Rd. Depew, NY 14043 while Amtrak Downtown Buffalo train depot is located at 75 Exchange St. Washington St. Buffalo, NY 14203. The station is staffed and features an enclosed waiting area, checked baggage service, quik-trak ticket machines, restrooms, payphones, and vending machines. Transportation options from the station include Hertz Car Rental toll-free (800) 654-3131 and local taxi service.

Trains serving Buffalo/Depew station are the Empire Service, Lake Shore Limited, and the Maple Leaf, while trains serving Downtown Buffalo station are the Empire Service and the Maple Leaf.

Niagara's train depot is located at 27 Lockport Rd. Niagara Falls, NY 14305. The station is staffed and features an enclosed waiting area, restrooms, payphones, and vending machines. Transportation from the station is local taxi service.

Trains serving Niagara station are the Empire Service and the Maple Leaf

Visitor Information center

Buffalo Niagara Visitor Center, at the Market Arcade 617 Main Street Buffalo, NY 14203 toll-free (800) BUFFALO.

Buffalo Niagara Visitor Center, at the Walden Galleria Walden Avenue Cheektowaga, NY 14225 Tel: (716) 686-9430.

Places to See and Things to Do

Buffalo Area

Visit the site of **Buffalo's Underground Railroad** located at 511 Michigan Avenue Buffalo, New York. Visit the oldest indoor market in the United States established in 1888, the **Broadway Market** located at 999 Broadway Buffalo, NY 14212 Tel: (716) 893-0705. **Theodore Roosevelt Inaugural National Historic Site,** located at 641 Delaware Avenue Buffalo, NY 14202 Tel: (716) 884-0095, exhibits memorabilia of President Roosevelt's inauguration; the museum also celebrates the 100-year anniversary of the "Teddy Bear." The third oldest zoo in the US, the **Buffalo Zoo** is located at 300 Parkside Ave. Buffalo, NY 14214-1999 Tel: (716) 837-3900 and houses more than 300 species of exotic and wild animals.

Part of the **Erie Canal,** originally opened in 1825, was recently renovated in the Buffalo Canal District. The canal was 425 miles long expanding from Buffalo to Albany New York. The canal was recently designated as the nation's 23rd National Heritage Corridor and was recognized as one of the great engineering marvels of the 19th Century. **QRS Music Technologies,** located at 1026 Niagara Street Buffalo, NY 14213 toll-free (800) 247-6557, is the largest and oldest manufacturer of piano rolls.

Cofeld Judaic Muesum of Temple Beth Zion, located at 805 Delaware Avenue Buffalo, NY 14209 Tel: (716) 836-6565, exhibits thousands of Judaic artifacts. **Mark Twain Room,** located in Buffalo & Erie County Public Library 1 Lafayette Avenue Buffalo, NY 14203-1887 Tel: (716) 858-8900, exhibits original memorabilia of the famous writer. **Buffalo Transportation/Pierce-Arrow Museum,** located at 263 Michigan Avenue at 201 Seneca Street Buffalo, NY 14203 Tel: (716) 853-0084, exhibits automobiles and motorcycles from the early 1900's to the 1960's. **Buffalo and Erie County Naval and Military Park,** located in One Naval Park Cove Buffalo, NY 14202 Tel: (716) 847-1773, exhibits a destroyer, WWII submarine, missile cruiser and more; the park is the largest of its kind in the US. **Buffalo Fire Historical Museum,** located at 1850 William Street Buffalo, NY 14206-1449 Tel: (716) 892-8400, exhibits history of fire fighting.

The Iron Island Museum, located at 131 West Main Street Batavia, NY 14020 Tel: (585) 343-4727, exhibits railroad memorabilia. **Lower Lakes Marine Historical Society Museum,** located at 66 Erie Street Buffalo, NY14202 Tel: (716) 849-0914, features artifacts relating the history of the creation of the Erie Canal. **Buffalo Museum of Science,** located at 1020 Humboldt Parkway Buffalo, NY 14211 Tel: (716) 896-5200, has hands-on exhibits, known as one of the best in the US. **The Karpeles Manuscript Library Museum,** located at 453 Porter Avenue Buffalo, NY 14201 Tel: (716) 885-4139, features an extensive collection of the historical documents.

<u>Niagara Area</u>

The Niagara Falls

The <u>American falls</u> is 56 meters (180 ft) high and 328 meters (1,075 ft) wide. The American falls is higher than the Canadian Horse Shoe Falls. It is said that 75,000 meters of water flow each second at the falls. For many years the American falls has undergone several facelifts to contain the natural erosion of the falls bedrock.

The <u>Canadian Falls</u> or the "Horse Shoe Falls" is 52 meters (170 ft) high and 675 meters (2,200 ft) wide. The depth of the river is said to be 56 meters (184 ft) and an estimated 168,000 cubic meters water flow across the falls per second. Part of the Canadian fall can be seen in the American Territory. Geologists have estimated that each year the falls erode about 3 feet and predicted that in the future the falls will finally erode.

The Daredevil Museum, located at 303 Rainbow Boulevard Niagara Falls, NY 14303 Tel: (716) 282-4046, exhibits many daredevil memorabilia. **Schoellkopf Geological Museum,** located on Robert Moses Parkway Niagara Falls, NY 14303 Tel: (716) 278-1780, exhibits the 435 million years of Niagara geological history. Visit the **Honeymoon Capital Souvenirs**, a shop which has various selections of souvenirs and hospitable people, ask for Janelle. The shop is located in downtown Niagara at 16 Rainbow Blvd. Niagara Falls, Tel: (716) 285-6117.

The Niagara Aerospace Museum, located at 345 Third Street Niagara Office Building Niagara Falls, NY 14303 Tel: (716) 278-0060, exhibits Niagara's aerospace memorabilia and artifacts. **Niagara's Wax Museum of History,** located at 303 Prospect Street Niagara Falls, NY 14303 Tel: (716) 285-1271, exhibits life-size figures portraying the history of Niagara.

Niagara County Historical Society, located at 215 Niagara Street Lockport, NY 14094 Tel: (716) 434-7433, houses a civil war room, Tuscarora Nation, Erie Canal exhibits, and many more. **Aquarium of Niagara,** located at 701 Whirlpool Street Niagara Falls, NY 14301-1094 toll-free (800) 500-4609, exhibits harbor seals, Peruvian penguins, and California sea lions.

Accommodations

<u>Buffalo Area</u>

Holiday Inn located at 620 Delaware Ave, Buffalo, NY 14202 Tel: (716) 886-2121. **Holiday Inn** located at 1881 Niagara Falls Blvd, Buffalo, NY 14228 Tel: (716) 691-8181. **Quality Inn** located at 4217 Genesee St, Buffalo, NY 14225 Tel: (716) 633-5500. **Radisson Hotel Airport** located at 4243 Genesee St, Buffalo, NY 14225 Tel: (716) 634-2300. **Holiday Inn** located at 601 Dingens St, Buffalo, NY 14206 Tel: (716) 896-2900. **Best Western Inn** located at 510 Delaware Ave, Buffalo, NY 14202 Tel: (716) 886-8333.

Homewood Suites located at 760 Dick Rd, Buffalo, NY 14225 Tel: (716) 685-0700. **Radisson Suites Downtown** located at 601 Main St, Buffalo, NY 14203 Tel: (716) 854-

5500. **Sleep Inn** located at 75 Inn Keepers Ln, Buffalo, NY 14228 Tel: (716) 691-6510. **Comfort Inn** located at 901 Dick Rd, Buffalo, NY 14225 Tel: (716) 633-6000. **Days Inn** located at 4345 Genesee St, Buffalo, NY 14225 Tel: (716) 631-0800. **Hampton Inn** located at 210 Delaware Ave, Buffalo, NY 14202 Tel: (716) 855-2223.

Hotel Lafayette located at 391 Washington St # 3, Buffalo, NY 14203, Tel: (716) 852-5470. **Hyatt Hotels & Resorts** located in 2 Fountain Plz, Buffalo, NY 14202 Tel: (716) 856-1234. **Olympic Management Systems Inc** located in 2 Fountain Plz, Buffalo, NY 14202 Tel: (716) 855-4901. **Sheraton** located at 2040 Walden Ave, Buffalo, NY 14225 Tel: (716) 681-2400. **Travelodge** located at 3612 Main St, Buffalo, NY 14226 Tel: (716) 837-3344. **Buffalo Comfort Lodge** located at 1159 Main St, Buffalo, NY 14209 Tel: (716) 882-3490.

Niagara Falls Area

Econo Lodge Niagara Falls located at 7708 Niagara Falls Blvd, Niagara Falls NY 14304 Tel: (716) 283-0621 expect to pay $30-$250. **Niagara Falls Thriftlodge** located at 9401 Niagara Falls Blvd Niagara Falls NY 14304 toll-free (800) 578-7878 expect to pay $20-$150. **Knight's Inn Niagara Falls** located at 9900 Niagara Falls Blvd. Niagara Falls NY 14304 Tel: (925) 473-2230 expect to pay $70-$100. **Comfort Inn The Pointe Niagara Falls** located at 1 Prospect Pointe Niagara Falls NY 14304 toll-free (800) 228-5150 expect to pay $50-$250.

Holiday Inn Select Niagara Falls located at 231 3rd St. Niagara Falls NY 14303 Tel: (716) 282-2211 expect to pay $50-$300. **Best Western Summit Inn Niagara Falls** located at 9500 Niagara Falls Boulevard Niagara Falls NY 14304 Tel: (716) 297-5050 expect to pay $50-$100. **Days Inn Riverview at the Falls Niagara Falls** located at 401 Buffalo Ave. Niagara Falls NY 14301 toll-free (800) DAYS INN expect to pay $50-$1000.

Rochester (NY)

Rochester is located on Lake Ontario in western New York State. The native Indian Iroquois were the first to settle in the area for many generations. Named after Colonel Nathaniel Rochester, the settlement was rediscovered in 1803 and was incorporated as a city in 1834. It has an area of 22.6 sq. miles (58 sq. kilometers) and a population of roughly 220,000. Like Buffalo, Rochester is part of the Erie Canal network which is largely responsible for the early development of the city's economy. Rochester is known as the "World Image Center" because of the city's contribution to the development of optics and photography. Rochester is home to Xerox Corp, Eastman Kodak Co, and Bausch & Lomb.

Places of interest: The International Museum of Photography and Film is located at 900 East Ave Rochester, NY 14607 Tel: (716) 271-3361. The 1822 Charlotte/Genesee Lighthouse is one of the oldest in the great lakes area, the lighthouse houses a museum, located at 70 Lighthouse St Rochester, NY 14612 Tel: (716) 621-6179. Other attractions are the Genesee River waterfalls and Lake Ontario.

Rochester's train depot is located at 320 Central Ave. Rochester, NY 14605. The station is staffed and features an enclosed waiting area, checked baggage service, restrooms, quik-trak ticket machine, payphones, and vending machines. Transportation options from the station include Hertz Car Rental toll-free (800) 654-3131, local transit and taxi services.

Trains serving Rochester station are the Empire Service, Lake Shore Limited, and the Maple Leaf.

Syracuse (NY)

Syracuse is located in central New York State 127 miles northwest of Albany. Syracuse has a land area of 25 sq. miles (65 sq. kilometers) and a population of roughly 170,000. The early settlers of the area were the Native American Indians. The site was first settled and later abandoned in mid 1600's by the Jesuits. It was only in 1805 when the city of Syracuse was founded. Syracuse was the US's leading supplier of salt for many years until the 1920's. Syracuse is the only city in the US with a green traffic signal on the top.

Places of interest: the Museum of Automobile History located at 321 North Clinton Street Syracuse, NY 13202 Tel: (315) 478-CARS, Everson Museum of Art located at 401 Harrison St. Syracuse, New York Tel: (315) 474-6064, and the Erie Canal Museum located at 318 Erie Blvd. E. Syracuse, New York Tel: (315) 471-0593.

Syracuse's train depot is located at 131 P + C Pkwy. Syracuse, NY 13208. The station is staffed and features an enclosed waiting area, checked baggage service, quik-trak ticket machine, restrooms, payphones, and a restaurant. Transportation options from the station include Hertz Car Rental toll-free (800) 654-3131, local transit, bus, and taxi services.

Trains serving Syracuse station are the Empire Service, Lake Shore Limited, and the Maple Leaf.

Utica (NY)

Utica is located in the center of the state of New York and is the western gateway to the Adirondack Mountains. Utica has a land area of 16 sq. miles (42 sq. kilometers) and a population of approximately 70,000.

Places of interest: the Munson-Williams-Proctor Institute located at 310 Genesee Street Utica, NY 13502 Tel: (315) 797-0000, and the Utica Blue Sox minor league baseball team located at 1700 Sunset Ave, Utica, NY 13502 Tel: (315) 738-0999.

Utica's train depot is located at 321 Main St. Utica, NY 13501. The station is staffed and features an enclosed waiting area, checked baggage service, restrooms, payphones, and a snack bar. Transportation options from the station include local transit, bus, and taxi services.

Trains serving Utica station are the Empire Service, Lake Shore Limited, and the Maple Leaf.

Schenectady (NY)

Schenectady, a native Indian word meaning "near the pines," is located in the beautiful Mohawk River Valley, just 11 miles from the state capital Albany. Schenectady has an area of 10 sq. miles (28 sq. kilometers) and a population of more than 65,000. Just like many other cities along the Erie Canal, Schenectady emerged due to the economic development brought by the historical Erie Canal.

Schenectady's train depot is located at 332 Erie Blvd. Schenectady, NY 12305. The station is staffed and features an enclosed waiting area, checked baggage service, quik-trak ticket machine, restrooms, payphones and vending machines. Transportation options from the station include local transit and taxi services.

Trains serving Schenectady station are the Adirondack, Empire Service, Ethan Allen Express, Lake Shore Limited, and the Maple Leaf.

Albany (NY)

Albany is the capital city of the state of New York, located on the Hudson River just 150 miles north of New York City. Albany has a land area of 21 sq. miles (55 sq. kilometers) and a population of more than 100,000. Albany is one of the oldest cities in the US; it was first sighted in 1609 by Henry Hudson and first settled in 1624 and was called Fort Orange. Albany was incorporated as a city in 1686 and later became the state capital in 1797. Albany is New York's historical center rich in architectural splendors.

Getting Around

Airport

Albany International Airport is located at 737 Albany-Shaker Road Albany, NY 12211 Tel: (518) 242-2299. There are local and regional bus services at the airport, ask the airport information center located in the terminal. Taxi service is available at the taxi stand located outside the baggage claim area. Major rental car services are available at the airport's new parking garage.

Bus

The Capital District Transportation Authority (CDTA), 110 Watervliet Avenue Albany, NY 12206 Tel: (518) 482-8822, offers local bus services throughout the region.

Taxi

Yellow Cab, 137 Lark Street Albany, NY 12210 Tel: (518) 434-2222, provides taxi services around the capital region.

Rent-A-Car

Budget toll-free (800) 527-0700, Thrifty toll-free (800) THRIFTY, Hertz toll-free (800) 654-3131, National toll-free (800) 227-7368, Enterprise toll-free (800) Rent-A-Car, Avis toll-free (800) 331-1212.

Train and Commuter

Albany-Rensselaer train depot is located at 555 East St. Rensselaer, NY 12144. The station is staffed and features an enclosed waiting area, quik-trak ticket machine, checked baggage service, restrooms, payphones, ATM machines, and a snack bar. Transportation options from the station include Hertz Car Rental Tel: (518) 434-6911, Yellow Cab Co. Tel: (518) 433-0300, and local transit service.

Trains serving Albany-Rensselaer station are the Adirondack, Empire Service, Ethan Allen Express, Lake Shore Limited, and the Maple Leaf.

Visitor Information Center

The Albany Heritage Area Visitors Center, 25 Quackenbush Sq. Albany, NY 12207 Tel: (518) 434-0405.

Places to see and Things to Do

Visit the oldest Neo-Gothic Cathedral structure in the US, the **Cathedral of the Immaculate Conception,** located at 25 Eagle St. Albany, NY 12202 Tel: (518) 463-4447. **Shrine of North American Martyrs** is the birthplace of blessed Kateri Tekakwitha; the shrine is located at 136 Shrine Rd. Auriesville, NY 12016 Tel: (518) 853-3033. The 1761 Georgian architecture **Schuyler Mansion,** located at 32 Catherine St. Albany, NY 12202 Tel: (518) 434-0834, is home of the American revolutionary general Philip Schuyler. **Albany Institute of History & Art** located at 125 Washington Avenue Albany, NY 12210 Tel: (518) 463-4478.

Empire State Aerosciences Museum, located at 250 Rudy Chase Dr. Glenville, NY 12302 Tel: (518) 377-2191, exhibits aviation models, memorabilia, and an airpark. **New York State Museum,** located at Empire State Plaza, Madison Avenue Albany, NY 12230 Tel: (518) 474-5877, has extensive exhibit collections for adult and children. **Irish American Heritage Museum,** located at 2267 Rte. 145 East Durham, NY 12207 Tel: (518) 634-7497, exhibits educational programs.

Henry Hudson Planetarium located in the Albany Visitors Center at 25 Quackenbush Square Albany, NY 12207 Tel: (518) 434-0405. **USS Albany Heritage Exhibit** located at the Albany Visitors Center, 25 Quackenbush Sq. Albany, NY 12207 Tel: (518) 434-0405. **USS Slater/DEHF** located in Broadway at Quay St. Albany, NY 12201 Tel: (518) 431-1943. **American Museum of Firefighting** located at 117 Harry Howard Ave. Hudson, NY 12534 Tel: (518) 828-7695.

Accommodations

Econo Lodge Albany located at 1632 Central Ave. Albany NY 12205 toll-free (800) 553-2666 expect to pay $40-$120. **Howard Johnson Hotel Albany** located at 1614 Central Ave Albany NY 12205 toll-free (800) I-GO-HOJO expect to pay $40-$90. **Holiday Inn Express Albany** located at 1442 Western Ave. Albany NY 12205 Tel: (518) 438-0001 expect to pay $60-$180. **Ramada Inn Downtown Albany** located at 300 Broadway Albany NY 12207 toll-free (800) 2-RAMADA expect to pay $80-110.

Hilton Garden Inn Albany Airport located at 800 Albany Shaker Road Albany NY Tel: (518) 464-6666 expect to pay $80-$180. **Crowne Plaza Hotel Albany** located on State Lodge Streets Albany NY 12205 Tel: (518) 462-6611 expect to pay $80-$250. **The State House Morgan, Albany** located at 393 State Street Albany NY 12205 toll-free (888) 427-6063 expect to pay $135-$260. **Albany Marriott** located at 189 Wolf Road Albany NY 12205 Tel: (518) 458-8444 expect to pay $70-$200.

Howard Johnson Hotel Albany Airport Central located at 1614 Central Ave, Albany Tel: (518) 869-0281. **Western Motel** located at 2019 Western Ave, Albany Tel: (518) 456-7241. **Howard Johnson Hotel and Conference Center** located at 1375 Washington Ave, Albany Tel: (518) 459-3100 **Holiday Inn Express Turf On Western Ave.** located at 205 Wolf Rd, Albany (518) 438-0001.

Lakeshore Limited- Albany (NY) to Boston (MA) connection

Pittsfield (MA)

Pittsfield is located on the westernmost part of the state of Massachusetts. Pittsfield has a land area of 40.9 sq. miles (105 sq. kilometers) and a population of roughly 50,000.

Point of interest: the Hancock Shaker Village is located in Route 20, Pittsfield, MA 01201 Tel: (413) 443-0188 and the Berkshire Museum is located at 39 South Street, Pittsfield, MA 01201 Tel: (413) 443-7171.

Pittsfield's train depot is located at Depot St. Pittsfield, MA 01201. The station is un-staffed and features an enclosed waiting area and payphones. Transportation options from the station include local transit, bus, and taxi services.

Pittsfield station is served by Lake Shore Limited.

Springfield (MA)

Springfield is located in southwestern Massachusetts just 82 miles from Boston. Springfield has a land area of 32.5 sq. miles (83 sq. kilometers) and a population of more than 150,000. Springfield is known as the home of the Basketball Hall of Fame located at 1150 West Columbia Ave Springfield, Massachusetts 01105 Tel: (413) 781-6500.

Springfield's train depot is located at 66 Lyman St. Springfield, MA 01103. The station is staffed and features an enclosed waiting area, checked baggage service, a quik-trak ticket machine, restrooms, payphones, vending machines, a snack bar, and restaurant. Transportation options from the station include Hertz Car Rental toll-free (800) 654-3131, local transit, bus, and taxi service.

Trains serving Springfield station are the Lake Shore Limited, Northeast Direct, and the Vermonter.

Worcester (MA)

Worcester is located just 40 miles west of Boston with a land area of 37.8 sq. miles (97 sq. kilometers) and a population of roughly 170,000. Worcester is the second largest city in Massachusetts.

Worcester's train depot is located at 2 Washington SQ. Worcester, MA 01604. The station is staffed and features an enclosed waiting area, checked baggage service, restrooms, payphones, and vending machines. Transportation options from the station include Hertz Car Rental toll-free (800) 654-3131, local transit, and taxi services.

Trains serving Worcester station are the Lake Shore Limited and the Northeast Direct.

Framingham (MA)

Framingham is located 22 miles west of Boston with a land area of 25 sq. miles (65 sq. kilometers) and a population of almost 65,000.

Framingham's train depot is located at 443 Waverly St. Framingham, MA 01701. The station is un-staffed and features payphones and a snack bar. Transportation options from the station include local transit and taxi services.

Trains serving Framingham station are the Lake Shore Limited and the Northeast Direct.

Boston - Back Bay Station (MA)

Boston Back Bay train depot is located at 145 Dartmouth St. Boston, MA 02116. The station is staffed and features an enclosed waiting area, checked baggage service, restrooms, payphones, and vending machines. Transportation options from the station include Hertz Car Rental toll-free (800) 654-3131, Massachusetts Bay Transportation Authority Tel: (617) 222-3200, and local taxi service.

Trains serving Boston Back Bay station are the Acela Express, Acela Regional, Lake Shore Limited, Northeast Direct, and the Twilight Shoreliner.

Boston South Station is located on Atlantic Ave. and Summer St. Boston, MA 02110. The station is staffed and features an enclosed waiting area, metropolitan lounge, checked baggage service, quik-trak ticket machine, restrooms, payphones, a snack bar and restaurant. Transportation options from the station include Hertz Car Rental toll-free (800) 654-3131, Budget Rent a Car toll-free (800) 527-0700, Avis Rent A Car toll-free (800) 230-4898, Massachusetts Bay Transportation Authority Tel: (617) 222-3200, local bus, and taxi services.

Trains serving Boston South Station are the Acela Express, Acela Regional, Lake Shore Limited, Northeast Direct, and the Twilight Shoreliner.

Lakeshore Limited- Albany (MA) to New York City (NY) connection

Croton-Harmon (NY)

Croton-Harmon train depot is located at Croton Point Ave. Croton-on-Hudson, NY 10520. The station is staffed and features an enclosed waiting area, quik-trak ticket machine, restrooms, payphones, and a snack bar. Transportation options from the station include Avis Rent-A-Car toll-free (800) 230-4898, J and S Taxi Stand Tel: (914) 271-4000, and local transit service.

Trains serving Croton-Harmon station are the Adirondack, Empire Service, Ethan Allen Express, Lake Shore Limited, and the Maple Leaf.

New York (NY)

Connecting train to: **Poughkeepsie (NY), Albany (NY), Hudson (NY),** and **Rhinecliff-Kingston (NY)**

New York, also known as "The Big Apple," is the largest city in the United States. New York City is located at the southern tip of the state of New York 137 miles south of the state capital Albany. It has a land area of 309 sq. miles (800 sq. kilometers) and a population of approximately 8 million.

Native American Indians first occupied the site of what is now New York City for thousands of years. It was in 1609 when Henry Hudson claimed the area, and in 1624 the Dutch established the first white settlement in the region. The settlement was later ceded to the British in 1664. It was here in New York in 1789 that the United States' first president George Washington was sworn in.

New York (NY)

Capital: Albany (Population: 18,976,457)
Size: 54,475 sq mi. (141,090 sq km)
Nickname: The Empire State
Joined the union on: July 26, 1788 (11th state)
Motto: Excelsior
Flower: Rose
Bird: Bluebird
Song: I Love New York
Famous for: Statue of Liberty, Niagara Falls, Manhattan
Major industries: Tourism, foreign trade, publishing, entertainment, farm and agriculture.

In 1892 Ellis Island Immigration Station was officially opened, since then thousands of new immigrants from Europe and other parts of the world arrived in the US to find new hope of a better life in the new world. The city's fast-growing population, economy, and improvements to the transportation system have resulted in the consolidation of the cities of Manhattan, Queens, Brooklyn, Bronx, and Staten Island into New York City in 1898.

Each year there are more than 35 million people visiting the Big Apple, injecting more than $24 billion dollars to the city's economy. New York has something to offer everybody: world-class museums, theaters, from street market to world-class boutique, from self-service restaurant to the most elegant fine dining in the country, from bed and breakfast to the most lavish five star hotels, New York has it all!

There are approximately 19,000 restaurants in the city so you will never have a hard time getting what you want to eat. With a very diverse population New York has every cuisine that you can imagine. If you are looking for something to bring back home, New York has more than 10,000 shops that will fit anyone's budget.

New York has an average temperature of 55 degrees F. (14 degree C.) with an average annual rain fall of 47 inches and an average annual snowfall of 29 inches.

Getting Around

Airport

John F. Kennedy International Airport, Building 14, Jamaica, New York 11430 Tel: (718) 244 4444, is located 15 miles (24 kilometers) southeast of central Manhattan. Local taxi is available at the airport terminals. Courtesy phones are located next to the ground transportation information desk in the baggage claim area. Major car rental companies are located at the arrivals level.

New York Airport Express Bus Service operates bus services every 30 minutes from the airport to Manhattan areas at Port Authority Bus Terminal (West Manhattan) and Grand Central Station (East Manhattan). There are free shuttles that take passengers to Howard Beach Subway Station that will connect passengers to several stations in the Central Manhattan area.

La Guardia Airport, Hangar Center, Third Floor, Flushing, New York 11371 Tel: (718) 533-3400, is located 8 miles (13 kilometers) east of New York City. Major car rental companies and taxi services are located at the arrival area. There are several local bus and regional bus services serving the airport.

Bus

Metropolitan Transit Authority (MTA)/New York City Transit, Tel: (718) 330-3000, operates public bus services around the city of New York. Basic fare is $1.50. Passengers can pay (exact fare) in coins, token, or by Metro Card. Bus and subway transfers are allowed for MetroCard holders; you can purchase your MetroCard pass at the subway station, visitor information centers, or at thousands of other merchants throughout the city.

Taxi

New York City Taxi & Limousine Commission operates public taxi around New York City. For information contact the Taxi and Limousine Commission at Tel: (212) NYC-TAXI or (212) 692-8294.

Rent-A-Car

Enterprise Rent A Car toll-free (800) 736-8222, Dollar Rent A Car toll-free (800) 800-4000, Budget toll-free (800) 527-0700, National Car Rental toll-free (800) 227-7368, New York Rent-A-Car toll-free (800) 697-2227, Avis toll-free (800) 230-4898, and Hertz toll-free (800) 654-3131.

Ferry

The Staten Island Ferry, St. George Ferry Terminal, Staten Island, New York 10301 Tel: (718) 815-BOAT, offers free harbor tours including around the statue of Liberty.

NY Waterway, toll-free (800) 53-FERRY, offers sightseeing cruises and operates ferry services between Manhattan and New Jersey, and Yankee and Shea Stadiums.

Train and Commuter

The Metropolitan Transit Authority (MTA) Tel: (718) 330-1234 operates the New York subway system. Basic fare is $1.50. Visitors are encouraged to purchase a MetroCard that will allow you multiple rides. Metro card cost $4 for one-day pass, $17 for a week pass, and $63 for a month pass. Subway and bus transfers are allowed for MetroCard holders; you can purchase your MetroCard pass at the subway station, visitor information centers, or at thousands of other merchants throughout the city.

New York's train depot is located in Penn Station near Madison Square garden at 7th Ave. and W. 32nd St. New York, NY 10001. The station is staffed and features an enclosed waiting area, quik-trak ticket machine, checked baggage service, restrooms, payphones, and restaurants. Transportation options from the station include Hertz Car Rental toll-free (800) 654-3131, Avis Rent A Car toll-free (800) 230-4898, New York City Bus and Subways Tel: (718) 330-1234, Long Island Rail Road Tel: (718) 217-5477, and local taxi service.

Trains serving New York station are the Acela Express, Acela Regional, Metroliner, Adirondack, Carolinian and Piedmont, Crescent, Empire Service, Ethan Allen Express,

New York City Skyline 407

Keystone, Lake Shore Limited, Maple Leaf, Northeast Direct, Silver Service, Three Rivers, Vermonter, and the Twilight Shoreliner.

Visitor Information Center

The Dairy, Central Park Visitor Center, (Uptown) Central Park near 65th St. New York City Tel: (212) 794-6564.

NYU Info Center, (Downtown) 50 West 4th Street at Greene Street New York City Tel: (212) 988-4636.

Manhattan Mall Info Booth, (Midtown) 6th Avenue & 33rd Street, 1st floor Herald Square New York City Tel: (212) 465-0500.

Lady Liberty

Places to See and Things to Do

The Statue of Liberty and Ellis Island Immigration Museum

The Statue of Liberty is located on Liberty Island, in the New York Harbor Tel: (212) 363-3200. Lady Liberty was a gift from France to the people of the United States and was dedicated on October 28, 1886. The statue is made of copper and measures 305 ft. (92.99 m) from the ground to the tip of the torch. Frederic Auguste Bartholdi designed the statue of Liberty with the help of Alexandre Gustave Eiffel; the statue was completed in 1884 and was sent to the United States the following year.

The Statue of Liberty was designated a National Monument on October 15, 1924 and as a World Heritage Site in 1984. The statue underwent an extensive renovation in preparation for Lady Liberty's 100-year anniversary in 1986. The **Ellis Island Immigration Museum** is located on Ellis Island in Lower New York Harbor, just a mile from lower Manhattan.

Ferry services to Liberty Island and Ellis Island are located in Battery Park at the southern tip of Manhattan; a single ticket includes both islands. Visitors are advised to take public transportation since parking areas are limited and very expensive. Subway trains stop at the Battery Park Station a few feet away from the ferry station. The ferry operates from 9:00 am - 5:30 pm daily. Tickets cost: adults $10.00, seniors $8.00, children $4.00, and children under 4 are free. For more information call Tel: (212) 269-5755.

Ellis Island Immigration Museum

As of this writing visitors are only allowed to visit the grounds of Liberty Island. The statue, pedestal, museum, and crown are closed to the public. Call Tel: (212) 363-3200 for information.

Around New York City

Central Park is located in the middle of Manhattan. This 843 acres park is said to be the lungs of New York City. Central Park is a popular recreational place for many locals and visitors. Each year various festivals and performances are staged at the park. Avoid visiting the park at night. Central Park Visitor Information Centers are located at the Belvedere Castle, Mid-Park at 79th Street, Tel: (212) 772-0210, The Dairy, Mid-Park at 65th Street, Tel: (212) 794-6564, Charles A. Dana Discovery Center, Inside the Park at 110th Street and Lenox Avenue, Tel: (212) 860-1370, and the North Meadow Recreation Center, Mid-Park at 97th Street, Tel: (212) 348-4867.

Explore the 92-acre **Battery Park City** located in One World Financial Center New York, NY 10281 Tel: (212) 416-5300. Admired by many, the **Grand Central Terminal** is a Beaux architecture designed by architect Whitney Warren in 1913, located at 42nd Street and Park Avenue, New York City, New York. **United Nations** is located at 1st Avenue at 46th Street New York, NY Tel: (212) 963-7713. **St. Patrick's Cathedral** is located on 5th Avenue between 50th and 51st Streets New York, NY.

Times Square at Broadway & 7th Avenue / 42nd through 47th Streets New York, NY, Time Square is one of New York's major destinations for shops, restaurants, theaters, street artists, anything that you can imagine. **Madison Square Garden** is located on Seventh Avenue between 31st and 33rd Streets New York City, New York 10001 Tel: (212) 465-6741, Amtrak station is located in Madison Square Garden, there are various shops and restaurants under the garden, an interesting place to visit.

Central Park Wildlife Center, located at 830 Fifth Avenue in New York, NY 10021. Tel: (212) 439-6574, is home to exotic land and marine animals. **New York Aquarium** is located on Surf Avenue & West 8th Street in Brooklyn, NY 11224 Tel: (718) 265-3426 and exhibits more than 300 species of marine animals, featuring the Sea Cliffs and the Aquatheater. The **Bronx Zoo,** located in Fordham Road and Bronx River Park way Tel: (718) 367-1010, the urban zoo is the largest in the US and is home to more than 4,000 animals.

New York Botanical Garden located at Bronx River Parkway at Fordham Road Bronx, New York 10458 Tel: (718) 817-8700. This beautiful garden is a National Historic Landmark which features exotic plants from different parts of the world and houses the largest Victorian glasshouse in the US. Located in Brooklyn, **Coney Island** is one of the most popular places in New York. It's famous for its boardwalk, roller coaster, and sandy beach, Tel: (718) 266-1234.

Chrysler Building, located at 405 Lexington Avenue at 42nd Street New York City, was designed by architect William Van Alen and was completed in 1930 at the height of 1046 feet. Chrysler Building is the world's 18th tallest building. **The Empire State Building,** located at 350 Fifth Avenue, between 33rd and 34th Streets, Midtown Manhattan, once again is the current tallest building in New York. Visit the observatory on the 86th floor. The New York Skyride Tel: (212) 564-2224 motion simulator movie thrill ride is located on the second floor of the Empire State building. **Rockefeller Center,** located at 30 Rockefeller Plaza New York, NY 10112 Tel: (212) 664-3700, is one of New York's architectural marvels.

American Folk Art Museum, located in Two Lincoln Square New York, NY 10023-7015 Tel: (212) 595-9533, exhibits 18th century folk arts. **The Bronx County Historical Society,** located at 3309 Bainbridge Avenue Bronx, NY 10467 Tel: (718) 881-8900, is dedicated to the history of Bronx and New York City. **American Museum of Natural History** located in Central Park West at 79th Street New York, NY 10024 Tel: (212) 769-5100. The museum is one of the largest in the US; it houses dinosaur halls, Rose Center, Hall of Planet Earth, and more. **Children's Museum of Manhattan,** located in the Ticsh Building at 212 West 83rd Street New York, NY 10024 Tel: (212) 721-1223, features hands-on exhibits for the whole family.

The Jewish Museum located at 1109 Fifth Avenue New York, NY 10128 Tel: (212) 423-3200 exhibits ancient and modern Jewish arts and culture. **Museum of Jewish Heritage A Living Memorial to the Holocaust,** located at 18 First Place Battery Park City New York, NY 10280 Tel: (212) 968-1800, exhibits memorabilia of the victims of the Holocaust. **Yeshiva University Museum** located at 15 West 16th Street New York, NY 10011 Tel: (212) 294-8330 exhibits Jewish arts, culture, and history.

Madame Tussaud's, located at 234 West 42nd Street New York, NY 10036 Tel: (212) 512-9600, features wax figures of world-known personalities. General Washington's **Morris-Jumel Mansion** is Manhattan's oldest house, located at 65 Jumel Terrace New York, NY 10032 Tel: (212) 923-8008. The **Museum of American Financial History** is the only one of its kind, dedicated to capitalism and free enterprise. The museum is located at 28 Broadway New York, NY 10004 Tel: (212) 908-4110.

Museum of Sex, located at 233 Fifth Avenue New York, NY 10016 Tel: (212) 308-5991, is dedicated to the continuing history and evolution of human sexuality. **Whitney Museum,**

located at 945 Madison Avenue New York, NY 10021 Tel: (212) 570-3676, exhibits modern American art, visual arts, video, and films. **DIA Center for the Arts,** located at 542 West 22nd Street New York, NY 10011 Tel: (212) 989-5566, exhibits large collections of contemporary arts.

Museum of Modern Art, located at 11 West 53rd Street New York, NY 10019 Tel: (212) 708-9400, has extensive collections of modern art. The museum also houses a restaurant, bar, and gardens. **Museum of the City of New York,** located at 1220 Fifth Avenue New York, NY 10029 Tel: (212) 534-1672, is dedicated to the history of New York City. The museum has permanent and seasonal exhibits. **New Museum of Contemporary Art,** located at 583 Broadway New York, NY 10012 Tel: (212) 219-1222, exhibits contemporary arts of international artists. **Museum for African Art,** located at 593 Broadway New York, NY 10012 Tel: (212) 966-1313, exhibits traditional and contemporary African arts.

National Academy of Design Museum & School of Fine Arts, located at 1083 Fifth Avenue New York, NY 10128 Tel: (212) 369-4880, has seasonal arts exhibits. **The Studio Museum in Harlem,** located at 144 West 125th Street New York, NY 10027 Tel: (212) 864-4500, exhibits Africa American arts. **The New York Historical Society,** located at 2 West 77th Street New York, NY 10024 Tel: (212) 873-3400, features New York history museum and library.

New York Hall of Science, located at 47-01 111th Street Corona, NY 11368 Tel: (718) 699-0005, features hands-on exhibits. **Valentine-Varian House,** located in Varian Park 3266 Bainbridge Avenue Bronx, NY 10458 Tel: (718) 881-5900, feature a cultural gallery. **Stand-Up New York,** located at 236 W 78th Street New York, NY 10024 Tel: (212) 595-0850, features live comedy entertainment. **NBC Experience Store / Studio Tours,** located at 30 Rockefeller Plaza at 49th Street New York, NY 10112 Tel: (212) 664-3700, offers studio tours and features an interactive store.

The United Nations Headquarters

Staten Island Children's Museum located at 1000 Richmond Terrace Staten Island, NY 10301 Tel: (718) 273-2060. **Staten Island Institute of Arts & Science,** located at 75 Stuyvesant Place Staten Island, NY 10301-1998 Tel: (718) 727-1135, exhibits history, culture, and arts of Staten Island. The **Historic Richmond Town** located in Staten Island Historical Society 441 Clarke Avenue Staten Island, NY 10306 Tel: (718) 351-1611. The town has some of the oldest residents of the island.

411

Accommodations

Belleclaire Hotel located at 250 West 77th Street New York NY 10024 Tel: (212) 362-7700 expect to pay $70-$250. **The Algonquin** located at 59 West 44th Street New York NY 10030 Tel: (212) 840-6800 expect to pay $170-$490. **Americana Inn** is located in the heart of Central New York at 69 West 38th St New York NY 10018 Tel: (212) 840-7106 expect to pay $70-$100. **Astor on the Park** located at 465 Central Park West New York NY 10025 Tel: (212) 866-1880 expect to pay $70-$200. **Holiday Inn Manhattan Downtown** located at 138 Lafayette Street New York NY 10013 Tel: (212) 966-8898 expect to pay $100-$350.

Belvedere Hotel located in the New York City Theater District 319 W 48th St New York NY 10036 Tel: (212) 245-7000 expect to pay $100-$250. **Broadway Plaza Hotel** located at 1155 Broadway New York NY 10001 Tel: (212) 679-7665 expect to pay $110-$350. **Cosmopolitan** located at 95 West Broadway (at Chambers) New York NY 10007 Tel: (212) 566-1900 expect to pay $100-$150. **Helmsley New York** located near major financial and entertainment centers at 212 East 42nd Street New York NY 10017 toll-free (800) 221-4982 expect to pay $100-$250. **West Side Inn** located on the upper West Side of Manhattan at 237 West 107 St New York NY 10025 Tel: (212) 866-0061 expect to pay $50-$150.

Seaport Suites located at 129 Front St New York NY 10005 Tel: (212) 742-0003 expect to pay $100-$450. **Best Western Woodward** located near Broadway Theatre and Central Park at 210 West 55th Street New York NY 10019 toll-free (800) 336-4110 expect to pay $70-$450. **Clarion Hotel Fifth Avenue** located at 3 E. 40th Street New York NY 10016 toll-free (800) 252-7466 expect to pay $150-$400. **Comfort Inn Manhattan** located at 42 West 35th Street New York NY 10001 toll-free (800) 228-5150 expect to pay $90-$300. **Crowne Plaza Manhattan** located at 1605 Broadway between 48th and 49th Streets New York NY 10019 toll-free (800) 243-6969 expect to pay $170-$450.

Grand Hyatt New York adjacent to the Chrysler Building and Grand Central Station, located in Park Avenue at Grand Central Station New York City NY 10017 Tel: (212) 883 1234 expect to pay $150-$550. **Comfort Inn Central Park West** located at 31 West 71st St New York NY 10023 toll-free (800) 228-5150 expect to pay $70-$400. **Crowne Plaza at the United Nations** located one block from the United Nations headquarters at 304 East 42nd Street New York NY 10017 toll-free (800) 879-8836 expect to pay $150-$600. **Helmsley Carlton** located at 680 Madison Ave New York NY 10021 Tel: (212) 838-3000 expect to pay $350-$650.

Amsterdam Court located at 226 W 50th St New York NY 10019 Tel: (212) 459-1000 expect to pay $90-$1000. **Embassy Suites Hotel New York** located at 102 North End Ave New York NY 10281 Tel: (212) 945-0100 expect to pay $150-$1100. **Hotel Inter-Continental New York** located in midtown Manhattan 111 East 48th Street New York NY 10017 Tel: (212) 755-5900 expect to pay $150-$950. **Millenium Hilton** located at 55 Church Street New York NY 10007 Tel: (212) 693-2001 expect to pay $90-$900.

Inter-Continental Central Park located at 112 Central Park South New York NY 10019 Tel: (212) 757-1900 expect to pay $150-$1150. **Bryant Park** located at 40 W 40th St New York NY 10018 Tel: (212) 869-0100 expect to pay $180-$950. **Bentley Hotel** located at 500 E 62nd St New York NY 10021 Tel: (212) 644-6000 expect to pay $90-$950. **Ameritania**

Hotel located at 230 W 54th St New York NY 10019 Tel: (212) 247-5000 expect to pay $110-$1000. **Bedford Hotel** few yards from Rockefeller Center, Fifth Avenue and United Nations located at 118 E. 40th St. New York NY 10016 toll-free (800) 221-6881 expect to pay $130-$950.

Three Rivers and Pennsylvanian

The Pennsylvanian and Three Rivers travel through some of America's most historical places. They connect the states of Illinois, Indiana, Ohio, Pennsylvania, New Jersey, and New York. The Pennsylvanian and the Three Rivers routes cover more than 900 miles.

Route Destination Highlights

Chicago, IL- Home to America's tallest building Sears Tower, visit the Museum of Science and Industry and other outstanding museums; admire the charming Centennial Fountain and take a romantic stroll along Lake Michigan; and enjoy Chicago's attractive and busy nightlife.

Harrisburg, PA- See the Pennsylvania State Capitol, the State Museum of Pennsylvania, the National Civil War Museum, Pennsylvania Dutch Folk Festival, or visit the Hershey's Chocolate World Visitor Center and Hershey Park.

Cleveland, OH- See the Rock and Roll Hall of Fame and Museum, the International Women's Air & Space Museum dedicated to the success of women in aviation history. The rare car exhibits of the Crawford Auto-Aviation Museum, the Dunham Tavern Museum that depicts life of the early settlers in Cleveland, or the NASA John Glenn Research Center and the WWII submarine USS Cod.

Pittsburgh, PA- Visit one of the best observatories in the world the Allegheny Observatory; the English Gothic Tudor mansion and gardens of Hartwood; the Pittsburgh Zoo & Aquarium, home to thousands of animals and housing Asian Forest, African Savanna, and Kids Kingdoms; the Carnegie Museum of Art and the Carnegie Science Center; and the Rodef Shalom Biblical Botanical Garden that exhibits plants related to the bible and plants with biblical names.

Philadelphia, PA- See the world's largest mint the U.S. Mint, the oldest zoo in the US the Philadelphia Zoo, pay a visit to the body of Saint John Neumann at National Shrine of Saint John Neumann, visit the birthplace of the nation Independence Hall and the Liberty Bell, spend one afternoon and stroll Fairmount Park or shop in Philadelphia's upscale district Rittenhouse Square.

New York, NY- See and admire the most popular statue in the world the Statue of Liberty, explore the Ellis Island Immigration Museum, Central Park, Times Square, United Nations, and see some of the tallest buildings in the world. Visit the 1913 Beaux architecture Grand Central Terminal, the Museum of Sex, and the Museum of Modern Art.

Scenery along the Route

From Chicago to the Amish farmland of Nappanee, Indiana you will travel along the Ohio River; near the city of Pittsburgh you will see the Golden Triangle where the Ohio, Allegheny, and Monongahela rivers meet. You will pass the great Horseshoe Curve on your way to the Allegheny Mountains, and in Pennsylvania you'll see Dutch Country homes of the Amish People.

Train Schedules

The Pennsylvanian travels daily from Chicago, Illinois to Philadelphia, Pennsylvania. The trip between the two cities takes approximately 18 hours of travel time. The Three Rivers travels daily from Chicago, Illinois to New York City, New York. The trip between the two cities takes 20 hours of travel time.

Accommodations

Three Rivers accommodations are Reserved Coach and Viewliner Sleeping Cars. There is a Lounge and Cafe car that serves local cuisine, snacks, soups, sandwiches, and drinks. Pennsylvanian accommodation is Reserved Coach. There is a Dinette car that serves snacks, soups, sandwiches, and drinks.

Three Rivers		
12:15 pm-D	New York (NY)	7:10 pm-A
12:34 pm	Newark (NJ)	6:45 pm
1:20 pm	Trenton (NJ)	6:01 pm
1:55 pm-A	Philadelphia (PA)*	5:25 pm-D
2:25 pm-D		4:25 pm-A
2:54 pm	Paoli (PA)	3:49 pm
3:45 pm	Lancaster (PA)	2:58 pm
4:30 pm-A	Harrisburg (PA)	2:20 pm-D
4:45 pm-D		1:55 pm-A
5:58 pm	Lewistown (PA)	12:13 pm
6:37 pm	Huntingdon (PA)	11:34 am
7:22 pm	Altoona (PA)	10:52 am
8:22 pm	Johnstown (PA)	9:51 am
9:03 pm	Latrobe (PA)	9:09 am
9:15 pm	Greensburg (PA)	8:58 am
9:55 pm-A	Pittsburgh (PA)*	8:15 am-D
10:23 pm-D		8:00 am-A
12:13 am	Youngstown (OH)	5:38 am
1:14 am	Akron (OH)	4:30 am
3:00 am	Fostoria (OH)	2:45 pm
4:24 am	Nappanee (IN)	11:18 pm
6:03 am	Hammond Whiting (IN)	9:45 pm
7:45 am-A	Chicago (IL)	9:00 pm-D
D-Departure	**A**- Arrival	
*Connecting Train to Washington (Vise-Versa)		
--Philadelphia (PA)		
--Baltimore (MD)		
--Washington D.C		

Three Rivers.

Fostoria (OH)

Three Rivers Route

All Aboard!

Chicago (IL) See Illinois and Missouri Service, page 268

Hammond-Whiting (IN)
See International Service, page 344- 347.

Nappanee (IN)

Nappanee is located in Elkhart County in the far north of Indiana. It has a land area of 2 sq. miles (9 sq. kilometers) and a population of more than 6,000. Nappanee has one of the largest Amish communities in the US and was chosen as a Heritage Tourism Pilot area by the National Trust for Historic Preservation.

Nappanee's train depot is located at 252 S. Main St. Nappanee, IN 46550. The station is un-staffed. Nappanee station is served by the

Fostoria is located in Northwest Ohio just 40 miles southeast of Toledo. It has a land area of 7 sq. miles (18 sq. kilometers) and a population of roughly 15,000. Fostoria's economy is based mainly in manufacturing industries of automobiles, machinery, building materials, and others.

Fostoria's train depot is located at 500 S. Main St. Fostoria, OH 44830. The station is unstaffed and features an enclosed waiting area, restrooms, and payphones. Transportation from the station is local taxi service.

Fostoria station is served by the Three Rivers.

Akron (OH)

Akron, the name comes from a Greek word meaning "High," is located south of Cleveland along the Ohio-Erie Canal. Founded in 1825, Akron has a land area of 71.9 sq. miles (161 sq. kilometers) and a population of more than 220,000. Akron was once known as the "Rubber Center of the World" and the birthplace of trucking industry. Akron is home to James Ingram, Rita Dove (Pulitzer Prize Winner-Poet Laureate), and other known personalities.

Akron's train depot is located at 906 E. Bowery St. Akron, OH 44308. The station is unstaffed and features an enclosed waiting area, restrooms, and payphones. Transportation from the station is local taxi service.

Akron station is served by the Three Rivers.

Youngstown (OH)

Youngstown is located in northeastern Ohio halfway between New York City and Chicago. Youngstown was named after John Young who purchased the town in 1797. During the early days the town of Youngstown became a center for the iron and steel industries. The arrival of the railroad in the early 1800's dramatically increased the population of Youngstown. Today Youngstown has very diverse industries, from automobile assembly to other small businesses. Youngstown has a land area of 33.9 sq. miles (87.5 sq. kilometers) and a population of roughly 100,000.

Places of interest: the **War Vet Museum,** located at 23 East Main Street Canfield, OH 44406 Tel: (330) 533-6311, features memorabilia from American wars and other war collections including a model train. **Lanterman's Mill & Covered Bridge,** located at Canfield Road & Old Mill Road Youngstown, OH 44511 Tel: (330) 740-7115, is a restored 1846 grist mill; its worth visiting. **National Shrine of Our Lady of Lebanon** is located at 2759 North Lipkey Road North Jackson, OH 44451 Tel: (330) 538-3351; the shrine was dedicated to the Immaculate Conception in 1908.

Ohio (OH)
Capital: Columbus (Population: 11,353,140)
Size: 44,828 sq mi. (116,104 sq km)
Nickname: The Buckeye State
Joined the union on: March 1, 1803 (17th state)
Motto: With God, all things are possible
Flower: Scarlet carnation
Bird: Cardinal
Song: Beautiful Ohio
Famous for: The first airplane
Major industries: Manufacturing, jet engines and metal products.

Built in 1829, **St. James Meeting House** is one of the oldest standing Episcopal Churches in the US. The church is located at 375 Boardman-Poland Road Boardman, OH 44512 Tel: (330) 726-8107. **Butler Institute of American Art,** located at 524 Wick Avenue Youngstown, OH 44502 Tel: (330) 743-1711, exhibits more than 10,000 American original artworks, such as works of Audubon, Remington, and Homer. And **Mahoning County Courthouse** is located at 120 Market Street Youngstown, OH 44503 Tel: (330) 740-2130.

Youngstown's train depot is located at 530 Mahoning Ave. Youngstown, OH 44502. The station is un-staffed and features an enclosed waiting area, restrooms, and payphones. Transportation from the station is local taxi service.

Youngstown station is served by Three Rivers.

Pittsburgh (PA) See Capitol Limited service, page 437.
See Pennsylvania for the rest of the route

Pennsylvania Route

All Aboard!

Chicago (IL) See Illinois and Missouri service, page 268

Hammond-Whiting (IN) See Michigan- International Service, pages 344- 347

South Bend (IN) See Capitol Limited service, page 431.

Elkhart (IN) See Lake Shore Limited service, page 393- 395.

Waterloo (IN) See Lake Shore Limited service, page 393- 395

Bryan (OH) See Lake Shore Limited service, page 393- 395

Toledo (OH) See Capitol Limited service, page 432.

Sandusky (OH) See Lake Shore Limited service, page 393-395

Elyria (OH) See Capitol Limited service, page 433.

Cleveland (OH) See Capitol Limited service, page 434.

Alliance (OH) See Capitol Limited service, 436

Pennsylvanian		
8:00 am-D	**Philadelphia (PA)***	8:00 pm-A
8:31 am	Paoli (PA)	7 :21 pm
9 :21 am	Lancaster (PA)	6:32 pm
10 :00 am-A 10:30 am-D	Harrisburg (PA)	5:50 pm-D 5:20 pm-A
11:35 am	Lewistown (PA)	3:36 pm
12:14 pm	Huntingdon (PA)	2:57 pm
12:41 pm	Tyrone (PA)	2:30 pm
1:02 pm	Altoona (PA)	2:11 pm
2:02 pm	Johnstown (PA)	1:10 pm
2:43 pm	Latrobe (PA)	12:28 pm
2:55 pm	Greensburg (PA)	12:17 am
3:40 pm-A 3:55 pm-D	**Pittsburgh (PA)***	11:35 am-D 11:23 am-A
5:33 pm	Alliance (OH)	9:30 am
7:35 pm	**Cleveland (OH)**	8:20 am
8:05 pm	Elyria (OH)	7:22 am
8:39 pm	Sandusky (OH)	6:49 am
9:45 pm	Toledo (OH)	6:00 am
9:59 pm	Waterloo (IN)	3:25 am
10:50 pm	Elkhart (IN)	2:29 am
11:17 pm	South Bend ((IN)	2:00 am
12:19 pm	Hammond Whiting (IN)	12:50 am
1:44 am-A	**Chicago (IL)**	11:55pm-D

D-Departure **A**-Arrival

*Connecting Train to Washington
--Philadelphia (PA)
--Baltimore (MD)
--Washington D.C

Connecting Train to New York City
--Trenton (NJ)
--Metropark (NJ)
--Newark (NJ)
--New York (NY)

Pittsburgh (PA) See Capitol Limited service, page 437

Greensburg (PA)

Greensburg is located on the Allegheny Plateau in the foothills of the Appalachian Mountains southeast of Pittsburgh. It has a land area of 4.2 sq. miles (10.9 sq. kilometers) and a population of approximately 16,500. Greensburg was originally known as Newtown, because of the request of the local postal service the town's name was changed to its present name in 1786. Greensburg was a railroad transport and mining center during the late 1800's and early 1900's, and during the 1970's the city's economy relied on service, banking, and professional services.

Greensburg's train depot is located on Harrison Ave. Greensburg, PA 15601. The station is un-staffed and features an enclosed waiting area and payphones. Transportation from the station is local taxi service.

Trains serving Greensburg station are the Pennsylvanian and the Three Rivers.

Latrobe (PA)

Latrobe is located 35 miles southeast of Pittsburgh; it has a land area of 2.2 sq. miles (5.7 sq. kilometers) and a population of roughly 10,000. The area of what it is now Latrobe was first sighted by an explorer/surveyor Christopher Gist, but it was only in 1852 that the formal plans for the town of Latrobe were laid out by Oliver Barnes. The town was incorporated in 1854. Latrobe was an important railroad industrial hub during the early days of the town's history.

Latrobe's train depot is located at 329 Mckinley Ave. Latrobe, PA 15650. The station is un-staffed and features an enclosed waiting area, payphones, and restaurant. Transportation from the station is local taxi service.

Trains serving Latrobe station are the Pennsylvanian and the Three Rivers.

Johnstown (PA)

Joseph Johns is said to be the first settler of the town of Johnstown in the early 1800's. Many of Johnstown's elderly are enthusiastic in sharing the story of the great flood of 1889 that swept most of Johnstown and the surrounding areas. Johnstown is located in southwestern Pennsylvania east of Pittsburgh; it has a land area of 5.8 sq. miles (15.15 sq. kilometers) and a population of approximately 30,000.

Places of interest: If you are visiting Johnstown on Labor Day see the 3 day-long annual **Johnstown Folk Fest** featuring live entertainment, tours, and local cuisine. **Bottle Works Ethnic Arts Center,** located at 411 Third Ave. Johnstown, PA 15906 Tel: (814) 536-5399, exhibits hands-on ethnic cooking classes; the center also houses a gallery and studios. **Johnstown Flood Museum,** 304 Washington St. / P.O. Box 1889, Johnstown, PA 15907-1889 Tel: (814) 539-1889, commemorates the horrific flood that leveled the city of Johnstown in 1889. And the **Allegheny Portage Railroad National Historic Site,** located at 110 Federal Park Road Gallitzin, PA 16641 Tel: (814) 886-6156, is an inclined plane railroad that provides a link between the Pennsylvania Mainline Canal System and the western railroad.

Johnstown's train depot is located at 47 Walnut St. Johnstown, PA 15901. The station is staffed and features an enclosed waiting area, checked baggage service, restrooms, vending machines, and payphones. Transportation from the station is local taxi service.

419

Trains serving Johnstown station are the Pennsylvanian and the Three Rivers.

Pennsylvania (PA)
Capital: Harrisburg (Population: 12,281,054)
Size: 46,058 sq mi. (119,290 sq km)
Nickname: The Keystone State
Joined the union on: December 12, 1787 (2nd state)
Motto: Virtue, liberty, and independence
Flower: Mountain laurel
Bird: Ruffed grouse
Song: Pennsylvania
Major industries: Metal industries, machinery and chemicals.

Altoona (PA)

Altoona is located in Blair County northeast of Johnstown. It has a land area of 9.7 sq. miles (25 sq. kilometers) and a population of more than 51,000.

If visiting Altoona, see the **Altoona Railroaders Memorial Museum** located at 1300 North Avenue Altoona, PA 16602 Tel: (814) 946-0834; the museum is dedicated to railroaders. The museum exhibits railroad memorabilia, hands-on entertainments, railroad films, and books.

Altoona's train depot is located at 1231 11th Ave. Altoona, PA 16601. The station is staffed and features an enclosed waiting area, checked baggage service, restrooms, payphones, and a snack bar. Transportation options from the station include local transit, bus, and taxi services. Trains serving Altoona station are the Pennsylvanian and the Three Rivers.

Tyrone (PA)

Tyrone is located in Blair County north of Altoona just 17 miles west of Harrisburg. Known as the origin of the Valentine's heart chocolate box, Tyrone has a land area of 1.9 sq. miles (5 sq. kilometers) and a population of approximately 6,000.

Tyrone's train depot is located at 10th and Logan Ave. Tyrone, PA 16686. The station is un-staffed and features payphones. Tyrone station is served by the Pennsylvanian.

Huntingdon (PA)

Huntingdon is located in central Pennsylvania east of Altoona and 61 miles west of Harrisburg. Huntingdon has a land area of 3.4 sq. miles (8.9 sq. kilometers) and a population of roughly 7,000. Huntingdon was originally called "Standing Stone" by the local Indians because of the stone totem pole that was found at the site.

Huntingdon's train depot is located at 402 Allegheny St. Huntingdon, PA 16652. The station is un-staffed and features an enclosed waiting area, payphones, and a snack bar. Trains serving the Huntingdon station are the Pennsylvanian and the Three Rivers.

Lewistown (PA)

Lewistown is located in south central Pennsylvania, northwest of Harrisburg in Mifflin County. It has a land area of 1.9 sq. miles (5 sq. kilometers) and a population of roughly 9,000.

Lewiston's train depot is located at Helen St. Lewistown, PA 17044. The station is un-staffed and features an enclosed waiting area, restrooms, and payphones. Transportation from the station is local taxi service.

Trains serving Lewiston station are the Pennsylvanian and the Three Rivers.

Harrisburg (PA)

Harrisburg is the capital of the state of Pennsylvania, located in eastern Pennsylvania 106 miles from Washington, D. C. Harrisburg has a land area of 8.9 sq. miles (21 sq. kilometers) and a population of 53,000. The early European settlers first founded Harrisburg in 1710; the site was first named Harrisburg in 1785 after the famous local "Harris" family. The town of Harrisburg was incorporated in 1791 and later in 1860 as a city.

Harrisburg's train depot is located at 4th and Chestnut Sts. Harrisburg, PA 17101. The station is staffed and features an enclosed waiting area, checked baggage service, restrooms, payphones, and a snack bar. Transportation options from the station include Avis Rent A Car toll-free (800) 230-4898, Capitol Area Transit Tel: (717) 238-8304, and local bus and taxi services.

Trains serving Harrisburg station are the Keystone, Pennsylvanian, and the Three Rivers.

Places of Interest

Pennsylvania State Capitol is located in N. Third & State St, Harrisburg, PA 17120 Tel: (717) 787-6810. **The Susquehanna Art Museum** is located at 301 Market Street Harrisburg, Pa. 17101 Tel: (717) 233-8668. **John Harris-Simon Cameron Mansion Museum** is located at 219 S. Front St, Harrisburg, PA 17104 Tel: (717) 233-3462. **The State Museum of Pennsylvania** is located at 300 North St. Harrisburg, PA 17120 Tel: (717) 787-4979. **Art Association of Harrisburg** is located at 21 N. Front St, Harrisburg, PA 17101 Tel: (717) 236-1432.

National Civil War Museum is located in Lincoln Circle at Reservoir Park, Harrisburg, PA 17101 Tel: (717) 260-1861. **Fire Museum of Greater Harrisburg** located at 1820 N 4th St, Harrisburg, PA 17102 Tel: (717) 232-8915. **Felicita** is located at 550 Lakewood Dr, Harrisburg, PA 17112 Tel: (717) 599-5301. **Historic Harrisburg Resource Center** is located at 1230 N. Third Street, Harrisburg, PA 17102 Tel: (717) 233-4646. **Pennsylvania Dutch Folk Festival** at the Fair Rd, Schuylkill County Fairgrounds, Summit Station, PA 17979 Tel: (215) 679-9610. **Water Golf at City Island** is located in City Island, Harrisburg, PA 17101 Tel: (717) 232-8533.

Hershey's Chocolate World Visitor Center is located at 800 Park Blvd, Hershey, PA 17033 Tel: (717) 534-4900; **Hershey Theater** is located at 15 East Caracas Avenue, P.O. Box 395, Hershey, PA 17033 Tel: (717) 534-3405; **Hershey Gardens** is located at 170 Hotel Road, Hershey, PA 17033 Tel: (717) 534-3492; **Hershey Park** is located at 100 W. Hersheypark Dr, Hershey, PA 17033 Tel: (800) HERSHEY; the **Hershey Museum** is located at 170 W. Hersheypark Drive, Hershey, PA 17033 Tel: (717) 534-3439; and **The Zoo America** is located at 100 W. Hersheypark Dr, Hershey, PA 17033 Tel: (800) HERSHEY.

Accommodations

Best Western Inn located at 150 Nationwide Dr, Harrisburg, PA 17110 Tel: (717) 545-9089. **Clarion Inn & Suites** located at 5680 Allentown Blvd, Harrisburg, PA 17112 Tel: (717) 657-2200. **Windham Garden Hotel** located at 765 Eisenhower Blvd, Harrisburg, PA 17111 Tel: (717) 558-9500. **Crowne Plaza** located at 23 S 2nd St, Harrisburg, PA 17101 Tel: (717) 234-5021.

Fairfield Inn located at 1018 Briarsdale Rd, Harrisburg, PA 17109 Tel: (717) 412-4326. **Ramada Inn** located at 7975 Jonestown Rd, Harrisburg, PA 17112 Tel: (717) 545-6944. **Hampton Inn** located at 4230 Union Deposit Rd, Harrisburg, PA 17111 Tel: (717) 545-9595. **Travelodge** located at 631 Eisenhower Blvd, Harrisburg, PA 17111 Tel: (717) 564-3876. **Days Inn** located at 3919 N Front St, Harrisburg, PA 17110 Tel: (717) 233-3100. **Econo Lodge** located at 495 Eisenhower Blvd, Harrisburg, PA 17111 Tel: (717) 561-1885. **Comfort Inn** located at 4021 Union Deposit Rd, Harrisburg, PA 17109 Tel: (717) 561-8100.

Hilton Hotel located at 1 N 2nd St, Harrisburg, PA 17101 Tel: (717) 233-6000. **Holiday Inn** located at 4751 Lindle Rd # 104, Harrisburg, PA 17111 Tel: (717) 939-7841. **Marriott Hotels & Resorts** located at 4650 Lindle Rd, Harrisburg, PA 17111 Tel: (717) 564-5511. **Red Roof Inn** located at 950 Eisenhower Blvd, Harrisburg, PA 17111 Tel: (717) 939-1331. **Sheraton Hotel** located at 800 E Park Dr, Harrisburg, PA 17111 Tel: (717) 561-2800. **Fairview Inn** located at 1350 Eisenhower Blvd, Harrisburg, PA 17111 Tel: (717) 939-9531. **Crowne Plaza Harrisburg** located at 23 S 2nd St, Harrisburg, PA 17101 Tel: (717) 234-5021.

Elizabethtown (PA)

Elizabethtown is located in Lancaster County 17 miles southeast of Harrisburg with a land area of 2.6 sq. miles (6.7 sq. kilometers) and a population of approximately 10,000. Elizabethtown is one of the oldest towns in Pennsylvania. A visit to the town will bring you to a journey back in time.

Elizabethtown's train depot is located at Wilson Ave. Elizabethtown, PA 17022. The station is un-staffed and features payphones. Transportation options from the station include Red Rose Transit Tel: (717) 397-4246 and Diamond Cab Tel: (717) 939-7805.

Trains serving the Elizabethtown are the Keystone and the Pennsylvanian.

Lancaster (PA)

Lancaster is located in southeastern Pennsylvania just 70 miles west of the city of Philadelphia. Lancaster has a land area of 7.4 sq. miles (19 sq. kilometers) and a population of more than 55,000. Lancaster is the seat of Lancaster County, the fourth largest in the state of Pennsylvania. The earliest settlers of the area were the Mennonites in the early 1700's. It was John Wright who named the town Lancaster after his homeland Lancaster in England. Lancaster was the capital of Pennsylvania from 1799 to 1812.

Many historic places and buildings of Lancaster County towns are listed in National Historic Landmark. The Hans Herr House is the oldest building in the County, and Wheatland was the home of the 15th President of the United States James Buchanan from 1848 to 1868.

Places of interest

At Penn Square the historic **Central Market Towers** is one of the most distinctive buildings, call Tel: (717) 291-4739 for information. **Heritage Center Museum,** located at Penn Square Lancaster, PA Tel: (717) 299-6440, features 18th and 19th century furniture and house decorations. James Buchanan's **Wheatland** located at 1120 Marietta Avenue Lancaster, PA Tel: (717) 392-8721 was the home of the US 15th President; the mansion features authentic furniture of the era. The 1852 **Fulton Opera House,** located at 12 North Prince Street, Lancaster, PA 17603-1865 Tel: (717) 394-7133, is a national historic landmark.

The **North Museum of Natural History & Science**, located at 400 College Ave. Lancaster, PA 17603, exhibits live animals and more; it also houses the third largest planetarium in Pennsylvania. **Hands-on House** Children's Museum is located at 2380 Kissel Hill Road Lancaster, PA 17601 Tel: (717) 569-KIDS. **Lancaster Museum of Art** located at 135 N. Lime Street Lancaster, PA 17602 Tel: (717) 394-3497. **The Rockford Plantation and Museum** is an elegant 1794 mansion of Gen. Edward Hand, the Adjutant General of the Continental Army, and also see the Kauffman Museum of Pennsylvania there.

Lancaster's train depot is located at 53 Mcgovern Ave. Lancaster, PA 17602. The station is staffed and features an enclosed waiting area, quik-trak ticket machine, restrooms, payphones, and vending machines. Transportation options from the station include Avis Rent A Car toll-free (800) 230-4898, National Car Rental Tel: (717) 394-2158, Friendly Cab Tel: (717) 392-7329, Yellow Cab Tel: (717) 397-8108, and local transit and bus services.

Trains serving Lancaster station are the Pennsylvanian, Keystone, and Three Rivers.

Downingtown (PA)

Downingtown is located in Chester County just 32 miles west of Philadelphia. Downingtown has a land area of 1.9 sq. miles (5.6 sq. kilometers) and a population of roughly 8,000. During the early 1700's the area was called Milltown and was renamed Downingtown after the war of 1812. Downingtown is rich in historical structures and Downingtown's East Lancaster Avenue Historic District exhibits the city's rich history. There are 20 historical structures registered as National Historic Places in the district.

Downingtown's train depot is located on Viaduct Ave. Downingtown, PA 19335. The station is un-staffed and features payphones. Transportation options from the station include Krapf's Coaches Tel: (610) 431-1500, SEPTA Commuter Service Tel: (215) 580-7800, and local transit service.

Trains serving Downingtown station are the Pennsylvanian and the Keystone.

Paoli (PA)

Paoli is located in Chester County just 19 miles west of Philadelphia. Paoli has a land area of 3 sq. miles (5 sq. kilometers) and a population of approximately 6,000. The Historic Paoli Memorial was dedicated to the war heroes of the American Revolution.

Paoli's train depot is located at Lancaster Pike and S. Valley Rd. Paoli, PA 19301. The station is staffed and features an enclosed waiting area, restrooms, payphones, and a restaurant. Transportation options from the station include Paoli Cab Tel: (610) 644-0200 and SEPTA Commuter Service Tel: (215) 580-7800.

Trains serving Paoli station are the Pennsylvanian, Three Rivers, and the Keystone.

Ardmore (PA)

Ardmore was originally called Athensville in 1811 by Dr. Anderson, but was changed to Ardmore in 1873. Ardmore has a land area of 1.9 sq. miles (4.9 sq. kilometers) and a population of around 13,000.

Ardmore's train depot is located at Station Rd. and Lancaster Ave. Ardmore, PA 19003. The station is un-staffed and features an enclosed waiting area, quik-trak ticket machines, restrooms, and payphones. Transportation options from the station include City Taxi Tel: (215) 492-6500, Main Line Taxi Tel: (610) 664-0444, and SEPTA Commuter Service Tel: (215) 580-7800.

Trains serving Ardmore station are the Pennsylvanian and the Keystone.

Philadelphia (PA)

Philadelphia is the first capital of the United States making the city a pioneer of American culture. It was here in Philadelphia where the first paper mill was introduced, the first bank, the first medical college, the first zoo, the first US mint, and many more. Philadelphia was also home to many great American icons like Benjamin Franklin making Philadelphia one of the most historical cities of the United States.

Philadelphia has a land area of 135 sq. miles (349.9 sq. kilometers) and a population of more than 1.5 million. Philadelphia is the county seat of Philadelphia County and is located in the southeastern-most part of the state of Pennsylvania. William Penn, a Quaker, founded Philadelphia in 1682. Since then the town grew dramatically and played an important role in the American Revolution.

Known as the birthplace of American Independence, it was here in Philadelphia where the Constitution of the United States was written in 1787. Today Philadelphia is the fifth largest city in the United States and one of America's cultural centers where many of the city's historical landmarks are well preserved. It is here in Philadelphia where two of the country's most important monuments of independence are situated, the "Liberty Bell," the symbol of America's freedom, and Independence Hall, also known as the birthplace of the nation.

Philadelphia is known as "America's friendliest city."

Getting Around

Airport

Philadelphia International Airport, 8500 Essington Avenue, Philadelphia, Pennsylvania 19153 Tel: (215) 937-5499, is located just 7 miles (11 kilometers) from downtown Philadelphia. Major car rental companies are available in zone 2 outside the baggage claim areas. SEPTA's R1 high-speed train provides service between the airport and Philadelphia city center. Taxi services are available throughout the airport.

Bus

The Southeastern Pennsylvania Transportation Authority (SEPTA), 1234 Market Street Philadelphia, Pennsylvania 19107-3780 Tel: (215) 580-7800, operates the elevated subway, train, trolley and bus services in the city of Philadelphia and outlying areas.

Taxi

Taxi services are offered by: A-1 Express Transportation, Co., 141 Durham Road Penndel, PA 19047 Tel: (215) 741-9500, City Cab Company, Inc., 6821 Norwitch Drive Philadelphia, PA 19153 Tel: (215) 492-6600, Southeastern Pennsylvania Transportation Authority, 1234 Market Street, 10th Floor Philadelphia, PA 19107 3701 Tel: (215) 580-7071, and the American Coach, 205 W. Lancaster Avenue Wayne, PA 19087 Tel: (610) 520-1300.

Rent-A-Car

Alamo Rent-a-Car toll-free (800) 327-9633, Hertz Rent-a-Car toll-free (800) 654-3131, Dollar Rent-a-Car toll-free (800) 800-4000, National Rent-a-Car toll-free (800) 227-7368, Budget Rent-a-Car toll-free (800) 527-0700, and Avis Rent-a-Car toll-free (800) 331-1212.

Train and Commuter

Philadelphia Union Station is located at 30th and Market Sts. Philadelphia, PA 19104. The station is staffed and features an enclosed waiting area, quik-trak ticket machines, checked baggage service, restrooms, payphones, and a snack bar. Transportation options from the station include National Car Rental toll-free (800) 328-4567, Budget Rent a Car toll-free (800) 642-0408, Southeastern Pennsylvania Transportation Authority Tel: (215) 580-7800, local bus, and taxi services. Subway trains also serve the station.

Trains serving the Philadelphia Union Station are the Twilight Shoreliner, Three Rivers, Silver Service, Vermonter, Pennsylvanian, Acela Express, Acela Regional, Metroliner, Crescent, Carolinian and Piedmont, Northeast Direct, and the Keystone.

Visitor Information Center

Community Information Center, 3107 Kensington Ave Philadelphia, PA 19134-2420 Tel: (215) 291-1810.

Philadelphia Convention & Visitors Bureau, 1515 Market Street, Suite 2020 Philadelphia, PA, 19102 Tel: (215) 636-3300.

Places to See and Things to Do

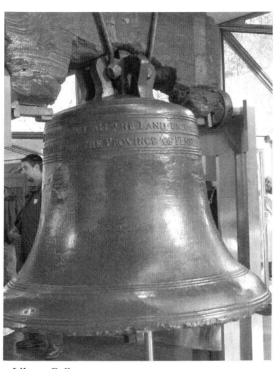

Liberty Bell

See the world's largest mint, the **U.S. Mint,** located at Fifth and Arch Sts. Tel: (215) 408-0114. The **Philadelphia Zoo,** located at 3400 W Girard Ave Philadelphia, PA 19104-1139 Tel: (215) 243-1100, is the oldest in the US. The zoo is home to more than 2,000 animals and was opened to public in 1874. **Horticulture Center,** located in Montgomery Drive, east of Belmont Ave, Fairmount Park Tel: (215) 685-0000, features greenhouses and gardens. **Penn's Landing,** located in Waterfront Park, Columbus Blvd, between Lombard and Market Streets Tel: (215) 922-2386, is the site where William Penn landed in 1682; the site features several historical water vessels and cruisers. **Reading Terminal Market** is located at 12th and Arch Sts. Tel: (215) 922-2317; the farmer's market features several stalls selling local produce since 1892.

Cathedral Basilica of Saints Peter and Paul, located at Benjamin Franklin Pkwy and N. 18th St. Tel: (215) 561-1313, has an imposing façade and copper dome. **National Shrine of Saint John Neumann,** located in St. Peter the Apostle Shrine Church, 1019 North Fifth Street Philadelphia PA 19123 Tel: (215) 627-3080, houses the body of Saint John Neumann. **St. Mark's Church,** located at 1625 Locust St. Tel: (215) 735-1416, is a fine example of English Rural Gothic architecture.

Rodelph Shalom Synagogue is the oldest Ashkenazic temple in the western hemisphere. It houses a museum and ceremonial art. The synagogue is located at 615 N. Broad St. Tel: (215) 627-6747.

Historic and Waterfront District begins on 6th Street to Penn's Landing located along the banks of the Delaware River. A must-see historical area of Philadelphia, many historical buildings and sites are located within the district. **Independence Hall** National Historic Park is located at 313 Walnut Street Philadelphia, PA 19106 and was the birthplace of the nation. The **Liberty Bell** is located between 5th and 6th Streets on Market Street, Philadelphia Tel: (215) 597-8974. Philadelphia's first commercial district was the **Old City**

located just north of Market Street. The district houses galleries and shops, and is known as the one of the oldest residential street in the US.

South Street is well known as Philadelphia's hippest district: there are shops, restaurants, and great nightlife. **Chinatown**, located between N. 8th and N. 11th Sts. and Vine and Arch Sts, is known as one of the best China towns in the US; there are various shops, restaurants, arts and cultural collections. **Convention Center District** located at 12th St and Arch Streets is home to the state-of-the-art convention center, one of the finest in the US. **Sesame Place,** located at 100 Sesame Road, Langhorne Tel: (215) 752-7070, is the only Sesame Street theme park in the US.

Washington Square District is located between Locust St. and 7th St.; there are antique shops, jewelry shops, and many other interesting shops around the area. **Rittenhouse Square District** is Philadelphia's upscale district, located at the corner of 16th and Walnut St. The district has several world-class restaurants and boutiques. **University City District** is home to the University of Pennsylvania and Drexel University. The district is located across the Schuylkill River west of Center City.

Fairmount Park is located along the Schuylkill River. It has more than 8,900 acres of recreation trails. The park also houses some of the larges' and oldest mansions in the US, the Philadelphia Museum of Art, and the Japanese Garden. Call Tel: (215) 685-0000 for information. **Philadelphia Museum of Art** is located at 26th Street and Benjamin Franklin Parkway, Philadelphia, PA 19130 Tel: (215) 763-8100.

Accommodations

Crowne Plaza Hotel Center City located at 1800 Market Street Philadelphia PA 19103 Tel: (215) 561-7500 expect to pay $80-$250. **Embassy Suites Philadelphia** located at 1776 Benjamin Franklin Parkway Philadelphia PA 19103 Tel: (215) 561-1776 expect to pay $70-$200. **Best Western Hotel - Philadelphia Northeast** located at 11580 Roosevelt Blvd. Philadelphia PA 19116 Tel: (215) 464-9500 expect to pay $60-$150. **The Westin Philadelphia** located at 17th and Chestnut at Liberty Place Philadelphia PA 19103 Tel: (215) 563-1600. **Doubletree Hotel Philadelphia** located in

Independence Hall

427

Broad and Locust Streets Philadelphia PA 19107 Tel: (215) 893-1600 expect to pay $110-$250.

Sheraton Inn Harrisburg located in the suburbs of Harrisburg at 800 East Park Drive Harrisburg PA 17111 toll-free (800) 325-3535 expect to pay $70-$100. **Clarion Suites Philadelphia** located at 1010 Race Street Philadelphia PA 19107 Tel: (215) 922-1730 expect to pay $50-$300. **The Rittenhouse Hotel** located in the Historic Park, Rittenhouse Square at 210 West Rittenhouse Square Philadelphia PA 19103 Tel: (215) 546-9000. **Hilton Garden Inn** located at 1100 Arch Street Philadelphia PA 19107 Tel: (215) 923-0100. **Comfort Inn Downtown Historic Area** located at 100 North Christopher Columbus Blvd. Philadelphia PA 19106 Tel: (215) 627-7900 expect to pay $80-$150.

Marriott Philadelphia Downtown located at 1201 Market Street Philadelphia PA 19107 Tel: (215) 625-2900 expect to pay $100-$300. **The Ritz-Carlton Philadelphia** located at 10th Avenue of the Arts Philadelphia PA 19102 Tel: (215) 735-7700. **Hyatt Regency Penn's Landing** located near the popular Dock Street, at 200 North Columbus Road Blvd. Philadelphia PA 19106 Tel: (215) 928-1234 expect to pay $100-$300. **Holiday Inn Express** located at 1305 Walnut Street Philadelphia PA 19107 Tel: (215) 735-9300 expect to pay $70-$150.

Omni Hotel at Independence Park located at 401 Chestnut Street Philadelphia PA 19106 toll-free (800) THE-OMNI expect to pay $100-$290. **Sheraton Rittenhouse Square Hotel** located at 18th at Locust Street Philadelphia PA 19103 Tel: (215) 546-9400. **Wyndham Philadelphia at Franklin Plaza** located at 17th and Race Streets Philadelphia PA 19103 Tel: (215) 448-2000 expect to pay $70-$250. **Radisson Plaza - Warwick Hotel Philadelphia** is a National Register of Historic Places site, located at 1701 Locust Street Philadelphia PA 19103 toll-free (800) 523-4210 expect to pay $200-$250.

New Jersey (NJ)

Capital: Trenton (Population: 8,414,350)
Size: 8,722 sq mi. (22,589 sq km)
Nickname: The Garden State
Joined the union on: December 18, 1787 (3rd state)
Motto: Liberty and Prosperity
Flower: Purple Violet
Bird: Eastern Goldfinch
Song: None
Famous for: Drive in theater
Major industries: Chemicals, oil refinery, machinery, fashion, and tourism

Trenton (NJ)

Trenton is the state capital of New Jersey and is located in west central New Jersey on the Delaware River. It has a land area of 4.6 sq. miles (12 sq. kilometers) and a population of more than 85,000. Trenton was founded in 1680 and it was originally named The Falls.

Places of interest: the Trent House built in 1719 is the oldest in Trenton, the house is located at 15 Market St. Trenton, NJ Tel: (609) 989-3027; the New Jersey State Museum, located at 205 W. State St. Trenton, NJ Tel: (609) 292-6464, has seasonal exhibits and houses a planetarium; and the only surviving British barracks in the US, the Old Barracks Museum is located on Barrack St. Trenton, NJ Tel: (609) 396-1776.

Trenton's train depot is located at 72 S. Clinton Ave. Trenton, NJ 08609. The station is staffed and features an enclosed waiting area, quik-trak ticket machines, restrooms, payphones, and a snack bar. Transportation options from the station include local transit and taxi services.

Trains serving Trenton station are the Twilight Shoreliner, Vermonter, Metroliner, Acela Express, Acela Regional, Carolinian and Piedmont, Northeast Direct, Silver Service, Three Rivers, Keystone, and the Crescent.

Newark (NJ)

Newark is located just 8 miles west of New York City and 46 miles northeast of Trenton. Newark has a land area of 23 sq. miles (61.6 sq. kilometers) and a population of 273,546. Newark has the largest Portuguese community in the US, is the most populous city in New Jersey, and is the third oldest major city in the US. It was founded by the Puritans in 1666.

Newark's train depot is located at Raymond Plaza West Newark, NJ 07102. The station is staffed and features an enclosed waiting area, checked baggage service, restrooms, payphones, and a snack bar. Transportation options from the station include local transit, bus, and taxi services.

Trains serving Newark station are the Carolinian and Piedmont, Northeast Direct, Three Rivers, Silver Service, Metroliner, Crescent, Vermonter, Twilight Shoreliner, Keystone, and the Acela Express.

New York (NY) See Lake Shore Limited- Albany to New York service, page 405.
Connecting Train to **Washington D.C., Philadelphia (PA), Baltimore (MD)**

Capitol Limited

7:00 pm-**D**	**Chicago (IL)**	8:40 am-**A**
8:53 pm	Hammond Whiting (IN)	6:01 am
10:01 pm	South Bend (IN)	4:52 am
12:28 am-A 12:43 am-D	Toledo (OH)	4:40 am-D 4:16 am-A
2:00 am	Elyria (OH)	2:35 am
2:26 am-A 2:30 am-D	**Cleveland (OH)**	2:05 am-D 2:00 am-A
3:39 am	Alliance (OH)	12 :59 am
5 :40 am-A 6 :00 am -D	**Pittsburgh (PA)***	11 :20 pm D 11 :01 pm-A
7 :39 am	Connellsville (PA)	9 :00 pm
10 :06 am	Cumberland (MD)	6:31 pm
11:35 am	Martinsburg (WV)	5:00 pm
12:00 N	Harpers Ferry (WV)	4:31 pm
12:45 pm	Rockville (MD)	3:44 pm
1:45 pm-**A**	**Washington D.C****	3:20 pm-**D**

D-Departure   **A**- Arrival

*Connecting Train to New York (NY)
--Pittsburgh (PA) --Philadelphia (PA) --**New York (NY)**

**Connecting Train to New York (NY)
--**Washington D.C** --Baltimore (MD) --Philadelphia (PA) --**New York (NY)**

**Connecting Train to Miami (FL)
--**Washington D.C** --Savannah (GA) --**Jacksonville (FL)** --**Orlando (FL)** --**West Palm Beach (FL)** --**Miami (FL)**

Capitol Limited

The Capitol Limited takes travelers to some of most beautiful sceneries, historical towns, and great cities of the Eastern United States. The Capitol Limited links the states of **Illinois, Indiana, Ohio, Pennsylvania, West Virginia, Maryland**, and the **District of Columbia**. The Capitol Limited uses the bi-level Superliner cars with wider seats and luxurious sleeping cars.

Route Destination and Highlights

Chicago, IL- Home to America's tallest building Sears Tower, visit the Museum of Science and Industry and other outstanding museums; admire the charming Centennial Fountain and take a romantic stroll along Lake Michigan; and enjoy Chicago's attractive and busy nightlife.

South Bend, IN- Visit the University of Notre Dame, the Northern Indiana Center for History, and the Studebaker National Museum.

Toledo, OH- Visit the only Plateresque architecture in the world, the Queen of the Most Holy Rosary Cathedral; shop for your Christmas gifts and trimmings at the Christmas Manor; or take the 1880 streetcar Historic Toledo/Maumee Group Trolley Tour and explore the old town of Toledo.

Cleveland, OH- See the Rock and Roll Hall of Fame and Museum, the International Women's Air & Space Museum dedicated to the success of women in aviation history, the rare car exhibits of the Crawford Auto-Aviation Museum, the Dunham Tavern Museum that depicts life of the early settlers in Cleveland, or the NASA John Glenn Research Center and the WWII submarine USS Cod.

Pittsburgh, PA- Visit one of the best observatories in the world the Allegheny Observatory; the English Gothic Tudor mansion and gardens of Hartwood; the Pittsburgh Zoo & Aquarium home to thousands of animals and housing the Asian Forest, the African Savanna, and Kids Kingdom; the Carnegie Museum of Art and the Carnegie Science Center; and the Rodef Shalom Biblical Botanical Garden that exhibits plants related to bible and plants with biblical names.

Washington, DC- The capital city of the US, explore the National Mall and visit the United States Capitol Building, the Library of Congress, the Washington Monument, Vietnam Veterans Memorial, Thomas Jefferson Memorial, and the Lincoln Memorial. Take a tour of the White House or visit the world's largest office building the Pentagon. Shop at the Eastern Market, explore the Union Station, see the world's largest chair, or visit Georgetown University and George Washington University. Washington D.C. has it all!

Scenery along the Route

From the state of Indiana to the capital city of Washington D.C. the views are dominated by breathtaking landscape with scenery of greenery, hills, mountains, rivers, and fields. The Capitol Limited follows the original B&O rail line that takes passengers to some of the most beautiful landscapes of the eastern United States.

Train Schedules

The Capitol Limited travels daily from Chicago, Illinois to Washington D.C. The trip between the two cities takes approximately 19 hours of travel time.

Accommodations

Accommodations are Superliner Reserved Coach and Superliner Sleeping Car. There is a Lounge Car that has a Bistro located on the first level that serves local cuisine, snacks, soups, sandwiches, and drinks. Restaurant style meals are served in the Dining Car. Other amenities include movies, rail phones, and electrical outlets. Bicycle storage rooms are available.

All Aboard!

Chicago (IL) See Illinois and Missouri service, page 268.

Hammond-Whiting (IN) See Michigan- International service, page 344- 347.

South Bend (IN)

South Bend is the fourth largest city in Indiana, located in north-central Indiana just 10 miles south of the Michigan and Indiana border, 96 miles east of Chicago. South Bend has a land area of 36.6 sq. miles (94 sq. kilometers) and a population of 105,511.

Places of interest: Northern Indiana Center for History, located at 808 West Washington South Bend, IN 46601 Tel: (574) 235-9664, is a Victorian mansion exhibiting South Bend history. Studebaker National Museum, located at 525 South Main St. South Bend, IN 46601 Tel: (574) 235-9714, exhibits transportation history.

South Bend's train depot is located at 2702 W. Washington Ave. South Bend, IN 46628. The station is staffed and features an enclosed waiting area, checked baggage service, restrooms, payphones, and vending machines. Transportation from the station is local taxi service.

Trains serving South Bend station are the Capitol Limited, Lake Shore Limited, and the Pennsylvanian.

Waterloo (IN) See Lakeshore Limited service, page 393- 395.

Ohio (OH)
Capital: Columbus (Population: 11,353,140)
Size: 44,828 sq mi. (116,104 sq km)
Nickname: The Buckeye State
Joined the union on: March 1, 1803 (17th state)
Motto: With God, all things are possible
Flower: Scarlet carnation
Bird: Cardinal
Song: Beautiful Ohio
Famous for: The first airplane
Major industries: Manufacturing, jet engines and metal products.

Toledo (OH)

Toledo is located along the border of the states of Michigan and Ohio at Lake Erie. It has a land area of 81 sq. miles (208.6 sq. kilometers) and a population of almost half a million.

Toledo's economy mainly depends on automotive assembly and parts production and manufacturing industries. In addition, the Port of Toledo is one of the busiest on the Great Lakes/Saint Lawrence Seaway system. Toledo was voted in 1998 as an All-American city.

Toledo's train depot is located at 415 Emerald Ave. Toledo, OH 43602. The station is staffed and features an enclosed waiting area, checked baggage service, restrooms, payphones, and vending machines. Transportation options from the station include local transit and taxi services.

Trains serving Toledo station are the Capitol Limited, Lake Shore Limited, and the Pennsylvanian.

Places to See and Things to Do

Visit the **Farmers Market** located at 525 Market St, Toledo, OH 43602 Tel: (419) 255-6765 or the **Erie Street Market** located at 237 South Erie Street, Toledo, Ohio 43697 Tel: (419) 936-3743 for local produce and crafts. **Christmas Manor** located at 317 W Butler Street Bryan OH 43506 Tel: (419) 636-3082 opens only during the months of October, November, and December. Christmas Manor has thousands of Christmas trimmings and gifts. **The Toledo Zoo** houses more than 4000 animals, located at 2700 Broadway Street Toledo OH 43609 Tel: (419) 385-5721. **Toledo Botanical Garden** is located at 5403 Elmer Dr, Toledo, OH 43615 Tel: (419) 936-2986.

Visit the only Plateresque architecture in the world, the **Queen of the Most Holy Rosary Cathedral** Tel: (419) 244-9575 located near the Toledo Museum of Art in the heart of the Old West End. Visit the **Historic Old West End** which features some of the most beautiful Victorian houses in the US. **Historic Toledo/Maumee Group Trolley Tours** offers a street tour of downtown Toledo using TARTA's 1880 streetcar replica. Call Tel: (419) 245-5225 for information. **Rutherford B. Hayes Presidential Center** is the largest presidential library in the US. It is also the site of 19th US President Rutherford B. Hayes graveyard. The center is located at 1337 Hayes Ave, Fremont, OH 43420 toll-free (800) 998-7737.

Toledo Firefighters Museum exhibits firefighter equipment, the museum is located at 918 Sylvania Ave, Toledo, OH 43612 Tel: (419) 478-3473. **The Toledo Museum of Art** exhibits some of the finest collections of ancient civilization in the US. The museum is located at 2445 Monroe St, Toledo, OH 43620 Tel: (419) 255-8000. **Toledo, Lake Erie & Western Railway & Museum, Inc.** offers train trips along Toledo, Lake Erie and Western Railways. Call Tel: (419) 255-7100 for information. **S.S. Willis B. Boyer Maritime Museum** located at 26 Main St, Toledo, OH 43605, Tel: (419) 936-3070.

COSI is located in downtown Toledo on the riverfront at 1 Discovery Way Toledo, OH 43604 Tel: (419) 244-2674. There many things to learn and discover at the COSI Discovery. **Sauder Farm & Craft Village** depicts 1800's rural Ohio, features live craftsmen, blacksmiths, and many more. The village is located on State Rte. 2, Archbold, OH 43502 toll-free (800) 590-9755. **Sandpiper Canal Boat**, 2144 Fordway, Toledo, OH 43606 Tel: (419) 537-1212, is a replica of an 1850's Miami & Erie canal boat offering lunch or dinner cruises. **Maumee Brewing Company** is a German Brew Pub/Restaurant that produces lagers, ales, and specialty brews located in the Historic Oliver House at 27 Broadway, Toledo, OH 43602 Tel: (419) 243-1302.

Accommodations

Clarion Hotel Westgate located at 3536 Secor Road Toledo OH 43606 Tel: (419) 535-7070 expect to pay $50-$350. **Days Inn Toledo** located at 1800 Miami Street Toledo OH 43605 toll-free (800) DAYS INN expect to pay $50-$100. **Hilton Toledo** located at 3100 Gendale Avenue Toledo OH 43614 Tel: (419) 381-6800. **Wyndham Hotel Toledo** located at 2 Summit Street Toledo OH 43604 Tel: (419) 241-1411. **Holiday Inn Toledo** located at 2340 South Reynolds Road Toledo OH 43614 Tel: (419) 865-1361 expect to pay $50-$150.

Hampton Inn and Suites Toledo North located at 5865 Hagman Road Toledo OH 43612 Tel: (419) 727-8725 expect to pay $80-$200. **Red Roof Inn Toledo Secor Westgate** located at 3530 Executive Parkway Toledo OH 43606 toll-free (800) RED-ROOF expect to pay $50-$80. **Comfort Inn North** located at 445 East Alexis Road Toledo OH 43612 toll-free (800) 228-5150 expect to pay $50-$150.

Elyria (OH)

Elyria is located 22 miles west of Cleveland and 107 miles northeast of Columbus. It has a land area of 19 sq. miles (50 sq. kilometers) and a population of approximately 60,000.

Elyria's train depot is located at 410 E. River Rd. Elyria, OH 44035. The station is un-staffed and features an enclosed waiting area, restrooms, and payphones. Transportation options from the station include local transit and taxi services.

Trains serving Elyria station are the Capitol Limited, Lake Shore Limited, and the Pennsylvanian.

Cleveland (OH)

Cleveland is located in northeastern Ohio along the shore of Lake Erie. It has a land area of 77.6 sq. miles (199 sq. kilometers) and a population of roughly half a million. Moses Cleaveland founded the town of Cleaveland in 1796, and later the named was changed to Cleveland just to fit the name in the local Gazette by removing one letter. When the Ohio and Erie Canal was completed in 1832, Cleveland's economic and population growth increased dramatically. Many of today's large companies trace their roots to Cleveland.

The town of Cleveland was an important part of the slave underground railroad system. Many slaves who were able to reach the port of Cleveland made it to Canada for freedom.

Getting Around

Airport

Cleveland Hopkins International Airport, 5300 Riverside Drive, Terminal Building, Cleveland, Ohio 44135 Tel: (216) 265-6000 is located 10 miles (16 kilometers) southwest of Cleveland. Major car rental companies are located in off-site consolidated car hire areas on the baggage claim level. RTA Rapid Metro Train Tel: (216) 566-5227 red line connects the airport to Cleveland.

Bus

The Regional Transit Authority Tel: (216) 621-9500 operates local bus service and rapid service in Cleveland and the rest of the region. Bus fare is $1.25. Greyhound, Chester Avenue at East 13th Street Tel: (216) 781-1400, connects Cleveland and the rest of the country.

Taxi

Amerycab Tel: (216) 881-1111, Ace Taxi Service Tel: (216) 361-4700, Yellow Cab Co. of Cleveland Tel: (216) 623-1550, Southwest Cabs Tel: (440) 237-3100, and North East Cab Co. Tel: (440) 953-0000.

Rent-A-Car

Hertz Car Rental toll-free (800) 654-3131, Alamo Rent a Car toll-free (800) 327-9633, Budget Rent A Car toll-free (800) 233-3416, Dollar Rent A Car toll-free (800) 800-4000, Thrifty Car Rental toll-free (800) 367-2277, Avis Rent a Car toll-free (800) 831-2847, and Enterprise Rent-A-Car toll-free (800) 325-8007.

Train and Commuter

Trolley Tours of Cleveland Tel: (216) 771-4484 offers a 20-mile historic city tour, call for information.

Cleveland's train depot is located at 200 Clev. Mem. Shoreway Cleveland, OH 44114. The station is staffed and features an enclosed waiting area, checked baggage services, restrooms, payphones, and vending machines. Transportation options from the station include rental car, local transit, and taxi services.

Trains serving Cleveland train station are the Capitol Limited, Lake Shore Limited, and the Pennsylvanian.

Visitor Information Center

Cleveland Visitor Information Center, East Bank of the Flats at 1170 Old River Road beneath the Main Avenue Bridge Tel: (216) 621-2218.

Cleveland Visitor Information Center, Tower City Center at 50 Public Square, rotunda of Terminal Tower Tel: (216) 621-7981.

Cleveland Visitor Information Center, Star Plaza & C-tix discount tickets adjacent from Playhouse Square Center at 1302 Euclid Avenue Tel: (216) 771-9118.

Places to See and Things to Do

City of Cleveland Greenhouse, Rockefeller Park located at 750 E. 88th St. Cleveland, OH Tel: (216) 664-3103. **Botanical Garden** located at 11030 East Blvd Cleveland, OH Tel: (216) 721-1600. **Great Lakes Science Center** located at 601 Erie side Avenue Cleveland, Ohio 44114 Tel: (216) 694-2000; the science center has hands-on exhibits and educational programs. **NASA John Glenn Research Center** located at 21000 Brookpark Road, Cleveland Tel: (216) 433-4000. **USS Cod** located at North Marginal Drive, Cleveland Tel: (216) 566-8770, the national historic landmark is a WWII submarine on display.

The Cleveland Museum of Art exhibits more than 30,000 works of art from the masters. The museum is located at 11150 East Blvd. Cleveland, OH Tel: (216) 421-7340. **Museum of Natural History** houses the Reinberger Hall of Earth and Planetary Exploration, planetarium, an observatory, and more. The museum is located at 1 Wade Oval Cleveland, OH Tel: (216) 231-4600. **Children's Museum** located at 10730 Euclid Ave. Cleveland, OH Tel: (216) 791-5437 features hands-on exhibits for children.

Rock and Roll Hall of Fame and Museum located at 1 Key Plaza Cleveland, OH 44114 Tel: (216) 781-7625 features rock n' roll films, music, and much more. **Cleveland Center for Contemporary Art** located at 8501 Carnegie Avenue, Cleveland Tel: (216) 421-8671. **Polka Hall of Fame** located at Shore Cultural Center, 291 E. 222nd St, Euclid Tel: (216) 261-FAME, features polka artists. **Cleveland Metroparks Zoo** located at 3900 Brookside Park Dr. Cleveland, OH 44109 Tel: (216) 661-6500; the zoo is home to more than 3,000 animals.

International Women's Air & Space Museum, located in Burke Lakefront Airport terminal building at 1501 N. marginal Road, Cleveland Tel: (216) 623-1111, exhibits the success of women in aviation history. Crawford Auto-Aviation Museum, located at 10825 East Blvd, Cleveland Tel: (216) 721-5722, exhibits rare cars and other interesting modes of transportation. Dunham Tavern Museum, located at 6709 Euclid Avenue, Cleveland Tel: (216) 431-1060, depicts the life of the early settlers of Cleveland. Lake View Cemetery is located at 12316 Euclid Avenue, Cleveland Tel: (216) 421-2687; the graveyard is considered an outdoor historical museum cemetery. Western Reserve Historical Society, located at 10825 East Blvd, Cleveland Tel: (216) 721-5722, houses a Research Library, the Crawford Auto-Aviation Museum, and the History Museum.

Accommodations

Hilton Cleveland South located at 6200 Quarry Lane Cleveland OH 44131 Tel: (216) 447-1300 expect to pay $50-$200. Sheraton Cleveland City Center Hotel located in downtown Cleveland at 777 St. Clair Avenue Cleveland OH 4114 toll-free (800) 325-3535 expect to pay $100-$350. Hyatt Regency Cleveland at the Arcade located at 420 Superior Avenue Cleveland OH 44114 toll-free (800) 233-1234 expect to pay $80-$350. Wyndham Cleveland Hotel Playhouse Square located in center of Cleveland's business and entertainment districts at 1260 Euclid Avenue Cleveland OH 44115 Tel: (216) 615-7500 expect to pay $70-$250.

Holiday Inn Cleveland Mayfield located at 780 Beta Drive Cleveland OH 44143 Tel: (440) 461-9200 expect to pay $70-$150. Embassy Suites Cleveland Downtown located at 1701 East 12th Street Cleveland OH 44114 Tel: (216) 523-8000 expect to pay $80-$250. Hilton Garden Inn Cleveland Airport located at 4900 Emerald Court S.W. Cleveland OH 44135 Tel: (216) 898-1898 expect to pay $60-$150. Sheraton Airport Hotel located at 5300 Riverside Drive Cleveland OH 44135 toll-free (800) 325-3535 expect to pay $80-$250.

Marriott Cleveland Airport located at 4277 West 150th Street Cleveland OH 44135 toll-free (800) MARRIOTT expect to pay $60-$200. Inter-Continental Suite Hotel Cleveland Clinic located near downtown at 8800 Euclid Avenue Cleveland OH 44106 Tel: (216) 707-4300 expect to pay $100-$350. The Ritz-Carlton Cleveland located in downtown at 1515 West Third Street Cleveland OH 44113 toll-free (800) 241-3333 expect to pay $150-$450. Renaissance Cleveland Hotel Tower City Center located at 24 Public Square Cleveland OH 44113 toll-free (800) HOTELS-1 expect to pay $80-$300.

Alliance (OH)

Alliance is located 56 miles southeast of Cleveland and 84 miles northwest of Pittsburgh. It has a land area of 8.4 sq. miles (21.6 sq. kilometers) and a population of approximately 24,000.

Alliance's train depot is located at Main and Webb Sts. Alliance, OH 44601. The station is un-staffed and features payphones.

Trains serving Alliance station are the Capitol Limited and the Pennsylvanian.

Pittsburgh (PA)

Pittsburgh is located in western Pennsylvania 165 miles west of Harrisburg. It has a land area of 34 sq. Miles (89 sq. kilometers) and a population of approximately 350,000. Pittsburgh was founded in 1758 and named after the British statesman, William Pitt; the city was incorporated in 1816. Pittsburgh was an industrial city during the 1800's and was called the "Smoky City" by many. Today Pittsburgh is the US's 13th largest city and is visited by more than 3.9 million tourists each year.

Pennsylvania (PA)

Capital: Harrisburg (Population: 12,281,054)
Size: 46,058 sq mi. (119,290 sq km)
Nickname: The Keystone State
Joined the union on: December 12, 1787 (2nd state)
Motto: Virtue, liberty, and independence
Flower: Mountain laurel
Bird: Ruffed grouse
Song: Pennsylvania
Major industries: Metal industries, machinery and chemicals.

Getting Around

Airport

Pittsburgh International Airport, Landside Terminal Suite 4000 P.O. Box 12370 Pittsburgh, PA 15231 Tel: (412) 472-3525 is located 16 miles west of downtown Pittsburgh. There are major rental car services on the baggage claim level. Local taxi and bus connect the airport to Pittsburgh and the outlying areas.

Bus

Port Authority Transit (PAT) Tel: (412) 442-2000 provides local bus services in Pittsburgh and the rest of the area. Basic fare is $1.95.

Taxi

Checker Cab-Pittsburgh Tel: (412) 381-5600 and Yellow Cab Co. of Pittsburgh Tel: (412) 665-8100.

Rent-A-Car

Alamo rent-a-car toll-free (800) 327-9633, Budget rent-a-car toll-free (800) 527-0700, Avis rent-a-car Tel: (412) 472-5200, Hertz rent-a-car toll-free (800) 654-3131, Enterprise rent-a-car Tel: (412) 472-3490, Thrifty rent-a-car Tel: (412) 472-5288, National rent-a-car Tel: (412) 472-5045, and Dollar rent-a-car toll-free (800) 800-4000.

Train and Commuter

Pittsburgh's train depot is located at 1100 Liberty Ave. Pittsburgh, PA 15222. The station is staffed and features an enclosed waiting area, checked baggage service, restrooms, payphones, and vending machines. Transportation options from the station include local bus, transit, and taxi services.

Trains serving Pittsburgh station are the Capitol Limited, Pennsylvanian, and the Three Rivers.

Visitor Information Center

<u>Pittsburgh Visitor and Convention Information</u>, Greater Pittsburgh, PA Convention and Visitor Bureau, Four Gateway Center 1800 Pittsburgh, PA 15222 Tel: (412) 281-7711 or toll-free (800) 359-0758.

Places to See and Things to Do

One of the best observatories in the world, the **Allegheny Observatory,** is located at Riverview Park Pittsburgh PA 15214 Tel: (412) 321-2400; the area surrounding the observatory has several recreational activities. **Hartwood,** located at 215 Saxonburg Blvd Pittsburgh, PA Tel: (412) 767-9200, features the English Gothic Tudor mansion and gardens.

Pittsburgh Zoo & Aquarium located at One Wild Place Pittsburgh, PA 15206 Tel: (412) 665-3640. The zoo and aquarium is home to thousand of animals: it houses the Asian Forest, the African Savanna, Kids Kingdom, and many others. **Pittsburgh Children's Museum** located at 10 Children's Way, Allegheny Square Pittsburgh, PA 15212 Tel: (412) 322-5058. The museum has Hands-on exhibits, arts, and other educational entertainment.

Carnegie Museum of Natural History, located at 4400 Forbes Ave Pittsburgh, PA 15213 Tel: (412) 622-3131, exhibits history of earth's natural inhabitants. **Carnegie Museum of Art,** located at 4400 Forbes Avenue Pittsburgh, PA 15213 Tel: (412) 622-3131, exhibits modern works of art and was the first contemporary art museum in the US. **Carnegie Science Center** located at One Allegheny Avenue Pittsburgh, PA 15212 Tel: (412) 237-3400. The center features hands-on exhibits, a planetarium, WWII submarine tour, and Omnimax Theater.

Rodef Shalom Biblical Botanical Garden, located at 4905 Fifth Avenue Pittsburgh PA 15213 Tel: (412) 621-6566, exhibits plants that are related to the Bible and plants with biblical names. **Phipps Conservatory and Botanical Gardens,** located at One Schenley Park Pittsburgh, PA 15213-3830 Tel: (412) 622-6914, features a Victorian glass house. **Pittsburgh Theological Seminary: Bible Lands Museum** located at 616 North Highland Ave. Pittsburgh, PA Tel: (412) 362-5610.

Other places of interest: **The University of Pittsburgh** located at Bigelow Blvd, 5th Ave, Bellefield Ave. and Forbes Ave. Pittsburgh. **University Art Gallery, University of Pittsburgh** 104 Frick Fine Arts Building (412) 648-2400. **Fort Pitt Museum** located at 101 Commonwealth Place Pittsburgh, PA Tel: (412) 281-9284.

Accommodations

Marriott Pittsburgh City Center located at 112 Washington Place Pittsburgh PA 15219 Tel: (412) 471-4000 expect to pay $50-$150. **Days Inn Pittsburgh** located at 1150 Banksville Road Pittsburgh PA 15216 Tel: (412) 531-8900 expect to pay $50-$150. **Holiday Inn - Pittsburgh North Hills** located at 4859 McKnight Road Pittsburgh PA 15237 Tel: (412) 366-5200 expect to pay $50-$150. **Ramada Inn Pittsburgh** located near downtown Pittsburgh at 2898 Banksville Road Pittsburgh PA 15216 Tel: (412) 343-3000 expect to pay

$50-$100. **Econo Lodge Pittsburgh** located at 4800 Steubenville Pike Pittsburgh PA 15205 Tel: (412) 922-6900 expect to pay $30-$100.

Hilton Pittsburgh and Towers located at 600 Commonwealth Place Pittsburgh PA 15222 Tel: (412) 391-4600 expect to pay $70-$250. **Ramada Plaza Hotel** located in downtown Pittsburgh at 1 Bigelow Square Pittsburgh PA toll-free (888) 298-2054 expect to pay $50-$200. **Holiday Inn Pittsburgh International Airport** located at 1406 Beers School Road Pittsburgh PA 15108-2591 Tel: (412) 262-3600 expect to pay $50-$150. **The Westin Convention Center Pittsburgh** located at 1000 Penn Avenue Pittsburgh PA 15222 Tel: (412) 281-3700 expect to pay $70-$450. **Holiday Inn - Pittsburgh North Hills** located at 4859 McKnight Road Pittsburgh PA 15237 Tel: (412) 366-5200 expect to pay $50-$150.

Wyndham Garden Hotel - Pittsburgh University Place located at 3454 Forbes Avenue, Pittsburgh, PA 15213 Tel: (412) 683-2040. **Comfort Inn** located at 1340 Lebanon Church Rd, Pittsburgh, PA 15236 Tel: (412) 653-6600. **Hyatt Regency Pittsburgh International Airport** located at Pittsburgh, PA 15231 Tel: (724) 899-1234. **Sheraton Station Square Hotel** located at 7 Station Square Drive Pittsburgh, PA 15219 Tel: (412) 261-2000 expect to pay $70-$250. **Holiday Inn Pittsburgh Central** located in downtown at 401 Holiday Drive Pittsburgh, PA 15220 Tel: (412) 922-8100. **Days Inn** located at 6 Landings Dr, Pittsburgh, PA 15238 Tel: (412) 828-5400.

Connellsville (PA)

Connellsville is located in southwestern Pennsylvania 144 miles west of Harrisburg. It has a land area of 2.2 sq. miles (5.8 sq. kilometers) and a population of approximately 10,000. Zachariah Connell founded Connellsville in 1806 and it was incorporated as a city in 1909. At the beginning of the 20th century Connellsville was known as the coke (a solid residue of coal) capital of the world.

Ohiopyle State Park is located a few miles from Connellsville, call Tel: (724) 329-8591 for directions and other information. Youghiogheny River Trail is one of the best hiking/biking trails in the US. The trail also offers a great view of the Youghiogheny River Valley, Tel: (724) 628-5500 for information.

Connellsville's train depot is located at Front and Water St. Connellsville, PA 15425. The station is un-staffed and features an enclosed waiting area and payphones. Transportation options from the station include local transit and taxi services.

Connellsville station is served by the Capitol Limited.

Cumberland (MD)

Cumberland is located 100 miles southeast of Pittsburgh, PA and 136 miles northwest of the state capital, Annapolis. It has a land area of 8.1 sq. miles (21 sq. kilometers) and a population of 23,700.

Cumberland's train depot is located at E. Harrison St. and Queen City Dr. Cumberland, MD 21502. The station is un-staffed and features an enclosed waiting area, restrooms, and payphones. Transportation options from the station include local transit and taxi services.

Cumberland station is served by the Capitol Limited.

Martinsburg (WV)

General Adam Stephen founded Martinsburg in 1778 and the city was incorporated in 1868. Martinsburg has a land area of 4.5 sq. miles (11.6 sq. kilometers) and a population of roughly 14,000.

Martinsburg's train depot is located at 229 E. Martin St. Martinsburg, WV 25401. The station is un-staffed and features an enclosed waiting area, restrooms, and payphones. Transportation options from the station include local transit and taxi services.

Martinsburg station is served by the Capitol Limited.

Harpers Ferry (WV)

Harpers Ferry is located at the state boundaries of Maryland, Virginia, and West Virginia at the junction of the Potomac and the Shennandoah Rivers, just 50 miles from Washington D.C. It has a land area of 0.5 sq. miles (1.4 sq. kilometers) and a population of just over 300.

Harpers' train depot is located at Potomac St. Harpers Ferry, WV 25425. The station is self-serve and features an enclosed waiting area, payphone, and restrooms. Transportation from the station is local transit service.

Harpers station is served by the Capitol Limited.

Rockville (MD)

Rockville is located jus 14 miles north of Washington D.C. It has a land area of 12 sq. miles (31.4 sq. kilometers) and a population of roughly 45,000. Rockville played some important roles during the early years of the American Revolution, and today many of Rockville's old buildings and districts are still well preserved and designated as national historic landmarks. The B & O Railroad Station, West Montgomery Avenue historic district, and the Wire Hardware Company are some of the best examples.

Rockville's train depot is located at Hungerford Dr. and Park St. Rockville, MD 20850. The station is un-staffed and features payphones. Transportation options from the station include local transit and taxi services.

Rockville station is served by the Capitol Limited.

Washington D.C.

Connecting Train to: **New York (NY), Pittsburgh (PA), Philadelphia (PA), New York (NY), Baltimore (MD), Savannah (GA), Jacksonville (FL), Orlando (FL), West Palm Beach (FL) and Miami (FL)**

Washington D.C. is located on the Potomac River enclosed by the states of Virginia and Maryland. It has a land area of 61 sq. miles (157 sq. kilometers) and a population of 572,059. Washington D.C was founded in 1790. The D.C. stands for "District of Columbia" which is an administrative district created to function as the permanent US capital city. The land of what is now the District of Columbia was donated by the states of Virginia and Maryland and was designed by Major Pierre Charles L' Enfant. The land given by the state of Virginia was later returned back to Virginia.

Washington D.C. is the center of US governmental and political power. Many US historical government buildings are located in the city, such as the White House, US Capitol Building, and the Pentagon among others. Washington D.C. is also home to some of the most important US historical monuments, such as the Washington Monument, Lincoln Memorial, and the Jefferson Memorial. Each year millions of people visited the capital city, exploring the city's many national monuments, museums, and historical places.

Washington D.C. has many inexpensive accommodations, wide choices of cuisine, restaurants, and places to shop. Washington D.C. has an average temperature of 37 degrees F. (3 degrees C.) during winter, 56 degrees F. (12 degrees C.) during spring, 77 degrees F. (26 degrees C.) during summer, and 60 degrees F. (17 degrees C.) during fall.

Getting Around

Airport

Ronald Reagan Washington National Airport, Washington, DC 20001 Tel: (703) 417-8000, is located 4 miles (7 kilometers) south of Washington D.C. Major rental car companies are located in car park A area. Taxis are available at the terminal exits. Washington Flyer Express Bus serves both National and Washington Dulles airports and the Metrorail stops at terminals B and C.

Washington Dulles International Airport, Washington, DC 20041 Tel: (703) 572-2700, is located 26 miles (42 kilometers) west of Washington D.C. There are major car rental companies located at the ground transportation center on the lower level of the main terminal. Washington Flyer Taxicabs are available throughout the airport. Washington Flyer Express Bus Tel: (703) 417-8000 and Greyhound provides services to the airport and the Washington D.C. Metrorail stops at the West Falls Metro Station near the airport.

Bus

Metrobus operated by Washington Metropolitan Area Transit, 600 Fifth Street, NW Washington, DC 20001 Tel: (202) 637-7000, provides local bus services around Washington D.C. and the rest of the region. Basic fare is $1.10, $2 express-routes, and 50 cents for senior and disabled.

Taxi

Checker Cab Association Tel: (202) 398-0532, American Cab Association Tel: (202) 398-0529, DC Express Auto Shop Inc. Tel: (202) 526-5656, Gold Star Cab Company Tel: (202) 484-5555, Hill Top Cab Association Tel: (202) 529-1212, Courtesy Cabs Inc. Tel: (202) 269-2600, Elite Cab Association Tel: (202) 529-0222.

Alexandria Yellow Cab Tel: (703) 549-2500, Delta Cab Association Tel: (202) 543-0084, Empire Cab Tel: (202) 488-4844, Family Transportation Tel: (202) 291-4788, Globe Cab Company Tel: (202) 232-3700, Dial Taxicab Radio Service Tel: (202) 829-4222, City Cab Tel: (202) 269-0990, Capitol Cab Co-Op Association Tel: (202) 546-2400, Best Cab Association Tel: (202) 265-7834, Red Top of Arlington Tel: (703) 522-3333, Dulles Taxi Service Tel: (703) 481-8181.

For complains contact the D.C. Taxicab Commission, 2041 Martin Luther King Jr. Ave. SE, Washington, D.C., Tel: (202) 645-6018.

Rent-A-Car

Alamo Rent A Car toll-free (800) 327-9633, Budget Car & Truck toll-free (800) 527-0700, Enterprise Rent-A-Car toll-free (800) 227-7368, Avis Rent A Car toll-free (800) 831-2847, Harley Davidson rentals Tel: (703) 218-4004, and Thrifty Rental Car toll-free (800) 367-2277.

The State Capitol

Train and Commuter

Metrorail serving the US capital and the outlying regions is operated by Washington Metropolitan Area Transit, 600 Fifth Street, NW Washington, DC 20001 Tel: (202) 637-7000. Basic fare is from $1.50 to $3.25, there is a $5 One-Day Pass of unlimited Metrorail travel on weekdays after 9:30 am. Metrorail opens at 5:30 a.m. during weekdays and 8 am on the weekends.

Washington D.C. Union Station is located at 50 Massachusetts Ave. N.E. Washington, DC 20002. The station is staffed and features an enclosed waiting area, checked baggage service, quik-trak ticket machine, ATM machines, restrooms, payphones, restaurants, and food court. Transportation options from Union Station include Wa,hington Metropolitan Area Transit Authority Tel: (202) 637-7000 and local taxi services.

Trains serving Washington D.C. Union Station are the Acela Express, Acela Regional, Metroliner, Capitol Limited, Cardinal, Carolinian and Piedmont, Crescent, Northeast Direct, Silver Service, Vermonter, and the Twilight Shoreliner.

Visitor Information Center

DC Visitor Information Center, 1300 Pennsylvania Avenue, NW the Ronald Reagan International Trade Center Building Ground Floor Washington, DC 20004 Tel: (202) 328-4748.

Washington DC Convention and Tourism Corporation, 1212 New York Avenue, NW, Suite 600, Washington, DC 20005 Tel: (202) 789-7000.

Places to See and Things to Do

At the National Mall

Perhaps one of the most admired buildings in the US, the **United States Capitol,** is located at the east end of the National Mall Washington, DC Tel: (202) 225-6827, call for tour information. **United States Botanic Gardens,** located at the foot of Capitol Hill at First and Maryland Streets, SW Washington, DC Tel: (202) 225-8333, features exotic plants and flowers. **The Library of Congress** is known as the world's largest, it exhibits numerous American and world treasures such as

The Mall

musical instruments and compositions. The library is located at First and Independence Avenue SE, Washington, DC 20540 Tel: (202) 707-8000. **The Washington Monument** is located at Constitution Avenue and 15th Street NW, Washington, DC Tel: (202) 426-6841. Dedicated to George Washington, the first US president, it took 40 years to complete due to lack of funds; it was finally completed in 1885.

Korean War Veterans Memorial was dedicated to the American war heroes of the Korean War. The memorial features life size figures depicting the war. The memorial is located at Daniel French Drive and Independence Avenue SW, Washington, DC Tel: (202) 619-7222. **Vietnam Veterans Memorial** is a beautiful black granite wall with inscribed names of the thousands of Americans soldiers missing and killed in the Vietnam War. The memorial is located at Constitution Avenue & Henry Bacon Drive, NW Washington, DC Tel: (202) 634-1568. **Vietnam Women's Memorial is** dedicated to the women who served in the Vietnam War, the memorial is located at 21st Street and Constitution Washington, DC Tel: (202) 426-6841.

The Lincoln Memorial is located on the West end of the National Mall at 23rd Street between Constitution and Independence Avenue NW, Washington, DC Tel: (202) 426-6841. The memorial was dedicated to President Abraham Lincoln. Inside the memorial building at the center is a huge statue of president Lincoln, and on the wall is engraved Lincoln's famous Gettysburg address.

Built in 1942 to honor Thomas Jefferson the third US president, the **Thomas Jefferson Memorial** is one of the most beautiful memorials in Washington. The memorial is located at 15th Street SW on the Tidal Basin Washington, DC Tel: (202) 426-6841. **Franklin Delano Roosevelt Memorial,** located at West Potomac Park near the Lincoln memorial on Ohio Drive Washington, DC Tel: (202) 426-6841, has four outdoor galleries.

Around the City

The White House is located at 1600 Pennsylvania Ave. Washington D.C, Tel: (202) 456-7041, contact the White House Historical Association (WHHA) at 740 Jackson Place NW Washington, D.C. 20503 Tel: (202) 737-8292 for information. The **Old Post Office Pavilion** is located between the U.S. Capitol and the White House on Pennsylvania Ave. at 12th Street NW, Washington, DC 20004 Tel: (202) 289-4224. **The Pentagon** is located on I-395 South at Boundary Channel Drive exit Arlington, VA Tel: (703) 695-1776. The Pentagon is the world's largest office building and the center of the US defense intelligence. **United States Supreme Court** is located at First and East Capitol Streets, NE Washington, DC Tel: (202) 479-3499 call for court tour information.

Fort Stevens is the site where President Lincoln was besieged during the Civil War. The fort is located at 13th and Quakenbos Street, NW, Washington, DC. Founded in 1861 **Fort Dupont Park** is one of the many other forts built to defend the capital from the Confederate attack. The park is located at Randle Circle, SE, Washington, DC Tel: (202) 426-7723.

Eastern Market located at Seventh & C Streets, SE, Washington, DC Tel: (202) 546-2698 is home to several artists and talented performers; there are antique shops and other items sold along streets. Built in 1921 the **Lincoln Theatre** features musical programs, the theater is located at 1215 U Street, NW Washington, DC Tel: (202) 328-6000. **Carter Barron Amphitheater** features outdoor Shakespeare performances. The amphitheater is located on Rock Creek Park at 16th Street and Colorado Avenue, NW Washington, DC Tel: (202) 619-7222. **John F. Kennedy Center for the Performing Arts** is located at New Hampshire and F Street, NW Washington, DC Tel: (202) 416-8340.

C & O Canal located at 30th and Jefferson Streets, NW Washington, DC Tel: (202) 653-5190. This 184.5-mile canal stretches from Georgetown to Cumberland, MD and is popular both to visitors and locals alike. The Beaux architecture **Union Station** is located at 50 Massachusetts Avenue, NE Washington, DC 20002 Tel: (202) 289-1908. Built in 1908 it is one of the most popular tourist sites in Washington D.C. There are several shops, restaurants, and theaters located at the station. The Union Station is Amtrak's stop for Washington D.C.

Built to honor the thousands of law enforcement officers killed in duty is the **National Law Enforcement Officers Memorial** located in Judiciary Square between E & F Streets, 4th & 5th Streets, NW Washington, DC Tel: (202) 737-3400. **World's Largest Chair** is located in V Street and Martin Luther King, Jr. Avenue, SE Washington, DC. This 19.5-foot tall chair was a gift from Bassett Furniture Industries to honor the Curtis Brothers. **African-American Civil War Memorial** was dedicated to the African American soldiers who fought in the civil war. The memorial is located at 10th & U Streets, NW Washington, DC Tel: (202) 667-2667.

Parks and Gardens

Kenilworth Aquatic Gardens features exotic water lilies, lotuses, and wildlife. The garden is located at 1900 Anacostia Avenue and Douglas Avenue, NE Washington, DC Tel: (202) 426-6905. **Lincoln Park** is located on East Capitol Street and Massachusetts Avenue, NE between 11th and 13th Streets Washington, DC Tel: (202) 690-5155. The park exhibits beautiful statues of Mary McLeod Bethune and Abraham Lincoln. **The US National Arboretum** located at 24th and R Street, NE Washington, DC Tel: (202) 245-2726 houses a Japanese Garden, the National Bonsai Collection, and more. **National Zoological Park** is home to thousands of animals, including two pandas. The zoo is located at 3001 Connecticut Avenue, NW Washington, DC Tel: (202) 673-4717.

Historical Cemetery

The Battleground National Cemetery is located at 6625 Georgia Avenue, NW Washington, DC. The cemetery was dedicated to the union soldiers who died in defense of Washington, DC. The US first national cemetery founded in 1807 the **Historic Congressional Cemetery** is located at 1801 E Street, SE Washington, DC Tel: (202) 543-0539. **Arlington National Cemetery** is the final resting place of some of the most famous figures in the US such as the late President John F. Kennedy. The cemetery is located across Memorial Bridge, less than a mile from the Lincoln Memorial in Arlington, VA. Founded in 1895 the **Woodlawn Cemetery** is the final resting place of some famous African Americans such as John Mercer Langston and Winfield Scott Montgomery. The cemetery is located at 4611 Benning Road, SE Washington, DC.

Universities

The most predominant African American school in the world, **Howard University,** is located at 2400 6th Street, NW Washington, DC Tel: (202) 806-6100. **Southeastern University** is located at 501 I Street SW Washington, DC Tel: (202) 488-8162. **Trinity College** is located at 125 Michigan Avenue, NE Washington, DC Tel: (202) 884-9000. The oldest catholic university in the US, **Georgetown University,** is located at 37th and O Streets, NW Washington, DC Tel: (202) 687-0100. **George Washington University** is located at 2121 Eye Street Washington, DC 20052 Tel: (202) 994-1000.

Accommodations

Allen Lee Hotel located at 2224 F Street NW Washington DC 20037 Tel: (202) 331-1224 expect to pay $50-$100. **Days Inn - Washington, DC** located at 4400 Connecticut Avenue NW, Washington DC 20008 toll-free (800) 544-8313 expect to pay $50-$250. **Hilton Garden Inn Washington DC, Franklin Square** located near the White House at 815 14th Street, NW Washington DC 20005 Tel: (202) 783-7800 expect to pay $50-$350. **Clarion Hotel Hampshire** located at 1310 New Hampshire Avenue Washington DC 20036 toll-free (800) 252-7466 expect to pay $70-$250. **Courtyard Convention Center** located at 900 F Street NW Washington DC 20004 Tel: (202) 638-4600 expect to pay $50-$250.

Four Seasons Hotel located at 2800 Pennsylvania Ave. NW Washington DC 20007 Tel: (202) 342-0444 expect to pay $400-$450. **Grand Hyatt Washington** located at 1000 H Street NW Washington DC 20001 Tel: (202) 582-1234 expect to pay $100-$400. **Crownplaza Hotel** located downtown at 14th and K Streets NW Washington DC 20005 Tel: (202) 682-0111 expect to pay $80-$500. **The Hay-Adams Hotel** (with view of the White House) located at One Lafayette Square Washington DC 20006 toll-free (800) 323-7500 expect to pay $200-$700.

Holiday Inn Washington Downtown located at 1155 14th Street NW Washington DC 20005 Tel: (202) 737-1200 expect to pay $50-$280. **Hilton Washington Embassy Row** located at 2015 Massachusetts Avenue Washington DC 20036 toll-free (800) 445-8667 expect to pay $100-$300. **Doubletree Guest Suites Washington/New Hampshire Avenue** located at 801 New Hampshire Avenue, NW Washington DC 20037 Tel: (202) 785-2000 expect to pay $100-$250.

Morrison-Clark Inn located six miles from the National Airport at 1015 L Street Northwest Washington DC 20001 Tel: (202) 898-1200 expect to pay $80-$250. **Holiday Inn Capitol at the Smithsonian** located at 550 C Street, SW Washington DC 20024 Tel: (202) 479-4000 expect to pay $100-$250. **City Center Hotel** located near the METRO Station at 1143 New Hampshire Avenue Washington DC 20037 Tel: (202) 775-0800 expect to pay $70-$250.

Hyatt Regency Washington DC on Capitol Hill located at 400 New Jersey Avenue NW Washington DC 20001 Tel: (202) 737-1234 expect to pay $70-$400. **Park Hyatt Washington** located at 24th and M Street NW Washington DC 20037 Tel: (202) 789-1234 expect to pay $160-$500. **The Westin Grand Washington DC** located near the White House at 2350 M Street NW Washington DC 20037 Tel: (202) 429-0100 expect to pay $150-$550. **J.W Marriott Hotel on Pennsylvania** located at 1331 Pennsylvania Avenue Washington DC 20004 toll-free (800) MARRIOTT expect to pay $100-$400.

Omni Shoreham Hotel located at 2500 Calvert Street NW Washington DC 20008 Tel: (202) 234-0700 expect to pay $100-$600. **The Ritz-Carlton Washington DC** (up-scale) located at 1150 22nd Street NW Washington DC 20037 Tel: (202) 835-0500 expect to pay $100-$800. **Hotel George** located at 15 E St. NW Washington DC 20001 Tel: (202) 347-4200 expect to pay $100-$1000. **The Madison** located at 15th & M Sts. NW Washington DC 20005 toll-free (800) 424-8577 expect to pay $150-$1000.

Other Hotels: **The Washington Monarch Hotel** located at 2401 M Street NW Washington DC 20037 Tel: (202) 429-2400. **The Jefferson - Camberley Hotel** located at 1200 16th Street NW Washington DC 70036 toll-free (800) 555-8000. **The Watergate Hotel** (Historical Hotel) located at 2650 Virginia Avenue Washington DC 20037 Tel: (202) 965-2300. **Willard Inter-Continental Washington** (Historic landmark) located a few minutes from the White House at 1401 Pennsylvania Ave. NW Washington DC 20004 Tel: (202) 628-9100. **The St. Regis Washington** (up scale) located at 923 16th Street NW Washington DC 20006 Tel: (202) 638-2626.

Cardinal

	Cardinal	
7:55 pm-D	**Chicago (IL)**	8:37 am-**A**
9:07 pm	Dyer (IN)	6:49 am
9:56 pm	Rensselaer (IN)	6:05 am
11:03 pm	Lafayette (IN)	5:06 am
11:35 pm	Crawfordsville (IN)	4:32 am
12:55 am-**A**	**Indianapolis (IN)**	2:50 am-**A**
1:05 am-D		2:40 am-D
2:36 am	Connersville (IN)	1:01 am
4:41 am	Hamilton (OH)	12:55 am
5:30 am-**A**	**Cincinnati (OH)**	11:59 pm-**A**
5:39 am-D		11:56 pm-D
7:01 am	Maysville (KY)	10:29 pm
7:45 am	SO. Portsmouth SO. Shore (KY)	9:34 pm
8:29 am	Ashland (KY)	9:01 pm
8:55 am	Huntington (WV)	8:38 pm
10:02 am	**Charleston (WV)**	7:39 pm
10:31am	Montgomery (WV)	7:07 pm
11:22 am	Thurmond (WV)	6:16 pm
11:39 am	Prince (WV)	6:00 pm
12:09 pm	Hinton (WV)	5:30 pm
1:07 pm	White Sulphur Springs (WV)	4:33 pm
1:56 pm-**A**	Clifton Forge (VA)	3:41 pm-**A**
2:01 pm-D		3:38 pm-D
3:31 pm	Stauton (VA)	12:15 pm
4:47 pm	**Charlotttesville (VA)**	1:13 pm
5:52 pm	Culpeper (VA)	12:02 pm
6:27 pm	Manassas (VA)	11:29 am
7:11 pm	Alexandria (VA)	10:54 am
7:45 pm-**A**	**Washington D.C ***	10:35 am-**D**

D-Departure   **A**- Arrival

*Connecting Train to New York (NY)

--**Washington D.C**
--New Carrollton (MD)
--BWI Airport (MD)
--Baltimore (MD)
--Wilmington (DE)
--Philadelphia (PA)
--Trenton (NJ)
--Newark (NJ)
--**New York (NY)**

Cardinal

The Cardinal brings passengers to some of the most scenic landscape, towns, and cities of the southeastern United States. It links the states of **Illinois**, **Indiana, Ohio, Kentucky, West Virginia, Virginia,** and the nation's capital **Washington D.C**.

The Cardinal covers more than 900 miles of beautiful scenery along the Ohio River and the lovely countryside of the state of West Virginia. It uses the double deck Superliner cars.

Route Destination Highlights

Chicago, IL- Home to America's tallest building Sears Tower, visit the Museum of Science and Industry and other outstanding museums; admire the charming Centennial Fountain and take a romantic stroll along lake Michigan; and enjoy Chicago's attractive and busy nightlife.

Indianapolis, IN- Visit the Indianapolis Motor Speedway which has the largest collection of racing cars, vintage cars, and racing memorabilia in the US; the National Art Museum of Sport which exhibits the largest sports art collection in the US; Hoosier Park and Indianapolis Raceway Park are some of the best multi-purpose motor sports facilities in the world. Visit the Indiana Basketball Hall of Fame, the Historic State Capitol, Medal of Honor Memorial and Indiana War Memorial, or relax and enjoy performances of the Indianapolis Jazz Orchestra and the Indianapolis Symphony Orchestra, recognized as one of the best in the US.

Cincinnati, OH- Visit the restored 19th century German neighborhood MainStrasse Village, the first observatory in the US Mt. Lookout Observatory, or the William Howard Taft Birthplace. Take the Turtle Creek Valley Railway train tour around the southwestern Ohio countryside or visit the National Railway Historical Society Library and Museum. Explore the Ohio River and take the B&B Riverboats cruise or try your luck at Caesars Indiana Riverboat Casino.

Charlottesville, VA- Visit the Monticello home of President Thomas Jefferson, and the home of James Monroe.

Alexandria, VA- Visit the Home of General Robert E. Lee, the Alexandria Archaeology Museum, and the Stabler-Leadbeater Apothecary Shop Museum. Learn about the history of Alexandria's African-American community at the Black History Resource Center or see the Masonic National Memorial and the Torpedo Factory Art Center.

Washington, DC- The capital city of the US, explore the National Mall and visit the United States Capitol Building, the Library of Congress, the Washington Monument, Vietnam Veterans Memorial, Thomas Jefferson Memorial, and the Lincoln Memorial. Take a tour of the White House or visit the world's largest office building the Pentagon. Shop at the Eastern Market, explore the Union Station, see the world's largest chair, or visit Georgetown University and George Washington University. Washington D.C. has it all!

Scenery along the Route

The Cardinal will take you to some of the most alluring scenery of the eastern United States, the landscape of Indiana is dominated by farmland; from Cincinnati you will explore the beauty of the mighty Ohio River. West Virginia is a land of endless natural beauty where you will explore the enchanting view of the Allegheny Mountains, wild white-water rivers and falls, Blue Ridge, Shenandoah Valley, historic towns, cities, and grasslands.

Train Schedules

The Cardinal travels three times weekly from Chicago, Illinois to Washington D.C. The trip between the two cities takes approximately 23 hours of travel time.

Accommodations

Accommodations are Reserved Coach and Sleeping Car. There is a Lounge and Cafe car that serves local cuisine, snacks, soups, sandwiches, and drinks and on-board entertainment and scenic commentary. A Dining Car serves complete meals.

All Aboard!

Chicago (IL) See Illinois and Missouri service, page 268.

Dyer (IN) See Kentucky Cardinal service, page 363- 364.

Rensselaer (IN) See Kentucky Cardinal Service, page 363- 364.

449

Lafayette (IN) See Kentucky Cardinal Service, page 363- 364.

Crawfordsville (IN) See Kentucky Cardinal Service, page 363- 364.

Indianapolis (IN) See Kentucky Cardinal Service, page 364

Indiana (IN)

Capital: Indianapolis
(Population: 6,080,485)
Size: 36,420 sq mi. (94,327 sq km)
Nickname: The Hoosier State
Joined the union on: December 11, 1816 (19th state)
Motto: The Crossroads of America
Flower: Peony
Bird: Cardinal
Song: On the Banks of the Wabash
Famous for: Racing Car, David Letterman
Major industries: Minerals, Oil

Connersville (IN)

Connersville is located 57 miles (92 kilometers) east of Indianapolis and is the seat of Fayette County. It has a land area of 7.4 sq. miles (19 sq. kilometers) and a population of 15,550. It was John Conner who first established a trading post at the site of what is now the city of Connersville in 1808.

It was here in Connersville where the first high school band and industrial park in the US was established. Today Connersville is known as "Little Detroit" due to the city's many auto parts manufacturing companies. Indiana's most scenic railroad the Whitewater Valley Railroad, P.O. Box 406 Connersville, Indiana 47331 Tel: (765) 825-2054, offers guided scenic tours around the region.

Connersville's train depot is located at 1012 Eastern Ave. Connersville, IN 47331. The station is un-staffed and features payphones. Transportation from the station is local taxi service.

The Cardinal serves Connersville station.

Hamilton (OH)

Hamilton is located in the southwestern corner of the State of Ohio, north of the city of Cincinnati. It has a land area of 261 sq. miles (670 sq. kilometers) and a population of 845,268. The development and growth of Hamilton was closely associated with that of the city of Cincinnati. Hamilton County was named after Alexander Hamilton in 1790.

Hamilton's train depot is located at M. L. King Blvd. at Henry St. Hamilton, OH 45012. The station is un-staffed. Transportation options from the station include local transit and taxi services.

The Cardinal serves Hamilton station.

Ohio (OH)

Capital: Columbus (Population: 11,353,140)
Size: 44,828 sq mi. (116,104 sq km)
Nickname: The Buckeye State
Joined the union on: March 1, 1803 (17th state)
Motto: With God, all things are possible
Flower: Scarlet carnation
Bird: Cardinal
Song: Beautiful Ohio
Famous for: The first airplane
Major industries: Manufacturing, jet engines and metal products.

450

Cincinnati (OH)

Home of the 27th President of the United States, William Howard Taft, Cincinnati is located along the Great Ohio River it the southwestern corner of the state of Ohio just 104 miles southwest of the state capital Columbus. Cincinnati has a land area of 78 sq. miles (200 sq. kilometers) and a population of less than half a million.

Cincinnati was founded in 1790; the early growth of the city was attributed to the construction of the Miami and Erie Canals in the 1820's. The city population grew gradually and many new businesses flourished and efficient movement of goods became possible. By early 1800's the city of Cincinnati became the world's largest pork packaging center and gained the title, "The Porkopolis."

Cincinnati has an average high temperature of 76 degrees F (24 degrees C), average low temperature of 31 degrees F (1 degree C) and an average annual rainfall of 40 inches.

Getting Around

Airport

Cincinnati-Northern Kentucky International Airport, PO Box 752000, Cincinnati, Ohio 45275 Tel: (859) 767-3151, is located 13 miles (20 kilometers) southwest of Cincinnati. Local taxis are available at every terminal and can be arranged at the airport taxi desk located near the terminal exits. Taxi fare from the airport to downtown Cincinnati costs approximately $24. Jet Port Express Shuttle provides services from the airport to central Cincinnati and the Kentucky River area. TANK bus services connect the airport to central Cincinnati and Covington. Major car rental companies are available at the airport terminal.

Bus

Southwest Ohio Regional Transit Authority, 1014 Vine Street Suite 2000 Cincinnati, OH 45202-1122 Tel: (513) 632-7510 and SORTA, 120 W. Fifth St, Suite 1201 Cincinnati, OH 45202 Tel: (513) 651-3020 provides local bus services around Cincinnati and nearby areas.

Taxi

Quick Service Taxi Co., Inc. Tel: (610) 434-8132 provides local taxi service around Cincinnati.

Rent-A-Car

Express Car & Truck Rental Tel: (610) 782-0850 and National Car Rental Tel: (610) 264-5535.

Train and Commuter

Cincinnati's train depot is located at 1301 Western Ave. Cincinnati, OH 45203. The station is staffed and features an enclosed waiting area, checked baggage service, restrooms, payphones, and a restaurant. Transportation from the station is local taxi service.

The Cardinal serves the Cincinnati station.

Visitor Information Center

Greater Cincinnati Convention and Visitors Bureau located at 300 West 6th St Cincinnati, OH 45202-2361 toll-free (800) CINCY-USA.

Places to See and Things to Do

MainStrasse Village is a five-block restored 19th century German neighborhood. There are shops, restaurants, and live entertainment venues in the area. The village is located in Covington, KY; Tel: (859) 491-0458. **Cathedral Basilica of the Assumption** located at 1140 Madison Ave, Covington, KY, 41011 Tel: (859) 431-2060. The cathedral basilica is one of the few basilicas in the US and has the world's largest stained glass window. **Mt. Lookout Observatory** is the first observatory in the US, located at 3489 Observatory Pl. Cincinnati, OH 45208 Tel: (513) 321-5186.

One of Cincinnati's newest attractions, the **Newport Aquarium,** features glass tunnels and more than 11,000 species of animals. Admissions are: adults $14.95, seniors $12.95, and children $8.95. The aquarium is located across the Great Ohio River in Newport at One Aquarium Way, Newport, KY, 41071 Tel: (859) 261-7444. **Cincinnati Zoo & Botanical Gardens** is home to 700 species of animals and thousands of world exotic plants. The zoo and garden is located at 3400 Vine St, Cincinnati, OH 45220 Tel: (513) 281-4700. Admissions are: adult $10, seniors $7, and children $4.75.

Ohio Renaissance Festival features 16th century England with live entertainment. The festival is located in Harveysburg, OH 45032-0068 Tel: (513) 897-7000. Admissions are: adults $13.95 and children $7. **Coney Island** features live shows, entertainment, rides, miniature golf, and shops. Coney Island is located at 6201 Kellogg Ave, Cincinnati, OH, 45228 Tel: (513) 232-8230. **Surf Cincinnati Water Park** features pools, entertainment, and sports recreation activities. The park is located at 11460 Sebring Dr, Cincinnati, OH, 45240 Tel: (513) 742-0620. Admissions are: $15 general admission, children under four feet $9.95.

Sharon Woods Village features a 19th century Ohio village. There is an old train depot, houses, barns, and entertainment. The village is located at U.S. Highway 42, Sharon Woods Park, Cincinnati, OH Tel: (513) 563-9484. Admissions are: adults $5, seniors $3, and children $2. **The Beach Water Park** features more than 30 waterslides and family entertainment, admission is $22.95. The water park is located at 2590 Water Park Dr, Mason, OH, 45040 Tel: (513) 398-2040.

Cinergy Children's Museum houses Water Works, Energy Zone, the Animal Spot, and Kids at Work. The museum is located at 1301 Western Ave, Cincinnati, OH 45203 Tel: (513) 287-7000. **Museum of Natural History and Science** exhibits geography and biology of the Ohio Valley. It houses a walk-through ice cave, Dino Hall, and more. The museum is located at 1301 Western Ave, Cincinnati, OH 45203 Tel: (513) 287-7000. **Museum Center at**

Union Terminal houses three museums, a theater, and library. The museum center is located at 1301 Western Ave, Cincinnati, OH 45203 Tel: (513) 287-7000.

The 1808 **Betts House Research Center** has temporary exhibits year-round. The center is located at 416 Clark St, Betts-Longworth Historic District Cincinnati, OH 45203 Tel: (513) 651-0734. **William Howard Taft Birthplace** has daily tours and memorabilia of the US president; there are also various yearly activities, located at 2038 Auburn Ave, Cincinnati 45219 Tel: (513) 684-3262. **Wolf Planetarium** is located on Burnet Woods, at Clifton Ave. and Martin Luther King Dr, Cincinnati, OH Tel: (513) 321-6070.

Cincinnati Fire Museum exhibits the history of Cincinnati fire control and prevention. The museum is located at 315 W. Court St, Cincinnati, OH 45202 Tel: (513) 621-5553. **National Railway Historical Society Library and Museum** exhibits model trains; the museum is located at 10151 Springfield Pike, Woodlawn, OH 45215 Tel: (513) 772-7557. Visit the **Cincinnati Railroad Club** at the Historic Tower A, fifth floor of the Museum Center Union Terminal at 1301 Western Ave, Cincinnati, OH 45203 Tel: (513) 651-7245. **Turtle Creek Valley Railway** offers train tours around the southwestern Ohio countryside. Fares are adults $10, seniors $9, children $6. Turtle Creek Valley Train Tour is located at 198 South Broadway, Lebanon, OH, 45036 Tel: (513) 398-8584.

Riverboat Cruises

B&B Riverboats offers cruises with entertainment, located at 1 Madison Ave, Covington, KY, 41011 Tel: (859) 261-8500.

Casinos

Grand Victoria Casino Resort located at 600 Grand Victoria Dr, Rising Sun, IN, 47040 toll-free (800) GRAND-11; **Caesars Indiana Riverboat Casino** located at 11999 Avenue of the Emperors, Elizabeth, IN, 47117 toll-free (877) G0-2-ROME; and **Argosy Casino** located at 777 Argosy Parkway, Lawrenceburg, IN, 47025 toll-free (888) ARGOSY-7.

Accommodations

Homewood Suites located at 2670 E Kemper Rd, Cincinnati, OH 45241 Tel: (513) 772-8888. **Embassy Suites** located at 10 East River Center Blvd, Covington, KY Tel: (606) 261-8400. **Holiday Inn** located at Cincinnati Riverfront, 800 W. 3rd Street, Covington, KY Tel: (606) 291-4300. **Econo Lodge** located at 11620 Chester Rd, Cincinnati, OH 45246 Tel: (513) 771-0370. **Days Inn** located at 2880 Central Parkway, Cincinnati, OH Tel: (513) 559-0400. **Holiday Inn** located in downtown Cincinnati at 800 W. 8th Street, Cincinnati, OH Tel: (513) 241-8660. **Westin Hotels & Resorts** located at 21 E 5th St # A, Cincinnati, OH 45202 Tel: (513) 621-7700.

Ameri Suites located at 11435 Reed Hartman Hwy, Cincinnati, OH 45241 Tel: (513) 489-3666. **Country Inn & Suites** located at 2463 E Sharon Rd, Cincinnati, OH 45241 Tel: (513) 771-9309. **Courtyard by Marriott** located at 4625 Lake Forest Dr, Cincinnati, OH 45242 Tel: (513) 733-4334. **Embassy Suites Hotel** located at 4554 Lake Forest Dr, Cincinnati, OH 45242 Tel: (513) 733-8900. **Best Western Inn** located at 11160 Dowlin Dr, Cincinnati, OH 45241 Tel: (513) 771-9080.

Holiday Inn located at 130 E Mitchell Ave, Cincinnati, OH 45217 Tel: (513) 242-1010. **Hyatt Hotels & Resorts** located at 151 W 5th St, Cincinnati, OH 45202 Tel: (513) 579-1234. **Radisson Hotel** located at 11320 Chester Rd, Cincinnati, OH 45246 Tel: (513) 772-1720. **Red Roof Inn** located at 11345 Chester Rd, Cincinnati, OH 45246 Tel: (513) 771-5141. **Omni Netherland Plaza Hotel** located at 35 W 5th St, Cincinnati, OH 45202 Tel: (513) 421-9100.

Comfort Inn located at 9011 Fields Ertel Rd, Cincinnati, OH 45249 Tel: (513) 683-9700. **Best Western Inn** located at 5901 Pfeiffer Rd, Cincinnati, OH 45242 Tel: (513) 793-4500. **Howard Johnson** located at 400 Glensprings Dr, Cincinnati, OH 45246 Tel: (513) 825-3129. **Marriott Hotels & Resorts** located at 151 Goodman St, Cincinnati, OH 45219 Tel: (513) 487-3800. **Residence Inn** located at 11401 Reed Hartman Hwy, Cincinnati, OH 45241 Tel: (513) 530-5060. **Travelodge** located at 3244 Central Pkwy, Cincinnati, OH 45225 Tel: (513) 559-1800.

Kentucky (KY)
Capital: Frankfort (Population: 4,041,769)
Size: 39,732 sq mi. (102,907 sq km)
Nickname: The Bluegrass State
Joined the union on: June 1, 1792 (15th state)
Motto: United We Stand, Divided We Fall
Flower: Goldenrod
Bird: Kentucky cardinal
Song: My Old Kentucky Home
Famous for: Abraham Lincoln, Muhammad Ali, and the Louisville Slugger
Major industries: Machinery, tourism, minerals

Maysville (KY)

Maysville is located in northeastern Kentucky at the bank of the Ohio River just 51 miles east of Cincinnati. Maysville is the county seat of Mason County; it has a land area of 9.7 sq. miles (24.9 sq. kilometers) and a population of almost 8,000.

Maysville has several stations on the Underground Railroad system used by the black slaves trying to escape to freedom. The National Underground Railroad Museum, located at 115 E. 3rd St. in Maysville, exhibits stories and facts to help visitors better understand the importance of the underground railways to the history of America's slaves.

Maysville's train depot is located at W. Front St. Maysville, KY 41056. The station is un-staffed and features an enclosed waiting area, restrooms, payphones, and restaurants. Transportation from the station is local taxi service.

The Cardinal serves Maysville station.

S. Portsmouth- S. Shore (KY)

South Shore is located in the northeastern corner of the state of Kentucky. It has a land area of 0.6 sq. miles (1.6 sq. kilometers) and a population of more than 1,000.

South Portsmouth-South Shore train depot is located on Rte. 23 at Main St. South Shore South Portsmouth, KY 41174. The station is un-staffed and features an enclosed waiting area. Transportation from the station is local taxi service.

The Cardinal serves South Shore-South Portsmouth train station.

Ashland (KY)

The Poage family founded the site of what is now the present city of Ashland in 1786. The town's development was slow until 1854 when the first plan of the city was laid out and it was called Ashland. Ashland has a land area of 10.8 sq. miles (27.8 sq. kilometers) and a population of around 25,000.

Ashland's train depot is located at 99 15th St. Ashland, KY 41101. The station is un-staffed and features an enclosed waiting area, restrooms, payphones, and vending machines. Transportation options from the station include local transit and taxi services.

The Cardinal serves Ashland station.

Huntington (WV)

Huntington is located along the Ohio River on the southwestern border of West Virginia. Huntington has a land area of 14.8 sq. miles (38 sq. kilometers) and a population of more than half a million. Collis P. Huntington founded Huntington in 1871 and in 1893 the city was incorporated.

Places of Interest

Heritage Village, located in downtown Huntington's former B & O Railway Station, features old locomotives, Pullman cars, shops, and restaurants. For information: Greater Huntington Park and Recreation District, 11th St. and Veterans Memorial Blvd. I-64 Exit 8 Tel: (304) 696-5954. The Huntington Museum of Art exhibits 19th and 20th century American and European art. The museum is located at 2033 McCoy Road. I-64 Exit 8 Tel: (304) 529-2701. Museum of Radio & Technology exhibits the largest collections of old radios and TVs in the eastern US. The museum is located at 1640 Florence Avenue WV Tel: (304) 525-8890.

Blenko Glass Company features live artisans creating handmade glassware, located in east Huntington on I-64 exit 28, Milton, WV Tel: (304) 743-9081. The Mountain State Mystery Train has year-round train tours with theatrical entertainment; the mystery train is located at 10th Street & 8th Avenue I-64 Exit 8, toll-free (800) CALL – WVA. Benjy's Harley-Davidson Motorcycle Museum located at 408 4th Street, Huntington, WV 25701. Tel: (304) 523-1340. The museum exhibits vintage motorcycles.

Huntington's train depot is located at 8th Ave. and 10th St. Huntington, WV 25701. The station is staffed and features an enclosed waiting area, checked baggage service, restrooms, and payphones. Transportation from the station is local taxi service.

The Cardinal serves Huntington station.

West Virginia (WV)	
Capital: Charleston (Population: 1,808,344)	
Size: 24,087 sq mi. (62,384 sq km)	
Nickname: The Mountain State	
Joined the union on: June 20, 1863 (35th state)	
Motto: The Mountaineers are Always Free	
Flower: Rhododendron	
Bird: Cardinal	
Song: My Home Sweet Home; The West Virginia Hills; and This is My West Virginia	
Famous for: Rugged Mountain Recreations and the Alppalachian highland culture.	
Top industries: Coal mining, chemical manufacturing and service industries.	

455

Charleston (WV)

Charleston is the capital of West Virginia with a land area of 29.6 sq. miles (76 sq. kilometers) and a population of more than half a million. Fort Lee was the first structure in Charleston built in 1788. The town of Charleston was officially founded only in 1794 named after the father of Col. George Clendenin the builder of Fort Lee. In 1885 Charleston was officially made the state capital of West Virginia. Charleston is known for its 293-foot high capitol dome glistening over the Kanawha River. The capitol was designed by one of the famous American architects of the time, Cass Gilbert.

Getting Around

Airport

Yeager Airport Charleston, 100 Airport Road - Suite 175 Charleston, WV 25311 Tel: (304) 344-8033, just an eight-minute drive from downtown Charleston.

Bus

Kanawha Valley Regional Transportation Authority, 1550 4th Ave, Charleston, WV Tel: (304) 343-3840, the KRT Tel: (304) 343-7586, and KAT (Kanawha Alternative Transit) Tel: (304) 343-0489 serves the city Charleston and the neighboring areas. Greyhound Bus Lines, 300 Reynolds Ave, Charleston Tel: (304) 357-0056 or toll-free (800) 231-2222.

Taxi

Yellow Top Cab Tel: (304) 345-7777, C & H Taxi Co Tel: (304) 344-4902, and Gary's Taxi Tel: (304) 727-9342.

Rent-A-Car

Enterprise Rent-A-Car, Riverwalk Plaza. Tel: (304) 744-3644; and Newsome Limousine Services, South Charleston Tel: (304) 727-1390.

Train and Commuter

Charleston's train depot is located at 350 Maccorkle Ave. S.E. Charleston, WV 25314. The station is staffed and features an enclosed waiting area, checked baggage service, restrooms, payphones, and vending machines. Transportation options from the station include local transit and taxi services.

The Cardinal serves Charleston station.

Visitor Information Center

Charleston, WV Convention and Visitors Bureau, 200 Civic Center Drive Charleston, WV 25301 Tel: (304) 344-5075 or toll-free (800) 733-5469.

Place to See and Things to Do

Governor's Mansion is located at 1900 East Kanawha Boulevard, Charleston Tel: (304) 558-3809. The **City Hall** is located at Court and Virginia Streets. **Shrewsbury Street** between the 1000 block of Washington Street and Lewis Street features West Virginia's African American historical site. The East side of **Capitol Street** between Virginia & Quarrier Streets has some of the oldest building in Charleston.

Haddad Riverfront Park features an amphitheater with many outdoor local activities. The park is located in the 700 Block of Kanawha Blvd Charleston. Built in 1905 the **C & O Railroad Depot** remains one of Charleston's historical landmarks. The train depot also houses Amtrak located at 350 SE MacCorkle Ave. Charleston.

Built in 1915, the **Masonic Building,** located at 107 Hale Street Charleston, is one of Charleston's unique examples of Gothic architecture. Famous for its marble façade, the **Payne Building** is one of Charleston's most appreciated structures. The building is located at 819 Lee Street, Charleston. **Sunrise Museum** houses a Science Hall and art museum. The museum is located at 746 Myrtle Road, Charleston Tel: (304) 344-8035.

Davis Park located on Capitol and Lee Streets is the local's favorite place for leisure. Around the area at Lee and Court Streets is the **St. George Orthodox Church,** easily recognized by its onion-shaped dome. Built between 1873 and 1885 the Victorian Gothic architecture **Kanawha Presbyterian Church** is one of the oldest in Charleston that is still in use. The church is located at 1009 East Virginia Street, Charleston.

Built in 1915 the **First Presbyterian Church** is known for its impressive Byzantine interior and its 52-foot diameter dome. The church is located at 16 Broad Street, Charleston. The Romanesque-style **Sacred Heart Co-Cathedral** located at 1032 East Virginia Street, Charleston is known for its tower and great arches. **St. John's Episcopal Church** is a Gothic and Romanesque architecture built between 1883 and 1901; the cathedral is one of the most beautiful in the city, located at 1105 Quarrier Street, Charleston.

Hale Street Antique Mall built in 1930 houses several antique shops, located at 213 Hale Street Charleston. **Capitol Center** located at 123 Summers Street features various entertainments. **Capitol Market** is located at 800 Smith Street, Charleston Tel: (304) 344-1905. **Farmer's Market** is located at 2809 Kanawha Boulevard, East Charleston, Tel: (304) 925-5341.

Accommodations

Embassy Suites Hotel located at 300 Court St, Charleston, WV 25301 Tel: (304) 347-8700. **Budget Host Inn** located at 3313 Kanawha Blvd E, Charleston, WV 25306, Tel: (304) 925-2592. **Fairfield Inn** located at Washington St & Broad St, Charleston, WV 25301 Tel: (304) 343-4661. **Holiday Inn** located at 100 Civic Center Dr, Charleston, WV, 25301 Tel: (304) 345-0600. **Kanawha City Motor Lodge** located at 3103 Maccorkle Ave SE, Charleston, WV 25304, Tel: (304) 344-2461. **Days Inn** located at 6400 Maccorkle Ave SE, Charleston, WV 25304, Tel: (304) 925-1010.

Hampton Inn located at 1 Virginia St W, Charleston, WV 25302, Tel: (304) 343-9300. Marriott Hotels & Resorts located at 200 Lee St E, Charleston, WV 25301, Tel: (304) 345-6500. Red Roof Inn located at located at 4006 Maccorkle Ave SW, Charleston, WV 25309, Tel: (304) 744-1500. Valley View Motel located at 5222 Kanawha Blvd E, Charleston, WV 25306, Tel: (304) 926-0880. Sleep Inn located at 2772 Pennsylvania Ave, Charleston, WV 25302, Tel: (304) 345-5111. Holiday Inn located at 600 Kanawha Blvd E, Charleston, WV 25301, Tel: (304) 344-4092.

Montgomery (WV)

Montgomery is located 21 miles west of Charleston. It has a land area of 1.5 sq. miles (3.9 sq. kilometers) and a population of 2449.

Montgomery's train depot is located at Washington St. and 3rd Ave. Montgomery, WV 25136. The station is un-staffed and features payphones. Transportation options from the station include local transit and taxi services.

The Cardinal serves Montgomery station.

Thurmond (WV)

Thurmond is located just 65 miles west of Charleston, with a land area of 0.06 sq. miles (0.16 sq. kilometers) and no permanent population density. Thurmond was incorporated in 1903 and was an important coal-railroading center during the early days. Thurmond does not have a Main St, there are a few buildings that remain standing and in perfect condition.

Thurmond's train depot is located at C&O Railroad Station Thurmond, WV 25936. The station is self-serve.

The Cardinal serves Thurmond station.

Prince (WV)

Prince is located 79 miles south of Charleston. Prince also serves Amtrak stops for the city of Berkley, West Virginia.

Prince's train depot is located at Rte. 41 North Prince, WV 25907. The station is staffed and features an enclosed waiting area, checked baggage service, restrooms, and payphones. Transportation option from the station is local taxi service.

The Cardinal serves Prince station.

Hinton (WV)

Hinton is located in the southern part of West Virginia, and is the seat of the Summer County. It was incorporated in 1880, has a land area of 2.1 sq. miles (5.4 sq. kilometers), and a population of around 3,500. The town of Hinton was an important stop for the C & O Railways; it served as the company's train maintenance and repair center. Downtown Hinton has many architectural beauties and in 1984 it was registered on the US National Register of Historic Places.

Hinton's train depot is located at Front St. Hinton, WV 25951. The station is un-staffed and features an enclosed waiting area. Transportation option from the station is local taxi service.

The Cardinal serves Hinton station.

Places of Interest

The world famous Hinton Railroad Days & New River Train Excursion offers a round-trip river train excursion around the region. This unique train travel experience is highly recommended for train enthusiasts. Contact C/O Summers County CVB at 206 Temple Street Hinton, WV 25951 or PO Box 451, Kenova, Tel: (304) 466-5420 or (304) 453-1641 for information. Hinton Railroad Museum located at 206 Temple Street Hinton, WV 25951 Tel: (304) 466-5420. The museum exhibits memorabilia and artifacts from the C & O Railway. John Henry Woodcarving Exhibit, located at 206 Temple Street, Hinton WV 25951 Tel: (304) 466-5420, has a collection of more than 100 railroading wood carved figurines by John Henry.

White Sulfur Spring (WV)

White Sulfur Springs is located 84 miles southeast of Charleston. It has a land area of 1.6 sq. miles (4.3 sq. kilometers) and a population of roughly 3,000. White Sulfur Springs is home to the world known Greenbrier Resort; many have claimed that the resort's healing water does wonders for many who are suffering from rheumatism. White Sulfur Springs is also a great place for many outdoor activities, including trail hiking or biking, fishing, boating, and canoeing.

White Sulfur Springs' train depot is located at 315 W. Main St. White Sulfur Springs, WV 24986. The station is self-serve. Transportation from the station is local taxi service.

The Cardinal serves White Sulfur Springs station.

Clifton Forge (VA)

Virginia (VA)

Capital: Richmond (Population: 7,078,515)
Size: 42,769 sq mi. (110,771 sq km)
Nickname: The Old Dominion, Mother of Presidents
Entered the union: June 25, 1788 (10th state)
Motto: Thus always to tyrants
Flower: American Dogwood
Bird: Cardinal
Song: Carry Me Back to Old Virginia
Famous for: Presidents, Aristocracy and guess what "Ham"
Major industries: Government, agriculture, and manufacturing.

Clifton Forge is located east of the city Covington, Virginia just 134 miles west of Richmond. It has a land area of 3 sq. miles (8 sq. kilometers) and a population of approximately 5,000. Clifton Forge is part of the Alleghany Highlands area. Clifton Forge was founded way back in the 1700's and was incorporated in 1906.

Just like Hinton, West Virginia, Clifton Forge was a major maintenance center for C & O Railroad Company and the town's rich history and development were closely related to development the railroad industry.

Clifton's train depot is located at 400 Ridgeway St. Clifton Forge, VA 24422. The station is self-serve and features an enclosed waiting area and restrooms. Transportation from the station is local taxi service.

The Cardinal serves Clifton station.

Staunton (VA)

Staunton is located 99 miles northwest of Richmond, the state capital. It has a land area of 19.8 sq. miles (51 sq. kilometers) and a population of more than 25,000. Founded by John Lewis in 1732 and incorporated in 1801, Staunton became a train transportation hub for the state of Virginia during the mid 1800's. Many of Staunton's historic Victorian, Greek, and Federal architecture buildings remained intact and have survived the blaze of the civil war.

Places of interest are the Museum of American Frontier Culture Tel: (540) 332-7850, and the Woodrow Wilson Birthplace and Museum located at Coalter and Frederick Streets Tel: (540) 885-0897.

Staunton's train depot is located at 1 Middlebrook Ave. Staunton, VA 24401. The station is un-staffed and features an enclosed waiting area and payphones. Transportation options from the station include local transit, bus, and taxi services.

Staunton station is served by the Cardinal.

Charlottesville (VA)

Charlottesville is located in the foothills of the Blue Ridge Mountains just 68 miles west of Richmond. It has a land area of 10 sq. miles (26.5 sq. kilometers) and a population of approximately 50,000. Named after Princess Charlotte, the wife of King George III of England, Charlottesville was founded by Peter Jefferson, the father of Thomas Jefferson, in 1737. The city of Charlottesville was established as a town in 1762 and was incorporated as a city in 1888.

The beauty of the Blue Ridge Mountains illuminates the city of Charlottesville; the city is the economic, cultural, and educational center of the region. Charlottesville is home to the well-recognized University of Virginia established by Thomas Jefferson. The region is also known for its grapes and wine production, many local wines are nationally recognized.

Places of interest: Monticello, the home of President Thomas Jefferson located two miles south of Charlottesville Tel: (434) 984-9800; and the home of James Monroe, the 5th president of the United States, Ash Lawn-Highland is located at 1000 James Monroe Parkway Charlottesville, VA 22902 Tel: (434) 293-9539.

Charlottesville's train depot is located at 810 W. Main St. Charlottesville, VA 22901. The station is staffed and features an enclosed waiting area, checked baggage service, restrooms, payphones, and vending machines. Transportation options from the station include local transit and taxi services.

Trains serving Charlottesville station are the Cardinal and the Crescent.

Culpaper (VA)

Culpaper is located in the rolling hills of Piedmont Virginia just 63 miles northwest of Richmond. It has a land area of 6.6 sq. miles (17 sq. kilometers) and a population of approximately 9,000. Culpaper's history is visible in the town's many historical buildings that still dominate its historic downtown area. Places of interest: Commonwealth Park Equestrian located at 13256 Commonwealth Parkway, Culpaper, VA 22701 Tel: (540) 825-7469; The Museum of Culpaper History located in historic Downtown at 140 E. Davis Street Curlpaper, VA 22701 Tel: (703) 825-1973; and the Civil War Battlefields of Kelly's Ford, Cedar Mountain, and Brandy Station.

Culpaper's train depot is located at 109 S. Commerce St. Culpaper, VA 22701. The station is self-serve and features payphones. Transportation options from the station include local taxi and bus services.

Trains serving Culpaper station are the Cardinal and the Crescent.

Manassas (VA)

Manassas is located 32 miles west of Washington D.C. It has a land area of 5 sq. miles (25.9 sq. kilometers) and a population of approximately 35,000. Manassas was incorporated in 1873 as a town and again in 1975 as a city. Manassas played a significant role in the civil war as two major battles were fought in the area.

Manassas is home to Lockheed-Martin, Dominion Semiconductor (a computer chip manufacturer), and IBM. Places of interest: Manassas Museum located at 9101 Prince William St Manassas, VA 20110-5615 Tel: (703) 368-1873 and the Rohr's Store & Museum located at 9122 Center St Manassas, VA 20110-5534 Tel: (703) 368-3000. Downtown Manassas offers several accommodations, museums, shops and restaurants.

Manassas' train depot is located at 9500 West St. Manassas, VA 20110. The station is un-staffed and features payphones. Transportation options from the station include local transit and taxi services.

Trains serving Manassas station are the Cardinal and the Crescent.

Alexandria (VA)

Alexandria is located just 6 miles southwest of Washington D.C. in northeast Virginia. It has a land area of 15.4 sq. miles (39.5 sq. kilometers) and a population of roughly 120,000. Captain John Smith first founded the site in 1608, but it was only in 1669 when the town was settled and called Alexandria. It was incorporated in 1779 and was a major port of entry for foreign ships.

Alexandria was one of the sites of the early black slave trade coming from Africa. It also played an important role in America's campaign for independence against the British. George Washington trained his army at Alexandria's Market Square in 1754 and Alexandria was occupied by the Union troops during the civil war. And from 1863 to 1865 the city of Alexandria became the capital of the Restored Government of Virginia. It also housed a torpedo and munitions factory that was used during World War I and II.

Today Alexandria is home to the American Society for Training and Development, American Diabetes Association, AT&T, Softec, and Fokker Aircraft USA. A visit to Alexandria's old town historic district will reward you with architectural beauty, museums, local entertainment, fine restaurants and hotels.

Alexandria's train depot is located at 110 Callahan Dr. Alexandria, VA 22301. The station is staffed and features an enclosed waiting area, checked baggage service, restrooms, payphones, and vending machines. Transportation options from the station include local transit and taxi services.

Trains serving the Alexandria station are the Cardinal, Carolinian and Piedmont, Crescent, Northeast Direct, Silver Service, and the Twilight Shoreliner.

Visitor Information Center

Alexandria Visitors & Convention Center, 221 King Street, Alexandria, VA 22314 Tel: (703) 838-4200.

Places of Interest

Black History Resource Center located at 638 North Alfred St. Alexandria, VA 22314 Tel: (703) 838-4356. The center exhibits the history of Alexandria's African-American community. **Alexandria African American Heritage Park** is dedicated to the African Americans for their contribution to the growth of the city of Alexandria. The park is located on Holland Avenue between Duke Street and Eisenhower Avenue, Alexandria Tel: (703) 838-4356.

George Washington Masonic National Memorial, dedicated to President George Washington, was patterned after the ancient lighthouse of Alexandria in Egypt. The memorial is located at King Street at Callahan Drive, Alexandria, Virginia 22314 Tel: (703) 683-2007. **Friendship Firehouse** is located at 107 S. Alfred St. Alexandria, VA 22314 Tel: (703) 838-3891. The firehouse exhibits old historical firefighting gear. **Ramsay House Visitors Center,** built in 1724, was the original house of Alexandria's city founder William Ramsay. The center is located at 221 King Street, Alexandria, Virginia 22314 Tel: (703) 838-4200.

Alexandria Seaport Foundation's Seaport Center, located on Alexandria Waterfront, south of Founders Park, Alexandria, Tel: (703) 549-7078, houses a marine sciences lab and a boat building program. **Gadsby's Tavern Museum** is an 18th century restored historical inn. The museum is located at 134 N. Royal St. Alexandria, VA 22314 Tel: (703) 838-4242. **Torpedo Factory Art Center** located at 105 N. Union Street, Alexandria, Virginia 22314 Tel: (703) 838-4565 exhibits 160 live artists.

Lloyd House exhibits civil war memorabilia and Virginia's history. The Lloyd house is located at 220 N. Washington St. Alexandria, Virginia 22314 Tel: (703) 838-4577. Visit the elegant childhood Home of General Robert E. Lee built in 1795 located at 607 Oronoco St. Alexandria, VA 22314 Tel: (703) 548-8454. River Farm located at 7931 E. Boulevard, Alexandria, Virginia 22314 Tel: (703) 768-5700 was once owned by George Washington, the farm houses gardens and woods. Old Presbyterian Meeting House was the site of George Washington's memorial services; the house is located at 321 S. Fairfax Street, Alexandria, Virginia 22314 Tel: (703) 549-6670.

Alexandria Archaeology Museum, located in the Torpedo Factory Art Center at 105 N. Union Street, Alexandria, Virginia 22314, Room 327, Tel: (703) 838-4399, exhibits the history of Alexandria. The Lyceum, Alexandria's History Museum exhibits the city's history and artifacts. The museum is located at 201 S. Washington Street, Alexandria, Virginia 22314 Tel: (703) 838-4994. Stabler-Leadbeater Apothecary Shop Museum, located at 105-107 S. Fairfax Street, Alexandria, Virginia 22314 Tel: (703) 836-3713, exhibits the factory's preserved herbs, potions, paper labels, and more than 8,000 early medical care items. Fort Ward Museum & Historic Site located at 4301 W. Braddock Rd Alexandria, VA 22304 Tel: (703) 838-4848. The museum exhibits historical collections of the civil war.

Accommodations

Best Western Inn located at 615 1st St, Alexandria, VA 22314 Tel: (703) 739-2222. Econo Lodge located at 8849 Richmond Hwy, Alexandria, VA 22309 Tel: (703) 780-0300. Days Inn located at 6100 Richmond Hwy, Alexandria, VA 22303 Tel: (703) 329-0500. Hilton Alexandria Old Town located at 1767 King St, Alexandria, VA 22314 Tel: (703) 837-0440. Intercontinental Hotel located at 6573 Medinah Ln, Alexandria, VA 22312 Tel: (703) 642-5877. Red Roof Inn located at 5975 Richmond Hwy, Alexandria, VA 22303 Tel: (703) 960-5200.

Embassy Suites Hotel located at 1900 Diagonal Rd, Alexandria, VA 22314 Tel: (703) 684-5900. Comfort Inn located at 6254 Duke St, Alexandria, VA 22312 Tel: (703) 642-3422. Holiday Inn located at 2460 Eisenhower Ave, Alexandria, VA 22314 Tel: (703) 960-3400. Hilton Hotel located at 1767 King St, Alexandria, VA 22314 Tel: (703) 837-0440. Best Western Inn located at 8751 Richmond Hwy, Alexandria, VA 22309 Tel: (703) 360-1300. Travelers Motel located at 5916 Richmond Hwy, Alexandria, VA 22303 Tel: (703) 329-1310.

Radisson-Old Town located at 901 N Fairfax St, Alexandria, VA 22314 Tel: (703) 683-6000. Days Inn located at 110 S Bragg St, Alexandria, VA 22312 Tel: (703) 354-4950. Holiday Inn located at 480 King St, Alexandria, VA 22314 Tel: (703) 549-6080. Washington Suites located at 100 S Reynolds St, Alexandria, VA 22304 Tel: (703) 370-9600. Hampton Inn located at 4800 Leesburg Pike, Alexandria, VA 22302 Tel: (703) 671-4800.

Washington D.C See Capitol Limited service, page 441.
Connecting Train to New York (NY), New Carrollton (MD), BWI Airport (MD), Baltimore (MD), Wilmington (DE), Philadelphia (PA), Trenton (NJ), Newark (NJ), and New York (NY).

Maple Leaf

7:15 am-**D**	**New York (NY)**	9:50 pm-**A**
7:39 am	Yonkers (NY)	9:17 pm
8:00 am	Croton Harmon (NY)	8:58 pm
8:39 am	Poughkeepsie (NY)	8:21 pm
8:54 am	Rhinecliff Kingston (NY)	8:06 pm
9:15 am	Hudson (NY)	7:45 pm
9:40 am-**A** 10:00 am-**D**	Albany Rensselaer (NY)	7:20 pm-**D** 7:05 pm-**A**
10:22 am	Schenectady (NY)	6:39 pm
10:39 am	Amsterdam (NY)	6:19 pm
11:37 am	Utica (NY)	5:23 pm
11:51 am	Rome (NY)	5:06 pm
12:40 pm	Syracuse (NY)	4:27 pm
1:56 pm	Rochester (NY)	3:12 pm
2:52 pm	Buffalo Depew (NY)	2:15 pm
3:04 pm	Buffalo Exchange St. (NY)	2:00 pm
3:55 pm-**A**	Niagara Falls (NY)*	1:25 pm-**D**

*Cross border Canada

--Niagara Falls (ON)
--St. Catharines (ON)
--Grimsby (ON)
--Aldershot (ON)
--Oakville (ON)
--Toronto (ON)

Maple Leaf

Maple Leaf takes passengers from New York City, New York to Toronto, Canada, connecting the rest of Canada's rail system "VIA Rail Canada."

Route Destination Highlights

New York, NY- See and admire the most popular statue in the world the Statue of Liberty, explore the Ellis Island Immigration Museum, Central Park, Times Square, the United Nations, and see some of the tallest buildings in the world. Visit the 1913 Beaux architecture Grand Central Terminal, the Museum of Sex, and the Museum of Modern Art.

Albany, NY- Visit the oldest Neo-Gothic Cathedral structure in the US, the Cathedral of The Immaculate Conception or the Shrine of North American Martyrs the birthplace of blessed Kateri Tekakwitha. See the 1761 Georgian architecture Schuyler Mansion, the home of the American revolutionary general Philip Schuyler. The Empire State Aerosciences Museum exhibits aviation models and houses galleries and an airpark.

Rochester, NY- See the International Museum of Photography and Films; the 1822 Charlotte-Genesee Lighthouse, one of the oldest in the great lakes area; the Genesee River waterfalls, or enjoy water sports at Lake Ontario.

Buffalo, NY- Visit the site of Buffalo's underground railroad at the Michigan Street Baptist Church, see part of the Erie Canal recognized as one of the great engineering marvels of the 19th Century, the Lower Lakes Marine Historical Society Museum that features artifacts relating the history of the creation of the Erie Canal. Visit the Mark Twain Room and the

Buffalo and Erie County Naval and Military exhibits destroyer, WWII submarine, and missile cruiser.

Niagara, NY- Visit the magnificent Niagara Falls (the American Falls and the Horseshoe Falls), the Daredevil Museum, Schoellkopf Geological Museum, the Niagara Aerospace Museum, Niagara's Wax Museum of History, the Aquarium of Niagara, and shop at the Honeymoon Capital Souvenirs Shop.

Scenery along the Route

Along the route you'll see the beautiful Finger Lakes Region of upstate New York, the lovely Hudson River, and the breathtaking American Falls and Horseshoe Falls of Niagara.

Train Schedules

Maple Leaf travels daily from Toronto, Canada to New York City, New York. The trip between the two cities takes approximately 12 hours of travel time.

Accommodations

Accommodations are Business Class and Reserved Coach. There is a Cafe Car that serves local cuisine, snacks, soups, sandwiches, and drinks. There is a Railfone available in the Lounge Car.

Boarder Crossing

If you travel north to Niagara, New York you will cross the boarder to Canada.

All Aboard!

Toronto (Canada) (Optional Destination)

Niagara Falls (NY)
Connecting train to and from **Toronto, Canada**

Niagara Falls is located in northwestern New York, at the US/Canada border. Niagara has a land area of 14 sq. miles (36 sq. kilometers) and a population of approximately 62,000. The Europeans first settled Niagara in the early 19th century, and the town of Niagara Falls was incorporated in 1892. Niagara Falls is a famous honeymoon spot.

Places to See and Things to Do

The American Falls is 56 meters (180 ft) high and 328 meters (1,075 ft) wide. The American falls is taller than the Canadian Horse Shoe Falls. It is said that 75,000 meters of water flow each second at the falls. For many years the American falls has undergone several facelifts to contain the natural erosion of the falls bedrocks.

The Canadian Falls or the "Horse Shoe Falls" is 52 meters (170 ft) high and 675 meters (2,200 ft) wide. The depth of the river is said to be 56 meters (184 ft) and an estimated 168,000 cubic meters water flow through the falls per second. Part of the Canadian fall can be seen in the American Territory.

Geologists have estimated that each year the falls erodes about 3 feet and predicts that in the future the falls will finally erode completely.

The Daredevil Museum, located at 303 Rainbow Boulevard Niagara Falls, NY 14303 Tel: (716) 282-4046, exhibits daredevil memorabilia. **Schoellkopf Geological Museum,** located on Robert Moses Parkway Niagara Falls, NY 14303 Tel: (716) 278-1780, exhibits the 435 million years of Niagara's geological history. Visit the **Honeymoon Capital Souvenirs** shop which has various selections of souvenirs and hospitable people, ask for Janelle. The shop is located in downtown Niagara at 16 Rainbow Blvd. Niagara Falls, Tel: (716) 285-6117.

The Niagara Aerospace Museum, located at 345 Third Street Niagara Office Building Niagara Falls, NY 14303 Tel: (716) 278-0060, exhibits Niagara's aerospace memorabilia and artifacts. **Niagara's Wax Museum of History,** located at 303 Prospect Street Niagara Falls, NY 14303 Tel: (716) 285-1271, exhibits life-size figures portraying the history of Niagara.

Niagara County Historical Society, located at 215 Niagara Street Lockport, NY 14094 Tel: (716) 434-7433, houses a civil war room, Tuscarora Nation, and Erie Canal exhibits and many more. **Aquarium of Niagara,** located at 701 Whirlpool Street Niagara Falls, NY 14301-1094 toll-free (800) 500-4609, exhibits harbor seals, Peruvian penguins, and California sea lions.

Accommodations

Econo Lodge Niagara Falls located at 7708 Niagara Falls Blvd, Niagara Falls NY 14304 Tel: (716) 283-0621 expect to pay $30-$250. **Niagara Falls Thriftlodge** located at 9401 Niagara Falls Blvd Niagara Falls NY 14304 toll-free (800) 578-7878 expect to pay $20-$150. **Knight's Inn Niagara Falls** located at 9900 Niagara Falls Blvd. Niagara Falls NY 14304 Tel: (925) 473-2230 expect to pay $70-$100. **Comfort Inn The Pointe Niagara Falls** located at 1 Prospect Pointe Niagara Falls NY 14304 toll-free (800) 228-5150 expect to pay $50-$250.

Holiday Inn Select Niagara Falls located at 231 3rd St. Niagara Falls NY 14303 Tel: (716) 282-2211 expect to pay $50-$300. **Best Western Summit Inn Niagara Falls** located at

The American Falls

9500 Niagara Falls Boulevard Niagara Falls NY 14304 Tel: (716) 297-5050 expect to pay $50-$100. **Days Inn Riverview at the Falls Niagara Falls** located at 401 Buffalo Ave. Niagara Falls NY 14301 toll-free (800) DAYS INN expect to pay $50-$1000.

Buffalo - Depew (NY) See Lake Shore Limited service, page 395.

Rochester (NY) See Lake Shore Limited service, page 399- 400.

Syracuse (NY) See Lake Shore Limited service, page 399- 400.

Rome (NY)

Rome is located along the Mohawk River Valley in western Oneida County just 97 miles from Albany, the state capital. Rome has a land area of 75.6 sq. miles (194 sq. kilometers) and a population of approximately 45,000. It was the Oneida people who first settled and occupied the area for 10,000 years. It was the English who first built permanent forts in the area in 1750 as a protection against the French. Rome was the point of origin of the 425 mile-long Erie Canal that expanded across the state of New York.

Rome's train depot is located at 6599 Martin St. Rome, NY 13440. The station is un-staffed and features an enclosed waiting area, restrooms, payphones, and a restaurant. Transportation options from the station include local transit and taxi services.

Trains serving Rome station are the Empire Service and the Maple Leaf.

Utica (NY) See Lake Shore Limited service, page 399- 400.

Amsterdam (NY)

Amsterdam is located 28 miles north of Albany. It has a land area of 5.8 sq. miles (15 sq. kilometers) and a population of 25,700 making Amsterdam the 18th most populated city in the state of New York. Amsterdam was incorporated in 1830, and was chartered as a city in 1885.

Amsterdam's train depot is located at Railroad and 26 W. Main Sts. Amsterdam, NY 12010. The station is un-staffed and features an enclosed waiting area, restrooms, and payphones. Transportation options from the station include local transit and taxi services.

Trains serving Amsterdam station are the Empire Service and the Maple Leaf.

Schenectady (NY) See Lake Shore Limited service, page 399- 400.

New York (NY)
Capital: Albany (Population: 18,976,457)
Size: 54,475 sq mi. (141,090 sq km)
Nickname: The Empire State
Joined the union on: July 26, 1788 (11th state)
Motto: Excelsior
Flower: Rose
Bird: Bluebird
Song: I Love New York
Famous for: Statue of Liberty, Niagara Falls, Manhattan
Major industries: Tourism, foreign trade, publishing, entertainment, farm and agriculture.

467

Hudson (NY)

Hudson is the home of the 8th President of the United States, Martin Van Buren. Hudson is located just 28 miles south of Albany and it has a land area of 2.1 sq. miles (5.6 sq. kilometers) and a population of more than 8,000. Visitors should visit Warren Street to glance at the city's many architectural beauties and history. Hudson is known for its many antique shops and rare art collections.

Hudson's train depot is located at 69 S. Front St. Hudson, NY 12534. The station is staffed and features an enclosed waiting area, restrooms, payphones, and a snack bar. Transportation options from the station include Stan Martin Ford Car Rental Tel: (518) 828-9915, Howard's Taxi Tel: (518) 828-3355, Decker Taxi Tel: (518) 828-7673, Hudson Mini-Bus System Tel: (518) 828-9458, and Commuter Rail toll-free (800) METRO-INFO.

Trains serving Hudson station are the Maple Leaf, Empire Service, Ethan Allen Express, and the Adirondack.

Rhinecliff - Kingston (NY)

The Rhinecliff-Kingston stop serves the city of Kingston and the town of Rhinecliff. Kingston is located where the Rondout Creek and the Hudson River meet, 50 miles north of New York City. Kingston has a land area of 7.4 sq. miles (19 sq. kilometers) and a population of more than 23,000. The site of what is today Kingston was first settled in 1652 by the Dutch settlers who named it Esopus, and later was renamed to Wiltwyck (wild woods), and again to Kinston in 1664. Kingston became the first capital of the state of New York in 1777; the city's long history made Kingston one of the most diverse cities of New York in terms of architectural beauty.

Rhinecliff-Kingston train depot is located at Hutton and Charles Sts. Rhinecliff, NY 12574. The station is staffed and features an enclosed waiting area, restrooms, quik-trak ticket machines, payphones, and vending machines. Transportation options from the station include Hertz Car Rental Tel: (914) 339-7036, Avis Rent A Car toll-free (800) 230-4898, Red Hook Transportation Tel: (914) 876-2010, Kingston Kabs Tel: (914) 331-8294, LOOP Bus System Tel: (914) 876-5255, and Commuter Rail toll-free (800) METRO-INFO.

Trains serving Rhinecliff-Kingston station are the Maple Leaf, Empire Service, Ethan Allen Express, and the Adirondack.

Poughkeepsie (NY)

Poughkeepsie is located along the Hudson River Valley southeast of the State of New York. Poughkeepsie is the county seat of Dutchess County; it has a population of approximately 29,000 and a land area of 5 sq. miles (13 sq. kilometers). The Dutch and English traders first settled Poughkeepsie in 1670. The town of Poughkeepsie was founded in 1687 and was incorporated in 1854 as a city. Briefly during the American Revolution in late 1700's the city of Poughkeepsie was posted as temporary US capital.

Poughkeepsie's train depot is located at 41 Main St. Poughkeepsie, NY 12601. The station is staffed and features an enclosed waiting area, quik-trak ticket machine, restrooms, payphones, and a snack bar. Transportation options from the station include Avis Rent A Car toll-free (800) 230-4898, LOOP Bus System Tel: (914) 485-4690, Commuter Rail: toll-free (800) METRO-INFO, and local taxi service.

Trains serving Poughkeepsie station are the Maple Leaf, Empire Service, Ethan Allen Express, and the Adirondack.

Croton - Harmon (NY) See Lake Shore Limited – Albany to New York City service, page 405.

Yonkers (NY)

Yonkers is located along the Hudson River north of New York City. Yonkers is the fourth largest city in the state of New York and it has a land area of 11.5 sq. miles (29.6 sq. kilometers) and a population of approximately 200,000. The town of Yonkers was incorporated in April 1872 and later in June of the same year Yonkers was designated as a city. It was here in Yonkers that the first street light was introduced in 1861.

Yonkers' train depot is located at Foot of Dock St. and Wells Ave Yonkers, NY 10701. The station is staffed and features an enclosed waiting area, quik-trak ticket machine, restrooms, payphones, and a snack bar. Transportation options from the station include Avis Rent-A-Car toll-free (800) 230-4898, Metro Taxi Service Tel: (914) 968-4444 and local transit service.

Trains serving Yonkers station are the Maple Leaf, Empire Service, Ethan Allen Express, and the Adirondack.

New York (NY) See Lake Shore Limited- Albany to New York City service, page 405
Connecting train to **Philadelphia (PA)** and **Washington D.C**

Adirondack

Canadian Routes

--Montreal (QC)
--ST. Lambert (QC)
--Cantic (QC)

12:25 pm-D	Rouses Point (NY)	3 :17 pm-A
12:53 pm	Plattsburgh (NY)	2:46 pm
	Port Kent (NY)	
1:57 pm	Westport (NY)	1:34 pm
2:15 pm	Port Henry (NY)	1:16 pm
2:36 pm	Ticonderoga (NY)	12:55 pm
3:08 pm	Whitehall (NY)	12:22 pm
3:31 pm	Fort Edward (NY)	11 :59 am
3 :52 pm	Saratoga Springs (NY)	11:39 am
4:27 pm	Schenectady (NY)	11:13 am
4:50 pm-A 5:20 pm-D	Albany Rensselaer (NY)	10:50 am-D 10:40 am-A
5:45 pm	Hudson (NY)	10:13 am
6:06 pm	Rhinecliff Kingston (NY)	9:50 am
6:21 pm	Poughkeepsie (NY)	9:35 am
6:58 pm	Croton Harmon (NY)	8:56 am
7: 17 pm	Yonkers (NY)	
7:50 pm-A	New York (NY)*	8:15 am-D

D-Departure   **A**- Arrival

*Connecting Train

--**New York (NY)**
--Newark (NJ)
--Trenton (NJ)
--**Philadelphia (PA)**
--Wilmington (DE)
--**Baltimore (MD)**
--BWI Airport (MD)
--New Carrollton (MD)
--**Washington D.C**

Adirondack

Adirondack links New York City, New York and the city of Montreal, Canada with train connections to the rest of Canada on VIA Rail Canada. Adirondack is jointly financed and operated by Amtrak and the State of New York.

Route Destination Highlights

Saratoga Springs, NY- Visit the Congress Park, the National Bottle Museum, Grant Cottage State Historic Site, or have a refreshing and relaxing time at the Saratoga Spa State Park, Crystal Spa, and the Lincoln Bathhouse.

Albany, NY- Visit the oldest Neo-Gothic Cathedral structure in the US, the Cathedral of The Immaculate Conception or the Shrine of North American Martyrs, the birthplace of blessed Kateri Tekakwitha. See the 1761 Georgian architecture Schuyler Mansion, the home of the American revolutionary general Philip Schuyler. The Empire State Aerosciences Museum exhibits aviation models and houses galleries, and an airpark.

New York, NY- See and admire the most popular statue in the world the Statue of Liberty, explore the Ellis Island Immigration Museum, Central Park, Times Square, the United Nations, and see some of the tallest buildings in the world. Visit the 1913 Beaux architecture Grand Central Terminal, the Museum of Sex, and the Museum of Modern Art.

Scenery along the Route

You will travel some of the most scenic views in the state of New York, the wine country of the Hudson Valley, and the charming shoreline of Lake Champlain.

470

Train Schedules

Adirondack travels daily from Montreal, Canada to New York City, New York. The trip between the two cities takes approximately 10 hours of travel time.

Accommodations

Accommodation is Reserved Coach. There is a Lounge Car that serves local cuisine, sandwiches, soups, and drinks. Other amenities are Railfone and seasonal national park guide presentations.

Boarder Crossing

If you travel north of Rouses Point, New York you will cross the border into Canada.

All aboard!

The Canadian Routes:

Montreal (QC) (Optional)

ST. Lambert (QC) (Optional)

Cantic (QC) (Optional)

Rouses Point (NY)

Rouses Point is located in Clinton County, less than a mile from the US/Canadian boarder. Rouses Point has a land area of 1.7 sq. miles (4.6 sq. kilometers) and a population of more than 2,000.

Rouses Point train depot is located on Pratt St. Rouses Point, NY 12979. The station is un-staffed and features an enclosed waiting area, restrooms, and payphones. Transportation from the station is local taxi service.

Rouses Point station is served by the Adirondack.

Plattsburgh (NY)

The city of Plattsburgh was a part of the land granted by Governor Clinton, the first governor of the state of New York to Zephaniah Platt in 1784 as part of the "Land Grants" Program. Plattsburgh has a land area of 5 sq. miles (13 sq. kilometers) and a population of more than 21,000.

Plattsburgh's train depot is located on Bridge St. Plattsburgh, NY 12901. The station is un-staffed and features an enclosed waiting area, restrooms, and payphones. Transportation from the station is local taxi service.

Plattsburgh station is served by the Adirondack.

Port Kent (NY)

Port Kent is located in the Adirondack region on Lake Champlain. Port Kent is known as the Grand Canyon of the East, admired for its natural rock formations carved by centuries of the powerful force of running water.

Port Kent's train depot is located on Rt. 9 North Port Kent, NY 12975. The station is un-staffed. Transportation from the station is local taxi service.

Port Kent station is served by the Adirondack.

Westport (NY)

Westport is located 106 miles north of Albany along Lake Champlain near the New York and Vermont state border. It has a land area of 0.9 sq. miles (2.5 sq. kilometers) and a population of roughly 1,000. Westport is a gateway to the Adirondack State Park. Adirondack State Park has more than 6 million acres of preserved wilderness popular for hiking, canoeing, skiing, and other recreational activities.

Westport's train depot is located at Highway 9 N and D+H Railroad Tracks Westport, NY 12993. The station is un-staffed and features an enclosed waiting area, restrooms, and payphones.

Westport station is served by the Adirondack.

New York (NY)

Capital: Albany (Population: 18,976,457)
Size: 54,475 sq mi. (141,090 sq km)
Nickname: The Empire State
Joined the union on: July 26, 1788 (11th state)
Motto: Excelsior
Flower: Rose
Bird: Bluebird
Song: I Love New York
Famous for: Statue of Liberty, Niagara Falls, Manhattan
Major industries: Tourism, foreign trade, publishing, entertainment, farm and agriculture.

Port Henry (NY)

Port Henry is located on the eastern side of the Adirondack Mountains along Lake Chaplain. Port Henry has a land area of 1.1 sq. miles (3 sq. kilometers) and a population of more than 1,000. Port Henry was known for the sighting of the Lake Champlain monster also known as "Champ," like the Loch Ness Monster in the UK, many have claimed that a creature with an elongated shape like snake or horse head was sighted in the Bulwagga Bay area in southern part of Port Henry. See it for yourself!

Port Henry's train depot is located on Rte. 9 North Port Henry, NY 12974. The station is un-staffed and features an enclosed waiting area, restrooms, and payphones. Transportation from the station is local taxi service.

Port Henry station is served by the Adirondack.

Ticonderoga (NY)

Ticonderoga, an Iroquois word meaning "Land between the waters," is located 100 miles north of Albany with a land area of 1.1 sq. miles (3 sq. kilometers) and a population of approximately 6,000. Ticonderoga is a site of many historical events; the city was constantly attacked during the early history of the nation. Memories of the early war days are still visible at Fort Ticonderoga and Fort Crown Point.

Ticonderoga's train depot is located on Rte. 74 Ticonderoga, NY 12883. The station is un-staffed and features an enclosed waiting area, restrooms, and payphones. Transportation from the station is local taxi service.

Ticonderoga station is served by the Adirondack.

Whitehall (NY)

Whitehall is known as the gateway to Lake Champlain Valley, located just 63 miles north of Albany in northern Washington County in the Glens Falls area. Whitehall was founded in 1759 and was originally named Skenesborough. Whitehall has a land area of 4.6 sq. miles (12 sq. kilometers) and a population of more than 3,000. Whitehall is the birthplace of the American Navy.

Whitehall's train depot is located on Main St. Whitehall, NY 12887. The station is un-staffed and features an enclosed waiting area and payphones. Transportation from the station is local taxi service.

Whitehall station is served by the Adirondack.

Fort Edward (NY)

Fort Edward is located in Washington County four miles southeast of Glenn Falls across the Hudson River. The Native American Indians called the site Wahcoloosencoochaleva, or the "Great Carrying Place." Just like other cities in the area, Fort Edward played a vital role in US early history, many wars were fought there. Fort Edward was incorporated as a town in 1818; today Fort Edward has a land area of 1.7 sq. miles (4.5 sq. kilometers) and a population of approximately 4,000.

Fort Edward's train depot is located at East St. Fort Edward, NY 12828. The station is un-staffed and features payphones. Transportation from the station is Joes Taxi Company Tel: (518) 792-1234 and County Taxi Company Tel: (518) 793-9601.

Trains serving Forth Edward station are the Adirondack and the Ethan Allen Express.

Saratoga Springs (NY)

Saratoga Springs is one of the oldest and most historical cities in the state of New York; it is located just 27 miles north of Albany and has a land area of 28.7 sq. miles (73.6 sq.

kilometers) and a population of more than 25,000. The site of what is today Saratoga County was originally a hunting ground for Iroquois Indians.

Saratoga is a popular tourist destination, famous for its numerous spas and bathhouses. Many of America's known figures come to Saratoga for relaxation and leisure. During the 1800's Saratoga was known as the "Queen of the Spas." Visitors should visit the city's many well-preserved 19th century buildings.

Places of Interest: Congress Park located in the heart of downtown, Saratoga Lake, National Bottle Museum Tel: (518) 885-7589, Grant Cottage State Historic Site Tel: (518) 587-8277, Saratoga Spa State Park Tel: (518) 584-2000, Saratoga Performing Arts Center located on the grounds of the Spa State Park Tel: (518) 587-9330, the Crystal Spa Tel: (518) 584-2556, and the Lincoln Bathhouse Tel: (518) 584-2001.

Saratoga Springs' train depot is located at West Ave and Station Lane, Saratoga Springs, NY 12866. The station is staffed and features an enclosed waiting area, restrooms, and payphones. Transportation options from the station include Enterprise Rent-A-Car toll-free (800) RENT-A-CAR, Thrifty Car Rental Tel: (518) 583-4601, AAA Apple Cab Tel: (518) 583-7577, Saratoga Taxi Tel: (518) 584-2700, and local transit service.

Trains serving Saratoga station are the Adirondack and the Ethan Allen Express.

Schenectady (NY) See Lake Shore Limited service, page 399- 400.

Albany-Rensselaer (NY) See Lake Shore Limited service, page 401.

Hudson (NY) See Maple leaf service, page 467- 469.

Rhinecliff-Kingston (NY) See Maple leaf service, page 467- 469.

Poughkeepsie (NY) See Maple leaf service, page 467- 469.

Croton-Harmon (NY) See Lake Shore Limited – Albany to New York City service, page 405.

Yonkers (NY) See Maple leaf service, page 467- 469.

New York (NY) See Lake Shore Limited service, page 405
Connecting Train to New York (NY), Newark (NJ), Trenton (NJ), Philadelphia (PA), Wilmington (DE), Baltimore (MD), BWI Airport (MD), New Carrollton (MD) and Washington D.C.

Vermonter		
8:10 am-**D**	St. Albans (VT)	9:05 pm-**A**
8:40 am	Burlington Essex (VT)	8:20 pm
9 :08 am	Waterbury Stowed (VT)	7:51 pm
9:22 am	**Montpelier Barre (VT)**	7:37 pm
9:57 am	Randolph (VT)	7:02 pm
10:40 am-**A** 10:45 am-**D**	White River Jct. (VT)	6:20 pm-**D** 6:15 pm-**A**
11:03 am	Windsor Mt. Ascutney (VT)	5:55 pm
11:14 am	Claremont (NH)	5:43 pm
11:36 am	Bellows Falls (VT)	5:20 pm
12:11 pm	Brattleboro (VT)	4:45 pm
12:59 pm	Amherst (MA)	3:55 pm
2:20 pm-**A** 2:30 pm-**D**	Springfield (MA)	2:50 pm-**D** 2:40 pm-**A**
3:11 pm	Hartford (CT)	1:58 pm
3: 56 pm-**A** 4:11 pm-**D**	**New Heaven (CT)**	1:17 pm-**D** 1:06 pm-**A**
4:31 pm	Bridgeport (CT)	12:42 pm
4:56 pm	Stamford (CT)	12: 18 pm
6:00 pm-**A** 6:20 pm-**D**	**New York (NY)**	11:30 am-**D** 10:55 am-**A**
6:36 pm	Newark (NJ)	10:35 am
6:46 pm	Metropark (NJ)	10:17 am
7:12 pm	Trenton (NJ)	9:55 am
7:45 pm	**Philadelphia (PA)**	9:25 am
8:08 pm	Wilmington (DE)	9:01 am
9:00 pm	**Baltimore (MD)**	8:31 am
9:13 pm	BWI Airport, (MD)	7:57 am
9:27 pm	New Carrollton (MD)	7:41 am
9:45 pm-**A**	**Washington D.C**	7:30 am-**D**

Vermonter

Vermonter brings passengers to the beautiful state of Vermont. It connects the cities of Washington D.C. and St. Albans, Vermont with a throughway bus connection to Montreal, Canada. The Vermonter is jointly financed and operated by Amtrak and the State of Vermont.

Route Destination Highlights

Montpelier, VT- See the State Capitol known for its Gold-leaf dome, the Thomas Waterman Wood Art Gallery, and the Pavilion Hotel which houses the Vermont Historical Society Museum.

New Haven, CT- Visit the Yale University Art Gallery, Yale Center for British Art, and the Yale Collection of Musical Instruments at Yale University; one of the largest libraries in the world the Beinecke Rare Book and Manuscript Library; Knights of Columbus Headquarters Museum and Archives; the New Haven Crypt; and the Shoreline Trolley Museum.

New York, NY- See and admire the most popular statue in the world, the Statue of Liberty; explore the Ellis Island Immigration Museum, Central Park, Times Square, the United Nations, and some of the tallest buildings in the world. Visit the 1913 Beaux architecture Grand Central Terminal, the Museum of Sex, and the Museum of Modern Art.

Philadelphia, PA- See the world's largest mint the U.S. Mint, the oldest zoo in the US the Philadelphia Zoo, pay a visit to the body of Saint John Neumann at National Shrine of Saint John Neumann, visit the birthplace of the nation Independence Hall and the Liberty Bell, spend one afternoon and stroll Fairmount Park or shop in Philadelphia's upscale district Rittenhouse Square.

Baltimore, MD- Visit the oldest Catholic Church in Baltimore, St. Vincent de Paul Church; Baltimore's oldest restored historic cathedral and the oldest cemetery, Westminster Hall and Burying Ground; visit the home of the first American Roman Catholic canonized saint at the Mother Seton House. The Baltimore Street Car Museum, the B and O Railroad Museum,

National Museum of Dentistry, the birthplace of the American national anthem at Fort McHenry National Monument and Historic Shrine, and the home of Mary Pickersgill creator of the Star-Spangled Banner at the Star-Spangled Banner Flag House and Museum.

Washington, DC- The capital city of the US, explore the National Mall and visit the United States Capitol Building, the Library of Congress, the Washington Monument, Vietnam Veterans Memorial, Thomas Jefferson Memorial, and the Lincoln Memorial. Take a tour of the White House or visit the world's largest office building the Pentagon. Shop at the Eastern Market, explore the Union Station, see the world's largest chair, or visit Georgetown University and George Washington University. Washington D.C. has it all!

Train Schedules

Vermonter travels daily from Washington D.C. to St. Albans, Connecticut. The trip between the two cities takes approximately 14 hours of travel time. Vermonter has a throughway bus connection to Montreal, Canada.

Accommodations

Accommodations are Business Class and Reserved Coach. There is a Cafe Car that serves sandwiches, snacks, and drinks. Other amenities are Railfone, bicycle racks, and ski racks.

All Aboard!

Vermont (VT)

Capital: Montpelier (Population: 608,827)
Size: 9,615 sq mi. (24902 sq km)
Nickname: The Green Mountain State
Joined the union on: March 4, 1791 (14th state)
Motto: Vermont, Freedom and Unity
Flower: Red clover
Bird: Hermit Thrush
Song: Hail, Vermont
Major industries: Farm, manufacturing and tourism

St. Albans (VT)

St. Albans is located in the northwestern corner of the state of Vermont near the US/Canadian border just 46 miles northwest of Montpelier the state capital and 26 miles south of Montreal, Canada. St. Albans has a land area of 1.9 sq. miles (5 sq. kilometers) and a population of over 13,000.

St. Albans is known as the "Capital of the Maple Sugaring Industry." A visit to St. Albans' Main Street reveals a very picturesque town setting with beautiful shops, restaurants, parks, museums, and warm people.

Places of interest: the Missisquoi Valley Rail Trail, Brick School House Historical Museum, Burton Island State Park, St. Albans Historical Museum, Taylor Park, and the Vermont Maple Festival from June through September.

St. Albans' train depot is located at 40 Federal Street, St. Albans, VT 05478. The station is staffed and features an enclosed waiting area, checked baggage service, restrooms, payphones, and restaurants. Transportation options from the station include Thrifty Car Rental Tel: (802) 524-1400, Dussault Auto Rental Tel: (802) 524-2189, and Yellow Cab Tel: (802) 864-7411.

St Albans is served by the Vermonter.

Burlington-Essex (VT)

Burlington is located on the eastern shore of Lake Champlain between the Adirondack and Green Mountains, 37 miles west of Montpelier. Known as Vermont's cultural and education center, Burlington has a land area of 10.5 sq. miles (27 sq. kilometers) and a population of roughly 40,000. Essex Junction has a land area of 5 sq. miles (13 sq. kilometers) and a population of more than 8,000.

Burlington-Essex train depot is located at 29 Railroad Ave. Essex Junction, VT 05452. The station is staffed and features an enclosed waiting area, checked baggage service, restrooms, payphones, and vending machines. Transportation options from the station include Hertz Car Rental Tel: (802) 864-7409, Thrifty Car Rental Tel: (802) 863-5500, Avis Rent A Car toll-free (800) 230-4898, Benways Taxi Tel: (802) 862-1010, and local transit service.

Burlington-Essex station is served by the Vermonter.

Waterbury-Stowe (VT)

Waterbury is located 10 miles northwest of Montpelier; it has a land area of 1.1 sq. miles (3 sq. kilometers) and a population of approximately 3,500. Founded in 1763, Waterbury is a tourism and ski resort destination. Stowe is located near Mt. Mansfield, the highest point in the state of Vermont. It has a land area of 0.7 sq. mile (1.8 sq. kilometers) and a population of roughly 500.

Points of interest are: the Ben & Jerry's Ice-cream factory and the Waterbury Center State Park. Route 100 is one of the most scenic roads in the state of Vermont. Mount Mansfield at 4393 feet is a popular year-round ski resort area.

Waterbury-Stowe's train depot is located at Park Row, Waterbury - Stowe, VT 05676. The station is un-staffed and features an enclosed waiting area, restrooms, and payphones. Transportation options from the station include Avis Rent A Car toll-free (800) 230-4898, Thrifty Car Rental Tel: (802) 244-8800, Valley Rent-ALL Tel: (802) 244-5161, Mad River Taxi Tel: (802) 496-4279, Lamoille Taxi Tel: (802) 253-9433, and local bus service.

Waterbury-Stowe station is served by the Vermonter.

Montpelier-Barre (VT)

Montpelier is located in central Vermont; it is the state capital and the region's center for government, entertainment, and arts. Montpelier has a land area of 10 sq. miles (26.5 sq. kilometers) and a population of approximately 10,000. The American Indians first inhabited the Montpelier area 6,000 years ago while the European settlers arrived in the area in 1787. Barre is located just a few minutes from Montpelier and is home to more than 10,000 residents.

Places of interest: the State Capitol is known for its Gold-leaf dome, the Thomas Waterman Wood Art Gallery on the Vermont College campus, and the Pavilion Hotel houses the Vermont Historical Society Museum.

Montpelier's train depot is located on Montpelier Jct. Rd. Montpelier, VT 05602. The station is un-staffed and features an enclosed waiting area, restrooms, and payphones. Transportation options from the station include Avis Rent A Car toll-free (800) 230-4898, Thrifty Car Rental Tel: (802) 476-3535, Enterprise Rent-A-Car Tel: (802) 479-5400, Garretts Taxi Tel: (802) 479-2127, and Norm's Taxi Tel: (802) 223-5226.

Montpelier station is served by the Vermonter.

Randolph (VT)

Randolph is located south of Montpelier, and is home to approximately 5,000 residents. Randolph's train depot is located in Depot Square Randolph, VT 05060. The station is un-staffed and features an enclosed waiting area, restrooms, payphones, and snack bar. Transportation options from the station include Especially Imports car rental Tel: (802) 728-4455, and local transit service.

Randolph station is served by the Vermonter.

White River Jct. (VT)

White River Junction is located 44 miles south of Montpelier along the Connecticut River on the Vermont and New Hampshire border. White River Junction has a land area of 1.6 sq. miles (4.2 sq. kilometers) and a population of roughly 3,000. White River Junction is a popular ski resort destination.

White River Junction train depot is located in Railroad Row, White River Junction, VT 05001. The station is staffed and features an enclosed waiting area, checked baggage service, restrooms, and payphones. Transportation options from the station include Avis Rent-A-Car toll-free (800) 230-4898, Thrifty Car Rental Tel: (802) 295-6611, Enterprise Rent-A-Car Tel: (603) 448-3337, New Face Taxi Tel: (802) 295-1500, Big Yellow Taxi Tel: (603) 643-TAXI, and local transit service.

White River Junction station is served by the Vermonter.

Windsor (VT)

Windsor is located at the foot of Mt. Ascutney along the banks of the Connecticut River and was founded in 1761. Windsor was incorporated in 1761 and was the birthplace of the independent state of Vermont; visit the old Constitution House located at the north end of Windsor's Main Street. Windsor has a land area of 12 sq. miles (32 sq. kilometers) and a population of roughly 4,000.

Windsor's train depot is located on Depot Ave. east of Main, Windsor, VT 05089. The station is un-staffed and features payphones. Transportation from the station is local bus service.

Windsor station is served by the Vermonter.

Claremont (NH)

Claremont is a small city located on the western border of New Hampshire near the New Hampshire and Vermont border. Claremont is home to approximately 14,000 residents.

Claremont's train depot is located on Plains Road, Claremont, NH 03743. The station is un-staffed and features payphones. Transportation options from the station include Claremont Auto Rentals Tel: (603) 542-6514, National Car Rental Tel: (802) 254-6067, Paul Sun Ford Motors Car Rental Tel: (603) 543-1221, Yellow Taxi Tel: (603) 643-8294, and Ed's Taxi Stand Tel: (603) 542-1500.

Claremont station is served by the Vermonter.

Bellows Falls (VT)

Bellows Falls is located along the banks of the Connecticut River. It has a land area of 1.3 sq. miles (3.5 sq. kilometers) and a population of approximately 3,500. Founded in 1792 Bellows Falls is popularly known as home to the Great Falls and its canals.

Bellows Falls' train depot is located on Depot St, Bellows Falls, VT 05101. The station is un-staffed and features an enclosed waiting area, restrooms, and payphones. Transportation from the station is Bellows Falls Taxi Tel: (802) 463-4600.

Bellows Falls station is served by the Vermonter.

Brattleboro (VT)

Brattleboro is located 96 miles south of Montpelier near the Vermont and Massachusetts state border. Brattleboro has a land area of 9.5 sq. miles (24.6 sq. kilometers) and a population of roughly 12,000. Brattleboro was first settled in 1724; the town was named after George Brattle Jr. and was chartered by King George II of England in 1753.

Places of interest: the Rudyard Kipling's home, the Retreat Tower, Brattleboro Museum and Art Center, and Brattleboro's covered bridges.

Brattleboro's train depot is located at Vernon Rd. Brattleboro, VT 05301. The station is un-staffed and features an enclosed waiting area and restrooms. Transportation options from the station include Avis Rent A Car toll-free (800) 230-4898, National Car Rental Tel: (802) 254-6067, Thrifty Car Rental Tel: (802) 254-9900, and Federal Taxi Tel: (802) 254-5411.

Brattleboro station is served by the Vermonter.

Amherst (MA)

Amherst is located in the Pioneer Valley of Western Massachusetts just 79 miles west of Boston, the state capital. Amherst has a land area of 4.9 sq. miles (12.6 sq. kilometers) and a population of approximately 18,000. Amherst is home to the Hampshire Colleges and the University of Massachusetts.

Amherst's train depot is located on Railroad St, Amherst, MA 01002. The station is un-staffed and features an enclosed waiting area and payphones. Transportation options from the station include local transit and taxi services.

Amherst station is served by the Vermonter.

Springfield (MA) See Lake Shore Limited- Albany to Boston service, page 403 -404.

Hartford (CT)

Hartford is located along the Connecticut River, centrally located a hundred miles from both Boston and New York City. Hartford is the state capital of Connecticut. Hartford has a land area of 17 sq. miles (44.8 sq. kilometers) and a population of roughly 140,000; it was first explored in 1614 by Adraien Block, a Dutch mariner, and was settled in 1636. Hartford was incorporated in 1784.

Hartford is the Insurance Capital of the World, home of many insurance companies including Hartford Fire Insurance Group, established in 1810, the nation's oldest insurance company. Hartford is also home to the US oldest continuously published newspaper the Hartford Courant, founded in 1764, and the oldest public art museum the Wadsworth Athenaeum.

Connecticut (CT)
Capital: Hartford (Population: 3,405,565)
Size: 5,544 sq mi. (14,358 sq km)
Nicknames: The Constitution State
Joined the union on: January 9, 1788 (5th state)
Motto: He Who Transplanted Still Sustains
Flower: Mountain Laurel
Bird: American Robin
Song: "Yankee Doodle"
Famous for: Webster Dictionaries
Major industries: Agriculture, tourism

Places of interest: The State Capitol is located on Capitol Avenue, Hartford; City Hall is located at 550 Main Street, Hartford; The Old State House, located at 800 Main Street, Hartford, is the oldest state house in the US; The Soldiers & Sailors Memorial Arch is located at Bushnell Park, Hartford; Keney Clock Tower is located in North Main Street, Hartford; Armsmear/Colt Estate is located at 80 Wethersfield Avenue Hartford; The Wadsworth Atheneum Art Museum is located at 600 Main Street, Hartford; and Main Street downtown Hartford has many beautiful and historic buildings and Churches.

Hartford's train depot is located at 1 Union Place Hartford, CT 06103. The station is staffed and features an enclosed waiting area, checked baggage service, quik-trak ticket machine, restrooms, payphones, restaurants, snack bar, and vending machines.

Transportation options from the station include Hertz Car Rental toll-free (800) 654-3131, local transit, bus, and taxi services.

Trains serving Hartford station are the Northeast Direct and the Vermonter.

New Haven (CT)

New Haven is located in south-central Connecticut 35 miles south of Hartford. New Haven has a land area of 18.8 sq. miles (48.8 sq. kilometers) and a population of approximately 128,000. New Haven was home to the Native Americans Indians the Quinnipiack for many generations and in 1638 the English Puritans settled in the area. New Haven was incorporated in 1784, and from 1701 to 1873 New Haven was a co-capital with Hartford.

Today, New Haven is a center for production of high-tech electronics, aerospace technology, biopharmaceuticals, and home to world-renowned Yale University, one of the most visited attractions in the city.

New Haven's train depot is located at 50 Union Ave. New Haven, CT 06519. The station is staffed and features an enclosed waiting area, checked baggage service, quik-trak ticket machine, restrooms, payphones, and a snack bar. Transportation options from the station include Enterprise Rent-A-Car (203) 789-2252, Hertz Car Rental (203) 777-6861, Budget/Sears Car Rental Tel: (203) 787-1143, Yellow Cab Tel: (203) 562-4123, Metro Taxi Tel: (203) 777-7777, local Bus Tel: (203) 624-0151, and Metro North toll-free (800) 638-7646.

Trains serving New Haven station are Vermonter, Acela Regional, Acela Express, Northeast Direct, and Twilight Shoreliner.

Places of Interest

Yale University

Yale University Art Gallery, located at 1111 Chapel Street, New Haven, CT 06510 Tel: (203) 432-0600, is the oldest college art museum in the US; the museum houses thousands of ancient and modern arts. **Yale Center for British Art,** located at 1080 Chapel Street, New Haven, CT 06510 Tel: (203) 432-2800, exhibits Elizabethan period arts and books. **Yale Collection of Musical Instruments,** located at 15 Hillhouse Avenue, New Haven, CT 06511 Tel: (203) 432-0822, exhibits hundreds of musical instruments from the 16th through 20th centuries. **Peabody Museum of Natural History,** located at 170 Whitney Avenue, New Haven, CT 06511 Tel: (203) 432-5050, is one of the largest and oldest in the US; the museum has permanent exhibits of fossils, mammals, and many others

481

<<http://www.peabody.yale.edu >>.

Around New Haven

Beinecke Rare Book and Manuscript Library, located at 121 Wall Street, New Haven, CT 06511 Tel: (203) 432-2977, is one of the largest in the world; it houses millions volumes of books and manuscripts. **Eli Whitney Museum,** located at 915 Whitney Avenue, Hamden, CT 06517 Tel: (203) 777-1833, houses an 1816 barn, water laboratory, and features various activities <<http://www.eliwhitney.org>>. **Connecticut Children's Museum,** located at 22 Wall Street, New Haven, CT 06511 Tel: (203) 562-5437, features many educational activities and displays for children.

Connecticut Afro-American Historical Society is located in Southern Connecticut State University (SCSU), Wintergreen Building 117, at 501 Crescent Street, New Haven, CT 06515 Tel: (203) 392-6126. The society is dedicated to New Haven's African American heritage. **Irish-American Historical Society,** located in Southern Connecticut State University (SCSU), Wintergreen Building 117, 501 Crescent Street, New Haven, CT 06515 Tel: (203) 392-6126, tracks the history of Irish Americans. **Ethnic Heritage Center,** located in Southern Connecticut State University (SCSU), Wintergreen Building 117, 501 Crescent Street, New Haven, CT 06515 Tel: (203) 392-6126, represents various American ethnic communities.

Amistad Memorial located in front of the city hall at 165 Church Street, New Haven, CT 06510 Tel: (203) 387-0370 was dedicated to the incidence of the kidnapped black slave from Sierra Leone in 1839. One of New Haven's scariest sites is the **New Haven Crypt** located at 311 Temple Street, New Haven, CT 06511Tel: (203) 787-0121; the crypt features tombstones dating back to the late 1600's. One of the finest English Gothic churches in the US is the 1897 **Christ Church on Broadway** located at 84 Broadway, New Haven, CT 06511 Tel: (203) 865-6354.

Shoreline Trolley Museum, located at 17 River Street, East Haven, CT 06513 Tel: (203) 467-6927, exhibits trolleys from 1903 to 1939, and offers an authentic vintage trolley tour. **102nd Infantry Regiment Museum and National Guard Armory,** located at 290 Goffe Street, New Haven, CT 06511 Tel: (203) 784-6851, exhibits rare military artifacts and artilleries. **New Haven Colony Historical Society,** located at 114 Whitney Avenue, New Haven, CT 06510 Tel: (203) 562-4183, exhibits the history of New Haven.

Accommodations

Fairfield Inn at Long Wharf located at 400 Sargent Drive, New Haven, CT 06511 Tel: (203) 562-1111. **Regal Inn** located at 1605 Whalley Avenue, New Haven, CT 06515 Tel: (203) 389-9504. **The Colony** located at 1157 Chapel Street, New Haven, CT 06511 Tel: (203) 776-1234. **Quality Inn & Conference Center** located at 100 Pond Lily Avenue, New Haven, CT 06515 toll-free (800) 228-5151.

New Haven Hotel located at 229 George Street, New Haven, CT 06510 Tel: (203) 498-3100. **Holiday Inn at Yale** located at 30 Whalley Avenue, New Haven, CT 06511 Tel: (203) 777-6221. **Omni New Haven Hotel** (at Yale) located at 155 Temple Street, New Haven, CT 06477 toll-free (800) 843-6664. **Hotel Duncan** located at 1151 Chapel Street, New

Haven, CT 06511 Tel: (203) 787-1273. **Residence Inn by Marriott** located at 3 Long Wharf Drive, New Haven, CT 06511 Tel: (203) 777-5337.

Bridgeport (CT)

Bridgeport is located 50 miles southwest of Hartford. It has a land area of 15.9 sq. miles (41 sq. kilometers) and a population of just over 140,000. Bridgeport is home to Singer sewing machines and the original Frisbie pie company.

Places of Interest: Housatonic Museum of Art located at 900 Lafayette Blvd, Bridgeport Tel: (203) 332-5000, The Barnum Museum located at 820 Main St, Bridgeport Tel: (203) 331-1104, The Discovery Museum located at 4450 Park Ave, Bridgeport Tel: (203) 372-3521, and the Beardsley Zoological Gardens located at 1875 Noble Ave, Bridgeport Tel: (203) 394-6565.

Bridgeport's train depot is located at 525 Water St. Bridgeport, CT 06604. The station is staffed and features an enclosed waiting area, quik-trak ticket machine, restrooms, payphones, and a snack bar. Transportation options from the station include local transit, bus, and taxi services.

Trains serving Bridgeport station are the Northeast Direct and the Vermonter.

Stamford (CT)

Stamford is located along Connecticut's shoreline, 90 miles southwest of Hartford and just 24 miles northeast of New York City. Stamford has a land area of 19.8 sq. miles (50.9 sq. kilometers) and a population of more than 100,000. Stamford was founded in 1641 and was originally called Rippowam by the native Indians.

Places of Interest: Whitney Museum of American Art located at Atlantic Street at Tresser Boulevard Tel: (203) 358-7652, Stamford Museum & Nature Center located at 39 Scofieldtown Road Tel: (203) 322-1646, and the Stamford Historical Society Museum located at 1508 High Ridge Road Tel: (203) 329-1183.

Stamford's train depot is located at Wash. Blvd. and E. State St. Stamford, CT 06902. The station is staffed and features an enclosed waiting area, quik-trak ticket machine, restrooms, payphones, and a snack bar. Transportation options from the station include Hertz Car Rental toll-free (800) 654-3131, local transit and taxi services.

Vermonter serves Stamford train station.

New York (NY) See Lake Shore Limited- Albany to New York City service, page 405.

Newark (NJ) See Pennsylvania service, page 428- 429.

Metropark (NJ) See Carolinian/Piedmont service, page 513- 515.

Trenton (NJ) See Pennsylvania service, page 428- 429.

Philadelphia (PA) See Pennsylvania service, page 424

Wilmington (DE)

Wilmington is centrally located between New York City and Washington D.C. It has a land area of 10.8 sq. miles (27.9 sq. kilometers) and a population of approximately 73,000. Wilmington was founded by the Swedish in 1638 and later occupied by the Dutch and the British. Wilmington was incorporated in 1731.

Wilmington is known as the "Chemical capital of the world" and the city is the industry and shipping hub of the state of Delaware. Wilmington is also known as the "Corporate Capital of the World" since the city houses many Fortune 500 companies. A visit to downtown Wilmington is a delightful experience of old and new. There are many restored Victorian buildings and houses but also many state-of-the-art buildings in the city.

Places of interest: Old Town Hall located on the 500 block of Market Street, Willingtown Square located between Fifth and Sixth Streets on the Market Street Mall, and the Brandywine Zoo located at 1001 North Park Dr, Wilmington, DE 19802 Tel: (302) 571-7747.

Wilmington's train depot is located at M. L. King Blvd and French Street, Wilmington, DE 19801. The station is staffed and features an enclosed waiting area, checked baggage service, quik-trak ticket machine, restrooms, payphones, and a snack bar. Transportation options from the station include Hertz Car Rental toll-free (800) 654-3131, Budget Rent a Car Tel: (302) 764-3300, DART First State Public Bus Service toll-free (800) 652-DART, SEPTA Commuter Rail Service Tel: (215) 580-7800, taxi and local bus services.

Trains serving Wilmington station are Crescent, Metroliner, Acela Regional, Acela Express, Carolinian and Piedmont, Northeast Direct, Silver Service, Twilight Shoreliner, and Vermonter.

Baltimore (MD)

Baltimore is located 35 miles northeast of Washington D.C. and 23 miles north of Annapolis, the state capital of Maryland. Baltimore has a land area of 81.5 sq. miles (209 sq. kilometers) and a population of approximately 74,000. Popularly known as the "Charm City," Baltimore was founded in 1729. Baltimore's rich history is preserved in its many museums, historical sites, and several architectural marvels.

Getting Around

Airport

Baltimore-Washington International Airport Tel: (410) 859-7111 is located 10 miles (16 Kilometers) south of Baltimore. Major car rentals companies are located at the airport arrival areas. The BWI Supershuttle offers bus services from the airport and central Baltimore areas;

a train station is located nearby connecting the airport to the rest of the region. Taxi services are available anywhere in the airport.

Bus

Maryland Public Transportation toll-free (800) 543-9809 serves the city of Baltimore and the outlying areas. Maryland Transit Administration (MTA), 6 St. Paul Street Baltimore MD, 21202-1614 Tel: (410) 539-5000, operates local commuter bus services throughout Baltimore and the surrounding areas.

Taxi

Yellow Cab Tel: (410) 727-7300 and Checker Cab Tel: (410) 685-1212.

Rent-A-Car

Avis Rent a Car Tel: (410) 859-1680, Thrifty Car Rental Tel: (410) 787-9267, and Enterprise Rent-a-Car Tel: (410) 412-4620.

Trains and Commuter

Maryland Transit Administration (MTA), 6 St. Paul Street Baltimore MD, 21202-1614 Tel: (410) 539-5000, operates local light rail, metro subway, and MARC train throughout Baltimore and the surrounding areas.

Baltimore's train depot is located on Amtrak Way, off Rt. 170 South Baltimore, MD 21240. The station is staffed and features an enclosed waiting area, quik-trak ticket machine, restrooms, payphones, and a snack bar. Transportation options from the station include Hertz Car Rental toll-free (800) 654-3131, local transit and taxi services.

Trains serving Baltimore station are the Carolinian and Piedmont, Acela Regional, Acela Express, Northeast Direct, Twilight Shoreliner, and Vermonter.

Maryland (MD)
Capital: Annapolis (Population: 5,296,486)
Size: 12,407 sq mi. (32,134 sq km)
Nickname: The Free State, Old Line State
Joined the union on: April 28, 1788 (7th state)
Motto: Manly deeds, womanly words
Flower: Black-eyed Susan
Bird: Baltimore Oriole
Song: Maryland! My Maryland!
Famous for: Johns Hopkins, Baltimore Orioles
Major industries: Sea Freight, marine food, Johns Hopkins Hospital

Visitor Information Center

Baltimore Area Convention and Visitors Association, 100 Light Street, 12th Floor Baltimore, Maryland 21202 Tel: (410) 659-7300 or toll-free (800) 343-3468.

Baltimore Area Visitors Center, 301 East Pratt Street Constellation Pier Baltimore, Maryland 1202 Tel: (410) 837-INFO or toll-free (800) 282-6632.

Places to See and Things to Do

St. Vincent de Paul Church, located at 120 N. Front Street, Baltimore MD, 21202 Tel: (410) 962-5078, is listed as a national historic place; the church is the oldest Catholic Church in Baltimore. **St. Luke's at Franklin Square** located at 623 N. Carrollton Avenue, Baltimore MD, 21217 Tel: (410) 669-6790. **The Washington Monument and Museum at Mt. Vernon Place,** located at 2600 Madison Avenue, Baltimore MD, 21217 Tel: (410) 396-7837, is the first civil monument in the US. **Harbor Place and the Gallery at Harbor Place,** located at 200 E. Pratt Street, Baltimore MD, 21202 Tel: (410) 332-4191, features more than a hundred shops and restaurants.

Baltimore Zoo, located at Druid Hill Park, Baltimore MD, 21217 Tel: (410) 396-7102, is home to more than 2,000 animals of different species. **U.S. Naval Academy,** located at 52 King George Street, Annapolis MD, 21402 Tel: (410) 263-6933, offers guided tours of the US navy college. **USS Constellation,** located at Pier 1301 E. Pratt Street, Baltimore MD, 21202 Tel: (410) 539-1797, is the only surviving civil war naval warship. The historic 1782 **Lexington Market,** located at 400 W. Lexington Street, Baltimore MD, 21201 Tel: (410) 685-6169, has more than 100 various food shops.

Maryland Science Center, located at 601 Light Street, Baltimore MD, 21230 Tel: (410) 685-2370, also houses an IMAX 3D five-story theatre, Davis Planetarium, restaurant, and gift shops. **National Aquarium in Baltimore,** located at Pier 3501 E. Pratt Street, Baltimore MD, 21202 Tel: (410) 576-3800, is home to more than 10,000 marine creatures. The Aquarium also features a walk-through living rain forest.

Westminster Hall and Burying Ground, located at 500 W. Baltimore Street, Baltimore MD, 21201 Tel: (410) 706-2072, is one of the oldest restored historic Cathedrals in Baltimore; the Westminster is surrounded by Baltimore's oldest cemetery. **The Baltimore Street Car Museum,** located at 1901 Falls Road P.O. Box 4881, Baltimore MD, 21211 Tel: (410) 547-0264, exhibits permanent street car collections; the museum also offers tours and rides. **Jewish Museum of Maryland,** located at 15 Lloyd Street, Baltimore MD, 21202 Tel: (410) 732-6400, houses two galleries and synagogues. **Pride of Baltimore,** located in World Trade Center 401 E. Pratt Street Suite 222, Baltimore MD, 21202 Tel: (410) 539-1151, is a replica of an 1812-era Baltimore Clipper topsail schooner.

Baltimore Public Works Museum, located at 751 Eastern Avenue, Baltimore MD, 21202 Tel: (410) 396-1509, exhibits local artifacts. **Baltimore Museum of Industry,** located at 1415 Key Highway Inner Harbor South, Baltimore MD, 21230 Tel: (410) 727-4808, offers a guided tour; the museum is dedicated to the industrial heritage of Baltimore. **B and O Railroad Museum,** located at 901 W. Pratt Street, Baltimore MD, 21223-2699 Tel: (410) 752-2490, exhibits early American trains and the history of American railroading.

Port Discovery, the Kid-Powered Museum, located at 35 Market Place, Baltimore MD, 21202 Tel: (410) 727-8120, features hands-on exhibits. **National Museum of Dentistry** located at 31 S. Greene Street Baltimore MD, 21201 Tel: (410) 706-0600. **Mother Seton House of Paca Street,** located at 600 N. Paca Street, Baltimore MD, 21201 Tel: (410) 523-3443, is home of the first American Roman Catholic canonized saint. **Robert Long House,** built in 1765, is located in Fell's Point historic district at 812 S. Ann Street, Baltimore MD, 21231 Tel: (410) 675-6750.

Fort McHenry National Monument and Historic Shrine, located at 2400 E. Fort Avenue, Baltimore MD, 21230 Tel: (410) 962-4290, is the birthplace of the American national anthem. Star-Spangled Banner Flag House and Museum, located at 844 E. Pratt Street, Baltimore MD, 21202 Tel: (410) 837-1793, was home to Mary Pickersgill, creator of the Star-Spangled Banner that inspired the rebirth of the United States. Baltimore Civil War Museum located at 601 President Street, Baltimore MD, 21202 Tel: (410) 385-5188.

Baltimore Maritime Museum, located at 802 S. Caroline Street, Baltimore MD, 21231 Tel: (410) 396-3453, features WWII submarines and other historic marine vessels. The 1760 Mount Claire Museum House, located at 1500 Washington Boulevard Carroll Park, Baltimore MD, 21230 Tel: (410) 837-3262, exhibits collections of 1,000 rare 18th and 19th century objects. National Historic Seaport of Baltimore, located at 802 S. Caroline Street, Baltimore MD, 21231 Tel: (410) 675-4814, exhibits Baltimore's more than 300 year-old maritime history.

Accommodations

The Admiral Fell Inn located at 888 South Broadway Baltimore MD 21231 Tel: (410) 522-7377 expect to pay $150-$200. Clarion Hotel Mount Vernon Square located at 612 Cathedral Street, Baltimore MD, 21201 Tel: (410) 727-7101 expect to pay $70-$450. Doubletree Inn at the Colonnade Baltimore located at 4 West University Parkway, Baltimore MD, 21218 Tel: (410) 235-5400 expect to pay $90-$200. Harbor Court Hotel located at 550 Light Street, Baltimore MD, 21202 Tel: (410) 234-0550 expect to pay $110-$800.

Biltmore Suites located at 205 West Madison Street, Baltimore MD, 21201 Tel: (410) 728-6550 expect to pay $100-$150. Holiday Inn Baltimore Inner Harbor located at 301 West Lombard Street Baltimore MD, 21201 Tel: (410) 685-3500 expect to pay $120-$250. Hilton Garden Inn White Marsh located at 5015 Campbell Boulevard, Baltimore MD, 21236 Tel: (410) 427-0600 expect to pay $90-$150. Hyatt Regency Baltimore located at 300 Light Street, Baltimore MD, 21202 Tel: (410) 528-1234 expect to pay $150-$350.

Sheraton Inner Harbor located at 300 South Charles Street, Baltimore MD, 21201 Tel: (410) 962-8300 expect to pay $110-$1500. Days Inn Baltimore East located at 8801 Loch Raven Boulevard, Baltimore MD, 21286 Tel: (410) 882-0900 expect to pay $50-$100. Renaissance Harborplace Hotel located at 202 East Pratt Street, Baltimore MD, 21202 Tel: (410) 547-1200 expect to pay $110-$350. Marriott Baltimore Inner Harbor located at 110 South Eutaw Street, Baltimore MD, 21201 Tel: (410) 962-0202 expect to pay $90-$300.

BWI Airport (MD)

Baltimore Washington International Airport station is located on Amtrak Way, off Rt. 170 South Baltimore, MD 21240. The station is staffed and features an enclosed waiting area, quik-trak ticket machine, restrooms, payphones, and a snack bar. Transportation options from the station include Hertz Car Rental toll-free (800) 654-3131, local transit and taxi services.

Trains serving BWI station are the Twilight Shoreliner, Vermonter, Northeast Direct, Carolinian and Piedmont, Acela Regional, and the Acela Express.

New Carrollton (MD)

New Carrollton is located in Prince George's County, Maryland just 9 miles northeast of Washington D.C. and 21 miles west of Annapolis. It has a land area of 1.5 sq. miles (3.9 sq. kilometers) and a population of more than 12,000. New Carrollton was incorporated in 1953.

New Carrollton's train depot is located at 4300 Garden City Dr, New Carrollton, MD 20785. The station is staffed and features an enclosed waiting area, quik-trak ticket machine, restrooms, payphones and a snack bar. Transportation options from the station include local transit and taxi services.

Trains serving New Carrollton station are the Metroliner, Acela Regional, Avela Express, Carolinian and Piedmont, Northeast Direct, Twilight Shoreliner, and the Vermonter.

Washington D.C See Capitol Limited service, page 441.

Ethan Allen Express

1:20 pm-**D**	Rutland (VT)	11:03 am-**A**
1:40 pm	Fair Heaven (VT)	10:56 am
2:38 pm	Fort Edwards (NY)	9 :59 am
2 :58 pm	Saratoga Springs (NY)	9:39 am
3:33 pm	Schenectady (NY)	9:13 am
4:00 pm-**A**	Albany (NY)	8:50 am-**D**
4:20 pm-**D**		8:40 am-**A**
4:45 pm	Hudson (NY)	8:13 am
5:06 pm	Rhinecliff-Kingston (NY)	7:50 am
5:21 pm	Poughkeepsie (NY)	7:35 am
5:58 pm	Croton Harmon (NY)	6:56 am
6:17 pm	Yonkers (NY)	
6:45 pm-**A**	**New York (NY)***	6:15 am-**D**

D- Departure   **A**-Arrival

*Connecting Train

--**New York (NY)**
--Newark (NJ)
--Metropark (NJ)
--Trenton (NJ)
--Philadelphia (PA)
--Wilmington (DE)
--Baltimore (MD)
--New Carrollton (MD)
--**Washington D.C**

Ethan Allen Express

Ethan Allen Express connects New York City to Rutland, Vermont with motor-coach connections to Killington and Okemo, Vermont.

Train Schedule

Ethan Allen travels daily from New York City, New York to Rutland, Vermont. The trip between the two cities takes approximately 5 hours of travel time.

Accommodations

Accommodations are Business Class and Reserved Coach. There is a Cafe Car that serves local cuisine, sandwiches, snacks, and drinks. Other amenities are Railfone and ski racks.

All Aboard!

Rutland (VT)

Rutland is located in central Vermont near the Green Mountains. Rutland has a land area of 7.6 sq. miles (19.7 sq. kilometers) and a population of more than 18,000. Rutland was first settled in 1770 and was incorporated in 1892.

Rutland's train depot is located in Merchants' Row Rutland, VT 05701. The station is un-staffed and features an enclosed waiting area, restrooms, payphones, and vending machines. Transportation options from the station include Thrifty Car Rental Tel: (802) 773-5901, Enterprise Rent-A-Car Tel: (802) 773-0855, Big Yellow Taxi Tel: (802) 747-8395, local transit and bus services.

The Ethan Allen Express serves Rutland station.

Fair Haven (VT)

Fair Haven is located in western Vermont near the Vermont and New York state border. Fair Haven has a land area of 2.7 sq. miles (7 sq. kilometers) and a population of roughly 2,900.

Fair Haven's train depot is located at Depot and Water Sts. Fair Haven, VT 05743. The station is un-staffed.

Fair Heaven station is served by Ethan Allen Express.

Fort Edwards (NY) See Adirondack service, page 471- 473.

Saratoga Springs (NY) See Adirondack service, page 471- 473.

Schenectady (NY) See Lake Shore Limited service, page 399- 400.

Albany (NY) See Lake Shore Limited service, page 401.

Hudson (NY) See Maple Leaf service, page 467- 469.

Rhinecliff-Kingston (NY) See Maple Leaf service, page 467- 469.

Poughkeepsie (NY) See Maple Leaf service, page 467- 469.

Croton-Harmon (NY) See Lakeshore Limited- Albany to New York City service, page 405.

Yonkers (NY) See Maple Leaf service, page 467- 469.

New York (NY) See Lake Shore Limited service, page 405.
Connecting train to **Newark (NJ), Metropark (NJ), Trenton (NJ), Philadelphia (PA), Wilmington (DE), Baltimore (MD), New Carrollton (MD),** and **Washington D.C**

Downeaster

Downeaster	
Multiple Daily Train Departure	**Multiple Daily Train Departure**

Portland (ME)
Old Orchard Beach (ME)
Saco-Biddeford (ME)
Wells (ME)
Dover (NH)
Durham (NH)
Exeter (NH)
Haverhill (MA)
Woburn (MA)
Boston (MA)

Route Destination Highlights

Boston, MA- Take a walk and explore the Freedom Trail, visit the Massachusetts State House built in 1798, see the Boston Irish Famine Memorial, beautiful Beacon Street, the Old State House, the Museum of Fine Arts Boston, the Museum of Transportation, and the Museum of Bad Arts. Climb the Skywalk Observation Deck, or meet the locals at Harvard Square; visitors should also visit Harvard University and the Massachusetts Institute of Technology.

Portland, ME- Experience and see Maine's well known natural phenomenon the Desert of Maine, the Maine Narrow Gauge RR Co. and Museum, the Maine Toy Train Museum, the Children's Museum Of Maine, the Portland Harbor Museum, and one of the oldest lighthouses in the US the Portland Head Light. Visit the home of American poet Henry Wadsworth Longfellow, the Tate House Museum, and the famous Victoria Mansion.

Train Schedules

Downeaster travels four times daily from Boston, Massachusetts to Portland, Maine. The trip between the two cities takes approximately 3 hours.

Accommodations

Accommodations are Coastal Club Service (Business Class) and Reserved Coach. There is a Café Car that serves sandwiches, snacks, and drinks. Other amenities are bicycle racks.

All Aboard!

Portland (ME)

Portland is located in southern Maine along the Atlantic coastline, 50 miles southwest of the state capital, Augusta. Portland has a land area of 22.8 sq. miles (58.6 sq. kilometers) and a population of approximately 65,000.

Getting Around

Airport

Portland International Jetport, 1001 Westbrook Street Portland, ME 04102 Tel: (207) 772-0690, is located just five miles from downtown Portland. The airport is served by various public transportations that connect the airport to the rest of the region.

Bus

GR Portland Transit District Tel: (207) 774-0351, Concord Trailways Tel: (207) 828-1151, and Vermont Transit Co. Inc Tel: (207) 772-6587 serve Portland and the outlying areas.

Taxi

Airport Limo & Taxi Express, toll-free (800) 517-9442.

Rent-A-Car

Maine (ME)
Capital: Augusta (Population: 1,274,923)
Size: 35,387 sq mi. (91,652 sq km)
Nickname: The Pine Tree State
Joined the union on: March 15, 1820 (23rd state)
Motto: I direct
Flower: White Pine cone and tassel
Bird: Chickadee
Song: State of Maine Song
Famous for: Pine Trees
Major industries: Banking and finance, tourism, manufacturing, agriculture, Marine products, paper products.

Budget Rent-A-Car Tel: (207) 775-6508 and Hertz Corporation Tel: (207) 774-6391.

Train and Commuter

Portland's train depot is located in Portland Transportation Center at 100 Thompson Point Road Portland, ME 04102. The station is staffed and features an enclosed waiting area, quik-trak ticket machines, restrooms, and payphones. Transportation options from the station include Hertz toll-free (800) 654-3131, Avis toll-free (800) 230-4898, Concord Trailways toll-free (800) 639-3317, Portland Metro Tel: (207) 774-0351, Inter Terminal Shuttle Tel: (207) 774-0351, and local taxi service.

The Downeaster serves Portland station.

Visitor Information Center

Portland Visitor Information Center, 305 Commercial St, Portland Maine Tel: (207) 772-5800.

Places to See

Desert of Maine, located at 95 Desert Rd Freeport, ME 04032 Tel: (207) 865-6962, is Maine's well known natural phenomenon; see and explore it for yourself. **Maine Narrow Gauge RR Co. and Museum** is located at 58 Fore St Portland, ME 04101 Tel:(207) 828-0814; the museum exhibits historic train equipment, artifacts, and offers train tours along the Casco Bay. The **Maine Toy Train Museum** located at 151 Congress St 5 Portland, ME 04101 Tel: (207) 874-6641.

Children's Museum of Maine located at 142 Free St Portland, ME 04101 Tel: (207) 828-1234. **Portland Museum of Art** located at 7 Congress Sq. Portland, ME 04101 Tel: (207)

775-6148. The **Portland Harbor Museum** Fort Road, S. Portland, Maine 04106 Phone: (207) 799-6337. **Portland Head Light,** located at 1000 Shore Road Cape Elizabeth, Maine 04107 Tel: (207) 799-2661, is one of the oldest lighthouses in the US. **Portland Observatory** is located at 138 Congress St. Portland, ME 04101 Tel: (207) 774-5561.

Wadsworth Longfellow House, located at 489 Congress St Portland, ME 04101 Tel: (207) 879-0427, is home of the American poet Henry Wadsworth Longfellow. The **Tate House Museum** located at 2 Waldo St Portland, ME 04102 Tel: (207) 774-6177. **Victoria Mansion** located at 109 Danforth St Portland, ME 04101 Tel: (207) 772-4841.

Accommodations

Harbor Plaza Hotel located on Fore St, Portland, ME 04101 Tel: (207) 774-5512. **Inn at St John** located at 939 Congress St, Portland, ME 04102 Tel: (207) 773-6481. **Holiday Inn** located at 81 Riverside St, Portland, ME 04103 Tel: (207) 774-5601. **Portland Regency Inn** located at 20 Milk St, Portland, ME 04101 Tel: (207) 774-4200. **Howard Johnson** located at 155 Riverside St, Portland, ME 04103 Tel: (207) 774-5861. **Doubletree Hotel** located at 1230 Congress St, Portland, ME 04102 Tel: (207) 774-5611.

West End Inn located at 146 Pine St, Portland, ME 04102 Tel: (207) 772-1377. **Eastland Park Hotel** located at 157 High St, Portland, ME 04101 Tel: (207) 775-5418. **Holiday Inn** located at 88 Spring St, Portland, ME 04101 Tel: (207) 775-2311. **Embassy Suites Hotel** located at 1050 Westbrook St, Portland, ME 04102 Tel: (207) 775-2200. **Oak Leaf Inn** located at 51 Oak St #A, Portland, ME 04101 Tel: (207) 773-7882. **Susse Chalet Inn** located at 340 Park Ave, Portland, ME 04102 Tel: (207) 871-0611. **Back Cove Inn** located at 575 Forest Ave, Portland, ME 04101 Tel: (207) 772-2557.

Old Orchard Beach (ME)

Old Orchard Beach is located a few miles south of the city of Portland. It has a land area of 7.4 sq. miles (19 sq. kilometers) and a population of approximately 8,000.

Old Orchard Beach's train depot is located at First Street Old Orchard Beach, ME 04064. The Downeaster serves Old Orchard Beach station.

Saco (ME)

Saco is located in southwestern Maine 65 miles southwest of the city of Augusta, the state capital. It has a land area of 38.8 sq. miles (99.6 sq. kilometers) and a population of approximately 17,000.

Saco's train depot is located in Saco Island on Main Street Saco, ME 04072. The Downeaster serves Saco station.

Wells (ME)

Wells' train depot is located at 696 Sanford Wells, ME 04090. The station is un-staffed and features an enclosed waiting area, restrooms, payphones, and an ATM machine.

The Downeaster serves Wells station.

Dover (NH)

Dover is located in the southeastern part of the state near the New Hampshire/Maine state border. It has a land area of 26.9 sq. miles (69 sq. kilometers) and a population of more than 25,000.

Dover's train depot is located at Chestnut and Third Streets Dover, NH 03820. The station is un-staffed and features an enclosed waiting area, restrooms, and payphones. Transportation options from the station include C+J Trailways toll-free (800) 258-7111, Wildcat Transit Tel: (603) 862-2328, COAST Transit Tel: (603) 743-5777, and local taxi service.

The Downeaster serves Dover station.

Durham (NH)

Durham is located in southeastern New Hampshire just 32 miles from the state capital the city of Concord. It has a land area of 2.6 sq. miles (6.8 sq. kilometers) and a population of approximately 10,000.

Durham's train depot is located at 3 Depot Road Durham, NH 03824. The station is un-staffed and features an enclosed waiting area, payphones, and restrooms. Transportation options from the station include Merchants Rent-A-Car Tel: (603) 868-2997, Wildcat Transit Tel: (603) 862-2328, UNH Shuttle Tel: (603) 862-1010, C+J Trailways toll-free (800) 258-7111, and local taxi service.

The Downeaster serves Durham station.

Exeter (NH)

Exeter is located 37 miles southeast of the city of Concord, New Hampshire's state capital. It has a land area of 4.7 sq. miles (12.3 sq. kilometers) and a population of approximately 10,000.

Exeter's train depot is located at 60 Lincoln Street Exeter, NH 03833. The station is un-staffed and features an enclosed waiting area and payphones. Transportation options from the station include Hurlbert rent-a-car Tel: (603) 778-8134, Budget rent-a-car Tel: (603) 772-0205, Enterprise rent-a-car toll-free (800) RENT-A-CAR, Ed's Taxi toll-free (866) 766-0070, Exeter Taxi Tel: (603) 778-7778, and COAST Trolley Tel: (603) 743-5777.

Exter station is served by the Downeaster.

Massachusetts (MA)

Capital: Boston
(Population: 6,340,843)
Size: 10,555 sq mi. (27,337 sq km)
Nickname: The Bay State
Joined the Union On: February 6, 1788 (6th state)
Motto: By the sword we seek peace, but peace only under liberty
Flower: Mayflower
Bird: Chickadee
Song: All Hail To Massachusetts
Famous for: Harvard University, MIT, Ben Franklin, John Adams, Freedom Trail, etc.
Major industries: Tourism, Education, Fishing, Publishing, etc.

Haverhill (MA)

Haverhill is located in northeastern Massachusetts along the Merrimack River, 31 miles north of Boston, the state capital. Once the Shoe Capital of the world, Haverhill was first founded in 1640 and was incorporated in 1870. Haverhill has a land area of 33.5 sq. miles (86 sq. kilometers) and a population of more than 55,000.

Haverhill's train depot is located on Washington Street at Railroad Tracks Haverhill, MA 01832. The station is un-staffed and features an enclosed waiting area and payphones. Transportation options from the station include Merrimack Valley Regional Transit Authority Tel: (978) 373-1184 and local taxi service.

The Downeaster serves Haverhill station.

Boston (MA) See Twilight Shoreliner service, page 497.

495

Twilight Shoreliner

8:45 pm-D	Boston (MA) South Sta.	6:25 am-A
8:50 pm	Boston (MA) Black Bay Sta.	6:15 am
9 :04 pm	Route 128 ((MA)	6 :00 am
9:33 pm-A	Providence (MA)	5:30 am-D
9:42 pm-D		5:17 am-A
10:03 pm	Kingston (MA)	4:53 am
10:24 pm	Westerly (RI)	4:35 am
10:35 pm	Mystic (CT)	4:25 am
10:50 pm	New London (CT)	4:12 am
11:12 pm	Old Saybrook (CT)	3:50 am
11:50 pm-A	New Heaven (CT)	3:16 am-D
12:05 am-D		2:46 am-A
12:48 am	Stamford (CT)	1:59 am
1:40 am-A	New York (NY)	1:10 am-D
2:10 am-D		12:41 am-A
2:30 am	Newark (NJ)	12:18 am
2:44 am	Metropark (NJ)	12:01 am
3:08 am	Treton (NJ)	11:38 pm
3:55 am-A	Philadelphia (PA)	11:07 pm-D
4:05 am-D		10:57 pm-A
4:28 am	Wilmington (DE)	10:35 pm
5:33 am	Baltimore (MD)	9:48 pm
5:46 am	BWI Airport Rail Sta. (MD)	9:28 pm
6:02 am	New Carrollton (MD)	9:11 pm
6:20 am-A	Washington DC	9:00 pm-D
7:00 am-D		8:35 pm-A
7:16 am	Alexandria (VA)	8:10 pm
7:46 am	Quantico (VA)	7:38 pm
8:05 am	Fredericksburg (VA)	7:19 pm
8:45 am	Ashland (VA)	6 :37 pm
9 :04 am-A	Richmond (VA)	6 :25 pm-D
9 :10 am-D		6 :17 pm-A
10 :25 am	Williamsburg (VA)	5:00 pm
11:05 am-A	Newport News (VA)	4:35 pm-D

Twilight Shoreliner

Twilight Shoreliner brings you to some of the most historic cities and places of the Eastern United States. It connects the city of Boston, Massachusetts and Newport News, Virginia.

Route Destination Highlights

Boston, MA- Take a walk and explore the Freedom Trail, visit the Massachusetts State House built in 1798, see the Boston Irish Famine Memorial, beautiful Beacon Street, the Old State House, the Museum of Fine Arts Boston, the Museum of Transportation, and the Museum of Bad Arts. Climb the Skywalk Observation Deck, or meet the locals at Harvard Square; visitors should also visit Harvard University and the Massachusetts Institute of Technology.

Washington, DC- The capital city of the US, explore the National Mall and visit the United States Capitol Building, the Library of Congress, the Washington Monument, Vietnam Veterans Memorial, Thomas Jefferson Memorial, and the Lincoln Memorial. Take a tour of the White House or visit the world's largest office building the Pentagon. Shop at the Eastern Market, explore the Union Station, see the world's largest chair, or visit Georgetown University and George Washington University. Washington D.C. has it all!

Alexandria, VA- Visit the Home of General Robert E. Lee, the Alexandria Archaeology Museum, and the Stabler-Leadbeater Apothecary Shop Museum. Learn about the history of Alexandria's African-American community at the Black History Resource Center, or see the Masonic National Memorial and the Torpedo Factory Art Center.

Richmond, VA- See one of the finest Victorian Gothic buildings in the US, the Old City Hall; Richmond Main Street Station; the Canal Walk; Edgar Allan Poe Museum; and the beautiful Monument Avenue.

Newport News, VA- Relax and spend some time at Newport News Park, see the Victory Arch dedicated to the men and women of the US military, the Historic Hilton Village, and the Historic North End/Huntington Heights district. Also see the Virginia War Museum, Virginia Living Museum, the James River Reserve Fleet or the "ghost fleet."

Train Schedule

The Twilight Shoreliner travels daily from Boston, Massachusetts to Newport News, Virginia. The trip between the two cities takes approximately 15 hours of travel time.

Accommodations

Accommodations are Viewliner Sleeping Car, Business Class, and Reserved Coach. There is a Cafe Car that serves sandwiches, snacks, and drinks. Complementary meals are served for Sleeping Car passengers. Other amenities include audio / video entertainment in Sleeping Car, Railfone, and the Metropolitan Lounges.

All Aboard!

Boston (MA)

Boston is one of the most popular and visited cities in the US with more than 10 million visitors each year. Boston is located in eastern Massachusetts and is the state capital. It has a land area of 48.7 sq. miles (125 sq. kilometers) and a population of approximately 600,000. Boston was first settled in the early 1620's and was called the Trimountains because of its three hills.

Boston is the birthplace of the American Revolution and the site of the many significant historical events that shaped the foundation of the United States. Boston is home to two of the most famous and respected universities and institutes in the world: Harvard University and Massachusetts Institute of Technology in Cambridge.

Getting Around

Airport

Massachusetts (MA)
Capital: Boston (Population: 6,340,843)
Size: 10,555 sq mi. (27,337 sq km)
Nickname: The Bay State
Joined the Union On: February 6, 1788 (6th state)
Motto: By the sword we seek peace, but peace only under liberty
Flower: Mayflower
Bird: Chickadee
Song: All Hail To Massachusetts
Famous for: Harvard University, MIT, Ben Franklin, John Adams, Freedom Trail, etc.
Major industries: Tourism, Education, Fishing, Publishing, etc.

Logan International Airport, One Harborside Drive, Massport, East Boston, Massachusetts 02128 Tel: (617) 561-1800, is located 4 miles (6 Kilometers) northeast of Boston. Major car rental companies are available at the airport arrival terminal areas. Taxis are easy accessible throughout the terminal. There are three bus companies serving the airport and outlying areas. Massachusetts Bay Transportation Authority (MBTA) Tel: (617) 222-5000 Blue Line subway connects the airport to the city of Boston.

Bus

Massachusetts Bay Transportation Authority (MBTA) Tel: (617) 222-5000 serves public bus transportation around the Boston Area. Basic bus fare is 75 cents, half fare for children. Call MBTA for special passes and information.

Taxi

Cambridge Limo Tel: (617) 491-5964, College Rides toll-free (877) 920-7433, Red Cab Tel: (617) 734-5000.

Rent-A-Car

Revolution Rent-A-Car, 33 Mystic Avenue Medford, MA Tel: (781) 391-1144; Verc Rentals, 1489 Main Street Brockton, MA Tel: (508) 580-0507; Rent-A-Wreck Revere, 2022 Commonwealth Ave. Boston, MA Tel: (617) 542-8700; Select Car Rental, 40 Lee Burbank Hwy Revere, MA Tel: (781) 289-8882; and Rodman Car & Truck Rentals, Route 44 Raynham, MA Tel: (508) 884-8448.

Trains and Commuters

Massachusetts Bay Transportation Authority (MBTA) Tel: (617) 222-5000 operates Boston's subway services; basic subway fare is $1 for all subway stations except Red line and Green line which cost $2 and $2.50. Call MBTA for information on special passes.

Boston's train depot is located at Atlantic Ave. and Summer St. Boston, MA 02110. The station is staffed and features an enclosed waiting area, quik trak ticket machine, metropolitan lounge, checked baggage service, restrooms, payphones, a restaurant, and snack bar. Transportation options from the station include Avis Rent A Car toll-free (800) 230-4898, Hertz Car Rental toll-free (800) 654-3131,

Budget Rent a Car toll-free (800) 527-0700, and Massachusetts Bay Transportation Authority Tel: (617) 222-3200, local bus and taxi services.

Trains serving Boston station are the Twilight Shoreliner, Northeast Direct, Lake Shore Limited, Acela Regional, and the Acela Express.

Boston - Back Bay Station (BBY) is located at 145 Dartmouth St. Boston, MA 02116. The station is staffed and features an enclosed waiting area, restrooms, payphones, and vending machines. Transportation options from the station include Hertz Car Rental toll-free (800) 654-3131, Massachusetts Bay Transportation Authority Tel: (617) 222-3200 and local taxi services.

Trains serving Boston - Back Bay station are the Twilight Shoreliner, Northeast Direct, Lake Shore Limited, Acela Regional, and the Acela Express.

Visitor Information Center

Greater Boston Convention & Visitors Bureau, 2 Copley Place Suite 105, Boston MA, 02116 toll-free (888) See-Boston.

Places to See and Things to Do

Freedom Trail

Visitors must take the **Freedom Trail** at 15 State St Boston, MA 02109 Tel: (617) 242-5642. This self-guided walking tour following the red line across the city will take visitors to some of Boston's historical landmarks and sites. Part of the Freedom Trail includes the

Boston City Skyline

499

Massachusetts State House. Built in 1798, it is a classic example of Bullfinch design. The **Boston Irish Famine Memorial,** located on the corner of Washington & School Street, is dedicated to the over one million Irish victims of the famine of 1845-1849.

Beacon Hill & Downtown

Beacon Street is known for its many architectural beauties and magnificent state houses; a visit to Beacon Street will reward visitors with a glimpse of the old historical city of Boston. **Old State House,** located at 206 Washington St. Tel: (617) 727-3676, is known as one of the most majestic classical architecture buildings in the US.

Museums

Museum of Science located close to the Science Park T stop, Science Park, Boston, MA Tel: (617) 723-2500. **DeCordova Museum & Sculpture Park,** located at 51 Sandy Pond Road, Lincoln, MA Tel: (781) 259-8355, has extensive collections of sculpture and contemporary art. **The Institute of Contemporary Art** located on Green Line, Hynes Convention Center/ICA T stop 955 Boylston St, Boston, MA Tel: (617) 266-5152. **Arthur M. Sackler Museum,** located at 485 Broadway Tel: (617) 495-9400, exhibits an outstanding collection of arts from the Middle and Far East.

Children's Museum, located at 300 Congress St. Tel: (617) 426-8855, has interactive exhibits for every member of the family. **Museum of Fine Arts Boston,** located at 465 Huntington Avenue Boston, MA 02115-5523 Tel: (617) 267-9300, exhibits extensive collections of art from 19th-century Boston collectors. **Museum of Transportation** located at 15 Newton St, Brookline, MA Tel: (617) 522-6547.

Massachusetts State House

The New Museum at the John F. Kennedy Library, Columbia Point, take the red line to JFK University of Massachusetts, then free shuttle bus. The museum was dedicated to the late president. Museum of Bad Art, located at 580 High St, West Roxbury, MA Tel: (617) 325-8224, is a unique museum that houses collections of what many have considered dreadful art. Museum of Science, Science Park at the Charles River Dam Tel: (617) 723-2500, offers hands-on exhibits of different disciplines of science.

Other Attractions

Visitors should explore the 1.6-mile Black Heritage Trail located between Pinckney and Cambridge, Joy and Charles streets; the trail narrates stories and life of the African American before the civil war. The trail features the Smith Court Residences, George Middleton House, African Meeting House, and others. The New England Aquarium is located at the Boston harbor. The aquarium is home to more than 600 marine creatures. Located in Charleston is the 220-foot Bunker Hill Monument Tel: (617) 242-5641 built to commemorate the 1775 Battle of Bunker Hill.

The Bull and Finch Pub, located on Beacon Street, is said to be the original bar patterned for the hit TV series, *Cheers*. See it for yourself. Skywalk Observation Deck, located at 800 Boylston St Boston, MA 02199 Tel: (617) 236-3318, offers a panoramic view of the city of Boston and the Charles River.

Harvard Square in Cambridge, MA is a favorite site of the locals and visitors alike; there are various restaurants and shops. Harvard Museum of Natural History located at 26 Oxford St, Cambridge, MA Tel: (617) 495-3045. The Fogg Museum is located at 32 Quincy Street Tel: (617) 495-9400. The museum was founded in 1891 and is Harvard's oldest museum. The museum has wide collections of western arts.

Harvard Square

501

Massachusetts Institute of Technology is located just 2 miles southeast of Harvard Square along Massachusetts Avenue. Visit the visitor information center and ask for a walking guided tour, Tel: (617) 253-4795. **MIT Museum and Gift Store** is located at 265 Massachusetts Ave, Cambridge, MA Tel: (617) 253-4444.

Accommodations

Eliot Hotel located at 370 Commonwealth Ave, Boston, MA 02215 Tel: (617) 267-1607. **Four Seasons Hotel** located at 200 Boylston St, Boston, MA 02116 Tel: (617) 338-4400. **Best Western Inn** located at 342 Longwood Ave, Boston, MA 02115 Tel: (617) 731-4700. **International Hall** located at 237 Beacon St, Boston, MA 02116 Tel: (617) 375-5400. **Hotel Meridien** located at 250 Franklin St, Boston, MA 02110 Tel: (617) 451-1900. **Buckminster Hotel** located at 645 Beacon St, Boston, MA 02215 Tel: (617) 236-7050. **Copley Inn** located at 19 Garrison St, Boston, MA 02116 Tel: (617) 236-0300.

Hilton located at 40 Dalton St, Boston, MA 02115 Tel: (617) 236-1100. **Radisson Hotel** located at 200 Stuart St # L1, Boston, MA 02116 Tel: (617) 482-1800. **Marriott Boston Long Wharf** located at 296 State St, Boston, MA 02109 Tel: (617) 227-0800. **Regal Bostonian Hotel** located at 24 North St, Boston, MA 02109 Tel: (617) 523-3600. **Holiday Inn** located at 55 Ariadne Rd, Dedham, MA 02026, (781) 329-1000. **Colonnade Hotel** located at 120 Huntington Ave, Boston, MA 02116 Tel: (617) 424-7000. **Boston Intl Youth Hostel** located at 12 Hemenway St, Boston, MA 02115 Tel: (617) 536-1027.

Lenox Hotel located at 710 Boylston St, Boston, MA 02116 Tel: (617) 536-5300. **Sonesta Beach Resort Bermuda** located at 11 Beacon St #1205, Boston, MA 02108 Tel: (617) 421-5454. **Wyndham Boston Hotel** located at 89 Broad St, Boston, MA 02110 Tel: (617) 556-0006. **Howard Johnson** located at 1271 Boylston St, Boston, MA 02215 Tel: (617) 267-8300. **Holiday Inn** located at 5 Blossom St, Boston, MA 02114 Tel: (617) 742-7630. **Sonesta International Hotels** located at 200 Clarendon St, Boston, MA 02116 Tel: (617) 421-5400. **Copley Plaza Hotel** located at 138 Saint James Ave, Boston, MA 02116 Tel: (617) 267-5300.

Mount Vernon Place located at 6 Mount Vernon Pl, Boston, MA 02108 Tel: (617) 248-8707. **Swissotel Boston** located at 1 Avenue De Lafayette, Boston, MA 02111 Tel: (617) 451-2600. **Ritz Carlton Hotels** located at 15 Arlington St, Boston, MA 02116 Tel: (617) 536-5700. **Westin Hotels & Resorts** located at 10 Huntington Ave, Boston, MA 02116 Tel: (617) 262-9600. **Marriott Hotels & Resorts** located at 110 Huntington Ave, Boston, MA

02116 Tel: (617) 236-5800. **Boston Harbor Hotel** located at 70 Rowes Wharf, Boston, MA 02110 Tel: (617) 439-7000.

Boston-Route 128 (MA)

Boston Route 128 train depot is located at University Ave. and Route 128 Westwood, MA 02090. The station is staffed and features an enclosed waiting area, restrooms, payphones, and vending machines. Transportation options from the station include Hertz Car Rental toll-free (800) 654-3131, local transit and taxi services.

Trains serving Westwood station are the Twilight Shoreliner, Northeast Direct, Acela Regional, and the Acela Express.

Providence (RI)

Providence is the state capital and is located in eastern Rhode Island. It has a land area of 11.8 sq. miles (30.5 sq. kilometers) and a population of more than 160,000. The site of the present Providence was first inhabited by the Narragansett Indians, it was in 1636 that the first white settlement arrived in the area.

Providence is home to Brown University, one of the most respected educational institutions in the United States. Today Providence is a thriving metropolis with an economy that is based on manufacturing, health services, and tourism. Rhode Island is the smallest state in the US, however the state has more than 20% of the entire US registered historic landmarks.

Places of Interest: Founded in 1821 the First Universal's Church in Providence, located at 250 Washington Street Providence Tel: (401) 751-1821, is listed in the national historic landmark register. The Museum of Rhode Island History, Aldrich House 110 Benevolent Street, Providence, RI 02906 Tel: (401) 331-8575, exhibits galleries depicting the history of Rhode Island. The John Brown House located at 52 Power Street Providence Tel: (401) 331-8575. The Meeting House, First Baptist Church in America located at 75 North Main Street Providence. Built in 1775 the church is the first Baptist church in America. And the John Brown House Museum, located at 52 Power Street, Providence, RI 02906 Tel: (401) 331-8575, exhibits the finest example of the 18th century Rhode Island lifestyle.

Rhode Island (RI)
Capital: Providence (Population: 1,048,319)
Size: 1,045 sq mi. (2,706 sq km)
Nickname: The Ocean State
Joined the union on: May 29, 1790 (13th state)
Motto: Hope
Flower: Violet
Bird: Rhode Island Red
Song: Rhode Island
Famous for: Steamed Power Mills, first state to declare independence to the British
Major industries: Metals manufacturing, jewelry, silverware, and textiles.

Providence's train depot is located at 100 Gaspee St. Providence, RI 02903. The station is staffed and features an enclosed waiting area, quik-trak ticket machines, restrooms, payphones, and a snack bar. Transportation options from the station include Hertz Car Rental toll-free (800) 654-3131, Massachusetts Bay Transportation Authority Tel: (617) 222-3200, and local taxi service.

Trains serving Providence station are the Twilight Shoreliner, Metroliner, Northeast Direct, Acela Regional and the Acela Express.

Kingston (RI)

Kingston station is the stop serving several Kingston and Wakefield areas. Kingston was incorporated in 1723. Places of interest: the Great Swamp Monument located off Route 2. West Kingston is the site of the Battle of 1675. Historic Main Street in Wakefield will take visitors back in time. Built in 1875, Kingston Train Station located on Route 138, West Kingston is one of the oldest continuously operating stations in the US.

Main Street at Kingston Village retains a charming 18th century Rhode Island feel. Old Washington County Jail located at 2636 Kingstown Rd, in Kingston Village depicts Kingston's 300 years of history. Located in West Kingston, The Old Washington County Courthouse is an impressive granite building. Built in 1707, the Old Narragansett Church located in Church Lane, Wickford is one of the oldest Episcopal Churches in America.

Kingston's train depot is located on Railroad Ave. West Kingston, RI 02892. The station is staffed and features an enclosed waiting area, restrooms, and payphones. Transportation options from the station include Rhode Island Public Transit Authority Tel: (401) 781-9400, Block Island Ferry Tel: (401) 783-4613, and local taxi service.

Trains serving Kingston station are the Twilight Shoreliner and the Northeast Direct.

Westerly (RI)

Westerly is located in the southwestern corner of the state of Rhode Island. The Town of Westerly was incorporated in 1669, and today Westerly is home to approximately 23,000 residents. Places of Interest: Flying Horse Carousel located on Bay St, Watch Hill; the carousel is the oldest in the US. Watch Hill Lighthouse Keepers Association, located at 14 Lighthouse Road, Watch Hill, was built in 1858 and the lighthouse exterior is open to the public.

Westerly's train depot is located at 14 Railroad Ave. Westerly, RI 02891. The station is staffed and features an enclosed waiting area, restrooms, payphones, and vending machines. Transportation options from the station include Rhode Island Public Transit Authority Tel: (401) 781-9400 and local taxi services.

The Twilight Shoreliner and Northeast Direct serve Westerly station.

Mystic (CT)

Mystic is located in southeastern Connecticut; it has a land area of 3 sq. miles (7.7 sq. kilometers) and a population of just 2,600. Places of interest: Olde Mistick Village, located on Coogan Boulevard, just off I-95 at Exit 90, will bring visitors back to the early 1700's Mystic Connecticut. Mystic Seaport, located on Greenmanville Avenue, Route 27, is one of the best maritime museums in the US.

The seaport exhibits galleries, several sea vessels, and marine artifacts. Denison Pequotsepos Nature Center, located at 109 Pequotsepos Road, offers an all seasons Connecticut woodland nature adventure. And Mystic Aquarium, located at 55 Coogan Boulevard, is home to more than 3,500 marine animals, including a beluga whale and seals.

Mystic's train depot is located on Rte. 1 Mystic, CT 06355. The station is un-staffed and features an enclosed waiting area, restrooms, and payphones. Transportation options from the station include Valenti Chevrolet Car Rental toll-free (860) 536-4931 and local taxi service.

Trains serving Mystic station are the Northeast Direct and the Twilight Shoreliner.

Connecticut (CT)
Capital: Hartford (Population: 3,405,565)
Size: 5,544 sq mi. (14,358 sq km)
Nicknames: The Constitution State
Joined the union on: January 9, 1788 (5th state)
Motto: He Who Transplanted Still Sustains
Flower: Mountain Laurel
Bird: American Robin
Song: "Yankee Doodle"
Famous for: Webster Dictionaries, and Yale University.
Major industries: Agriculture, tourism

New London (CT)

New London was founded in 1659 and was incorporated in 1784. New London has a land area of 5.4 sq. miles (14 sq. kilometers) and a population of roughly 29,000. Being situated in a long, deep shoreline of Thames River, New London has a rich maritime history.

Places of interest: New London Harbor Lighthouse, built in 1760, was the fourth oldest lighthouse in the United States; it was destroyed in 1799 and was rebuilt and completed in 1801.

New London's train depot is located at 27 Water St. New London, CT 06320. The station is staffed and features an enclosed waiting area, quik-trak ticket machine, restrooms, and payphones. Transportation options from the station include Budget Rent a Car Tel: (860) 446-1965, Avis Rent A Car toll-free (800) 230-4898, local bus Tel: (203) 624-0151, local transit - S.E.A.T. toll-free (860) 886-2631, and taxi service.

Trains serving New London station are the Northeast Direct and the Twilight Shoreliner.

Old Saybrook (CT)

Old Saybrook is located at the mouth of the Connecticut River and is one of the oldest towns in the lower Connecticut River Valley. Old Saybrook has a land area of 1.9 sq. miles (5 sq. kilometers) and a population of roughly 2,000. Places of interest: Fort Saybrook, built in 1636, is Connecticut's first British military fort. Lynde Point Lighthouse, built in 1803, is a 71-foot octagonal tower lighthouse.

Old Saybrook's train depot is located at 455 Boston Post Rd. Old Saybrook, CT 06475. The station is staffed and features an enclosed waiting area, restrooms, and payphones. Transportation options from the station include local taxi and transit services.

Trains serving Old Saybrook station are the Northeast Direct and Twilight Shoreliner.

New Heaven (CT) See Vermonter service, page 481.

Stamford (CT) See Vermonter service, page 483- 484.

New York (NY) See Lake Shore Limited- Albany to New York City service, page 405.

Newark (NJ) See Three Rivers and Pennsylvania- Pennsylvania service, page 428- 429.

Metropark (NJ) See Carolinian/Piedmont service, page 513- 515.

Trenton (NJ) See Three Rivers and Pennsylvania- Pennsylvania service, page 428- 429.

Philadelphia (PA) See Three Rivers and Pennsylvania- Pennsylvania service, page 424.

Wilmington (DE) See Vermonter service, page 483- 484.

Baltimore (MD) See Vermonter service, page 484.

BWI Airport Rail Sta. (MD) See Vermonter service, page 487- 488

New Carrollton (MD) See Vermonter service, page 487- 488.

Washington D.C See Capitol Limited service, page 441

Virginia (VA)
Capital: Richmond (Population: 7,078,515)
Size: 42,769 sq mi. (110,771 sq km)
Nickname: The Old Dominion, Mother of Presidents
Entered the union: June 25, 1788 (10th state)
Motto: Thus always to tyrants
Flower: American Dogwood
Bird: Cardinal
Song: Carry Me Back to Old Virginia
Famous for: Presidents, Aristocracy and guess what "Ham"
Major industries: Government, agriculture, and manufacturing.

Alexandria (VA) See Cardinal service, page 461.

Quantico (VA)

Quantico, an Indian word which means "By the large stream," is located along the Potomac River just 70 miles north of Richmond the state capital. Quantico has a land area of just 0.07 sq. miles (0.18 sq. kilometers) and a population of 670. Quantico is site to many historical events and was part of the American revolutionary movement. Home to the Marine Corps Schools founded in 1920, Quantico houses the largest Marine Corps installation in the US.

Quantico's train depot is located on Railroad Ave. Quantico, VA 22134. The station is un-staffed and features payphones. Transportation options from the station include local transit and taxi services.

Trains serving Quantico station are the Northeast Direct, Carolinian and Piedmont, and the Twilight Shoreliner.

Fredericksburg (VA)

Fredericksburg is located in northeastern Virginia just 49 miles southwest of Washington D.C. and 52 miles north of Richmond. Fredericksburg has a land area of 10.5 sq. miles (27 sq. kilometers) and a population of approximately 20,000 residents. Much of Fredericksburg's history is deeply associated with the history of American Revolution; the city was the center for manufacturing of ammunitions, many important leaders of the revolution met here and planned the success of the revolutionary war.

During the civil war the city was the site of one of the bloodiest battles in the history of the American civil war. A visit to Fredericksburg's downtown historic district will give visitors the spirit of the old colonial city.

Fredericksburg's train depot is located at Caroline St. and Lafayette Blvd, Fredericksburg, VA 22401. The station is un-staffed and features payphones and restaurants. Transportation options from the station include local transit and taxi services.

Trains serving Fredericksburg station are the Twilight Shoreliner, Northeast Direct, and the Carolinian and Piedmont.

Ashland (VA)

Ashland is located in the heart of Virginia, just 15 miles north of Richmond. Like Fredericksburgm, Ashland was a scene of some of the bloodiest battles in the history of American civil war. Ashland has a land area of 3.9 sq. miles (10 sq. kilometers) and a population of 5900.

Ashland's train depot is located at 112 N. Railroad Ave. Ashland, VA 23005. The station is un-staffed and features an enclosed waiting area. Transportation from the station is local taxi service.

Trains serving Ashland station are the Twilight Shoreliner and the Northeast Direct.

Richmond (VA)

Richmond is the state capital of Virginia and is located in eastern Virginia. Richmond was home to the Indian tribes of the Powhatan for many years and in 1737 Colonel William Byrd II rediscovered the site. Richmond became the state capital in 1779 and confederate capital in 1861 during the American civil war. Richmond has a land area of 60.7 sq. miles (155.7 sq. kilometers) and a population of more than 200,000.

Richmond's train depot is located at 7519 Staples Mill Rd. Richmond, VA 23228. The station is staffed and features an enclosed waiting area, quik-trak ticket machines, checked baggage service, restrooms, payphones, snack bar and vending machines. Transportation options from the station include Budget Rent a Car toll-free (800) 527-0770, Enterprise Rent-A-Car toll-free (800) 325-8007, and local transit service.

Trains serving Richmond station are the Twilight Shoreliner, Silver Service, Northeast Direct, and the Carolinian and Piedmont.

Places to See and Things to Do

The Old City Hall is located at 1001 E. Broad Street and is a fine Victorian Gothic building built in 1894. **Main Street Station**, located at 1520 E. Main Street, is listed on the national register of historic places; the historic station was once the city's grand train station. **Canal Walk**, located in Riverfront between Seventh and 12th streets, features part of the 197-mile James River and Kanawha Canal system. **Federal Reserve Money Museum** is located at the Federal Reserve headquarters at Seventh and Byrd streets Tel: (804) 697-8000; the museum exhibits the history of money printing and old collections of paper money and coins.

Edgar Allan Poe Museum, located at 1914-16 E. Main Street Tel: (804) 648-5523, is one of the oldest buildings in Richmond; it is dedicated to the famous writer Edgar Alan Poe. **The Library of Virginia,** located at 800 E. Broad St. Tel: (804) 692-3592, has rare collections of written documents and records of Virginia's history. **Marine Raider Museum and American Historical Foundation Museum,** located at 1142 W. Grace St. Tel: (804) 353-1812, exhibits marine artifacts and the history of the US military. **Museum of the Confederacy and the Confederate Executive Mansion,** located at 1201 E. Clay St. Tel: (804) 649-1861, exhibits one of the largest collections of US civil war artifacts in the US.

Linden Row (Inn), located at 100-114 E. Franklin Street, was a former girls school and is one of the city's best districts. **Monument Avenue** known as one of the most beautiful street in the US is situated in Lombardy to Roseneath Road. **Maymont,** located at 1700 Hampton St. Tel: (804) 358-7166, is a Victorian estate that houses lovely gardens and a museum. **Masonic Hall,** located on Franklin Street between 18th and 19th streets, is a historic building built in 1787. The **Monumental Church,** located at 1224 E. Broad Street, is the site of the 1811 fire that leveled the former Richmond Theater along with the many of the city's prominent resident. Many of the victims' remains were buried inside the church vault.

Accommodations

AmeriSuites Richmond Arboretum located at 201 Arboretum Place Richmond VA toll-free (800) 833-1516. **Jefferson Hotel** located at 101 West Franklin Street Richmond VA 23225 toll-free (800) 424-8014. **Wyndham Hotel Richmond Airport** located at 4700 South Laburnum Avenue Richmond VA 23231 Tel: (804) 226-4300. **Linden Row Inn** located at 100 East Franklin Street Richmond VA 23219 Tel: (804) 783-7000. **Comfort Inn Corporate Gateway** located at 8710 Midlothian Turnpike Richmond VA 23235 Tel: (804) 320-8900.

Comfort Inn Executive Center located at 7201 West Broad Street Richmond VA 23294 Tel: (804) 672-1108. **Econo Lodge** located at 2125 Willis Rd, Richmond, VA 23237 Tel: (804) 271-6031. **Courtyard Richmond West** located at 6400 West Broad Street Richmond VA 23230 Tel: (804) 282-1881. **Days Inn** located at 1600 Robin Hood Rd, Richmond, VA 23220 Tel: (804) 353-1287. **Econo Lodge Richmond** located at 8350

Brook Road Richmond VA 23227 Tel: (804) 262-7070. **Super 8 Motel Richmond Broad Street** located at 7200 West Broad Street Richmond VA 23294 Tel: (804) 672-8128.

Sheraton Richmond West Hotel located at 6624 West Broad Street Richmond VA 23230 Tel: (804) 285-1234. **Crowne Plaza Hotel Richmond-E Canal** located at 555 East Canal Street Richmond VA 23219 Tel: (804) 788-0900. **Best Western Governors Inn** located at 9826 Midlothian Tpke, Richmond, VA 23235 Tel: (804) 323-0007. **Holiday Inn Richmond Central** located at 3207 North Boulevard Richmond VA 23230 Tel: (804) 359-9441. **Holiday Inn Express Richmond** located at 9933 Mayland Drive Richmond VA 23233 Tel: (804) 934-9300.

Williamsburg (VA)

Williamsburg is located between Richmond and Newport. Williamsburg was Virginia's center for politics, economy, and culture during the colonial era. Named after King William III of England, Williamsburg was the state capital of Virginia during the early 1700's until 1780 when the capital was moved to Richmond. Williamsburg is home to the historical College of William & Mary and the Historic Triangle, also known as the largest living museum in the world. Williamsburg has a land area of 8.5 sq. miles (22 sq. kilometers) and a population of just over 12,000.

Places of interest: the Williamsburg Historic District, also known as the largest museum in the world, exhibits well-preserved structures. The College of William & Mary located at the end of Duke of Gloucester Street in the Historic District is where Thomas Jefferson went to study; the college is the second oldest in the US. Historic Jamestown is the first English settlement in the United States; there are several historical sites in the area. Busch Gardens, located at 8550 Richmond Road Tel: (757) 253-3350, has roller coaster rides, entertainment, and games for every member of the family; a fun place to visit. And the Music Theatre of Williamsburg, located at 7575 Richmond Road Tel: (757) 564-0200, features live entertainment shows.

Williamsburg's train depot is located at 468 N. Boundary St. Williamsburg, VA 23185. The station is staffed and features an enclosed waiting area, restrooms, payphones, quik-trak ticket machines, and vending machines. Transportation options from the station include Thrifty Car Rental Tel: (757) 877-5745, Avis Rent A Car toll-free (800) 230-4898, Budget Rent a Car Tel: (757) 847-5794, J.C.C.T. Transit Authority Tel: (757) 220-1621, local bus and taxi services.

Trains serving Williamsburg station are the Twilight Shoreliner, Northeast Direct and the Acela Regional.

Newport News (VA)

Newport News is located in southeastern Virginia 62 miles southeast of Richmond near Norfolk and Hampton. Newport News has a land area of 68.9 sq. miles (176.9 sq. kilometers) and a population of approximately 170,000. It was founded in 1621 and played a major role in the campaign of the American civil war. It was here in Newport News where the renowned "Battle of the Ironclads" took place in 1862. Also some of the most famous battleships and aircraft carriers of the modern American war fleet were built here including the Roosevelt, Enterprise, and the Kennedy.

Newport News' train depot is located at 9304 Warwick Blvd. Newport News, VA 23601. The station is staffed and features an enclosed waiting area, quik-trak ticket machine, restrooms, and payphones. Transportation options from the station include Budget Rent a Car Tel: (757) 847-5794, Enterprise Rent-A-Car Tel: (757) 872-9536, Hops Taxi Tel: (757) 245-3005, Independent Taxi Tel: (757) 245-8378, and Pentran City Bus Tel: (757) 723-3344.

Trains serving Newport News station are the Northeast Direct and the Twilight Shoreliner.

Places of Interest

Virginia War Museum is located at 9285 Warwick Boulevard Tel: (757) 247-8523; the museum exhibits more than 6,000 artifacts of American military history. **The Mariners' Museum** is located at 100 Museum Drive Tel: (757) 596-2222 and exhibits maritime artifacts and miniature marine vessels. **Virginia Living Museum**, located at 524 J. Clyde Morris Boulevard Tel: (757) 595-1900, exhibits live wild animals in their natural habitats. The **James River Reserve Fleet,** or the "ghost fleet," is best viewed along Harrison Road on Ft.

Governors Palace, Williamsburg

Eustis. Visitors can also join the James River Ghost Fleet Cruise toll-free: (800) 853-5002.

Newport News Park is located at 13564 Jefferson Avenue Tel: (757) 886-7912; the park is the local favorite recreational park for hiking, biking, canoeing, camping, and more. **Victory Arch,** located at West Avenue and 25th Street, was dedicated to the men and women of the US armed forces.

Historic Hilton Village, extending from Warwick Boulevard to the James River, is listed on the national register of historic places; the village features English architecture buildings of the early 1900's. The **Historic North End/Huntington Heights** district is located between Huntington Avenue and Warwick Boulevard. The district features several beautiful homes of the early 1900's.

Accommodations

Executive Inn located at 6069 Jefferson Ave, Newport News, VA 23605 Tel: (757) 247-5330. **Travelodge** located at 13700 Warwick Blvd, Newport News, VA 23602 Tel: (757) 874-4100. **Ramada Inn** located at 950 J Clyde Morris Blvd, Newport News, VA 23601 Tel: (757) 599-4460. **Ft Eustis Inn** located at 16924 Warwick Blvd, Newport News, VA 23603 Tel: (757) 887-9122. **Days Inn** located at 11829 Fishing Point Dr, Newport News, VA 23606 Tel: (757) 873-6700.

Budget Lodge located at 930 J Clyde Morris Blvd, Newport News, VA 23601 Tel: (757) 599-5647. **Econo Lodge** located at 15237 Warwick Blvd, Newport News, VA 23608 Tel: (757) 874-9244. **Comfort Inn** located at 12330 Jefferson Ave, Newport News, VA 23602 Tel: (757) 249-0200. **Newport News Inn** located at 6128 Jefferson Ave, Newport News, VA 23605 Tel: (757) 826-9654. **Holiday Inn** located at 16890 Warwick Blvd, Newport News, VA 23603 Tel: (757) 887-3300.

Hampton Inn located at 12251 Jefferson Ave, Newport News, VA 23602 Tel: (757) 249-0001. **Warwick Motel** located at 12304 Warwick Blvd, Newport News, VA 23606 Tel: (757) 599-4444. **King James Motor Hotel** located at 6045 Jefferson Ave, Newport News, VA 23605 Tel: (757) 245-2801. **Omni Newport News Hotel** located at 1000 Omni Blvd, Newport News, VA 23606 Tel: (757) 873-6664.

Carolinian/Piedmont

6:05 am- **D**	**New York (NY)**	10:10 pm-**A**
6:24 am	Newark (NJ)	9:48 pm
6;38 am	Metropark (NJ)	9:31 pm
7:03 am	Trenton (NJ)	9:10 pm
1:31 am	Philadelphia (PA)	8:40 pm-D
7:43 am		8:19 pm-A
8:06 am	Wilmington (DE)	7:58 pm
9:10 am	Baltimore (MD)	7:10 pm
9:25 am	BWI Airport Rail Sta.(MD)	6:54 pm
9:41 am	New Carrollton (MD)	6:37 pm
9:55 am	**Washington DC**	6:25 pm-D
10:25 am		5:32 pm-A
10:42 am	Alexandria (VA)	5:06 pm
11:14 am	Quantico (VA)	4:37 pm
11:32 am	Fredericksburg (VA)	4:17 pm
12:32 am- A	Richmond (VA)	3:23 pm-D
12:42 am- D		3:16 pm-A
1 :13 pm	Petersburg (VA)	2 :42 pm
2 :40 pm	Rocky Mount (NC)	1 :20 pm
2:58 pm	Wilson (NC)	1:01 pm
3:26 pm	Selma (NC)	12:32 pm
4:05 pm-A	Raleigh (NC)	11:57 am-D
4:17 pm-D		11:49 am-A
4:31 pm	Cary (NC)	11:33 am
4:58 pm	Durham (NC)	11:08 am
5:43 pm	Burlington (NC)	10:20 am
6:29 pm	Greensboro (NC)	9:44 am
6:43 pm	High Point (NC)	9:24 am
7:24 pm	Salisbury (NC)	8:45 am
7:41 pm	Kannapolis (NC)	8:27 am
8:16 pm - **A**	Charlotte (NC)	8:00 am-**D**

D-Departure
A-Arrival
Multiple Daily Train Departure

Carolinian/ Piedmont

Carolinian and Piedmont brings passengers to some of the most historical, exciting, and beautiful cities of the eastern United States. It connects the cities of New York, Philadelphia, Washington D.C., Richmond, Raleigh, and Charlotte. The Carolinian and Piedmont are jointly operated and financed by Amtrak and the State of North Carolina.

Route Destination Highlights

Charlotte, NC- Visit the Charlotte Museum of History/Hezekiah Alexander Homesite, the Mint Museum of Art, the Mint Museum of Craft and Design, take a trolley tour on the Charlotte Historic Trolley Museum, or take a trip to nearby Great Smokey Mountain National Park.

Raleigh, NC- Visit the North Carolina Museum of Art, the Raleigh City Museum, and the Joel Lane Museum House. Take the Historic Trolley Tour at Mordecai Historic Park and tour around the historic city of Raleigh. Visit the birthplace of President Andrew Johnson, the St. Mary's School, and the Historic Oakwood district both listed on the National Register of Historic Places.

Baltimore, MD- Visit the oldest Catholic Church in Baltimore, St. Vincent de Paul Church; Baltimore's oldest restored historic cathedral and the oldest cemetery, Westminster Hall and Burying Ground; visit the home of the first American Roman Catholic canonized saint at the Mother Seton House. The Baltimore Street Car Museum, the B and O Railroad Museum, National Museum of Dentistry, the birthplace of the American national anthem at Fort McHenry National Monument and Historic Shrine, and the home of Mary Pickersgill creator of the Star-Spangled Banner at the Star-Spangled Banner Flag House and Museum.

Philadelphia, PA- See the world's largest mint the U.S. Mint, the oldest zoo in the US the Philadelphia Zoo, pay a visit to the body of Saint John Neumann at National Shrine of Saint John Neumann, visit the birthplace of the nation Independence Hall and the Liberty Bell, spend one afternoon and stroll Fairmount Park or shop in Philadelphia's upscale district Rittenhouse Square.

New York, NY- See and admire the most popular statue in the world, the Statue of Liberty; explore the Ellis Island Immigration Museum, Central Park, Times Square, the United Nations, and some of the tallest buildings in the world. Visit the 1913 Beaux architecture Grand Central Terminal, the Museum of Sex, and the Museum of Modern Art.

Train Schedules

Carolinian and Piedmont travels daily from New York City, New York to Charlotte, South Carolina. The trip between the two cities takes approximately 14 hours of travel time.

Accommodations

Both services have a Reserved Coach accommodation. Other accommodations are Dinette Car, Business Class Coach available in Carolinian, and Cafe Lounge available in Piedmont. Carolinian has entertainment and amenities served for Business Class, while Piedmont has hot meals and other snacks served at the Café Lounge.

All Aboard!

New York City (NY) See Lake Shore Limited, page 405.

Newark (NJ) See Three Rivers and Pennsylvania- Pennsylvania service, page 428- 429.

Metropark (NJ)

Metropark's train depot is located at 100 Middlesex-Essex Tpk. Garden State Pkw. Exit 131 Iselin, NJ 08830. The station is staffed and features an enclosed waiting area, quik-trak ticket machine, restrooms, and payphones. Transportation options from the station include local transit and taxi services.

Trains serving Metropark station are the Metroliner, Keystone, Vermonter, Twilight Shoreliner, Carolinian and Piedmont, Northeast Direct, Acela Regional, and the Acela Express.

Trenton (NJ) See Three Rivers and Pennsylvania – Pennsylvania Route, page 428 -429.

Philadelphia (PA) See Three Rivers and Pennsylvania – Pennsylvania Route, page 424.

Wilmington (DE) See Vermonter service, page 483- 484.

Baltimore (MD) See Vermonter service, page 484.

BWI Airport (MD) See Vermonter service, page 487–488.

New Carrollton (MD) See Vermonter service, page 487–488.

Washington DC See Capitol Limited service, page 441.

Alexandria (VA) See Cardinal service, page 461.

Quantico (VA) See Twilight Shoreline service, page 503–507.

Fredericksburg (VA) See Twilight Shoreline service, page 503–507.

Richmond (VA) See Twilight Shoreline service, page 507.

Petersburg (VA)

Petersburg is located 23 miles south of Richmond; it has a land area of 23 sq. miles (59 sq. kilometers) and a population of approximately 40,000. Petersburg is known as the site of the Battle of the Crater during the civil war. Native American Indians were living at the site of what is now Petersburg for many years. European settlers gradually moved to the area and in 1748 the town of Petersburg was formally established.

Petersburg's train depot is located at 3516 South St, Ettrick Petersburg, VA 23803. The station is staffed and features an enclosed waiting area, checked baggage service, restrooms, payphones, and restaurants. Transportation from the station is local taxi service.

Trains serving Petersburg station are the Carolinian and Piedmont and the Silver Service.

Rocky Mount (NC)

Rocky Mount is located in eastern North Carolina just 45 miles east of Raleigh. It has a land area of 25 sq. miles (64.7 sq. kilometers) and a population of approximately 55,000. The town of Rocky Mount was incorporated as a town in 1867 and as a city in 1907. In 1970 Rocky Mount was named an All-American city.

Rocky Mount's train depot is located at 101 Hammond St. Rocky Mount, NC 27801. The station is staffed and features an enclosed waiting area, checked baggage service, restrooms, payphones, and vending machines. Transportation options from the station include local bus and taxi services.

Trains serving Rocky Mount station are the Carolinian and Piedmont, and Silver Service.

Wilson (NC)

Wilson is recognized as one of North Carolina's most beautiful cities. It was the native Indian tribe called the Tuscaroras who first lived and ruled the land of what is now Wilson County. Wilson was incorporated in 1849 with a land area of 18.6 sq. miles (47.9 sq. kilometers) and a population of roughly 37,000. Wilson is located just 42 miles east of Raleigh.

Places of interest: Dean's Farm Market located at 4273 NC 42 W. Wilson, NC 27893 Tel: (252) 237-0967. Wilson Area Railroad Modelers, Inc. at the Antique Barn 2810 Forest Hills Rd. Wilson, NC 27893 Tel: (252) 237-6778. Tobacco Farm Life Museum is located on Hwy 301 N. Kenly, NC 27542 Tel: (919) 284-3431. And Country Doctor Museum is located at 6642 Peele Rd. Bailey, NC 27807 Tel: (252) 235-4165.

North Carolina (NC)
Capital: Raleigh (Population: 8,049,313)
Size: 53,821 sq mi. (139,396 sq km)
Nickname: The Tar Heel State
Joined the union on: November 21, 1789 (12th state)
Motto: To be rather than to seem
Flower: Dogwood
Bird: Cardinal
Song: The Old North State
Famous for: the first English colony in America
Major industries: Furniture manufacturing, tobacco, textile, chemicals, agriculture

Wilson's train depot is located at 401 E. Nash St. Wilson, NC 27893. The station is unstaffed and features an enclosed waiting area, payphones, and restrooms. Transportation options from the station include local bus and taxi services.

Trains serving Wilson station are the Carolinian and Piedmont, and Silver Service.

Selma-Smithfield (NC)

Selma and Smithfield are located 28 miles southeast of Raleigh. Selma has a land area of 4.9 sq. miles (8 sq. kilometers) and a population of just over 5,000. Smithfield has a land area of 6.9 sq. miles (17.7 sq. kilometers) and a population of approximately 11,000. Selma is popularly known for its many antique shops in its downtown area while Smithfield is known as the home of Ava Gardner (movie star); the actress was honored with the town's Ava Gardner Museum located at 325 E. Market Street.

Selma's train depot is located at 401 E. Railroad St. Selma, NC 27576. The station is unstaffed and features payphones. Transportation from the station is local taxi service.

Carolinian and Piedmont serve Selma-Smithfield station.

Raleigh (NC)

Raleigh is the state capital and is located in north central North Carolina. The city of Raleigh was named after Sir Walter Raleigh; the city is also known as the City of Oaks. Raleigh is one of the oldest cities in the United States and was founded as the state capital 1792.

Raleigh was home to the seventeenth president of the United States, Andrew Johnson. Raleigh has a land area of 88.9 sq. miles (228 sq. kilometers) and a population of approximately 280,000.

Getting Around

Airport

Raleigh-Durham International Airport Tel: (919) 840-2123 is located 10 miles (16 Kilometers) south of Raleigh. Major car rental services are located within the airport. Taxi services are available on the lower level at the arrival area. Airport shuttle bus is available at the baggage claim area; local transit also serves the airport.

Bus

Capital Area Transit Triangle serves the city of Raleigh and the outlying areas, call Transit Authority Tel: (919) 549-9999 for information. Greyhound connects the city of Raleigh to the rest of the country toll-free (800) 231-2222.

Taxi

Alpha Cab Company Tel: (919) 385-4953, Metro Cab Company Tel: (919) 479-4785, Dixon Cab Tel: (919) 688-9593, American Cab Company Tel: (919) 821-0095, Cardinal Cab Company Tel: (919) 828-3228, DART, Inc. Tel: (919) 688-6121, Diamond Cab Company Tel: (919) 302-5557, and Silver Cab Company Tel: (919) 319-5403.

Rent-A-Car

Budget toll-free (800) 527-0700, Avis toll-free (800) 331-1212, Alamo toll-free (800) 327-9633, National toll-free (800) 227-7368, Hertz toll-free (800) 654-3131, Thrifty toll-free (800) 847-4389, Triangle toll-free (800) 643-7368, and Dollar toll-free (800) 800-4000.

Train and Commuter

Raleigh's train depot is located at 320 W. Cabarrus St. Raleigh, NC 27601. The station is staffed and features an enclosed waiting area, checked baggage service, restrooms, payphones, and vending machines. Transportation options from the station include local transit and taxi services.

Trains serving Raleigh station are the Carolinian and Piedmont and Silver Service.

Visitor Information Center

Capital Area Visitor Center, 301 N. Blount St. Raleigh, NC Tel: (919) 733-3456.

Places to See and Things to Do

North Carolina Museum of Art is located at 2110 Blue Ridge Road Raleigh, NC 27607 Tel: (919) 839-NCMA. **Raleigh City Museum** is located at 220 Fayetteville Street Mall Briggs Building Raleigh, NC Tel: (919) 832-3775. **Joel Lane Museum House,** located on the corner of St. Mary's and W. Hargett Streets Raleigh, NC Tel: (919) 833-3431, is the oldest residential house in Raleigh built in 1760. **Contemporary Art Museum** located at 409 W. Martin Street, Raleigh, NC. Tel: (919) 836-0088 exhibits contemporary modern arts.

The North Carolina Symphony located in the Memorial Auditorium at 2 E. South St. Raleigh, NC Tel: (919) 733-2750. **The Carolina Ballet** located at 3101 Glenwood Ave, Suite 265 Raleigh, NC Tel: (919) 303-6303. **Historic Trolley Tours**, at Mordecai Historic Park Tel: (919) 834-4844, offers a narrated tour around the city of Raleigh. **North Carolina Museum of History,** located at 5 E. Edenton St, Bicentenial Plaza Tel: (919) 715-0200, features the history of North Carolina. **Martin Luther King Jr. Memorial Gardens** is located on the Corner of Rock Quarry Rd. and Martin Luther King Blvd Raleigh 27611 Tel: (919) 834-6264; the park was dedicated to the civil rights activist Martin Luther King Jr.

Birthplace of President Andrew Johnson is located at Corner of Mimosa St. and Wake Forest Rd. Raleigh, NC Tel: (919) 834-4844. **Oakwood Cemetery** is located adjacent to Historic Oakwood, at 701 Oakwood Ave, Raleigh 27601 Tel: (919) 832-6077; built in 1869, the cemetery is the final resting place to many of Confederate Army and other prominent people. **St. Mary's School,** located at 900 Hillsborough St, Raleigh 27603 Tel: (919) 424-4000, is listed on the national register of historic places. The school was founded in 1842 as a preparatory school for young girls.

Historic Oakwood district bordered by Franklin, Watauga, Linden, Jones, and Person Streets Tel: (919) 733-3456 is listed on the National Register of Historic Places. The district has many restored 19th century houses. **North Carolina State Capitol,** located in Capitol Square, 1 E. Edenton St, Raleigh 27601 Tel: (919) 733-4994, is a national historic landmark; the state capitol was built between 1833 and 1840 in Greek Revival-style architecture. **Saint Augustine's College Chapel** is located at 1315 Oakwood Ave, Raleigh 27610 Tel: (919) 516-4189; this historic Norman Gothic-style chapel was built in 1896.

Accommodations

Sheraton Capital Center Hotel Raleigh located at 421 South Salisbury Street, Raleigh NC 27601 Tel: (919) 834-9900, expect to pay $50-$300. **Days Inn Crabtree Raleigh** located at 6329 Glenwood Avenue, Raleigh NC toll-free (800) 544-8313, expect to pay $30-$110. **Marriott Crabtree Valley Raleigh** located at 4500 Marriott Drive, Raleigh NC 27612 Tel: (919) 781-7000, expect to pay $50-$150. **Hampton Inn Capital Blvd Raleigh** located at 3621 Spring Forest Road, Raleigh NC 27616 Tel: (919) 872-7111, expect to pay $50-$100.

Hilton North Raleigh located at 3415 Wake Forest Road, Raleigh NC 27609 Tel: (919) 872-2323. **Embassy Suites Crabtree Valley Raleigh** located at 4700 Creedmoor Road, Raleigh NC 27612 toll-free (800) 362-2779, expect to pay $70-$200. **Clarion Hotel Crabtree** located at 4501 Creedmoor Road, Raleigh NC 27612 Tel: (919) 787-7111, expect to pay $50-$200. **Brownestone Hotel Raleigh** located at 1707 Hillsborough Street, Raleigh NC 27605 toll-free (800) 331-7919, expect to pay $70-$150. **Comfort Inn North Raleigh** located at 2910 Capital Blvd, Raleigh NC 27604 Tel: (919) 878-9550, expect to pay $50-$150.

Holiday Inn Crabtree Raleigh located at 4100 Glendwood Avenue, Raleigh NC 27612 Tel: (919) 782-8600, expect to pay $50-$150. **Red Roof Inn South Garner Raleigh** located at

1813 South Saunders Street, Raleigh NC 27603 toll-free (800) RED-ROOF, expect to pay $50-$80. **Wingate Inn Raleigh** located at 2610 Westinghouse Blvd, Raleigh NC 27604 toll-free (800) 993-7232, expect to pay $50-$150. **Comfort Inn Six Forks Raleigh** located at 4220 Six Forks Road, Raleigh NC 27609 Tel: (919) 787-2300, expect to pay $40-$100.

Cary (NC)

Cary is located just 8 miles west of Raleigh adjacent to the Research Triangle Park. Cary was first settled in 1750 and was called Bradford's Ordinary; in 1850 the name was changed to Cary and the town was incorporated in 1871. Cary has a land area of 31 sq. miles (80.7 sq. kilometers) and a population of more than 100,000.

Place of interest: Cary historic train depot in downtown has been serving the town for many years, and the Page-Walker Arts and History Center, located in Town Hall Campus, is listed on the National Register of Historic Places.

Cary's train depot is located at 211 North Academy Street Cary, NC 27511. The station is un-staffed and features an enclosed waiting area, restrooms, payphones, and vending machines. Transportation options from the station include local transit and taxi services.

Carolinian and Piedmont serve Cary station.

Durham (NC)

Durham, also known as the "Bull City" or the "City of Medicine," is located 18 miles northwest of Raleigh, part of the Research Triangle Park. Research Triangle Park is a triangular region that encompasses the cities of Durham, Raleigh, and Chapel Hill where major world companies are conducting research in various areas of science. Durham is also home to the renowned Duke University Medical School. Durham has a land area of 69.8 sq. miles (179 sq. kilometers) and a population of 187,035.

The site of what is now the city of Durham was once home to native Indians the Eno and Occaneechi for many generations. The town was founded in 1853 and was first called Durhamville, later it was shortened to Durham's and again was officially shortened to Durham. The town of Durham was incorporated in 1869.

Durham's train depot is located on Pettigrew St. Durham, NC 27704. The station is un-staffed and features an enclosed waiting area, restrooms, payphones, and vending machines. Transportation from the station is local taxi service.

Durham station is served by the Carolinian and Piedmont.

North Carolina (NC)	
Capital: Raleigh (Population: 8,049,313)	
Size: 53,821 sq mi. (139,396 sq km)	
Nickname: The Tar Heel State	
Joined the union on: November 21, 1789 (12th state)	
Motto: To be rather than to seem	
Flower: Dogwood	
Bird: Cardinal	
Song: The Old North State	
Famous for: the first English colony in America	
Major industries: Furniture manufacturing, tobacco, textile, chemicals, agriculture	

Burlington (NC)

Burlington is located 48 miles northwest of Raleigh. The town of Burlington was incorporated in 1893 and it has a land area of 20 sq. miles (52 sq. kilometers) and a population of more than 39,000. The historic Burlington train depot was built in the mid 1800's, for many years it served as a meeting place to the community.

The Burlington Historic District, located around West Davis and West Front Streets and Fountain Place area, is listed in the National Register of Historic Places. Several houses and buildings of Victorian architecture are still well preserved. Other places of interest are: the Dentzel Menagerie Carousel located in City Park and the Alamance Battleground and Museum located five miles south of Burlington.

Burlington's train depot is located at 110 E. Webb Ave. Burlington, NC 27216. The station is un-staffed and features payphones. Transportation options from the station include local transit and taxi services.

Burlington station is served by the Carolinian and Piedmont.

Greensboro (NC)

Greensboro is located in north central North Carolina just 67 miles northwest of Raleigh. The Saura and Keyauwee Indians first inhabited the area until 1740 when the permanent European settlement came to the area. Greensboro has a land area of 68.64 sq. miles (176 sq. Kilometers) and a population of 209,000.

Places of interest: the Blandwood Mansion and Carriage House, located at 447 W. Washington St. Tel: (910) 272-5003, is listed as a National Historic Landmark; the mansion is a 19th century Italian Villa, home of the former North Carolina Governor John Motley Morehead. The Greensboro Historical Museum is located at 130 Summit Ave. Tel: (336) 373-2043. Water spoon Art Gallery, located on the corner of Spring Garden and Tate St in the Anne and Benjamin Cone Building on the UNCG campus Tel: (910) 334-5770, exhibits American arts and houses a museum and galleries. And the Mattyed Reed African Heritage Museum, located in NC A&T State University at 1601 E. Market St. Tel: (910) 334-7874, has one of the best collections of African art and culture in the US.

Greensboro's train depot is located at 2603 Oakland Ave. Greensboro, NC 27403. The station is staffed and features an enclosed waiting area, checked baggage service, restrooms, payphones, and vending machines. Transportation from the station is local taxi service.

Greensboro station is served by the Carolinian and Piedmont and the Crescent.

High Point (NC)

High Point is located just 13 miles southwest of Greensboro in north central North Carolina. High Point has a land area of 43 sq. miles (111 sq. kilometers) and a population of approximately 79,000. High Point was named for being the highest point on the North Carolina railroad. The city is known as the world's center for "Home Furnishing Market."

Places of interest: The World's Largest Chest of Drawers built 1926 is High Point's testimony as the world furnishing capital, located at 508 N. Hamilton St. Tel: (336) 883-2016. The Atrium Furniture Mall, located at 430 S. Main St. Tel: (336) 882-5599, has various old and modern galleries. The Furniture Discovery Center, located at 101 W. Green Dr. Tel: (336) 887-3876, features and illustrates modern furniture manufacturing. Bernice Bienenstock Furniture Library, located at 1009 N. Main St. Tel: (336) 883-4011, has the world's largest book collection about the history of furniture. Angela Peterson Doll and Miniature Museum, 101 W. Green Dr. Tel: (336) 885-3655, exhibits more than 2,000 dolls and dollhouses. And the High Point Museum & Historical Park, located at 1859 E. Lexington Ave. Tel: (336) 885-1859, exhibits the history of High Point and its industries.

High Point's train depot is located at 100 W. High St. High Point, NC 27260. The station is un-staffed and features an enclosed waiting area, restrooms, payphones, and vending machines. Transportation options from the station include local transit and taxi services.

Trains serving High Point station are the Carolinian and Piedmont and Crescent.

Salisbury (NC)

Salisbury is located in the center of Rowan County in north central North Carolina. Salisbury has a land area of 16 sq. miles (42 sq. kilometers) and a population of more than 23,000.

Places of interest: Salisbury's Historic Downtown District was listed in the National Register of Historic Places, there are many residential and commercial buildings from the early 1900 still preserved. The O.O. Rufty's General Store & Market, located at 126 East Innes St. Salisbury, NC Tel: (704) 633-4381, is a 1905 general merchandise store run by the Ruffy's for 3 generations. History/Genealogy Room at Rowan Public Library is located at 201 W. Fisher St. Salisbury, NC Tel: (704) 638-3021. Waterworks Visual Arts Center, located at One Water St. Salisbury, NC Tel: (704) 636-1882, exhibits national art gallery exhibitions, amongst others. And the Piedmont Players Theatre, located at 213 S. Main St. Salisbury, NC Tel: (704) 633-5471, is one of the oldest operating theaters in North Carolina.

Salisbury's train depot is located at Depot and Liberty streets, Salisbury, NC 24142. The station is un-staffed and features an enclosed waiting area and payphones. Transportation options from the station include local transit and taxi services.

Trains serving Salisbury station are the Carolinian and Piedmont and the Crescent.

Kannapolis (NC)

Kannapolis is a thriving city with a population of 36,910 and a land area of 15.8 sq. miles (40.6 sq. kilometers). Kannapolis' train depot is located at 306 N. Main St. Kannapolis, NC 28081. The station is un-staffed and features an enclosed waiting area, restrooms, and payphones. Transportation from the station is local taxi service.

Kannapolis station is served by the Carolinian and Piedmont.

Charlotte is located in southern North Carolina near the North and South Carolina state boarder. Charlotte has a land area of 175 sq. miles (451 sq. kilometers) and a population of more than 500,000. Charlotte was founded by the Scotch-Irish settlers in the mid 1700's and named after the queen of England. Charlotte was incorporated in 1768.

Charlotte's train depot is located at 1914 N. Tryon St. Charlotte, NC 28206. The station is staffed and features an enclosed waiting area, checked baggage service, restrooms, payphones, and vending machines. Transportation options from the station include Hertz Car Rental toll-free (800) 654-3131, local transit and taxi service.

Trains serving Charlotte station are the Carolinian and Piedmont and Crescent.

Visitor Information Center

Charlotte Visitor Information Center, Charlotte Convention & Visitors Bureau 122 E. Stonewall Street Charlotte, NC 28202 Tel: (704) 331-2700 or toll-free (800) 231-4636.

Places to See and Things to Do

Carolina Historic Aviation Commission Air Museum is located at Airport Drive Charlotte, NC 28219 Tel: (704) 359-8442. **Charlotte Museum of History/Hezekiah Alexander Homesite** is located at 3500 Shamrock Drive Charlotte, NC 28215 Tel: (704) 568-1774. **Mint Museum of Art** is located at 2730 Randolph Rd Charlotte, NC 28207-2012 Tel: (704) 337-2000. **Mint Museum of Craft and Design** is located at 220 North Tryon Street Charlotte, NC 28202 Tel: (704) 337-2000. **Charlotte Historic Trolley Museum**, located at 2100 South Boulevard Charlotte, NC Tel: (704) 375-0850, exhibits old Charlotte's trolley memorabilia and offers trolley rides.

Historic Rosedale Plantation, located at 3427 North Tryon Street Charlotte, NC 28206 Tel: (704) 335-0325, is listed on the National Register and features an 1815 manor house and gardens. **Vietnam War Memorial Wall at Thompson Park** is located at 1129 East Third Street Charlotte, NC 28202 Tel: (704) 336-4200. The 18th century **Settler's Cemetery,** located on the corner of Fifth Street & Church Street Charlotte, NC 28202 Tel: (704) 331-2700, is the oldest city-owned cemetery. Information on **Great Smokey Mountain National Park** is available by calling Tel: (615) 436-1200.

Accommodations

Ameri Suites Charlotte located at 7900 Forest Point Blvd, Charlotte, NC 28273, Tel: (704) 522-8400. **Country Inn & Suites-Carlson** located at 2541 Little Rock Rd, Charlotte, NC 28214 Tel: (704) 394-2000. **Days Inn** located at 118 E Woodlawn Rd, Charlotte, NC 28217 Tel: (704) 525-5500. **Hampton Inn** located at 530 E 2nd St, Charlotte, NC 28202 Tel: (704) 373-0917. **Hilton Charlotte** located at 8629 J M Keynes Dr, Charlotte, NC 28262 Tel: (704) 547-7444. **Travelodge** located at 2812 Beatties Ford Rd, Charlotte, NC 28216 Tel: (704)

394-4817.

Best Inn & Suites located at 219 Archdale Dr, Charlotte, NC 28217 Tel: (704) 527-8500. **Courtyard by Marriott** located at 15660 John J Delaney Dr, Charlotte, NC 28277 Tel: (704) 341-0041. **Econo Lodge** located at 1415 Tom Hunter Rd, Charlotte, NC 28213 Tel: (704) 597-0470. **Embassy Suites Hotel** located at 4800 S Tryon St, Charlotte, NC 28217 Tel: (704) 527-8400. **Ramada Inn** located at 3000 E Independence Blvd, Charlotte, NC 28205 Tel: (704) 377-1501.

Townplace Suites by Marriott located at 7805 Forest Point Blvd, Charlotte, NC 28217 Tel: (704) 227-2000. **Comfort Inn** located at 4040 S Interstate 85 Serv Rd, Charlotte, NC 28208 Tel: (704) 394-4111. **Best Western Inn** located at 3024 E Independence Blvd, Charlotte, NC 28205 Tel: (704) 358-3755. **Hilton Garden Inn Charlotte** located at 508 E 2nd St, Charlotte, NC 28202 Tel: (704) 347-5970. **La Quinta Inn** located at 7900 Nations Ford Rd, Charlotte, NC 28217 Tel: (704) 522-7110. **Sheraton** located at 3315 S Interstate 85 Serv Rd, Charlotte, NC 28208 Tel: (704) 392-1200.

Courtyard by Marriott located at 6023 Park South Dr, Charlotte, NC 28210 Tel: (704) 552-7333. **Fairfield Inn** located at 3400 S Interstate 85 Serv Rd, Charlotte, NC 28208 Tel: (704) 392-0600. **Clarion Hotel** located at 321 W Woodlawn Rd, Charlotte, NC 28217 Tel: (704) 523-1400. **Howard Johnson** located at 6426 N Tryon St, Charlotte, NC 28213 Tel: (704) 596-0042. **Econo Lodge** located at 4325 S Interstate 85 Serv Rd, Charlotte, NC 28214 Tel: (704) 394-0172. **Manor House Aptel** located at 2800 Selwyn Ave, Charlotte, NC 28209 Tel: (704) 377-2621. **Quality Inn** located at 4330 N Interstate 85 Service, Charlotte, NC 28206 Tel: (704) 596-0182.

Doubletree Hotel located at 895 W Trade St, Charlotte, NC 28202 Tel: (704) 347-0070. **Holiday Inn** located at 2707 Little Rock Rd, Charlotte, NC 28214 Tel: (704) 394-4301. **Hyatt Hotels & Resorts** located at 5501 Carnegie Blvd, Charlotte, NC 28209 Tel: (704) 554-1234. **Holiday Inn** located at 212 W Woodlawn Rd, Charlotte, NC 28217 Tel: (704) 525-8350. **Wyndham Garden Hotel** located at 2600 Yorkmont Rd, Charlotte, NC 28208 Tel: (704) 357-9100. **Marriott Hotels & Resorts** located at 5700 Westpark Dr, Charlotte, NC 28217 Tel: (704) 527-9650.

Crescent

2:25 pm-D	**New York (NY)**	2:12 pm
2:43 pm	Newark (NJ)	1:46 pm
3:30 pm	Trenton (NJ)	1:03 pm
4:35 pm	**Philadelphia (PA)**	12:25 pm
4:57 pm	Wilmington (DE)	11:32 am
5:59 pm	Baltimore (MD)	10:40 am
6:45 pm-A	**Washington DC**	10:05 am
7:10 pm-D		9:50 am
7:29 pm	Alexandria (VA)	9:22 am
8:02 pm	Manassas (VA)	8:31 am
8:35 pm	Culpeper (VA)	7:57 am
9:27 pm-A	Charlottesville (VA)	7:05 am
9:32 pm-D		6:59 am
10:50 pm	Lynchburg (VA)	5:51 am
11:52 pm	Danville (VA)	4:41 am
12:58 am-A	Greensboro (NC)	3:39 am
1:03 am-D		3:34 am
1:17 am	High Point (NC)	3:16 am
1:57 am	Salisbury (NC)	2:35 am
3:00 am-A	Charlotte (NC)	1:49 am
3:30 am-D		1:23 am
3:57 am	Gastonia (NC)	12:43 am
4:59 am	Spartanburg (SC)	11:43 pm
5:39 am-A	Greenville (SC)	11:00 pm
5:46 am-D		10:55 pm
6:24 am	Clemson (SC)	10:18 pm
7:00 am	Toccoa (GA)	9:42 pm
7:43 am	Gainesville (GA)	9:01 pm
8:58 am-A	**Atlanta (GA)**	8:06 pm
9:18 am-D		7:36 pm
10:40 am	Anniston (AL)	4:00 pm
12:24 pm-A	**Birmingham (AL)**	2:27 pm
12:39 pm-D		2:19 pm
1:47 pm	Tuscaloosa (AL)	12:50 pm
3:28 pm	Meridian (MS)	11:16 am
4:25 pm	Laurel (MS)	10:14 am
4:55 pm	Hattiesburg (MS)	9:40 am
5:56 pm	Picayune (MS)	8:36 am
6:18 pm	Slidell (LA)	8:15 am
7:50 pm-A	**New Orleans (LA)**	7:20 am

D-Departure
A-Arrival

Crescent

Route Destination Highlights

New York, NY- See and admire the most popular statue in the world, the Statue of Liberty; explore the Ellis Island Immigration Museum, Central Park, Times Square, the United Nations, and some of the tallest buildings in the world. Visit the 1913 Beaux architecture Grand Central Terminal, the Museum of Sex, and the Museum of Modern Art.

Baltimore, MD- Visit the oldest Catholic Church in Baltimore, St. Vincent de Paul Church; Baltimore's oldest restored historic cathedral and the oldest cemetery, Westminster Hall and Burying Ground; visit the home of the first American Roman Catholic canonized saint at the Mother Seton House. The Baltimore Street Car Museum, the B and O Railroad Museum, National Museum of Dentistry, the birthplace of the American national anthem at Fort McHenry National Monument and Historic Shrine, and the home of Mary Pickersgill creator of the Star-Spangled Banner at the Star-Spangled Banner Flag House and Museum.

Charlotte, NC- Visit the Charlotte Museum of History/Hezekiah Alexander Homesite, the Mint Museum of Art, the Mint Museum of Craft and Design, take a trolley tour on the Charlotte Historic Trolley Museum, or take a trip to nearby Great Smokey Mountain National Park.

Atlanta, GA- Visit the Martin Luther King Jr. National Historic site, the birthplace of the human rights activist. Join a tour at the CNN Center or watch one of the finest symphony orchestras in the US, the Atlanta Symphony, and the oldest ballet company in the US, the Atlanta Ballet. See the Georgia State Capitol, the Centennial Olympic Park and its "Fountain of Rings" the largest fountain in the world. Learn about the history of the Coca-Cola Company at the World of

Coca-Cola, or enjoy Atlanta's exciting nightlife at Underground Atlanta. Visit the Virginia-Highland area for dining, shopping, galleries, or simply meeting the locals.

Birmingham, AL- See the largest cast iron statue in the world at the Vulcan Statue and Park Alabama, the Sports Hall of Fame, Barber Vintage Motorsports Museum, the Alabama Mining Museum, and the Alabama Jazz Hall of Fame.

New Orleans, LA- Visit the famous French Quarter, the French Market, the Mardi Gras Fountains, the Louisiana Superdome, and the Old U.S. Mint. Or explore art galleries, antique shops, and restaurants on Magazine Street. See the famous Louisiana white alligator at the Audubon Zoological Gardens, Aquarium of the Americas known as one of the best in the US, or be amazed at the New Orleans Historic Voodoo Museum. Take the educational and fun Cajun cooking lesson at Bayou Country's "Cookin' on the River," or explore Mardi Gras World located near Algiers, or try your luck at the casinos.

Train Schedules

Crescent travels daily from New York City, New York to New Orleans, Louisiana. The trip between the two cities takes approximately 30 hours of travel time.

Accommodations

Accommodations are Viewliner Sleeping Car, Dining Car, Lounge Car, and Reserved Coach. There is a Lounge Car that serves local cuisine, sandwiches, drinks, and snacks. Restaurant style meals are served in the dining car. Other amenities include audio and video entertainment and seasonal Trails and Rails National Park guide presentations.

All Aboard!

New York City (NY) See lakeshore Limited, page 405.

Newark (NJ) See Pennsylvania service, page 428-429.

Trenton (NJ) See Pennsylvania service, page 428-429.

Philadelphia (PA) See Pennsylvania service, page 424.

Wilmington (DE) See Vermonter service, page 483-484.

Baltimore (MD) See Vermonter service, page 484.

Washington DC See Capitol Limited service, page 441.

Alexandria (VA) See Cardinal service, page 461.

Manassas (VA) See Cardinal service, page 458-461.

Culpeper (VA) See Cardinal service, page 458-461

Charlotesville (VA)

Charlottesville is located in central Virginia, 70 miles northwest of Richmond. It has a land area of 10 sq. miles (26.5 sq. kilometers) and a population of more than 40,000. Named after the princess of England, Charlottesville was incorporated in 1888. Charlottesville is home to Thomas Jefferson, his estate Monticello is located two miles southwest of Charlottesville. Call Tel: (434) 984-9800 for information.

Charlottesville's train depot is located at 810 W. Main St. Charlottesville, VA 22901. The station is staffed and features an enclosed waiting area, restrooms, payphones, and vending machines. Transportation options from the station include local transit and taxi services.

Trains serving Charlottesville station are the Cardinal and the Crescent.

Lynchburg (VA)

Lynchburg is located in western-central Virginia, 97 miles west of Richmond. Lynchburg has a land area of 49.8 sq. miles (127.9 sq. kilometers) and a population of approximately 70,000. Like Charlottesville, Thomas Jefferson visited Lynchburg frequently, and during the civil war Lynchburg was a major storage depot. Lynchburg has five historic districts; each one is rich in 18th to 20th century architectural and historical treasures.

Lynchburg's train depot is located at 825 Kemper St. Lynchburg, VA 24501. The station is staffed and features an enclosed waiting area, checked baggage service, restrooms, and payphones. Transportation from the station is local taxi service.

Virginia (VA)
Capital: Richmond (Population: 7,078,515)
Size: 42,769 sq mi. (110,771 sq km)
Nickname: The Old Dominion, Mother of Presidents
Entered the union: June 25, 1788 (10th state)
Motto: Thus always to tyrants
Flower: American Dogwood
Bird: Cardinal
Song: Carry Me Back to Old Virginia
Famous for: Presidents, Aristocracy and guess what "Ham"
Major industries: Government, agriculture, and manufacturing.

Lynchburg station is served by the Crescent.

Danville (VA)

Danville is located in south-central Virginia near the Virginia and North Carolina state border. Danville has a land area of 43 sq. miles (111.5 sq. kilometers) and a population of approximately 55,000.

Danville's train depot is located at 1201 Craghead St. Danville, VA 24541. The station is un-staffed and features an enclosed waiting area, restroom, and payphones. Transportation options from the station include local transit and taxi services.

Danville station is served by the Crescent.

Greensboro (NC) See Carolinian and Piedmont service, page 518-520.

525

High Point (NC) See Carolinian and Piedmont service, page 518-520

Salisbury (NC) See Carolinian and Piedmont service, page 518-520

Charlotte (NC) See Carolinian and Piedmont service, page 521

Gastonia (NC)

Gastonia is located in west North Carolina near the state boarder of the two Carolinas, 22 miles west of Charlotte. Gastonia has a land area of 30 sq. miles (78.6 sq. kilometers) and a population of more than 66,000. The city of Gastonia was incorporated in 1877 and is the seat of Gastonia County.

Gastonia's train depot is located at 350 Hancock St. Gastonia, NC 28054. The station is un-staffed and features an enclosed waiting area, restrooms, and payphones. Transportation from the station is local taxi service.

Crescent serves Gastonia train depot.

Spartanburg (SC)

Spartanburg is located in northwest South Carolina at the foothills of the Great Smokey Mountains, 88 miles from the state capital Columbia. Spartanburg has a land area of 18 sq. miles (46.8 sq. kilometers) and a population of approximately 44,500.

Spartanburg is part of the Cherokee Nation, for many generations the Cherokee Indians have been living in the region. In 1755 the English occupied the area and ceded the land from the Cherokee Indians. Today Spartanburg is a thriving city that takes pride in its hospitality, economic success, and history.

Spartanburg's train depot is located at 290 Magnolia St. Spartanburg, SC 29303. The station is un-staffed and features payphones.

Crescent serves Spartanburg train depot.

Greenville (SC)

Greenville is in northwestern South Carolina at the base of the Appalachian Mountains, 104 miles northwest of Columbia. Greenville has a land area of 25 sq. miles (65 sq. kilometers) and a population of 60,000. Greenville was incorporated in 1831.

Places of interest: Greenville Town Square is located in historic downtown Greenville at the corner of Main and Court streets; a visit to the square will bring visitors back in time to the rich history of the town. Greenville County Museum of Art, located at 420 College St, Greenville, SC 29601 Tel: (864) 271-7570, exhibits several master works of art. Roper Mountain Science Center, located at 402 Roper Mountain Rd, Greenville SC 29615 Tel: (864) 281-1188, houses the largest planetarium in South Carolina and a large telescope.

South Carolina (SC)	
Capital: Columbia (Population: 4,012,012)	
Size: 32,007 sq mi. (82,898 sq km)	
Nickname: The Palmetto State	
Joined the union on: May 23, 1788 (8th state)	
Mottoes: Prepared in mind and resources and While I breathe, I hope	
Flower: Carolina yellow jessamine	
Bird: Carolina wren	
Song: Carolina	
Famous for: Museums, First Public Library and Steam Rail Road	
Major industries: Textile, chemicals and agriculture.	

Two of the most admired churches in Greenville are the Christ Episcopal Church (great architecture), located at 10 N. Church St, Greenville, SC 29601 Tel: (864) 271-8773, and the Downtown Baptist Church located at 101 W. McBee Ave, Greenville, SC 29601 Tel: (864) 235-5746. Bob Jones University Museum & Gallery, located at 1700 Wade Hampton Blvd, Greenville, SC 29614 Tel: (864) 242-5100, has some of the finest collections of religious art in the US. Furman University Thompson Gallery, located at 3300 Poinsett Hwy, Greenville, SC 29613 Tel: (864) 294-2074, exhibits art works from local and regional artists.

Listed on the National Register of Historic Places is the Beattie House located at 8 Bennett St, Greenville, SC 29601 Tel: (864) 233-9977. It is an 1834 Italian Gothic architecture house. Gassaway Mansion, located at 106 Dupont Drive, Greenville, SC 29607 Tel: (864) 271-0188, is a classic example of the wealthy Southern Carolinian's homes. Kilgore-Lewis House, located at 560 N. Academy St, Greenville, SC 29601 Tel: (864) 232-3020, is listed on the National Register of Historic Places; the house is surrounded by several beautiful gardens.

Greenville's train depot is located at 1120 W. Washington St. Greenville, SC 29601. The station is staffed and features an enclosed waiting area, checked baggage service, restrooms, payphones, and vending machines. Transportation from the station is local taxi service.

Greenville station is served by Crescent.

Clemson (SC)

Clemson is located in the northwestern part of South Carolina, 123 miles from the state capital Columbia, with a land area of 7 sq. miles (18 sq. kilometers) and a population of more than 11,000. The town of Clemson was incorporated in 1946.

Clemson's train depot is located at US Hwy 123 / US Hwy 133 Clemson, SC 29631. The station is un-staffed and features an enclosed waiting area, restrooms, and payphones.

Clemson station is served by Crescent.

Toccoa (GA)

Toccoa, a native Indian word for "the beautiful," is located in the foothills of the Smokey Mountains in northeastern Georgia. The city of Toccoa was founded in 1874; it has a land area of 7 sq. miles (18.8 sq. kilometers) and a population of approximately 9,000.

Toccoa's train depot is located at 47 N. Alexander St. Toccoa, GA 30577. The station is un-staffed and features an enclosed waiting area, restrooms, and payphones. Transportation from the station is local taxi service.

Toccoa station is served by Crescent.

Gainesville (GA)

Gainesville is located 50 miles northeast of the state capital of Georgia, Atlanta. The city of Gainesville was originally called the Mule Camp Spring until November 1821 when the city was chartered and was given a new name, Gainesville. By 1849 Gainesville was a well-known resort center in the northern Georgia region, but in 1851 a devastating fire destroyed much of the city and left Gainesville in ruins. During the 1996 Atlanta Summer Olympics, Gainesville participated and was recognized as one of Georgia's prime cities. Gainesville has a land area of 22.9 sq. miles (58.8 sq. kilometers) and a population of approximately 18,000.

Gainesville's train depot is located at 116 Industrial Blvd. Gainesville, GA 30501. The station is un-staffed and features an enclosed waiting area, restrooms, payphones, and vending machines. Transportation options from the station include Enterprise Rent-A-Car toll-free (800) RENT-A-CAR and local taxi service.

Gainesville station is served by Crescent.

Atlanta (GA)

Atlanta is the state capital and is located in the northwest part of the state of Georgia. It has a land area of 132.9 sq. miles (341 sq. kilometers) and a population of more than 430,000. Atlanta was founded during the era of railroad expansion in 1837. Today Atlanta is a leading tourism, manufacturing, and finance center. Atlanta has an average temperature of 25-60 degrees F during winter; 50-70's degrees F during spring and fall; and 90+ degrees F during summer.

Getting Around

Airport

Hartsfield Atlanta International Airport, Atlanta GA 30320 Tel: (404) 209-1700, is located 10 miles (16 Kilometers) south of Atlanta. Courtesy phones of major rental car companies are located in the ground transportation division at the west end of the baggage claim areas. Local taxi and bus also operate at the airport. Rapid train services connect the airport and city of Atlanta.

Bus

Metropolitan Atlanta Rapid Transit Authority

Georgia (GA)

Capital: Atlanta (Population: 8,186,453)
Size: 59,441 sq mi. (153,952 sq km)
Nickname: The Empire State of the South, the Peach State
Joined the union on: January 2, 1788 (4th state)
Motto: Wisdom, justice, and moderation
Flower: Cherokee Rose
Bird: Brown Thrasher
Song: Georgia on My Mind
Famous for: Mansion of Savannah
Major industries: Textiles

528

(MARTA) Tel: (404) 848-4711 operates public bus services throughout the city of Atlanta and outlying areas. Basic fare is $1.75; call MARTA for special fares and the Visitors Pass. Greyhound toll-free (800) 231-2222 connects Atlanta to the rest of the country.

Taxi

Crown Taxi Tel: (404) 898-0554, Allied Nations Cab, Inc. Tel: (404) 758-2007, Star Tel: (404) 758-6616, Amigo Tel: (404) 248-0106, National Tel: (404) 752-6834, Yellow Cab Tel: (404) 521-0200, Wilson Tel: (404) 758-8299, Assurance Taxi Tel: (404) 874-7139, Ambassador Tel: (404) 724-0220, Atlanta Royal Cabbies Tel: (404) 584-6655, Omega Taxicab Company Tel: (404) 249-9830, United Express Tel: (404) 658-1638, Checker Tel: (404) 351-8255, and Citywide Tel: (404) 875-1223.

Rent-A-Car

Alamo Rent-a-Car toll-free (800) 327-9633, Budget Ret-a-Car toll-free (800) 527-0700, Thrifty Rent-a-Car toll-free (800) 367-2277, National Ret-a-Car toll-free (800) 227-7368, Dollar Rent-a-Car toll-free (800) 800-4000, Hertz Ret-a-Car toll-free (800) 654-3131, and Avis Rent-a-Car toll-free (800) 331-1212.

Train and Commuter

Metropolitan Atlanta Rapid Transit Authority (MARTA) Tel: (404) 848-4711 operates the subway train system throughout Atlanta. Basic one-way fare is $1.75; call MARTA for special fares and Visitors Pass.

Atlanta's train depot is located at 1688 Peachtree St. N. W. Atlanta, GA 30309. The station is staffed and features an enclosed waiting area, checked baggage service, restrooms, payphones, and vending machines. Transportation options from the station include Hertz Car Rental toll-free (800) 654-3131, local transit and taxi services.

Atlanta station is served by the Crescent.

Visitors Information Center

Atlanta Convention & Visitors Bureau, 233 Peachtree Street NE Suite 100 Atlanta, GA 30303 Tel: (404) 521-6600.

Places to See and Things to Do

Fernbank Museum of Natural History, located at 767 Clifton Rd. N.E. Atlanta, GA Tel: (404) 370-0906, is dedicated to the history of Georgia; the museum also features an IMAX theater. **Metropolitan Museum of Art** located at 3393 Peachtree Rd NE # 3096 Atlanta, GA 30326 Tel: (404) 264-1424. The **High Museum of Art - Folk Art and Photography Galleries** located in Georgia-Pacific Center at 133 Peachtree St, Atlanta Tel: (404) 577-6940. **William Breman Jewish Heritage Museum** is located in the Selig Center at 1440 Spring St, NW, Atlanta Tel: (404) 873-1661. The museum is dedicated to Atlanta's Jewish community.

High Museum of Art, located at 1280 Peachtree St NE Atlanta, GA 30309 Tel: (404) 733-4400, exhibits contemporary art from different parts of the world. **The Road to Tara Museum,** located at 659 Peachtree St, Suite 600 Atlanta, GA Tel: (404) 897-1939, has an extensive collection of memorabilia from the movie "Gone with the Wind." **Atlanta International Museum** located at 285 Peachtree Center Ave NE Atlanta, GA 30303 Tel: (404) 688-2467.

Georgia State Capitol is located on Washington St. between Mitchell St. and Martin Luther King, Jr. Dr. Tel: (404) 656-2844. This magnificent state capitol was patterned after the US Capitol Building in Washington D.C. **Carter Presidential Center and Museum of the Jimmy Carter Library** is located at 1 Copenhill Ave. NE Atlanta, GA 30307 Tel: (404) 331-3942. The library has an extensive collection of documents and memorabilia of the Jimmy Carter presidency. **Martin Luther King Jr. National Historic Site,** located on Auburn Avenue Tel: (404) 331-3920, is the site of the birthplace of the human rights activist. **Atlanta Cyclorama,** located at 800 Cherokee Ave, S.E. Atlanta, GA 30315 Tel: (404) 624-1071, features the history of Atlanta during the civil war.

Centennial Olympic Park, located in the heart of downtown at 265 Luckie Street, NW Atlanta GA 30313 Tel: (404) 223-4412, is the reminder of the 1996 Olympic Games held in Atlanta. The park houses the "Fountain of Rings," the largest fountain in the world. **The Georgia Dome,** located at One Georgia Dome Drive, N.W. Atlanta GA 30313 Tel: (404) 223-9200, is the largest cable supported dome in the world and hosts major international events including the Atlanta Olympics. **Philips Arena,** located at One Philips Drive Atlanta, GA 30303 Tel: (404) 878-3000, is the home of NBA Atlanta Hawks and the NHL Atlanta Thrashers; Philips Arena is Atlanta's major sports and entertainment complex.

Zoo Atlanta is located at 800 Cherokee Ave. S.E. Atlanta, GA 30315 Tel: (404) 624-5600. The zoo is home to more than 1,000 animals. **Atlanta Botanical Gardens**, located in Piedmont Park Tel: (404) 876-5859, features exotic plants from different regions of the world, and the garden house conservatory. **Six Flags over Georgia,** located 12 miles west of downtown Atlanta Tel: (770) 739-3400, is the local favorite theme park. Six Flags features rides and entertainment for every member of the family.

The World of Coca-Cola, located at 55 Martin Luther King Jr. Dr. Atlanta, GA Tel: (404) 676-5151, exhibits the history of the Coca-Cola Company. **CNN Center,** located at One CNN Center Atlanta, GA 30303 Tel: (404) 827-2491, offers studio tours to one of America's top news channels; make sure to book early.

Watch one of the finest symphony orchestras in the US, the **Atlanta Symphony** Orchestra, at the Woodruff Arts Center, 1280 Peachtree St, NE Atlanta Tel: (404) 733-5000. Also at the Woodruff Arts Center is the **Alliance Theater,** one of the largest in the US. Nearby is the **Fox Theatre,** located at 660 Peachtree St, NE, Atlanta Tel: (404) 881-2100, it houses the **Atlanta Ballet** Tel: (404) 873-5811, the oldest ballet company in the US. The **Atlanta Broadway Series,** also in Fox Theatre Tel: (404) 873-4300, has seasonal performances featuring world-class artists.

Stone Mountain Park, located 16 miles from Downtown Atlanta - take Highway 78 East to Stone Mountain Tel: (770) 498-5600, features a large mountain carving, Antebellum plantation, scenic railroad, sky lift, and many more attractions. **Virginia-Highland,** spanning between Elizabeth St. and University Ave at 1026 North Highland Avenue NE, Atlanta GA 30306 Tel: (404) 876-7249, is Atlanta's exiting nightlife area; enjoy dining and shopping, see galleries, or simply meet the locals. **Underground Atlanta,** located in the heart of Atlanta, is a six city-block area featuring a marketplace, restaurants, shops, and entertainment. It's the place to be, call Tel: (404) 523-2311 for information.

Accommodations

Clarion Suites Hotel Atlanta located at 4900 Circle 75 Parkway, Atlanta GA 30339 Tel: (770) 956-1504 expect to pay $40-$150. **Crowne Plaza Hotel Atlanta Airport** located at 1325 Virgina Avenue, Atlanta GA 30344 Tel: (404) 768-6660 expect to pay $50-$200. **Hyatt Regency Atlanta** located at 265 Peachtree Street NE, Atlanta GA 30303 Tel:(404) 577-1234 expect to pay $100-$300. **Renaissance Concourse Hotel Atlanta** located at one Hartsfield Centre Parkway, Atlanta GA 30354 Tel: (404) 209-9999 expect to pay $60-$200.

Country Hearth Inn Atlanta Perimeter North located at 5793 Roswell Road N.E., Atlanta GA 30328 Tel: (404) 252-6400 expect to pay $60-$100. **Days Inn Atlanta Midtown Peachtree Street** located at 683 Peachtree Street N.E., Atlanta GA 30308 Tel: (404) 874-9200 expect to pay $60- $150. **Econo Lodge Atlanta** located at 4275 NE Expressway, Atlanta GA 30340 Tel: (770) 934-2770 expect to pay $30-$80. **Embassy Suites Atlanta Buckhead** located at 3285 Peachtree Road Northeast, Atlanta GA 30305 Tel: (404) 261-7733 expect to pay $100-$250. **Holiday Inn Express Hotel and Suites** located at 765 Hammond
Drive, Atlanta GA 30328 Tel: (404) 250-4450 expect to pay $70-$150.

Doubletree Guest Suites Atlanta Perimeter located at 6120 Peachtree Dunwoody Road, Atlanta GA 30328 Tel: (770) 668-0808 expect to pay $60-$300. **The Georgian Terrace** located at 659 Peachtree Street, Atlanta GA 30308 Tel: (404) 897-1991 expect to pay $70-$350. **Crowne Plaza Hotel Atlanta Ravina** located at 4355 Ashford-Dunwoody Road, Atlanta GA 30346 Tel: (770) 395-7700 expect to pay $90-$350. **AmeriSuites Atlanta Perimeter Center** 1005 Crestline Parkway, Atlanta GA 30328 Tel: (770) 730-9300 $40-$100. **Swissotel Atlanta** located at 3391 Peachtree Road, Atlanta GA 30326 Tel: (404) 365-0065 expect to pay $100-$770. **Doubletree Club Atlanta Airport** located at 3400 Norman Berry Drive, Atlanta GA 30344 Tel: (404) 763-1600 expect to pay $50-$180.

Quality Inn Northeast located at 2960 N.E. Expressway, Atlanta GA 30341 Tel: (770) 451-5231 expect to pay $30-$70. **The Highland Inn** located at 644 North Highland Avenue, Atlanta GA 30306 toll-free (888) 256-7221 expect to pay $50-$100. **Courtyard Atlanta Midtown** 1132 Techwood Drive, Atlanta GA 30318 Tel: (404) 607-1112 expect to pay $50-$200. **Grand Hyatt Atlanta** located at 3300 Peachtree Road, Atlanta GA 30305 Tel: (404) 365-8100 expect to pay $130-$300. **Hilton Atlanta Airport and Towers** located at 1031 Virginia Avenue, Atlanta GA 30354 Tel: (404) 767-9000 expect to pay $50-$350.

Capital: Montgomery
(Population: 4,447,100)
Size: 57,919 sq mi. (150,010 sq km)
Nickname: The Heart of Dixie, The Cotton State, the Camellia State
Joined the union on: December 14, 1819 (22nd state)
Motto: We Dare Defend Our Rights
Flower: Camellia
Bird: Yellowhammer
Song: "Alabama"
Famous for: Nat King Cole, Lionel Ritchie and Joe Lewis
Major industries: Paper, Chemicals, and Rubber and Plastics

Anniston (AL)

Anniston is located along the foothills of the Appalachian Mountains, 60 miles east of the city of Birmingham. Anniston has a land area of 20 sq. miles (52 sq. kilometers) and a population of approximately 27,000.

Places of interest: the Berman Museum is located at 840 Mimosa Dr Anniston, AL 36206 Tel: (256) 237-6261 and the Anniston Museum of History is located at 800 Mimosa Dr Anniston, AL 36206 Tel: (256) 237-6766.

Anniston's train depot is located at 126 W. 4th St. Anniston, AL 36201. The station is un-staffed and features an enclosed waiting area, restrooms, and payphones. Transportation from the station is local taxi service.

Anniston station is served by the Crescent.

Birmingham (AL)

Birmingham is located in central Alabama, 86 miles north of Montgomery the state capital. Birmingham has a population of 170,000 residents and a land area of 149 sq. miles (384.5 sq. kilometers); it was founded and incorporated in 1871. Birmingham's average annual temperature is 62 degrees F with an average annual rainfall of 52.16 inches.

Getting Around

Airport

Birmingham International Airport, 5900 Airport Highway Birmingham, AL 35212 Tel: (205) 595-0533, is located just five miles from downtown Birmingham. Major rental car companies serve the airport, local taxi are also available at the airport arrival area. Ask the airport visitor information desk for other transportation services in the airport.

Bus

Metro Area Express (MAX) Central Station is located at 1735 Morris Avenue Tel: (205) 521-0101; MAX operates and serves the city of Birmingham and outlying areas. Basic fare is $1.15 for transfer and 50 cents for elderly and disabled passengers. There are special fares for students and monthly passes, call MAX for information. Greyhound, 618 N 19th St. Birmingham, AL 35203 Tel: (205) 322-0321, connects Birmingham to the rest of the country.

Taxi

Yellow Cab, 2316-B 1st Avenue South Birmingham, AL 35233 Tel: (205) 252-1131.

Rent-A-Car

Alabama Limousine Tel: (205) 592-2001, Alamo Tel: (205) 591-4395, National Tel: (205) 592-7259, Hertz Tel: (205) 591-6090, Avis Tel: (205) 592-8901, Budget Tel: (205) 322-3596, Enterprise Tel: (205) 591-1925, and Dollar Tel: (205) 595-8802.

Train and Commuter

Birmingham's train depot is located at 1819 Morris Ave. Birmingham, AL 35203. The station is staffed and features an enclosed waiting area, checked baggage service, restrooms, payphones, and vending machines. Transportation from the station is local taxi service.

Birmingham station is served by Crescent.

Visitor Information Center

Greater Birmingham Convention & Visitors Bureau, 2200 Ninth Avenue North, Birmingham, Alabama 35203-1100 toll-free (800) 458-8085 or Tel: (205) 458-8000.

Places of Interest and Things to Do

Birmingham Botanical Gardens, located at 2612 Lane Park Road, Birmingham Tel: (205) 879-1227, exhibits exotic plants and houses a Japanese Garden. **Birmingham Zoo,** located at 2630 Cahaba Road, Tel: (205) 879-0408, is home to almost 1,000 animals. **Arlington Antebellum Home and Gardens,** located at 331 Cotton Avenue SW, Birmingham, Jefferson County Tel: (205) 780-5656, was a former Civil War Headquarters. **Vulcan Statue and Park** is located at 20th Street South at Valley Avenue, on Red Mountain, Birmingham Tel: 205-254-6020. At 56 feet tall, this is the largest cast iron statue in the world. The statue represented the state of Alabama at the 1904 St. Louis World Fair.

Red Mountain Cut and Geological Walkway, located at 1422 22nd Street South, east of Highway 280, Birmingham, is a natural window of Birmingham geological history and the cut walkway is designated as a National Natural Landmark. **Alabama Sports Hall of Fame,** located at 2150 Civic Center Boulevard, Birmingham Tel: (205) 323-6665, has collections of Alabama's sports heroes. **Birmingham Public Library (BPL)** is located at 2100 Park Place, Birmingham, 3520. **Historic Fourth Avenue Visitor Center,** located at 319 17th Street North Tel: (205) 328-1850, is a social and cultural center of African Americans since the early 20th century.

Southern Museum of Flight, located near the Birmingham International Airport at 4343 73rd Street North Tel: (205) 833-8226, exhibits the history of aircraft starting as early as the Wright Brothers to the modern jet plane. **McWane Center-Adventures in Science** is located at 210 19th Street North, Birmingham Tel: (205) 714-8314; the science center also houses an IMAX Dome theater. **Birmingham Civil Rights Institute,** located at 520 16th

Street North, exhibits historical documents and memorabilia of Alabama's African-American civil right movements.

Alabama Mining Museum, located at 120 East Street, Dora, Walker County Tel: (205) 648-2442, exhibits history and memorabilia of coal mining in Alabama. **Barber Vintage Motorsports Museum,** located at 2721 Fifth Avenue South, Birmingham Tel: (205) 252-8377, features more than 300 sports vehicles including a motorcycle collection. **Birmingham Museum of Art,** located at 2000 8th Avenue North, Birmingham Tel: (205) 254-2565, has more than 21,000 works of art from all over the world. **Sixteenth Street Baptist Church,** located at 1530 Sixth Avenue North, Birmingham, Jefferson County Tel: (205) 251-9402, is a striking Beaux architecture church and the church also housed part of the civil rights movement. **Sloss Furnaces National Historic Landmark,** located in Second Avenue North and 32nd Street, Birmingham Tel: (205) 324-1911, is a museum dedicated to the economic history of Birmingham.

Alabama Theatre, located at 1817 3rd Avenue North Birmingham Tel: (205) 252-2262, is the region's most elegant movie house. **Alabama Jazz Hall of Fame** is located in the historic Carver Theater at 1631 4th Avenue north, Birmingham Tel: (205) 254-2731; the hall exhibits memorabilia of Alabama's famous jazz musicians. **Samuel Ullman-Morris Newfield House,** located at 2150-15th Avenue South, Birmingham, Jefferson County Tel: (205) 934-5634, is the site where the famous poem the "Youth" was written by Samuel Ullman. Established in 1871 is the **Oak Hill Cemetery** located at 1120 19th Street North, Birmingham, Tel: (205) 251-6532, the cemetery is the final resting place to many of Birmingham's founding fathers.

Accommodations

Amerisuites located at 4686 Highway 280 E, Birmingham, AL 35242 Tel: (205) 995-9242. **Budget Inn** located at 2224 5th Ave N, Birmingham, AL 35203 Tel: (205) 324-6107. **Clarion Hotel** located at 5216 Messer Airport Hwy, Birmingham, AL 35212 Tel: (205) 591-7900. **Courtyard by Marriott** located at 4300 Colonnade Pkwy, Birmingham, AL 35243 Tel: (205) 967-4466. **Embassy Suites Hotel** located at 2300 Woodcrest Pl, Birmingham, AL 35209 Tel: (205) 879-7400. **Comfort Inn** located at 7905 Crestwood Blvd, Birmingham, AL 35210 Tel: (205) 957-0084. **Radisson Hotel** located at 808 20th St S. #A, Birmingham, AL 35205 Tel: (205) 933-9000.

Holiday Inn located at 1548 Montgomery Hwy, Birmingham, AL 35216 Tel: (205) 822-4350. **Best Western Inn** located at 2230 Civic Center Blvd, Birmingham, AL 35203 Tel: (205) 328-6320. **Best Inn & Suites** located at 9225 Parkway E, Birmingham, AL 35206 Tel: (205) 836-5400. **Red Roof Inn** located at 151 Vulcan Rd, Birmingham, AL 35209 Tel: (205) 942-9414. **Suburban Lodge** located at 1902 Highway 31 S, Birmingham, AL 35244 Tel: (205) 985-9117. **Holiday Inn** located at 4627 Highway 280 S, Birmingham, AL 35242 Tel: (205) 991-9977. **Quality Inn** located at 260 Goodwin Crest Dr, Birmingham, AL 35209 Tel: (205) 290-8000.

Motel Birmingham located at 7905 Crestwood Blvd, Birmingham, AL 35210 Tel: (205) 956-4440. **Hampton Inn** located at 1940 Edwards Lake Rd, Birmingham, AL 35235 Tel: (205) 655-9777. **Royal Inn** located at 821 20th St S, Birmingham, AL 35205 Tel: (205) 252-8041. **Villager Lodge** located at 1313 3rd Ave N, Birmingham, AL 35203 Tel: (205) 323-

8806. **Days Inn** located at 5101 Messer Airport Hwy, Birmingham, AL 35212 Tel: (205) 592-6110.

Sheraton located at 2101 Civic Center Blvd, Birmingham, AL 35203 Tel: (205) 324-5000.
Holiday Inn located at 7941 Crestwood Blvd, Birmingham, AL 35210 Tel: (205) 956-8211.
Suburban Lodge located at 90 W Oxmoor Rd, Birmingham, AL 35209 Tel: (205) 945-9154.
La Quinta Inn located at 905 11th Ct W, Birmingham, AL 35204 Tel: (205) 324-4510.
Travelers Rest Motel located at 1066 Forestdale Blvd. Birmingham, AL 35214 Tel: (205) 798-3831.

Tuscaloosa (AL)

Tuscaloosa is located in western Alabama along the Black Warrior River, 55 miles west of Birmingham. The site of the present city of Tuscaloosa was part of the native Indian's trade route along the Black Warrior River. The name Tuscaloosa was taken from the native Indian words "Tushka" meaning warrior and "Lusa" meaning black. The town of Tuscaloosa was incorporated in 1819 and since then the city grew and became a capital of commerce and trade in the region.

Tuscaloosa is home to the University of Alabama and other major educational institutions, Mercedes Benz assembly plant, and other major industries. Tuscaloosa has a land area of 47.5 sq. miles (121.9 sq. kilometers) and a population of approximately 78,000.

Tuscaloosa's train depot is located at 2105 Greensboro Ave. Tuscaloosa, AL 35401. The station is staffed and features an enclosed waiting area, restrooms, payphones, and vending machines. Transportation from the station is local taxi service.

Tuscaloosa station is served by the Crescent.

Mississippi (MS)

Capital: Jackson (Population: 2,844,658)
Size: 48,434 sq mi. (125,444 sq km)
Nickname: The Magnolia State
Joined the union on: December 10, 1817 (20th state)
Motto: By valor and arms
Flower: Magnolia
Bird: Mockingbird
Song: Go, Mississippi
Famous for: Blues, Elvis Presley, and Kermit the Frog!
Major industries: Agriculture, Fisheries, and Manufacturing

Meridian (MS)

Meridian was originally a Choctaw Indian territory, located in eastern Mississippi near the Mississippi and Alabama state border. Meridian was first settled in 1831 as a result of the Treaty of Dancing Rabbit Creek. Meridian was greatly involved in the civil war and the city was one of the Confederate army's headquarters. General William Sherman nearly destroyed much of the city and before the civil war ended much of Meridian's railroad was destroyed. Soon after the civil war the rebuilding of Meridian began; its railroad lines were repaired and the city slowly recovered. Today Meridian is home to approximately 42,000 residents in an area of 35.8 sq. miles (92 sq. kilometers). The city is one of Mississippi's centers for art, education, medicine, and commerce.

Places of interest: the Hamasa Shrine Temple Theater, located at 2320 8th Street Meridian, MS Tel: (601) 693-1361, is listed on the National Register of Historic Places and houses a rare pipe organ. The Grand Opera House of Mississippi, 2206 Fifth Street Meridian, MS 39302 Tel: (601) 693-5239. Meridian Museum of Art, 628 25th Avenue, Meridian, MS 39302 Tel: (601) 693-1501. Merrehope Victorian Mansion, located at 905 Martin Luther King Jr. Memorial Drive Meridian, MS 39301 Tel: (601) 483-8439, is one of the few buildings in the city to survive the civil war. Highland Park, located at 19th Street and 41st Avenue Meridian, MS Tel: (601) 485-1808, is the home of Jimmie Rodgers, the father of country music. The house exhibits memorabilia from the great country music artist.

Meridian's train depot is located at 1901 Front St. Meridian, MS 39301. The station is staffed and features an enclosed waiting area, checked baggage service, restrooms, payphones, and a restaurant. Transportation options from the station include local transit, bus, and taxi services.

Meridian station is served by the Crescent.

Laurel (MS)

Laurel is located in southeastern Mississippi, 76 miles from Jackson City the state capital. Laurel has a land area of 15.5 sq. miles (39.8 sq. kilometers) and a population of approximately 19,000. Places of interest: Lauren Rogers Museum of Art, located in Laurel historic district, is the state's oldest museum of art.

Laurel's train depot is located at 230 N. Maple St. Laurel, MS 39440. The station is un-staffed and features an enclosed waiting area, restrooms, and payphones. Transportation from the station is local taxi service.

Laurel station is served by the Crescent.

Hattiesburg (MS)

Hattiesburg is in southeast Mississippi, 87 miles from Jackson City. Hattiesburg has a land area of 25.6 sq. miles (65.8 sq. Kilometers) and a population of approximately 45,000. The city of Hattiesburg was founded in 1882 and was named Twin Forks, it was named again as Gordonville and finally Hattiesburg after it was incorporated in 1884. Hattiesburg is home to the University of Southern Mississippi.

Hattiesburg's train depot is located at 308 Newman St. Hattiesburg, MS 39401. The station is un-staffed and features an enclosed waiting area, restrooms, payphones, and vending machines. Transportation from the station is local taxi service.

Hattiesburg station is served by the Crescent.

Picayune (MS)

Picayune was named after the Spanish coins circulated in the area during the colonial era. Picayune is located on the south end of Mississippi near the state border with Louisiana, just 54 miles north of New Orleans. Picayune has a land area of 11.7 sq. miles (30 sq. kilometers) and a population of approximately 12,000. The city of Picayune was incorporated in 1904.

Picayune's train depot is located at 100 S. Hwy. 11 Picayune, MS 39466. The station is un-staffed. Transportation from the station is local taxi service.

Picayune station is served by the Crescent.

Louisiana (LA)
Capital: Baton Rouge (Population: 4,468,976)
Size: 51,843 sq mi. (134273 sq km)
Nickname: The Pelican State, the Sugar State, Creole State
Joined the union on: April 30, 1812 (18th state)
Motto: Union, Justice, and Confidence
Flower: Magnolia
Bird: Pelican
Song: Give Me Louisiana and You Are My Sunshine
Famous for: Creole and Cajun Cuisine, Mardi Gras, French Quarters
Major industries: Tourism, manufacturing, minerals, petroleum products, marine

Slidell (LA)

Slidell is located at the southeastern tip of St. Tammany Parish Louisiana, 35 miles north of New Orleans. Slidell was founded around 1852 during the expansion of the railroad in the area and was incorporated in 1888. Slidell has a land area of 9.3 sq. miles (24 sq. kilometers) and a population of approximately 32,000. Slidell is home to NASA Slidell Computer Complex.

Slidell's train depot is located at 1827 Front St. Slidell, LA 70458. The station is un-staffed and features an enclosed waiting area and payphones. Transportation from the station is local taxi service.

Slidell station is served by the Crescent.

New Orleans (LA) See City of New Orleans service, page 384

Silver Meteor/Silver Star/Silver Palm

Silver Meteor/Silver Star/Silver Palm		
Multiple Train Departure Daily	New York (NY)	**Multiple Train Departure Daily**
	Newark (NJ)	
	Metropark (NJ)	
	Trenton (NJ)	
	Philadelphia (PA)	
	Wilmington (DE)	
	Baltimore (MD)	
	BWI Airport Rail Sta. (MD)	
	New Carrollton (MD)	
	Washington DC	
	Alexandria (VA)	
	Quantico (VA)	
	Fredericksburg (VA)	
	Richmond (VA)	
	Petersburg (VA)	
	Rocky Mount (NC)	
	Wilson (NC)	
	Selma (NC)	
	Raleigh (NC)	
	Fayetteville (NC)	
	Dillon (SC)	
	Florence (SC)	
	Kingstree (SC)	
	Charleston (SC)	
	Yemassee (SC)	
	South Pines (SC)	
	Hamlet (SC)	
	Camden (SC)	
	Columbia (SC)	
	Denmark (SC)	
	Savannah (GA)	
	Jesup (GA)	
	Jacksonville (FL)	

D-Departure
A-Arrival
Multiple Daily Train Departure

The Silver Meteor, Silver Star, Silver Palm bring passengers to some of the most visited, most beautiful cities and destinations of the eastern United States. The Silver Services and the Carolinian and Piedmont service connect the cities of New York City, New York and Miami, Florida.

Route Destination Highlights

New York, NY- See and admire the most popular statue in the world, the Statue of Liberty; explore the Ellis Island Immigration Museum, Central Park, Times Square, the United Nations, and some of the tallest buildings in the world. Visit the 1913 Beaux architecture Grand Central Terminal, the Museum of Sex, and the Museum of Modern Art.

Charleston, SC- Shop at the Old City Market; visit the Charles Towne Landing State Park, the oldest English settlement in the area; and the College of Charleston, founded in 1770, which was the first municipal college in the US. Visit some of the most historic and impressive houses in Charleston; the Aiken-Rhett House; and Heyward-Washington House. The Calhoun Mansion, a post-civil war Victorian Baronial Manor House; and the Drayton Hall pre-civil war house of Georgian Palladian architecture.

Savannah, GA- Visit the Ships of the Sea Maritime Museum, the Savannah History Museum, the Savannah Science Museum, the Roundhouse Railroad Museum, and the Savannah Ogeechee Canal Museum & Nature Center. See the historic City Market, the Old Fort Jackson, and the Juliette Gordon Low Birthplace.

Jacksonville, FL- Visit Jacksonville's Historical Center and learn about the history of Jacksonville; see the Treaty Oak, the oldest living thing in Jacksonville and one of the oldest in the state of Florida; take a relaxing walk at the Riverwalk and visit the Friendship Park and Fountain, one of the largest in the world. Enjoy a romantic dinner with entertainment by taking a river cruise, explore the Big Talbot Island, see the Mayport Lighthouse, American Lighthouse and Maritime Museum, or explore the historic St. Augustine district.

Orlando, FL- Explore some of the world's greatest theme parks like Walt Disney World, Universal Studios Florida, Sea World, Skull Kingdom, and Discovery Island - the world's largest aviary amongst others. See the Mennello Museum of American Folk Art, the Central Florida Railroad Museum, and the Kennedy Space Center, or sit and relax and be amazed by the world's most enchanting and artistic circus, the Cirque du Soleil.

Tampa, FL- Spend a day at Adventure Island, one of Tampa's favorite water parks, or ride the roller coasters at Busch Gardens Tampa Bay. Visit the Florida Gulf Coast Art Center, the Florida Aquarium, and the Lowry Park Zoo which is home to many exotic animals. Go to the historic district of Ybor City and explore the Pier and visit the Great Explorations Hands-On Museum. The Salvador Dali Museum exhibits Spanish works of art, and the St. Petersburg Museum of History is dedicated to the history of St. Petersburg.

Miami, FL- Visit the Port of Miami, the "Cruise Capital of the World," and see some of the world's finest and largest cruise ships. Take an ocean drive along Miami Beach and experience the vibrant city of Miami. See the Ancient Spanish Monastery built in Spain in 1141, the Lowe Art Museum, the Holocaust Memorial, Miami Museum of Science Planetarium, Gold Coast Railroad Museum, the Black Heritage Museum, the Miami Beach Garden Conservancy, and the Parrot Jungle and Gardens. Visit the nearby Everglades National Park, the Everglades Alligator Farm, and the Everglades Safari Park. Take the Miccosukee Indian Village & Everglades cultural, farm and ecosystem Airboat Tours.

Train Schedules

The Silver Meteor, Silver Star, and Silver Palm, travel daily between New York City, New York and Miami, Florida. The trip between the two cities takes approximately 27 hours.

Accommodations

Accommodations on the Silver Services are the Viewliner Sleeping Car and Reserved Coach. There is a Lounge Car that serves local cuisine, soup, snacks, sandwiches, and drinks. Restaurant style meals are served in the Dining Car.

All Aboard!

New York City (NY) See Lakeshore Limited, page 405

Metropark (NJ) See Carolinian/Piedmont, page 513-515

Trenton (NJ) See Pennsylvania service, page 428-429

Philadelphia (PA) See Pennsylvania service, page 425

Wilmington (DE) See Vermonter service, page 483-484

Baltimore (MD) See Vermonter service, page 484

New Carrollton (MD) See Vermonter service, page 487-488

Washington DC See Capitol Limited service, page 441

Alexandria (VA) See Cardinal service, page 461

Quantico (VA) See Twilight Shoreline service, page 503-507

Richmond (VA) See Twilight Shoreline service, page 507

Petersburg (VA) See Carolinia/Piedmont service, page 513-515

Rocky Mount (NC) See Carolinia/Piedmont service, page 513-515

Wilson (NC) See Carolinia/Piedmont service, page 513-515

Raleigh (NC) See Carolinia/Piedmont service, page 515

North Carolina (NC)
Capital: Raleigh (Population: 8,049,313)
Size: 53,821 sq mi. (139,396 sq km)
Nickname: The Tar Heel State
Joined the union on: November 21, 1789 (12th state)
Motto: To be rather than to seem
Flower: Dogwood
Bird: Cardinal
Song: The Old North State
Famous for: the first English colony in America
Major industries: Furniture manufacturing, tobacco, textile, chemicals, agriculture

Fayetteville (NC)

Fayetteville is located in south-central North Carolina, just 53 miles south of Raleigh. Fayetteville has a land area of 40.9 sq. miles (105 sq. kilometers) and a population of approximately 125,000. Fayetteville was established in 1778 and was originally named upper and lower Campbellton until 1783 when a town official changed the town's name to Fayetteville in honor of the French General Marquis de LaFayette. The town of Fayetteville was razed and leveled to ground during the devastating fire of 1831, and in 1885 railroad tracks arrived in the town and linked Fayetteville to the rest of the region.

Fayetteville's train depot is located at 472 Hay St. Fayetteville, NC 28301. The station is staffed and features an enclosed waiting area, checked baggage service, restrooms, and payphones. Transportation from the station is local taxi service.

Fayetteville station is served by the Silver Service.

Dillon (SC)

Dillon is a small town located in northeast South Carolina near the border of the two Carolinas. It has a land area of 4.2 sq. miles (11 sq. kilometers) and a population of approximately 7,000.

Dillon's train depot is located at 100 N. Railroad Ave. Dillon, SC 29536. The station is unstaffed and features an enclosed waiting area and payphones. Transportation from the station is local taxi service.

Dillon station is served by the Silver Service.

Florence (SC)

Florence is located in eastern South Carolina just 80 miles from the state capital Columbia. It has a land area of 14.8 sq. miles (38 sq. kilometers) and a population of 33,000. Florence was founded as a railroad center in 1871 and was incorporated in 1890.

Places of interest: The War Between the States Museum Tel: (843) 669-1266, the Francis Marion University Planetarium Tel: (843) 661-1250, and the Pee Dee State Farmers Market Tel: (843) 665-5154.

Florence's train depot is located at 807 E. Day St. Florence, SC 29506. The station is staffed and features an enclosed waiting area, checked baggage service, restrooms, payphones, and vending machines. Transportation options from the station include Hertz Rent-A-Car toll-free (800) 654-3131 and local taxi service.

Florence station is served by the Silver Service.

South Carolina (SC)
Capital: Columbia (Population: 4,012,012)
Size: 32,007 sq mi. (82,898 sq km)
Nickname: The Palmetto State
Joined the union on: May 23, 1788 (8th state)
Mottoes: Prepared in mind and resources and While I breathe, I hope
Flower: Carolina yellow jessamine
Bird: Carolina wren
Song: Carolina
Famous for: Museums, First Public Library and Steam Rail Road
Major industries: Textile, chemicals and agriculture.

Kingstree (SC)

Kingstree is located in eastern South Carolina, 68 miles from the city of Columbia and 75 miles northeast of Charleston. It has a land area of 3 sq. miles (8 sq. kilometers) and a population of approximately 4,000. Places of interest: Williamsburg County Art Gallery Tel: (843) 354-7247 and Williamsburg Historical County Museum Tel: (843) 354-3306.

Kingstree's train depot is located at 101 E. Main St. Kingstree, SC 29556. The station is un-staffed and features an enclosed waiting area, restrooms, and payphones. Transportation options from the station include local transit and taxi services.

Kingstree station is served by the Silver Service.

Charleston (SC)

Charleston is one of the oldest and one of the most historical cities of the United States. Charleston is located in southeastern South Carolina on the Atlantic Coast. It has a land area of 43.6 sq. miles (111.9 sq. kilometers) and a population of more than 80,000. Charleston's rich history and architectural beauty are still seen in the city's many historical sites and narrow streets. Take a day or two and explore the historical city of Charleston.

Charleston's train depot is located at 4565 Gaynor Ave, N. Charleston SC 29406. The station is staffed and features an enclosed waiting area, checked baggage service, restrooms, payphones, and vending machines. Transportation options from the station include Hertz Car Rental toll-free (800) 654-3131 and local taxi service.

Charleston station is served by the Silver Service.

Places of Interest

The 1841 Old City Market, located on Market St. between Meeting and East Bay St. Charleston, SC, features restaurants, shops, and a flea market. **Old Exchange** is located at 122 East Bay Street Charleston, SC 29401 Tel: (843) 727-2165. One of the most historical places in the US, it was built in 1771 by the British as the exchange and custom house. **Charles Towne Landing State Park,** located at 1500 Old Towne Road Charleston, is the site of the oldest English settlements in the area. The park houses a zoo, gardens, and recreational areas. **The Powder Magazine,** located at 79 Cumberland Street Charleston, SC 29401 Tel: (843) 805-6730, was built in the late 1600's and is the oldest in both north and south Carolinas.

The historical **Dock Street Theatre** is located at 135 Church Street Charleston, SC Tel: (843) 720-3968. **The Avery Research Center for African-American History and Culture** is dedicated to the preservation of South Carolina's historical and cultural heritage. The museum is located at 125 Bull St. Charleston, SC 29424 Tel: (843) 727-2009. **The College of Charleston,** located in St. Philip and George Streets Charleston, SC Tel: (843) 953-5507, was founded in 1770 and was the first municipal college in the US. **The Charleston Museum,** located at 360 Meeting St, Charleston, SC 29403 Tel: (843) 722-2996, exhibits collections of the region's historical artifacts.

Historical Houses

Aiken-Rhett House, located at 48 Elizabeth St. Charleston, SC Tel: (843) 724-8481, was built in 1818 and is Charleston's most impressive residence. **The Nathaniel Russell House,** located at 51 Meeting St. Charleston, SC 29401 Tel: (843) 724-8481, is one of America's most recognized neoclassical houses. **Heyward-Washington House,** located at 87 Church Street Charleston, SC 29401 Tel: (843) 722-2996, is a historical landmark; George Washington stayed in the house during his visit to Charleston in 1791.

Calhoun Mansion, located at 16 Meeting Street Charleston, SC 29401 Tel: (843) 722-8205, is a fine example of the post-civil war Victorian Baronial Manor House. **The Drayton Hall,** located at 3380 Ashley River Rd. Charleston, SC 29414 Tel: (843) 769-2600, is a pre-civil war house of Georgian Palladian architecture, one of the few remaining plantation houses that survived the civil war in the region.

Accommodations

Comfort Inn located at 144 Bee St, Charleston, SC 29401 Tel: (843) 577-2224. **Historic Charleston B & B** located at 57 Broad St, Charleston, SC 29401 Tel: (843) 722-6606. **Courtyard by Marriott** located at 35 Lockwood Dr, Charleston, SC 29401 Tel: (843) 722-

7229. **Days Inn** located at 155 Meeting St, Charleston, SC 29401 Tel: (843) 722-8411. **Econo Lodge** located at 2237 Savannah Hwy, Charleston, SC 29414 Tel: (843) 571-1880. **Westin Francis Marion** located at 387 King St, Charleston, SC 29403 Tel: (843) 722-0600. **Battery Inc** located at 20 S Battery St, Charleston, SC 29401 Tel: (843) 722-3337.

Arlington-Rhettsbury Inn located at 19 Pinckney St, Charleston, SC 29401 Tel: (843) 958-8000. **Charleston Place** located at 205 Meeting St, Charleston, SC 29401 Tel: (843) 722-4900. **Hampton Inn** located at 39 John St, Charleston, SC 29403 Tel: (843) 723-4047. **Meeting Street Inn** located at 173 Meeting St, Charleston, SC 29401 Tel: (843) 723-1882. **Barksdale House Inn** located at 27 George St, Charleston, SC 29401 Tel: (843) 577-4800. **Holiday Inn** located at 125 Calhoun St, Charleston, SC 29401 Tel: (843) 805-7900.

Wingate Inn Charleston located at 5219 N Arco Ln, Charleston, SC 29418 Tel: (843) 308-9666. **Embassy Suites Hotel** located at 337 Meeting St, Charleston, SC 29403 Tel: (843) 723-6900. **Doubletree Guest Suites** located at 181 Church St, Charleston, SC 29401 Tel: (843) 577-2644. **Best Western Inn** located at 1540 Savannah Hwy, Charleston, SC 29407 Tel: (843) 571-6100. **Radisson Charleston Hotel** located at 170 Lockwood Blvd, Charleston, SC 29403 Tel: (843) 723-3000.

Yemassee (SC)

Yemassee is located in central South Carolina, 92 miles from the state capital Columbia. Yemassee has a land area of 4.5 sq. miles (11.6 sq. kilometers) and a population of less than 1,000. The name Yemassee was taken from the Indian tribe of the area.

Yemassee's train depot is located on Main St. Yemassee, SC 29945. The station is un-staffed and features an enclosed waiting area, restrooms, and payphones. Transportation from the station is local taxi service.

Yemassee station is served by the Silver Service.

Southern Pines (NC)

Southern Pines was founded in 1887 by John Patrick, and is located in south-central North Carolina. South Pines has a land area of 6 sq. miles (26.8 sq. kilometers) and a population of less than 10,000.

Places of interest: the Union Station located in downtown Aberdeen Tel: (910) 944-5902, the North Carolina Literary Hall of Fame located in Weymouth Center, 555 E. Connecticut Ave, Southern Pines Tel: (910) 692-6261, and the Shaw House Property located at Morganton Road and SW Broad Street, Southern Pines Tel: (910) 692-2051.

Southern Pines' train depot is located on N. W. Broad St. Southern Pines, NC 28387. The station is un-staffed and features an enclosed waiting area, restrooms, and payphones. Transportation from the station is local taxi service.

Southern Pines station is served by the Silver Service.

Hamlet (NC)

Hamlet is located in south-central North Carolina, 88 miles from the city of Raleigh. Hamlet has a land area of 4 sq. miles (10.7 sq. kilometers) and a population of approximately 7,000. Hamlet is known as a railroad town; it was in 1870 when the railroad track from Wilmington arrived in Hamlet. Hamlet was founded by John Shortridge and was incorporated in 1897.

Places of interest: The National Railroad Museum and Hall of Fame, located at 2 Main St, Hamlet Tel: (910) 582-3317, is in Victorian architecture. The museum exhibits locomotives, railroad memorabilia, and more.

Hamlet's train depot is located on Main St. Hamlet, NC 28345. The station is un-staffed and features an enclosed waiting area, restrooms, and payphones. Transportation from the station is local taxi service.

Hamlet station is served by the Silver Service.

Camden (SC)

Camden is located in central South Carolina, 22 miles northeast of Columbia. Camden has a land area of 6.7 sq. miles (17.2 sq. kilometers) and a population of approximately 8,000. Camden is the site of the historic Battle of Camden in August 1780.

Camden's train depot is located at 1060 W. Dekalb St. Camden, SC 29020. The station is un-staffed and features an enclosed waiting area and restrooms. Transportation from the station is local taxi service.

Camden station is served by the Silver Service.

Columbia (SC)

Columbia is the capital of South Carolina. It has a land area of 118 sq. miles (303 sq. kilometers) and a population of approximately 116,000. Columbia was founded in 1786, incorporated as a town in 1805, and as a city in 1854. Places of interest: Fort Jackson, and Columbia City Hall which is listed on the National Register of Historic Places.

Columbia's train depot is located at 850 Pulaski St. Columbia, SC 29201. The station is staffed and features an enclosed waiting area, checked baggage service, restrooms, payphones and vending machines. Transportation from the station is local taxi service.

Columbia station is served by the Silver Service.

Denmark (SC)

Denmark is located 50 miles south of Columbia. It has a land area of 3 sq. miles (7.8 sq. kilometers) and a population of approximately 4,000.

Denmark's train depot is located at 200 W. Baruch St. Denmark, SC 29042. The station is un-staffed and features an enclosed waiting area, restrooms, and payphones. Transportation from the station is local taxi service.

Denmark station is served by Silver Service.

Savannah (GA)

Savannah is situated at the mouth of the Savannah River in eastern Georgia and is the county seat of Chatham County. Savannah has a land area of 63 sq. miles (162 sq. kilometers) and a population of approximately 140,000. Savannah has a rich cultural heritage and many historical sites are still present. Enjoy the city's beautiful and richly decorated architectures, monuments, and streets.

Savannah was the first planned city in the United States. General James Edward Oglethorpe and 120 travelers founded the site of what is now the city of Savannah in 1733. General Oglethorpe named their newfound land "Georgia" in honor of King George of England, and Savannah became the first city in the state of Georgia. The new settlers were immediately welcomed and earned the trust of the native Indians, thus, the long history of Savannah begun.

Savannah also had its low points in its long history. During the American Revolution the city of Savannah was the site of bloody battles in the late 1700's. The city was leveled twice and almost left in ruins during the city's fires of 1796 and 1820. On the other hand, Savannah was spared and avoided devastation by the forces of General Sherman during the civil war of the 1860's.

Getting Around

Airport

Savannah Hilton Head International Airport Tel: (912) 964-0514 is located 15 minutes from downtown Savannah. Major rental car and taxi services are available at the airport.

Bus

Chatham Area Transit (CAT) Tel: (912) 233-5767 operates local bus routes around Savannah and the outlying areas. The Shuttle offers free shuttles in Savannah's historic district. Greyhound Bus Lines Tel: (912) 232-2135 connects Savannah to the rest of the country.

Taxi

Yellow Cab Tel: (912) 236-1133, Philip's Taxi Cab Tel: (912) 659-0917, and Toucan Taxi Tel: (912) 233-3700.

Georgia (GA)
Capital: Atlanta (Population: 8,186,453)
Size: 59,441 sq mi. (153,952 sq km)
Nickname: The Empire State of the South, the Peach State
Joined the union on: January 2, 1788 (4th state)
Motto: Wisdom, justice, and moderation
Flower: Cherokee Rose
Bird: Brown Thrasher
Song: Georgia on My Mind
Famous for: Mansion of Savannah
Major industries: Textiles

Rent-A-Car

Thrifty Rent-a-Car Tel: (912) 966-2277, Alamo Rent-a-Car Tel: (912) 964-7364, National Rent-a-Car Tel: (912) 964-1771, Avis Rent-a-Car Tel: (912) 964-1781, Hertz Rent-a-Car Tel: (912) 964-9595, Enterprise Rent-a-Car Tel: (912) 920-1093, and Budget Rent-a-Car Tel: (912) 964-4600.

Train and Commuter

Savannah's train depot is located at 2611 Seaboard Coastline Dr. Savannah, GA 31401. The station is staffed and features an enclosed waiting area, checked baggage service, restrooms, payphones, and vending machines. Transportation options from the station include Hertz Car Rental toll-free (800) 654-3131 and local taxi service.

Savannah station is served by the Silver Service.

Visitor Information Center

Savannah Visitor Information Center, 301 Martin Luther King Blvd. Savannah, GA 31401 Tel: (912) 944-0455.

River Street Hospitality Center, 1 River Street Savannah, GA 31401 Tel: (912) 651-6662.

Places to See and Things to Do

Ships of the Sea Maritime Museum located at 41 Martin L. King Jr. Blvd. Savannah Tel: (912) 232-1511. **Savannah History Museum** located at 303 Martin L. King, Jr Blvd. Savannah Tel: (912) 238-1779. **Savannah Science Museum** located at 4405 Paulsen St Savannah, GA 31405-3637 Tel: (912) 355-6705. **The Roundhouse Railroad Museum** located at 601 W. Harris St. Savannah Tel: (912) 651-6823. **Savannah Ogeechee Canal Museum & Nature Center** located at 681 Fort Argyle Road Savannah Tel: (912) 748-8068.

City Market located at Jefferson at West Saint Julian St. Savannah, GA 31401 Tel: (912) 232-4903. **The Andrew Low House** located at 329 Abercorn St. Savannah Tel: (912) 233-6854. **King-Tisdell Cottage** located at 502 E. Harris St. Savannah Tel: (912) 234-8000. **Old Fort Jackson** located at 1 Fort Jackson Road Savannah Tel: (912) 232-3945. **Georgia Historical Society** located at 501 Whitaker St. Savannah Tel: (912) 651-2125. **Coastal Heritage Society** located at 303 Martin L. King, Jr. Blvd. Savannah Tel: (912) 651-6840. **Juliette Gordon Low Birthplace** located at 10 E. Oglethorpe Ave. Savannah Tel: (912) 233-4501.

Accommodations

Econo Lodge Gateway located at 7 Gateway Boulevard, West Savannah GA 31419 toll-free (800) 553-3666 expect to pay $30-$80. **Days Inn and Suites Savannah Historic District** located at 201 West Bay Street, Savannah GA 31401 toll-free (800) 544-8313 expect to pay $50-$170. **Baymont Inn and Suites Savannah** located at 8484 Abercorn Street, Savannah GA 31406 toll-free (800) 301-0200 expect to pay $60-$90. **Wingate Inn Savannah** located at 11 Gateway Boulevard East, Savannah GA 31419 Tel: (912) 925-2525 expect to pay $60-$130. **Best Western Savannah Historic District** located at 412 West Bay Street, Savannah Georgia 31401 Tel: (912) 233-1011 expect to pay $70-$140.

Hyatt Regency Savannah located at 2 West Bay Street, Savannah GA 31401 toll-free (800) CHECK-IN expect to pay $140-$370. **River Street Inn** located at 115 East River Street, Savannah GA 31401 Tel: (912) 234-6400 expect to pay $100-$250. **Holiday Inn Savannah Midtown** located at 7100 Abercorn Street, Savannah GA 31406 Tel: (912) 352-7100 expect to pay $80-$200. **Comfort Inn and Suites Midtown** located at 211 Stephenson Avenue, Savannah GA 31405 toll-free (800) 228-5150 expect to pay $70-$130. **Marriot Savannah Riverfront** located at 100 General McIntosh Boulevard, Savannah GA 31401 Tel: (912) 233-7722 expect to pay $90-$290.

Jesup (GA)

Jesup is the county seat of Wayne County, Georgia. The city of Jesup is located in southeast Georgia, 212 miles from Atlanta. Jesup has a land area of 16 sq. miles (42 sq. kilometers) and a population of roughly 9,000. The town of Jesup was born out of the development of the railroad industry. It was said that in the late 1800's Jesup became one of the major train centers in the region. Jessup was incorporated in 1870.

Jesup's train depot is located at 176 N.W. Broad St. Jesup, GA 31545. The station is un-staffed and features an enclosed waiting area, restrooms, and payphones. Transportation options from the station include local bus and taxi services.

The Silver Service serves Jesup station.

Florida (FL)
Capital: Tallahassee (Population: 15,982,378)
Size: 65,758 sq mi. (170,313 sq km)
Nickname: The Sunshine State
Joined the Union On: March 3, 1845 (27th state)
Motto: In God we trust
Flower: Orange Blossom
Bird: Mockingbird
Song: The Suwanee River
Major industries: Tourism, agriculture, manufacturing, mining, marine

Jacksonville (FL)

Jacksonville, also known as the "River City," is located in the northeastern corner of Florida near the Florida/Georgia state border, 157 miles east of Tallahassee, the state capital. Jacksonville has a population of approximately 700,000 and a land area of 759 sq. miles (1965.8 sq. kilometers) making Jacksonville is the largest city in lower 48 states of the US by area.

The site of what is now Jacksonville was first inhabited by the Timucuan Indians; the Spanish led by Juan Ponce de Leon arrived in the area in 1513 and later built a settlement called St. Augustine. Jacksonville was named after General Andrew Jackson, the first military governor of the province. Jacksonville has a temperate year-round temperature of 72.8 degrees F (23 degree C).

Getting Around

Airport

Jacksonville International Airport, 2400 Yankee Clipper Drive, Suite 102, Jacksonville, Florida Tel: (904) 741 2000. The airport is located 15 miles (24 kilometers) north of Jacksonville. Major rental car services, taxi and minibuses area available at the arrival terminal near the baggage claim area.

Bus

Jacksonville Transportation Authority (JTA), 100 N. Myrtle Avenue Jacksonville, FL 32203 Tel: (904) 630-3181. JTA provides various mass transit including express and local transit services in the city of Jacksonville and the surrounding area.

Taxi

Checker Cab Co. of Jacksonville Tel: (904) 764-2472 and Citi Cab Tel: (904) 425-2222.

Rent-A-Car

Annette Auto Rental, 2238 Atlantic Blvd. Jacksonville, FL 32207 Tel: (904) 399-8877.

Train and Commuter

Jacksonville Transportation Authority (JTA), 100 N. Myrtle Avenue Jacksonville, FL 32203 Tel: (904) 630-3181. JTA runs the downtown Skyway monorail and the Trolley service.

Jacksonville's train depot is located at 3570 Clifford Lane Jacksonville, FL 32209. The station is staffed and features an enclosed waiting area, checked baggage service, restrooms, payphones and vending machines. Transportation options from the station include local transit and taxi services.

Jacksonville station is served by the Sunset Limited and Silver Service.

Visitors Information Center

Jacksonville and the Beaches Convention & Visitors Bureau, 201 East Adams Street Jacksonville, FL 32202 toll-free (800) 733-2668.

Places to See and Things to Do

Jacksonville

Jacksonville Zoological Gardens is located at 8605 Zoo Parkway, (Northside) Jacksonville Tel: (904) 757-4463. The zoo is home to hundreds of animals; it also houses a reptile house and the "great apes of the world." The **Jacksonville Museum of Contemporary Art,** located at 4160 Boulevard Center Drive (Southside) Jacksonville Tel: (904) 398-8336, has wide collections of contemporary art. **Jacksonville Historical Center,** located in Southbank Riverwalk Tel: (904) 398-4301, exhibits the history of Jacksonville.

Treaty Oak, located in Southbank, downtown Jacksonville, is the oldest living thing in Jacksonville and one of the oldest in the state. Take a relaxing walk at the **Riverwalk** at Southbank and Northbank in downtown Jacksonville; stroll the 1.2-mile boardwalk and catch a glimpse of the city of Jacksonville. **Friendship Park and Fountain** is located at Southbank Riverwalk in Downtown Jacksonville. At the height of 100 feet, the Friendship Fountain is one of the largest in the world. **Museum of Science and History** is located at Southbank Jacksonville at 1025 Museum Circle Tel: (904) 396-7062.

Karpeles Manuscript Library Museum is located in downtown Jacksonville at 101 W. 1st Street Tel: (904) 356-2992; the library museum features extensive collections of rare documents. **River Cruises,** located in downtown Jacksonville Tel: (904) 396-2333, offers a romantic dinner cruise with entertainment along the St. Johns River. **Veterans Memorial Wall,** located in downtown Jacksonville at 1145 East Adams Street, is a black granite wall dedicated in 1995 to the veterans of the two world wars. **The Florida Theatre** is located in downtown area at 128 E. Forsyth Street Tel: (904) 355-2787. This charming 20th century theater hosted more than a hundred events each year.

Places to Stroll and Jog

Tree Hill, Jacksonville's Nature Center, located in Arlington at 7152 Lone Star Road Tel: (904) 724-4646, the park houses the Natural History Museum, hall, gardens, and more. **Alexander Brest Museum,** located on the campus of Jacksonville University at 800 University Boulevard North Tel: (904) 745-7371, has various art exhibits specializing in glass, porcelain, and ivory arts. **Alhambra Dinner Theatre,** located at 12000 Beach Blvd. Jacksonville Tel: (904) 641-1212, offers a musical and comedy dinner; a fun place to spend a romantic evening.

Big Talbot Island, located in northeast Jacksonville taking Heckscher Drive via Little Talbot Island, is a favorite spot for those looking for a little privacy; the beach is still untouched by development. Built in 1859 the **Mayport Lighthouse** is listed on the National Register of Historic Places, access to the lighthouse is via the Naval Station Mayport Tel: (904) 247-8688.

American Lighthouse and Maritime Museum, located in Jacksonville Beach at 1011 North 3rd Street Tel: (904) 241-8845, exhibits memorabilia of the lighthouse's history. **Pablo Historical Park,** located in Jacksonville Beach at 425 Beach Blvd. Tel: (904) 246-0093, features historic landmarks and buildings, museums, and a historic railroad track.

Jacksonville Beach Fishing Pier, located in Jacksonville Beach at 3 Sixth Avenue South Tel: (904) 246-6001, is a favorite relaxation and recreation spot for locals and visitors.

St. Augustine

Oldest Store Museum, Inc., located at 4 Artillery Lane St. Augustine FL 32084-4463 Tel: (904) 829-9729, exhibits thousands of antique objects. **The Ximenez- Patio House,** located at 20 Aviles Street St. Augustine Florida 32084 Tel: (904) 829-3575, is a perfectly preserved 19th century inn; the house is an example of the rich architectural history of St. Augustine. **Potters Wax Museum** is located at 17 King St. St. Augustine FL 32084 Tel: (904) 829-9056; the museum features more than 100 wax figures of popular personalities. **Ripley's Believe It or Not! Museum** is located at 19 San Marco Ave. St. Augustine FL 32084-3278 Tel: (904) 824-1606.

Anastasia Riverboat, located at 303-A Anastasia Boulevard Tel: (904) 824-3463, offers historic paddlewheel sunset dinner cruises along St. Augustine Marina. **St. Augustine Sightseeing Trains,** located at 170 San Marco Avenue St. Augustine Tel: (904) 829-6545, offers guided tours around the historic city of St. Augustine.

Spanish Quarter Village, located at 29 St. George St. Augustine FL, features the 18th century local lifestyle of St. Augustine. **Old Florida Museum,** located at 254-D San Marco Ave, St. Augustine, toll-free (800) 813-3208, exhibits St. Augustine history of pre-European to early European time. **Castillo de San Marcos** is a 1695 Spanish fort that played a major role in the defense of the Spanish possession of Florida. The fort is accessible via Highway A1A South Tel: (904) 829-6506. **Ft. Matanzas National Monument** is located at 8635 A1A South St. Augustine Tel: (904) 471-0116. **St. Augustine Lighthouse** is located on SR A1A, Old Beach Rd. Anastasia Island, St. Augustine Florida Tel: (904) 829-0745. The view at the top of the 165-foot lighthouse is rewarding.

Accommodations

Jacksonville Area

Courtyard Butler Boulevard located at 4670 Lenoir Avenue South, Jacksonville Fl 32216 Tel: (904) 296-2828 expect to pay $50-$150. **Holiday Inn Express Hotel & Suites** located at 4675 Salisbury Road, Jacksonville Fl 32256 Tel: (904) 332-9500 expect to pay $40-$150. **SpringHill Suites Jacksonville/Deerwood** located at 4385 Southside Blvd, Jacksonville FL 32246 Tel: (904) 997-6650 **Holiday Inn Airport Rd** located at I-95 & Airport Rd, Jacksonville Fl 32229 Tel: (904) 741-4404 expect to pay $50-$130. **Days Inn Airport Jacksonville** located at 1181 Airport Road, Jacksonville Fl 32218 Tel: (904) 741-4000 expect to pay $40-$130. **Candlewood Suites** located at 4990 Belfort Road, Jacksonville FL 32256 Tel: (904) 296-7785 expect to pay $40-$130.

Comfort Suites Airport located at 1180 Airport Road, Jacksonville Fl 32218 Tel: (904) 741-0505 expect to pay $70-$130. **Motel 6 Orange Park** located at 6107 Youngerman Circle, Jacksonville Fl Tel: 925 473-2230 expect to pay $30-$70. **Holiday Inn Commonwealth** located at 6802 Commonwealth Ave, Jacksonville Fl 32236 Tel: (904) 781-6000 expect to pay $50-$150. **Hilton Jacksonville and Towers** located in Hilton Jacksonville and Towers, Jacksonville Fl 32207 toll-free (800) HILTONS, expect to pay $70-

$200. **Best Western Executive Inn** located at 10888 Harts Road, Jacksonville Fl 32118 Tel: (904) 751-5600 expect to pay $60-$150. **Clarion Hotel Airport Conference Center** located at 2101 Dixie Clipper Rd, Jacksonville Fl 32218 Tel: (904) 741-1997 expect to pay $50-$150. **Baymont Inn & Suites** located at 3199 Hartley Rd, Jacksonville Fl 32257 Tel: (904) 268-9999 expect to pay $50-$70.

St. Augustine Area

Holiday Inn St. Augustine Beach located at 860 A1A Beach Blvd, St. Augustine FL 32080 Tel: (904) 471-2555 expect to pay $60-$200. **Quality Inn Alhambra St. Augustine** located at 2700 Ponce De Leon Blvd, St. Augustine FL 32084 Tel: (904) 824-2883 expect to pay $50-$300. **Hampton Inn St. Augustine** located at 2050 N Ponce de Leon, St. Augustine FL 32084 Tel: (904) 829-1996 expect to pay $50-$150. **Days Inn West St. Augustine** located at 2560 State Road 16, St. Augustine FL 32092 Tel: (904) 824-4341 expect to pay $30-$150. **Sleep Inn St. Augustine** located at 601 Anastasia Blvd, St. Augustine FL 32084 Tel: (904) 825-4535 expect to pay $50-$150.

Howard Johnson Express Inn located at 137 San Marco Avenue, St. Augustine FL 32084 Tel: (904) 824-6181 expect to pay $50-$150. **Holiday Inn Express I-95 St. Augustine** located at 2310 SR 16 & I-95, St. Augustine FL 32095 Tel: (904) 823-8636 expect to pay $60-$200. **Ramada Limited St. Augustine** located at 2535 State Road 16, St. Augustine FL Tel: (904) 829-5643 expect to pay $30-$150. **Best Western Spanish Quarters Inn St. Augustine** located at 6 Castillo Drive, St. Augustine FL 32084 Tel: (904) 824-4457 expect to pay $60-$200. **Hilton Garden Inn St. Augustine** located at 401 A1A Beach Boulevard, St. Augustine FL 32080 Tel: (904) 471-5559 expect to pay $60-$200.

Silver Meteor/Silver Star/Silver Palm- Jacksonville to Miami Route

All Aboard!

Jacksonville (FL)

Palatka (FL)

Palatka is located in northeastern Florida, 170 miles from the state capital Tallahassee. Palatka has a land area of 6.2 sq. miles (16 sq. kilometers) and a population of more than 11,000. Visit the David Browning RR Museum, located at Reid & 11th Streets Palatka, Florida 32178 Tel: (386) 328-1539, exhibiting railroad memorabilia and model trains. If you are coming to Palatka during the Memorial Day weekend, see the "Blue Crab Festival" and have some fun!

Palatka's train depot is located at 11th and Reid Sts. Palatka, FL 32077. The station is un-staffed and features an enclosed waiting area, restrooms, and payphones. Transportation from the station is local taxi service.

Trains serving Palatka station are the Silver Service and the Sunset Limited.

Deland (FL)

Deland is known for its friendly people and historical Main Street. The city of Deland is proud to be bestowed as "Main Street America" for its well-preserved historic district. Deland is located in the general Orlando area in Volusia County, Florida. It has a land area of 9.7 sq. miles (24.9 sq. kilometers) and a population of approximately 17,000. Deland is home to Stetson University, the oldest private school in Florida.

Deland's train depot is located at 2491 Old New York Ave. Deland, FL 32720. The station is staffed and features an enclosed waiting area, checked baggage service, restrooms, payphones, and vending machines. Transportation from the station is local taxi service.

Trains serving Deland station are the Silver Service and Sunset Limited.

Sanford (FL)

Sanford is located near the south shore of Lake Monroe, just 25 miles north of Orlando. Sanford has a land area of 17 sq. miles (44.8 sq. kilometers) and a population of approximately 34,000. Visitors should visit the Seminole County Museum located at 300 Bush Blvd Sanford, FL 32773-6135 Tel: (407) 321-2489, and the Sanford Commercial District and Residential District, both are registered on the National Register of Historic Places.

Sanford's train depot is located at 800 Persimmon Ave. Suite 100 Sanford, FL 32771. The station is un-staffed and features an enclosed waiting area, restrooms, payphones and vending machines. Transportation options from the station include Hertz Car Rental toll-free (800) 654-3131 and local taxi service.

Trains serving Sanford station are the Silver Service and the Sunset Limited.

Winter Park (FL)

Winter Park is located just 5 miles northeast of Orlando. Winter Park has a land area of 7 sq. miles (18 sq. kilometers) and a population of approximately 25,000. Winter Park is appreciated for its brick streets, vibrant beauty, and people. Winter Park is a good alternative to Orlando's soaring accommodations.

Winter Park's train depot is located at 150 W. Morse Blvd. Winter Park, FL 32789. The station is staffed and features an enclosed waiting area, checked baggage service, restrooms, payphones, and a restaurant. Transportation options from the station include local transit and taxi services.

Trains serving Winter Park station are the Silver Service and Sunset Limited.

Accommodations

Langford Resort Hotel located at 300 E New England Ave, Winter Park, FL 32789 Tel: (407) 644-3400. **Park Plaza Hotel** located at 307 S Park Ave, Winter Park, FL 32789 Tel: (407) 647-1072. **Mt Vernon Best Western Inn** located at 110 S Orlando Ave, Winter Park, FL 32789 Tel: (407) 647-1166. **Langford Corp** located at 300 E New England Ave, Winter Park, FL 32789 Tel: (407) 647-4117. **Tropical Court Motel** located at 271 S Orlando Ave, Winter Park, FL 32789 Tel: (407) 644-6099. **Fairfield Inn** located at 951 N Wymore Rd, Winter Park, FL 32789 Tel: (407) 539-1955. **Days Inn** located at 901 N Orlando Ave, Winter Park, FL 32789 Tel: (407) 644-8000.

Florida (FL)

Capital: Tallahassee (Population: 15,982,378)
Size: 65,758 sq mi. (170,313 sq km)
Nickname: The Sunshine State
Joined the Union On: March 3, 1845 (27th state)
Motto: In God we trust
Flower: Orange Blossom
Bird: Mockingbird
Song: The Suwanee River
Famous for: Beaches, Amusement Parks, and Everglades
Major industries: Tourism, agriculture, manufacturing, mining, marine

Orlando (FL)

Motor-coach connection to **St. Petersburg (FL)**, Train Connection via Silver Service to **Miami (FL)**

Orlando is located in central Florida and has a land area of 67.8 sq. miles (174 sq. kilometers) and a population of around 185,000. Orlando is one of the most popular destinations in the US; more than 25 million people visit the city and its outlying areas each year. Orlando's strategic location, comfortable weather, natural wonders, and state-of-the-art theme parks have made this city a wonderland for many vacationers.

Getting Around

Airport

Orlando International Airport, One Airport Boulevard, Orlando, Florida 32827 Tel: (407) 825-2001 is 6.5 miles (10 Kilometers) southeast of Orlando. Local taxi, LYNX buses, and major car rental companies are available in the airport level 1 ground terminal building.

Bus

LYNX, Tel: (407) 841-8240, provides bus services throughout the region. Basic fare is $1. I-Ride Trolley Service, Tel: (407) 354-5656, operates in the International Drive area. Basic fare is 75 cents. Ask for Unlimited Day Pass if you are planning to use the trolley more than once in a day.

Taxi

Advantage Limousine Tel: (407) 438-8888 and A central Florida Limo Tel: (407) 862-6400. Both companies provide taxi services around the region.

Rent-A-Car

Dollar Rent-A-Car Tel: (407) 825-3265, Alamo Rent-A-Car Tel: (407) 857-8200, and Avis Rent-A-Car Tel: (407) 825-3700. Note: it is cheaper and more convenient to rent a car while exploring Orlando.

Train and Commuter

Orlando's Train depot is located at 1400 Sligh Blvd. Orlando, FL 32806. The station is staffed and features an enclosed waiting area, restrooms, payphones, and vending machines. Transportation options from the station include Hertz Car Rental toll-free (800) 654-3131, local transit and taxi services.

Trains serving Orlando station are the Silver Service and Sunset Limited.

Visitor Information Center

Orlando/Orange County, Florida Convention and Visitors bureau, 6700 Forum Drive No. 100 Orlando, Florida 32821 Tel: (407) 363-5800.

Orlando Visitor Center, 8723 International Drive, Suite 101, Orlando Fl 32819 Tel: (407) 363-5872.

Places to See and Things to Do

Kennedy Space Center is located on the east coast of Florida 35 miles east of Orlando International Airport. KSC Visitor Complex is open everyday from 9:00 am to 5:30 pm. Tickets are $26 for adults and $16 for children. 12-month passes are available at the visitor complex at $44 for adults and $28 for children. Contact the KSC Visitor Complex at Tel: (321) 449-4444; for Space Shuttle launch viewing information call toll-free (800) 572-4636.

Walt Disney World is located on Lake Buena Vista Florida Drive, south of Interstate 4. The biggest Disneyland park, there are several themed lands featuring your favorites classic Disney characters, attractions, live entertainment, and parades at downtown Main Street U.S.A. in late afternoon. There are numerous restaurants, gift shops, and shops. Admission prices are, adult (10-59 yrs.) - $43.00; senior (60 and over) - $41.00; child (3-9 yrs.) - $33.00. Multi-day tickets (3 days) are, adult - $111.00; child - $87.00. Prices include all rides. Call Tel: (407) 824-4321 for information. Included inside Disney World Resort are Epcot, Disney MGM Studios, the Magic Kingdom, Walt Disney World Swan and Dolphin Resort Complex, and more.

Other Theme Parks

Universal Studios Florida is located at 1000 Universal Studios Plaza, Orlando, Florida 32819 Tel: (407) 363-8000. See behind-the-scenes movie and T.V. action, special effects, and exciting rides. Tickets are $43 adult, $32.00 senior, and $32 kids. Tel: (818) 508-9600 for current information. **Sea World** is located at 7007 Sea Harbor Dr Orlando, FL 32821-8009 Tel: (407) 363-2200. Open from 9 a.m.-7 p.m. daily, admission fees are: adult - $42.95; child (3-11) - $32.95; and senior (55+) - $39.95. **Skull Kingdom** is located at 5933 American Way, Orlando, FL 32819 Tel: (407) 354-1564.

Typhoon Lagoon, located on E. Buena Vista Dr, Lake Buena Vista Florida, features water attractions. Admission prices are $23.95 for adults; child (3-9 years) $17.95. **River Country** located on E. Vista Blvd, Lake Buena Vista Florida, features water adventures, slides, and recreation. Admissions are $14.75 for adults; child (3-9 years) $11.50. **Discovery Island,** located in Lake Buena Vista Florida, houses the world's largest aviary. Discovery Island features wildlife and exotic plants. **Gatorland** is located at 14501 South Orange Blossom Trail, Orlando, FL 32837 Tel: (407) 855-5496.

Other Attractions

Orlando Museum of Art is located at 2416 Mills Ave Orlando, Florida. The museum exhibits 19th and 20th century American arts. **Mennello Museum of American Folk Art**, located at 900 East Prineton Street, Orlando, FL 32803 Tel: (407) 246-4278. **Central Florida Railroad Museum** is located at 1225 Marcastle Ave. Orlando, FL 32812. **Titanic, Ship of Dreams** located in "The Mercado" at 8445 International Drive, Orlando, FL 32819 Tel: (407) 248-1166. **Orlando Science Center** located at 777 East Princeton Street, Orlando, FL 32803 Tel: (407) 514-2000.

Ripley's Believe It Or Not! is located at 8201 International Drive, Orlando, FL 32819 Orlando Tel: (407) 363-4418. **Mystery Fun House** located at 5767 Major Boulevard, Orlando, FL 32819 Tel: (407) 351-3355. **Cirque du Soleil** located at 1478 Buena Vista Drive, Lake Buena Vista, FL 32830 Tel: (407) 939-7600. **Guinness World of Records Attractions** located at 8437 International Drive, Orlando, FL 32819 Tel: (407) 351-5803. **Church Street Station** at 129 W. Church St, downtown Orlando has exiting and fun nightlife; there are several restaurants, nightclubs, and shops that are located along the street.

Accommodations

Downtown

Comfort Suites Downtown located at 2416 N. Orange Ave, Orlando FL 32804 Tel: (407) 228-4007 expect to pay $70-$150. **Marriott Downtown Orlando** located at 400 West Livingston Street, Orlando FL 32801 Tel: (407) 843-6664. **Four Points by Sheraton Downtown Orlando** located at 151 East Washington Street, Orlando FL 32801 Tel: (407) 841-3220 expect to pay $50-$200. **Embassy Suites Orlando Downtown** located at 191 East Pine Street, Orlando FL 32801 Tel: (407) 841-1000. **Courtyard Downtown Orlando** located at 730 North Magnolia Avenue, Orlando FL 32803 Tel: (407) 996-1000.

Disney World Area

Walt Disney World Swan and Dolphin located at 1500 Epcot Resorts Blvd, Lake Buena Vista FL 32830 Tel: (407) 934-4000 expect to pay $120-$500. **Grosvenor Resort Walt Disney World Resort** located at 1850 Hotel Plaza Boulevard, Lake Buena Vista FL 32830 Tel: (925) 473-2230 expect to pay $50-$200. **Doubletree Hotels GS Orlando-Walt Disney World FL** located at 2305 Hotel Plaza Boulevard, Lake Buena Vista FL 32830 Tel: (407) 934-1000 expect to pay $100-$200. **Walt Disney World Swan (Westin)** located at 1200 Epcot Resorts Boulevard, Lake Buena Vista FL 32830 Tel: (407) 934-3000. **Hilton at Walt Disney World Resort** located at 1751 Hotel Plaza Boulevard, Lake Buena Vista FL 32830 Tel: (407) 827-4000 expect to pay $90-$450.

Kissimmee (FL)

Kissimmee is located in central Florida 18 miles southwest of Orlando. It has a land area of 12 sq. miles (32 sq. kilometers) and a population of more than 30,000. The name Kissimmee is an Indian name meaning "Heaven's Place." Originally named Allendale, Kissimmee was incorporated and renamed in 1883. Just like Winter Park, Kissimmee is a good alternative for Orlando's towering accommodations, especially during summer.

Kissimmee's train depot is located at 111 Dakin St. Kissimmee, FL 34741. The station is staffed and features an enclosed waiting area, checked baggage service, restrooms, payphones, and vending machines. Transportation options from the station include transit, bus, and taxi service.

Kissimmee station is served by the Silver Service.

Places of interest

Splendid China, located at 3000 Splendid China Blvd, Kissimmee, Florida Tel: (407) 397-8800, features China's famous landmarks and wonders. **Water Mania,** located at 6730 W. Irlo Bronson Memorial Hwy, Kissimmee, Florida Tel: (407) 396-2626, features water slides, flumes, and other water recreations. **Jungle Land,** located at 4580 W. Irlo Bronson Memorial Hwy Tel: (407) 396-1012, exhibits rare and exotic animals. **Flying Tigers Warbird Restoration Museum,** located at 231 N. Hoagland Blvd. Kissimmee, Florida Tel: (407) 933-1942, exhibits war planes of World War II and war memorabilia. And **The World**

of Orchids, located on Old Lake Wilson Rd. Tel: (407) 396-1887, exhibits different varieties of rare and exotic orchids.

Accommodations

Best Western Inn located at 5565 W Irlo Bronson Meml Hwy, Kissimmee, FL 34746 Tel: (407) 396-0707. Holiday Inn located at 2009 W Vine St, Kissimmee, FL 34741 Tel: (407) 846-2713. Budget Inn East located at 307 E Vine St, Kissimmee, FL 34744 Tel: (407) 847-8010. Comfort Suites located at 2775 Florida Plaza Blvd, Kissimmee, FL 34746 Tel: (407) 397-7848. Hostelling International Rsrt located at 4840 W Irlo Bronson Meml Hwy, Kissimmee, FL 34746 Tel: (407) 396-8282. Thriftlodge Eastgate located at 4624 W Irlo Bronson Meml Hwy, Kissimmee, FL 34746 Tel: (407) 396-2151.

Comfort Inn located at 7571 W Irlo Bronson Meml Hwy, Kissimmee, FL 34747 Tel: (407) 396-7500. Best Inn-Maingate located at 7571 W Irlo Bronson Meml Hwy, Kissimmee, FL 34747 Tel: (407) 396-7500. Magic Castle Inn & Suites located at 5055 W Irlo Bronson Meml Hwy, Kissimmee, FL 34746 Tel: (407) 396-2212. Econo Lodge located at 4311 W Vine St, Kissimmee, FL 34746 Tel: (407) 396-7100. Quality Inn located at 4944 W Irlo Bronson Meml Hwy, Kissimmee, FL 34746 Tel: (407) 396-4455.

Ramada Plaza Hotel Gateway located at 7470 W Irlo Bronson Mem Hwy, Kissimmee, FL 34747 Tel: (407) 396-4400. Sheraton located at 7769 W Irlo Bronson Mem Hwy, Kissimmee, FL 34747 Tel: (407) 396-7448. Red Roof Inn located at 4970 Kyngs Heath Rd, Kissimmee, FL 34746 Tel: (407) 396-0065. Ramada East Gate Fountain Park located at 5150 W Irlo Bronson Memorial, Kissimmee, FL 34746 Tel: (407) 396-1111. Hampton Inn located at 3000 Maingate Ln, Kissimmee, FL 34747 Tel: (407) 396-6300.

Travelodge located at 2407 W Vine St, Kissimmee, FL 34741 Tel: (407) 933-2400. Knights Inn located at 7475 W Irlo Bronson Mem Hwy, Kissimmee, FL 34747 Tel: (407) 396-4200. Holiday Inn - Main Gate East 5678 Irlo Bronson Memorial Highway Kissimmee, Florida 34746 Tel: (407) 396-4488. Days Inn located at 4104 W Irlo Bronson Meml Hwy, Kissimmee, FL 34741 Tel: (407) 846-4714.

Waldo (FL)

Waldo is located in north-central Florida 137 miles from Tallahassee. It has a land area of 1.5 sq. miles (3.9 sq. kilometers) and a population of more than 1,000.

Waldo's train depot is located at Hwy 301 and State Rd 24, Waldo, FL 32694. The station is un-staffed and features an enclosed waiting area, restrooms, and payphones. Transportation from the station is local taxi service.

Waldo station is served by the Silver Service.

Ocala (FL)

Ocala is located in north-central Florida approximately 67 miles northwest of Orlando. It has a land area of 29 sq. miles (74.7 sq. kilometers) and a population of 45,000. The Timucua

557

Indians first inhabited the site of what is now Ocala and it was in 1846 that Ocala was incorporated and became the county seat of Marion County.

Places of interest: the Appleton Museum of Art located at 4333 NE Silver Springs Blvd Ocala, FL 34470 Tel: (352) 236-7100. Silver River Museum & Ed Center located at 7189 NE 7th St Ocala, FL 34470 Tel: (352) 236-5401. The Discovery Science Center located at 50 S Magnolia Ave Ocala, FL 34474-4153 Tel: (352) 620-2555. And the Marion County Museum of History located at 306 SE 26th Ter Ocala, FL 34471 Tel: (352) 629-2773.

Ocala's train depot is located at 531 N.E. 1st Ave. Ocala, FL 34470. The station is staffed and features an enclosed waiting area, checked baggage service, restrooms, payphones, and vending machines. Transportation options from the station include local bus and taxi service.

Ocala station is served by the Silver Service.

Wildwood (FL)

Wildwood is located in north-central Florida. Wildwood has a land area of 3.3 sq. miles (8.6 sq. kilometers) and a population of roughly 3,500.

Wildwood's train depot is located at 601 N. Main St. Wildwood, FL 34785. The station is un-staffed and features an enclosed waiting area, restrooms, and payphones. Transportation from the station is local taxi service.

Wildwood station is served by the Silver Service.

Dade City (FL)

Florida (FL)

Capital: Tallahassee (Population: 15,982,378)
Size: 65,758 sq mi. (170,313 sq km)
Nickname: The Sunshine State
Joined the Union On: March 3, 1845 (27th state)
Motto: In God we trust
Flower: Orange Blossom
Bird: Mockingbird
Song: The Suwanee River
Famous for: Beaches, Amusement Parks, and Everglades
Major industries: Tourism, agriculture, manufacturing, mining, marine

Dade City is located in Eastern Pasco County, less than an hour drive from Tampa. Dade City was incorporated in 1889. It has a land area of 3 sq. miles (7.9 sq. kilometers) and a population of approximately 6,000. Dade City was named after Major Francis Dade and has been admired for the oak trees that dominate its many streets giving the city the title of "Tree City, USA." Visit the historic Edwinola, a former city hotel.

Dade City's train depot is located on E. Meridian Ave. at Hwy. 98 Bypass, Dade City, FL 33525. The station is un-staffed and features payphones. Transportation from the station is local taxi service.

Dade City station is served by the Silver Service.

Tampa (FL)

Ponce De Leon first discovered Tampa in 1513. Tampa is located on the western coast of Florida at Tampa Bay. It has a land area of 109 sq. miles (281 sq. kilometers) and a population of more than 190,000. Tampa's economy is very diverse but largely depends on its port and tourism. Tampa enjoys a moderate semi-tropical climate and has an annual rainfall of 46.7 inches per year.

Getting Around

Airport

Tampa International Airport Tel: (813) 870-8750 is located 5 miles (8 Kilometers) west of Tampa. Major rental car company services are available at the airport. Bus and taxi services are available at the baggage claim area.

Bus

Sarasota–Tampa Express and HART line operate in Tampa and the rest of the region. Call Tel: (813) 870-8700 for information.

Taxi

United Cab Company Tel: (813) 253-2424, Yellow Cab Tel: (813) 253-0121, and United Cab Tel: (813) 253-2424.

Rent-A-Car

Avis Rent-A-Car Tel: (813) 396-3500, Budget Rent-A-Car Tel: (813) 877-6051, and Dollar Rent-A-Car Tel: (813) 877-5507

Train and Commuter

Tampa's train depot is located at 601 Nebraska Ave. Tampa, FL 33602. The station is staffed and features an enclosed waiting area, restrooms, payphones, and vending machines. Transportation options from the station include local taxi and transit services.

Tampa station is served by the Silver Service.

Visitors Information Center

Tampa Bay Convention and Visitors Center, 615 Channelside Dr. Ste. 108-A Tampa FL, 33602 Tel: (813) 233-2752.

Places to See and Things to Do

Tampa Area

Adventure Island, located at 1001 McKinley Dr, Tampa, Florida Tel: (813) 987-5660, is one of Tampa's favorite water parks. **Busch Gardens - Tampa Bay,** located at 3000 East Busch Blvd, Tampa, Florida Tel: (813) 987-5082, features roller coasters, a zoo, and entertainment. **Museum of Science & Industry (MOSI),** located at 4801 E. Fowler Ave, Tampa, Florida

Tel: (813) 987-6100, houses Florida's only IMAX dome theater. **Florida Gulf Coast Art Center** is located in Heritage Park Tel: (813) 584-8634.

The Florida Aquarium, located at 701 Channelside Dr, Tampa, Florida Tel: (813) 273-4000, exhibits Florida's rare Marine habitats. **Lowry Park Zoo,** located at 7530 North Blvd, Tampa, Florida Tel: (813) 935-8552, is home to many exotic animals; the zoo houses aquatic and wildlife centers. The historic district of **Ybor City** located between Interstate 4, 5th Avenue, Nebraska Avenue, and 22nd Street, Tampa, Florida 33605 Tel: (813) 248-3712. The historic district of **Old Hyde Park Village,** located at 1509 West Swann Avenue, Tampa, Florida 33606 Tel: (813) 251-3500, has a great deal of shopping opportunities.

Busch Gardens located at 3605 East Bougainvillea Avenue, Tampa, Florida 33612 Tel: (813) 987-5209. **Tampa Museum of Art** located at 600 North Ashley Drive, Tampa, Florida 33602 Tel: (813) 274-8130. **Tampa Bay History Center** located at 225 South Franklin Street, Tampa, Florida 33602 Tel: (813) 228 0097. **Tampa Bay Performing Arts Center** located at 1010 North Macinnes Place, Tampa, Florida 33602 Tel: (813) 229-7827.

St. Petersburg Area

The Pier, located at 800 2nd Ave. N.E, St. Petersburg Tel: (813) 821-6164, has various entertainments, shops, and restaurants - a fun place to visit. Also at the Pier is the **Great Explorations Hands-On Museum**, located on the third floor at 800 2nd Street N.E. St. Petersburg, Florida 33701727 Tel: (813) 821-8992. **Museum of Fine Arts,** located at 255 Beach Dr. N.E, St. Petersburg, Florida Tel: (727) 896-2667, has fine collections of world arts. **Salvador Dali Museum,** located at 1000 Third Street South St. Petersburg, Florida Tel: (727) 823-3767, exhibits Spanish works of art.

St. Petersburg Museum of History, located at 335 2nd Ave. N.E., St. Petersburg, Florida Tel: (727) 894-1052, is dedicated to the history of St. Petersburg. **Gulf Beaches Historical Museum,** located at 115 10th Ave, St. Petersburg Beach, Florida Tel: (813) 360-2491, exhibits the history of the Barrier Islands. **Great Explorations**, located on the Pier in downtown St. Petersburg, Florida Tel: (813) 821-8992, is a childrens museum that has hands-on exhibits for children of all ages. **Florida International Museum** is located at 100 2nd Street North, St. Petersburg, Florida 33701 Tel: (727) 821-1448.

Accommodations

Econo Lodge located at 1020 S Dale Mabry Hwy, Tampa, FL 33629 Tel: (813) 254-3005. **La Quinta Inn** located at 2904 Melburne Blvd, Tampa, FL 33605 Tel: (813) 623-3591. **Residence Inn** located at 13420 Telecom Dr, Tampa, FL 33637 Tel: (813) 972-4400. **University Motel** located at 9408 N Nebraska Ave, Tampa, FL 33612 Tel: (813) 931-4566. **Sheraton** located at 4400 W Cypress St, Tampa, FL 33607 Tel: (813) 873-8675. **Wingate Inn** located at 3751 E Fowler Ave, Tampa, FL 33612 Tel: (813) 979-2828.

Holiday Inn located at 111 W Fortune St, Tampa, FL 33602 Tel: (813) 223-1351. **Hyatt Regency Tampa** located at 2 Tampa City Ctr, Tampa, FL 33602 Tel: (813) 225-1234. **Courtyard by Marriott** located at 10152 Palm River Rd, Tampa, FL 33619 Tel: (813) 661-9559. **Holiday Inn** located at 3025 N Rocky Point Dr, Tampa, FL 33607 Tel: (813) 287-

8585. **Budget Host Tampa Motel** located at 3110 W Hillsborough Ave, Tampa, FL 33614 Tel: (813) 876-8673.

Radisson Hotel located at 7700 W Courtney Campbell Cswy, Tampa, FL 33607 Tel: (813) 281-8900. **Marriott Tampa Airport** located at the Tampa International Airport, Tampa, FL 33607 Tel: (813) 879-5151. **Hyatt Hotels & Resorts** located at 6200 W Courtney Campbell Cswy, Tampa, FL 33607 Tel: (813) 874-1234. **Hilton** located at 1700 E 9th Ave, Tampa, FL 33605 Tel: (813) 769-9267. **Courtyard by Marriott** located at 13575 Cypress Glen Ln, Tampa, FL 33637 Tel: (813) 978-9898.

Red Roof Inn located at 10121 Horace Ave, Tampa, FL 33619 Tel: (813) 681-8484. **Doubletree Guest Suites** located at 11310 N 30th St, Tampa, FL 33612 Tel: (813) 971-7690. **Best Western Inn** located at 3001 University Center Dr, Tampa, FL 33612 Tel: (813) 971-8930. **Days Inn** located at 2522 N Dale Mabry Hwy, Tampa, FL 33607 Tel: (813) 877-6181. **Crowne Plaza** located at 700 N West Shore Blvd, Tampa, FL 33609 Tel: (813) 289-8200. **Travelodge Hotel** located at 820 E Busch Blvd, Tampa, FL 33612 Tel: (813) 933-4011.

Wyndham Harbour Island Hotel located at 725 S Harbour Island Blvd, Tampa, FL 33602 Tel: (813) 229-5000. **Tampa Marriott Waterside** located at 400 N Tampa St #24440, Tampa, FL 33602 Tel: (813) 221-4900. **Ramada Limited** located at 2106 E Busch Blvd, Tampa, FL 33612 Tel: (813) 931-3313. **Hampton Inn** located at 3035 N Rocky Point Dr, Tampa, FL 33607 Tel: (813) 289-6262. **Howard Johnson** located at 2055 N Dale Mabry Hwy, Tampa, FL 33607 Tel: (813) 875-8818. **Quality Inn** located at 1200 N West Shore Blvd, Tampa, FL 33607 Tel: (813) 282-3636.

Lakeland (FL)

Named as the 10th "Best Place to Live in America" in 1998 by Money magazine, Lakeland is located on the western side of central Florida between Tampa and Orlando. Lakeland is home to more than 75,000 residents and it has a land area of 38.6 sq. miles (99 sq. kilometers).

Places of interest: Lakeland's downtown area is an interesting place of antiques shops and many other places of interest including the Polk Museum Of Art located at 800 E Palmetto St Lakeland, FL 33801 Tel: (941) 688-7743, the Bok Tower Garden Tel: (863) 679-1408 listed on National Register of Historic Places, and near the Bok Tower Garden is Spook Hill known for its famous Indian ghosts.

Lakeland's train depot is located at 600 Lake Mirror Dr. Lakeland, FL 33801. The station is staffed and features an enclosed waiting area, checked baggage service, restrooms, payphones, and vending machines. Transportation from the station is local taxi service.

Lakeland station is served by the Silver Service.

Winter Heaven (FL)

Winter Haven is known as the "water Skiing Capital of the World." There are 23 lakes surrounding Winter Haven most of which are connected by navigable canals. Winter Heaven is located near Cypress Gardens, the oldest theme park in the US and one of Florida's most beautiful. Winter Heaven is located east of Tampa and it has a land area of 12 sq. miles (31 sq. kilometers) and a population of more than 25,000. Winter Haven was incorporated in 1911.

Winter Heaven's train depot is located at 1800 7th St. S. W. Winter Haven, FL 33880. The station is staffed and features an enclosed waiting area, checked baggage service, restrooms, payphones, and vending machines. Transportation from the station is local taxi service.

Winter Heaven station is served by the Silver Service.

Sebring (FL)

Sebring was named "Florida Main Street Community" in 1996; this vibrant small community is home to approximately 9,000 residents. Also known as "The City on the Circle," Sebring was founded in 1911 by George Sebring. Visit Downtown Sebring, listed on the National Register of Historic Places.

Sebring's train depot is located at 601 E. Center St. Sebring, FL 33870. The station is staffed and features an enclosed waiting area, restrooms, payphones, and vending machines. Transportation from the station is local taxi service.

Sebring station is served by the Silver Service.

Okeechobee (FL)

Okeechobee is located 61 miles northwest of West Palm Beach. It has a land area of 4 sq. miles (10.5 sq. kilometers) and a population of approximately 5,000.

Okeechobee's train depot is located at 801 N. Parrott Ave. Okeechobee, FL 33474. The station is un-staffed and features payphones. Transportation from the station is local taxi service.

Okeechobee station is served by the Silver Service.

West Palm Beach (FL)

West Palm Beach is located in southeastern Florida, 65 miles north of Miami. Henry Morrison Flagler founded the site in 1893 and the following year West Palm Beach was incorporated. Flagler laid the city plan and named the streets for native plants. The city of West Palm Beach is popularly known for its beautiful beaches, resorts, museums of art, and its great weather. West Palm Beach has a land area of 49.5 sq. miles (127.7 sq. kilometers) and a population of approximately 68,000.

Getting Around

Airport

Palm Beach International Airport, 1000 PBIA, West Palm Beach, Florida 33406, Tel: (561) 471 7412, is located 2.5 miles (4 Kilometers) west of central West palm Beach. Major rental car companies are available at the airport. Local taxi and bus services serve the airport and outlying areas.

Bus

PalmTran, Palm Beach County's public bus transportation Tel: (561) 841-4200 operates bus services throughout Palm Beach County. Greyhound Lines connect Palm Beach to the rest of the country, toll-free (800) 231-2222.

Taxi

Palm Beach Transportation Taxi and Limo Service Tel: (561) 684-9900 and Yellow Cab Tel: (561) 689-2222.

Rent-A-Car

Hertz Car Rental toll-free (800) 654-3131, Alamo Rent-A-Car toll-free (800) GO-ALAMO, Budget Rent-A-Car toll-free (800) 527-0700, and Dollar Rent-A-Car toll-free (800) 800-3665.

Train and Commuter

West Palm Beach's train depot is located at 201 S. Tamarind Ave. West Palm Beach, FL 33402. The station is staffed and features an enclosed waiting area, restrooms, payphones, and vending machines. Transportation options from the station include Hertz Car Rental toll-free (800) 654-3131, local bus, transit, and taxi services.

West Palm Beach station is served by the Silver Service.

Visitor Information Center

Palm Beach County Convention and Visitors Bureau, 1555 Palm Beach Lake Boulevard, Suite 800 West Palm Beach Fl 33401 Tel: (561) 233-3000.

Places to See and Things to Do

Okeeheelee Nature Center, located on Forest Hill Boulevard West Palm Beach Tel: (516) 233-1400, is a nature preserve and sanctuary, the center has more than two miles of trails. **Mounts Botanical Gardens,** located at 531 North Military Trail, West Palm Beach Tel: (516) 233-1749, exhibits exotic tropical and subtropical plants. **Palm Beach Zoo at Dreher Park,** located at 1301 Summit Boulevard, West Palm Beach Tel: (516) 533-0887, is home to exotic and rare animals from different parts of the world.

South Florida Science Museum, located at 4801 Dreher Trail North, West Palm Beach, Tel: (516) 832-1988, has hands-on exhibits and houses an observatory, aquarium, and planetarium. **Yester Year Village,** located in South Flo:ida Fairgrounds, West Palm Beach Tel: (561) 793-0333, brings visitors to the old Florida, there are local entertainments, reenactors, and more. **Rapids Water Park,** located at 6566 N. Military Trail, West Palm Beach Tel: (516) 842-8756, is south Florida's favorite water park, there are several water pools and slides. **Christopher's Christmas Shoppe,** located in North Palm Beach Tel: (516) 848-4500, is a year around Christmas store; hear your favorite carol sung by the local choir.

Accommodations

Best Western Inn located at 1800 Palm Beach Lakes Blvd, West Palm Beach, FL 33401 Tel: (561) 683-8810. **Crown Plaza Hotel** located at 1601 Belvedere Rd, West Palm Beach, FL 33406 Tel: (561) 689-6400. **Embassy Suites Hotel** located at 4350 Pga Blvd, West Palm Beach, FL 33410 Tel: (561) 622-1000. **Knights Inn** located at 2200 45th St, West Palm Beach, FL 33407 Tel: (561) 478-1554. **Residence Inn** located at 2461 Metrocentre Blvd, West Palm Beach, FL 33407 Tel: (561) 687-4747. **Radisson Palm Beach Shores** located at 181 S Ocean Ave, West Palm Beach, FL 33404 Tel: (561) 863-4000.

Royal Inn located at 675 Royal Palm Beach Blvd, West Palm Beach, FL 33411 Tel: (561) 793-3000. **Radisson Hotel** located at 1808 S Australian Ave, West Palm Beach, FL 33409 Tel: (561) 689-6888. **Comfort Inn** located at 1901 Palm Beach Lakes Blvd, West Palm Beach, FL 33409 Tel: (561) 689-6100. **New Port Inn** located at 5901 Broadway, West Palm Beach, FL 33407 Tel: (561) 845-6467. **Sheraton** located at 630 Clearwater Park Rd, West Palm Beach, FL 33401 Tel: (561) 833-1234.

Hilton located at 150 Australian Ave, West Palm Beach, FL 33406 Tel: (561) 684-9400. **Tropical Isle Motel & Apt** located at 106 Inlet Way, West Palm Beach, FL 33404 Tel: (561) 842-2447. **Red Roof Inn** located at 2421 Metrocentre Blvd, West Palm Beach, FL 33407 Tel: (561) 697-7710. **Economy Inn** located at 6915 S Dixie Hwy, West Palm Beach, FL 33405 Tel: (561) 585-7501. **Holiday Inn** located at 1301 Belvedere Rd, West Palm Beach, FL 33405 Tel: (561) 659-3880.

Mirage Resorts located at 3801 Pga Blvd # 508, West Palm Beach, FL 33410 Tel: (561) 624-7700. **Courtyard by Marriott** located at 600 Northpoint Pkwy, West Palm Beach, FL 33407 Tel: (561) 640-9000. **Days Inn** located at 2300 45th St, West Palm Beach, FL 33407 Tel: (561) 689-0450. **Hampton Inn** located at 1505 Belvedere Rd, West Palm Beach, FL 33406 Tel: (561) 471-8700.

Delray Beach (FL)

Theodore Roosevelt founded Delray Beach in 1894 and in the same year a group of settlers from Michigan arrived and settled in the area. Delray is a Spanish word which means "Of the King;" the city was named an "All-America City" by the National Civic League in 1993. Delray has a land area of 14.8 sq. miles (38 sq. kilometers) and a population of approximately 48,000. Delray is has two miles of beach front with various entertainments, restaurants, and recreational facilities within the area.

Places of interest: the Rapids Water Park located at 6566 N. Military Trail, W.P.B. Tel: (561) 842-8756. The Morikami Park & Museum located at 400 Morikami Park Rd. off Jog/Carter Rd, Tel: (561) 495-0233. And the Cornell Museum located in the Old School Square at 51 N. Swinton Ave Tel: (561) 243-7922.

Delray's train depot is located at 345 South Congress Ave. Delray Beach, FL 33444. The station is un-staffed and features an enclosed waiting area, restrooms, payphones, and vending machines. Transportation from the station is local taxi and transit services.

Delray station is served by the Silver Service.

Deerfield Beach (FL)

Deerfield Beach is located between Palm Beach and Miami in southeastern Florida. First settled in 1877, the area of what is now Deerfield was originally called Hillsboro. The town was incorporated in 1925, and in 1939 the name was changed to Deerfield Beach because of the numbers of wild deer wandering around the area. Deerfield has a land area of 10.5 sq. miles (27 sq. kilometers) and a population of over 50,000. The city's economy is largely dependant on tourism. Visit the Freedom Marine Center located at 790 NW 1 Avenue - Deerfield Beach, FL 33441 Tel: (954) 418-0777.

Deerfield's train depot is located at 1300 W. Hillsboro Blvd. Deerfield Beach, FL 33442. The station is staffed and features an enclosed waiting area, checked baggage service, restrooms, payphones, vending machines, and a restaurant. Transportation options from the station include local transit and taxi services.

Deerfield station is served by the Silver Service.

Ft. Lauderdale (FL)

Fort Lauderdale is located just 30 miles north of Miami. Ft. Lauderdale has a land area of 31.5 sq. miles (81 sq. kilometers) and a population of approximately 150,000. Ft. Lauderdale has 23 miles of beach front and is blessed with a sub-tropical climate and moderate temperatures. Not surprisingly, Ft. Lauderdale's economy is mainly based on tourism industries.

Fort Lauderdale's train depot is located at 200 S.W. 21st Terrace Fort Lauderdale, FL 33312. The station is staffed and features an enclosed waiting area, checked baggage service, restrooms, payphones, and vending machines. Transportation options from the station include Hertz Car Rental toll-free: (800) 654-3131, local transit and taxi services.

Fort Lauderdale station is served by the Silver Service.

Places of interest: The Riverwalk in downtown Ft. Lauderdale, from SW 7th Avenue to SW 2nd Avenue, is popular to both tourist and locals. There are lots of restaurants, shops, and attractions. Port Everglades is the second busiest cruise port in the world. Club Nautico Boat Rentals located on Pier 66 Marina Tel: (954) 523-0033. Downtown Trolley, in downtown Fort Lauderdale Tel: (954) 761-3543, offers rides between downtown and beautiful Las Olas Blvd. Stranahan House, located in Las Olas at SE 6th Ave, Fort Lauderdale Tel: (954) 524-4736, is the oldest house in the area. To experience swimming and interacting with Dolphins take the Dolphin Swim Keys Adventure Tour Tel: (954) 525-4441;

it's a unique and fun experience. Take an adventure tour of the Everglades, contact Everglades Day Safari Tel: (941) 472-1559 or Everglades Holiday Park-Airboat Tours toll-free (800) 226-2244 for information.

Accommodations

Days Inn located at 1595 W Oakland Park Blvd, Fort Lauderdale, FL 33311 Tel: (954) 484-9290. **Marriott Hotels & Resorts** located at 6650 N Andrews Ave, Fort Lauderdale, FL 33309 Tel: (954) 771-0440. **Sea Lord Resort Motel** located at 4140 El Mar Dr, Fort Lauderdale, FL 33308 Tel: (954) 776-1505. **Three Palms Resort** located at 710 N Birch Rd, Fort Lauderdale, FL 33304 Tel: (954) 566-7429. **Travelodge** located at 1251 E Sunrise Blvd, Fort Lauderdale, FL 33304 Tel: (954) 763-6601. **Budget Inn** located at 1317 S Federal Hwy, Fort Lauderdale, FL 33316 Tel: (954) 523-5280.

Ramada Sea Club Hotel located at 619 N Atlantic Blvd, Fort Lauderdale, FL 33304 Tel: (954) 564-3211. **Palm Plaza Apartment Motel** located at 2801 Riomar St, Fort Lauderdale, FL 33304 Tel: (954) 565-7250. **Ocean Manor Resort Hotel** located at 4040 Galt Ocean Dr, Fort Lauderdale, FL 33308 Tel: (954) 566-7500. **Holiday Inn** located at 1711 N University Dr, Fort Lauderdale, FL 33322 Tel: (954) 472-5600. **Courtyard by Marriott** located at 5001 N Federal Hwy, Fort Lauderdale, FL 33308 Tel: (954) 771-8100. **Best Western Inn** located at 1180 Seabreeze Blvd, Fort Lauderdale, FL 33316 Tel: (954) 525-8115.

Winwood Motor Lodge located at 505 SE 18th St, Fort Lauderdale, FL 33316 Tel: (954) 524-7448. **Bahamas Princess Resort** located at 1170 Lee Wagener Blvd, Fort Lauderdale, FL 33315 Tel: (954) 359-9898. **Villa Venice Motel** located at 2900 Terramar St, Fort Lauderdale, FL 33304 Tel: (954) 564-7855. **Tropic Cay Resort Motel** located at 529 N Atlantic Blvd, Fort Lauderdale, FL 33304 Tel: (954) 564-5900.

Hollywood (FL)

Hollywood, also called the "Diamond of the Gold Coast," is located between Ft. Lauderdale and Miami. Hollywood is known for its beautiful beaches, very diverse community, and its international atmosphere. Joseph Young founded Hollywood in 1920. Hollywood has a land area of 27.5 sq. miles (70.6 sq. kilometers) and a population of more than 120,000.

Places of Interest: Visit Downtown Hollywood and experience the vitality of the city of Hollywood; there are various shops, restaurants, bars, and entertainment for everybody. Hollywood's six-mile beach is one of the most vibrant in Florida. Enjoy the sun, sand, and beautiful people. Hollywood North Beach is Hollywood's best kept secret.

Hollywood's train depot is located at 3001 Hollywood Blvd. Hollywood, FL 33021. The station is staffed and features an enclosed waiting area, checked baggage service, restrooms, payphones, and vending machines. Transportation options from the station include Hertz Car Rental toll-free (800) 654-3131, local transit and taxi services.

Hollywood station is served by the Silver Service.

Miami (FL)

Miami is the city of life, fun, beautiful beaches, and gorgeous bodies! Miami is located in southern Florida and has a land area of 35.8 sq. miles (92 sq. kilometers) and a population of more than 370,000. The city was incorporated in 1896 and is the only city founded by a woman named Julian Tuttle. However, it was the Tequesta Indians who first lived in the area for thousands of years.

Like many other American cities of the time, Miami is a city that progressed through the arrival of the railway system. Today Miami is one of the most dynamic and diverse cities in the US. Sixty percent of its approximately 370,000 residents are foreigners. Over 5 million visitors arrived in the city each year making it one of the world's gateways to the US.

Getting Around

Airport

Miami International Airport Tel: (305) 876 7000 is located 9 miles (14 Kilometers) west of Miami. Major rental car companies can be reached by taking a shuttle bus located at the ground transportation area. Taxis and Super Shuttle Bus are available at the ground terminal.

Bus

The South Miami-Dade Busway serves the Miami areas. Fare is $1.25 for Metro Bus and $1.50 for Express Bus. Make sure that you have exact change when boarding the bus as the bus does not provide change. Change Token Machines are available at the station. Call Tel: (305) 770-3131 for more information.

Taxi

Metro Taxi Company Tel: (305) 888-8888, Key Biscayne Taxi Tel: (305) 365-2222, Central Cab Tel: (305) 532-5555, Doral Area Taxi Tel: (305) 888-8856, and Dolphin Taxi Tel: (305) 948-6666.

Rent-A-Car

Miami Rent-A-Car Tel: (305) 754-2929, Hertz Car Rental toll-free (800) 654-3131, and Inter American Car Rental Tel: (305) 871-6060.

Train and Commuter

The Miami-Dade County's 21-mile Metro Rail transit system runs from Kendall through South Miami, Coral Gables, downtown Miami, and the rest of the area; fares are $1.25. Call Tel: (305) 770-3131 for information.

Miami's train depot is located at 8303 N.W. 37th Ave. Miami, FL 33147. The station is staffed and features an enclosed waiting area, checked baggage service, restrooms, payphones, and vending machines. Transportation options from the station include Hertz Car Rental toll-free (800) 654-3131, local transit and taxi services.

Miami station is served by the Silver Service.

Visitor Information Center

Greater Miami Convention & Visitors Bureau, 701 Brickell Ave, Suite 2700, Miami 33131 Tel: (305) 539-3000.

Bayside Marketplace, 401 Biscayne Blvd, Miami 33132 Tel: (305) 539-8070.

Places to See and Things to Do

Game Works, located at "The Shops" at Sunset Place 5701 Sunset Dr, Suite 330 Miami, FL 33143 Tel: (305) 667-4263, features game entertainment by Steven Spielberg. See some amazing films at **IMAX Theatre at Sunset Place** located at 5701 Sunset Dr, Suite 134 South Miami, FL 33143 Tel: (305) 663-4629 **Miami Museum of Science & Space Transit Planetarium,** located in Coconut Grove at 3280 S. Miami Ave. Miami, FL 33129 Tel: (305) 854-4247, has hands-on exhibits and live animals. **Weeks Air Museum,** located in Tamiami Airport at 14710 SW 128th St. Miami, FL 33196 Tel: (305) 233-5197, displays historic aircraft and artifacts.

Miami Beach Garden Conservancy Inc., located at 2000 Convention Center Dr, Miami Beach, FL 33139 Tel: (305) 673-7256, features a botanical garden. **Parrot Jungle and Gardens,** located at 11000 SW 57th Ave. Miami, FL 33156 Tel: (305) 666-7834, exhibits unique animals and houses a botanical garden and bird sanctuary. **Miami Seaquarium,** located at 4400 Rickenbacker Cswy. Key Biscayne, FL 33149 Tel: (305) 361-5705, has exhibits and live marine animals. **Miccosukee Indian Village & Everglades Airboat Tours** offers cultural, farm, and ecosystem tours, located in the Everglades Area, P.O. Box 440021 Tamiami Station Miami, FL 33144 Tel: (305) 223-8380.

The **Port of Miami** is known as the "Cruise Capital of the World;" several cruise liners operate from the port taking passengers to different parts of the world. **Norwegian Cruise Lines** is located at 7655 Corporate Center Drive Miami, FL 33126 toll-free (800) 327-7030. **Royal Caribbean International** is located at 1050 Caribbean Way Miami, FL 33132 toll-free (800) 539-6000. **Cunard Line** is located at 6100 Blue Lagoon Drive Miami, FL 33126 Ph: (800) 728-6273.

Miami Beach Marina is located at 300 Alton Road Miami Beach. Take **Ocean Drive** between 5th Street and 14th Place Miami Beach and experience the vibrant city of Miami. **Wolfsonian Museum** is located at 1001 Washington Avenue Miami Beach (305) 531-1001. The **Sanford L. Ziff Jewish Museum** is located at 301 Washington Avenue Miami Beach (305) 672-5044. **The Ancient Spanish Monastery** is located at 16711 W. Dixie Hwy. North Miami Beach, FL 33160 Tel: (305) 945-1461. Built in Spain in 1141, the monastery was shipped to the US and assembled in Miami during the early 1950's. **Museum of Contemporary Art** is located at 770 NE 125th Street North Miami (305) 893-6211.

Lowe Art Museum is located at the University of Miami at 1301 Stanford Drive, Coral

Gables FL (305) 284-3535. **Historical Museum of Southern Florida** is located at 101 West Flagler Street Miami (305) 375-1492. **Holocaust Memorial** is located at 1933-1945 Meridian Avenue Miami Beach (305) 538-1663. **Miami Art Museum** is located at 101 W. Flagler Street, Miami (305) 375-1700. **Miami Museum of Science Planetarium** is located at 3280 S. Miami Avenue, Miami (305) 854-4247. **Gold Coast Railroad Museum** is located at 12450 SW 152 Avenue Miami Tel: (305) 253-0063. **Black Heritage Museum** is located at 20900 SW 97th Ave Miami Tel: (305) 252-3535.

Nearby Miami

Everglades National Park has 1.5 million acres of a rich and rare ecosystem, located near Homestead Florida. For information call Tel: (305) 242-7700. **Everglades Alligator Farm,** located in Homestead/Florida City Area at 40351 SW 192nd Ave. Homestead, FL 33034 Tel: (305) 247-2628, offers airboat tours and live alligator and snake shows. **Everglades Safari Park** features an alligator farm and guided tours. Located in Everglades Area, contact Tel: (305) 226-6923 for information.

Accommodations

AmeriSuites Miami Kendall located at 11520 S.W. 88th Street, Miami FL 33176 Tel: (305) 718-8292 expect to pay $70-$200. **Doubletree Grand hotel Biscayne Bay** located at 1717 North Bayshore Drive, Miami FL 33132-1180 Tel: (305) 372-0313 expect to pay $60-$300. **Everglades Hotel** located at 244 Biscayne Blvd, Miami FL 33132 Tel: (305) 379-5461 expect to pay $70-$150. **Homewood Suites Miami Airport Blue Lagoon** located at 5500 Blue Lagoon Dr, Miami FL 33126 Tel: (305) 261-3335 expect to pay $70-$150. **Marriott Miami Dadeland** located at 9090 S. Dadeland Blvd, Miami FL 33156 Tel: (305) 670-1035 expect to pay $70-$200. **Clarion Hotel and Suites** located at 100 SE 4th St, Miami FL 33131 Tel: (925) 473-2230 expect to pay $80-$200. **Sheraton Biscayne Bay Hotel** located at 495 Brickell Ave, Miami FL 33131 Tel: (305) 373-6000 expect to pay $70-$350.

Courtyard Miami Airport South located at 1201 NW LeJeune Road, Miami FL 33126 Tel: (305) 642-8200 expect to pay $50-$150. **Candlewood Suites - Miami Airport** located at 8855 NW. 27th Street, Miami FL 33172 Tel: (305) 591-9099 expect to pay $70-$130. **Crowne Plaza Miami Airport** located at 950 NW LeJeune Rd, Miami FL 33126 Tel: (305) 446-9000 expect to pay $70-$200. **Baymont Inns and Suites** located at 3501 N.W. Le Jeune Rd, Miami FL 33142 Tel: (305) 871-1777 expect to pay $50-$100. **Airport Regency Hotel** located at 1000 NW 42 Ave, Miami FL 33126 Tel: (305) 441-1600 expect to pay $50-$100. **Travelodge Convention Center Miami** located at 1170 NW 11th St, Miami FL 33136 Tel: (305) 324-0800 expect to pay $50-$100.

Days Inn Civic Center Miami located at 1050 NW 14th St, Miami FL 33136 Tel: (305) 324-0200 expect to pay $50-$130. **Howard Johnson Hotel Miami** located at 1100 Biscayne Blvd, Miami FL 33132 Tel: (305) 358-3080 expect to pay $50-$100. **Doubletree Hotel Coconut Grove** located at 2649 South Bayshore Drive, Miami FL 33133 Tel: (305) 858-2500 expect to pay $70-$200. **Holiday Inn Miami Downtown** located at 200 SE 2 Ave, Miami FL 33131 Tel: (305) 374-3000 expect to pay $40-$150. **Hilton Miami Airport and Towers** located at 5101 Blue Lagoon Dr, Miami FL 33126 Tel: (305) 262-1000 expect to pay $50-$250. **Quality Inn South Kendall** located at 14501 S. Dixie Hwy, Miami FL 33176-7925 Tel: (305) 251-2000 expect to pay $60-$150.

Other Florida city connections and services: Charlotte (NC), Salisbury (NC), Greensboro (NC), Burlington (NC), Durham (NC), Raleigh (NC), Wilson (NC), Raleigh (NC)

Connecting Train: Jacksonville (FL), Orlando (FL), Tampa (FL), Winter Heaven (FL), West Palm Beach (FL), Ft. Lauderdale (FL), Miami (FL), via Cross Florida Services. Tampa (FL), Lakeland (FL), Lake Buena Vista (FL), Orlando (FL), Kissimmee (FL), Winter Heaven (FL), Sebring (FL), Okeechobee (FL), West Palm Beach (FL), Delray Beach (FL), Dearfield Beach (FL), Ft. Lauderdale (FL), Hollywood (FL), Miami (FL)

Sand Sculpture, Miami Beach

Useful Information and Tips

Other Trains and Railroads in the US

Alaska

White Pass & Yukon Route Railroad, PO Box 23343, Ketchikan, AK 99901; Tel: (800) 343-7373 or (888) 320-9049. The WP&YR was serving most of the scenic southern part of Alaska for more than a hundred years. Built to take gold miners of the Klondike Gold Rush, today the WP & YR serves exclusively as a passenger rail service. WP & YR offers three-hour round trip train journey from Skagway that climbs 2865 feet in just 20 miles. <<http://www.whitepassrailroad.com/index.html>>.

Alaska Railroad 431 West First Avenue, Anchorage, AK 99501; Tel: (907) 265-2494 or (907) 265-2620 TDD or toll-free (800) 544-0552. Alaska railroad bring passengers to more than 500 miles of routes from tidewater at Whittier and Seward to the heart of Interior Alaska. There are seasonal trip schedules, be sure to make inquiries and book yourself as far as possible before your intended departure. The Alaska Railroad fleet is composed of state-of-the-art locomotives, custom-built passenger coaches, and vista dome-style coaches for great viewing <<http://www.akrr.com>>.

Arizona

Grand Canyon Railway, 233 N. Grand Canyon Blvd Williams, AZ 86046; Tel: (800) 843 8724 or (800) THE-TRAIN. The restored 1901 steam train takes tourists daily from the historic Williams train depot to the south rim of the Grand Canyon

<<http://www.thetrain.com>>.

Verde Canyon Railroad, 300 North Broadway, Clarkdale, AZ 86324; toll-free (800) 320-0718, gives the only access to the protected wild life of North Verde River and a chance to view the Sinagua Indian Ruins. There is a 680 ft. tunnel along the route <<http://www.verdecanyonrr.com/packages.cfm>>.

Arkansas

Eureka Springs & North Arkansas Railway Company, 299 North Main Street Highway 23, Eureka Springs, AR 72632-0310; Tel: (501) 253-9623. **Offers** steam train dinner excursions <<http://www.railterminal.com/arrr.html>>.

California

Napa Valley Wine Train, 1275 McKinstry Street, Napa, California 94559 (train is located at downtown Napa, off Soscol and First St.) Tel: (707) 253 2111 toll-free (800) 427-412, offers 3-hours and 36 miles of gourmet-dining excursions that take tourists to some of California's popular wineries and vineyards. This magnificent excursion has several daily schedules and dining package options <<http://www.winetrain.com/wtginfo.html>>.

Fillmore and Western Railway, 351 Santa Clara, Fillmore, CA 93015; Tel: (805) 524 2546 toll-free (800) 773 8724. Offer 2½ hour excursion with panoramic views between Fillmore and Santa Paula. The fleet consists of vintage and antique rolling stock with open and enclosed coach cars <<http://www.fwry.com>>.

McCloud Railway Company, P.O. Box 1199 / 328 Main Street, McCloud, California 96057; Tel: (530) 964 2142 toll-free (800) 733 2141, operates a seasonal one-hour open-air excursion through the forest slopes of the southern side of Mt. Shasta. The fleets consist of a 1925

Alco built locomotive, 1914 Baldwin locomotive, and diesel locomotives <<http://www.shastasunset.com/index.shtml>>.

Niles Canyon Railway (NCRY), 6 Kilkare Road-5550 Niles Canyon Road Sunol, CA; Tel: (925) 862-9063. NCRY has seasonal scenic excursions the Polar Express and the Flower from downtown Sunol <<http://www.ncry.com/contactus.htm>>.

Roaring Camp Railroads (RC&BTNGRR), P.O. Box G-1, Felton, CA 95018; Tel: (831) 335-4484. Built as early as 1857, the Roaring Camp Railroad operates daily excursion through some of central California's beautiful scenery and historical places <<http://www.roaringcamprr.com/map.html>>.

Sierra Railroad's Golden Sunset Dinner Train, 220 South Sierra Oakdale, CA; toll-free (800) 866-1690, offers daily three-hour, 38-mile dinner excursions from central valley to Sierra foothill to Cooperstown. The Golden Sunset dinner train excursion uses the historic Sierra Railroad made famous in movies and T.V. <<http://www.sierrarailroad.com/fares.html>>.

Yosemite Mountain Sugar Pine Railroad, 56001 Hwy 41, Fish Camp, CA 93623; Tel: (559) 683 7273, offers a 4-mile railroad excursion into the forest of the Sierra Mountains, located near Yosemite Park's south gate on highway 41. They operate two vintage Shay steam locomotives built in 1931 and 1928 (which used to provide transportation for logging) and antique trolley-like "Jenny" cars which use Model "A" Ford gas engines <<http://www.ymsprr.com/about.html>>.

Colorado

Cumbres & Toltec Scenic Railroad, Antonito, Colorado, toll-free (888) 286 2737, offers daily steam excursions between Antonio Colorado & Chama New Mexico for $40 (round trip) with a chance to visit a Ghost Town at the midway point

<<http://www.cumbrestoltec.com>>.

Royal Gorge Route Railroad P.O. Box 859, Georgetown, CO 80444; Tel: (888) RAILS-4-U or (888) 724-5748. The Royal Gorge Route Railroad operates year-round along the Royal Gorge Route also known as "The most spectacular 12 miles of railroad in America" <<http://www.royalgorgeroute.com>>.

Durango & Silverton Narrow Gauge Railroad, 479 Main Ave, Durango, CO 81301; Tel: (888) 872 4607 or (888) TRAIN-07, is one of the most popular steam trains that takes tourists to the Rocky Mountains of Colorado. The Silverton takes visitors to some of the most beautiful and dramatic scenery of canyons and San Juan National Forest <<http://www.durangotrain.com/historytour>>.

Georgetown Loop Railroad, 1106 Rose Street in Georgetown (Old Georgetown Station) Tel: (800) 691-4386 or (303) 569-2403, operates a little more than one hour round trip train excursion between the town of Georgetown and Silver Plume, both rich in railroad and mining history <<http://www.gtownloop.com>>.

Connecticut

The Essex Steam Train, One Railroad Avenue, P.O. Box 452, Essex, CT 06426; toll-free (860) 767-0103 or (800) 377-3987, operates a 12-mile round-trip excursion to some of the most beautiful scenery of New England, traveling from Essex train depot to the towns of Deep River and Chester using two coal-fired locomotives and restored railroad coaches <<http://www.essexsteamtrain.com>>.

Delaware

Wilmington and Western Railroad, P.O. Box 5787, Wilmington, DE 19808-0787; Tel: (302) 998-1930 or (302) 998-7408. Delaware's oldest tourist steam railroad, the Wilmington and Western Railroad, takes tourists to the historic Red Clay Valley

<<http://www.wwrr.com>>.

Florida

Seminole Gulf Railway 4110 Centerpointe Drive-Suite 207, Fort Myers, FL 33916; Tel: (239) 275 6060 toll-free (800) SEM-GULF, operates a dinner theatre train where passengers join the crew in solving a murder mystery on the train

<<http://www.semgulf.com/default.htm>>.

Georgia

Blue Ridge Scenic Railway, 241 Depot Street, Blue Ridge, Georgia 30513; Tel: (706) 632-9833 toll-free (800) 934-1898, operates a 26-mile round trip excursion on a more than 100 year old railroad taking passengers to historic Murphy Junction along the gorgeous Toccoa River <<http://www.brscenic.com>>.

Indiana

Whitewater Valley Railroad, Grand Central Station Connersville, Indiana; Tel: (765) 825-2054. Indiana's Longest Scenic Railroad, the Whitewater Valley Railroad takes passengers on a two-hour, 32-mile round trip from Connersville to Metamora, Indiana

<<http://www.whitewatervalleyrr.org>>.

Iowa

Boone and Scenic Valley Railroad, P.O. Box 603/ 225 10th Street Boone, IA 50036; Tel: (515) 432-4249 toll-free (800) 626-0319, operates an electric trolley and Chinese steam engine along the 15-miles (round trip) of beautiful scenery between Des Moines River Valley and Boone, Iowa <<http://www.scenic-valleyrr.com>>.

Kentucky

Bluegrass Scenic Railroad, P.O. Box 27 Versailles, KY 40383 (Located 15 miles from Lexington); Tel: (606) 873-2476 toll-free (800) 755-2476, offers a 90-minute trip through the hills and charming farmland also known as the Bluegrass Region of central Kentucky <<http://www.bgrm.org>>.

Maryland

Western Maryland Scenic Railroad, 13 Canal Street Cumberland, MD 21502; toll-free (800) TRAIN-50, operates restored early 20th century rolling stock steams taking tourists on a 32 mile round trip through the beautiful mountains of Western Maryland between Cumberland and Frostburg <<http://www.wmsr.com>>.

Walkersville Southern Railroad P.O. Box 651, Walkersville, Maryland 21793; toll-free (877) 363-WSRR or (877) 363-9777, offers an excursion from Walkersville around Fountain Rock and neighboring areas visiting breathtaking landscape, rivers, farms, and a railroad-bridge <<http://www.wsrr.org>>.

Michigan

The Huckleberry Railroad, 5045 Stanley Road, Flint, Michigan 48506; Tel: (810) 736-7100. Huckleberry Railroad offers a 45-minute train ride using a historic Baldwin steam locomotive and wooden passenger cars taking passengers to Crossroads Village with 32 historic structures and friendly locals.

<<http://www.geneseecountyparks.org/crossroadsvillage.htm>>.

Michigan Star Clipper Dinner Train, 840 North Pontiac Trail, Walled Lake, Michigan, 48390; Tel: (248) 960-9440. One of the finest dinner trains in the US, the Star Clipper offers a 3-hour excursion serving five full courses of delicious cuisine freshly prepared onboard <<http://www.michiganstarclipper.com>>.

The Michigan State Trust for Railway Preservation Inc, P.O. Box 665, Owosso, Michigan 48864; Tel: (989) 725-9464, operates seasonal excursions in the Michigan region using the Pere Marquette 2-8-4 No.1225 steam locomotive engine <<http://www.mstrp.com>>.

Minnesota

Lake Superior Railroad Museum and North Shore Scenic Railroad, 506 West Michigan Street Duluth, MN 55802; Tel: (218) 733-7590 toll-free (800) 423-1273, offers a 90-minute 14-mile roundtrip excursion along the shores of Lake Superior, scenic bridges, and Lester River <<http://www.duluth.com/lsrm>>.

NorthernRail Traincar Suites, Ltd., P.O. BOX 117 Two Harbors, MN 55616; Tel: (218) 834-6084, takes passengers along the beautiful north shore of Lake Superior using authentic train cars <<http://www.northernrail.net>>.

Missouri

St Louis Iron Mountain and Southern Railway, Intersection of Highway 61 & 25 Jackson, Missouri; Tel: (573) 243 1688 toll-free (800) 455-7245, is the region's only steam passenger train still in use. It takes passengers through historic southeast Missouri using the "Shelby Brown" steam engine built in 1946 with narrated stories about Jesse James, Civil war battles, and the pioneering spirit <<http://rosecity.net/trains/station.html>>. The Frisco No. 1522, 1901 Mistflower Glen Court, Chesterfield, MO 63005; Here you'll find a seasonal train tour using a restored Frisco 1522, a 4-8-2 'Mountain Type,' steam locomotive built in 1926 by the Baldwin Locomotive Works of Philadelphia <<http://www.frisco1522.org>>.

Montana

Charlie Russell Chew-Choo, 408 NE Main Lewistown, MT 59457/PO Box 818; Tel: (406) 735-7886 or (406) 538-2527, offers a 28-mile dinner train ride with expedition through the heart of Montana << http://www.lewistownchamber.com/chewchoo.htm >>.

Ohio

Amish Steam Train, P.O. Box 427, Sugarcreek, OH 44681; toll-free (866) 850-4676. This offers a one-hour steam locomotive train trip around Sugarcreek, the largest Amish community in the world <<http://www.amishsteamtrain.com/>>.

Oregon

Southern Pacific Steam Locomotive No. 4449, Friends of 4449, P.O Box 42486, Portland, OR 97242 or PO Box 19342, Portland, OR 97280; Tel: (503) 244-4449. SP 4449 offers seasonal steam train excursions from Portland around the northern Pacific region; call for trip information <<http://www.4449.com>>.

Spokane, Portland & Seattle Steam Locomotive No. 700, 23440 NW Pubols Rd, Hillsboro, OR 97124-9349; Tel: (503) 804-7772, operates a seasonal steam train excursion trip using steam locomotive 4449 No. 700 between Portland and Washington states <<http://www.sps700.org>>.

Tennessee

Tennessee Valley Railroad, 4119 Cromwell Road, Chattanooga TN 37421; Tel: (423) 894-8028, operates the largest historic railroad in southeastern United States. The Tennessee valley railroad uses an 1854 steam and diesel engine taking passengers on a six-mile roundtrip train excursion <<http://www.tvrail.com>>.

Washington

Mt. Rainier Scenic Railroad, P.O Box 921, Elbe, WA 98330; Tel: (360) 569-2588 toll-free (888) STEAM-11. Mt. Rainier Scenic Railroad operates tours from the majestic Mt. Rainer to Mineral Lake using a vintage steam locomotive <<http://www.mrsr.com>>.

West Virginia

Cass Scenic Railroad P.O. Box 107 Cass, WV 24927; Tel: (304) 456-4300 toll-free (800) CALL-WVA, operates a 10-mile railroad using an old steam locomotive used to carry logs during the early days. Today Cass Scenic Railroad takes tourists to some of West Virginia's historic sites <<http://www.cassrailroad.com>>.

Wisconsin

The Milwaukee Road 261 steam locomotive takes passengers to various places in Illinois and Wisconsin; visit the friends of the 261 for scheduled trips at <<http://www.261.com>>.

Soo Line 4-6-2 No. 2719, Locomotive & Tower Preservation Fund, Ltd., P.O. Box 1266, Eau Claire, WI 54702-1266, operates a seasonal tour within Wisconsin and surrounding areas <<http://www.2719.com>>.

Wyoming

Union Pacific Steam 4-6-6-4 and Challenger No. 3985 (by Alco, 1943), 1800 Westland Road Cheyenne, Wyoming, 82001; Tel: (307) 637-3376 or (307) 638-8535, operates seasonal excursions between Denver and Wyoming; call for information <<http://www.upsteam.com>>.

Other Train Excursions in the US

American Orient Express 5100 Main Street, Suite 300, Downers Grove, IL 60515; toll-free (800) 320-4206. This private luxury train offers several excursions both in Canada and the US using classic cars equipped with Pullman sleeper cars and a fine dinning car ornamented with fine china, a chandelier, and piano entertainment. Traveling on the American Orient Express, with its fine and luxurious appointments, is pricey. Call for information or visit the American Orient Express website at <<http://www.americanorientexpress.com>>.

Montana Rockies Rail Tours (MRRT), 1055 Baldy Park Ave. Sandpoint, ID, 83864; Tel: (208) 265-8618 or toll-free (800) 519-7245, offers trips with spectacular views to southern and western Montana and northern Idaho; also linked motor coaches tour Glacier, Yellowstone, and Grand Teton National Parks. Traveling 478-miles of routes, the MRRT is the longest multiple day scenic rail journey in the US <<http://www.montanarailtours.com>>.

Amtrak Worldwide Sales Representatives

Argentina

Vanguard Marketing Tel: (54-11) 4328-9415

Australia

Asia Pacific Travel Marketing, St. David's Hall 17 Arthur St. Surry Hills Sydney, Australia 2010; Tel: (612) 9319-6624; Fax: (612) 9319-4151; <<http://www.aptms.com.au>>

Special Interest, 96 Canterbury Rd., Blackburn South, Melbourne; Tel: (03) 9877-3322

Destination Holidays, Suite 1 - 157 Main St Croydon VIC 3136 AUSTRALIA; Tel: (61 3) 9725-4655; Fax: (61 3) 9723-9211; Web: <<http://www.south-america.com.au>>

Rail Plus, Level 3, 459 Little Collins St. Melbourne; Tel: (03) 9642-8644; <<http://www.railplus.com.au>>

Austria

Austria Reiseservice, Hessgasse 7, A-1010 Vienna; Tel: (01) 310-7441

Bahamas

New Providence Travel, Peek Building, George Street, Nassau; Tel: (242) 322-2548

Barbados

Paul Foster/Travel Planners, Independence Square, Bridgetown; Tel: (246) 432-8900

Belgium

INCENTO B.V., Stationsweg 40, 1404 AP BUSSUM, The Netherlands; Tel: (31 35) 695 5111; Fax: (31 35) 695 5155; web: <<http://www.incento.nl->>

Bermuda

Meyer Agencies Limited, 35 Church Street, Hamilton; Tel: (441) 295-4176

Bolivia

Emete Ltda./Magri Turismo, Av. 16 de Julio, #1490, La Paz; Tel: (2) 317-140

Brazil

GSA Representacoes E Turismo, Ltda., Rua Nestor Pestana, 125-7o, Suite 71/72, Sao Paulo; Tel: (11) 3257-1177; Fax: (11) 3259-3824; (11) 3256-1791; <<http://www.gsarepresentacoes.com.br>>

Cayman Islands

International Travel, West Bay Road, Grand Cayman; Tel: (345) 947-4323

Chile

Masterhouse, Estado 10, Piso 11 Santiago, Chile; Tel: 56-2 633 4418; Fax: 56-2 639 7959

Colombia

Travel Club, Av. 19 No. 109-21, Bogota; Tel: (01) 618-4870

Costa Rica

Travel Mar/Agencia de Viajes TAM, Avenida 1, Calle 11, San Jose; Tel: 216695

Croatia

Mediteran International d.o.o, Kosovelova 2 SI - 6320 Portoroz; Tel: (386 5) 67 10 777; <<http://www.cruise-ferry-center.com>>

Denmark

Linda Engving, Scandinavian Cruise Center Strandvejen 6 2100 Copenhagen OE Denmark; Tel: 45 39 27 78 00; Fax: 45 39 27 78 10

Dominican Republic

Turinter, Leopoldo Navarro 4, Santo Domingo; Tel: (809) 686-4020

Ecuador

Klein Rep, Ave. Shyris 1000 y Holanda, Quito; Tel: (2) 469-286

Finland

Finland Travel Bureau, Kaivokatu 10A, Helsinki; Tel: (09) 182-664

Germany

North America Travel House, CRD International Stadthausbrucke 1-3 20355 Hamburg, Germany; Tel: (040) 300 616 0; fax (040) 300 616 55; <<http://www.crd.de/Amtrak>>

MESO Amerika-Kanada Reisen, Wilmersdorfer Str. 94, Berlin; Tel: 0180-525-4350; Fax: (0) 30/883 55 14

Guatemala

GTM, 20 Calle 5-35 Z 10, Plaza Los Arcos, 3er Nivel, Guatemala City; Tel: (2) 333-6915

Hong Kong

Travel Advisors, Ltd., Rm. 906, South Seas Centre, Tower 2, 75 Mody Road, Kowloon; Tel: (2) 312-7138

Hungary

Tradesco Tours, Rakoczi ut 14, Budapest; Tel: (1) 268-0038

India

TCI, 10 Veer Nariman Rd. Fort, Mumbai ; Tel: (22) 204-2032

Ireland

USIT, 19/21 Aston Quay, O'Connell Bridge, Dublin 2; Tel: (01) 602-1600

Israel

Tal Aviation, 29 Ben Yehuda Street; Tel: 972-3-7952128; Fax: 972-3-5107565

Italy

Tabb, S.R.L., Piazza della Repubblica 28, Milano; Tel: (02) 657-1141. Also at Via Pomba 29, Torino; Tel: (011) 562-3912 and Via Tommaseo 24, Padova; Tel: (049) 876-2760

Japan

H.I.S. Co. Ltd., Hotel & Rail Division, 1st Floor South Gate Building, 5-33-8 Sendagaya Shibuya-ku, Tokyo, Japan 151-0043; Tel: (81) 3-5360-4762; Fax: (81) 3-5360-4764

Korea

Hana Tour Service Inc., Seoul, Korea; Tel: (02) 725-1607; Fax: (02) 723-1828

Malaysia

Diners World Travel, 6th Floor, Wisma Clangor Dredging, Ku ala Lump; Tel: 61-3522

Mexico
Sales International, S.A., Rio Ni lo 80-501, Mexico City; Tel: (5) 208-1517

Netherlands
INCENTO B.V., Stationsweg 40, 1404 AP BUSSUM, The Netherlands; Tel: +31 35 695 5111; Fax: +31 35 695 5155; <<http://www.incento.nl>>

New Zealand
Gullivers Pacific Ltd., 5th Floor, Price Waterhouse Building, 66 Wyndham Street, Auckland New Zealand

Walshes World Ding Wall Building, 87 Queen Street, Auckland; Tel: (09) 379-3708

Norway
Nordmanns-Reiser A/S, Rädhusgaten 23b, 0158 Oslo; Tel: (47)-21609880 (Oslo); Fax: (47)-21609898

Geo tours/Nordic America Travel, P.O. Box 8, Sent rum, 0101 Oslo; Tel: (22) 825-500

NS Reseal, Storing 28, Oslo; Tel: (22) 838-850

Pakistan
Columbus Travel, Altar Hussar Rd., New Calif; Tel: (21) 212-218

Panama
Mar go Tours, Calle 51, Bell Vista 24, Panama City; Tel: 64-0111

Peru
Lima Reps, S.A., Av. Com andante Espionage, 349 Miraflores, Lima; Tel: (14) 444-7000

Portugal
Pinto Basto, Praca Duque Da Terdeia, Lisbon; Tel: (01) 346-0091

Poland
Alternativ Tours Polska, Spolka zo.o, 70-415 Szczecin, al. Jednosci Narodowej 49A, Poland; Tel: 091-812-31-70; Fax: 091-812-31-74

Singapore
Diners World Travel, 7500 E. Beach Road, The Plaza; Tel: 292-5522

Slovenia
Mediteran International d.o.o., Kosovelova 2, SI - 6320 Portoroz; Tel: (05) 67 10 777; Fax: (05) 67 10 762; <<http://www.cruise-ferry-center.com>>

AMZS Dunajska 128^a, SI - 1000Ljubljana; Tel: (01) 530 53 33

South Africa
World Travel Agency, PTY, Ltd., 8th Fl., Evrite Hse., 20 De Korte St., Braamfrontein, Johannesburg; Tel: 011-403-2638

Spain
Expomundo, Santa Cruz de Marcenado, 31, Oficina 10, Madrid; Tel: 542-1348

Diputacion, 238, Barcelona, Tel: 412-5956.

Sweeden

Scandinavian Cruise Center, Strandvejen 6, 2100 Copenhagen; Tel: (45) 39 27 78 00

Switzerland

Kuoni Travel, Ltd., Neue Hard 7, Neugasse 231, Zurich; Tel: (01) 277-4580

Sky Tours Ltd. , Freischutzgasse, 1 / PO Box CH-8021 Zurich Switzerland; Tel: 01 295 58 95; Fax: 01 295 5880 and Freischutzgassel, 3021 Zurich; Tel: (01) 295 58 85

SSR-Reisen, Ankerstrasse 112, Zurich; Tel: (01) 297-1111

Travac, Treichleistr. 10, Zurich; Tel: (01) 267-5757 and 25 Rue de Monthoux, Geneva; Tel: (022) 909-7810

Taiwan

Golden Formosa Travel Services, No. 142 Chung Hsiao East Rd., Sec. 4, Taipei, Taiwan 106; Tel: (02) 2775-1138; Fax: (02) 2721-2784

Thailand

T.V. Air Bookings, 795 Silom Rd. Bangkok, Thailand; Tel: (662) 233-5160

United Arab Emirates

Al Tayer Travel, Al Maktoum Street, Dubai; Tel: (4) 236-000

United Kingdom

Leisurail, P.O. Box 5, 12 Coningsby Road Peterborough, England, PE3 8XP; Tel: 0870 7500222; Fax: 0870 7500333

Destination Marketing Limited, Molasses House, Plantation Wharf, London; Tel: (0171) 253-9009

Trailfinders Limited:

>   -215 Kensington High Street, London; Tel: 0171) 937-5400

>   -58 Deansgate, Manchester; Tel: (0161) 839-6969

>   -48 Corn Street, Bristol; Tel: (0117) 929-9000

>   -22-24 The Priory Queensway, Birmingham; Tel: (0121) 236-1234

>   -254-284 Sauchiehall St., Glasgow; Tel: (0141) 353-2224 -

Venezuela

Tur-V Special Tours, Av. Fco. de Miranda Torre Provincial B, Piso 11, Chacao – Caracas Venezuela – 1060; Tel: 264-64-66 / 264-45-55 / 2643312/264-33-55 / 264-77-97; Fax: 264-11-76

Rail Road Parks and Museums in the US

Arizona Railway Museum, 399 N. Delaware St., Chandler, AZ 85224, Tel: (480) 821-1108. The Arizona Railway Museum is dedicated to the preservation and restoration of Arizona's Railroading history.

Best Friend Museum located in downtown Charleston, S.C., on Ann Street near the visitors information center Tel: (843) 973-7269, mailing address: 456 King Street Charleston, South Carolina 29403. The museum has a full-size replica of the Best Friend and other railroad artifacts.

California State Railroad Museum is located in Old Sacramento near the Amtrak train station, Tel: (916) 323-9280. The California State Railroad Museum is dedicated to the preservation of the history and artifacts of California Railroad.

Colorado Railroad Museum, 17155 West 44th Ave. Golden, Colorado 80403, toll-free (800) 365-6263. The Museum is dedicated to preserving the rich heritage of standard and narrow gauge railroading of the Rocky Mountains.

Connecticut Trolley Museum, 58 North Road, East Windsor, CT 06088, toll-free (860) 627-6540. Founded in 1940, the museum is owned and operated by the Connecticut Electric Railway Association, Inc., and is the oldest incorporated organization dedicated to the preservation of streetcars and the Trolley Era in the US.

Florida Gulf Coast Railway Museum is located in Manatee County in the town of Parrish on US 301, toll-free (877) 869-0800. The museum was founded in 1981 dedicated to preserve history and artifacts of railroads that served the state of Florida.

Golden Spike National Historic Site is located in Brigham City Utah, Tel: (435) 471-2209. The site is where the Central Pacific and Union Pacific Railroads first joined forming the transcontinental railroad on May 10, 1869.

Illinois Railway Museum is located on Union Road in Union Illinois, toll-free (800) BIG-RAIL. The museum is the largest railway museum in the US and it exhibits railroad equipment and the history of railroad development.

Indiana Transportation Museum is located in Forest Park, Noblesville, Indiana, about 20 miles north of downtown Indianapolis, Tel: (317) 773-6000. The museum is dedicated to the preservation of Indiana's railroad history and the experience of railroad travel.

Kentucky Railway Museum located at the Heartland of Kentucky, toll-free (800) 272-0152 is one of the oldest rail museums in the US. The museum exhibits the railroad history and heritage of Kentucky.

Lake Superior Railroad Museum, 506 West Michigan Street, Duluth, MN 55802; the museum is one of the largest railroad museums in the US.

Long Island Railroad Museum is located west of Greenport on North Fork, Long Island. The museum was built in 1892 and is dedicated to the preservation of the railroad history of Long Island.

Museum of Transportation, 3015 Barrett Station Road, St. Louis, MO 63122, is one of the oldest and best rail museums in the US. The museum has the largest collection of steam locos in North America.

National Railroad Museum, 2285 South Broadway St. Green Bay, WI 54304 Tel: (920) 437-7623. The museum exhibits and preserves collections of equipment, artifacts, and railroad historical documents of Green Bay Wisconsin.

North Alabama Railroad Museum is located in 694 Chase Road, Alabama, east of Huntsville Alabama 35815-4163 Tel: (256) 851-6276. The museum is dedicated to the preservation of railroad history.

Northwest Railway Museum is located in Snoqualmie-North Bend, Washington; the museum exhibits the importance of railroad on the development of the state of Washington.

Oregon Electric Railway Museum, 3995 Brook-lake Road NE Brooks, OR 97303; the museum houses the largest trolley collection in the US Pacific Northwest.

Saginaw Railway Museum, 900 Maple Street, at the tracks Saginaw, Mich. 48602-1175, Tel: (517) 790-7994, a small museum exhibits significant historical railroad collections.

Santa Maria Valley Railway Historical Museum is located on the southeast corner of Main and Broadway at the center of Santa Maria, Tel: (805) 714-4927. The museum is dedicated to the preservation of the railroad heritage of California, the Central Coast, and the Santa Maria Valley.

San Diego Model Railroad Museum is located at the heart of Balboa Park, 1649 El Prado San Diego, CA 92101-1621, Tel: (619) 696-0199. The museum has the largest operating model railroad exhibit in the world; the scale model railroad depicts the old southwestern railroading. <<http://www.globalinfo.com/noncomm/SDMRM/sdmrm.html>>

South Florida Railway Museum is located at the former Seaboard Air Line station building in Deerfield Beach, 1300 West Hillsboro Beach Blvd, Deerfield Beach, Fla. 33442, Tel: (954) 698-6620. The museum has collections of railroad artifacts <<http://www.sfrm.org/>>.

Southeastern Railway Museum is located in Duluth Georgia (suburb of Atlanta); the museum has collections of railway publications and memorabilia.

Steam-Town National Historic Site is located in Scranton, P.A. The museum is a 40-acre site created by congress in 1986 to exhibit the story of steam railroading of the early days.

Tennessee Central Railway Museum, 220 Willow Street Nashville, TN 37210-2159, Tel: (615) 244-9001. The museum has growing collections of Tennessee's historical railway equipment.

Texas State Railroad Historical Park, Anderson and Cherokee Counties, between the cities of Palestine and Rusk, Tel: (903) 683-2561. The park has train excursion, entertainment, and Texas railroad educational experience.

Texas Transportation Museum, 11731 Wetmore Road, San Antonio, Texas 78247, Tel: (210) 490-3554, the museum displays various transportation methods in the US.

The Twin City Model Railroad Museum, 1021 Bandana Blvd. East, Suite 222 Saint Paul, MN 55108, Tel: (651) 647-9628. The museum exhibits a scale model panorama of railroading of the 40s and 50s in the United States <<http://www.tcmrm.org/>>.

The National Toy Train Museum, 300 Paradise Lane Strasburg, PA 17579; Tel: (717) 687-8976. The museum exhibits huge collections of toy trains and equipments <<http://www.traincollectors.org/toytrain.html>>.

The Age of Steam Railroad Museum located at Fair Park Dallas, Texas; Tel: (214) 428-0101. The museum exhibits comprehensive collections of heavyweight passenger cars <<http://www.dallasrailwaymuseum.com/>>.

Virginia Museum of Transportation, 303 Norfolk Avenue, Roanoke, VA 24016 Tel: (540) 342-5670, the museum exhibits steam and diesel locomotives.

Wichita Falls Railroad Museum, 500 9th Street Wichita Falls, Texas, Tel: (940) 723-2661, the museum is dedicated to preserving the railroad heritage of Wichita Falls Texas.

Whippany Railway Museum, 1 Railroad Plaza Route 10 West & Whippany Road, Tel: (973) 887-8177, the museum is dedicated to the preservation of New Jersey's railroad heritage.

Wilmington Railroad Museum, 501 Nutt Street, downtown Wilmington, NC 28401, Tel: (910) 763-2634. The museum preserves the history of the Atlantic Coast Line Railroad and the US southeastern railroad system.

5070815R00332

Printed in Great Britain
by Amazon.co.uk, Ltd.,
Marston Gate.